# THE LOEB CLASSICAL LIBRARY

FOUNDED BY JAMES LOEB 1911

EDITED BY

## JEFFREY HENDERSON

# ATHENAEUS

# V

LCL 274

# ATHENAEUS

## THE LEARNED BANQUETERS

### BOOKS 10.420e–11

EDITED AND TRANSLATED BY

S. DOUGLAS OLSON

HARVARD UNIVERSITY PRESS
CAMBRIDGE, MASSACHUSETTS
LONDON, ENGLAND
2009

*First published 2009*

LOEB CLASSICAL LIBRARY® is a registered trademark
of the President and Fellows of Harvard College

Library of Congress Control Number 2006041321
CIP data available from the Library of Congress

ISBN 978-0-674-99632-8

*Composed in ZephGreek and ZephText by
Technologies 'N Typography, Merrimac, Massachusetts.
Printed on acid-free paper and bound by
The Maple-Vail Book Manufacturing Group*

# CONTENTS

# PREFACE

For a general introduction to Athenaeus and *The Learned Banqueters*, and to my citation conventions, see the beginning of Volumes I and III. I have altered Casaubon's numbering of the text at one point, where he chose to use 459a to refer to both one of the final sections of Book 10 and the very beginning of Book 11 (my 11.459d). In addition, I have (like all previous editors) tacitly added a handful of section-divisions accidentally omitted from Casaubon's text. Two passages missing from manuscript A have been supplied from the Epitome, one (referred to by Casaubon numbers 11.781b–784d) following the first part of 11.466d, and the other (unnumbered) following the first part of 11.502b.

Thanks are due my research assistant Timothy Beck, and my undergraduate students Joseph McDonald, William Blessing, and Andrew Gerstenberger for their many hours of reference-checking, proofreading, formatting assistance, and the like. Final work on the manuscript was completed at the National Humanities Center, an ideal research environment. This volume is dedicated to my beloved, brave, and beautiful Rachel for the same reasons that Volume I was and now for many more as well.

# ABBREVIATIONS

| | |
|---|---|
| O'Connor | J. B. O'Connor, *Chapters in the History of Actors and Acting in Ancient Greece together with a Prosopographia Histrionum Graecorum* (Chicago, 1908) |
| *PA* | J. Kirchner, *Prosopographia Attica* (Berlin, 1901–3) |
| *PAA* | J. Traill (ed.), *Persons of Ancient Athens* (Toronto, 1994– ) |
| *PMG* | D. L. Page (ed.), *Poetae Melici Graeci* (Oxford, 1962) |
| Poralla | P. Poralla, *A Prosopography of Lacedaimonians from the Earliest Times to the Death of Alexander the Great (X–323 B.C.)*[2] (revised by A. S. Bradford: Chicago, 1985) |
| *SH* | H. Lloyd-Jones and P. Parsons (eds.), *Supplementum Hellenisticum* (Texte und Kommentar, Band 11: Berlin and New York, 1983) |
| *SSR* | G. Giannantoni, *Socratis et Socraticorum Reliquiae* (4 vols.; n.p., 1990) |
| Stephanis | I. E. Stephanis, Διονυσιακοὶ Τεχνίται (Herakleion, 1988) |
| *SVF* | J. van Arnim (ed.), *Stoicorum Veterum Fragmenta* (3 vols.; Leipzig, 1921, 1903) |
| *TrGF* | B. Snell *et al.* (eds.), *Tragicorum Graecorum Fragmenta* (Göttingen, 1971–2004) |

# THE CHARACTERS

ATHENAEUS, the narrator; also a guest at the dinner party

TIMOCRATES, Athenaeus' interlocutor

AEMILIANUS MAURUS, grammarian (e.g. 3.126b)

ALCEIDES OF ALEXANDRIA, musician (1.1f; 4.174b)

AMOEBEUS, citharode (14.622d–e)

ARRIAN, grammarian (3.113a)

CYNULCUS, Cynic philosopher whose given name is Theodorus (e.g. 1.1d; 3.97c)

DAPHNUS OF EPHESUS, physician (e.g. 1.1e; 2.51a)

DEMOCRITUS OF NICOMEDIA, philosopher (1.1e; 3.83c)

DIONYSOCLES, physician (3.96d, 116d)

GALEN OF PERGAMUM, physician (e.g. 1.1e–f, 26c)

LARENSIUS, Roman official and also host of the party (e.g. 1.2b–3c; 2.50f)

LEONIDAS OF ELIS, grammarian (1.1d; 3.96d)

MAGNUS (e.g. 3.74c)

MASURIUS, jurist, poet, musician (e.g. 1.1c; 14.623e)

MYRTILUS OF THESSALY, grammarian (e.g. 3.83a)

PALAMEDES THE ELEATIC, lexicographer (9.379a)

PHILADELPHUS OF PTOLEMAIS, philosopher (1.1d)*

# CHARACTERS

PLUTARCH OF ALEXANDRIA, grammarian (e.g. 1.1c–d; 3.83b)

PONTIANUS OF NICOMEDIA, philosopher (1.1d; 3.109b)

RUFINUS OF NICAEA, physician (1.1f)*

ULPIAN OF TYRE, grammarian and also symposiarch (e.g. 1.1d–e; 2.49a)

VARUS, grammarian (3.118d)

ZOILUS, grammarian (e.g. 1.1d; 7.277c)

* Neither Philadelphus nor Rufinus is said to speak anywhere in the preserved text of *The Learned Banqueters*, and most likely some of the anonymous speeches in 1.2a–3.73e (represented in the Epitome manuscripts only) belong to them.

# THE LEARNED BANQUETERS

# I

Οἱ δὲ νῦν συνάγοντες ἐπὶ τὰ δεῖπνα καὶ μάλιστα οἱ ἀπὸ τῆς καλῆς Ἀλεξανδρείας βοῶσι, κεκράγασι, βλασφημοῦσι τὸν οἰνοχόον, τὸν διάκονον, τὸν μάγειρον· κλαίουσι δ᾽ οἱ παῖδες τυπτόμενοι κονδύλοις ἄλλος ἄλλοθεν. καὶ οὐχ οἷον οἱ κεκλημένοι μετὰ πάσης ἀηδίας δειπνοῦσιν, ἀλλὰ κἂν τύχῃ θυσία τις οὖσα, παρακαλυψάμενος ὁ θεὸς οἰχήσεται καταλιπὼν οὐ μόνον τὸν οἶκον, ἀλλὰ καὶ τὴν | πόλιν ἅπασαν· γελοῖον γάρ ἐστιν αὐτὸν ⟨τὸν⟩[1] εὐφημίαν κηρύξαντα καταρᾶσθαι τῇ γυναικὶ καὶ τοῖς τέκνοις. καὶ τοῖς δειπνοῦσι δ᾽ ἂν εἴποι ὁ τοιοῦτος·

> νῦν δ᾽ ἔρχεσθ᾽ ἐπὶ δεῖπνον, ἵνα ξυνάγωμεν Ἄρηα.

τῷ γὰρ τοιούτῳ ὁ οἶκος

> ὁμοῦ μὲν θυμιαμάτων γέμει, ‖
> ὁμοῦ δὲ παιάνων τε καὶ στεναγμάτων.

τούτων λεχθέντων ἔφη τις τῶν παρόντων· παραιτητέον εἰς ταῦτ᾽ ἀποβλέποντάς ἐστι τὸ γαστρίζεσθαι.

---

[1] add. Meineke

---

[1] Sc. in embarrassment at being associated with such a place.

# BOOK X.420e

People who invite guests to dinner nowadays, and in particular the inhabitants of the lovely city of Alexandria, shout, scream, and swear at the wine-steward, the waiter, and the cook, while their slaves cry out in pain throughout the room when they are punched. And not only are the guests thoroughly disgusted as they consume their meal, but if this is a sacrificial rite, the god will cover his face[1] and leave, abandoning not just the house, but the entire city; for it is ridiculous that the same person who called for "words of good omen only"[2] is now cursing his wife and his children. A man like this might say to the others eating with him (*Il.* 2.381):[3]

But now go to your dinner, so that we can join battle.

For the house of someone like this (S. *OT* 4–5)

> is simultaneously full of incense
> and of paeans and cries of lament.

After these remarks were made, one of the guests said: If we pay attention to this, we ought to refuse to stuff ourselves. Because

[2] Standard preliminary procedure when making a sacrifice.
[3] Quoted also at 8.364a, in a very similar context.

ἀτελὲς δὲ δεῖπνον οὐ ποεῖ παροινίαν,

ὡς Ἄμφις φησὶν ἐν Πανί, οὐδὲ ὕβρεις καὶ προπηλα-
κισμούς, ὡς Ἄλεξις ἐν Ὀδυσσεῖ Ὑφαίνοντι μαρτυρεῖ
διὰ τούτων·

      (Α.) φιλεῖ γὰρ ἡ μακρὰ συνουσία
καὶ τὰ συμπόσια τὰ πολλὰ καὶ καθ᾽ ἡμέραν |
b      ποεῖν
σκῶψιν, ἡ σκῶψις δὲ λυπεῖ πλεῖον ἢ τέρπει
     πολύ.
τοῦ κακῶς λέγειν γὰρ ἀρχὴ γίγνετ᾽· ἂν δ᾽ εἴπῃς
     ἅπαξ,
εὐθὺς ἀντήκουσας· ἤδη λοιδορεῖσθαι λείπεται,
εἶτα τύπτεσθαι δέδεικται καὶ παροινεῖν. (Β.)
     ταῦτα γὰρ
κατὰ φύσιν πέφυκεν οὕτως· καὶ τί μάντεως ἔδει;

καὶ Μνησίμαχος δὲ ἐν Φιλίππῳ διὰ τὸν ὑπερβάλλοντα
κόρον ἐν τοῖς δείπνοις παράγει τι συμπόσιον πολέμου
παρασκευὴν ἐπαγγελλόμενον καὶ ὡς ἀληθῶς κατὰ τὸν
c χαριέστατον Ξενοφῶντα πολέμου | ἐργαστήριον. λέ-
γει δ᾽ οὕτως·

ἆρ᾽ οἶσθ᾽ ὁτιὴ πρὸς ἄνδρας ἐστί σοι μάχη,
οἳ τὰ ξίφη δειπνοῦμεν ἠκονημένα,
ὄψον δὲ δᾷδας ἡμμένας καταπίνομεν;
ἐντεῦθεν εὐθὺς ἐπιφέρει τραγήματα
ἡμῖν ὁ παῖς μετὰ δεῖπνον ἀκίδας Κρητικάς,
ὥσπερ ἐρεβίνθους, δορατίων τε λείψανα
κατεαγότ᾽, ἀσπίδας δὲ προσκεφάλαια καὶ
θώρακας ἔχομεν, πρὸς ποδῶν δὲ σφενδόνας
καὶ τόξα, καταπάλταισι δ᾽ ἐστεφανώμεθα. |

4

An inexpensive dinner produces no bad, drunken
      behavior,

as Amphis says in *Pan* (fr. 29), nor any outrageous actions or abusive comments, as Alexis insists in *Odysseus
Weaving* (fr. 160), in the following passage:

      (A.) Since extended socializing
and lots of parties every day tend to produce
mockery; and mockery produces way more grief than
      pleasure.
This is how verbal abuse begins; the minute you say
      something,
you immediately hear it back. Next comes name-
      calling;
and then you see people punching each other and
      acting like drunken idiots. (B.) Yeah;
that's the natural course of events. What need was
      there for a seer?

So the overwhelming excess seen at banquets motivated
Mnesimachus in *Philip* to introduce a drinking party he
describes as a preparation for hostilities and a genuine
workshop of war, as the delightful Xenophon (*HG* 3.4.17)
puts it. Mnesimachus says the following (fr. 7):

So do you realize you'll be fighting men
who eat sharpened swords for dinner
and gobble down flaming torches as a side-dish?
Then right after that the slave brings us
Cretan arrowheads as an after-dinner snack,
like chickpeas, plus some shattered fragments
of javelins; and we use shields and breastplates
as pillows, and put slings and bows
by our feet, and wear catapults as garlands.

d  καὶ ὁ Κολοφώνιος δὲ Φοῖνιξ φησίν·

Νίνου κάδοι μάχαιρα καὶ κύλιξ αἰχμή,
κύμβη δὲ τόξα, δήιοι δὲ κρητῆρες,
ἵπποι δ' ἄκρητος, κἀλαλὴ "μύρον χεῖτε."

ἐν δὲ τῷ Παρασίτῳ Ἄλεξις περὶ πολυφάγου τινὸς
διαλεγόμενός φησι·

καλοῦσι δ' αὐτὸν πάντες οἱ νεώτεροι
Παράσιτον ὑποκόρισμα· τῷ δ' οὐδὲν μέλει.
δειπνεῖ δ' ἄφωνος Τήλεφος, νεύων μόνον
πρὸς τοὺς ἐπερωτῶντάς τι, ὥστε πολλάκις |
e  αὐτὸν ὁ κεκληκὼς τὰ Σαμοθρᾴκι' εὔχεται
λῆξαι πνέοντα καὶ γαληνίσαι ποτέ.
χειμὼν ὁ μειρακίσκος ἐστὶ τοῖς φίλοις.

Δίφιλος δ' ἐν Ἡρακλεῖ περί τινος τῶν ὁμοίων διαλεγόμενος διέξεισιν·

                    ἐμὲ μὲν οὐχ ὁρᾷς πεπωκότα
ἤδη τ' ἀκροθώρακ' ὄντα καὶ θυμούμενον,
τονδὶ δὲ ναστὸν Ἀστ<ερ>ίωνος μείζονα
ἤδη σχεδὸν δωδέκατον ἠριστηκότα;

διὸ καλῶς ἔλεγεν ὁ Βορυσθενίτης Βίων οὐ δεῖν ἀπὸ |
f  τῆς τραπέζης τὰς ἡδονὰς πορίζεσθαι, ἀλλ' ἀπὸ τοῦ

---

4 After Telephus murdered his maternal uncles (Hyg. *Fab.*
244.2), he fled to Mysia, where as a polluted murderer he was not
allowed to speak to anyone; cf. Amphis fr. 30 (quoted at 6.224d–e).

5 The "Samothracian gods" offered protection during storms
at sea; cf. Olson on Ar. *Pax* 276–9.

6 Apparently a reference to one of the Giants, who was killed
by Athena.

6

Phoenix of Colophon (fr. 3, p. 234 Powell) as well says:

> Wine-jars are Ninos' dagger; his spear is a drinking-
>      cup;
> his bow is a wine-bowl; his enemies are mixing-bowls;
> his horses are unmixed wine; and his battle-cry is
>      "Pour the perfume!"

In his *The Parasite* (fr. 183) Alexis discusses a gluttonous
individual and says:

> All the younger men refer to him
> by the nickname "Parasite"; but he doesn't care.
> He eats dinner like a mute Telephus,[4] nodding to
>      people
> who ask him a question, but not doing anything else,
>      so that his hosts
> routinely repeat the prayers offered to the gods from
>      Samothrace,[5]
> asking that he eventually stop blowing and calm
>      down.
> The boy affects his friends like a storm.

Diphilus in *Heracles* (fr. 45) discusses someone similar and
describes him as follows:

> Don't you see that I've been drinking,
> and that I'm a bit wrecked and angry now,
> and that this is now almost the twelfth cake
> bigger than Asterion[6] that I've had for lunch?

Bion of Borysthenes (fr. 14 Kindstrand) was therefore
right to argue that we ought to get our pleasure not from

φρονεῖν. ὁ δ' Εὐριπίδης φησί·

φαύλῃ διαίτῃ προσβαλὼν ἤσθη στόμα,

ὡς τῆς ἀπὸ τῶν προσφορῶν τέρψεως περὶ τὸ στόμα
μᾶλλον γινομένης. Αἰσχύλος τ' ἐν Φινεῖ·

καὶ ψευδόδειπνα πολλὰ μαργώσης γνάθου
ἐρρυσίαζον στόματος ἐν πρώτῃ χαρᾷ.

ἐν Σθενεβοίᾳ δ' ὁ Εὐριπίδης περὶ εὐτελείας λέγων·

βίος δὲ πορφυροῦς θαλάσσιος ‖
422     οὐκ εὐτράπεζος, ἀλλ' ἐπάκτιοι φάτναι.
ὑγρὰ δὲ μήτηρ, οὐ πεδοστιβὴς τροφὸς
θάλασσα· τήνδ' ἀροῦμεν, ἐκ ταύτης βίος
βρόχοισι καὶ πέδαισιν οἴκαδ' ἔρχεται.

μέγα γὰρ ἀνθρώποις κακὸν ἡ γαστήρ, περὶ ἧς φησιν
Ἄλεξις ἐν Συναποθνῄσκουσι·

μάθοις τ' ἂν οἷον ἀνθρώποις κακὸν
ἔστιν ἡ γαστήρ, διδάσκει δ' οἷ' ἀναγκάζει θ'
    ὅσα.
εἴ τις ἀφέλοι τοῦτ' ἀφ' ἡμῶν τὸ μέρος ἀπὸ τοῦ
    σώματος, |
b     οὔτ' ἂν ἀδικοῖτ' οὐδὲν οὐδεὶς οὔθ' ὑβρίζοι τἂν
    ἑκών.
νῦν δὲ διὰ ταύτην ἅπαντα γίγνεται τὰ δυσχερῆ.

Δίφιλος δ' ἐν Παρασίτῳ·

---

7 A longer version of the fragment is cited at Stob. 4.20.2,
where it is identified as coming from *Antiope*.

the dinner table, but from intellectual activity. Euripides (fr. 213.4)[7] says:

He made his mouth happy by attacking a nasty meal,

as if the pleasure derived from food was most closely associated with the mouth. Also Aeschylus in *Phineus* (fr. 258):[8]

They seized many cheating dinners from my ravening jaw as my mouth was about to enjoy them.

Euripides in *Stheneboea* (fr. 670), discussing thrift:

The living that comes from the surging sea
is not luxurious; our mangers are on the beach.
The sea is a moist mother, not an earth-trodding
nurse. We plow her, and our livelihood comes home
from her by means of our nets and traps.

For the belly causes people tremendous trouble. Alexis says the following about it in *Men Who Were Dying Together* (fr. 215):

And you could learn the sort of trouble
people's bellies
cause them, and the kind of lessons it teaches us, and
everything it forces us to do.
If you removed this part of our anatomy,
no one would deliberately commit a crime or abuse
anyone else.
But as it is, it's the cause of all our difficulties.

Diphilus in *The Parasite* (fr. 60):

8 Describing the Harpies, which snatched Phineus' food before he could consume it.

εὖ γ' ὁ κατάχρυσος εἶπε πόλλ' Εὐριπίδης·
"νικᾷ δὲ χρεία μ' ἡ ταλαίπωρός τέ μου
γαστήρ." ταλαιπωρότερον οὐδέν ἐστι γὰρ
τῆς γαστρός· εἰς ἣν πρῶτον ἐμβαλεῖς < ... >
ἀλλ' οὐχ ἕτερον ἀγγεῖον. ἐν πήρᾳ φέροις |
c   ἄρτους ἄν, ἀλλ' οὐ ζωμόν, ἢ διαφθερεῖς.
εἰς σπυρίδα μάζας ἐμβαλεῖς, ἀλλ' οὐ φακῆν·
οἰνάριον εἰς λάγυνον, ἀλλ' οὐ κάραβον.
εἰς τὴν θεοῖς ἐχθρὰν δὲ ταύτην εἰσφόρει
ἅπανθ' ἑαυτοῖς μηδὲν ὁμολογούμενα.
κοὐ προστίθημι τἆλλα, διότι πανταχοῦ
διὰ τὴν τάλαιναν πάντα ταύτην γίνεται.

  καὶ Κράτης δ' ὁ κυνικός, ὥς φησι Σωσικράτης ἐν ταῖς
d  Διαδοχαῖς, ἐπερράπισε Δημήτριον τὸν Φαληρέα | σὺν
τῇ πήρᾳ τῶν ἄρτων καὶ λάγυνον πέμψαντα οἴνου· "εἴθε
γάρ", ἔφη, "τὰς κρήνας καὶ ἄρτους ἦν φέρειν." Στίλπων δ' οὐ κατεπλάγη τὴν ἐγκράτειαν καταφαγὼν
σκόροδα καὶ κατακοιμηθεὶς ἐν τῷ τῆς μητρὸς τῶν
θεῶν ἱερῷ· ἀπείρητο δὲ τῷ τούτων τι φαγόντι μηδὲ
εἰσιέναι. ἐπιστάσης δὲ αὐτῷ τῆς θεοῦ κατὰ τοὺς
ὕπνους καὶ εἰπούσης ὅτι "φιλόσοφος ὤν, ὦ Στίλπων,
παραβαίνεις τὰ νόμιμα," καὶ τὸν δοκεῖν ἀποκρίνασθαι
κατὰ τοὺς ὕπνους[2]· "σὺ δέ μοι πάρεχε ἐσθίειν καὶ
σκορόδοις οὐ χρήσομαι." |

---

[2] κατὰ τοὺς ὕπνους del. Meineke

---

[9] = E. fr. 915.1–2.
[10] Very similar material is preserved at D.L. 6.90.
[11] Since all he actually wanted to drink was water.

The silver-tongued Euripides offered many fine
      remarks:
"Poverty and my miserable belly have got the upper
      hand
over me."[9] Because nothing's more miserable
than your belly. First of all, you'll put . . . into it,
but not into any other container. You could carry
      bread
around in a beggar's-bag, but not soup; if you do,
      you'll ruin it.
You'll put barley-cakes in a basket, but not lentil-
      porridge;
and wine in a wine-flask, but not a crayfish.
Whereas you toss anything, in a complete jumble,
into this goddamned part of your anatomy.
Nothing else counts; because this rotten belly of ours
makes everything happen everywhere.

So too the Cynic Crates, according to Sosicrates in his *Successions* (fr. 22, *FHG* iv.503 = *SSR* V H 33), reprimanded Demetrius of Phaleron (fr. 58b Wehrli = 33a Fortenbaugh–Schütrumpf)[10] when the latter sent him a flask of wine along with his beggar's-bag stuffed full of bread. "If only the springs also produced bread!", he said.[11] Stilpo's (*SSR* II O 21) frugal lifestyle did not lead to him being terrified when he ate some garlic and fell asleep in the temple of the Mother of the Gods. (Anyone who ate food like this was forbidden to enter the place.) When the goddess appeared to him in his sleep and said, "Even though you're a philosopher, Stilpo, you're violating my rules!", he thought that he answered, while still asleep: "Well, give me something to eat, and I'll avoid garlic."

11

e    Ἐπὶ τούτοις ὁ Οὐλπιανὸς ἔφη· ἐπεὶ δεδείπναμεν (εἴρηκε δὲ οὕτως Ἄλεξις ἐν Κουρίδι·

    < . . . > ἐπεὶ πάλαι δεδείπναμεν.

Εὔβουλος Προκρίδι·

    < . . . > ἡμεῖς δ᾿ οὐδέπω δεδείπναμεν.

καὶ πάλιν·

    < . . . > ὃν χρὴ δεδειπνάναι πάλαι.

καὶ Ἀντιφάνης ἐν Λεωνίδῃ·

                  ἀλλὰ πρὶν δεδειπνάναι
    ἡμᾶς παρέσται.

καὶ Ἀριστοφάνης ἐν Προαγῶνι·

    ὥρα βαδίζειν μούστιν ἐπὶ τὸν δεσπότην·
    ἤδη γὰρ αὐτοὺς οἴομαι δεδειπνάναι.

καὶ ἐν Δαναίσιν· |

f    ἤδη παροινεῖς <εἰς> ἐμὲ πρὶν δεδειπνάναι.

καὶ Πλάτων Σοφισταῖς· < . . . >. καὶ Ἐπικράτης ὁ Ἀμβρακιώτης—μέσης δ᾿ ἐστὶ κωμῳδίας ποιητής—ἐν Ἀμαζόσιν·

    δεδειπνάναι γὰρ ἄνδρες εὐκαίρως πάνυ
    δοκοῦσί μοι.

---

12 Sc. rather than the expected *dedeipnēkamen* (infinitive *dedeipnēkenai*).

13 The quotation has dropped out of the text.

Ulpian responded by saying: Since we have finished our dinner (*dedeipnamen*)—this is the form of the verb used by Alexis in *The Female Barber* (fr. 114):[12]

since we finished dinner (*dedeipnamen*) long ago.

Eubulus in *Procris* (fr. 90):

We haven't finished dinner (*dedeipnamen*) yet.

And again (fr. 91):

who should have finished dinner (*dedeipnanai*) long
ago.

Also Antiphanes in *Leonides* (fr. 141):

But he'll be here before
we've finished dinner (*dedeipnanai*).

And Aristophanes in *The Proagon* (fr. 480):

It's time for me to go find my master;
I expect they've finished dinner (*dedeipnanai*) by
now.

And in *Danaids* (fr. 260):

You're already acting like a nasty drunk to me, even
before you've finished dinner (*dedeipnanai*)!

Also Plato in *Sophists* (fr. 157):[13] . . . And Epicrates of Ambracia (test. 2)—he is a Middle Comic poet—in *Amazons* (fr. 1):

Because my impression is that the men have had a
very leisurely dinner (*dedeipnanai*).

ATHENAEUS

καὶ ἠρίσταμεν δ' εἴρηκεν Ἀριστοφάνης ἐν Ταγη-
νισταῖς·

　　ὑποπεπώκαμεν < ... >, ὦνδρες, καὶ καλῶς
　　　ἠρίσταμεν. ‖

423　καὶ Ἕρμιππος ἐν Στρατιώταις· ἠριστάναι † καὶ παρ-
ιστάναι τουτί. † Θεόπομπος Καλλαίσχρῳ·

　　ἠρίσταμεν· δεῖ γὰρ συνάπτειν τὸν λόγον.

καταριστᾶν δὲ εἴρηκεν ἐν τῷ Πολιτικῷ Ἀντιφῶν
οὕτως· ὅτ' ἄν τις πράγματα τὰ ἑαυτοῦ ἢ τὰ τῶν φίλων
κατηρίστηκεν. παραδεδειπνημένος δ' εἴρηκεν Ἄμφις
ἐν Πλάνῳ οὕτως·

　　< ... > παραδεδειπνημένος, παῖδες, πάλαι.)—

τοῖς οὖν θεοῖς, κατὰ τὸν Πλάτωνα, ὡς ἐν Φιλήβῳ
b　φησίν, εὐχόμενοι κεραννύωμεν, | εἴτε Διόνυσος εἴθ'
Ἥφαιστος εἴθ' ὅστις θεῶν ταύτην τὴν τιμὴν εἴληχε
τῆς συγκράσεως. καθάπερ γὰρ ἡμῖν οἰνοχόοις τισὶν
παρεστᾶσιν κρῆναι, καὶ μέλιτος μὲν ἂν ἀπεικάζοι τις
τὴν τῆς ἡδονῆς, τὴν δὲ τῆς φρονήσεως νηφαντικὴν καὶ
ἄοινον αὐστηροῦ τινος καὶ ὑγιεινοῦ ὕδατος· ἃς προ-
θυμητέον ὡς κάλλιστα συμμιγνύναι. ὥρα οὖν πίνειν
ἡμῖν ἐστι, καὶ τῶν παίδων τις ἐκ τοῦ κυλικείου τῶν
ποτηρίων παραφερέτω· ὁρῶ γὰρ πλῆθος καλῶν καὶ

---

[14] Sc. rather than the expected ēristēkamen.
[15] Quoted again at 10.424d, where see n.

Aristophanes in *Frying-Pan Men* (fr. 513) also uses the form *ēristamen*:[14]

> We've had a bit to drink, gentlemen, and we've had a
> nice lunch (*ēristamen*).

Likewise Hermippus in *Soldiers* (fr. 60, corrupt and unmetrical): to have had lunch (*ēristanai*) † and to stand beside this †. Theopompus in *Callaeschrus* (fr. 23):

> We've had lunch (*ēristamen*); because I need to keep
> the story short.

Antipho in his *The Statesman* (87 B 73 D–K) uses *kataristan* ("to squander money on lunch"), as follows: Whenever someone's squandered his own property or that of his friends on lunch (*katēristēken*). And Amphis uses *paradedeipnēmenos* ("having gone without dinner") in *The Vagabond Actor* (fr. 31), as follows:

> having been dinnerless (*paradedeipnēmenos*) for a
> long time now, slaves.

Let us accordingly pray to the gods, as Plato puts it in the *Philebus* (61b–c),[15] and mix some wine, whether the honor associated with the mixing belongs to Dionysus, or Hephaestus, or some other deity. For two springs are set beside us, as they are sometimes beside wine-stewards, and one might compare the one that produces pleasure to a spring of honey, and the one that produces contemplation, and that sobers us up and contains no wine, to a spring of hard, healthy water; our task is to mix them together in the best possible proportion. It is therefore time for us to begin drinking. So let one of the slaves bring us a goblet from the cup-stand; for I see a large number of

c ποικίλων ἐκπωμάτων. δοθέντος | οὖν ποτηρίου μεγά-
λου ἔφη· ἀλλ᾽ ἀκρατέστερόν μοι, ὦ παῖ, τῷ κυάθῳ
πληρῶν ἔγχει εἰς τὴν κύλικα, μὴ κατὰ τὸν κωμῳδιοποιὸν Ἀντιφάνην, ὃς ἐν Διδύμοις φησί·

> τὸ ποτήριόν μοι τὸ μέγα προσφέρει λαβών.
> ἐπεχεάμην ἄκρατον· "ἔγχει, παιδίον,
> κυάθους θεῶν τε καὶ θεαινῶν μυρίους·
> ἔπειτ᾽ ἐπὶ τούτοις πᾶσι τῆς σεμνῆς θεᾶς
> καὶ τοῦ γλυκυτάτου βασιλέως διμοιρίαν."

ἐμοὶ οὖν, ὦ παῖ, ζωρότερον κέραιρε· οὔπω γὰρ |
d λέγομεν περὶ ἀριθμοῦ κυάθων. δείξω δὲ ὅτι καὶ ὁ
κύαθος εἴρηται καὶ τὸ ἀκρατέστερον, καὶ περὶ οἰνοχόων. πρότερον δέ μοι λελέξεται περὶ τοῦ ζωρότερον.
Ἀντιφάνης Μελανίωνι·

> τοῦτον ἐγὼ κρίνω μετανιπτρίδα τῆς Ὑγιείας
> πίνειν ζωροτέρῳ χρώμενον οἰνοχόῳ.

ἐν δὲ Λάμπωνι·

> ὁ δεῖν᾽, Ἰᾶπυξ, κέρασον εὐζωρέστερον.

Ἔφιππος Ἐφήβοις·

---

16 Presumably Alexander the Great (thus Meineke).

17 An echo of Il. 9.203 (quoted at 10.423e).

18 Sc. of wine and water required to produce an appropriate
mixture. The topic is eventually taken up at 10.426b.

19 Literally "[wine] mixed with less [water]".

20 Sc. by what the learned banqueters would have called "ancient authors".

beautiful, elaborately-wrought drinking vessels. Then after he was handed a large cup, he said: Fill your ladle (*kuathos*) with rather strong wine (*akratesteron*) for me, slave, and pour it into my cup! Do not follow the comic poet Antiphanes, who says in *Twins* (fr. 81):

> He gets the big cup and brings it to me.
> I poured unmixed wine into it for myself. "Pour us endless
> ladleful in honor of the gods and goddesses, slave!
> And then, after all of those, pour us one with twice as much
> in honor of the sacred goddess and our beloved king!"[16]

So then, slave, mix me some stronger (*zōroteros*) wine;[17] because we are not yet discussing the number of ladles.[18] I intend to demonstrate that the terms *kuathos* ("ladle, ladleful") and *akratesteron*[19] are used,[20] and I will also discuss wine-stewards. But first I will offer some remarks about the word *zōroteros* ("stronger"). Antiphanes in *Melanion* (fr. 147):

> I believe this guy should use a *zōroteros* wine-steward
> and consume an after-washing cup dedicated to Hygieia ("Health").

And in *Lampon* (fr. 137):

> Whatever your name is—Iapyx!—mix some nice *zōresteros* wine!

Ephippus in *Ephebes* (fr. 10):

φιάλην ἑκατέρᾳ |

e   ἔδωκε κεράσας ζωρότερον Ὁμηρικῶς.

τινὲς δὲ καὶ τὸ παρ' Ὁμήρῳ

ζωρότερον δὲ κέραιρε

οὐκ ἄκρατον σημαίνειν φασίν, ἀλλὰ θερμόν, ἀπὸ τοῦ
ζωτικοῦ καὶ τῆς ζέσεως· ἑταίρων γὰρ παρόντων νέον
ἐξ ὑπαρχῆς κεράννυσθαι κρατῆρα ἄτοπον. ἄλλοι δὲ τὸ
εὔκρατον, ὥσπερ τὸ δεξιτερὸν ἀντὶ τοῦ δεξιοῦ. τινὲς δέ,
ἐπεὶ οἱ ἐνιαυτοὶ ὧροι λέγονται καὶ τὸ ζα- ὅτι μέγεθος ἢ
πλῆθος σημαίνει, ζωρὸν τὸν πολυέτη λέγεσθαι. Δί-
φιλος δ' ἐν Παιδερασταῖς φησιν· |

f                 (Α.) ἔγχεον σὺ δὴ πιεῖν.
(Β.) εὐζωρότερόν γε νὴ Δί', ὦ παῖ, δός· τὸ γὰρ
ὑδαρὲς ἅπαν τοῦτ' ἐστι τῇ ψυχῇ κακόν.

Θεόφραστος δ' ἐν τῷ Περὶ Μέθης ζωρότερόν φησιν
εἶναι τὸ κεκραμένον, παρατιθέμενος Ἐμπεδοκλέους
τάδε· ‖

424   αἶψα δὲ θνήτ᾽ ' ἐφύοντο, τὰ πρὶν μάθον ἀθάνατ᾽
       εἶναι,

---

[21] I.e. *za-hōros*. The last two arguments, treated as alterna-
tives by Athenaeus (or his source), must instead be taken together:
*zōros* means "old," and the comparative form *zōroteros* stands in
for the positive, in the same way that comparative *dexiteros* sometimes stands in for positive *dexios*, allowing *zōroteros* to be understood as meaning simply "old". But these are in any case all false
etymologies.

18

> He mixed a *zōroteros*
> libation-bowl for each woman in the Homeric style
> and gave it to her.

Some authorities claim that the Homeric (*Il.* 9.203)

> and mix it *zōroteros*

refers not to wine with no water mixed in, but to hot wine, deriving the word from *zōtikos* ("full of life") and *zesis* ("boiling"), on the ground that it is unusual to have a fresh bowl mixed all over again when company is present. Others claim that the word means "well-mixed", comparing the use of *dexiteros* ("more to the right") in place of *dexios* ("to the right"). And some argue that years are referred to as *hōroi*, and that the prefix *za-* indicates size or number, so that old wine is called *zōros*.[21] Diphilus says in *Pederasts* (fr. 57):

> (A.) You! Pour us a drink!
> (B.) Give us some nice *zōroteros* wine, by Zeus, slave!
> All
> this watery stuff's bad for our souls.

Theophrastus in his *On Drunkenness* (fr. 574 Fortenbaugh) claims that anything mixed with another substance is *zōroteros*, citing the following passage from Empedocles (31 B 35.14–15 D–K):[22]

> And at once mortal substances, which they previously
> understood to be immortal, came into being,

[22] Part of a much larger quotation from *On Nature* preserved (with several variants from the text as quoted here) by Simplicius. Arist. *Po.* 1461a24–5 also cites portions of these two verses in isolation.

ζωρά τε τὰ πρὶν ἄκρητα, διαλλάξοντα κελεύθους.

κύαθον δ᾽ ἐπὶ τοῦ ἀντλητῆρος Πλάτων εἴρηκεν ἐν
Φάωνι οὕτως·

&lt; … &gt; τῷ στόματι τὸν κύαθον ὧδ᾽ εἰληφότες.

καὶ ἐν Πρέσβεσι·

&lt; … &gt; κυάθους ὅσους ἐκλέπτεθ᾽ ἑκάστοτε.

Ἄρχιππος Ἰχθύσι·

&lt; … &gt; κύαθον ἐπριάμην παρὰ Δαισίου. |

b  τοιοῦτόν ἐστιν καὶ τὸ ἐν Εἰρήνῃ Ἀριστοφάνους·

ὑπωπιασμέναι
&lt;ἀπαξάπασαι καὶ κυάθους προσκείμεναι&gt;[3].

τὰ γὰρ ὑπώπια τοῖς κυάθοις περιθλώμενα ἀμαυροῦται.
μνημονεύει τοῦ κυάθου καὶ Ξενοφῶν ἐν πρώτῳ Παιδείας καὶ Κρατῖνος, ἔτι δ᾽ Ἀριστοφάνης πολλαχοῦ καὶ
Εὔβουλος ἐν Ὀρθάννῃ. Φερεκράτης δ᾽ ἐν Λήροις ἀργυροῦν κύαθον ὠνόμασε. Τίμων δ᾽ ἐν δευτέρῳ Σίλλων
ἀρυσαίνας κέκληκε τοὺς κυάθους φάσκων οὑτωσί·

&lt; … &gt; ἀπληστοίνους τ᾽ ἀρυταίνας,

ἀπὸ τοῦ ἀρύσασθαι ὀνομάσας. καλοῦνται δὲ καὶ ἀρυ-
c  στῆρες καὶ | ἀρύστιχοι. Σιμωνίδης·

---

3 add. Schweighäuser

---

23 The discussion now moves on abruptly to the second topic
announced at 10.423d.        24 Cf. 10.452b–c with n.
25 An excerpt from a longer fragment quoted at 10.445e.

and substances that were previously unmixed became
*zōra*, changing course.

Plato in *Phaon* (fr. 192)[23] uses *kuathos* to refer to a vessel
used for ladling, as follows:

having seized the *kuathos* by its lip, like this.

Also in *Ambassadors* (fr. 128):

however many *kuathoi* you stole at any point.

Archippus in *Fish* (fr. 21):

I bought a *kuathos* from Daesius.

This is the type of vessel referred to in Aristophanes' *Peace*
(541–2):

each and every one of them
with black eyes and applying *kuathoi* to themselves.

Because black eyes disappear when pressure is applied to
them with a *kuathos*.[24] Xenophon also mentions a *kuathos*
in Book I of the *Education* (*Cyr.* 1.3.9), as does Cratinus
(fr. 464); Aristophanes (*Ach.* 1053; *Lys.* 444) also refers to
them frequently, as does Eubulus in *Orthannes* (fr. 79).
Pherecrates in *Frills* (fr. 112) mentioned a silver *kuathos*.
Timo in Book II of the *Silloi* (*SH* 778.3)[25] refers to *kuathoi*
as *arusainai*, saying the following:

and *arutainai* that could never be too full of wine,

deriving the word from *arusasthai* ("to draw liquid for oneself"). They are also referred to as *arustēres* and *arustichoi*.
Simonides (Sem. fr. 25 West[2]):

ἔδωκεν οὐδεὶς οὐδ᾽ ἀρυστῆρα τρυγός.

Ἀριστοφάνης δ᾽ ἐν Σφηξίν·

ἐγὼ γὰρ εἶχον τούσδε τοὺς ἀρυστίχους.

Φρύνιχος Ποαστρίαις·

< . . . > κύλικ᾽ ἀρύστιχον.

ἔνθεν καὶ ἡ ἀρύταινα. ἔλεγον δὲ καὶ ἔφηβον ⟨τὸ⟩ τοιοῦτον σκεῦος, ὡς Ζηνοφάνης ἐν τῷ Συγγενικῷ. Πολύβιος δ᾽ ἐν τῇ ἐνάτῃ τῶν Ἱστοριῶν καὶ ποταμόν d τινα ἀναγράφει Κύαθον καλούμενον περὶ | Ἀρσινόην πόλιν Αἰτωλίας. τῷ δὲ ἀκρατέστερον Ὑπερείδης κέχρηται ἐν τῷ Κατὰ Δημοσθένους γράφων οὕτως· εἰ μέν τις ἀκρατέστερον ἔπιεν, ἐλύπει σέ. τούτῳ ὅμοιόν ἐστι τὸ ἀνιηρέστερον καὶ τὸ ἐν Ἡλιάσιν Αἰσχύλου

< . . . > ἀφθονέστερον λίβα.

καὶ Ἐπίχαρμος δὲ ἐν Πύρρᾳ εὐωνέστερον ἔφη· καὶ ἐν τῷ Κατὰ Δημάδου δὲ ὁ Ὑπερείδης εἴρηκε ῥαδιεστέραν τὴν πόλιν. τῷ δὲ κεραννύειν κέχρηται Πλάτων μὲν ἐν Φιλήβῳ· τοῖς δὴ θεοῖς, ὦ Πρώταρχε, εὐχόμενοι κε- e ραννύωμεν. καὶ Ἀλκαῖος ἐν | Ἱερῷ Γάμῳ·

---

[26] Cf. 11.469a–b. [27] Aeschylus fr. 72 (cited below) is also quoted—although with the words in the nominative rather than the accusative—by the *Et.Gen.*, which identifies Philoxenus as its source. Theodorides accordingly attributed all the material that follows (to the end of the quote from Hyperides in 10.424d) to Philoxenus (= fr. *338) on that basis. [28] See 10.423d n.

[29] I.e. rather than *kerannunai* from the standard form of the verb, *kerannumi* (which would yield third-person plural present active indicative *kerannuasin* rather than *kerannuousin* [below]).

No one even gave me an *arustēr* of grape-must.

Aristophanes in *Wasps* (855):

Because I've got these *arustichoi*.

Phrynichus in *Female Grass-Cutters* (fr. 42):

an *arustichos* cup.

This is the source of the word *arutaina* ("cup" or "ladle"). They also referred to a vessel of this type as an *ephēbos*,[26] according to Zenophanes in his *Cognate Vocabulary*. Polybius in Book IX (vol. III p. 50 Buettner–Wobst) of his *History* records a river known as the Cyathus near the city of Arsinoe in Aetolia.[27] Hyperides uses the word *akratesteron*[28] in his *Against Demosthenes* (p. 24 Jensen), where he writes as follows: If anyone drank *akratesteron*, it upset you. The form *aniēresteron* ("more troublesome, annoying") is similar to this, as is the phrase

an *aphonesteron* ("less begrudging") stream

in Aeschylus' *Daughters of the Sun* (fr. 72). So too Epicharmus in *Pyrrha* (fr. 119) used the word *euōnesteron* ("cheaper"), while Hyperides in his *Against Demades* (fr. 86 Jensen) describes the city as *rhaidiestera* ("more easygoing"). Plato uses *kerannuein*[29] ("to mix") in the *Philebus* (61b–c):[30] Let's pray to the gods, Protarchus, and mix (*kerannuōmen*) (some wine)! Also Alcaeus in *The Sacred Marriage* (Alc. Com. fr. 15):

[30] Quoted also (in a slightly less direct form) at 10.423a–b, a context in which the observations that follow are more apposite.

23

< . . . > κεραννύουσιν ἀφανίζουσί τε.

Ὑπερείδης Δηλιακῷ· καὶ τὸν κρατῆρα τὸν Πανιώνιον κοινῇ οἱ Ἕλληνες κεραννύουσιν. ᾠνοχόουν τε παρὰ τοῖς ἀρχαίοις οἱ εὐγενέστατοι παῖδες, ὡς ὁ τοῦ Μενελάου υἱός·

οἰνοχόει δ' υἱὸς Μενελάου κυδαλίμοιο.

καὶ Εὐριπίδης δ' ὁ ποιητὴς ἐν παισὶν ᾠνοχόησε. Θεόφραστος γοῦν ἐν τῷ Περὶ Μέθης φησί· πυνθάνομαι δ' ἔγωγε καὶ Εὐριπίδην τὸν ποιητὴν οἰνοχοεῖν
f  Ἀθήνησι τοῖς ὀρχησταῖς καλουμένοις. ὠρχοῦντο | δὲ οὗτοι περὶ τὸν τοῦ Ἀπόλλωνος νεὼν τοῦ Δηλίου τῶν πρώτων ὄντες Ἀθηναίων καὶ ἐνεδύοντο ἱμάτια τῶν Θηραϊκῶν. ὁ δὲ Ἀπόλλων οὗτός ἐστιν ᾧ τὰ Θαργήλια ἄγουσι, καὶ διασῴζεται Φλυῆσιν ἐν τῷ Δαφνηφορείῳ γραφὴ περὶ τούτων. τὰ αὐτὰ ἱστορεῖ καὶ Ἱερώνυμος ὁ Ῥόδιος Ἀριστοτέλους ὢν μαθητής, καὶ οὗτος ἐν τῷ Περὶ Μέθης. Σαπφώ τε ἡ καλὴ πολλαχοῦ Λάριχον τὸν
425  ἀδελφὸν || ἐπαινεῖ ὡς οἰνοχοοῦντα ἐν τῷ πρυτανείῳ τοῖς Μυτιληναίοις. καὶ παρὰ Ῥωμαίοις δὲ οἱ εὐγενέστατοι τῶν παίδων τὴν λειτουργίαν ταύτην ἐκτελοῦσιν ἐν ταῖς δημοτελέσι τῶν θυσιῶν, πάντα τοὺς Αἰολεῖς μιμούμενοι, ὡς καὶ κατὰ τοὺς τόνους τῆς φωνῆς. τοσαύτη δ' ἦν ἡ τῶν παλαιοτέρων τρυφὴ περὶ

---

31 Cited (but not quoted) also at 1.18b; 5.192b–c.

32 Phlya was Euripides' ancestral deme, and "the Laurel-Bearer" was a cult-name of Apollo. The Thargelia festival was celebrated in Athens in late May and was common to a number of Ionian cities, hence presumably the connection to the temple specifically of Delian Apollo.

They mix (*kerannuousin*) (wine) and make it
   disappear.

Hyperides in *On Delos* (fr. 69 Jensen): And the Greeks col-
lectively mix (*kerannuousin*) the Panionian mixing-bowl.
Among the ancients, the boys from the best families used
to pour the wine, as for example Menelaus' son (*Od*.
15.141):[31]

And the son of famous Menelaus poured the wine.

The poet Euripides (test. 20) was also one of the boys who
poured wine. Theophrastus, at any rate, says in his *On
Drunkenness* (fr. 576 Fortenbaugh = E. test. 33b): I myself
have heard that the poet Euripides used to pour wine in
Athens for the so-called "dancers". These were members
of the most distinguished Athenian families, who danced
around the temple of Delian Apollo wearing Thracian
robes. This is the Apollo in whose honor they celebrate the
Thargelia festival, and a painting that depicts these events
is preserved in the sanctuary of the Laurel-Bearer in
Phlya.[32] Hieronymus of Rhodes, who was a pupil of Aristotle, tells the same story in his *On Drunkenness* (fr. 28
Wehrli). The lovely Sappho (fr. 203a) repeatedly praises
her brother Larichus for pouring wine in the town-hall for
the Mytileneans. Among the Romans as well, the sons of
the noblest families perform this duty at public sacrifices,
imitating the Aeolians in all respects, including in the accent with which they speak.[33] The luxury the ancients en-

[33] Latin was believed by some ancient authorities to be a dialect of Greek and in particular to be most closely related to Ae-
olian (in which Sappho wrote); cf. Stevens, *CJ* 102 (2006/7) 115–
44.

τὰς πολυτελείας ὥστε μὴ μόνον οἰνοχόους ἔχειν, ἀλλὰ
καὶ οἰνόπτας. ἀρχὴ γοῦν ἐστιν οἱ οἰνόπται παρὰ
Ἀθηναίοις, ἧς μνημονεύει ἐν ταῖς Πόλεσιν Εὔπολις ἐν
τούτοις· |

b     οὓς δ' οὐκ ἂν εἵλεσθ' οὐδ' ἂν οἰνόπτας πρὸ τοῦ,
    νυνὶ στρατηγοὺς < ... >. ὦ πόλις, πόλις,
    ὡς εὐτυχὴς εἶ μᾶλλον ἢ καλῶς φρονεῖς.

οἱ δὲ οἰνόπται οὗτοι ἐφεώρων τὰ ἐν τοῖς δείπνοις, εἰ
κατ' ἴσον πίνουσιν οἱ συνόντες. καὶ ἦν ἡ ἀρχὴ εὐ-
τελής, ὡς ὁ ῥήτωρ φησὶ Φιλῖνος ἐν τῇ Κροκωνιδῶν
Διαδικασίᾳ· καὶ ὅτι τρεῖς ἦσαν οἱ οἰνόπται, οἵτινες καὶ
παρεῖχον τοῖς δειπνοῦσι λύχνους καὶ θρυαλλίδας.

c ἐκάλουν δέ τινες τούτους καὶ ὀφθαλμούς. | παρὰ δὲ
Ἐφεσίοις οἱ οἰνοχοοῦντες ἤθεοι τῇ τοῦ Ποσειδῶνος
ἑορτῇ ταῦροι ἐκαλοῦντο, ὡς Ἀμερίας φησί. Ἑλλη-
σπόντιοι δ' ἐπεγχύτην ὀνομάζουσι τὸν οἰνοχόον καὶ
τὴν κρεανομίαν κρεωδαισίαν, ὥς φησι Δημήτριος ὁ
Σκήψιος ἐν ἕκτῳ καὶ εἰκοστῷ τοῦ Τρωϊκοῦ Διακόσμου.
τοῖς δὲ θεοῖς οἰνοχοοῦσάν τινες ἱστοροῦσι τὴν Ἁρ-
μονίαν, ὡς Καπίτων ἱστορεῖ ὁ ἐποποιός, Ἀλεξανδρεὺς
δὲ γένος, ἐν δευτέρῳ Ἐρωτικῶν. Ἀλκαῖος δὲ καὶ τὸν
Ἑρμῆν εἰσάγει αὐτῶν οἰνοχόον, ὡς καὶ Σαπφὼ λέ-
γουσα·

d     κῆ δ' | ἀμβροσίας μὲν

---

34 < epencheō, "pour in from above".
35 Various portions of the same fragment are quoted at 2.39a;
11.475a; cf. 5.192c.

joyed was so extravagantly expensive that they had not just wine-pourers, but wine-inspectors. The wine-inspectors, at any rate, were a class of magistrates in Athens, and the office is mentioned by Eupolis in his *Cities* (fr. 219), in the following passage:

> men you wouldn't have chosen previously as wine-
>     inspectors,
> but are now generals . . . Oh city, city!
> You're lucky rather than clever!

These wine-inspectors kept an eye on what went on at dinner parties, making sure that the guests drank equal amounts. The office was an undistinguished one, as the orator Philinus notes in his *Lawsuit Involving the Croconidae* (II, ii.219 Baiter–Sauppe); he also says that there were three wine-inspectors, who supplied the dinner-guests with lamps and wicks. Some people referred to them instead as "eyes". The young men who poured wine at the festival of Poseidon in Ephesus were known as "bulls", according to Amerias (p. 6 Hoffmann). The inhabitants of the Hellespont refer to the boy who pours wine as an *epenchutēs*,[34] and to the woman who divides the meat among the guests as a *kreōdaisia* ("meat-distributer"), according to Demetrius of Scepsis in Book XXVI of his *Trojan Battle-Order* (fr. 16 Gaede). Some authorities report that Harmonia pours wine for the gods, according to the epic poet Capito, whose family was from Alexandria, in Book II of the *Erotica*. But Alcaeus (fr. 447) introduces Hermes as their wine-pourer, as does Sappho (fr. 141.1–3)[35] when she says:

> A bowl of ambrosia

κράτηρ ἐκέκρατ᾽,
   Ἕρμαις δ᾽ ἔλων ὄλπιν θέοισ᾽ ἐοινοχόησε.

οἱ δὲ παλαιοὶ τοὺς πρὸς ταῖς ὑπηρεσίαις ταύταις
κήρυκας ἐκάλουν. Ὅμηρος·

κήρυκες δ᾽ ἀνὰ ἄστυ φέρον θεῶν[4] ὅρκια πιστά,
ἄρνε δύω καὶ οἶνον ἐύφρονα, καρπὸν ἀρούρης,
ἀσκῷ ἐν αἰγείῳ· φέρε δὲ κρητῆρα φαεινὸν
κῆρυξ Ἰδαῖος ἠδὲ χρύσεια κύπελλα.

καὶ πάλιν· |

e
                        ἀτὰρ κήρυκες ἀγαυοὶ
ὅρκια πιστὰ θεῶν σύναγον, κρητῆρι δὲ οἶνον
μίσγον, ἀτὰρ βασιλεῦσιν ὕδωρ ἐπὶ χεῖρας
    ἔχευαν.

Κλείδημος δὲ τοὺς μαγείρους κήρυκάς φησι καλεῖσθαι. καὶ τὴν Ἥβην δέ τινες ἀνέπλασαν οἰνοχοοῦσαν
αὐτοῖς, ἴσως διὰ τὸ ἡβητήρια καλεῖσθαι τὰ συμπόσια. Κλεινοῦς δὲ τῆς οἰνοχόου Πτολεμαίου τοῦ
βασιλέως, ἐπίκλην δὲ Φιλαδέλφου, μνημονεύει Πτο-
f λεμαῖος ὁ τοῦ Ἀγησάρχου | ἐν τῇ τρίτῃ τῶν Περὶ

---

[4] The manuscripts of Homer have θεῶν φέρον.

---

[36] The second half of the verse is quoted also at 2.40a.

[37] A much fuller account of Cleidemus' speculations is preserved at 14.660a–e.

[38] The remark ought to follow directly on the reference to
Hermes as wine-pourer in Alcaeus and Sappho above, marking
the material on heralds that intervenes as drawn from a different
source.

had been mixed up there,
> and Hermes picked up a vessel and poured wine
> > for the gods.

The ancients referred to the individuals assigned to provide these services as heralds. Homer (*Il.* 3.245–8):

> And heralds brought the gods' pledge-victims, by
> > which trust is established, through the city,
> that is, two lambs and cheerful wine, crop of the
> > field,[36]
> in a goatskin bag. And the herald Idaeus brought
> a shining mixing-bowl and gold goblets.

And again (*Il.* 3.268–70):

> > But the noble heralds
> assembled the gods' pledge-victims, by which trust is
> > established, and mixed
> wine in a bowl, and poured water over the kings'
> > hands.

Cleidemus (*FGrH* 323 F 5c)[37] claims that cooks were referred to as heralds. But some sources represented Hebe
as pouring wine for them instead,[38] perhaps because
drinking parties are referred to *hēbētēria*.[39] Cleino, the
woman who poured wine for King Ptolemy (nicknamed
Philadelphus),[40] is mentioned by Ptolemy son of Agesar-
chus in Book III of his *History Involving Philopator*

---

[39] Cf. Hdt. 2.133.4, quoted at 10.438b (although the traditional text of Herodotus has *enēbētēria*).

[40] Ptolemy II (reigned 285/3–246 BCE).

Φιλοπάτορα Ἱστοριῶν. Πολύβιος δὲ ἐν τῇ τεσσαρεσ-
καιδεκάτῃ τῶν Ἱστοριῶν καὶ ἀνδριάντας αὐτῆς ἐν
Ἀλεξανδρείᾳ ἑστάναι φησὶ κατὰ πολλὰ μέρη τῆς
πόλεως μονοχίτωνας, ῥυτὸν κρατοῦντας ἐν ταῖς χερσίν.

Ἐπὶ τούτοις τοῖς λόγοις ἐκπίνων τὸ ποτήριον ὁ
Οὐλπιανὸς ἔφη· ‖

426
     (A.) τήνδ᾽ ἐγὼ
μεστὴν ἅπαξ ἐπονομάσας προπίομαι
συγγενέσι πίστωμα φιλίας.

πρὸς ὃν ἔτι πίνοντα τῶν παρόντων τις προσέθηκε τὰ
λειπόμενα ἰαμβεῖα·

       πιὼν ἐρῶ
τὰ λοιπά· πνίγομαι γάρ. (Β.) ἀλλ᾽ ἐπιρρόφει.

καὶ ὁ Οὐλπιανὸς ἐκπιὼν ἔφη· ταῦτα μὲν Κλέαρχος ἐν
Κιθαρῳδῷ. ἐγὼ δὲ κατὰ τοὺς Ἄμφιδος Ἐρίθους παρα-
κελεύομαι·

ὁ παῖς σοβείτω τοῖς ποτηρίοις συχνούς.

καί· |

b  πίμπλα σὺ μὲν ἐμοί, σοὶ δ᾽ ἐγὼ δώσω πιεῖν·
ἀμυγδαλῆ μὲν παιζέτω παρ᾽ ἀμυγδαλῆν.

ταῦτα δ᾽ ἔφη Ξέναρχος ἐν Διδύμοις. αἰτούντων οὖν

---

41 Cleino is otherwise unknown. But her position as Ptolemy's
wine-pourer is unusual enough that, given his appreciation of her
physical beauty (cf. the report from Polybius that follows), the his-
torian must have mentioned her as one of the king's lovers; cf.
13.577f.

(*FGrH* 161 F 3).[41] Polybius in Book XIV (11.2) of his *History* reports that statues of her wearing nothing but a tunic and holding a drinking-horn in her hands stood in Alexandria in many parts of the city.[42]

After he made these remarks, Ulpian began to drain his cup and said:

> (A.) After I recite their names,
> I'm going to drink this cup full of wine as a toast
> that represents a pledge of my affection for my
>     relatives.

While he was still drinking, one of the other guests responded by adding the rest of the iambic passage:

> And after I empty it, I'll tell you
> the rest; because I'm choking. (B.) Well—bottoms
>     up!

After he finished his drink, Ulpian said: Clearchus (said) this in *The Citharode* (fr. 1). But I have some advice drawn from Amphis' *Day-Laborers* (fr. 18):

> Let the slave drive us on repeatedly with the cups!

And:

> You fill a cup for me, and I'll give you a drink!
> Let the almonds play side-by-side!

Xenarchus said this in *Twins* (fr. 3). Some members of the

---

[42] The same passage is quoted at 13.576f (in the course of a discussion specifically of Ptolemy's appreciation of beautiful women).

τῶν μὲν πλέον οἴνου, τῶν δὲ ἴσον ἴσῳ φασκόντων
κίρνασθαι, καὶ εἰπόντος τινὸς Ἄρχιππον εἰρηκέναι ἐν
δευτέρῳ Ἀμφιτρύωνι·

τίς ἐκέρασε σφῶν, ὦ κακόδαιμον, ἴσον ἴσῳ;,

καὶ Κρατῖνος ἐν Πυτίνῃ·

τὸν δ' ἴσον ἴσῳ φέροντ'· ἐγὼ δ' ἐκτήκομαι,

c  ἔδοξε πᾶσι λέγειν περὶ τῶν κράσεων | τῶν παρὰ τοῖς
ἀρχαίοις. καί τινος εἰπόντος ὅτι Μένανδρος ἐν Ἥρωι
ἔφη·

χοῦς κεκραμένου
οἴνου· λαβὼν ἔκπιθι τοῦτον,

ὁ Δημόκριτος ἔφη· Ἡσίοδος μέν, ὦ ἑταῖροι, παραινεῖ

τρὶς ὕδατος προχέειν, τὸ δὲ τέτρατον ἱέμεν οἴνου.

δι' ὃν καὶ Ἀναξίλας ἐν Νηρεῖ ἔφη·

καίτοι πολύ γ' ἐσθ' ἥδιον· οὐ γὰρ ἄν ποτε
ἔπινον ⟨ἂν⟩ τρὶς ὕδατος, οἴνου δ' ἓν μόνον.

Ἄλεξις δ' ἐν Τιτθῇ ἔτι σωφρονικώτερον κιρνάναι
παρακελεύεται· |

d  (A.) ἰδού, πάρεστιν οἶνος· οὐκοῦν ἐγχέω
† κρίτωνα †; (B.) πολὺ βέλτιον ἕνα καὶ τέτταρας.

group requested more wine, while others asked for it to
be mixed one-to-one; and after someone observed that
Archippus says in *Amphitryon II* (fr. 2):

> Which of them mixed the wine one-to-one, you
>       bastard?,

and that Cratinus says in *The Wine-Flask* (fr. 196):

> wine that can take being mixed one-to-one; but I'm
>       wasting away,

everyone agreed to discuss how the ancients mixed their
wine. When one person observed that Menander said in
*The Hero* (fr. 4 Sandbach):

> a pitcher of mixed
> wine; take it and drink it up!,

Democritus said: Hesiod (*Op.* 596), my friends, advises us

> to pour three parts of water, and put in the fourth of
>       wine.

Anaxilas in *Nereus* (fr. 23) was alluding to him when he
said:

> even though it's a lot more delicious; because I'd
>       never
> drink three parts of water and only one of wine.

But Alexis in *The Wet-Nurse* (fr. 228) encourages us to mix
it even more moderately:

> (A.) Look—here's some wine; should I pour it in
> [corrupt]? (B.) One-to-four's a lot better.

(A.) ὑδαρῆ λέγεις· ὅμως δὲ ταύτην ἐκπιὼν
† λέγε τι καὶ † διατριβήν τε τῷ πότῳ
ποιῶμεν.

καὶ Διοκλῆς ἐν Μελίσσαις·

(A.) πῶς δὲ καὶ κεκραμένον
πίνειν τὸν οἶνον δεῖ με; (B.) τέτταρα καὶ δύο.

ἡ δ' οὖν κρᾶσις αὕτη παρὰ τὸ ἔθος οὖσα ἐπέμνησε
τάχα καὶ τὴν θρυλουμένην παροιμίαν·

ἢ πέντε πίνειν ἢ τρί' ἢ μὴ τέτταρα·

e  ἢ γὰρ δύο πρὸς | πέντε πίνειν φασὶ δεῖν ἢ ἕνα πρὸς
τρεῖς. περὶ δὲ ταύτης τῆς κράσεως Ἴων ὁ ποιητὴς ἐν
τῷ Περὶ Χίου φησὶν ὅτι εὑρὼν ὁ μάντις Παλαμήδης
ἐμαντεύσατο πλοῦν ἔσεσθαι τοῖς Ἕλλησι πίνουσιν
τρεῖς πρὸς ἕνα κυάθους. οἱ δ' ἐπιτεταμένως χρώμενοι
τῷ ποτῷ δύο οἴνου ἔπινον πρὸς πέντε ὕδατος. Νικο-
χάρης γοῦν ἐν Ἀμυμώνῃ πρὸς τοὔνομα παίζων ἔφη·

f  Οἰνόμαος | οὗτος, χαῖρε· πέντε καὶ δύο,
κἀγώ τε καὶ σὺ συμπόται γενοίμεθα.

τὰ παραπλήσια εἴρηκε καὶ ἐν Λημνίαις. Ἀμειψίας δ' ἐν
Ἀποκοτταβίζουσιν· † ἐγὼ δὲ Διόνυσος πᾶσιν ὑμῖν εἰμὶ
πέντε καὶ δύο. † Εὔπολις Αἰξί·

Διόνυσε χαῖρε· μή τι πέντε καὶ δύο;

---

43 Sc. to Troy.
44 The first element in the other man's name is *oinos* ("wine"),
hence the speaker's enthusiasm at having met him.

34

(A.) That's a watery mixture you're describing. But all
       the same, after you drink this
† say something and † and let's get busy
drinking!

Also Diocles in *Honey-Bees* (fr. 7):

                (A.) How should I mix
the wine I'm drinking? (B.) Four-to-two.

Because this proportion was unusual, it immediately
reminded us of the well-known proverb (adesp. com. fr.
*732):

   Drink either five or three, but at any rate not four.

Because people claim that you should drink either five-to-
two or three-to-one. As for the latter proportion, the poet
Ion in his *On Chios* (*FGrH* 392 F 2) claims that after
the seer Palamedes discovered it, he prophesied that the
Greeks would have a successful voyage[43] if they drank
three ladles (of water) for each one (of wine). People who
were drinking hard, on the other hand, used to consume
two parts of wine to five of water. Nicochares in *Amymone*
(fr. 2), for example, played on a character's name and said:

   Hey Oenomaus[44]—greetings! Five-to-two;
   let's you and me become drinking buddies.

He says something similar in *Lemnian Women* (fr. 16).
Amipsias in *Cottabus-Players* (fr. 4, unmetrical): † But I
am Dionysus for all of you five-to-two. † Eupolis in *Nanny-
Goats* (fr. 6):

   Greetings, Dionysus! Maybe five-to-two?

Ἕρμιππος Θεοῖς·

> ἔπειθ᾽ ὅταν πινώμεθ᾽ ἢ διψώμεθα,
> εὐχόμεθα πρὸς τοῦθ᾽ † ὁ οἶνος ωκαιρας γενου ‖
427  οὐκ ἀστου καὶ πηλουγω † φέρω παίζων ἅμα
> καυθεὶς γεγένηται τοῦτο πέντε καὶ δύο.

παρὰ δὲ Ἀνακρέοντι εἷς οἴνου πρὸς δύο ὕδατος·

> ἄγε δὴ φέρ᾽ ἡμὶν ὦ παῖ
> κελέβην, ὅκως ἄμυστιν
> προπίω, τὰ μὲν δέκ᾽ ἐγχέας
> ὕδατος, τὰ πέντε δ᾽ οἴνου
> κυάθους ὡς ἂν † ὑβριστιῶς †
> ἀνὰ δηῦτε βασσαρήσω.

καὶ προελθὼν τὴν ἀκρατοποσίαν Σκυθικὴν καλεῖ πό-
σιν·

> ἄγε δηῦτε μηκέτ᾽ οὕτω
> πατάγῳ τε κἀλαλητῷ
b  Σκυθικὴν πόσιν | παρ᾽ οἴνῳ
> μελετῶμεν, ἀλλὰ καλοῖς
> ὑποπίνοντες ἐν ὕμνοις.

καὶ Λακεδαιμόνιοι δ᾽, ὥς φησιν Ἡρόδοτος ἐν τῇ ἕκτῃ,
Κλεομένη τὸν βασιλέα Σκύθαις ὁμιλήσαντα καὶ
ἀκρατοπότην γενόμενον ἐκ τῆς μέθης φασὶ μανῆναι.
καὶ αὐτοὶ δ᾽ οἱ Λάκωνες ὅταν βούλωνται ἀκρατέστερον
πίνειν, ἐπισκυθίσαι λέγουσι. Χαμαιλέων γοῦν ὁ Ἡρακλεώτης ἐν τῷ Περὶ Μέθης περὶ τούτων οὕτως γράφει·

---

45 A slightly shorter version of the fragment is quoted at
11.475c.     46 Cf. 11.499f.     47 Cleomenes I (Poralla
#436), reigned c.520–490 BCE. Cf. 10.436e.

Hermippus in *Gods* (fr. 24):

> Then whenever we drink or we're thirsty,
> we pray to this † the wine [corrupt]
> not [corrupt] and [corrupt] † I bring, joking that
>     when it
> got hot, it turned into five-to-two.

But in Anacreon (*PMG* 356(a))[45] the mixture is one part
wine to two parts water:

> Come on, slave—bring us
> a pot, so I can drink a toast
> without pausing to breathe, after I pour in ten
> ladles of water, followed by five of
> wine, letting me † violently †
> turn into a drunken madman.

And further on (*PMG* 356(b)) he refers to consuming unmixed wine as "Scythian drinking":[46]

> Come on—let's not practice
> Scythian drinking any longer,
> while we're consuming wine, with banging
> and shouting; instead, let's drink a bit
> to the accompaniment of beautiful hymns.

According to Herodotus in Book VI (84.1), the Spartans
too claim that after their king Cleomenes[47] spent time with
some Scythians and took up drinking unmixed wine, his
drunkenness drove him crazy. And whenever the Spartans
themselves want to drink particularly strong wine (*akratesteron*), they say that they are drinking Scythian style.
Chamaeleon of Heracleia in his *On Drunkenness* (fr. 10
Wehrli), at any rate, writes the following about them: since

ἐπεὶ καὶ Κλεομένη τὸν Σπαρτιάτην φασὶν οἱ Λάκωνες
c μανῆναι διὰ τὸ Σκύθαις ὁμιλήσαντα | μαθεῖν ἀκρα-
τοποτεῖν. ὅθεν ὅταν βούλωνται πιεῖν ἀκρατέστερον,
"ἐπισκύθισον" λέγουσιν. Ἀχαιὸς δ' ἐν Αἴθωνι σατυρικῷ τοὺς σατύρους ποιεῖ δυσχεραίνοντας ἐπὶ τῷ
ὑδαρῆ πίνειν καὶ λέγοντας·

(Α.) μῶν Ἀχελῷος ἦν κεκραμένος πολύς;
(Β.) ἀλλ' οὐδὲ λεῖξαι τοῦδε τῷ γένει θέμις.
(Α.) καλῶς μὲν οὖν † ἄγειν σκύθη † πιεῖν.

Ἦσαν δ' αἱ τῶν ἀκρατοποτῶν ἐπιχύσεις, ὥς φησι
d Θεόφραστος ἐν τῷ Περὶ Μέθης, οὐ παλαιαί· ἀλλ' | ἦν
ἀπ' ἀρχῆς τὸ μὲν σπένδειν ἀποδεδομένον τοῖς θεοῖς, ὁ
δὲ κότταβος τοῖς ἐρωμένοις. ἐχρῶντο γὰρ ἐπιμελῶς τῷ
κοτταβίζειν ὄντος τοῦ παιγνίου Σικελικοῦ, καθάπερ
καὶ Ἀνακρέων ὁ Τήιος πεποίηκε·

Σικελὸν κότταβον ἀγκύλῃ † δαΐζων †.

διὸ καὶ τὰ σκολιὰ καλούμενα μέλη τῶν ἀρχαίων
ποιητῶν πλήρη ἐστί· λέγω δ' οἷον καὶ Πίνδαρος πε-
ποίηκε·

χάριτάς τ' Ἀφροδισίων ἐρώτων,
ὄφρα σὺν Χειμάρῳ μεθύων Ἀγαθωνίδᾳ
βάλω κότταβον.

---

48 The longest Greek river; it ran between Acarnania and
Aetolia, and empties into the Ionian Sea at the extreme northwest
end of the Gulf of Corinth.

49 A drinking game that involved tossing wine-lees at a target;
discussed at length at 15.665d–8f.

50 Sc. of references to cottabus and love together (see above),
the preceding remark about the Sicilian origins of the game hav-

the Spartans claim that Cleomenes the Spartiate went crazy because he spent time with Scythians and learned to drink unmixed wine. As a consequence, whenever they want to drink particularly strong wine (*akratesteron*), they say "Mix it Scythian style!" Achaeus in the satyr play *Aethon* (*TrGF* 20 F 9) represents the satyrs as being unhappy about drinking watery wine and saying:

> (A.) A lot of Acheloüs[48] wasn't mixed into it, was it?
> (B.) Our family's not allowed even to soil our tongues
>        with this!
> (A.) Well, then, it's alright † to bring Scythian † to
>        drink.

According to Theophrastus in his *On Drunkenness* (fr. 570 Fortenbaugh), it was not the ancient practice to pour toasts while drinking unmixed wine. Instead, the initial libations were reserved for the gods, while cottabus[49] was for the people you were in love with. Because they devoted considerable attention to cottabus, which was a Sicilian game, according to a passage of Anacreon of Teos (*PMG* 415):

> † dividing † the Sicilian cottabus with his wrist.

This is why the lyrics of the ancient poets known as skolia are full (of this).[50] I am referring to passages like the one composed by Pindar (fr. *128):

> and the pleasures of physical love,
> so that I can get drunk with Cheimarus and throw
> cottabus for Agathonidas.

ing been inserted from a different source. For skolia, see 15.693f–6d.

e τοῖς δὲ τετελευτηκόσι τῶν φίλων | ἀπένεμον τὰ πίπτον-
τα τῆς τροφῆς ἀπὸ τῶν τραπεζῶν. διὸ καὶ Εὐριπίδης
περὶ τῆς Σθενεβοίας φησίν, ἐπειδὴ νομίζει τὸν Βελ-
λεροφόντην τεθνάναι·

πεσὸν δέ νιν λέληθεν οὐδὲν ἐκ χερός,
ἀλλ᾽ εὐθὺς αὐδᾷ· "τῷ Κορινθίῳ ξένῳ."

Οὐκ ἐμέθυον δ᾽ οἱ πάλαι, ἀλλὰ καὶ Πιττακὸς Περιάνδρῳ τῷ Κορινθίῳ παρήνει μὴ μεθύσκεσθαι μηδὲ
f κωμάζειν, "ἵν᾽", ἔφη, "μὴ γνωσθῇς | οἷος ὢν τυγχάνεις,
ἀλλ᾽ οὐχ οἷος προσποιῇ."

κάτοπτρον (γὰρ) εἴδους χαλκός ἐστ᾽, οἶνος δὲ
νοῦ.

διὸ καὶ καλῶς οἱ παροιμιαζόμενοι λέγουσι τὸν οἶνον
οὐκ ἔχειν πηδάλια. Ξενοφῶν γοῦν ὁ Γρύλου παρὰ
Διονυσίῳ ποτὲ τῷ Σικελιώτῃ πίνειν ἀναγκάζοντος τοῦ
οἰνοχόου προσαγορεύσας ὀνομαστὶ τὸν τύραννον, "τί
428 δή," ἔφη, "ὦ Διονύσιε, ‖ οὐχὶ καὶ ὁ ὀψοποιὸς ἀγαθὸς
ὢν καὶ ποικίλος ἀναγκάζει ἡμᾶς εὐωχουμένους ἐσθίειν
καὶ μὴ βουλομένους, ἀλλὰ κοσμίως ἡμῖν παρατίθησι
τὴν τράπεζαν σιγῶν;" καὶ ὁ Σοφοκλῆς δὲ ἐν σατυρικῷ
φησιν ὡς ἄρα

---

51 Stheneboea was the wife of King Proetus of Tiryns, but fell
in love with Bellerophon, a visitor from Corinth. When
Bellerophon refused to sleep with her, she accused him of rape,
and he was sent off to King Iobates of Lycia with orders that a way
be found to assure his death. The second verse of the fragment is
parodied at Cratin. fr. 299.4 (quoted at 11.782e).

52 Pittacus of Mitylene (c.650–570 BCE) was a politician and
one of the traditional Seven Sages, as was the less savory
Periander of Corinth (tyrant c.627–587 BCE).

They dedicated the bits of food that fell off the table to their dead friends. This explains what Euripides (fr. 664) says about Stheneboea, when she believes that Bellerophon is dead:[51]

> She notices every crumb that drops from her hand,
> and immediately says: "For the Corinthian stranger!"

People did not get drunk in the old days, and Pittacus in fact advised Periander of Corinth not to get drunk or become involved in wild parties, "So that no one realizes", he said, "the sort of person you actually are, letting you pretend to be the sort of person you aren't."[52] For (A. fr. 393)

> Bronze reflects your appearance, but wine reflects
> the mind.[53]

This is why people who like to quote proverbs are right to say that wine lacks rudders (Strömberg p. 30). When Xenophon the son of Gryllus,[54] at any rate, was visiting Dionysius of Sicily once, and the wine-pourer tried to force him to drink, he addressed the tyrant by name and said: "Why is it, Dionysius, that your chef, who's talented and inventive, doesn't force us to eat when we're at a feast and don't want anything, but instead keeps quiet and calmly sets the table beside us?" Sophocles as well says in a satyr play (fr. 735) that in fact

---

[53] The fragment is assigned to Aeschylus by Stobaeus.

[54] I.e. the famous Xenophon of Athens (*PAA* 734300). The Dionysius in question may well be Dionysius II (tyrant of Syracuse 367–357 BCE), who was both interested in philosophy and a heavy drinker, in which case the anecdote belongs to the final years of Xenophon's life.

τὸ πρὸς βίαν
πίνειν ἴσον πέφυκε τῷ διψῆν κακόν.

ὅθεν εἴρηται καὶ τὸ οἶνος ἄνωγε γέροντα καὶ οὐκ
ἐθέλοντα χορεύειν. Σθένελός τε ὁ ποιητὴς οὐ κακῶς
εἴρηκεν·

οἶνος καὶ φρονέοντας ἐς ἀφροσύνην ἀναβάλλει. |

b ὁ δὲ Φωκυλίδης ἔφη·

χρὴ δ᾽ ἐν συμποσίῳ κυλίκων περινισομενάων
ἡδέα κωτίλλοντα καθήμενον οἰνοποτάζειν.

ἔτι δὲ καὶ νῦν τοῦτο παραμένει παρ᾽ ἐνίοις τῶν Ἑλλήνων. ἐπεὶ δὲ τρυφᾶν ἤρξαντο καὶ χλιδῆσαι[5], κατερ-
ρύησαν ἀπὸ τῶν δίφρων ἐπὶ τὰς κλίνας καὶ λαβόντες
σύμμαχον τὴν ἀνάπαυσιν καὶ ῥαστώνην ἀνειμένως
ἤδη καὶ ἀτάκτως ἐχρῶντο τῇ μέθῃ, ὀδηγούσης οἶμαι
τῆς παρασκευῆς εἰς τὰς ἡδονάς. διὸ καὶ Ἡσίοδος ἐν
ταῖς Ἠοίαις εἶπεν· |

c οἷα Διώνυσος δῶκ᾽ ἀνδράσι χάρμα καὶ ἄχθος.
ὅστις ἄδην πίνῃ, οἶνος δέ οἱ ἔπλετο μάργος,
σὺν δὲ πόδας χεῖράς τε δέει γλῶσσάν τε νόον τε
δεσμοῖς ἀφράστοισι, φιλεῖ δέ ἑ μαλθακὸς ὕπνος.

καὶ Θέογνις δέ φησιν·[6]

ἥκω δ᾽ ὡς οἶνος χαριέστατος ἀνδρὶ πεπόσθαι·
οὔτε τι νήφων εἴμ᾽ οὔτε λίαν μεθύων.

---

[5] χλίδησαι Olson: χλιδῶσι A
[6] The version of the text preserved by Athenaeus varies widely
from the traditional one preserved in the manuscripts and printed
by West.

being forced to
drink is just as bad as being thirsty.

This is the source of the saying that wine encourages an old man to dance even when he does not want to.[55] The poet Sthenelus (*TrGF* 32 T 4 = *SH* 736) was not wrong to say:

> Wine drives even thoughtful people to thoughtless
>     behavior.

And Phocylides (fr. 14 Diehl³) said:

> As the cups are going around at a party, you should
> sit there and chatter pleasantly as you drink your
>     wine.

This is still the custom even today among some Greeks. But when they began to live a pampered, luxurious lifestyle, they slipped off their chairs onto couches; made relaxation and leisure their allies; and began to get drunk in a careless, sloppy way, being led into hedonism, in my opinion, by their possessions. This is why Hesiod in the *Ehoiai* (fr. 239) said:

> Just as Dionysus gave men both pleasure and trouble.
> If someone drinks as much as he wants, the wine
>     assaults him like a madman,
> and wraps his feet, hands, tongue, and mind
> in invisible bonds, and soft sleep welcomes him.

Theognis (477–86) as well says:

> I have come like wine a man is delighted to drink;
>     I am not the least bit sober, but neither am I too
>     drunk.

[55] Cf. Eriph. fr. 1 (quoted at 4.134c); Macar. 6.25.

43

ὃς δ᾽ ἂν ὑπερβάλλῃ πόσιος μέτρον, οὐκέτ᾽
ἐκεῖνος |

d     τῆς αὐτοῦ γνώμης καρτερὸς οὐδὲ νόου·
μυθεῖται δ᾽ ἀπάλαμνα, τὰ νήφοσι γίγνεται
αἰσχρά,
αἰδεῖται δ᾽ ἔρδων οὐδὲν ὅταν μεθύῃ,
τὸ πρὶν ἐὼν σώφρων τε καὶ ἤπιος. ἀλλὰ σὺ
ταῦτα
γιγνώσκων μὴ πῖν᾽ οἶνον ὑπερβολάδην,
πρὶν μεθύειν ἄρξῃ δ᾽, ἀπανίστασο, μή σε
βιάσθω
γαστὴρ ὥστε κακὸν λάτριν ἐφημέριον.

Ἀνάχαρσίς τε ὁ σοφὸς ἐπιδεικνύμενος τὴν τῆς ἀμπέλου δύναμιν τῷ τῶν Σκυθῶν βασιλεῖ καὶ τὰ κλή-
e ματα | αὐτῆς δεικνὺς ἔλεγεν ὡς εἰ μὴ καθ᾽ ἕκαστον
ἔτος ἔτεμνον οἱ Ἕλληνες τὴν ἄμπελον, ἤδη κἂν ἐν
Σκύθαις ἦν.

Οὐ καλῶς δὲ οἱ πλάττοντες καὶ γράφοντες τὸν
Διόνυσον, ἔτι τε οἱ ἄγοντες ἐπὶ τῆς ἁμάξης διὰ μέσης
τῆς ἀγορᾶς οἰνωμένον· ἐπιδείκνυνται γὰρ τοῖς θεαταῖς
ὅτι καὶ τοῦ θεοῦ κρείττων ἐστὶν ὁ οἶνος. καίτοι γ᾽ οὐδ᾽
ἄν, οἶμαι, ἄνθρωπος σπουδαῖος τοῦθ᾽ ὑπομείνειεν. εἰ δ᾽
ὅτι κατέδειξεν ἡμῖν τὸν οἶνον, διὰ τοῦτο ποιοῦσιν
f αὐτὸν οὕτως διακείμενον, δῆλον ὅτι καὶ τὴν | Δήμητρα
θερίζουσαν ἢ ἐσθίουσαν ποιήσουσιν. ἐπεὶ καὶ τὸν
Αἰσχύλον ἐγὼ φαίην ἂν τοῦτο διαμαρτάνειν· πρῶτος

---

56 A legendary Scythian wise man, mentioned already by
Herodotus (4.46.1, 76–7); cf. 4.159c; 10.437f–8a, 445f; 14.613d.

57 For Scythia as a land without grapevines, cf. Antiph. fr. 58
(quoted at 10.441d). But the Scythians certainly enjoyed wine
when they imported it from elsewhere (10.427a–c).

If someone drinks more than is appropriate, he is no
        longer
    in control of his thoughts and his mind;
he makes foolish remarks that embarrass sober
        people,
    and his behavior is shameless when he is drunk,
even if he was previously sensible and gentle. But
        since you understand
    this, do not drink excessive amounts of wine;
get up and leave before you start feeling drunk, so
        that your stomach
    does not turn on you, as if you were a low-born
        day-laborer.

When the wise Anacharsis[56] (fr. A24 Kindstrand) explained the power of the grapevine to the Scythian king, he
showed him its tendrils and said that if the Greeks did not
cut their vines back every year, they would already have
made their way to Scythia.[57]

The sculptors and painters who represent Dionysus as
intoxicated are making a mistake, as are the people who
drag him through the middle of the marketplace on a
wagon in the same condition;[58] because they are sending a
message to the audience that the god is less powerful than
his wine. No serious person, I am convinced, would accept
this. And if (the claim is) that they represent him in this
condition because he taught us about wine, they will obviously want to represent Demeter as harvesting or eating
grain! Since I would say that Aeschylus (test. 117a) makes

---

[58] Sc. as part of a festival procession in honor of the god.

45

γὰρ ἐκεῖνος καὶ οὐχ, ὡς ἔνιοί φασιν, Εὐριπίδης παρ-
ήγαγε τὴν τῶν μεθυόντων ὄψιν εἰς τραγῳδίαν· ἐν γὰρ
τοῖς Καβείροις εἰσάγει τοὺς περὶ τὸν Ἰάσονα μεθύ-
οντας. ἃ δ᾽ αὐτὸς ὁ τραγῳδιοποιὸς ἐποίει, ταῦτα τοῖς
ἥρωσι περιέθηκε· μεθύων γοῦν ἔγραφε τὰς τραγῳδίας.
διὸ καὶ Σοφοκλῆς αὐτῷ μεμφόμενος ἔλεγεν ὅτι "ὦ
Αἰσχύλε, εἰ καὶ τὰ δέοντα ποιεῖς, ἀλλ᾽ οὖν οὐκ εἰδώς γε
ποιεῖς," ὡς ἱστορεῖ Χαμαιλέων ἐν τῷ Περὶ Αἰσχύλου.
429  ἀγνοοῦσί τε οἱ λέγοντες πρῶτον Ἐπίχαρμον ‖ ἐπὶ τὴν
σκηνὴν παραγαγεῖν μεθύοντα, μεθ᾽ ὃν Κράτητα ἐν
Γείτοσι. καὶ Ἀλκαῖος δὲ ὁ μελοποιὸς καὶ Ἀριστοφάνης
ὁ κωμῳδιοποιὸς μεθύοντες ἔγραφον τὰ ποιήματα, πολλοὶ δὲ καὶ ἄλλοι μεθυσκόμενοι λαμπρότερον ἐν τῷ
πολέμῳ ἠγωνίσαντο. παρὰ δὲ Λοκροῖς τοῖς Ἐπιζεφυ-
ρίοις εἴ τις ἄκρατον ἔπιε μὴ προστάξαντος ἰατροῦ
θεραπείας ἕνεκα, θάνατος ἦν ἡ ζημία Ζαλεύκου τὸν
νόμον θέντος. παρὰ δὲ Μασσαλιήταις ἄλλος νόμος
τὰς γυναῖκας ὑδροποτεῖν. ἐν δὲ Μιλήτῳ ἔτι καὶ νῦν
b  φησι Θεόφραστος | τοῦτ᾽ εἶναι τὸ νόμιμον. παρὰ δὲ
Ῥωμαίοις οὔτε οἰκέτης οἶνον ἔπινεν οὔτε γυνὴ ἐλευ-
θέρα οὔτε τῶν ἐλευθέρων οἱ ἔφηβοι μέχρι τριάκοντα
ἐτῶν. ἄτοπος δὲ ὁ Ἀνακρέων ὁ πᾶσαν αὐτοῦ τὴν
ποίησιν ἐξαρτήσας μέθης· τῇ γὰρ μαλακίᾳ καὶ τῇ

---

59 Cf. Radt on Aeschylus' *Cabeiroi* (*TrGF* III p. 214).

60 A condensed (epitomized) version of the same material is
preserved at 1.22a–b.

61 According to Arist. *Po.* 1449[b]5–9 (drawing on what hard evidence, if any, we do not know), Crates' new, structurally more
sophisticated style of comedy was directly dependent on the work
of the Sicilian poets.

this mistake; because he—and not Euripides, as some authorities assert—was the first to bring the spectacle of drunks onto the tragic stage, given that he brings Jason's companions onstage drunk in his *Cabeiroi*.[59] The tragic poet attributed the same behavior to his heroes as he indulged in himself; at any rate, he used to write his tragedies drunk, which is why Sophocles (test. 52a) criticized him and said: "Aeschylus, even if you find the right words, you do so unconsciously," according to Chamaeleon in his *On Aeschylus* (fr. 40a Wehrli).[60] Those who claim that Epicharmus, followed by Crates in *Neighbors*,[61] was the first to bring a drunk on stage, are similarly ill-informed.[62] The lyric poet Alcaeus and the comic poet Aristophanes also produced their poetry while drunk, and many other men fought more brilliantly in war when drunk. In Epizypherian Locris, if anyone drank unmixed wine without a doctor requiring him to do so for medicinal purposes, the penalty was death; the law was proposed by Zaleucus.[63] In Massilia there is a different law, which specifies that women are to drink nothing but water; this is still the custom even today in Miletus, according to Theophrastus (fr. 579b Fortenbaugh). In Rome no slave or free woman used to drink wine, and neither did any free boy under the age of 30. Anacreon, who connected all his poetry to drunkenness, is an unusual case; he is maligned for surrendering

[62] The testimonium (like the mention of Aristophanes in the sentence that follows) is omitted in Kassel–Austin.

[63] Zaleucus (mid-7th century BCE) was the great lawgiver of Epizypherian Locris and was famous for his severity. Ael. *VH* 2.37–8 appears to be drawing on the same source (through the description of Roman drinking habits).

τρυφῇ ἐπιδοὺς ἑαυτὸν ἐν τοῖς ποιήμασι διαβέβληται,
οὐκ εἰδότων τῶν πολλῶν ὅτι νήφων ἐν τῷ γράφειν καὶ
ἀγαθὸς ὢν προσποιεῖται μεθύειν οὐκ οὔσης ἀνάγκης.

Οἱ δὲ ἀγνοοῦντες τὴν τοῦ οἴνου δύναμιν τὸν
Διόνυσον φάσκουσιν μανιῶν εἶναι αἴτιον τοῖς ἀνθρώ-
c  ποις, | βλασφημοῦντες οὐ μετρίως. ὅθεν ὁ Μελαν-
ιππίδης ἔφη·

πάντες δ᾽ ἀπεστύγεον ὕδωρ
τὸ πρὶν ἐόντες ἀίδριες οἴνου·
τάχα δὴ τάχα τοὶ μὲν οὖν ἀπωλλύοντο,
τοὶ δὲ παράπληκτον χέον ὀμφάν.

Ἀριστοτέλης δ᾽ ἐν τῷ Περὶ Μέθης φησίν· εἰ ὁ οἶνος
μετρίως ἀφεψηθείη, πινόμενος ἧττον μεθύσκει· τὴν
γὰρ δύναμιν ἀφεψηθέντος αὐτοῦ ἀσθενεστέραν γίγνε-
σθαι. μεθύσκονταί τε, φησίν, οἱ γεραίτεροι τάχιστα
δι᾽ ὀλιγότητα καὶ ἀσθένειαν τοῦ περὶ αὐτοὺς ἐνυπάρ-
d  χοντος φύσει θερμοῦ. καὶ οἱ παντελῶς δὲ | νέοι τάχιον
μεθύσκονται διὰ τὸ πλῆθος τοῦ ἐνυπάρχοντος θερμοῦ·
τῷ γὰρ ἐκ τοῦ οἴνου προσγινομένῳ κρατοῦνται ῥᾳδίως. μεθύσκονται δὲ κἂν τοῖς ἀλόγοις ζῴοις ὕες μὲν
σταφυλῆς στεμφύλων χορτασθέντες καὶ τὸ τῶν κοράκων καὶ τῶν κυνῶν γένος τὴν οἰνοῦτταν καλουμένην
φαγόντα βοτάνην, πίθηκος δὲ καὶ ἐλέφας πιόντες
οἶνον. διὸ καὶ τὰς θήρας ποιοῦνται τῶν πιθήκων καὶ
τῶν κοράκων μεθυσθέντων, τῶν μὲν οἴνῳ, τῶν δὲ τῇ
οἰνούττᾳ.

τὸ δ᾽ ἐνδελεχῶς μεθύειν,

himself to effeminate luxury in his poetry, but most people are unaware that he was sober when he composed, and merely pretended to be drunk, despite being a decent person, when there was no need to do so.

Those who misunderstand the power of wine claim that Dionysus is responsible for people going insane, which is an extraordinarily blasphemous assertion. This is why Melanippides (*PMG* 760) said:

> They all came to despise water,
> despite having previously known nothing of wine;
> and very very soon some of them died,
> while others began to talk like lunatics.

Aristotle says in his *On Drunkenness* (fr. 669): If wine is boiled down a bit, it is less intoxicating when consumed; because its strength is reduced when it is boiled. Older people, he claims, get drunk more rapidly, because they have less natural heat inside them and the heat is weaker. The very young, on the other hand, get drunk quite rapidly because of the large amount of heat inside them; for they are easily overpowered by the additional heat that comes from the wine. Of the irrational animals, pigs get drunk when fed grape pomace, as do ravens and dogs when they eat the plant known as *oinoutta*,[64] and monkeys and elephants when they drink wine. This is why people hunt monkeys and ravens when the animals are drunk, the former on wine, the latter on *oinoutta*.

But what pleasure is there,

[64] Cognate with *oinos* ("wine").

φησὶ Κρώβυλος ἐν Ἀπολειπούσῃ, |

e
τίν' ἡδονὴν ἔχει
ἀποστεροῦντα ζῶνθ' ἑαυτὸν τοῦ φρονεῖν,
ὃ μέγιστον ἡμῶν ἀγαθὸν ἔσχεν ἡ φύσις;

καὶ Ἄλεξις δὲ ἐν τῇ τοῦ Φρυγίου διασκευῇ φησιν·

εἰ τοῦ μεθύσκεσθαι πρότερον τὸ κραιπαλᾶν
παρεγίγνεθ' ἡμῖν, οὐδ' ἂν εἷς οἶνόν ποτε
προσίετο πλείω τοῦ μετρίου. νυνὶ δὲ τὴν
τιμωρίαν οὐ προσδοκῶντες τῆς μέθης
ἥξειν προχείρως τοὺς ἀκράτους πίνομεν. |

f τὸν δὲ Σαμαγόρειον οἶνον καλούμενόν φησιν ὁ
Ἀριστοτέλης ἀπὸ τριῶν κοτυλῶν κερασθεισῶν μεθύ-
σκειν ὑπὲρ τεσσαράκοντα ἄνδρας.

Ταῦτ' εἰπὼν ὁ Δημόκριτος καὶ πιὼν ἔφη· τούτοις εἴ
τις ἀντιλέγειν ἔχει, παρίτω. ἀκούσεται γὰρ κατὰ τὸν
Εὔηνον·

σοὶ μὲν ταῦτα δοκοῦντ' ἔστω, ἐμοὶ δὲ τάδε.

ἐγὼ δ' ἐπεὶ παρεξέβην περὶ τῶν ἀρχαίων κράσεων
διαλεγόμενος, ἐπαναλήψομαι τὸν λόγον τὰ ὑπὸ Ἀλ-
καίου τοῦ μελοποιοῦ λεχθέντα ἐπὶ νοῦν βαλλόμενος· ||
430 φησὶ γάρ που οὗτος·

< ... > ἔγχεε κέρναις ἕνα καὶ δύο.

---

65 Called *The Woman Who Left Her Husband* at 10.443f,
where the fragment is quoted again with a minor variant in the
first line.

66 A considerably longer version of the fragment is quoted in a
similar context at 9.367e. The entire section on Alcaeus that follows is treated by Voigt as fr. 464 (under the rubric "ad commen-
tationes antiquorum pertinentia").

says Crobylus in *The Woman Who Was Trying to Leave Her Husband*[65] (fr. 3),

> in being constantly drunk,
> if it means depriving yourself, while you're still alive,
> of the ability to think clearly,
> which is our best natural feature?

Alexis as well says in the revised version of his *The Phrygian* (fr. 257):

> If we had the hangover before
> we got drunk, no one would ever consume
> more wine than he should. But as it is, we
> don't expect there to be any penalty for
> getting drunk, so we readily drink unmixed wines.

Aristotle (fr. 670) claims that if as little as three cups of what is referred to as Samagoreian wine is mixed (with water), it can get more than 40 men drunk.

After he completed these remarks and had a drink, Democritus said: If anyone wants to object to anything I have said, let him step forward! Because the response he will get is, to quote Evenus (fr. 1.4 West[2]):[66]

> You can think that, but I think something else!

But since I digressed in my discussion of ancient mixing-proportions, I will return to my main topic, taking to heart the comment of the lyric poet Alcaeus (fr. 346.4), who says somewhere:[67]

> Mix it one-to-two, and pour it in the cup!

[67] The entire fragment is quoted at 10.430c–d, and most of it appears again at 11.481a.

ἐν τούτοις γάρ τινες οὐ τὴν κρᾶσιν οἴονται λέγειν
αὐτόν, ἀλλὰ σωφρονικὸν ὄντα καθ' ἕνα κύαθον[7] πίνειν
καὶ πάλιν κατὰ δύο. τοῦτο δὲ ὁ Ποντικὸς Χαμαιλέων
ἐκδέδεκται τῆς Ἀλκαίου φιλοινίας ἀπείρως ἔχων. κατὰ
γὰρ πᾶσαν ὥραν καὶ πᾶσαν περίστασιν πίνων ὁ
ποιητὴς οὗτος εὑρίσκεται· χειμῶνος μὲν ἐν τούτοις·

> ὕει μὲν ὁ Ζεύς, ἐκ δ' ὀράνω μέγας
> χείμων, πεπάγαισιν δ' ὑδάτων | ῥόαι

b

> \* \* \*
>
> κάββαλλε τὸν χείμων', ἐπὶ μὲν τίθεις
> πῦρ, ἐν δὲ κέρναις οἶνον ἀφειδέως
> μέλιχρον, αὐτὰρ ἀμφὶ κόρσᾳ
> μόλθακον ἀμφι< ... > γνόφαλλον.

θέρους δέ·

> τέγγε πλεύμονας οἴνῳ, τὸ γὰρ ἄστρον
> περιτέλλεται,
> ἀ δ' ὥρα χαλέπα, πάντα δὲ δίψαισ' ὑπὰ
> καύματος.

τοῦ δ' ἔαρος·

> ἦρος ἀνθεμόεντος ἐπάιον ἐρχομένοιο.

καὶ προελθών·

> ἐν δὲ κέρνατε τὼ μελιάδεος ὅττι τάχιστα
> κράτηρα.

---

[7] κύαθον ἄκρατον A: ἄκρατον del. Olson

For some authorities do not believe that he is referring in this passage to how the wine should be mixed, but insist that, being a temperate individual, he is encouraging his addressee to drink one ladleful at a time, and then two at a time. This is the interpretation of Chamaeleon of Pontus (fr. 12 Wehrli), who is unacquainted with Alcaeus' fondness for wine. Because this poet can be found drinking in every season and situation: during the winter (*cheimōn*), in the following passage (fr. 338.1–2, 5–8):

> Zeus is pouring rain, a great storm (*cheimōn*) is
>       descending
> from the sky, and the rivers' streams are frozen.
>
> \*       \*       \*
>
> Defeat the storm (*cheimōn*) by heaping wood on
> the fire and mixing up plenty of honey-like
> wine; and . . . soft wool
>       around your brow.

And in summer (fr. 347.1–2):[68]

> Moisten your lungs with wine. For the star[69] is rising,
> the season is a harsh one, and the heat makes
>       everything thirsty.

And in the spring (fr. 367.1):

> I realized that flowery spring was coming.

And further on (fr. 367.2–3):

> Mix up a bowl of honey-sweet wine as quick
> as you can!

[68] Quoted also at 1.22e–f.      [69] Sirius; see 1.22e n.

ἐν δὲ τοῖς συμπτώμασιν·

οὐ χρῆ κάκοισι θῦμον ἐπιτρέπην.
προκόψομεν γὰρ οὐδὲν ἀσάμενοι, |
ὦ Βύκχι· φάρμακον δ᾽ ἄριστον
οἶνον ἐνεικαμένοις μεθύσθην.

ἐν δὲ ταῖς εὐφρόναις·

νῦν χρῆ μεθύσθην καί τινα πρὸς βίαν
πώνην, ἐπεὶ δὴ κάτθανε Μύρσιλος.

καὶ καθόλου δὲ συμβουλεύων φησίν·

μηδὲν ἄλλο φυτεύσῃς πρότερον δένδρεον
ἀμπέλω.

πῶς οὖν ἔμελλεν ὁ ἐπὶ τοσοῦτον φιλοπότης νηφάλιος
εἶναι καὶ καθ᾽ ἕνα καὶ δύο κυάθους πίνειν; αὐτὸ γοῦν
τὸ ποιημάτιον, φησὶ Σέλευκος, ἀντιμαρτυρεῖ τοῖς οὕτως ἐκδεχομένοις. φησὶ γάρ·

πώνωμεν· τί τὰ λύχν᾽ | ὀμμένομεν; δάκτυλος
ἀμέρα.
κὰδ δ᾽ ἄερρε κυλίχναις μεγάλαις, ἄιτα,
ποικίλαις·
οἶνον γὰρ Σεμέλας καὶ Δίος υἶος λαθικάδεα
ἀνθρώποισιν ἔδωκ᾽. ἔγχεε κέρναις ἕνα καὶ δύο
πλήαις κὰκ κεφάλας, <ἀ> δ᾽ ἀτέρα τὰν ἀτέραν
κύλιξ
ὠθήτω,

In misfortune (fr. 335):

> We should not surrender our heart to troubles;
> for we'll get nowhere by being miserable,
> Bucchis. The best remedy
>     is to fetch some wine and get drunk.

And in happy times (fr. 332):

> Now everyone should get drunk and be forced
> to drink, since the fact is that Myrsilus is dead.

And in general his advice is (fr. 342):

> Plant no other tree before a grapevine.

How likely is it, then, that someone this fond of drinking is a teetotaler who consumes only one or two ladlesful at a time? The poem itself, at any rate, says Seleucus (fr. 79 Müller), contradicts those who interpret it this way. Because the poet says (Alc. fr. 346):[70]

> Let's drink! Why are we waiting for the lamps?
>         There's only a sliver of daylight left.
> Take down the fancy large cups, sweet boy;
> for the son of Semele and Zeus[71] gave human beings
>         wine
> to help them forget their troubles. Mix it one-to-two,
>         and pour it in the cup,
> filling it to the brim! Let the cups crowd against
> one another!,

[70] A shorter version of the fragment is quoted at 11.481a.
[71] Dionysus.

ἕνα πρὸς δύο ῥητῶς κιρνάναι κελεύων. ὁ δ᾽ Ἀνακρέων
ἔτι ζωρότερον ἐν οἷς φησι·

> καθαρῇ δ᾽ ἐν κελέβῃ πέντε ⟨τε⟩ καὶ τρεῖς
> ἀναχείσθω.

Φιλέταιρος δ᾽ ἐν Τηρεῖ δύο ὕδατος πρὸς τρεῖς ἀκράτου. λέγει δὲ οὕτως·

e >             πεπωκέναι δοκεῖ τὸν | κατὰ δύο
> καὶ τρεῖς ἀκράτου.

Φερεκράτης δ᾽ ἐν Κοριαννοῖ δύο ὕδατος πρὸς τέσσαρας οἴνου, λέγων ὧδε·

> (Α.) ἄποτος, ὦ Γλύκη.
> (Γλ.) ὑδαρῇ ᾽νέχεέν σοι; (Α.) παντάπασι μὲν οὖν
> ὕδωρ.
> (Γλ.) τί ἠργάσω; πῶς ὦ κατάρατε ⟨δ ᾽⟩ ἐνέχεας;
> (Β.) δύ᾽ ὕδατος, ὦ μάμμη. (Γλ.) τί δ᾽ οἴνου; (Γλ.)
> τέτταρας.
> (Γλ.) ἔρρ᾽ ἐς κόρακας. βατράχοισιν οἰνοχοεῖν σ ᾽
> ἔδει.

f Ἔφιππος δ᾽ ἐν Κίρκῃ | τρεῖς πρὸς τέτταρας·

> (Α.) οἶνον πίοις ἂν ἀσφαλέστερον πολὺ
> ὑδαρῆ. (Β.) μὰ τὴν γῆν, ἀλλὰ τρία καὶ τέτταρα.
> (Α.) οὕτως ἄκρατον, εἰπέ μοι, πίῃ; (Β.) τί φής;

ἴσον ἴσῳ δὲ Τιμοκλῆς ἐν Κονισάλῳ·

---

[72] The discussion of proportions of wine and water that follows
appears to come from the same source as the very similar collection of material that breaks off at 10.427a.

[73] Sc. "because *they* appreciate water!"

thus specifically ordering that the wine be mixed one-to-two.[72] Anacreon (*PMG* 409) asks for it to be even stronger in the passage where he says:

> Let five-to-three be poured into a clean cup!

Philetaerus in *Tereus* (fr. 15) (mentions) two parts water to three parts unmixed wine, putting it as follows:

> He appears to have drunk the combination of two
>     parts (water)
> with three parts unmixed wine.

Pherecrates in *Corianno* (fr. 76) (mentions) two parts water to four of wine, putting it this way:

> (A.) It's undrinkable, Glyce.
> (Glyce) Did she pour something watery into your
>     cup? (A.) Actually, it's *entirely* water.
> (Glyce) What did you do? How did you mix it for her,
>     you nasty creature?
> (B.) Two parts water, ma'am—(Glyce) And how much
>     wine? (B.) Four parts.
> (Glyce) Damn you to hell! You ought to be pouring
>     wine for frogs![73]

Ephippus in *Circe* (fr. 11) (mentions) three-to-four:

> (A.) You'd be much safer drinking watery
> wine. (B.) No, by earth! Three-to-four!
> (A.) Tell me—you really drink it that strong? (B.)
>     What do you mean?

Timocles in *Conisalus* (fr. 22) (mentions) a mix of one-to-one:

πατάξω τ᾽ ἴσον ἴσῳ ποτηρίοις
μεγάλοις ἅπασαν τὴν ἀλήθειαν φράσαι. ‖

431 καὶ Ἄλεξις ἐν Δορκίδι ἢ Ποππυζούσῃ·

τρεῖς φιλοτησίας ἐγὼ
μεστὰς προπίνω ⟨γ ᾽⟩ ἴσον ἴσῳ κεκραμένας.

καὶ Ξέναρχος ἢ Τιμοκλῆς ἐν Πορφύρᾳ·

μὰ τὸν Διόνυσον, ⟨ὃν⟩ σὺ λάπτεις ἴσον ἴσῳ.

Σώφιλος δ᾽ ἐν Ἐγχειριδίῳ·

συνεχὴς ἄκρατος ἐδίδοτ᾽ ἴσον ἴσῳ· πάλιν
τὴν μείζον᾽ ᾔτουν.

Ἄλεξις Τοκιστῇ ἢ Καταψευδομένῳ·

(Τρ.) μὴ παντελῶς αὐτῷ δίδου |
b  ὑδαρῆ. κατανοεῖς; ἴσον ἴσῳ μικροῦ. καλῶς.
(Α.) ἡδύ γε τὸ πῶμα. ποταπὸς ὁ Βρόμιος, Τρύφη;
(Τρ.) Θάσιος. (Α.) ὅμοιον. καὶ δίκαιον τοὺς
  ξένους
πίνειν ξενικόν, τοὺς δ᾽ ἐγγενεῖς ἐπιχώριον.

ἐν δὲ Ὑποβολιμαίῳ·

ἀπνευστί τ᾽ ἐκπιὼν
ὡς ἄν τις ἥδιστ᾽ ἴσον ἴσῳ κεκραμένον.

---

[74] Athenaeus (or his source) expresses similar doubts about
the authorship of the play at 7.319a (quoting fr. 8), but at 6.225c
(quoting fr. 7) assigns it unambiguously to Xenarchus.

[75] I.e. "Dionysus" (and thus here metonymically "wine").
Thasian wine (below) was regarded as being of particularly high
quality.

I'll smack you into telling me
the whole truth, by using big cups mixed one-to-one.

Also Alexis in *Dorcis or The Girl Who Popped Her Lips*
(fr. 59):

I'm proposing a toast of three
full friendship-cups mixed one-to-one.

And Xenarchus (fr. 9) or Timocles in *Porphyra*:[74]

No, by Dionysus—whom you lap up one-to-one!

Sophilus in *The Dagger* (fr. 4):

Strong wine mixed one-to-one was being offered
constantly; on top of that,
they kept asking for the larger cup.

Alexis in *The Loan-Shark or The Liar* (fr. 232):

(Tryphe) Don't offer him wine that's mixed real
watery. Do you understand? About one-to-one. Fine.
(A.) What I'm drinking tastes good! Where's your
Bromius[75] from, Tryphe?
(Tryphe) Thasos. (A.) It's all the same. It's right for
foreigners
to drink foreign wine, and for natives to drink the
local variety.

And in *The Supposititious Child* (fr. 246.3–4):[76]

emptying them without pausing for a breath,
mixed one-to-one, the most delicious proportion
possible.

Μένανδρος Ἀδελφοῖς·

    ὀκτώ τις ὑποχεῖν ἀνεβόα καὶ δώδεκα |
c    κυάθους, ἕως κατέσεισε φιλοτιμούμενος.

κατασείειν δὲ ἔλεγον ἐπὶ τῶν ἐν τοῖς πότοις προ-
πινόντων, τὴν μεταφορὰν λαμβάνοντες ἀπὸ τῶν τοὺς
καρποὺς κατασειόντων. Ἄλεξις δ᾽ ἐν Ἀποκοπτομένη·

    οὐ συμποσίαρχος ἦν γάρ, ἀλλὰ δήμιος
    ὁ Χαιρέας, κυάθους προπίνων εἴκοσιν.

Διόδωρος δ᾽ ὁ Σινωπεὺς ἐν Αὐλητρίδι·

    ἐπὰν κυάθους πίνῃ τις, ὦ Κρίτων, δέκα, |
d    ἀεὶ παρ᾽ ἕκαστον ἐνδελεχῶς ποτήριον
    πίνει τὸ λοιπόν, τοὺς λογισμοὺς δ᾽ ἐξεμεῖ.
    ταῦτα σκόπει πρὸς σαυτόν.

οὐκ ἀγλαφύρως δὲ Λύσανδρος ὁ Σπαρτιάτης, ὥς
φησιν Ἡγήσανδρος ἐν Ὑπομνήμασι, τὸν οἶνον ὑδαρῆ
πωλούντων τῶν καπήλων ἐν τῷ στρατοπέδῳ, κεκραμένον ἐκέλευσεν αὐτὸν πωλεῖν, ἵν᾽ αὐτὸν ἀκρατέστερον ὠνοῖντο. τὸ παραπλήσιον καὶ Ἄλεξις εἴρηκεν ἐν
Αἰσώπῳ οὕτως·

    (Αι.) κομψόν γε τοῦτ᾽ ἐστὶν παρ᾽ ὑμῖν, ὦ Σόλων, |
e    ἐν ταῖς Ἀθήναις, δεξιῶς θ᾽ εὑρημένον.
    (Σο.) τὸ ποῖον; (Αι.) ἐν τοῖς συμποσίοις οὐ πίνετε

---

76 A longer version of the fragment is quoted at 11.502b–c.
77 Literally "to shake down".
78 Cited at 13.562d as *The Man Who Was Mutilated*.
79 Lysander (Poralla #504) was Sparta's greatest commander
in the final phase of the Peloponnesian War; he died in 395 BCE.

Menander in *Brothers* (fr. 2):

> Someone kept shouting for them to pour eight ladles,
>     or
> twelve, until his taste for competition knocked them
>     down (*kateseise*) on the floor.

They used the verb *kataseiein*[77] to describe individuals who proposed toasts at drinking parties, borrowing the image from people who shake fruit out of trees. Alexis in *The Girl Who Was Mutilated*[78] (fr. 21):

> Because Chaereas wasn't a symposiarch, but a
> public executioner, proposing 20 cups as toasts.

Diodorus of Sinope in *The Pipe-Girl* (fr. 1):

> When someone drinks ten ladles, Crito,
> after that, along with each cup that he goes on
>     drinking, he pukes out his brains.
> Think about how that might apply to you.

According to Hegesander in his *Commentaries* (fr. 22, *FHG* iv.417), Lysander the Spartiate[79] was being quite subtle when he ordered the merchants selling diluted wine in the army camp to offer it as already mixed, in order to force them to buy it stronger in the first place. Alexis says something similar in *Aesop* (fr. 9), as follows:

> (Aesop) This is an ingenious idea you've got in
>     Athens,
> Solon, and cleverly conceived.
> (Solon) What specifically? (Aesop) You don't drink
>     unmixed wine

ἄκρατον. (Σο.) οὐ γὰρ ῥάδιον· πωλοῦσι γὰρ
ἐν ταῖς ἁμάξαις εὐθέως κεκραμένον,
οὐχ ἵνα τι κερδαίνωσι, τῶν δ᾽ ὠνουμένων
προνοούμενοι τοῦ τὰς κεφαλὰς ὑγιεῖς ἔχειν
ἐκ κραιπάλης. τοῦτ᾽ ἔσθ᾽, ὁρᾷς, Ἑλληνικὸς
πότος, μετρίοισι χρωμένους ποτηρίοις
λαλεῖν τι καὶ ληρεῖν πρὸς αὑτοὺς ἡδέως· |
f      τὸ μὲν γὰρ ἕτερον λουτρόν ἐστιν, οὐ πότος,
ψυκτῆρι πίνειν καὶ κάδοις. (Αι.) θάνατος μὲν οὖν.

πίνειν δ᾽ εἰς μέθην, φησὶν ἐν ἕκτῳ Νόμων Πλάτων,
οὔτε ἄλλοθί που πρέπει πλὴν ἐν ταῖς τοῦ τὸν οἶνον
δόντος θεοῦ ἑορταῖς οὐδ᾽ ἀσφαλές, οὔτ᾽ οὖν περὶ
γάμους ἐσπουδακότα, ἐν οἷς ἔμφρονα εἶναι πρέπει
μάλιστα νύμφην καὶ νυμφίον μεταβολὴν βίου οὐ
μικρὰν μεταλλάτοντας, ἅμα δὲ καὶ τὸ γεννώμενον
432    ὅπως ὅτι μάλιστα ἐξ ἐμφρόνων αἰεὶ γίγνεται· ‖ σχεδὸν γὰρ ἄδηλον ὁποία νὺξ ἢ φῶς αὐτὸ γεννήσει. κἂν
τῷ πρώτῳ δὲ τῶν Νόμων φησί· μέθης δὲ αὐτῆς, ὥσπερ
Λυδοὶ χρῶνται καὶ Πέρσαι καὶ Καρχηδόνιοι καὶ Κελτοὶ καὶ Ἴβηρες καὶ Θρᾷκες καὶ τὰ τοιαῦτα γένη,
καθάπερ ὑμεῖς, ὦ Λακεδαιμόνιοι, τὸ παράπαν ἀπ-
έχεσθε. Σκύθαι δὲ καὶ Θρᾷκες ἀκράτῳ παντάπασι
χρώμενοι, γυναῖκές τε καὶ πάντες αὐτοί, καὶ κατὰ τῶν
ἱματίων καταχεόμενοι καλὸν καὶ εὔδαιμον ἐπιτήδευμα
ἐπιτηδεύειν νενομίκασι. Πέρσαι δὲ καὶ σφόδρα μὲν
χρῶνται καὶ ταῖς ἄλλαις τρυφαῖς, ἃς ὑμεῖς ἀπο-

---

[80] I.e. in the marketplace.
[81] The text is slightly condensed and thus garbled.

at your parties. (Solon) Yeah—because it's not easy
    to! They sell it
in the wagons[80] already mixed—
not to make a profit, but because they're looking out
    for
the buyers, to keep them from having a headache
after they drink all night. You see, this is the Greek
way of drinking: use cups of a modest size,
and have a bit of banter and nice conversation with
    one another.
The other style amounts to bathing, not drinking—
I mean, drinking from a wine-cooling vessel or
    buckets. (Aesop) Actually, it amounts to death!

According to Plato in Book VI of the *Laws* (775b–c), drinking until you are intoxicated is not appropriate or safe anywhere except at the festivals celebrated in honor of the god
who gave us wine. Nor should it be encouraged at wed-
dings, where the bride and groom ought certainly to have
their wits about them, since a major change is taking place
in their lives, and in order that their offspring may be produced by the most thoughtful individuals possible; for it is
entirely unclear what day or night will produce them. And
in Book I of his *Laws* (637d–e) he says:[81] of drunkenness itself, as the Lydians, Persians, Carthaginians, Celts, Iberi-
ans, Thracians, and similar peoples engage in it, just as you,
Spartans, avoid it completely. The Scythians and Thracians
universally, men and women alike, drink wine with no water in it at all, and as they spill it over their clothing, they
think they are engaged in wonderful behavior that shows
how lucky they are. The Persians as well indulge in many
other luxuries you reject, but do so in a more orderly way

b βάλλετε, | ἐν τάξει δὲ μᾶλλον τούτων. ἔπινον πολλοὶ[8]
καὶ ἄλφιτα ἐπιβάλλοντες τῷ οἴνῳ, ὡς ὁ Δελφὸς
Ἡγήσανδρος φησίν. Ἐπίνικος γοῦν, Μνησιπτολέμου
ἀνάγνωσιν ποιησαμένου τῶν Ἱστοριῶν, ἐν αἷς ἐγέ-
γραπτο ὡς Σέλευκος ἐπηλφίτωσε, γράψας δρᾶμα
Μνησιπτόλεμον καὶ κωμῳδῶν αὐτὸν καὶ περὶ τῆς
πόσεως ταῖς ἐκείνου χρώμενος φωναῖς ἐποίησε λέ-
γοντα·

ἐπ' ἀλφίτου πίνοντα τοῦ θέρους ποτὲ |
c ἰδὼν Σέλευκον ἡδέως τὸν βασιλέα
ἔγραψα, καὶ παρέδειξα τοῖς πολλοῖς ὅτι,
κἂν τὸ τυχὸν ᾖ πραγμάτιον ἢ σφόδρ' εὐτελές,
σεμνὸν δύναται τοῦθ' ἡ δύναμις ἡ 'μὴ ποεῖν.
"γέροντα Θάσιον τόν τε γῆς ἀπ' Ἀτθίδος
ἑσμὸν μελίσσης τῆς ἀκραχόλου γλυκὺν
συγκυρκανήσας ἐν σκύφῳ χυτῆς λίθου,
Δήμητρος ἀκτῇ πᾶν γεφυρώσας ὑγρὸν
κατῃσίμωσε πῶμα, καύματος λύσιν."

ὁ δ' αὐτὸς ἱστορεῖ κἂν Θηράσι ταῖς νήσοις ἐπι-
πάττοντας λέκιθον ἀντὶ ἀλφίτου πίνειν, καὶ λέγεσθαι |
d ταύτην τὴν πόσιν καλλίονα τῆς ἐξ ἀλφίτων.
    Προπόσεις δὲ τὰς γινομένας ἐν τοῖς συμποσίοις
Λακεδαιμονίοις οὐκ ἦν ἔθος ποιεῖν οὐδὲ φιλοτησίας

---

[8] πολλοὶ tantum CE: οἱ πολλοὶ A

---

[82] The Seleucus in question might be either Seleucus II
(reigned 246/5–225 BCE) or Seleucus III (reigned 225–222 BCE).

[83] The "aged Thasian" is old Thasian wine (a particularly fine
variety); the "efflux of the bee" is honey (the Attic variety being

than these other nations. Many people used to sprinkle barley groats on the wine they drank, according to Hegesander of Delphi (fr. 23, *FHG* iv.418). When Mnesiptolemus (*FGrH* 164 T 2), for example, gave a reading of his *History*, in which he recorded that Seleucus[82] sprinkled barley groats on his wine, Epinicus wrote a play entitled *Mnesiptolemus* (fr. 1), in which he made fun of him and had a character quote what Mnesiptolemus said about Seleucus' drinking:

> In the summer once I saw King Seleucus
> happily drinking wine mixed with barley groats, and
> I wrote about it, making it clear to the masses that
> even if the event itself was no big deal, or utterly
>     insignificant,
> my powers can render it important.
> "Enmixing an aged Thasian and the
> sweet Attic efflux of the irascible
> bee in a vessel of cast stone,[83]
> and spanning the entire liquid drink with Demeter's
> corn, he sent it to its fate as a solution to solar
>     warmth."

The same author[84] records that in the Therad islands they sprinkle gruel rather than barley groats on their wine when they drink it, and that this way of consuming it is allegedly better than when groats are used.

It was not the Spartan custom to offer the toasts that are generally part of drinking parties, or to drink the associ-

generally judged the best in the world); and the "vessel of cast stone" is a ceramic cup.

[84] Hegesander.

ATHENAEUS

διὰ τούτων πρὸς ἀλλήλους ποιεῖσθαι. δηλοῖ δὲ ταῦτα
Κριτίας ἐν τοῖς Ἐλεγείοις·

καὶ τόδ' ἔθος Σπάρτῃ μελέτημά τε κείμενόν ἐστι·
   πίνειν τὴν αὐτὴν οἰνοφόρον κύλικα,
μηδ' ἀποδωρεῖσθαι προπόσεις ὀνομαστὶ λέγοντα |

e      μηδ' ἐπὶ δεξιτερὰν χεῖρα κύκλῳ θιάσου

\*      \*      \*

ἄγγεα Λυδὴ χεὶρ ηὗρ' Ἀσιατογενής,
καὶ προπόσεις ὀρέγειν ἐπιδέξια, καὶ
   προκαλεῖσθαι
ἐξονομακλήδην ᾧ προπιεῖν ἐθέλει.
εἶτ' ἀπὸ τοιούτων πόσεων γλώσσας τε λύουσιν
   εἰς αἰσχροὺς μύθους σῶμά τ' ἀμαυρότερον
τεύχουσιν· πρὸς δ' ὄμμ' ἀχλὺς ἀμβλωπὸς ἐφίζει,
   λῆστις δ' ἐκτήκει μνημοσύνην πραπίδων, |

f   νοῦς δὲ παρέσφαλται· δμῶες δ' ἀκόλαστον
      ἔχουσιν
ἦθος· ἐπεισπίπτει δ' οἰκοτριβὴς δαπάνη.
οἱ Λακεδαιμονίων δὲ κόροι πίνουσι τοσοῦτον
   ὥστε φρέν' εἰς ἱλαρὰν † ἀσπίδα † πάντ'
      ἀπάγειν
εἴς τε φιλοφροσύνην γλῶσσαν μέτριόν τε
      γέλωτα.
τοιαύτη δὲ πόσις σώματί τ' ὠφέλιμος

---

85 The reference is now to Athenians (rather than Spartans, as
in the first four verses and again below).

ated friendship cups in one another's honor. Critias makes this clear in his *Elegies* (fr. B 6 West[2], encompassing both quotations):

> This is an established custom and practice in Sparta:
>> to drink from one's own wine-cup,
> and not to offer toasts, mentioning individuals by
>> name
>>> or going from left to right in a circle around the
>>> party.
>
> \*　　\*　　\*
>
> An Asian-born Lydian hand invented their
>> vessels,[85]
> along with the idea of extending toasts from left to
>> right, and of calling
>> on the man one wishes to toast by name.
> Then the result of this sort of drinking is that their
>> tongues are set loose
>> to make ugly remarks, and their bodies are
>> rendered
> weaker. A dark mist settles over their eyes;
>> forgetfulness leaches memory from their minds;
> and their intelligence is hobbled. Their slaves behave
>> wildly, and the extravagance that lays a house
>> waste descends upon them.
> Sparta's young men, on the other hand, drink only
>> enough
>> to transport their mind entirely to cheerful †
>> shield †,
> and their tongue to friendly behavior and restrained
>> laughter.
>> This type of drinking is good for one's body,

γνώμῃ τε κτήσει τε· καλῶς δ᾽ εἰς ἔργ᾽ Ἀφροδίτης ‖

πρός θ᾽ ὕπνον ἥρμοσται, τὸν καμάτων λιμένα,
πρὸς τὴν τερπνοτάτην τε θεῶν θνητοῖς Ὑγίειαν,
καὶ τὴν Εὐσεβίης γείτονα Σωφροσύνην.

ἑξῆς τε πάλιν φησίν·

αἱ γὰρ ὑπὲρ τὸ μέτρον κυλίκων προπόσεις
παραχρῆμα
τέρψασαι λυποῦσ᾽ εἰς τὸν ἅπαντα χρόνον·
ἡ Λακεδαιμονίων δὲ δίαιθ᾽ ὁμαλῶς διάκειται, |

b
ἔσθειν καὶ πίνειν σύμμετρα πρὸς τὸ φρονεῖν
καὶ τὸ πονεῖν εἶναι δυνατούς· οὐκ ἔστ᾽ ἀπότακτος
ἡμέρα οἰνῶσαι σῶμ᾽ ἀμέτροισι πότοις.

Φίλοινος δ᾽ ἐστὶν ὁ πρὸς οἶνον ἕτοιμος, φιλοπότης
δὲ ὁ πρὸς πότους, κωθωνιστὴς δὲ ὁ μέχρι μέθης.
πλεῖστον δὲ ἔπινε τῶν μὲν ἡρώων Νέστωρ ὁ τριγέρων·
φανερῶς γὰρ αὐτὸς προσέκειτο τῶν ἄλλων μᾶλλον τῷ
οἴνῳ καὶ τοῦ Ἀγαμέμνονος αὐτοῦ, ὃν ὡς πολυπότην
ἐπιπλήσσει ὁ Ἀχιλλεύς. ὁ δὲ Νέστωρ καὶ τῆς μεγί-
c στης μάχης ἐνεστηκυίας οὐκ ἀπέχεται | καὶ τοῦ πίνειν.
φησὶ γοῦν Ὅμηρος·

Νέστορα δ᾽ οὐκ ἔλαθεν ἰαχὴ πίνοντά περ ἔμπης.

καὶ μόνου δὲ τούτου τῶν ἡρώων τὸ ποτήριον ἡρμή-

---

[86] Cognate with kōthōn (a wine-flask of some sort; see
11.483a–4c).

mind, and property; it is also nicely suited to
    sex and to sleep, which is the harbor for fatigue,
and to Health, who is the most pleasant god for
    mortals,
    and to Piety's neighbor Self-Restraint.

And again immediately after this, he says:

Because an excessive number of cups drunk as toasts
    offers pleasure
    in the short term, but causes pain in the long run.
The Spartan way of life rests on an even keel:
    eating and drinking moderate amounts, so that
    one can
think straight and work hard. No day is
    set aside to intoxicate one's body with endless
    drinking.

Someone who is eager for wine (*oinos*) is *philoinos*;
someone eager to have drinking parties (*potoi*) is *philopotos*;
and someone who drinks until he is drunk is a
*kōthōnistēs*.[86] Nestor drank more than any other hero, despite being extremely old; because he openly applied himself to wine more than the rest did, including Agamemnon
himself, whom Achilleus attacks for drinking so much (*Il.*
1.225). Even when an extremely important battle is going
on, Nestor does not stop drinking. Homer says, at any rate
(*Il.* 14.1):

Even though Nestor was drinking, he did not fail to
    hear the sound of battle.

Nestor's cup is also the only one Homer describes (*Il.*

νευκεν, ὡς τὴν ἀσπίδα·[9] ἐστρατεύετο γὰρ μετ᾽ αὐτοῦ
καθάπερ καὶ τῆς ἀσπίδος ἐκείνης, ἧς φησιν ὁ Ἕκτωρ
καὶ μέχρι οὐρανοῦ ἥκειν τὸ κλέος. οὐκ ἂν ἁμάρτοι δέ
τις καὶ τὸ ποτήριον αὐτοῦ λέγων φιάλην Ἄρεως κατὰ
τὸν Ἀντιφάνους Καινέα, ἐν ᾧ λέγεται οὕτως·

> εἶτ᾽ ἤδη δὸς φιάλην Ἄρεως,
d     κατὰ Τιμόθεον, ξυστόν τε | βέλος.

ἀλλὰ μὴν καὶ διὰ τὴν φιλοποσίαν ὁ Νέστωρ καὶ παρ᾽
Ἀχιλλέως φιάλην λαμβάνει δῶρον ἐν τῷ Ἐπὶ Πα-
τρόκλῳ Ἐπιτελουμένῳ Ἀγῶνι, † οὐχ ὅτι καὶ οὐχὶ τῷ
νικηθέντι ἔδωκε δέπας ὁ Ἀχιλλεύς (τοῖς γὰρ φιλο-
πόταις οὐ παρέπεται τὸ νικᾶν διὰ τὸ ῥᾴθυμον), ἢ ὅτι
διὰ δίψαν μάλιστα λείπονται οἱ πύκται διὰ τὸ βαρεῖ-
σθαι τὰς χεῖρας ἀνατείνοντες. ὁ δὲ Εὔμηλος λαμβάνει
θώρακα δραμὼν ἆθλον ἐπισφαλῶς καὶ ἀμυχθείς,
ἀσφαλείας ὅπλον.

e     Τῆς δὲ δίψης οὐδέν | ἐστι πολυποθητότερον. διόπερ
καὶ τὸ Ἄργος πολυδίψιον ὁ ποιητὴς ἔφη, τὸ πολυ-
πόθητον διὰ τὸν χρόνον· τὸ δίψος γὰρ πᾶσιν ἰσχυρὰν
ἐπιθυμίαν ἐμποιεῖ τῆς περιττῆς ἀπολαύσεως. διὸ καὶ ὁ
Σοφοκλῆς φησι·

---

[9] τὴν Ἀχιλλέως ἀσπίδα ACE: Ἀχιλλέως del. Olson

---

[87] The manuscripts have "in the same way he does Achilleus'
shield" (cf. *Il.* 18.478–608), which must represent a misguided
gloss that has intruded into the text, as the reference that follows
specifically to *Nestor's* shield makes clear.

[88] This passage is discussed at length at 11.487f–94b.

[89] Something has gone seriously wrong with the text at this
point, perhaps via a combination of intrusive notes and the loss of
some lines. Nestor does not take part in the chariot-racing contest

11.632–7), just as he does his shield;[87] because Nestor brought his cup with him on the expedition (*Il.* 11.632), precisely as he brought his famous shield, the reputation of which, according to Hector, "reached heaven" (*Il.* 8.192).[88] It would not be a mistake to refer to his cup as "Ares' libation-bowl", to quote Antiphanes' *Caineus* (fr. 110 = Timoth. *PMG* 797), where the following is said:

> Then at this point give me Ares' libation bowl,
> to quote Timotheus, and a shaved missile.

Nestor gets a libation-bowl, in fact, as a gift from Achilleus in *The Contest Celebrated in Honor of Patroclus* (*Il.* 23.615–24) because he liked to drink,[89] † not because Achilleus gave him a goblet when he was not defeated—for heavy drinkers tend not to win athletic contests, since they grow careless—or because boxers generally lose when they grow thirsty, because their hands grow heavy when they hold them out. Whereas Eumelus gets a breast-plate (*Il.* 23.560–2), which is a piece of protective equipment, because he fell during the course of the race and was injured (*Il.* 23.394–7).

No desire is more urgent than thirst. This is why the poet referred to Argos as "thirsty" (*Il.* 4.171), which is to say "much-longed-for" as a result of the lapse of time;[90] because thirst always produces a powerful desire for full satisfaction. This is why Sophocles (fr. 763 = adesp. com. fr. *120) says:

(although his son Antilochus did), and when Achilleus gives him a libation-bowl as a gift of honor afterward, he says that he does so because Nestor's advanced age renders him unable to compete in manly sports such as boxing.

90 Sc. "since the Achaeans had been gone from there".

διψῶντι γάρ τοι πάντα προσφέρων σοφὰ
οὐκ ἂν πλέον τέρψειας ἢ πιεῖν διδούς.

καὶ ὁ Ἀρχίλοχος·

       μάχης δὲ τῆς σῆς, ὥστε διψέων πιεῖν,
ὡς ἐρέω.

καὶ τῶν τραγικῶν δέ τις ἔφη· |

f   ἴσχειν κελεύω χεῖρα διψῶσαν φόνου.

καὶ Ἀνακρέων·

    φίλη γὰρ εἶς ξείνοισιν· ἔασον δέ με διψέοντα
    πιεῖν.

καὶ Ξενοφῶν δ' ἐν τῷ τρίτῳ τῆς Παιδείας ποιεῖ τὸν
Κῦρον τάδε λέγοντα· ἐγὼ ὑμῖν διψῶ χαρίσασθαι.
Πλάτων δ' ἐν τῇ Πολιτείᾳ· ὅταν, οἶμαι, δημοκρατουμένη πόλις ἐλευθερίας διψήσασα κακῶν οἰνοχόων
προστατούντων τύχῃ καὶ πορρωτέρω τοῦ δέοντος
434  ἀκράτου μεθυσθῇ. ‖ ἔπινε δὲ καὶ Πρωτέας ὁ Μακεδὼν
πλεῖστον, ὥς φησιν Ἔφιππος ἐν τῷ Περὶ τῆς Ἀλεξάνδρου καὶ Ἡφαιστίωνος Ταφῆς, καὶ εὐρώστῳ τῷ σώ-
ματι διῆγε, καίτοι τῷ πιεῖν ἐγγεγυμνασμένος ὤν.
Ἀλέξανδρος γοῦν αἰτήσας ποτὲ ποτήριον δίχουν καὶ
πιὼν προΰπιε τῷ Πρωτέᾳ. καὶ ὃς λαβὼν καὶ πολλὰ
ὑμνήσας τὸν βασιλέα ἔπιεν, ὡς ὑπὸ πάντων κρο-

---

91 Quoted at greater length at 10.443f–4a; cf. 11.505d.

92 Proteas (Berve i #664) grew up with Alexander the Great
and was one of his closest associates; cf. 4.129a (probably an
oblique reference to the passage of Ephippus cited here).

93 A *chous* was a liquid measure, equivalent (on the Attic standard) to about three quarts.

Because, let me assure you, if you offered a thirsty
      man wisdom of every sort,
you'd give him less pleasure than by offering him a
      drink.

Also Archilochus (fr. 125 West[2]):

               I'm as eager to fight you as a thirsty man
is for a drink.

So too one of the tragedians said (adesp. tr. fr. 96):

I urge you to restrain your hand, which is thirsty for
      bloodshed.

Also Anacreon (*PMG* 389):

For you are a friend to strangers; allow me, thirsty as
      I am, to drink.

Likewise Xenophon in Book III of his *Education* (*Cyr.*
5.1.1) represents Cyrus as saying the following: I'm thirsty
to do you favors. Plato in his *Republic* (562c–d):[91] whenever, I suppose, a democratically governed city thirsty
for freedom has bad wine-pourers in charge, and gets
more drunk on unmixed wine than it should. Proteas
of Macedon[92] was also a heavy drinker, according to
Ephippus in his *On the Burial of Alexander and
Hephaestion* (*FGrH* 126 F 3); he was in good physical
health his entire life, despite the fact that he spent much of
his time drinking. At one point, for example, Alexander
asked for a cup that could hold two *choēs*,[93] drained it, and
toasted Proteas. Proteas took the cup, praised the king at
length, and emptied it; and everyone applauded. Shortly

ταλισθῆναι. καὶ μετ᾽ ὀλίγον τὸ αὐτὸ ποτήριον αἰτήσας
ὁ Πρωτέας καὶ πάλιν πιὼν προύπιε τῷ βασιλεῖ. ὁ δὲ
b Ἀλέξανδρος λαβὼν | ἔσπασε μὲν γενναίως, οὐ μὴν
ὑπήνεγκεν, ἀλλ᾽ ἀπέκλινεν ἐπὶ τὸ προσκεφάλαιον
ἀφεὶς τῶν χειρῶν τὸ ποτήριον. καὶ ἐκ τούτου νοσήσας
ἀπέθανε, τοῦ Διονύσου, φησί, μηνίσαντος αὐτῷ, διότι
τὴν πατρίδα αὐτοῦ τὰς Θήβας ἐπολιόρκησεν. ἔπινε δὲ
ὁ Ἀλέξανδρος πλεῖστον, ὡς καὶ ἀπὸ τῆς μέθης συν-
εχῶς κοιμᾶσθαι δύο ἡμέρας καὶ δύο νύκτας. δηλοῦται
δὲ τοῦτο ἐν ταῖς Ἐφημερίσιν αὐτοῦ, ἃς ἀνέγραψαν
Εὐμένης τε ὁ Καρδιανὸς καὶ Διόδοτος ὁ Ἐρυθραῖος.
Μένανδρος δὲ ἐν Κόλακί φησι·

c (Βι.) κοτύλας | χωροῦν δέκα
ἐν Καππαδοκίᾳ κόνδυ χρυσοῦν, Στρουθία,
τρὶς ἐπέπιον μεστόν γε. (Στ.) Ἀλεξάνδρου πλέον
τοῦ βασιλέως πέπωκας. (Βι.) οὐκ ἔλαττον, οὐ
μὰ τὴν Ἀθηνᾶν. (Στ.) μέγα γε.

Νικοβούλη δὲ ἢ ὁ ἀναθεὶς ταύτῃ τὰ συγγράμματά
φησιν ὅτι παρὰ Μηδείῳ τῷ Θεσσαλῷ δειπνῶν ὁ
Ἀλέξανδρος εἴκοσιν οὖσιν ἐν τῷ συμποσίῳ πᾶσι
προύπιε, παρὰ πάντων τὰ ἴσα λαμβάνων, καὶ ἀναστὰς

---

94 Thebes was not just besieged, but destroyed and enslaved
by Alexander when it revolted from him in 335 BCE. Alexander
died in Babylon in 323 BCE.

95 Eumenes (Berve i #317) was probably the secretary (gram-
mateus) first of Alexander's father Philip, and then of Alexander
himself. Diodotus (Berve i #272) is otherwise unknown.

96 Bias is a braggart soldier, and Strouthias is the eponymous
flatterer. The first two verses are quoted also at 11.477f.

thereafter, Proteas asked for the same cup, and again drained it and toasted the king. Alexander took the cup and made a concerted effort to empty it, but could not manage the feat, and instead collapsed on his pillow and let the cup slip from his hands. He fell sick and died as a consequence, says Ephippus, because Dionysus was angry at him, since he besieged the god's native city of Thebes.[94] Alexander used to drink heavily, to the extent that he sometimes got so drunk that he slept for two days and nights straight. This is revealed in his *Journals* (*FGrH* 117 F 2b), which were composed by Eumenes of Cardia (*FGrH* 117 T 1) and Diodotus of Erythrae.[95] Menander says in *The Flatterer* (*Kolax* fr. 2 Sandbach):[96]

> (Bias) In Cappadocia, Strouthias, I
> drained a gold cup that held ten ladles—
> I did it three times, and it was full! (Strouthias)
> You've drunk
> more than King Alexander! (Bias) Certainly no less,
> by Athena! (Strouthias) That's a lot!

Nicoboule[97]—or whoever assigned her treatises to her— claims (*FGrH* 127 T 1, F 1) that when Alexander was having dinner with Medeius of Thessaly,[98] he drank a toast to everyone in the party. There were 20 of them, and they all

---

[97] Presumably a famous courtesan known to have associated with Alexander, and who could therefore be presented as an eyewitness of his final hours. Athenaeus cites the same treatise again at 12.537d.

[98] Medeius (or Medius) of Larissa (Berve i #521) was another member of Alexander's inner circle, and the party referred to is the one (also mentioned above) after which he fell sick and died.

⟨ἐκ⟩ τοῦ συμποσίου μετ᾽ οὐ πολὺ ἀνεπαύετο. Καλλισθένης δὲ ὁ σοφιστής, ὡς Λυγκεὺς ὁ Σάμιός φησιν

d ἐν τοῖς Ἀπομνημονεύμασι | καὶ Ἀριστόβουλος καὶ Χάρης ἐν ταῖς Ἱστορίαις, ἐν τῷ συμποσίῳ τοῦ Ἀλεξάνδρου τῆς τοῦ ἀκράτου κύλικος εἰς αὐτὸν ἐλθούσης ὡς διωθεῖτο, εἰπόντος τέ τινος αὐτῷ, "διὰ τί οὐ πίνεις;", "οὐδὲν δέομαι", ἔφη, "Ἀλεξάνδρου πιὼν τοῦ Ἀσκληπιοῦ δεῖσθαι." Δαρεῖος δὲ ὁ τοὺς μάγους ἀνελὼν ἐπιγεγραμμένον εἶχεν ἐπὶ τοῦ μνήματος· ἠδυνάμην καὶ οἶνον πίνειν πολὺν καὶ τοῦτον φέρειν καλῶς. Κτησίας δὲ παρ᾽ Ἰνδοῖς φησιν οὐκ εἶναι τῷ

e βασιλεῖ μεθυσθῆναι· | παρὰ δὲ Πέρσαις τῷ βασιλεῖ ἐφίεται μεθύσκεσθαι μιᾷ ἡμέρᾳ, ἐν ᾗ θύουσι τῷ Μίθρῃ. γράφει δὲ οὕτως περὶ τούτου Δοῦρις ἐν τῇ ἑβδόμῃ τῶν Ἱστοριῶν· ἐν μόνῃ τῶν ἑορτῶν τῶν ἀγομένων ὑπὸ Περσῶν τῷ Μίθρῃ βασιλεὺς μεθύσκεται καὶ τὸ Περσικὸν ὀρχεῖται· τῶν δὲ λοιπῶν οὐδεὶς κατὰ τὴν Ἀσίαν, ἀλλὰ πάντες ἀπέχονται κατὰ τὴν ἡμέραν ταύτην τῆς ὀρχήσεως. Πέρσαι γὰρ ὥσπερ ἱππεύειν οὕτω καὶ ὀρχεῖσθαι μανθάνουσι καὶ νομίζουσι τὴν |

f τῆς ἐργασίας ταύτης κίνησιν ἐμμελῆ τινα λαμβάνειν γυμνασίαν τῆς τοῦ σώματος ῥώμης. εἰς τοσοῦτον δὲ Ἀλέξανδρος ἐμέθυεν, ὥς φησι Καρύστιος ὁ Περγαμηνὸς ἐν Ἱστορικοῖς Ὑπομνήμασιν, ὡς καὶ ἐπὶ ὄνων ἅρματος κωμάζειν· ἐποίουν δὲ τοῦτο, φησί, καὶ οἱ τῶν

---

99 Or perhaps "died".          100 Callisthenes of Olynthus (Berve i #408) was a companion of Alexander from the beginning of his campaigns, but the outspokenness and lack of social grace evident in this anecdote eventually led to his downfall.

101 The god of medicine (as opposed to the supposedly divine Alexander).

responded in the same way; shortly thereafter he left the party and fell asleep.[99] According to Lynceus of Samos in his *Memoirs* (fr. 34 Dalby) and Aristobulus (*FGrH* 139 F 32) and Chares (*FGrH* 125 F 13) in their *Histories*, when the cup of unmixed wine came to the sophist Callisthenes[100] (*FGrH* 124 T 12) at a drinking party given by Alexander, and he tried to refuse it, someone said to him, "Why aren't you drinking?" He responded: "I've got no desire, when I'm drinking Alexander's wine, to need Asclepius'[101] assistance instead." The Darius who put the Magi to death[102] had inscribed on his tomb: "I was able to drink lots of wine and handle it well." Ctesias (*FGrH* 688 F 50) says that in India the king is not allowed to get drunk, whereas in Persia the king is allowed to get drunk on only one day, when they sacrifice to Mithra. Duris writes as follows about this topic in Book VII of his *History* (*FGrH* 76 F 5): At only one of the festivals the Persians celebrate, that in honor of Mithra, does the king get drunk and perform the Persian dance.[103] No one else in Asia does this; instead, they all avoid dancing on that day. For the Persians learn to dance in the same way they learn to ride horses,[104] and they believe that the movement this activity involves includes exercise that promotes physical strength. According to Carystius of Pergamum in the *Historical Commentary* (fr. 4, *FHG* iv.357), Alexander used to get so drunk, that he traveled on a donkey-cart when he went revelling; the Per-

---

[102] Darius I of Persia (reigned 522/1–486 BCE); implicitly distinguished here from Darius III, whom Alexander overthrew.

[103] Cf. 1.16a (quoting Xenophon); 14.629d.

[104] I.e. as a fundamental part of their education; cf. Hdt. 1.136.2.

Περσῶν βασιλεῖς. μήποτ' οὖν διὰ τοῦτο οὐδὲ πρὸς τὰ
ἀφροδίσια εἶχεν ὁρμήν· ἐξυδαροῦσθαι γάρ φησιν ὁ
Ἀριστοτέλης ἐν τοῖς Φυσικοῖς Προβλήμασι τῶν τοι-
435  ούτων τὴν γονήν. ‖ Ἱερώνυμός τε ἐν ταῖς Ἐπιστολαῖς
Θεόφραστόν φησι λέγειν ὅτι Ἀλέξανδρος οὐκ εὖ
διέκειτο πρὸς τὰ ἀφροδίσια, Ὀλυμπιάδος γοῦν καὶ
παρανακλινάσης αὐτῷ Καλλιξείναν τὴν Θετταλὴν
ἑταίραν περικαλλεστάτην οὖσαν, συνειδότος τοῦτο καὶ
τοῦ Φιλίππου (εὐλαβοῦντο γὰρ μὴ γύννις εἴη), πολλάκις ᾔτει αὐτῇ τὸν Ἀλέξανδρον συγγενέσθαι. καὶ
Φίλιππος δ' ὁ τοῦ Ἀλεξάνδρου πατὴρ φιλοπότης ἦν,
ὡς ἱστορεῖ Θεόπομπος ἐν τῇ ἕκτῃ καὶ εἰκοστῇ τῶν
b   Ἱστοριῶν. κἂν ἄλλῳ δὲ μέρει τῆς Ἱστορίας | γράφει·
Φίλιππος ἦν τὰ μὲν φύσει μανικὸς καὶ προπετὴς ἐπὶ
τῶν κινδύνων, τὰ δὲ διὰ μέθην· ἦν γὰρ πολυπότης καὶ
πολλάκις μεθύων ἐξεβοήθει. ἐν δὲ τῷ τρίτῃ καὶ πεντηκοστῇ περὶ τῶν ἐν Χαιρωνείᾳ γενομένων εἰπὼν καὶ ὡς
ἐπὶ δεῖπνον ἐκάλεσε τοὺς παραγενομένους τῶν Ἀθηναίων πρέσβεις φησίν· ὁ δὲ Φίλιππος ἀποχωρησάν-
των ἐκείνων εὐθέως μετεπέμπετό τινας τῶν ἑταίρων,
καλεῖν δ' ἐκέλευε τὰς αὐλητρίδας καὶ Ἀριστόνικον τὸν
c   κιθαρῳδὸν καὶ Δωρίωνα τὸν αὐλητὴν | καὶ τοὺς ἄλλους
τοὺς εἰθισμένους αὐτῷ συμπίνειν· περιήγετο γὰρ πανταχοῦ τοὺς τοιούτους ὁ Φίλιππος καὶ κατασκευασάμε-
νος ἦν ὄργανα πολλὰ συμποσίου καὶ συνουσίας. ὧν
γὰρ φιλοπότης καὶ τὸν τρόπον ἀκόλαστος καὶ βωμο-

---

105 Berve i #406 (otherwise unknown). Olympias (Berve i
#581) was Alexander's mother.

106 Where Philip crushed Athens and Thebes in 338 BCE.

107 Berve i #132; Stephanis #367.

sian kings, he claims, did the same. This may be why Alexander had no sex-drive; because Aristotle in his *Physical Problems* (872<sup>b</sup>20–5) reports that the semen of men who behave this way becomes watery. So too Hieronymus in his *Letters* (fr. 38 Wehrli) says that Theophrastus (fr. 578 Fortenbaugh) claims that Alexander was impotent. Olympias, at any rate, had the Thessalian courtesan Callixeina,[105] who was extremely beautiful, lie down beside him—Philip was also aware of what was going on—since they were worried that he was a pansy; and she frequently begged Alexander to have sex with the girl. Alexander's father Philip also liked to drink, according to Theopompus in Book XXVI of his *History* (*FGrH* 115 F 163). So too in another part of his *History* he writes (*FGrH* 115 F 282): Philip was manic and prone to rushing head-long into danger, in part because this was his nature, but in part because of his heavy drinking; for he consumed large amounts of wine and often went into battle drunk. And in Book LIII (*FGrH* 115 F 236), after describing what happened at Chaeronea[106] and how Philip invited the Athenian ambassadors who came to see him to dinner, he says: As soon as they were gone, Philip summoned some of the members of his inner circle, and told them to fetch the pipe-girls, Aristonicus the citharode,[107] Dorion the pipe-player,[108] and the others who routinely drank with him; for Philip took people like this around with him everywhere, and had plenty of equipment ready for drinking parties and festivities. Because since he liked to drink and was personally

---

[108] Stephanis #805; presumably to be identified with the Dorion about whom numerous anecdotes are preserved at 8.337b–8b.

λόχους εἶχε περὶ αὑτὸν συχνοὺς καὶ τῶν περὶ τὴν
μουσικὴν ὄντων καὶ τῶν τὰ γέλοια λεγόντων. πιὼν δὲ
τὴν νύκτα πᾶσαν καὶ μεθυσθεὶς πολὺ καὶ ἀφεὶς[10]
ἅπαντας τοὺς ἄλλους ἀπαλλάττεσθαι ἤδη πρὸς ἡμέ-
d   ραν ἐκώμαζεν ὡς τοὺς πρέσβεις | τοὺς τῶν Ἀθηναίων.
Καρύστιος δὲ ἐν τοῖς Ἱστορικοῖς Ὑπομνήμασιν, ὅτε,
φησί, μεθύειν προῃρεῖτο Φίλιππος, τοῦτ᾽ ἔλεγε· "χρὴ
πίνειν· Ἀντίπατρος γὰρ ἱκανός ἐστι νήφων." κυβεύ-
οντος δέ ποτε αὐτοῦ καί τινος ἀγγείλαντος ὡς Ἀντίπατρος πάρεστι, διαπορήσας ὦσεν ὑπὸ τὴν κλίνην τὸν
ἄβακα.

Φιλοπότας δὲ καὶ μεθύσους καταλέγει Θεόπομπος
Διονύσιον τὸν νεώτερον, Σικελίας τύραννον, ὃν καὶ τὰς
ὄψεις ὑπὸ τοῦ οἴνου διαφθαρῆναι. Ἀριστοτέλης δ᾽ ἐν
e   τῇ Συρακοσίων Πολιτείᾳ | καὶ συνεχῶς φησιν αὐτὸν
ἔσθ᾽ ὅτε ἐπὶ ἡμέρας ἐνενήκοντα μεθύειν· διὸ καὶ ἀμ-
βλυωπότερον γενέσθαι τὰς ὄψεις. Θεόφραστος δέ
φησι καὶ τοὺς ἑταίρους αὐτοῦ κολακεύοντας τὴν
τυραννίδα προσποιεῖσθαι μήτε τὰ παρατιθέμενα τῶν
ἐδεσμάτων μήτε τὰς κύλικας ὁρᾶν καὶ ὑπ᾽ αὐτοῦ τοῦ
Διονυσίου χειραγωγεῖσθαι·[11] διὸ κληθῆναι Διονυσιο-
κόλακας. ἔπινε δὲ πλεῖστον καὶ Νυσαῖος ὁ τυραννήσας Συρακοσίων καὶ Ἀπολλοκράτης· Διονυσίῳ δὲ

[10] καὶ πατάξας ἀφεὶς A: καὶ παίξας ἀφεὶς CE: πατάξας/
παίξας del. Olson

[11] προσποιεῖσθαι μὴ βλέπειν καὶ ὑπ᾽ αὐτοῦ τοῦ Διονυσίου
χειραγωγεῖσθαι καὶ μήτε τὰ παρατιθέμενα τῶν ἐδεσμάτων
μήτε τὰς κύλικας ὁρᾶν ACE

undisciplined, he was surrounded by large numbers of smart-asses, musicians, and comedians. After he drank all night and became extremely intoxicated, he let everyone else leave and now, as day was breaking, wandered off drunk to visit the Athenian ambassadors. Carystius says in his *Historical Commentaries* (fr. 3, *FHG* iv.357): When Philip decided to get drunk, he used to say the following: "We need to start drinking; because if Antipater's[109] sober, that's enough." On one occasion, when he was shooting dice and someone announced that Antipater had arrived, he had no idea what to do and shoved the board he was using to keep score under his couch.

Theopompus (*FGrH* 115 F 283a) includes in his list of people who liked to drink wine and get drunk the Sicilian tyrant Dionysius the Younger,[110] whose vision was damaged by the wine.[111] Aristotle in his *Constitution of the Syracusans* (fr. 605.1) claims that Dionysius was sometimes drunk for 90 days straight, which is why his vision deteriorated. Theophrastus (fr. 548 Fortenbaugh) says that the members of his inner circle, as a way of flattering his power, pretended to be unable to see the food they were served or the cups, and that Dionysius himself directed them to them; they were accordingly referred to as "Dionysius-flatterers".[112] The Syracusan tyrant Nysaeus also drank a great deal, as did Apollocrates; they were sons

109 Antipater (Berve i #94) was one of Philip's senior advisors and later served as Alexander's regent in Greece.

110 Reigned 367–357 BCE.

111 Cf. Ael. *VH* 6.12. A condensed version of what follows (to 10.440b) is preserved at Ael. *VH* 2.41.

112 Cf. 6.249e–f (drawing on Hegesander) with n.

f τοῦ | προτέρου οὗτοι υἱοί, ὡς ὁ Θεόπομπος ἱστορεῖ ἐν
τῇ τεσσαρακοστῇ κἂν τῇ ἑξῆς τῶν Ἱστοριῶν. γράφει
δὲ οὕτως περὶ τοῦ Νυσαίου· Νυσαῖος ὁ τυραννήσας
ὕστερον Συρακοσίων ὥσπερ ἐπὶ θανάτῳ συνειλημ-
μένος καὶ προειδὼς ὅτι μῆνας ὀλίγους ἤμελλε ἐπι-
βιώσεσθαι γαστριζόμενος καὶ μεθύων διῆγεν. ἐν δὲ τῇ
τριακοστῇ ἐνάτῃ φησίν· Ἀπολλοκράτης ὁ Διονυσίου
436 τοῦ τυράννου υἱὸς ἀκόλαστος ‖ ἦν καὶ φιλοπότης· καὶ
τῶν κολακευόντων τινὲς αὐτὸν παρεσκεύαζον ὡς ἔνι
μάλιστα ἀλλοτριώτατα πρὸς τὸν πατέρα διακεῖσθαι.
καὶ Ἱππαρῖνον δὲ τὸν Διονυσίου φησὶν ὑπὸ μέθης
τυραννοῦντα ἀποσφαγῆναι. περὶ δὲ τοῦ Νυσαίου καὶ
τάδε γράφει· Νυσαῖος ὁ Διονυσίου τοῦ προτέρου υἱὸς
κύριος τῶν ἐν Συρακούσαις γενόμενος πραγμάτων
κατεσκευάσατο τέθριππον καὶ τὴν ἐσθῆτα τὴν ποι-
κίλην ἀνέλαβεν, ἔτι δὲ καὶ τὴν ὀψοφαγίαν καὶ τὴν
b οἰνοφλυγίαν καὶ τὴν τῶν | παίδων καὶ τὴν τῶν γυναι-
κῶν ὕβριν καὶ τὴν τῶν ἄλλων ὅσα συντελῆ τούτοις
πέφυκε καὶ τὴν δίαιταν διῆγεν οὕτως. ἐν δὲ τῇ τεσσαρακοστῇ πέμπτῃ ὁ αὐτὸς περὶ Τιμολάου λέγων τοῦ
Θηβαίου φησίν· οὐκ ὀλίγων γὰρ ἤδη γενομένων
ἀσελγῶν περὶ τὸν βίον τὸν καθ᾽ ἡμέραν καὶ τοὺς
πότους οὐδένα νομίζω τῶν ἐν ταῖς πολιτείαις ὄντων
οὔτ᾽ ἀκρατέστερον οὔτε λιχνότερον οὔτε δοῦλον γεγονέναι μᾶλλον τῶν ἡδονῶν, εἰ μή, ὥσπερ εἶπον, Τιμό-
λαον. ἐν δὲ τῇ τρίτῃ καὶ εἰκοστῇ περὶ Χαριδήμου τοῦ
c Ὠρείτου | διηγούμενος, ὃν Ἀθηναῖοι πολίτην ἐποι-

---

113 Dionysius I was tyrant of Syracuse from the end of the 5th
century BCE until his death in 367. Hipparinus (who ruled Syracuse for several years beginning in 353) and Nysaeus (who took
over power after Hipparinus' assassination) were half-brothers of

of Dionysius I,[113] according to Theopompus in Books XL and XLI of his *History*. He writes as follows about Nysaeus (*FGrH* 115 F 188): Nysaeus, who later became tyrant of Syracuse, acted as if he had been arrested on a capital charge and knew beforehand that he had only a few months to live, and spent his time gorging himself and getting drunk. And in Book XXXIX he says (*FGrH* 115 F 185): Apollocrates, the son of the tyrant Dionysius, was out of control and liked to drink; some of his flatterers tried to make him as hostile as possible to his father. He also reports (*FGrH* 115 F 186) that Dionysius' son Hipparinus was murdered because he ran the city drunk. And as for Nysaeus, he writes the following (*FGrH* 115 F 187): After Nysaeus, the son of Dionysius I, took political control of Syracuse, he got a four-horse chariot for himself, adopted elaborately embroidered clothing, along with gluttony, wine-guzzling, sexual abuse of boys and women, and everything else that goes along with such behavior, and spent his time that way. In Book XLV (*FGrH* 115 F 210) the same author, in his discussion of Timolaus of Thebes,[114] says: For although there had already up to this point been quite a few individuals who showed no restraint in their day-to-day life and their drinking, in my opinion no one who exercised political power ever showed less self-control, or was more of a glutton or more enslaved to pleasure than, as I said, Timolaus. And in Book XXIII (*FGrH* 115 F 143), in his description of Charidemus of Oreus, whom the Athe-

Dionysius II, while Apollocrates was actually the son of Dionysius II rather than of Dionysius I.     [114] Timolaus was a (most likely pro-Macedonian) Theban general who was somehow held responsible for the disastrous revolt of 335 BCE.

ἤσαντο, φησίν· τήν τε γὰρ δίαιταν ἑωρᾶτο τὴν καθ᾽
ἡμέραν ἀσελγῆ καὶ τοιαύτην ποιούμενος ὥστε πίνειν
καὶ μεθύειν αἰεί, καὶ γυναῖκας ἐλευθέρας ἐτόλμα
διαφθείρειν· καὶ εἰς τοσοῦτον προῆλθεν ἀκρασίας
ὥστε μειράκιόν τι παρὰ τῆς βουλῆς τῆς τῶν Ὀλυν-
θίων αἰτεῖν ἐπεχείρησεν, ὃ τὴν μὲν ὄψιν ἦν εὐειδὲς καὶ
χάριεν, ἐτύγχανε δὲ μετὰ Δέρδου τοῦ Μακεδόνος
αἰχμάλωτον γεγενημένον. ἔπινε δὲ πλεῖστον καὶ
d  Ἀρκαδίων (ἄδηλον δ᾽ | εἰ ὁ Φιλίππῳ διεχθρεύσας), ὡς
τὸ ἐπίγραμμα δηλοῖ ὅπερ ἀνέγραψε Πολέμων ἐν τῷ
Περὶ τῶν Κατὰ Πόλεις Ἐπιγραμμάτων·

> τοῦ πολυκώθωνος τοῦτ᾽ ἠρίον Ἀρκαδίωνος
> ἄστεος ὤρθωσαν τᾷδε παρ᾽ ἀτραπιτῷ
> υἱῆες Δόρκων καὶ Χαρμύλος. ἔφθιτο δ᾽ ὡνήρ,
> ὤνθρωφ᾽, ἐκ χανδὸν ζωροποτῶν κύλικας.

Ἐρασίξενον δέ τινα πεπωκέναι πλεῖστόν φησι τὸ ἐπ᾽
αὐτῷ ἐπίγραμμα·

> οὐ[12] βαθὺν οἰνοπότην Ἐρασίξενον ἡ δὶς ἐφεξῆς |
e  ἀκρήτου φανερῶς ᾤχετ᾽ ἔχουσα κύλιξ.

ἔπινε δὲ πλεῖστον καὶ Ἀλκέτας ὁ Μακεδών, ὥς φησιν

---

12 Callimachus probably wrote τὸν (thus the corrrector to the
Palatine Anthology, followed by Gow–Page).

---

115 Charidemus of Oreus (Berve i #823), a city on the island
of Euboea, was a mercenary commander; the grant of Athenian
citizenship came most likely in 357/6 BCE (D. 23.65, etc.), but is
perhaps to be dated to the mid-360s instead.
116 Derdas was a member of the royal house of Elimeia, and

nians made a citizen,[115] he says: Because he openly led a depraved existence, to the extent that he was constantly drinking and in a stupor, and he went so far as to seduce free women. He became so reckless that he attempted to ask the Olynthian city council for a boy who was good-looking and graceful, and who had happened to be taken prisoner along with Derdas of Macedon.[116] Arcadion as well drank large amounts—it is unclear if this is Philip's bitter enemy[117]—as the epigram (anon. *FGE* 1624–7) copied by Polemon in his *On Epigrams by City* (fr. 79 Preller) makes clear:

> This tomb, which belongs to Arcadion of the many
> > cups,
> > > was erected here beside the path that leads to the
> > > city
> > by his sons Dorcon and Charmylus. The man died,
> > > sir, by gulping down six cups of strong wine.

A certain Erasixenus drank a lot, according to his epigram (Call. *HE* 1325–6 = *AP* 7.454):[118]

> Because Erasixenus was not a serious drinker, two
> > cups
> > in a row of unmixed wine patently carried him off.

Alcetas of Macedon[119] also drank large amounts, according

fought for Philip II of Macedon in his war with Olynthus in 349–348 BCE. [117] Arcadion of Achaea; cf. 6.249c–d.

[118] Athenaeus' version of the text is substantially different from that preserved elsewhere.

[119] A late 6th-century BCE king of Macedon (father of Amyntas I).

Ἄριστος ὁ Σαλαμίνιος, καὶ Διότιμος ὁ Ἀθηναῖος. οὗτος δὲ καὶ Χώνη ἐπεκαλεῖτο· ἐντιθέμενος γὰρ τῷ στόματι χώνην ἀπαύστως ἔπινεν ἐπιχεομένου οἴνου, ὅθεν καὶ Χώνη ἐπεκλήθη, ὥς φησι Πολέμων. Κλεομένης δὲ ὁ Λακεδαιμόνιος ὅτι καὶ ἀκρατοπότης ἦν προείρηται· ὅτι δὲ διὰ μέθην ἑαυτὸν καὶ μαχαίρᾳ
f κατέτεμεν Ἡρόδοτος | ἱστόρησε. καὶ Ἀλκαῖος δ᾽ ὁ ποιητὴς φιλοπότης ἦν, ὡς προεῖπον. Βάτων δ᾽ ὁ Σινωπεὺς ἐν τοῖς Περὶ Ἴωνος τοῦ Ποιητοῦ φιλοπότην φησὶ γενέσθαι καὶ ἐρωτικώτατον τὸν Ἴωνα. καὶ αὐτὸς δὲ ἐν τοῖς Ἐλεγείοις ἐρᾶν μὲν ὁμολογεῖ Χρυσίλλης τῆς Κορινθίας, Τελέου δὲ θυγατρός· ἧς καὶ Περικλέα τὸν Ὀλύμπιον ἐρᾶν φησι Τηλεκλείδης ἐν Ἡσιόδοις. Ξέναρχος δ᾽ ὁ Ῥόδιος διὰ τὴν πολυποσίαν Μετρητὴς ἐπεκαλεῖτο· μνημονεύει αὐτοῦ Εὐφορίων ὁ ἐποποιὸς ἐν Χιλιάσι. Χάρης δ᾽ ὁ Μυτιληναῖος ἐν ταῖς Περὶ
437 Ἀλέξανδρον Ἱστορίαις περὶ Καλάνου ‖ εἰπὼν τοῦ Ἰνδοῦ φιλοσόφου, ὅτι ῥίψας ἑαυτὸν εἰς πυρὰν νενημένην ἀπέθανε, φησὶν ὅτι καὶ ἐπὶ τῷ μνήματι αὐτοῦ διέθηκεν Ἀλέξανδρος γυμνικὸν ἀγῶνα καὶ μουσικὸν ἐγκωμίων. ἔθηκε δέ, φησί, καὶ διὰ τὴν φιλοινίαν τῶν Ἰνδῶν καὶ ἀκρατοποσίας ἀγῶνα, καὶ ἦν ἆθλον τῷ μὲν πρώτῳ τάλαντον, τῷ δὲ δευτέρῳ τριάκοντα μναῖ καὶ τῷ τρίτῳ δέκα. τῶν οὖν πιόντων τὸν οἶνον παραχρῆμα μὲν

---

120 *PAA* 365385; unidentified, but since the other men referred to in this section of Athenaeus were all prominent generals or politicians, most likely he was as well (cf. *PAA* 365395, 365850, 365865).     121 Cf. the modern "beer-bong".

122 The comic poets referred to the late 5th-century BCE Athenian statesman Pericles (*PAA* 772645) as "Olympian" because of the enormous power he exercised; cf. Ar. *Ach*. 530 with Olson ad loc.

to Aristus of Salamis (*FGrH* 143 F 3), as did Diotimus of
Athens.[120] The latter was nicknamed Funnel; because he
would put a funnel in his mouth and drink non-stop as
wine was poured into it,[121] as a consequence of which
he was nicknamed Funnel, according to Polemon (fr. 79
Preller, continued). That Cleomenes of Sparta drank unmixed wine was noted earlier (10.427b); Herodotus (6.75)
claimed that his drunkenness led to him castrating himself. The poet Alcaeus also liked to drink, as I noted earlier (10.429a, 430a–d). Bato of Sinope in his *On the Poet
Ion* (*FGrH* 268 F 6) claims that Ion liked to drink and was
very interested in sex. Ion himself in his *Elegies* (fr. 31
West[2]) admits to being in love with Chrysilla of Corinth,
the daughter of Teleus; according to Teleclides in *Hesiods*
(fr. 18), Olympian Pericles[122] was also in love with her.
Xenarchus of Rhodes was nicknamed Amphora because
he drank so much; the epic poet Euphorion mentions him
in the *Chiliads* (fr. 49, p. 39 Powell). Chares of Mytilene
in his *History Involving Alexander* (*FGrH* 125 F 19), after describing how the Indian philosopher Calanus threw
himself onto a heaped-up pyre and died, says that Alexander held athletic competitions and a musical contest in the
singing of praise-songs at his tomb.[123] Because the Indians
love wine, he claims, he also held a contest in drinking
it unmixed; first prize was a talent, second prize was 30
*minas*,[124] and third prize was 10. 35 of those who drank the

---

[123] A much fuller version of the anecdote is preserved at Plu.
*Alex.* 69.3–70.1. Calanus (Berve i #396) died near Susa in 324 BCE.

[124] I.e. ½ talent.

ἐτελεύτησαν ὑπὸ τοῦ ψύχους τριάκοντα καὶ πέντε,
μικρὸν δὲ διαλιπόντες ἐν ταῖς σκηναῖς ἕξ. ὁ δὲ
b πλεῖστον πιὼν καὶ | νικήσας ἔπιε μὲν ἀκράτου χοᾶς
τέσσαρας καὶ τὸ τάλαντον ἔλαβεν, ἐπεβίωσε δὲ ἡμέρας τέσσαρας· ἐκαλεῖτο δὲ Πρόμαχος. Τίμαιος δέ
φησιν ὡς Διονύσιος ὁ τύραννος τῇ τῶν Χοῶν ἑορτῇ τῷ
πρώτῳ ἐκπιόντι χοᾶ ἆθλον ἔθηκε στέφανον χρυσοῦν·
καὶ ὅτι πρῶτος ἐξέπιε Ξενοκράτης ὁ φιλόσοφος καὶ
λαβὼν τὸν χρυσοῦν στέφανον καὶ ἀναλύων τῷ Ἑρμῇ
τῷ ἱδρυμένῳ ἐπὶ τῆς αὐλῆς ἐπέθηκεν, ᾧπερ εἰώθει καὶ
τοὺς ἀνθινοὺς ἑκάστοτε ἐπιτιθέναι στεφάνους ἑσπέρας
ἀπαλλασσόμενος ὡς αὑτόν. καὶ ἐπὶ τούτῳ ἐθαυμάσθη.
c τὴν δὲ τῶν Χοῶν ἑορτὴν τὴν Ἀθήνησιν | ἐπιτελου-
μένην Φανόδημός φησι Δημοφῶντα τὸν βασιλέα
< . . . > βουλόμενον ὑποδέξασθαι παραγενόμενον τὸν
Ὀρέστην Ἀθήναζε. πρὸς δὲ τὰ ἱερὰ οὐ θέλων αὐτὸν
προσιέναι οὐδ' ὁμόσπονδον γενέσθαι μήπω δικασθέν-
τα ἐκέλευσε συγκλεισθῆναί τε τὰ ἱερὰ καὶ χοᾶ οἴνου
ἑκάστῳ παρατεθῆναι, τῷ πρώτῳ ἐκπιόντι εἰπὼν ἆθλον
δοθήσεσθαι πλακοῦντα. παρήγγειλέ τε καὶ τοῦ πότου
παυσαμένους τοὺς μὲν στεφάνους οἷς ἐστεφάνωντο
d πρὸς τὰ ἱερὰ μὴ τιθέναι διὰ | τὸ ὁμοροφους γενέσθαι
τῷ Ὀρέστῃ, περὶ δὲ τὸν χοᾶ τὸν ἑαυτοῦ ἕκαστον
περιθεῖναι καὶ τῇ ἱερείᾳ ἀποφέρειν τοὺς στεφάνους

---

125 Berve i #660.      126 Dionysius II of Syracuse (as in all
the anecdotes that follow), for whom cf. 10.435d n.

127 Xenocrates of Chalcedon, who became head of the Academy in 339 BCE and was famous for his *sōphrosunē*.

128 Philodemus preserves a very similar anecdote (= Timae.
*FGrH* 566 F 158b).

129 Demophon (a son of Theseus) was an early king of Athens,

wine died on the spot from a chill, and another six did so after lingering briefly in their tents. The man who drank the most and took the prize consumed four pitchers of unmixed wine and was awarded the talent, and survived for four days; his name was Promachus.[125] Timaeus (*FGrH* 566 F 158a) reports that the tyrant Dionysius[126] set a gold garland as the prize for the first man to drain his pitcher at the Choes festival; the first person to finish his wine was the philosopher Xenocrates,[127] who took the gold garland and hung it on the herm located in front of his courtyard, on which he normally hung his garlands made of flowers when he came home in the evening.[128] People were astonished at this. As for the Choes festival celebrated in Athens, Phanodemus (*FGrH* 325 F 11) claims that King Demophon . . . because he wanted to entertain Orestes when he visited Athens.[129] Because Demophon was unwilling to allow Orestes to enter the temples or participate in any libations, since his trial had not yet been held, he ordered that all the temples were to be locked and that each man was to be served his own pitcher (*chous*) of wine, and announced that a cake would be awarded as a prize to the first person to finish his pitcher. He also announced that, after they finished drinking, they were not to dedicate the garlands they were wearing in the temples, given that they had been under the same roof as Orestes. Instead, they were to put their garlands around their individual pitchers and take them to the sanctuary in the Marshes for the

where Orestes came to be tried for the murder of Clytaemestra. The story that follows is an aetiological myth intended to explain some of the odd features of the Athenian version of the Choes festival.

πρὸς τὸ ἐν Λίμναις τέμενος, ἔπειτα θύειν ἐν τῷ ἱερῷ τὰ
ἐπίλοιπα. καὶ ἔκτοτε τὴν ἑορτὴν κληθῆναι Χοάς. τῇ δὲ
ἑορτῇ τῶν Χοῶν ἔθος ἐστὶν Ἀθήνησι πέμπεσθαι δῶρά
τε καὶ τοὺς μισθοὺς τοῖς σοφισταῖς, οἵπερ καὶ αὐτοὶ
συνεκάλουν ἐπὶ ξένια τοὺς γνωρίμους, ὥς φησιν Εὐ-
βουλίδης ὁ διαλεκτικὸς ἐν δράματι Κωμασταῖς οὕτως·

σοφιστιᾷς, κάκιστε, καὶ Χοῶν δέῃ |

e     τῶν μισθοδώρων † οὐκ ἀδείπνων ἐν τρυφῇ †.

Ἀντίγονος δ' ὁ Καρύστιος ἐν τῷ Περὶ τοῦ Διονυσίου
Βίου τοῦ Ἡρακλεώτου τοῦ Ἐπικληθέντος Μεταθεμέ-
νου φησὶ τὸν Διονύσιον τοῖς οἰκέταις συνεορτάζοντα
ἐν τῇ τῶν Χοῶν ἑορτῇ καὶ μὴ δυνάμενον διὰ γήρας
χρῆσθαι ᾗ παρειλήφεσαν ἑταίρᾳ ὑποστρέψαντα εἰπεῖν
πρὸς τοὺς συνδειπνοῦντας·

< . . . > οὐ δύναμαι τανύσαι, λαβέτω δὲ καὶ
    ἄλλος.

ἦν δὲ ὁ Διονύσιος ἔτι ἐκ νέου, ὥς φησι Νικίας ὁ
Νικαεὺς ἐν ταῖς Διαδοχαῖς, πρὸς τὰ ἀφροδίσια |
f   ἐκμανὴς καὶ πρὸς τὰς δημοσίας εἰσῄει παιδίσκας
ἀδιαφόρως. καί ποτε πορευόμενος μετά τινων γνωρίμων ὡς ἐγένετο κατὰ τὸ παιδισκεῖον, εἰς ὃ τῇ προτε-
ραίᾳ παρεληλυθὼς ὤφειλε χαλκοῦς, ἔχων τότε κατὰ
τύχην ἐκτείνας τὴν χεῖρα πάντων ὁρώντων ἀπεδίδου.
Ἀνάχαρσις δ' ὁ Σκύθης παρὰ Περιάνδρῳ τεθέντος
ἄθλου περὶ τοῦ πίνειν ᾔτησε τὸ νικητήριον πρῶτος

---

130 Because he left the Stoa to follow Epicurus; see 7.281d–e.
He lived to be 80.
131 Adapted from *Od.* 21.152.

priestess, and were then to carry out the rest of the ritual inside the temple. Ever since that time, the festival has been known as the Choes. It is the custom in Athens for presents to be sent to the sophists during the Choes festival, along with their wages. The sophists for their part used to invite their students to dinner, according to Eubulides the dialectician in his play *Revellers* (fr. 1), as follows:

> You want to be a sophist, you bastard, and you're
> > eager for the Choes,
> when wages are given † not of dinnerless in luxury †.

Antigonus of Carystus in his *On the Life of Dionysius of Heracleia, Nicknamed Deserter*[130] (p. 126 Wilamowitz = fr. 41 Dorandi = Dion. Heracl. fr. 428, *SVF* i.94) says that when Dionysius was celebrating the Choes festival with the members of his household, and his advanced age prevented him from having sex with the prostitute they had invited to join them, he turned around and said to the men having dinner with him:

> I am unable to make it taut; someone else can have
> > her.[131]

Even as a young man, according to Nicias of Nicaea in his *Successions* (*FHG* iv.464), Dionysius was crazy about sex and visited common prostitutes indiscriminately. At one point, he was walking along the street with some students and came to the brothel he had visited the previous day, where he owed a small sum of money; since he happened to have it with him then, he extended his hand and paid his debt in full view of everyone. Anacharsis the Scythian was visiting Periander, and when a drinking-contest was held, he tried to claim the prize on the ground that he

91

438  μεθυσθεὶς τῶν συμπαρόντων, ‖ ὡς ὄντος τέλους τούτου καὶ τῆς ἐν τῷ πότῳ νίκης ὥσπερ καὶ τῆς ἐν τῷ
τρέχειν. Λακύδης δὲ καὶ Τίμων οἱ φιλόσοφοι κλη-
θέντες πρός τινα τῶν γνωρίμων ἐπὶ δύο ἡμέρας καὶ
βουλόμενοι συμπεριφέρεσθαι τοῖς παροῦσιν ἔπινον
προθυμότερον. τῇ μὲν οὖν πρώτῃ τῶν ἡμερῶν ὁ Λακύδης ἀπῄει πρότερος ἐπιπολάσαντος αὐτῷ τοῦ ποτοῦ,
καὶ ὁ Τίμων ὁρῶν αὐτὸν ἀπιόντα ἔφη·

> ἠράμεθα μέγα κῦδος· ἐπέφνομεν Ἕκτορα δῖον.

τῇ δ᾽ ὑστεραίᾳ προαπιόντος τοῦ Τίμωνος διὰ τὸ μὴ
b  δυνηθῆναι ἐκπιεῖν τὴν προποθεῖσαν αὐτῷ κύλικα ‖ ὁ
Λακύδης ἰδὼν αὐτὸν ἐπανάγοντα εἶπε·

> δυστήνων δέ τε παῖδες ἐμῷ μένει ἀντιόωσιν.

Μυκερῖνον δὲ τὸν Αἰγύπτιον ὁ Ἡρόδοτος ἱστορεῖ διὰ
τῆς δευτέρας ἀκούσαντα παρὰ τῶν μάντεων ὅτι ὀλι-
γοχρόνιός ἐστι, λύχνα ποιησάμενον πολλὰ ὁπότε
γένοιτο νὺξ πίνειν καὶ εὐπαθεῖν οὔτε ἡμέρας οὔτε
νυκτὸς ἀνιέντα· καὶ εἰς τὰ ἕλεα δὲ καὶ τὰ ἄλση
νεμόμενον, ἔτι τε ὅπου πύθοιτο ἡβητήρια εἶναι
μεθύσκεσθαι. καὶ Ἄμασιν δὲ τὸν καὶ αὐτὸν Αἰγυπτίων
βασιλέα Ἡρόδοτος πολλὰ πεπωκέναι φησίν. Ἑρμείας
c  δ᾽ ὁ Μηθυμναῖος ἐν τρίτῃ Σικελικῶν φιλοπότην φησὶ
γενέσθαι Νικοτέλη τὸν Κορίνθιον. Φαινίας δὲ ὁ Ἐρέ-

---

132 Plu. *Mor.* 155f–6a preserves a slightly fuller version of a
very similar anecdote. For Periander, see 10.427e n.

133 Lacydes (*PAA* 601060) became head of the Academy in
241/0 BCE and died in 206/5. Timo of Phlius (also a resident of
Athens; *PAA* 890905) died in 230 BCE.

134 Reigned 2539/2489–2511/2451 BCE.

92

was the first person there who got drunk, as if this were the goal and a drinking-contest could be won in the same way a footrace is.[132] The philosophers Lacydes and Timo[133] were invited to the house of one of their pupils for two days, and since they wanted to fit in with the other guests, they drank aggressively. On the first day, Lacydes left before anyone else, since the wine upset his stomach, and when Timo saw him going out, he said (*Il.* 22.393):

> We achieved great glory; we killed brilliant Hector.

The next day, Timo left before the others, because he was unable to finish the cup that was given to him as a toast, and when Lacydes saw him heading out, he said (*Il.* 6.127):

> Wretched are those whose children confront my
>     might!

Herodotus in Book II (133.4) reports that when Mycerinus of Egypt[134] heard from his seers that he was not going to live long, he surrounded himself with lamps when evening came, and drank and enjoyed himself constantly day and night; and he wandered around in the marshes, the woods, and anywhere he heard that parties (*hēbētēria*)[135] were going on, and got drunk. Herodotus (2.173.1, 174.1) also claims that Amasis, another king of Egypt,[136] drank large amounts. Hermeias of Methymna in Book III of the *History of Sicily* (*FGrH* 558 F 1) says that Nicoteles of Corinth[137] liked to drink. Phaenias of Eresus in his work

---

[135] Cf. 10.425e with n.     [136] Reigned 570–526 BCE.
[137] According to D.S. 14.10.3, Nicoteles of Corinth was one of the leaders of the Syracusan revolt again Dionysius I; he was killed in 404 BCE.

σιος ἐν τῷ ἐπιγραφομένῳ Τυράννων Ἀναίρεσις ἐκ
Τιμωρίας Σκόπαν φησὶ τὸν Κρέοντος μὲν υἱόν, Σκόπα
δὲ τοῦ παλαιοῦ υἱδοῦν φιλοποτοῦντα διατελέσαι καὶ
τὴν ἐπάνοδον τὴν ἀπὸ τῶν συμποσίων ποιεῖσθαι ἐπὶ
θρόνου καθήμενον καὶ ὑπὸ τεσσάρων βασταζόμενον
οὕτως οἴκαδε ἀπιέναι. Φύλαρχος δὲ ἐν τῇ ἕκτῃ τῶν
Ἱστοριῶν Ἀντίοχόν φησι τὸν βασιλέα φίλοινον γενό-
d μενον | μεθύσκεσθαί τε καὶ κοιμᾶσθαι ἐπὶ πλέον, εἶθ'
ἑσπέρας πάλιν ἀφυπνιζόμενον ἐπιπίνειν. ἐχρημάτιζέ
τε, φησί, νήφων μὲν βραχέα τελέως, μεθύων δὲ τὰ
πολλά. διὸ περὶ αὐτὸν δύο ἦσαν οἱ διοικοῦντες τὴν
βασιλείαν, Ἄριστος καὶ Θεμίσων, Κύπριοι μὲν γένος
καὶ ἀδελφοί, ἐρώμενοι δὲ ἀμφότεροι τοῦ Ἀντιόχου.
πολυπότης δὲ ἦν καὶ Ἀντίοχος ὁ βασιλεὺς ὁ κληθεὶς
Ἐπιφανής, ὁ ὁμηρεύσας παρὰ Ῥωμαίοις, ὃν ἱστορεῖ
Πτολεμαῖος ὁ Εὐεργέτης ἐν τῷ τρίτῳ τῶν Ὑπομνη-
e μάτων κἂν τῷ πέμπτῳ | φάσκων αὐτὸν εἰς τοὺς Ἰνδι-
κοὺς κώμους καὶ μέθας τραπέντα πολλὰ ἀναλίσκειν.
καὶ τὰ περιλειπόμενα δὲ τῶν χρημάτων μεθ' ἡμέραν
κωμάζων ὁτὲ μὲν ἐξέχει, ἄλλοτε δὲ ἐν ταῖς δημοσίαις
ὁδοῖς ἱστάμενος ἔλεγε· "τίνι ἡ τύχη δίδωσι, λαβέτω·"
καὶ ῥίψας τὸ ἀργύριον ᾤχετο. πολλάκις δὲ καὶ πλεκτὸν
στέφανον ῥόδων ἔχων ἐπὶ τῆς κεφαλῆς καὶ χρυσοϋφῆ
τήβενναν φορῶν μόνος ἐρέμβετο λίθους ὑπὸ μάλης
ἔχων, οἷς ἔβαλλε τῶν ἰδιωτῶν τοὺς ἀκολουθοῦντας

---

138 The Scopadae ruled the Thessalian city of Crannon in the
6th century BCE; cf. Pl. Prt. 339a–b (quoting a fragment of poetry
attributed to Simonides).

139 The location of this fragment in Book VI suggests that the
Antiochus in question is Antiochus II (reigned 261–246 BCE).

140 For Themison, cf. 7.289f–90a.

entitled *Revenge-Killings of Tyrants* (fr. 14 Wehrli) says
that Scopas,[138] who was the son of Creon and the grand-
son of the elder Scopas, enjoyed drinking throughout his
life and used to return from parties seated on a litter and
carried by four men, and that this is how he got home.
Phylarchus in Book VI of his *History* (*FGrH* 81 F 6) claims
that King Antiochus[139] liked wine, and that he got drunk
and slept a lot, and then in the evening would wake up
again and drink some more. Antiochus did not do much
business at all sober, he says, but instead did most of it
drunk. This is why he had two assistants who managed his
kingdom, Aristus and Themison,[140] who were brothers
from Cyprus and were both Antiochus' boyfriends. The
King Antiochus known as Epiphanes,[141] who was held hostage in Rome, also drank large amounts; Ptolemy Euer-
getes discusses him in Books III and V of his *Commentaries* (*FGrH* 234 F 3) and reports that after he became
interested in Indian parties and drinking-bouts, he began
to spend large amounts of money. When he was wandering
around drunk after the sun came up, he would sometimes
dump the rest of his money on the ground, while at other
times he would stand in the city streets and say: "Whoever
chance gives it to can have it!" And then he would throw his
money in the air and leave. He often wandered around
alone, with a garland woven out of roses on his head and
wearing a toga into which gold had been worked, and carrying stones under his arm, which he threw at the private
citizens who trailed him.[142] He used to bathe in the public

[141] Antiochus IV (reigned 175–164 BCE).
[142] Presumably waiting for the moment when he would
abruptly empty his pockets.

αὐτῷ. ἐλούετο δὲ καὶ εἰς τοὺς κοινοὺς λουτρῶνας

f μύροις | ἀλειφόμενος, ὅτε καί ποτε συνιδών τις αὐτὸν
ἰδιώτης ἔφη, "μακάριος εἶ, ὦ βασιλεῦ· πολυτελὲς
ὄζεις." καὶ ὃς ἡσθείς, "ἐγώ σε", φησίν, "ὑπέρκορον
τούτου ποιήσω." καὶ κατὰ τῆς κεφαλῆς αὐτοῦ ὑδρί-
σκην ὑπὲρ δύο χοᾶς ἔχουσαν παχέος μύρου κατα-
χυθῆναι ἐκέλευσεν, ὡς καὶ τὸ πλῆθος τῶν ἀγοραιο-
τέρων εἰς τὸ ἐκχυθὲν συγκυλισθῆναι. ὀλίσθου τε
γενομένου αὐτός τε ὁ Ἀντίοχος ἔπεσε καγχάζων καὶ οἱ

439 πλεῖστοι τῶν λουομένων τὸ αὐτὸ ἔπασχον. ‖ Πολύβιος
δ' ἐν τῇ ἕκτῃ καὶ εἰκοστῇ τῶν Ἱστοριῶν καλεῖ αὐτὸν
Ἐπιμανῆ καὶ οὐκ Ἐπιφανῆ διὰ τὰς πράξεις· οὐ μόνον
γὰρ μετὰ δημοτῶν ἀνθρώπων κατέβαινεν εἰς ὁμιλίας,
ἀλλὰ καὶ μετὰ τῶν παρεπιδημούντων ξένων τῶν εὐτελεστάτων[13] συνέπινεν. εἰ δὲ καὶ τῶν νεωτέρων, φησί,
αἴσθοιτό τινας συνευωχουμένους ὁπουδήποτε, παρῆν
μετὰ κερατίου καὶ συμφωνίας, ὥστε τοὺς πολλοὺς διὰ
τὸ παράδοξον ἀνισταμένους φεύγειν. πολλάκις δὲ καὶ

b τὴν βασιλικὴν ἐσθῆτα | ἀποβαλὼν τήβενναν ἀναλα-
βὼν περιῄει τὴν ἀγοράν. ἐν δὲ τῇ πρώτῃ καὶ τριακοστῇ ὁ αὐτὸς Πολύβιός φησι συντελοῦντα αὐτὸν ἐν τῇ
Ἀντιοχείᾳ ἀγῶνας συγκαλέσαι πάντας Ἕλληνας καὶ
τῶν βουλομένων τοὺς πολλοὺς ἐπὶ τὴν θέαν. καὶ
πλείστων παραγινομένων ἐν τοῖς γυμνασίοις, πάντας
ἐκ χρυσῶν ὁλκείων ἤλειφε κροκίνῳ μύρῳ καὶ κιννα-
μωμίνῳ καὶ ναρδίνῳ καὶ ἀμαρακίνῳ καὶ ἰρίνῳ. καὶ

13 καὶ τῶν εὐτελεστάτων A: καὶ μετὰ τῶν εὐτελεστάτων
CE; cf. 5.193d μετὰ τῶν παρεπιδημούντων . . . τῶν εὐτελεστάτων

baths and cover himself with perfume, and on one occasion a private citizen saw him and said: "You're a lucky man, your majesty; you smell like money!" Antiochus was pleased and responded: "I'll fill you to the brim with this!", and ordered a pitcher that contained more than two *choēs* of thick perfume to be dumped over the man's head, so that all the common people were able to roll around in the perfume that had been poured out. The floor became slippery, and Antiochus himself fell down laughing, as did most of those who were having a bath.[143] Polybius in Book XXVI (1ᵃ) of his *History*[144] refers to him as Epimanes ("the Madman") rather than Epiphanes ("God Apparent") because of his behavior; for not only did he associate with average people, but he drank with the least distinguished strangers who were visiting the country. And if he heard, says (Polybius), that some young men were having a feast somewhere, he showed up with a drinking-horn and a group of musicians, causing most of them to leap up in surprise and try to run away. He also frequently discarded his royal robes, put on a toga, and circulated through the marketplace. The same Polybius says in Book XXXI (Plb. 30.26) that when Antiochus held games in Antioch, he invited all the Greeks and many others who were interested to watch them.[145] Although there were large crowds in the competition sites, he covered them all with crocus-, cinnamon-, nard-, marjoram-, and iris-perfumes drawn from

---

[143] A different version of this anecdote is preserved at 5.194a–c, where it (like the material below) is attributed to Polybius Book XXVI.    [144] Cf. 5.193c–e (a fuller version).

[145] Material virtually identical to what follows is preserved at 5.194c, 195c–f.

συγκαλῶν αὐτοὺς εἰς εὐωχίαν ποτὲ μὲν χίλια τρίκλινα,
c ποτὲ δὲ χίλια πεντακόσια | συνεπλήρου μετὰ πολυ-
τελεστάτης κατασκευῆς. καὶ ὁ χειρισμὸς τῆς δια-
κονίας δι᾽ αὐτοῦ ἐγίνετο· κατὰ γὰρ τὰς εἰσόδους
ἐφιστάμενος οὓς μὲν εἰσῆγεν, οὓς δ᾽ ἀνέκλινεν, καὶ
τοὺς διακόνους δὲ τοὺς τὰς παραθέσεις εἰσφέροντας
αὐτὸς εἰσῆγε, καὶ περιπορευόμενος οὗ μὲν προσεκάθι-
ζεν, οὗ δὲ προσανέπιπτε. καὶ ποτὲ μὲν ἀποθέμενος
μεταξὺ τὸν ψωμόν, ποτὲ δὲ τὸ ποτήριον ἀνεπήδα καὶ
μετανίστατο καὶ περιῄει τὸν πότον προπόσεις λαμ-
d βάνων ὀρθὸς ἄλλοτε | παρ᾽ ἄλλοις, ἅμα δὲ τοῖς ἀκρο-
άμασι προσπαίζων. καὶ ὑπὸ τῶν μίμων εἰσεφέρετο
ὅλος συγκεκαλυμμένος καὶ ἐτίθετο εἰς τὴν γῆν ὡς εἷς
ὢν τῶν μίμων· καὶ τῆς συμφωνίας προκαλουμένης ὁ
βασιλεὺς ἀναπηδήσας ὠρχεῖτο καὶ προσέπαιζε τοῖς
μίμοις, ὥστε πάντας αἰσχύνεσθαι. τοιαῦτα ἀπεργάζεται τοὺς ταλαιπώρους ἡ πρὸς τῇ μέθῃ ἀπαιδευσία.
φιλοπότης δ᾽ ἦν καὶ ὁ ὁμώνυμος αὐτῷ Ἀντίοχος, ὁ ἐν
Μηδίᾳ πρὸς Ἀρσάκην πολεμήσας, ὡς ἱστορεῖ Ποσει-
e δώνιος ὁ Ἀπαμεὺς | ἐν τῇ ἑκκαιδεκάτῃ τῶν Ἱστοριῶν.
ἀναιρεθέντος γοῦν αὐτοῦ τὸν Ἀρσάκην θάπτοντα
αὐτὸν λέγειν· "ἔσφηλέν σε, Ἀντίοχε, θάρσος καὶ μέθη·
ἤλπιζες γὰρ ἐν μεγάλοις ποτηρίοις τὴν Ἀρσάκου
βασιλείαν ἐκπιεῖν." Ἀντίοχος δὲ ὁ μέγας ἐπικαλού-
μενος, ὃν Ῥωμαῖοι καθεῖλον, ὡς ἱστορεῖ Πολύβιος ἐν
τῇ εἰκοστῇ, παρελθὼν εἰς Χαλκίδα τῆς Εὐβοίας συν-
ετέλει γάμους, πεντήκοντα μὲν ἔτη γεγονὼς καὶ δύο τὰ
μέγιστα τῶν ἔργων ἀνειληφώς, τήν τε τῶν Ἑλλήνων

---

146 Antiochus VII Sidetes; he invaded Media in 130 BCE, and
was killed there in 129. Arsaces is the dynastic name of the
Parthian king Phraates II; cf. 4.153a n.

gold bowls. He also invited them to feasts, on one occasion filling 1000 banqueting-rooms with extremely expensive fixtures, on another 1500. In addition, he supervised all the serving himself: he stood at the entrance, and guided some people in and settled others in their couches; he personally led the servants who brought the food into the room; and he circulated around, sitting next to someone here and lying down next to someone else there. And sometimes he would put down a bit of food when he was halfway done with it, or a cup, and would leap up and change his position, or make his way around the party, standing beside various people and accepting toasts, while simultaneously participating in the entertainment. He was in fact carried in by the mimes, entirely wrapped up, and set on the ground as if he were one of them; and when the musicians gave a signal, the king leapt up and began to dance and act along with the mimes, which embarrassed everyone. This is what unsophisticated drunken behavior does to its unfortunate victims. The Antiochus who shared his name,[146] and who fought a war against Arsaces in Media, also liked to drink, according to Posidonius of Apameia in Book XVI of his *History* (*FGrH* 87 F 11 = fr. 63 Edelstein–Kidd). After he was killed, therefore, Arsaces said as he was burying him: "Your boldness and your drunkenness tripped you up, Antiochus; because you thought you were going to swallow up Arsaces' kingdom in large cups." According to Polybius in Book XX (8), after Antiochus (nicknamed the Great; this is the man the Romans overthrew)[147] arrived in Euboean Chalcis, he got married; he was 50 years old and had already undertaken his two greatest tasks, the liberation of

[147] Reigned 222–187 BCE.

f ἐλευθέρωσιν, ὡς αὐτὸς ἐπηγγέλλετο, καὶ τὸν | πρὸς
Ῥωμαίους πόλεμον. ἐρασθεὶς οὖν παρθένου Χαλκι-
δικῆς κατὰ τὸν τοῦ πολέμου καιρὸν ἐφιλοτιμήσατο
γῆμαι αὐτήν, οἰνοπότης ὢν καὶ μέθαις χαίρων· ἦν δ'
αὕτη Κλεοπτολέμου μὲν θυγάτηρ ἑνὸς τῶν ἐπιφανῶν,
κάλλει δὲ πάσας ὑπερβάλλουσα. καὶ τοὺς γάμους
συντελῶν ἐν τῇ Χαλκίδι αὐτόθι διέτριψε τὸν χειμῶνα,
τῶν ἐνεστώτων οὐδ' ἡντινοῦν ποιούμενος πρόνοιαν·
ἔθετο δὲ καὶ τῇ παιδὶ ὄνομα Εὔβοιαν. ἡττηθεὶς οὖν τῷ
πολέμῳ ἔφυγεν εἰς Ἔφεσον μετὰ τῆς νεογάμου. ἐν δὲ
440 τῇ δευτέρᾳ ὁ αὐτὸς Πολύβιος ἱστορεῖ ‖ Ἄγρωνα τὸν
Ἰλλυριῶν βασιλέα ἡσθέντα ἐπὶ τῷ νενικηκέναι τοὺς
μέγα φρονοῦντας Αἰτωλοὺς πολυπότην ὄντα καὶ εἰς
μέθας καὶ εὐωχίας τραπέντα πλευρίτιδι ληφθέντα
ἀποθανεῖν. ἐν δὲ τῇ ἐνάτῃ καὶ εἰκοστῇ ὁ αὐτὸς Γεν-
θίωνά φησι τὸν τῶν Ἰλλυριῶν βασιλέα διὰ τὴν πολυ-
ποσίαν πολλὰ ποιεῖν ἀσελγῆ κατὰ τὸν βίον, νύκτωρ τε
αἰεὶ καὶ μεθ' ἡμέραν μεθύοντα. ἀποκτείναντα δὲ καὶ
Πλεύρατον τὸν ἀδελφὸν γαμεῖν μέλλοντα τὴν Μονου-
νίου θυγατέρα αὐτὸν γῆμαι τὴν παῖδα καὶ ὡμῶς
b χρῆσθαι | τοῖς ἀρχομένοις. καὶ Δημήτριον δέ φησι
τὸν ἐκ τῆς Ῥώμης τὴν ὁμηρείαν διαφυγόντα ἐν τῇ
τρίτῃ καὶ τριακοστῇ βασιλεύσαντα Σύρων πολυπότην
ὄντα τὸ πλεῖστον τῆς ἡμέρας μεθύσκεσθαι. Ὀροφέρ-
νην τε ὀλίγον χρόνον Καππαδοκίας βασιλεύσαντα
καὶ παριδόντα τὰς πατρίους ἀγωγάς φησιν ἐν τῇ
τριακοστῇ δευτέρᾳ εἰσαγαγεῖν τὴν Ἰακὴν καὶ τεχνι-
τικὴν ἀσωτίαν.

---

148 In autumn 231 BCE.     149 c.181 BCE; Genthius' brother
was in fact probably named Plator rather than Pleuratus.
150 Demetrius I Soter of Syria (reigned 161–151/0 BCE).

the Greeks, as he himself referred to it, and his war against the Romans. He fell in love, then, with a young Chalcidian woman while this war was still going on, and became fixated on marrying her, even though he was a wine-drinker who liked to get drunk. She was a daughter of Cleoptolemus, who belonged to the upper class, and was the most beautiful woman in the city. He spent the winter there in Chalcis in order to complete the marriage, paying no attention whatsoever to larger developments; he referred to the girl as Euboea. After he lost the war, then, he escaped to Ephesus with his new bride. In Book II (4.6) the same Polybius reports that the Illyrian king Agron, who was delighted to have defeated the proud Aetolians, but who consumed large amounts of wine and spent his time at drinking parties and feasts, caught pneumonia and died.[148] In Book XXIX (13) the same author claims that the Illyrian king Genthion drank so much that he engaged in a great deal of ugly behavior throughout his life and was constantly intoxicated day and night. After he killed his brother Pleuratus,[149] who was about to marry Monounius' daughter, he married the girl himself and treated his subjects cruelly. In Book XXXIII (19) Polybius says that Demetrius, who escaped when he was being held hostage in Rome and became king of Syria,[150] drank large amounts and spent most of the day intoxicated. And in Book XXXII (11.10) he claims that Oropherenes, who was briefly king of Cappadocia[151] and rejected the traditional local customs, introduced the elaborate Ionian style of debauchery.[152]

[151] c.160–c.155 BCE.
[152] For the Ionians' alleged addiction to luxury, see 12.523e–4c, 524f–5e.

Διόπερ ὁ θειότατος Πλάτων καλῶς νομοθετεῖ ἐν τῷ
δευτέρῳ τοὺς παῖδας μέχρι ἐτῶν ὀκτωκαίδεκα τὸ
παράπαν οἴνου μὴ γεύεσθαι· οὐ γὰρ χρὴ πῦρ ἐπὶ πῦρ
c ὀχετεύειν. οἴνου δὲ μετρίου γεύεσθαι | μέχρι τριάκοντα
ἐτῶν, μέθης δὲ καὶ πολυοινίας τὸ παράπαν τὸν νέον
ἀπέχεσθαι. τετταράκοντα δὲ ἐπιβαίνοντα ἐτῶν ἐν τοῖς
συσσιτίοις εὐωχηθέντα καλεῖν τούς τε ἄλλους θεοὺς
καὶ δὴ <καὶ>[14] Διόνυσον παρακαλεῖν εἰς τὴν τῶν
πρεσβυτῶν τελετὴν ἅμα καὶ παιδιάν, ἣν τοῖς ἀνθρώποις ἐπίκουρον τῆς τοῦ γήρως αὐστηρότητος ἐδωρή-
σατο τὸν οἶνον[15] φάρμακον, ὥστε ἀνηβᾶν ἡμᾶς καὶ
δυσθυμίας λήθην γίγνεσθαι. καὶ ἑξῆς δέ φησι· λόγος |
d καὶ φήμη ὑπορρεῖ, ὡς ὁ θεὸς οὗτος ὑπὸ τῆς μητρυιᾶς
Ἥρας διεφορήθη τῆς ψυχῆς τὴν γνώμην· διὸ τάς τε
βακχείας καὶ τὴν μανικὴν πᾶσαν ἐμβάλλει χορείαν
τιμωρούμενος, ὅθεν καὶ τὸν οἶνον ἐπὶ τοῦτ' αὐτὸ δεδώ-
ρηται.

Φάλαικος δ' ἐν τοῖς Ἐπιγράμμασι γυναῖκά τινα
ἀναγράφει πολυπότιν Κλεὼ ὄνομα·

χρυσωτὸν κροκόεντα περιζώσασα χιτῶνα
τόνδε Διωνύσῳ δῶρον ἔδωκε Κλεὼ
οὔνεκα συμποσίοισι μετέπρεπεν, ἶσα δὲ πίνειν |
e οὔτις οἱ ἀνθρώπων ἤρισεν οὐδαμά πω.

ὅτι δὲ φίλοινον τὸ τῶν γυναικῶν γένος κοινόν. οὐκ

---

[14] added from the traditional text of Plato
[15] τὸν οἶνον (omitted in my translation) is also preserved in
the traditional text of Plato, but is difficult to incorporate into the
syntax of the sentence and most likely represents a misguided
superlinear note that made its way into the text.

102

This is why the wonderful Plato in Book II (*Lg.* 666a–b, condensed and adapted) is right to make it a law that boys are not even to taste wine until they are 18 years old; for there is no reason to add fire to fire.[153] A young man may consume a limited amount of wine up to the age of 30, but should completely avoid becoming intoxicated or drinking large quantities. Once a man reaches age 40, he may invoke the gods after he dines in the common mess, and in particular may summon Dionysus to the rite celebrated by the elders and to the good times they have; Dionysus granted this to human beings as a drug to help us deal with the bitterness of old age, allowing us to recover our youth and forget our discouragement. And immediately after this he says (*Lg.* 672b): A legend and a rumor circulate quietly, to the effect that this god's sanity was stripped from him by his stepmother Hera. This is why, when he punishes people, he forces them to act like bacchants and to engage in wild dancing of all kinds; he has accordingly given us wine for this very purpose.

Phalaecus in his *Epigrams* (*HE* 2935–8) describes a woman named Cleo who drinks large amounts:

> After she wrapped this gold-spangled, saffron-colored tunic about
>   herself, Cleo offered it as a gift to Dionysus
> because she stood out at drinking parties, and no one ever
>   came close to consuming as much wine as she did.

That women like wine is a commonplace. Xenarchus in his

---

153 I.e. "to bring coals to Newcastle".

ἀχαρίτως δὲ καὶ ὁ Ξέναρχος ἐν τῷ Πεντάθλῳ γυναῖκά
τινα παράγει φρικτότατον ὅρκον ὀμνύουσαν τόνδε·

⟨οὕτως⟩ ἐμοὶ γένοιτο σοῦ ζώσης, τέκνον,
ἐλευθέριον πιοῦσαν οἶνον ἀποθανεῖν.

παρὰ Ῥωμαίοις δέ, ὥς φησι Πολύβιος ἐν τῇ ἕκτῃ,
ἀπείρηται γυναιξὶ πίνειν οἶνον· τὸ δὲ καλούμενον
πάσσον πίνουσι. τοῦτο δὲ ποιεῖται μὲν ἐκ τῆς ἀστα-
φίδος καί ἐστι παραπλήσιος πινόμενος τῷ Αἰγοσθενεῖ
f    τῷ | γλυκεῖ καὶ τῷ Κρητικῷ· διὸ πρὸς τὸ κατεπεῖγον
τοῦ δίψους χρῶνται αὐτῷ. λαθεῖν δ' ἐστὶν ἀδύνατον
τὴν γυναῖκα πιοῦσαν οἶνον· πρῶτον μὲν γὰρ οὐδ' ἔχει
οἴνου κυρείαν ἡ γυνή· πρὸς δὲ τούτοις φιλεῖν δεῖ τοὺς
συγγενεῖς τοὺς ἑαυτῆς καὶ τοὺς τοῦ ἀνδρὸς ἕως ἐξανε-
ψιῶν καὶ τοῦτο ποιεῖν καθ' ἡμέραν, ὁπόταν ἴδῃ πρῶτον. λοιπὸν ἀδήλου τῆς ἐντυχίας οὔσης τίσιν ἀπαν-
τήσει φυλάσσεται· τὸ γὰρ πρᾶγμα κἂν γεύσηται
441  μόνον οὐ προσδεῖ διαβολῆς. ‖ Ἄλκιμος δ' ὁ Σικε-
λιώτης ἐν τῇ ἐπιγραφομένῃ τῶν βίβλων Ἰταλικῇ
πάσας φησὶ τὰς ἐν Ἰταλίᾳ γυναῖκας μὴ πίνειν οἶνον
ἀπὸ τοιαύτης αἰτίας· Ἡρακλῆς περὶ τὴν Κροτωνιᾶτιν
γενόμενος ἐπεὶ πρός τινα οἰκίαν οὖσαν παρὰ τὴν ὁδὸν
διψῶν ἀφίκετο, προσελθὼν ᾔτει πιεῖν ἐντεῦθεν. ἔτυχε
δ' ἡ γυνὴ τοῦ τὴν οἰκίαν κεκτημένου πίθον οἴνου
λαθραίως ὑποίξασα· καὶ πρὸς μὲν τὸν ἄνδρα δεινὸν
ἔφη ποιήσειν αὐτόν, εἰ ξένου χάριν τὸν πίθον τοῦτον
ἀνοίξειεν, ὕδωρ δ' ἐκέλευσεν αὐτὸν προσενεγκεῖν. |
b    Ἡρακλῆς δ' ἐπὶ θύραις ἑστὼς καὶ ἀκούσας ταῦτα τὸν
μὲν ἄνδρα αὐτῆς σφόδρα ἐπήνεσεν, ὃν ἐκέλευσεν

154 In place of the expected "water of freedom".
155 Latin passum.

*The Pentathlete* (fr. 5) quite amusingly brings a woman on-stage swearing the following absolutely horrifying oath:

> Thus might it be granted me, my child, while you are
>     still alive,
> to die once I drink the wine of freedom.[154]

In Rome, according to Polybius in Book VI (11a.4), women are forbidden to drink wine; they drink what is referred to as *passon*[155] instead. *Passon* is made from raisins, and when you drink it, it resembles Aegosthenic or Cretan grape-must; this is why people consume it when they are desperately thirsty. A woman cannot go undetected when she drinks wine; this is because, first of all, women are unable to hold their wine, and on top of that they are required to kiss their own relatives and their husband's relatives as far extended as first cousins once removed, and to do so every day, whenever they first see them. Moreover, since who she is going to run into is entirely a matter of chance, she stays on her guard; because even if she only has a taste, that is enough to ruin her reputation. Alcimus of Sicily in his book entitled *The History of Italy* (*FGrH* 560 F 2) claims that no Italian woman drinks wine for the following reason: Heracles was near Croton and was thirsty, and when he came to a house that stood beside the road, he went up to it and asked the people who lived there to give him a drink. The wife of the man whose house it was happened to have opened a storage-jar of wine without his knowledge, and she told her husband that it would be a terrible mistake to open this jar for the sake of a stranger, and encouraged him to offer their visitor water. Heracles was standing by the door and heard what she said, and he warmly praised

αὐτὸν παρελθόντα εἴσω σκοπεῖν τὸν πίθον· καὶ ὃς
εἰσελθὼν λίθινον εὗρε τὸν πίθον γεγονότα. τοῦτο δὲ τὸ
σημεῖον ἔτι καὶ νῦν ἐστιν ἐν ταῖς ἐπιχωρίαις γυναιξὶν
πάσαις ἐν αἰσχρῷ κεῖσθαι τὸ πίνειν οἶνον διὰ τὴν
προκειμένην αἰτίαν. οἶαι δ᾽ εἰσὶ παρὰ τοῖς Ἕλλησι
μεθύουσαι αἱ γυναῖκες παραδίδωσιν Ἀντιφάνης μὲν ἐν
τῇ Ἀκοντιζομένῃ οὕτω·

> γείτων ἐστί τις |

c  κάπηλος· οὗτος εὐθὺς ὅταν ἔλθω ποτὲ
διψῶσα, μόνος οἶδ᾽ ὥς γ᾽ ἐμοὶ κεράννυται.
οὔθ᾽ ὑδαρὲς οὔτ᾽ ἄκρατον οἶδ᾽ ἐγώ ποτε
πιοῦσα.

καὶ ἐν Μύστιδι· γυναῖκες δέ εἰσιν αἱ διαλεγόμεναι·

> (Α.) βούλει καὶ σύ, φιλτάτη, πιεῖν;
> (Β.) καλῶς ἔχει μοι. (Α.) τοιγαροῦν ⟨ἐμοὶ⟩ φέρε·
> μέχρι γὰρ τριῶν ⟨δεῖν⟩ φασι τιμᾶν τοὺς θεούς.

Ἄλεξις δὲ Ὀρχηστρίδι·

> (Α.) γυναιξὶ δ᾽ ἀρκεῖ πάντ᾽, ἐὰν οἶνος παρῇ
> πίνειν διαρκής. (Β.) ἀλλὰ μήν, νὴ τὼ θεώ, |
d  ἔσται γ᾽ ὅσον ἂν βουλώμεθ᾽, ἔσται καὶ μάλα
ἡδύς γ᾽, ὀδόντας οὐκ ἔχων, ἤδη σαπρός,
πέπων, γέρων γε δαιμονίως. (Α.) ἀσπάζομαι
γραῦν Σφίγγα· πρὸς ἐμὲ † ὡς αἰνίγματα.
λέγε καὶ τὰ λοιπά.

---

156 Sc. for resisting his wife's suggestion.

the woman's husband[156] and told him to go inside and have a look at the storage-jar; when the man did so, he discovered that the jar had turned to stone. Even today this is regarded as evidence among all the local women that drinking wine is unacceptable behavior, for the reason described above. Antiphanes in his *The Girl Who Was Hit by a Javelin* (fr. 25) conveys what Greek women are like when they get drunk, as follows:

> There's a neighborhood
> bartender; whenever I'm thirsty and I go in there, he's
> the only one who knows how I like my wine mixed.
> I don't think I've ever had it too watery or
> straight.

Also in *The Female Initiate* (fr. 163); women are speaking:

> (A.) Would you like a drink, my dear?
> (B.) That's fine by me! (A.) Alright then, bring me one;
> because people say we ought to honor the gods up to three times.

Alexis in *The Dancing-Girl* (fr. 172):

> (A.) Women have everything they need, provided there's enough
> wine to drink. (B.) Let me assure you, by the two goddesses,
> we'll have as much as we want, and it'll be absolutely
> delicious: no teeth, fully fermented,
> ripe, and devilishly old. (A.) Hello,
> you old Sphinx! To me † like riddles;
> tell me the rest!

ἐν δὲ Δὶς Πενθοῦντι Ζωπύρας τινὸς μνημονεύων φησί·

καὶ Ζωπύρα,

οἰνηρὸν ἀγγεῖον.

Ἀντιφάνης Βάκχαις·

ἐπεὶ δὲ τοῦτ' οὐκ ἔστι, κακοδαίμων σφόδρα
ὅστις γαμεῖ γυναῖκα, πλὴν ἐν τοῖς Σκύθαις·
ἐκεῖ μόνον γὰρ οὐχὶ φύετ' ἄμπελος. |

e   Ξέναρχος Πεντάθλῳ·

ὅρκον δ' ἐγὼ γυναικὸς εἰς οἶνον γράφω.

Πλάτων Φάωνι διηγούμενος ὅσα διὰ τὸν οἶνον συμβαίνει ταῖς γυναιξί φησιν·

εἶέν, γυναῖκες ‹ . . . › ὡς ὑμῖν πάλαι
οἶνον γενέσθαι τὴν ἄνοιαν εὔχομαι.
ὑμῖν γὰρ οὐδέν, καθάπερ ἡ παροιμία,
ἐν τῷ καπήλῳ νοῦς ἐνεῖναί μοι δοκεῖ.
εἰ γὰρ Φάωνα δεῖσθ' ἰδεῖν, προτέλεια δεῖ
ὑμᾶς ποῆσαι πολλὰ πρότερον τοιαδί· |

f   πρῶτα μὲν ἐμοὶ γὰρ Κουροτρόφῳ προθύεται
πλακοῦς ἐνόρχης, ἄμυλος ἐγκύμων, κίχλαι
ἑκκαίδεχ' ὁλόκληροι μέλιτι μεμιγμέναι,
λαγῷα δώδεκ' ἐπισέληνα. τἆλλα δὲ
ἤδη † ταῦτ' εὐτελέστατα· † ἄκουε δή.

---

157 In place of the expected "in water".

108

And in *Grieving Twice* (fr. 56) he mentions someone named Zopyra and says:

> and Zopyra,
>    who's a pot full of wine.

Antiphanes in *Bacchants* (fr. 58):

> But since this is impossible, anyone who gets married
> is in terrible trouble—except in Scythia;
> because that's the only place where grapevines don't
>     grow!

Xenarchus in *The Pentathlete* (fr. 6):

> I write a woman's oath in wine.[157]

Plato in *Phaon* (fr. 188), describing everything that happens to women because of wine, says:

> Alright, ladies . . . I've been praying for a long time
> for your foolishness to turn into wine;
> because your mind doesn't look to me to be
> in the wineshop, as the saying goes.
> If you want to see Phaon, you have to make
> lots of preliminary sacrifices of the following sort
>     first.
> Number one, a preliminary offering is made to me,
>     the Rearer of Children:
> an uncastrated cake, a pregnant wheat-paste cake, 16
> perfect thrushes in honey-sauce,
> and 12 moon-shaped bits of hare-meat. As for the
>     rest
> now † these items very cheap †. Pay attention!

βολβῶν μὲν Ὀρθάννῃ τρί' ἡμίεκτεα,
Κονισάλῳ δὲ καὶ παραστάταιν δυοῖν ‖
442    μύρτων πινακίσκος χειρὶ παρατετιλμένων·
λύχνων γὰρ ὀσμὰς οὐ φιλοῦσι δαίμονες.
† πυργης τετάρτης † Κυσί τε καὶ Κυνηγέταις,
Λόρδωνι δραχμή, Κυβδάσῳ τριώβολον,
ἥρῳ Κέλητι δέρμα καὶ θυλήματα.
ταῦτ' ἐστι τἀναλώματ'. εἰ μὲν οὖν τάδε
προσοίσετ', εἰσέλθοιτ' ἄν· εἰ δὲ μή, μάτην
ἔξεστιν ὑμῖν διὰ κενῆς βινητιᾶν.

Ἀξιόνικος δ' ἐν Φιλίννῃ φησί·

γυναικὶ δὴ πίστευε μὴ πίνειν ὕδωρ.

b    Καὶ ὅλα δὲ ἔθνη περὶ μέθας διατρίβοντα | μνήμης
ἠξίωται. Βαίτων γοῦν ὁ Ἀλεξάνδρου βηματιστὴς ἐν
τῷ ἐπιγραφομένῳ Σταθμοὶ τῆς Ἀλεξάνδρου Πορείας
καὶ Ἀμύντας ἐν τοῖς Σταθμοῖς τὸ τῶν Ταπύρων ἔθνος
φησὶν οὕτω φίλοινον εἶναι ὡς καὶ ἀλείμματι ἄλλῳ
μηδενὶ χρῆσθαι ἢ τῷ οἴνῳ. τὰ δ' αὐτὰ ἱστορεῖ καὶ
Κτησίας ἐν τῷ Περὶ τῶν Κατὰ τὴν Ἀσίαν Φόρων·

---

158 Thought to be an aphrodisiac (cf. 1.5c [quoting another passage from the same play]; 2.63e–4b); Orthannes was an ithyphallic fertility deity.    159 A pun on *murton* ("clitoris"), with an allusion to the partial pubic depilation practiced by fashionable Athenian women and accomplished either by plucking the hair by hand or singeing it off with a lamp. Conisalus was another ithyphallic fertility deity. But the word translated here as "attendants" can also mean "testicles" (cf. 9.395f), so that part of the joke is that Conisalus' name stands in for his most prominent physical feature: an erect penis.    160 Also mentioned in an early 4th-century Athenian inscription (*IG* II² 4962.9–10; deities associated

Three half-measures of hyacinth bulbs[158] for
    Orthannes,
and a little platter of myrtle berries[159] plucked
by hand for Conisalus and his two attendants;
because the deities dislike the smell of lamps.
† [corrupt] four † for the Hounds and the
    Huntsmen;[160]
a drachma for Lordon; three obols for Cybdasus;
a hide and sacrificial barley-cakes for the hero
    Celes.[161]
This is what you have to spend. If you brought
these items, you'd get in. Otherwise, you can
long in vain to be fucked.

Axionicus says in *Philinne* (fr. 5):

Trust a woman—not to drink water!

Whole peoples, moreover, have been thought to deserve being described as spending all their time drunk.
Alexander's quartermaster Baiton,[162] for example, in his
treatise entitled *Stages of Alexander's Journey* (*FGrH* 119
F 1), along with Amyntas in his *Stages* (*FGrH* 122 F 5),
claim that the Tapyrians like wine so much that they anoint
themselves with nothing else. Ctesias in his *On the Trib-*

with Asclepius). But exactly who the Hounds and Huntsmen
were—and thus the point of what must be another sexually ori-
ented joke—is obscure, although cf. Hsch. κ 4763 "Hound: this
refers to the male genitals".
[161] Lordon, Cybdasus, and Celes are invented names that re-
call terms for three sexual positions, in which the woman threw
her head back and her pelvis forward; bent forward "doggy style";
and sat astride the man, respectively.     [162] Berve i #198.

οὗτος δὲ καὶ δικαιοτάτους αὐτοὺς λέγει εἶναι. Ἁρμό-
διος δὲ ὁ Λεπρεάτης ἐν τῷ Περὶ τῶν Παρὰ Φιγαλεῦσι
Νομίμων φιλοπότας φησὶ γενέσθαι Φιγαλεῖς Μεσση-
c νίοις ἀστυγείτονας ὄντας | καὶ ἀποδημεῖν ἐθισθέντας.
Φύλαρχος δ᾽ ἐν ἕκτῃ Βυζαντίους οἰνόφλυγας ὄντας ἐν
τοῖς καπηλείοις οἰκεῖν, ἐκμισθώσαντας τοὺς ἑαυτῶν
θαλάμους μετὰ τῶν γυναικῶν τοῖς ξένοις, πολεμίας
σάλπιγγος οὐδὲ ἐν ὕπνοις ὑπομένοντας ἀκοῦσαι. διὸ
καὶ πολεμουμένων ποτὲ αὐτῶν καὶ οὐ προσκαρτε-
ρούντων τοῖς τείχεσι Λεωνίδης ὁ στρατηγὸς ἐκέλευσε
τὰ καπηλεῖα ἐπὶ τῶν τειχῶν σκηνοπηγεῖν, καὶ μόλις
ποτὲ ἐπαύσαντο λιποτακτοῦντες, ὥς φησι Δάμων ἐν
τῷ Περὶ Βυζαντίου. Μένανδρος δ᾽ ἐν Ἀρρηφόρῳ ἢ
Αὐλητρίδι· |

d                    πάντας μεθύσους τοὺς ἐμπόρους
   ποιεῖ τὸ Βυζάντιον. ὅλην ἐπίνομεν
   τὴν νύκτα διὰ σὲ καὶ σφόδρ᾽ ἄκρατόν μοὶ δοκῶ·
   ἀνίσταμαι γοῦν τέτταρας κεφαλὰς ἔχων.

   κωμῳδοῦνται δὲ ὡς μέθυσοι Ἀργεῖοι μὲν καὶ Τιρύνθιοι
   ὑπὸ Ἐφίππου ἐν Βουσίριδι. ποιεῖ δὲ τὸν Ἡρακλέα
   λέγοντα·

   (Ηρ.) οὐκ οἶσθά μ᾽ ὄντα, πρὸς θεῶν, Τιρύνθιον
   Ἀργεῖον; οἱ μεθύοντες αἰεὶ τὰς μάχας |
e  πάσας μάχονται. (Β.) τοιγαροῦν φεύγουσ᾽ ἀεί.

112

*utes Paid throughout Asia* (*FGrH* 688 F 54) records the same information; he also claims that they are the most honest people in the world. Harmodius of Lepreum in his *On the Customs in Phigaleia* (*FGrH* 319 F 2) claims that the Phigaleians, whose city is on the Messenian border and who are used to being away from home, like to drink. Phylarchus in Book VI (*FGrH* 81 F 7) (says) that because the inhabitants of Byzantium guzzle wine, they live in the bars and rent out their own bedrooms, wives and all, to foreigners, and cannot stand to hear a war-trumpet even in their dreams. This is why, when they were being attacked at one point and failed to show any courage in defending their walls, their general Leonides ordered bars to be set up under canopies on top of the walls, and even then they barely stopped deserting their positions, according to Damon in his *On Byzantium* (*FGrH* 389 F 1). Menander in *The Arrhephoros or The Pipe-Girl* (fr. 66):

> Byzantium gets all the
> merchants drunk. We drank all night
> long because of you—and awfully strong wine, it
>     seems to me!
> At any rate, I'm getting up with four heads.

The Argives and the Tirynthians are ridiculed for being drunks by Ephippus in *Bousiris* (fr. 2). He represents Heracles as saying:

> (Heracles) Aren't you aware, by the gods, that I'm a
>     Tirynthian
> Argive? They always fight all their
> battles drunk. (B.) Which is why they always run
>     away!

Μιλησίους δ᾽ Εὔβουλος ἐν Κατακολλωμένῳ ὑβριστὰς εἶναί φησι μεθυσθέντας. Πολέμων δὲ ἐν τῷ Περὶ τῶν Κατὰ Πόλεις Ἐπιγραμμάτων περὶ Ἠλείων λέγων παρατίθεται τόδε τὸ ἐπίγραμμα·

> Ἦλις καὶ μεθύει καὶ ψεύδεται. οἷος ἑκάστου
> οἶκος, τοιαύτη καὶ συνάπασα πόλις.

Θεόπομπος δ᾽ ἐν τῇ δευτέρᾳ καὶ εἰκοστῇ περὶ Χαλκιδέων ἱστορῶν τῶν ἐν Θρᾴκῃ φησίν· ἐτύγχανον γὰρ τῶν μὲν βελτίστων ἐπιτηδευμάτων ὑπερορῶντες, | ἐπὶ δὲ τοὺς πότους καὶ ῥᾳθυμίαν καὶ πολλὴν ἀκολασίαν ὡρμηκότες ἐπιεικῶς. ὅτι δ᾽ εἰσὶ πάντες οἱ Θρᾷκες πολυπόται ⟨κοινόν⟩[16]. διὸ καὶ Καλλίμαχος ἔφη·

> καὶ γὰρ ὁ Θρηϊκίην μὲν ἀπέστυγε χανδὸν
>     ἄμυστιν
> οἰνοποτεῖν, ὀλίγῳ δ᾽ ἥδετο κισσυβίῳ.

ἐν δὲ τῇ πεντηκοστῇ ὁ Θεόπομπος περὶ Μηθυμναίων τάδε λέγει· καὶ τὰ μὲν ἐπιτήδεια προσφερομένους πολυτελῶς, μετὰ τοῦ κατακεῖσθαι καὶ πίνειν, ἔργον δ᾽ οὐδὲν ἄξιον τῶν ἀναλωμάτων ποιοῦντας. ἔπαυσεν οὖν αὐτοὺς τούτων Κλεομένης ‖ ὁ τύραννος, ὁ καὶ τὰς μαστροποὺς τὰς εἰθισμένας προαγωγεύειν τὰς ἐλευθέρας γυναῖκας ⟨καὶ⟩[17] τρεῖς ἢ τέτταρας τὰς ἐπιφανέστατα πορνευομένας ἐνδήσας εἰς σάκκους καταποντί-

---

16 add. Kaibel     17 add. Wilamowitz

---

163 A rustic drinking-cup of some sort; cf. 11.477c (where these verses are quoted again, along with two more).

164 Probably in power by the 340s BCE.

165 Sc. for the local men.

Eubulus in *The Man Who Was Glued to the Spot* (fr. 49) claims that the Milesians get out of control when drunk. Polemon in his discussion of the Eleans in his *On Epigrams by City* (fr. 80 Preller) quotes the following epigram (*FGE* 1628–9):

> Elis is drunk and full of lies. The character of the
>> individual
>> households is the same as that of the city as a
>> whole.

Theopompus says in Book XXII (*FGrH* 115 F 139), in his account of the Chalcideans who live in Thrace: Because the fact was that they showed disdain for better habits, and had instead got deeply involved in drinking parties, laziness, and a considerable amount of undisciplined behavior. That all Thracians like to drink is a commonplace. This is why Callimachus (fr. 178.11–12 Pfeiffer) said:

> For he hated to drink wine greedily in a long
>> Thracian
>> draft, but enjoyed a small *kissubion*.[163]

In Book L (*FGrH* 115 F 227) Theopompus says the following about the inhabitants of Methymna: consuming their provisions in an expensive style, while lying down and drinking, but accomplishing nothing worth the amount of money they spent. The tyrant Cleomenes[164] made them stop behaving this way; he also ordered certain individuals to tie up the women who had made a business of arranging illicit sexual liaisons with the wives and daughters of free men,[165] along with three or four of those who had prostituted themselves most overtly, in sacks, and drown

σαι τισὶν προστάξας. καὶ Ἕρμιππος δὲ ἐν τοῖς Περὶ
τῶν Ἑπτὰ Σοφῶν Περίανδρον τὸ αὐτὸ ποιῆσαι. ἐν δὲ
τῇ δευτέρᾳ τῶν Φιλιππικῶν, Ἰλλυριοί, φησί, δειπνοῦσι καθήμενοι καὶ πίνουσιν, ἄγουσι δὲ καὶ τὰς γυναῖκας εἰς τὰς συνουσίας, καὶ καλὸν αὐταῖς προπίνειν οἷς
b    ἂν τύχωσι τῶν παρόντων· ἐκ δὲ τῶν συμποσίων | αὗται
τοὺς ἄνδρας ἀπάγουσι. καὶ κακόβιοι δὲ πάντες εἰσὶ
καὶ ζώννυνται τὰς κοιλίας ζώναις πλατείαις ὅταν
πίνωσι. καὶ τοῦτο μὲν πρῶτον μετρίως ποιοῦσιν, ἐπειδὰν δὲ σφοδρότερον πίνωσι, μᾶλλον αἰεὶ συνάγουσι
τὴν ζώνην. Ἀρδιαῖοι δέ, φησί, κέκτηνται προσπελα-
τῶν ὥσπερ εἱλώτων τριάκοντα μυριάδας. καθ᾽ ἑκάστην
δὲ ἡμέραν μεθύουσιν καὶ ποιοῦνται συνουσίας καὶ
διάκεινται πρὸς ἐδωδὴν καὶ πόσιν ἀκρατέστερον. διὸ
καὶ Κελτοὶ πολεμοῦντες αὐτοῖς καὶ εἰδότες αὐτῶν τὴν
c    ἀκρασίαν παρήγγειλαν | ἅπασι τοῖς στρατιώταις
δεῖπνον ὡς λαμπρότατον παρασκευάσαντας κατὰ
σκηνὴν ἐμβαλεῖν εἰς τὰ σιτία πόαν τινὰ φαρμακώδη
δυναμένην διακόπτειν τὰς κοιλίας καὶ διακαθαίρειν.
γενομένου δὲ τούτου οἱ μὲν αὐτῶν καταληφθέντες ὑπὸ
τῶν Κελτῶν ἀπώλοντο, οἱ δὲ καὶ εἰς τοὺς ποταμοὺς
αὐτοὺς ἔρριψαν, ἀκράτορες τῶν γαστέρων γενόμενοι.

Τοιαῦτα πολλὰ ἐφεξῆς καταλέξαντος τοῦ Δημοκρί-
του ὁ Ποντιανὸς ἔφη πάντων τούτων εἶναι τῶν δεινῶν
d    μητρόπολιν τὸν οἶνον, δι᾽ ὃν καὶ | τὰς μέθας καὶ τὰς

166 See 10.427e n.

167 Literally "neighbors".

168 The serf-class in Sparta, who were little better than slaves.
This sentence from Theopompus is quoted also at 6.271e.

169 Sc. where they drowned. The story as Athenaeus preserves
it is so truncated as to be almost incoherent. But the implication is

them in the sea. Hermippus in his *On the Seven Wise Men* (fr. 13 Wehrli) (reports that) Periander[166] did this as well. (Theopompus) says in Book II of his *History of Philip* (*FGrH* 115 F 39): The Illyrians eat dinner and drink sitting down, and bring their wives to their parties. It is acceptable for the women to drink toasts in honor of anyone who happens to be there, and they guide their husbands home from their drinking parties. They all live a hard life, and they wrap wide belts around their bellies when they drink. Initially they do not fasten them very tight; but once they start drinking more seriously, they constantly cinch their belts tighter and tighter. The inhabitants of Ardia, he claims, own 300,000 *prospelatai*,[167] who resemble helots[168]. They get drunk and have parties every day, and are completely undisciplined when it comes to food and drink. When the Celts, who were aware of the Ardians' lack of self-discipline, were at war with them, therefore, they sent around orders to all their soldiers to prepare the most fantastic dinner possible in their tents, but to add to the food an herb with a medicinal quality that caused it to disturb the intestines and empty them out. After this happened, some of the Ardians were captured by the Celts and executed, while others lost control of their bowels and threw themselves into the rivers.[169]

After Democritus offered a long series of remarks along these lines, Pontianus observed that wine is the fundamental source[170] of all these horrors, and is responsible

that the enemy were allowed to capture the Celtic camp; gorged themselves on the food they found there; and then became too sick to resist when a counter-attack was mounted.

[170] Literally "mother-city".

μανίας, ἔτι δὲ καὶ τὰς παροινίας γίνεσθαι· οὗ τοὺς
ἐκπαθῶς μεταλαμβάνοντας οὐ κακῶς ὁ Χαλκοῦς ἐπι-
καλούμενος Διονύσιος ἐν τοῖς Ἐλεγείοις κυλίκων ἐρέ-
τας ἔφη·

καί τινες οἶνον ἄγοντες ἐν εἰρεσίᾳ Διονύσου,
    συμποσίου ναῦται καὶ κυλίκων ἐρέται,
< ... > περὶ τοῦδε· τὸ γὰρ φίλον οὐκ ἀπόλωλε.

Ἄλεξις δ᾽ ἐν Κουρίδι περί τινος πλέον πίνοντος διαλεγόμενός φησιν·

ὁ μὲν οὖν ἐμὸς υἱός, οἷον ὑμεῖς ἀρτίως
εἴδετε, τοιοῦτος γέγονεν, Οἰνοπίων | τις ἢ
Μάρων τις ἢ Κάπηλος ἢ <καὶ> Τιμοκλῆς·
μεθύει γάρ, οὐδὲν ἕτερον. ὁ δ᾽ ἕτερος—τί ἂν
τύχοιμ᾽ ὀνομάσας; βῶλος, ἄροτρον, γηγενὴς
ἄνθρωπος.

χαλεπὸν οὖν ἐστιν, ἄνδρες φίλοι, τὸ μεθύειν· καὶ
καλῶς πρὸς τοὺς οὕτως λάπτοντας τὸν οἶνον ὁ αὐτὸς
Ἄλεξις ἐν Ὀπώρᾳ (ἑταίρας δ᾽ ὄνομα τὸ δρᾶμα ἔχει)
φησίν·

                              οἶνον πολὺν
οὐ κεκραμένον <σὺ> πίνεις μεστὸς ὢν κοὐκ
    ἐξεμεῖς;

κἂν Δακτυλίῳ·

---

171 Oenopion was a son of Dionysus (cf. 1.26b–c); Maron gave
Odysseus the extraordinarily strong wine that got the Cyclops
drunk (*Od.* 9.196–212); and Timocles may be the late 4th-century
comic poet (*PAA* 887000). Capelus is not an Athenian name and

for drunkenness and insanity, as well as for boorish behavior. The Dionysius nicknamed Chalcous was quite right to refer in his *Elegies* (fr. 5 West²) to those who consume it eagerly as "rowers of cups":

> And some who transport wine in Dionysus' oarage,
>     drinking-party sailors and rowers of cups,
> . . . about this; for what they love has not vanished.

Alexis in *The Female Barber* (fr. 113), discussing someone who drinks more than he should, says:

> As for my son, as you've just
> seen, this is what he's turned into: an Oenopion,
> a Maron, a Capelus, or even a Timocles.[171]
> Because he's drunk; that's all there is to it. And the
>     other guy—what
> would be the right word for him? A clod, a plow,
>     someone
> born from the earth!

Getting drunk, my friends, is accordingly problematic behavior. The same Alexis in *Opora* (fr. 169)—the play's title is the name of a courtesan—is quite right to say about people who lap up their wine this way:

>                           So you're drinking
> lots of unmixed wine, even though you're full—and
>     you're not throwing up?

And in *The Ring* (fr. 44):

ought perhaps to be printed without an initial capital and translated "and a bartender, wine-merchant".

εἶτ᾽ οὐχ ἁπάντων ἐστὶ τὸ μεθύειν κακὸν |

f    μέγιστον ἀνθρώποισι καὶ βλαβερώτατον;

κἂν Ἐπιτρόπῳ δ᾽ ἔφη·

πολὺς γὰρ οἶνος πόλλ᾽ ἁμαρτάνειν ποεῖ.

Κρωβύλός τ᾽ ἐν Ἀπολιπούσῃ·

τὸ γὰρ ἐνδελεχῶς μεθύειν τίν᾽ ἡδονὴν ἔχει
ἀποστεροῦντα ζῶνθ᾽ ἑαυτὸν τοῦ φρονεῖν,
ὃ μέγιστον ἡμῶν ἀγαθὸν ἔσχεν ἡ φύσις;

οὐ χρὴ οὖν μεθύειν. καὶ γὰρ <ὅταν>[18] δημοκρατουμένη
444    πόλις, φησὶν ὁ Πλάτων ἐν ὀγδόῳ Πολιτείας, || ἐλευ-
θερίας διψήσασα κακῶν οἰνοχόων προστατούντων
τύχῃ καὶ πορρωτέρω τοῦ δέοντος ἀκράτου αὐτῆς
μεθυσθῇ, τοὺς ἄρχοντας δή, ἂν μὴ πάνυ πρᾶοι ὦσι καὶ
πολλὴν παρέχωσι τὴν ἐλευθερίαν, κολάζει αἰτιωμένη
ὡς μιαρούς τε καὶ ὀλιγαρχικούς, τοὺς δὲ κατηκόους
τῶν ἀρχόντων προπηλακίζει. ἐν δὲ τῷ τῶν Νόμων ἕκτῳ
φησί· τὴν πόλιν εἶναι δεῖ δίκην κεκραμένην κρατῆρος,
οὗ μαινόμενος μὲν ὁ οἶνος ἐγκεχυμένος ζεῖ, κολαζό-
b    μενος δὲ ὑπὸ νήφοντος ἑτέρου θεοῦ καλὴν | κοινωνίαν
λαβὼν ἀγαθὸν πῶμα καὶ μέτριον ἀπεργάζεται. τὸ γὰρ
παροινεῖν ἐκ τοῦ μεθύειν γίνεται. διὸ καὶ Ἀντιφάνης ἐν
Ἀρκαδίᾳ φησίν·

[18] add. Kaibel ex Platone

---

[172] A slightly abbreviated version of this fragment is quoted at
10.429e.

[173] A shorter quotation from the same passage appears at
10.433f.

So isn't getting drunk the biggest problem
people have, and the one that does them the most
        damage?

And in *The Guardian* (fr. 82) as well he said:

Because lots of wine leads to lots of mistakes.

Also Crobylus in *The Woman Who Left Her Husband*
(fr. 3):[172]

Because what's so nice about being constantly drunk,
    when it means depriving yourself, while you're still
        alive, of the ability to think clearly,
which is our best natural feature?

You should therefore not get drunk. For according to Plato
in Book VIII of the *Republic* (562c–d),[173] whenever a democratically governed city thirsty for freedom has bad wine-
pourers in charge of it, and gets more drunk on strong wine
than it should, unless its officials are extremely mild and
give it considerable freedom, it punishes them, complain-
ing that they are nasty and oligarchically-inclined, and bru-
talizes any citizens who obey the officials. And in Book VI
of his *Laws* (773c–d) he says: The city needs to be tem-
pered like a mixing-bowl: when the wine is poured into
it, it bubbles madly, but when it is disciplined by a different, sober god, it yields a nice combination of the two
and produces something good and not too strong to drink.
For getting drunk leads to boorish behavior. This is why
Antiphanes in *Arcadia*[174] (fr. 42) says:

[174] The title of the play is given as *Arcas* (or *The Arcadian*) at
13.586a.

οὔτε γὰρ νήφοντα δεῖ
οὐδαμοῦ, πάτερ, παροινεῖν, οὔθ᾽ ὅταν πίνειν δέῃ
νοῦν ἔχειν. ὅστις δὲ μεῖζον ἢ κατ᾽ ἄνθρωπον
    φρονεῖ,
⟨ . . . ⟩ μικρῷ πεποιθὼς ἀθλίῳ νομίσματι,
εἰς ἄφοδον ἐλθὼν ὅμοιον πᾶσιν αὐτὸν ὄψεται, |

c   ἂν σκοπῇ τὰ τῶν ἰατρῶν τοῦ βίου τεκμήρια
τὰς φλέβας ⟨θ᾽⟩ ὅποι φέρονται, τὰς ἄνω καὶ τὰς
    κάτω
τεταμένας, δι᾽ ὧν ὁ θνητὸς πᾶς κυβερνᾶται βίος.

ἐν δὲ Αἰόλῳ διαβάλλων ὅσα δεινὰ πράττουσιν οἱ
πλέον πίνοντές φησι·

Μακαρεὺς ἔρωτι τῶν ὁμοσπόρων μιᾶς
πληγεὶς τέως μὲν ἐπεκράτει τῆς συμφορᾶς
κατεῖχέ θ᾽ αὑτόν· εἶτα παραλαβών ποτε
οἶνον στρατηγόν, ὃς μόνος θνητῶν ἄγει |

d   τὴν τόλμαν εἰς τὸ πρόσθε τῆς εὐβουλίας,
νύκτωρ ἀναστὰς ἔτυχεν ὧν ἠβούλετο.

καλῶς οὖν ἄρα καὶ Ἀριστοφάνης Ἀφροδίτης γάλα τὸν
οἶνον ἔφη εἰπών·

ἡδύς τε πίνειν οἶνος, Ἀφροδίτης γάλα,

---

175 Macareus, a son of Aeolus, the Homeric king of the winds,
fell in love with and eventually raped his sister Canace; cf. E.
*Aiolos* (frr. 13a–41) with testimonia; Ar. *Nu.* 1371–3; *Ra.* 1078–81;
Plu. *Mor.* 312c–d.

> Because when you're sober, you should
> never act like a drunken boor, honored sir, and when
>     you should be drinking,
> you shouldn't act sensibly. If someone's prouder than
>     a human being should be,
> and relies on a bit of nasty money,
> when he goes to the toilet, he'll see that he's just like
>     everyone else,
> if he examines the biological evidence the doctors
>     discuss
> and where his veins head, some of them extending
>     up,
> others down, which control our entire mortal
>     existence.

And in *Aeolus* (fr. 19), expressing his disgust for all the terrible behavior of people who drink too much, he says:

> Macareus[175] was stung with love for one of his
> sisters, and for a while he stayed in control of the
>     situation
> and restrained himself. But then one day he drafted
>     wine—
> which is the leading cause of mortal recklessness
>     getting
> out ahead of intelligent behavior—as his general,
> and he left his bed that night and got what he
>     wanted.

Aristophanes (fr. 613) was accordingly quite right to refer to wine as "Aphrodite's milk" when he said:

> and wine that's nice to drink, Aphrodite's milk,

ὃν πολὺν σπῶντες ἔνιοι παρανόμων ἀφροδισίων
ὄρεξιν λαμβάνουσιν.

Ἡγήσανδρος δ' ὁ Δελφὸς καὶ ἐξοίνους τινὰς κέκληκε λέγων οὕτως· Κόμων καὶ Ῥοδοφῶν τῶν ἐν Ῥόδῳ
πολιτευσαμένων ὄντες ἦσαν ἔξοινοι. καὶ ὁ Κόμων εἰς
e κυβευτὴν σκώπτων | τὸν Ῥοδοφῶντα ἔλεγεν·

ὦ γέρον, ἦ μάλα δή σε νέοι τείρουσι κυβευταί,

Ῥοδοφῶν ⟨τε ἐκείνῳ⟩[19] τὴν περὶ τὰς γυναῖκας σπου-
δὴν καὶ τὴν ἀκρασίαν ὠνείδιζεν οὐδεμιᾶς ἀπεχόμενος
λοιδορίας. Θεόπομπος δ' ἐν τῇ ἑκκαιδεκάτῃ τῶν Ἱστοριῶν περὶ ἄλλου Ῥοδίου διαλεγόμενός φησι τοῦ δὲ
Ἡγησιλόχου τὰ μὲν ἀχρείου γεγονότος ὑπὸ οἰνο-
φλυγίας καὶ κύβων καὶ παντάπασιν οὐκ ἔχοντος
ἀξίωμα παρὰ τοῖς Ῥοδίοις, ἀλλὰ διαβεβλημένου διὰ
f τὴν ἀσωτίαν τὴν τοῦ βίου καὶ παρὰ | τοῖς ἑταίροις καὶ
παρὰ τοῖς ἄλλοις πολίταις. εἶθ' ἑξῆς λέγων περὶ τῆς
ὀλιγαρχίας ἣν κατεστήσατο μετὰ τῶν φίλων ἐπιφέρει·
καὶ πολλὰς μὲν γυναῖκας εὐγενεῖς καὶ τῶν πρώτων
ἀνδρῶν ᾔσχυναν, οὐκ ὀλίγους δὲ παῖδας καὶ νεα-
νίσκους διέφθειραν. εἰς τοῦτο δὲ προέβησαν ἀσελ-
γείας, ὥστε καὶ κυβεύειν ἠξίωσαν πρὸς ἀλλήλους περὶ
τῶν γυναικῶν τῶν ἐλευθέρων καὶ διωμολογοῦντο τοὺς

---

[19] Ῥοδοφῶν ⟨τε ἐκείνῳ⟩ Schweighäuser: ῥοδοφῶντα ἔλεγεν A

---

176 For the word, cf. 8.349a (Macho); 14.613c; Arnott on Alex.
fr. 64.

177 Rhodophon (mid-2nd century BCE) was pro-Roman (Plb.
27.7.3 with Walbank ad loc.), and Comon was thus presumably a
member of Rhodes' anti-Roman faction.

since it gives some people an appetite for illicit sex, if they consume large quantities of it.

Hegesander of Delphi (fr. 20, *FHG* iv.417) refers to certain individuals as *exoinoi* ("complete drunks"),[176] saying the following: Comon and Rhodophon, who were members of the political class in Rhodes,[177] were *exoinoi*. Comon made fun of Rhodophon for shooting dice, saying:

> Old man, young dice-players are pressing you very
>     hard,[178]

while Rhodophon criticized Comon for his interest in women and his lack of self-control, insulting him in every possible way. Theopompus in Book XVI of his *History* (*FGrH* 115 F 121, encompassing both quotations) discusses another Rhodian and says:[179] since Hegesilochus was worthless because he guzzled wine, shot dice, and had a terrible reputation on Rhodes, and was instead criticized by the members of his own faction, as well as the other citizens, for the profligate life he led. Then immediately after this, discussing the oligarchy Hegesilochus and his friends established, he continues: They also disgraced many women who came from good families and from the houses of leading citizens, and corrupted substantial numbers of boys and young men. They became so depraved, that they considered it acceptable to shoot dice with one another for the control of free women, and made agreements among

---

[178] A parody of *Il.* 8.102 (Diomedes to Nestor), where the subject of the verb is "spearsmen".     [179] The reference is to events in the late 350s BCE, when an oligarchic faction on Rhodes, supported by the Carian satrap Mausolus, led the island into revolt from the Second Athenian League.

ἐλάττω τοῖς ἀστραγάλοις βάλλοντας ἥντινα χρὴ τῶν
445  πολιτίδων ‖ τῷ νικῶντι εἰς συνουσίαν ἀγαγεῖν, οὐδεμίαν ὑπεξαιρούμενοι πρόφασιν, ἀλλ᾽ ὅπως ἕκαστος[20]
εἴη δυνατὸς πείθων ἢ βιαζόμενος, οὕτω προστάττοντες
ἄγειν. καὶ ταύτην τὴν κυβείαν ἔπαιζον μὲν καὶ τῶν
ἄλλων Ῥοδίων τινές, ἐπιφανέστατα δὲ καὶ πλειστάκις
αὐτὸς ὁ Ἡγησίλοχος ὁ προστατεῖν τῆς πόλεως ἀξίων.
Ἀνθέας δὲ ὁ Λίνδιος, συγγενὴς δὲ εἶναι φάσκων
Κλεοβούλου τοῦ σοφοῦ, ὥς φησι Φιλόμνηστος ἐν τῷ
Περὶ τῶν Ἐν Ῥόδῳ Σμινθείων, πρεσβύτερος καὶ εὐ-
b  δαίμων ἄνθρωπος | εὐφυής τε περὶ ποίησιν ὢν πάντα
τὸν βίον ἐδιονυσίαζεν, ἐσθῆτά τε Διονυσιακὴν φορῶν
καὶ πολλοὺς τρέφων συμβάκχους, ἐξῆγέν τε κῶμον
αἰεὶ μεθ᾽ ἡμέραν καὶ νύκτωρ. καὶ πρῶτος εὗρε τὴν διὰ
τῶν συνθέτων ὀνομάτων ποίησιν, ᾗ Ἀσωπόδωρος ὁ
Φλιάσιος ὕστερον ἐχρήσατο ἐν τοῖς Καταλογάδην
Ἰάμβοις. οὗτος δὲ καὶ κωμῳδίας ἐποίει καὶ ἄλλα
πολλὰ ἐν τούτῳ τῷ τρόπῳ τῶν ποιημάτων, ἃ ἐξῆρχε
τοῖς μεθ᾽ αὑτοῦ φαλλοφοροῦσι.

c    Τούτων ἀκούσας ὁ Οὐλπιανός, ὁ δὲ πάροινος, | ἔφη,
καλέ μου Ποντιανέ, παρὰ τίνι κεῖται; καὶ ὃς ἔφη·

ἀπολεῖς μ᾽ ἐρωτῶν,

κατὰ τὸν καλὸν Ἀγάθωνα,

[20] ὅπως ἂν ἕκαστος ACE: del. Meineke

---

[180] Used like dice, except that they had only four sides.
[181] One of the Seven Wise Men; see 8.360d n.; 10.448b n.
[182] Although Kassel–Austin include Antheas among the comic
poets, no fragments of his comedies survive and Meineke was
rightly dubious that he wrote actual stage-dramas.

themselves that those who had the lowest total when they were playing knucklebones[180] had to bring whichever citizen-woman was requested for the winner to have sex with. Nor did they accept any excuses; instead, they ordered each man to bring them using whatever power of persuasion or physical force he could apply. Other Rhodians also played this game, but most overtly and most often Hegesilochus himself—who thought that he deserved to be the leading man in the city! According to Philomnestus in his *On the Smintheian Festival in Rhodes* (*FGrH* 527 F *2), Antheas of Lindus (*SH* 46), who claimed to be related to the sage Cleoboulus,[181] was very old and rich, and a talented poet. He imitated Dionysus throughout his entire life by wearing Dionysiac clothing and maintaining a large number of fellow-bacchants, and was always at the head of a revelling-band day and night. Antheas invented the style of poetry that featured compound words, which Asopodorus of Phlius later used in his *Prose Iambs* (*SH* 222). He also wrote comedies[182] and many other poems of this type, and performed the leading parts in them for the phallic processions that accompanied him.

When he heard this, Ulpian asked: Where is the word *paroinos* ("abusively drunk")[183] attested, my good Pontianus? And (Pontianus) responded:

You'll be the death of me with these questions,

to quote the noble Agathon (*TrGF* 39 F 13),

---

[183] Pontianus used the cognate verb *paroineō* twice at 10.444b, including in Antiph. fr. 42.2.

καὶ σὺ χὠ νέος τρόπος
ἐν οὐ πρέποντι τοῖς λόγοισι χρώμενος.

ἐπεὶ δὲ πάντων ἡμᾶς εὐθύνας σοι διδόναι κέκριται,
Ἀντιφάνης ἐν Λυδῷ εἴρηκε·

< . . . > Κολχὶς ἄνθρωπος πάροινος.

σὺ δὲ παροινῶν καὶ μεθύων οὐδέπω κόρον ἔχεις οὐδ᾽
ἐπὶ νοῦν λαμβάνεις ὅτι ὑπὸ μέθης ἀπέθανεν Εὐμένης ὁ
d Περγαμηνὸς ὁ | Φιλεταίρου τοῦ Περγάμου βασιλεύ-
σαντος ἀδελφιδοῦς, ὡς ἱστορεῖ Κτησικλῆς ἐν τρίτῳ
Χρόνων. ἀλλ᾽ οὐ Περσεὺς ὁ ὑπὸ Ῥωμαίων καθαι-
ρεθείς· κατ᾽ οὐδὲν γὰρ τὸν πατέρα Φίλιππον ἐμιμή-
σατο. οὔτε γὰρ περὶ γυναῖκας ἐσπουδάκει οὔτε φίλοινος ἦν, ἀλλὰ καὶ οὐ μόνον αὐτὸς μέτριον ἔπινε
δειπνῶν, ἀλλὰ καὶ οἱ συνόντες αὐτῷ φίλοι, ὡς ἱστορεῖ
Πολύβιος ἐν τῇ ἕκτῃ καὶ εἰκοστῇ. σὺ δέ, ὦ Οὐλπιανέ,
ἀρρυθμοπότης μὲν εἶ κατὰ τὸν Φλιάσιον Τίμωνα·
e οὕτως γὰρ ἐκεῖνος ὠνόμασε τοὺς τὸν πολὺν | σπῶντας
οἶνον ἄκρατον ἐν τῷ δευτέρῳ τῶν Σίλλων·

ἠὲ βαρὺν βουπλῆγα τομώτερον ἢ Λυκόοργος,
ὅς ῥα Διωνύσου ἀρρυθμοπότας ἐπέκοπτεν,
ἐκ δὲ ῥυτὰ ῥίπτασκεν ἀπληστοίνους τ᾽
ἀρυταίνας·

---

184 Reigned 263–241 BCE; Philetaerus preceded him on the
throne.

185 Perseus was the last king of Macedon (reigned 179–168
BCE); his father was Philip V (reigned 222–179).

186 The final portion of the third verse is quoted also at
10.424b.

187 A mythological Thracian king, who attacked the young Di-

you and your modern fashion
of using words inappropriately.

But since a decision has been made that we must be scruti-
nized by you on every subject, Antiphanes says in *The
Lydian* (fr. 144):

a *paroinos* Colchian.

You, however, never have enough of being *paroinos* and
drunk, and you fail to take into account the fact that
Eumenes of Pergamum,[184] the nephew of Philetaerus,
king of Pergamum, died from excessive drinking, according to Ctesicles in Book III of the *Annals* (*FGrH* 245 F 2).
The Perseus[185] who was deposed by the Romans, on the
other hand, did not; because he did not resemble his father
Philip in any way. For he was uninterested in women, and
did not like wine; instead, not only did he himself drink
only a modest amount at dinner, but the same was true
of the friends who were with him, according to Polybius
in Book XXVI (XXV.3.7). Whereas you, Ulpian, are an
"arrhythmic drinker", to quote Timo of Phlius. Because
this is how he referred in Book II of the *Silloi* (*SH* 778)[186]
to people who gulp down large amounts of unmixed wine:

or a heavy ax for killing bulls, sharper than
        Lycurgus,[187]
who of course cut down Dionysus' arrhythmic
        drinkers
and tossed away the drinking-horns and the ladles
        that could never be too full of wine.

onysus and his nurses with an ax of the sort referred to here and
was driven mad as a consequence (*Il.* 6.130–40).

οὐ ποτικὸς δέ. ὠνόμασε δὲ ποτικὸν Ἀλκαῖος Γανυμήδει οὕτως < ... > ὅτι δὲ τὸ μεθύειν καὶ τὰς ὄψεις ἡμῶν
f πλανᾷ σαφῶς ἔδειξεν Ἀνάχαρσις | δι᾽ ὧν εἴρηκε,
δηλώσας ὅτι ψευδεῖς δόξαι τοῖς μεθύουσι γίγνονται.
συμπότης γάρ τις ἰδὼν αὐτοῦ τὴν γυναῖκα ἐν τῷ
συμποσίῳ ἔφη· "ὦ Ἀνάχαρσι, γυναῖκα γεγάμηκας
αἰσχράν." καὶ ὃς ἔφη· "πάνυ γε κἀμοὶ δοκεῖ· ἀλλά μοι
ἔγχεον, ὦ παῖ, ποτήριον ἀκρατέστερον, ὅπως αὐτὴν
καλὴν ποιήσω."

Μετὰ ταῦτα ὁ Οὐλπιανὸς προπιών τινι τῶν ἑταίρων
ἔφη· ἀλλὰ κατὰ τὸν Ἀντιφάνην, ὦ φιλότης, ὃς ἐν
Ἀγροίκοις φησίν· ||

446    (Α.) ὅλην μύσας ἔκπινε. (Β.) μέγα τὸ φορτίον.
       (Α.) οὐχ ὅστις αὐτῆς ἐστιν ἐμπείρως ἔχων,

πῖθι οὖν, ὦ ἑταῖρε. καὶ

              (Α.) μὴ μεστὰς ἀεὶ
ἕλκωμεν,

ὁ αὐτός φησιν Ἀντιφάνης ἐν τῷ Τραυματίᾳ,

       ἀλλὰ καὶ λογισμὸς εἰς μέσον
παταξάτω τις, καί τι καὶ μελίσκιον,
στροφὴ λόγων παρελθέτω τις. ἡδύ τοι
ἔστιν μεταβολὴ παντὸς ἔργου πλὴν ἑνὸς
< ... > παραδίδου δ᾽ ἑξῆς ἐμοὶ

---

188 A rare adjective formed from the verb *pinō* ("drink
[wine]"), here apparently to be taken in the sense "merely fond of
drinking", or perhaps "fun to drink with".
189 The quotation has fallen out of the text.
190 Sex.

On the other hand, you are not *potikos*.[188] Alcaeus in *Ganymede* (fr. 9) used the word *potikos*, as follows:[189] . . . That being drunk confuses our vision was made clear by Anacharsis' remark (fr. A31A Kindstrand), when he brought out the fact that drunks perceive the world incorrectly. Someone who was at a drinking party with him saw his wife there and said: "Anacharsis, you're married to an ugly woman." And Anacharsis said: "I agree entirely. Pour me a cup full of stronger wine, slave, so I can make her attractive!"

After this, Ulpian drank a toast to one of the other guests and said: To quote Antiphanes, my friend, who says in *Rustics* (fr. 4):

(A.) Shut your eyes and drink the whole cup! (B.)
      That's a big load.
(A.) Not for someone who's got experience with it.

So drink up (*pithi*), my friend, and

                  (A.) Let's not always keep emptying
      full cups,

as the same Antiphanes puts it in *The Wounded Man* (fr. 205),

            but let's have a bit of conversation
      bounce around between us instead, and a little
            singing;
      and let's have some clever remarks present
            themselves! It's nice
      to have a change from activities of all kinds—except
            one.[190]

. . . And after that, hand me

131

τὸν ἀρκεσίγυιον, ὡς ἔφασκ' Εὐριπίδης.

b    (Β.) Εὐριπίδης γὰρ τοῦτ' ἔφασκεν; | (Α.) ἀλλὰ
τίς;
(Β.) Φιλόξενος δήπουθεν. (Α.) οὐθὲν διαφέρει,
ὦ τᾶν· ἐλέγχεις μ' ἕνεκα συλλαβῆς μιᾶς.

καὶ ὅς, τὸ δὲ πῖθι τίς εἴρηκεν; ἀπεσκοτώθης, φίλτατε,
ἔφη ὁ Οὐλπιανός, σπάσας οἴνου τοσοῦτον. παρὰ Κρα-
τίνῳ ἔχεις ἐν Ὀδυσσεῦσι·

τῇ νῦν τόδε πῖθι λαβὼν ἤδη, καὶ τοὔνομά μ'
εὐθὺς ἐρώτα.

καὶ Ἀντιφάνης ἐν Μύστιδι· |

c    (Α.) σὺ δ' ἀλλὰ πῖθι. (Β.) τοῦτο μέν σοι
πείσομαι·
καὶ γὰρ ἐπαγωγόν, ὦ θεοί, τὸ σχῆμά πως
τῆς κύλικός ἐστιν ἄξιόν τε τοῦ κλέους
τοῦ τῆς ἑορτῆς. οὗ μὲν ἦμεν ἄρτι γὰρ
ἐξ ὀξυβαφίων κεραμεῶν ἐπίνομεν·
τούτῳ δέ, τέκνον, πολλὰ κἀγάθ' οἱ θεοὶ
τῷ δημιουργῷ δοῖεν ὃς ἐποίησέ σε, |
d    τῆς συμμετρίας καὶ τῆς ἀφελείας οὕνεκα.

καὶ Δίφιλος ἐν Βαλανείῳ·

ἔγχεον μεστήν· τὸ θνητὸν περικάλυπτε τῷ θεῷ.
πῖθι· ταῦτα γὰρ <παρ'> ἡμῶν Διὸς Ἑταιρείου,
πάτερ.

---

191 *PMG* 832.
192 Odysseus addresses the Cyclops.
193 Quoted again at 11.494d.

the limb-strengthener, as Euripides put it.
(B.) Euripides actually said that? (A.) Who else?
(B.) Philoxenus,[191] I imagine. (A.) It doesn't make any
    difference,
buddy; you're criticizing me because of a single
    syllable.

But the other man said: Who uses the form *pithi*
("drink!")? You blacked out, my dear sir, replied Ulpian,
from gulping down so much wine. You can find the word in
Cratinus' *Odysseuses* (fr. 145):[192]

Here—take this now, and drink (*pithi*) it, and
    immediately ask me my name!

Also Antiphanes in *The Female Initiate* (fr. 161):[193]

(A.) But as for you—drink (*pithi*)! (B.) I'll do what
    you say;
because the fact is, by the gods, that the shape of the
    cup
is rather attractive and fits the reputation
of the festival. Because where we were just now,
we were drinking out of ceramic cruets!
May the gods grant many blessings, my child,
to the craftsman who produced you,
on account of your simple, symmetrical shape.

And Diphilus in *The Bathman* (fr. 20):

Pour a full cup! Wrap your mortal part in the god!
Drink (*pithi*)! Because this is what we have to offer
    from Zeus Patron of Comrades, old sir!

Ἀμειψίας Σφενδόνῃ·

λαγὸν ταράξας πῖθι τὸν θαλάσσιον.

Μένανδρος Αὐλητρίσι·

(Α.) ἐλλέβορον ἤδη πώποτ᾽ ἔπιες, Σωσία;
(Σω.) ἅπαξ. (Α.) πάλιν νῦν πῖθι· μαίνει γὰρ
κακῶς.

Πίομαι δὲ ἄνευ τοῦ ῡ λεκτέον, ἐκτείνοντας δὲ τὸ ῑ. οὕτω γὰρ ἔχει καὶ τὸ Ὁμηρικόν·

πιόμεν᾽ ἐκ βοτάνης.

καὶ Ἀριστοφάνης Ἱππεῦσιν· |

e     οὔποτ᾽ ἐκ ταὐτοῦ <μεθ᾽ ἡμῶν πίεται> ποτηρίου.

καὶ ἐν ἄλλοις·

πικρότατον οἶνον τήμερον πίῃ τάχα.[21]

ἐνίοτε δὲ καὶ συστέλλουσι τὸ ῑ, ὡς Πλάτων ἐν Ταῖς Ἀφ᾽ Ἱερῶν·

οὐδ᾽ ὅστις αὐτῆς ἐκπίεται τὰ χρήματα.

καὶ ἐν Σύρφακι·

< ... > καὶ πίεσθ᾽ ὕδωρ πολύ.

---

[21] πίε. τάχα ὡς ἀπὸ τοῦ πιοῦμαι A: τάχα κτλ. del. Dindorf

---

[194] Quoted (but without the name of the poet or the play) also at 9.400c.     [195] Referred to as *The Arrhephoros or The Pipe-Girl* at 10.442c; 13.559d.     [196] I.e. not *pioumai*.

[197] The metrical value of the *iota* cannot in fact be determined in this line.

134

Amipsias in *The Sling* (fr. 17):[194]

Stir up the sea-hare and drink (*pithi*) it!

Menander in *Pipe-Girls*[195] (fr. 69):

(A.) Did you ever drink hellebore at any point,
Sosias?
(Sosias) Just once. (A.) Drink (*pithi*) it again now;
because you're seriously insane!

The word should be pronounced *piomai* ("I will
drink"), without the *upsilon*[196] and with the *iota* length-
ened. Because this is how the Homeric form is spelled (*Il.*
13.493):

in order to drink (*piomen'*), leaving the grass.

Also Aristophanes in *Knights* (1289):

Never will he drink (*pietai*) with us from the same
cup.

And in another passage (fr. 614):[197]

You may perhaps drink (*piēi*) very bitter wine today.

But sometimes they shorten the *iota*, for example Plato in
*Women Coming from a Sacrifice* (fr. 9):

and not someone who'll drink up (*ekpietai*) her
money.

And in *The Rabble* (fr. 179):

And you'll drink (*piesth'*) lots of water.

πίε δὲ δισυλλάβως Μένανδρος ἐν Ἐγχειριδίῳ·

    (Α.) <πίε.> (Β.) πιεῖν ἀναγκάσω
τὴν ἱερόσυλον πρῶτα. |

f  καί·

    < . . . > τῇ, πίε.[22]

καὶ σὺ οὖν, ὦ ἑταῖρε, κατὰ τὸν Ἄλεξιν, ὃς ἐν Διδύμοις
φησί·

    τούτῳ πρόπιθ᾽, ἵνα καὐτὸς ἄλλῳ·

καὶ γένηται ἡ παρ᾽ Ἀνακρέοντι καλουμένη ἐπίστιος.
φησὶ γὰρ ὁ μελοποιός· ||

447    μηδ᾽ ὥστε κῦμα πόντιον
    λάλαζε, τῇ πολυκρότῃ
    σὺν Γαστροδώρῃ καταχύδην
    πίνουσα τὴν ἐπίστιον.

τοῦτο δ᾽ ἡμεῖς ἀνίσωμά φαμεν. σὺ δὲ πιὼν μὴ φοβη-
θῇς ὡς εἰς τοὐπίσω μέλλων καταπεσεῖσθαι· τοῦτο γὰρ
παθεῖν οὐ δύνανται οἱ τὸν κατὰ Σιμωνίδην πίνοντες
οἶνον

    < . . . > ἀμύντορα δυσφροσυνάων.

ἀλλ᾽, ὥς φησιν Ἀριστοτέλης ἐν τῷ Περὶ Μέθης, εἰς τὰ

---

[22] πίε καὶ πῖνε Α: καὶ πῖνε del. Meineke

---

[198] If Dindorf's correction of the manuscripts' *anisōna* is right,
the word (otherwise unattested) would seem to mean "an equal
share" (cognate with *anisoō*), i.e. "[a cup] shared by everyone".

Menander uses the disyllabic form *pie* in *The Dagger* (fr. 138 Koerte):

> (A.) Drink (*pie*)! (B.) First I'm going to force
> the woman who committed sacrilege to drink.

Also (*Od*. 9.347):

> Here! Drink (*pie*)!

So you too (should drink), my friend, to quote Alexis, who says in *Twins* (fr. 55):

> Drink a toast to him, so he can drink one to someone
> else!

Then we could have what is referred to in Anacreon as an *epistios* ("hearthside [cup], fireside [cup]"). Because the lyric poet says (*PMG* 427):

> And don't jabber like the sea's
> wave, drinking your
> *epistios* in great gulps in the company
> of the wily Gastrodora.

We, on the other hand, refer to this as an *anisōma*.[198] As for you, do not worry that you are likely to fall over backward after you drink; because this is impossible for people who drink the wine Simonides (fr. 23 West[2]) refers to as

> a bulwark against unhappy thoughts.

According to Aristotle in his *On Drunkenness* (fr. 671),[199] it

---

[199] Cf. 1.34b, where the philosopher's remarks are quoted more briefly.

νῶτα καταπίπτουσιν οἱ τὸν κρίθινον πεπωκότες, ὃν
πῖνον καλοῦσι, λέγων οὕτως· πλὴν ἴδιόν τι συμβαίνει
b περὶ τὰς τῶν κριθῶν, | τὸ καλούμενον πῖνον. ὑπὸ μὲν
γὰρ τῶν λοιπῶν τε καὶ μεθυστικῶν οἱ μεθυσθέντες ἐπὶ
πάντα τὰ μέρη πίπτουσιν· καὶ γὰρ ἐπὶ τὰ ἀριστερὰ καὶ
δεξιὰ καὶ πρηνεῖς καὶ ὕπτιοι. μόνοι δὲ οἱ τῷ πίνῳ
μεθυσθέντες εἰς τοὐπίσω καὶ ὕπτιοι κλίνονται. τὸν δὲ
κρίθινον οἶνον καὶ βρῦτόν τινες καλοῦσιν, ὡς Σοφοκλῆς ἐν Τριπτολέμῳ·

> βρῦτον δὲ τὸν χερσαῖον † οὐ δυεῖν †.

καὶ Ἀρχίλοχος·

> ὥσπερ αὐλῷ βρῦτον ἢ Θρέϊξ ἀνὴρ
> ἢ Φρὺξ ἔμυζε· κύβδα δ᾽ ἦν πονεομένη.

c μνημονεύει | τοῦ πώματος Αἰσχύλος ἐν Λυκούργῳ·

> κἀκ τῶνδ᾽ ἔπινε βρῦτον ἰσχναίνων χρόνῳ
> κἀσεμνοκόμπει τοῦτ᾽ ἐν ἀνδρείᾳ τιθείς.

Ἑλλάνικος δ᾽ ἐν Κτίσεσι, καὶ ἐκ ῥιζῶν, φησί, κατα-
σκευάζεται τὸ βρῦτον, γράφων ὧδε· πίνουσι δὲ βρῦτον
ἔκ τινων ῥιζῶν, καθάπερ οἱ Θρᾷκες ἐκ τῶν κριθῶν.
Ἑκαταῖος δ᾽ ἐν δευτέρῳ Περιηγήσεως εἰπὼν περὶ
Αἰγυπτίων ὡς ἀρτοφάγοι εἰσὶν ἐπιφέρει· τὰς κριθὰς ἐς
τὸ πῶμα καταλέουσιν. ἐν δὲ τῇ τῆς Εὐρώπης Περιόδῳ

---

[200] Beer.

[201] Used when drinking beer, to avoid swallowing the barley-
lees. Archilochus, however, is describing a blowjob.

[202] The word is here treated as neuter rather than masculine.

[203] Cf. 10.418e.

is instead those who drink barley-wine[200] (known as *pinos*) who collapse on their backs. He puts it as follows: except that something peculiar happens in the case of substances derived from barley, by which I mean what is referred to as *pinos*. For individuals who get drunk on other intoxicants collapse onto various parts of their anatomy, to the left, or the right, or onto their faces or their backs. By contrast, only those who get drunk on *pinos* fall over backward and lie supine. Some authorities refer to barley-wine as *brutos*, for example Sophocles in *Triptolemus* (fr. 610):

> and the mainland *brutos* † not to go down †.

Also Archilochus (fr. 42 West²):

> She was sucking away like a Thracian or a Phrygian
>     consuming
> *brutos* with a straw;[201] she was bent over and working
>     hard.

Aeschylus mentions the drink in *Lycurgus* (fr. 124):

> He was drinking *brutos* from them, and eventually
>     drained them dry;
> and he swaggered around, acting like he'd
>     accomplished a brave deed.

Hellanicus in the *Foundations* (*FGrH* 4 F 66), on the other hand, claims that *bruton*[202] is made from roots. He writes as follows: They drink *bruton* made from certain roots, in the same way that the Thracians drink it made from barley. Hecataeus in Book II of the *Tour* (*FGrH* 1 F 323a)[203] reports that the Egyptians eat bread, and then continues: They grind up barley to produce the substance they drink. And in his *Journey through Europe* (*FGrH* 1 F 154)

d  Παίονάς φησι | πίνειν βρῦτον ἀπὸ τῶν κριθῶν καὶ
παραβίην ἀπὸ κέγχρου καὶ κονύζης[23]· ἀλείφονται δέ,
φησίν, ἐλαίῳ ἀπὸ γάλακτος. καὶ ταῦτα μὲν ταύτῃ.
   Τῷ δ' ἡμετέρῳ χορῷ οἶνος φίλος † ον †

      θυρσοφόρος μέγα πρεσβεύων Διόνυσος,

φησὶν Ἴων ὁ Χῖος ἐν τοῖς Ἐλεγείοις·

      αὕτη γὰρ πρόφασις παντοδαπῶν λογίων,
   αἵ τε Πανελλήνων ἀγοραὶ θαλίαι τε ἀνάκτων,
   ἐξ οὗ βοτρυόεσσ' οἰνὰς ὑπὸ χθονίων |
e    πτόρθον ἀνασχομένη θαλερῷ ἐπτύξατο πήχει
   αἰθέρος· ὀφθαλμῶν δ' ἐξέθορον πυκινοὶ
   παῖδες, φωνήεντες ὅταν πέσῃ ἄλλος ἐπ' ἄλλῳ,
   πρὶν δὲ σιωπῶσιν· παυσάμενοι δὲ βοῆς
   νέκταρ ἀμέλγονται, πόνον ὄλβιον ἀνθρώποισιν,
   ξυννὸν τοῦ χαίρειν φάρμακον αὐτοφυές.
   τοῦ θαλίαι, φίλα τέκνα, φιλοφροσύναι τε χοροί
   τε |
f    τῶν ἀγαθῶν

            *   *   *
         βασιλεὺς οἶνος ἔδειξε φύσιν.
   τῷ σύ, πάτερ Διόνυσε, φιλοστεφάνοισιν ἀρέσκων

---

[23] κονύζης Musurus: κόνυζαν A

---

[204] Butter.

140

he says that the Paeonians drink *brutos* made from barley, and *parabiē* made from millet and fleabane; and they smear themselves, he claims, with oil made from milk.[204] So much for these topics.

To our group friendly wine † [corrupt] †

thyrsus-bearing, widely powerful Dionysus,

says Ion of Chios in his *Elegies* (fr. 26 West[2]);

> because this is an excuse for eloquence of all
>     kinds,
> along with the gatherings of all the Greek peoples
>     and feasts celebrated by their kings,
> ever since the grape-cluster-covered vine raised its
>     shoot,
> assisted by the earth-gods, and enwrapped the air in
>     its
> vigorous arm; and children leapt forth, one after
>     another,
> from its eyes, crying out when they fell on top of each
>     other,
> although formerly silent. But after they cease to
>     shout,
> they are pressed to produce nectar, hard work that
>     brings human beings blessings,
> a natural drug associated with happiness.
> Feasts belong to it, as do beloved children, and
>     friendliness, and dances
> performed by good people.

\*     \*     \*

> King Wine reveals character.
> Therefore, Father Dionysus, you who please garland-
>     loving

ἀνδράσιν, εὐθύμων συμποσίων πρύτανι,
χαῖρε· δίδου δ' αἰῶνα, καλῶν ἐπήρανε ἔργων,
πίνειν καὶ παίζειν καὶ τὰ δίκαια φρονεῖν.

Ἄμφις δ' ἐν Φιλαδέλφοις ἐπαινῶν τὸν τῶν φιλοποτῶν
φησι βίον· ||

448
κατὰ πόλλ' ἐπαινῶ μᾶλλον ἡμῶν τὸν βίον
τὸν τῶν φιλοποτῶν ἤπερ ὑμῶν τῶν μόνον
ἐν τῷ μετώπῳ νοῦν ἔχειν εἰωθότων.
ἡ μὲν γὰρ ἐπὶ τοῦ συντετάχθαι διὰ τέλους
φρόνησις οὖσα διὰ τὸ λεπτῶς καὶ πυκνῶς
πάντ' ἐξετάζειν δέδιεν ἐπὶ τὰ πράγματα
ὁρμᾶν προχείρως, ἡ δὲ διὰ τὸ μὴ σαφῶς
τί ποτ' ἀφ' ἑκάστου πράγματος συμβήσεται
διαλελογίσθαι δρᾷ τι καὶ νεανικὸν |
b      καὶ θερμόν.

Μέλλοντος δέ τι τούτοις προστιθέναι τοῦ Οὐλπια-
νοῦ ὁ Αἰμιλιανὸς ἔφη· ὥρα ἡμῖν, ἄνδρες φίλοι, ζητεῖν
τι καὶ περὶ γρίφων, ἵνα τι κἂν βραχὺ διαστῶμεν ἀπὸ
τῶν ποτηρίων, οὐ κατὰ τὴν Καλλίου τοῦ Ἀθηναίου
ἐπιγραφομένην Γραμματικὴν Τραγῳδίαν. ἀλλ' ἡμεῖς
ζητήσωμεν πρότερον μὲν τίς ὁ ὅρος τοῦ γρίφου, τίνα
δὲ Κλεοβουλίνη ἡ Λινδία προὔβαλλεν ἐν τοῖς Αἰ-
νίγμασιν· ἱκανῶς γὰρ εἴρηκε περὶ αὐτῶν ὁ ἑταῖρος |
c      ἡμῶν Διότιμος ὁ Ὀλυμπηνός· ἀλλὰ πῶς οἱ κωμῳδιο-

---

205 A glancing allusion to the next topic to be taken up (cf.
10.459b; 11.460a–b).

206 For *The Literal Tragedy*, see 7.276a; 10.453c–4a with nn.

207 The daughter of Cleoboulus of Lindus (8.360d n.; cf.
10.445a). For her lost *Obscure Sayings* (in dactylic hexameter, like
many riddles), see D.L. 1.89.

men, president of cheerful drinking parties—
hail to you! Grant us the time, assistant in good
deeds,
to drink, and to play, and to have just thoughts!

Amphis in *Men Who Loved Their Brothers* (fr. 33) praises
the life of people who like to drink and says:

I've got lots of reasons for recommending the life
of us who like to drink over the life of you who're
merely
used to maintaining a sensible attitude inside your
heads.
Because the mentality that always stresses
order, since it examines everything in
a careful, thoughtful way, lacks the courage to rush
into matters headlong. Whereas the opposite
mentality, since it
doesn't calculate the likely outcome of every
eventuality
precisely, accomplishes something fresh
and bold.

As Ulpian was on the verge of adding further remarks to
the above, Aemilianus said: It is time, my friends, for us to
take up the question of riddles (*griphoi*), allowing us a
break, even if a brief one, from our cups,[205] although (we
will) not (pursue the matter) in the style of the play by
Callias of Athens entitled *The Literal Tragedy*.[206] Instead,
let us first consider what the definition of a riddle is, and
what riddles Cleoboulina of Lindus[207] posed in her *Obscure Sayings*—for our friend Diotimus of Olympene discusses them at considerable length—and also what refer-

143

ποιοὶ αὐτῶν μέμνηνται, καὶ τίνα κόλασιν ὑπέμενον οἱ
μὴ λύσαντες. καὶ ὁ Λαρήνσιος ἔφη· ὁ μὲν Σολεὺς
Κλέαρχος οὕτως ὁρίζεται· γρῖφος πρόβλημά ἐστι
παιστικόν, προστακτικὸν τοῦ διὰ ζητήσεως εὑρεῖν τῇ
διανοίᾳ τὸ προβληθὲν τιμῆς ἢ ἐπιζημίου χάριν εἰρη-
μένον. ἐν δὲ τῷ Περὶ Γρίφων ὁ αὐτὸς Κλέαρχός φησιν
ἑπτὰ εἴδη εἶναι γρίφων. ἐν γράμματι μέν, οἷον ἐροῦμεν
ἀπὸ τοῦ ᾱ, ὡς ὄνομά τι ἰχθύος ἢ φυτοῦ, ὁμοίως δὲ κἂν |

d  ἔχειν τι κελεύῃ τῶν γραμμάτων ἢ μὴ ἔχειν, καθάπερ οἱ
ἄσιγμοι καλούμενοι τῶν γρίφων· ὅθεν καὶ Πίνδαρος
πρὸς τὸ σ̄ ἐποίησεν ᾠδήν, οἱονεὶ γρίφου τινὸς ἐν
μελοποιίᾳ προβληθέντος. ἐν συλλαβῇ δὲ λέγονται
γρῖφοι, οἷον ἐροῦμεν ἔμμετρον ὁτιδήποτε οὗ ἡγεῖται
βα-, οἷον βασιλεύς, ἢ ὧν ἔχει τελευτὴν τὸ -ναξ, ὡς
Καλλιάναξ, ἢ ὧν τὸν λέοντα καθηγεῖσθαι, οἷον Λεωνίδης, ἢ ἔμπαλιν τελικὸν εἶναι, οἷον Θρασυλέων. ἐν
ὀνόματι δέ, οἷον ἐροῦμεν ὀνόματα ἁπλᾶ ἢ σύνθετα

e  δισύλλαβα, | οὗ μορφή τις ἐμφαίνεται τραγικὴ ἢ
πάλιν ταπεινή, ἢ ἄθεα ὀνόματα, οἷον Κλεώνυμος, ἢ
θεοφόρα, οἷον Διονύσιος, καὶ τοῦτο ἤτοι ἐξ ἑνὸς θεοῦ ἢ
πλεόνων, οἷον Ἑρμαφρόδιτος· ἢ ἀπὸ Διὸς ἄρχεσθαι,
Διοκλῆς, ἢ Ἑρμοῦ, Ἑρμόδωρος· ἢ λήγειν εἰ τύχοι εἰς -

---

208 See 10.455b–c, 467b (quoting part of the poem).
209 Literally "a metrical word".
210 Like Leonides and Thrasyleon (below), a personal name.
211 Genitive *Dios*, whence Diocles.

ence the comic poets make to them, and how individuals
who failed to solve them were punished. Larensius responded: Clearchus of Soli (fr. 86 Wehrli, including the
material from *On Riddles* below) offers the following
definition: A *griphos* is a facetious question that requires
one to use a process of intellectual inquiry to discover what
is being referred to, and that is articulated with an eye to a
reward or a punishment. In his *On Riddles*, on the other
hand, the same Clearchus claims that there are seven types
of riddles. First are those that involve an individual letter,
for example when we are asked to come up with words that
begin with *alpha*, such as the name of a fish or a plant, or
similarly if (the riddle-poser) specifies that the word is to
contain a particular letter, or not contain it, as in the case
of what are referred to as asigmatic riddles. This is why
Pindar (fr. 79) composed a song directed against *sigma*,[208]
posing a riddle, as it were, within a lyric poem. Next, riddles are posed syllabically, for example when we are asked
to come up with some word used in poetry[209] that begins
with *ba-*, such as *basileus* ("king"), or with words that end
with *-nax*, like Callianax,[210] or that begin with *leōn* ("lion"),
for example Leonides, or alternatively that end with it, for
example Thrasyleon. Next (are riddles that) involve specific nouns, for example when we are asked to come up
with simple or compound bisyllabic nouns whose form
appears to be tragic or the opposite, colloquial; or with
names that have no divine element in them, for example
Cleonymus, or that contain a divine name, for example
Dionysius, and in the latter case either the name of one
god or of more than one, for example Hermaphroditus; or
with names that begin with Zeus,[211] for example, Diocles,
or with Hermes, for example, Hermodorus; or perhaps

ATHENAEUS

νικος. οἱ δὲ μὴ εἰπόντες ὡς προσετάττετο ἔπινον τὸ
ποτήριον. καὶ ὁ μὲν Κλέαρχος οὕτως ὡρίσατο· τί δέ
ἐστι τοῦτο τὸ ποτήριον, καλέ μου Οὐλπιανέ, ζήτει.
περὶ δὲ τῶν γρίφων Ἀντιφάνης μὲν ἐν Κνοιθιδεῖ ἢ
f Γάστρωνί | φησιν·

   ἐγὼ πρότερον μὲν τοὺς κελεύοντας λέγειν
   γρίφους παρὰ πότον ᾠόμην ληρεῖν σαφῶς
   λέγοντας οὐδέν· ὁπότε προστάξειέ τις
   εἰπεῖν ἐφεξῆς ὅ τι φέρων τις μὴ φέρει,
   ἐγέλων νομίζων λῆρον, οὐκ ἂν γενόμενον
   οὐδέποτέ γ᾽, οἶμαι, πρᾶγμα παντελῶς λέγειν, ‖
449   ἐνέδρας δ᾽ ἕνεκα. νυνὶ δὲ τοῦτ᾽ ἔγνωχ᾽ ὅτι
   ἀληθὲς ἦν· φέρομεν γὰρ ἄνθρωποι δέκα
   ἔρανόν τιν᾽, οὐ φέρει δὲ τούτων τὴν φορὰν
   οὐδείς. σαφῶς οὖν ὅ τι φέρων τις μὴ φέρει,
   τοῦτ᾽ ἔστιν, ἦν θ᾽ ὁ γρῖφος ἐνταῦθα ῥέπων.
   καὶ τοῦτο μὲν δὴ κἄστι συγγνώμην ἔχον·
   ἀλλ᾽ οἷα λογοποιοῦσιν ἐν τῷ πράγματι
   οἱ τἀργύριον μὴ κατατιθέντες. ὡς σφόδρα |
b   ὁ Φίλιππος ἆρ᾽ ἦν εὐτυχής τις, νὴ Δία.

ἐν δὲ Ἀφροδισίῳ·

---

212 E.g. Hellanicus.
213 The discussion of cups is ultimately put off until the next
day; cf. 10.459b.
214 There may be a lacuna in the text after verse 14 (thus
Dindorf). If not, the point is obscure, but the reference must be to
Philip II of Macedon, who was—from the Athenian perspective,
at any rate—a notorious liar.
215 A learned cook is speaking with the man who has hired him
to produce a meal.

146

with one that ends in *-nikos*.[212] Anyone who failed to respond as requested drank the contents of the cup. This is how Clearchus defined the word; but you, my good Ulpian, must take up the question of what the cup in question is.[213] On the subject of riddles, Antiphanes in *The Man from Mt. Cnoithideus or Pot-Belly* (fr. 122) says:

> Before this, I thought that people who tried to get
>       others to respond to riddles
> while they were drinking were talking nonsense and
>       obviously
> making no sense. Whenever someone ordered me
> to answer and tell him what a man doesn't carry when
>       he's carrying it,
> I laughed, because I thought he was talking
>       nonsense, describing
> something that could absolutely never happen, as far
>       as I could tell,
> just to trick me. But now I realize this
> was true! Because there are ten of us bearing the cost
> of a dinner party, and not one of the ten is carrying
>       his share
> of the burden. So this is obviously a case of someone
>       carrying something
> but not carrying it, which is what the riddle was
>       hinting at.
> There's an excuse for this, however;
> but the wild stories the people who don't pay
> their money tell in the course of the business . . .
>       What a
> really lucky guy Philip is, by Zeus![214]

And in *The Sex-Fiend* (fr. 55):[215]

147

(Α.) πότερ᾽ ὅταν μέλλω λέγειν σοι τὴν χύτραν,
⟨χύτραν⟩ λέγω
ἢ τροχοῦ ῥύμαισι τευκτὸν κοιλοσώματον κύτος,
πλαστὸν ἐκ γαίης, ἐν ἄλλῃ μητρὸς ὀπτηθὲν
στέγῃ,
νεογενοῦς ποίμνης δ᾽ ἐν αὐτῇ πνικτὰ
γαλατοθρέμμονα,
τακερόχρωτ᾽ εἴδη κύουσαν; (Β.) Ἡράκλεις,
ἀποκτενεῖς
ἆρά μ᾽, εἰ μὴ γνωρίμως μοι πάνυ φράσεις κρεῶν
χύτραν.

c     (Α.) εὖ λέγεις. | ξουθῆς μελίσσης νάμασιν δὲ
συμμιγῆ
μηκάδων αἰγῶν ἀπόρρουν θρόμβον, ἐγκαθειμένον
εἰς πλατὺ στέγαστρον ἁγνῆς παρθένου Δηοῦς
κόρης,
λεπτοσυνθέτοις τρυφῶντα μυρίοις καλύμμασιν,
ἢ σαφῶς πλακοῦντα φράζω σοι; (Β.) πλακοῦντα
βούλομαι.
(Α.) Βρομιάδος δ᾽ ἱδρῶτα πηγῆς; (Β.) οἶνον εἰπὲ
συντεμών.
(Α.) λιβάδα νυμφαίαν δροσώδη; (Β.) παραλιπὼν
ὕδωρ φάθι. |

d     (Α.) κασιόπνουν δ᾽ αὔραν δι᾽ αἴθρας; (Β.)
σμύρναν εἰπέ, μὴ μακράν,
μηδὲ τοιοῦτ᾽ ἄλλο μηδέν, μηδὲ τοὔμπαλιν λέγων,
ὅτι δοκεῖ τοῦτ᾽ ἔργον εἶναι μεῖζον, ὥς φασίν
τινες,
αὐτὸ μὲν μηδέν, παρ᾽ αὐτὸ δ᾽ ἄλλα συστρέφειν
πυκνά.

148

# BOOK X

(A.) When I'm about to mention the cookpot to
        you—should I say "a cookpot"
or "a hollow-bodied concavity, forged under the
        impulse of a wheel,
moulded of earth, baked in a separate chamber
        sprung from its mother,
and pregnant within with casseroled, milk-nourished
        portions of a new-born
flock, tender-fleshed forms"? (B.) Heracles! You'll be
        the death
of me, if you don't refer in a perfectly intelligible way
        to a "cookpot full of meat".
(A.) Very good. Should I refer to "a curdled mass that
        flows from bleeting she-goats,
mingled with streams spawned by a tawny honeybee,
        nested
in a broad wrapper belonging to Deo's sacred virgin
        daughter,
and luxuriant with countless fine-textured veilings";
or should I describe it clearly to you as "a cake"? (B.)
        I prefer "a cake".
(A.) "The sweat of Bromius' spring"? (B.) Keep it
        short—say "wine"!
(A.) "A dewy nymphaic font"? (B.) Drop that and use
        the word "water"!
(A.) "A cassia-breathing trans-ethereal waft"? (B.) Say
        "incense"; don't stretch it out,
and don't say anything else like that—or the opposite,
        either;
because this looks like a lot of work, to talk like some
        people do,
not actually naming anything, but putting together a
        mass of other words that allude to it.

καὶ Ἄλεξις δὲ ἐν Ὕπνῳ τοιούτους γρίφους προβάλλει·

(A.) οὐ θνητὸς οὐδ᾽ ἀθάνατος, ἀλλ᾽ ἔχων τινὰ
σύγκρασιν, ὥστε μήτ᾽ ἐν ἀνθρώπου μέρει
μήτ᾽ ἐν θεοῦ ζῆν, ἀλλὰ φύεσθαί τ᾽ ἀεὶ |
e   καινῶς φθίνειν τε τὴν παρουσίαν πάλιν,
ἀόρατος ὄψιν, γνώριμος δ᾽ ἅπασιν ὤν.
(B.) ἀεὶ σὺ χαίρεις, ὦ γύναι, μ᾽ αἰνίγμασι—
(A.) καὶ μὴν ἁπλᾶ γε καὶ σαφῆ λέγω μαθεῖν.
(B.) τίς οὖν τοιαύτην παῖς ἔχων ἔσται φύσιν;
(A.) ὕπνος, βροτείων, ὦ κόρη, παυστὴρ πόνων.

Εὔβουλος δ᾽ ἐν Σφιγγοκαρίωνι τοιούτους γρίφους
προβάλλει, αὐτὸς καὶ ἐπιλύων αὐτούς·

(A.) ἔστι λαλῶν ἄγλωσσος, ὁμώνυμος ἄρρενι
θῆλυς,
οἰκείων ἀνέμων ταμίας, δασύς, ἄλλοτε λεῖος, |
f   ἀξύνετα ξυνετοῖσι λέγων, νόμον ἐκ νόμου ἕλκων·
ἓν δ᾽ ἐστὶν καὶ πολλὰ καὶ ἂν τρώσῃ τις ἄτρωτος.
τί ἔστι τοῦτο; τί ἀπορεῖς; (B.) Καλλίστρατος.
(A.) πρωκτὸς μὲν οὖν οὗτός ⟨γε⟩· σὺ δὲ ληρεῖς
ἔχων.

οὗτος γὰρ αὐτός ἐστιν ἄγλωττος λάλος,

---

216 Since, as Speaker B sees it, Callistratus (*PAA* 561575; a
prominent Athenian politician in the first half of the 4th century
BCE) is a babbler (verses 1–3), an effeminate (verse 1), devoted to
generating endless legislation (verse 3), and impervious to criticism (verse 4).

217 Sc. when it produces farts.

Alexis in *Sleep* (fr. 242) also poses riddles of this type:

> (A.) Not mortal or immortal, but containing a
> mixture, so as to live neither in the human sphere
> nor in the divine, but to always both be coming into
>> being
> afresh and nonetheless diminishing its presence,
> unseen by eyes, but recognized by all.
> (B.) You're always happy to use riddles, woman, to
>> make me—
> (A.) In fact, what I'm saying is simple and easy to
>> understand.
> (B.) So what child could ever be like this?
> (A.) Sleep, my girl, who puts an end to mortal
>> troubles.

Eubulus in *Sphinx-Carion* (fr. 106) poses riddles of this
type, but solves them himself:

> (A.) It is something that lacks a tongue, but speaks;
>> the female shares a name with the male;
> it safeguards many winds; is hairy, but at other times
>> hairless;
> says what makes no sense to the sensible; and extracts
>> one law from another.
> It is one and many; and if someone wounds it, it
>> remains unwounded.
> What is it? Why are you puzzled? (B.) It's
>> Callistratus![216]
> (A.) No—it's an asshole. You're always talking
>> nonsense.
> An asshole's both tongueless and capable of
>> speech;[217]

151

ἐν ὄνομα πολλοῖς, τρωτὸς ἄτρωτος, δασὺς
λεῖος. τί βούλει; πνευμάτων πολλῶν φύλαξ ‖

\*    \*    \*

450    ἀττελεβόφθαλμος, † μὴ πρόστομος †,
     ἀμφικέφαλος,
αἰχμητής, παίδων ἀγόνων γόνον ἐξαφανίζων.

ἰχνεύμων Αἰγύπτιος·

τῶν γὰρ κροκοδίλων οὗτος ᾠὰ λαμβάνων
πρὶν θηριοῦσθαι τὸν γόνον καταγνύει,
ἔπειτ' ἀφανίζει. διότι δ' <ἔστ'> ἀμφίστομος;
κεντεῖ κάτωθε, τοῖς δὲ χείλεσιν δάκνει

\*    \*    \*

οἶδ' ἐγὼ ὃς νέος ὢν ἔστιν βαρύς, ἂν δὲ γέρων ᾖ,
ἄπτερος ὢν κούφως πέταται καὶ γῆν ἀφανίζει.

πάππος ἀπ' ἀκάνθης· οὗτος γὰρ

b    νέος μὲν ὢν | ἔστηκεν ἐν τῷ σπέρματι,
ὅταν δ' ἀποβάλῃ τοῦτο, πέτεται κοῦφος ὤν,
δήπουθεν ὑπὸ τῶν παιδίων φυσώμενος.

\*    \*    \*

ἔστιν ἄγαλμα μεμυκὸς ἄνω, τὰ κάτω δὲ κεχηνός,
εἰς πόδας ἐκ κεφαλῆς τετρημένον ὀξὺ διαπρό,
ἀνθρώπους τίκτον κατὰ τὴν πυγὴν ἕν' ἕκαστον,

---

218 Sc. when penetrated by a penis.

219 The solution to the riddle, which follows in the next four
verses, is in iambic trimeter, unlike the riddle itself (above), which
is—as often; cf. 10.448b n.—in dactylic hexameter. Cf. below.

220 Sc. by eating them. But the sense of the line-and-a-half
that follows is obscure.      221 The solution to the riddle is
again in iambic trimeter rather than dactylic hexameter; cf. above.

they all share a single name;
when wounded,[218] it's unwounded; it's hairy and
hairless. What more do you want? It's a guardian of
       many winds.

      *    *    *

locust-eyed, † without protruding lips †, two-headed,
a spearsman, which makes the spawn of unborn
       young vanish.

An Egyptian mongoose;[219]

    Because this creature gets crocodile eggs
    and breaks them before the spawn turns into a beast,
    and then makes them vanish.[220] Why is it two-
           mouthed?
    It stings from beneath, and it bites with its lips.

        *    *    *

    I know something that is heavy when young; but
           when it is old,
    it flies off lightly, despite lacking wings, and makes
           the earth disappear.

Thistle-down; because this[221]

    is attached to the seed when young;
    but once it releases its seed, it flies off lightly,
    when children blow on it, obviously.

        *    *    *

    There is an extraordinary object that is closed tight
           on top, but wide open on the bottom,
    and is pierced straight through from head to foot,
    and produces one person at a time from its butt.

ὧν οἱ μὲν μοίρας ἔλαχον βίου, οἱ δὲ πλανῶνται,
† αὐτὸ δ' ἕκαστος ἔχων αὐτόν, καλέω δὲ
        φυλάττειν †. |

c  ταῦτα δ' ὅτι κληρωτικὸν σημαίνει ὑμεῖς διακρίνατε,
ἵνα μὴ πάντα παρὰ τοῦ Εὐβούλου λαμβάνωμεν. Ἀντιφάνης δ' ἐν τῷ Προβλήματί φησιν·

(Α.) ἰχθύσιν ἀμφίβληστρον ἀνὴρ πολλοῖς
        περιβάλλειν
οἰηθεὶς μεγάλη δαπάνη μίαν εἵλκυσε πέρκην·
καὶ ταύτην ψευσθεὶς ἄλλην κεστρεὺς † ἴσον
        αὐτὴν
ἦγεν. βουλομένη δ' ἔπεται πέρκη μελανούρῳ.
(Β.) κεστρεύς, ἀνήρ, μελάνουρος, οὐκ οἶδ' ὅ τι
        λέγεις·
οὐδὲν λέγεις γάρ. (Α.) ἀλλ' ἐγὼ σαφῶς φράσω. |
d  ἔστι τις ὃς τὰ μὲν ὄντα διδοὺς οὐκ οἶδε δεδωκὼς
οἷσι δέδωκ' οὐδ' αὐτὸς ἔχων ὧν οὐδὲν ἐδεῖτο.
(Β.) διδούς τις οὐκ ἔδωκεν οὐδ' ἔχων ἔχει;
οὐκ οἶδα τούτων οὐδέν. (Α.) οὐκοῦν ταῦτα καὶ
ὁ γρῖφος ἔλεγεν. ὅσα γὰρ οἶσθ' οὐκ οἶσθα νῦν

---

222 I.e. a *klērōtērion*, used to allot jurors to particular courts in
Athens by means of balls dropped in from the top; see Rhodes on
[Arist.] *Ath.* 64.2–3 (with further bibliography). Jurors who were
chosen to serve were paid for their time; others could return and
try again the next day.

223 "A perch follows a *melanouros*" (an unidentified fish) is
identified as a proverb at 7.319c.

224 These two verses (like the second exchange between the
speakers below) are in iambic trimeter, whereas the various riddles and mock-riddles are all in dactylic hexameter; cf. 10.448b n.

Some of them are allotted the right to life, while
      others are made to wander off.
† itself each one having him, and I summon to stand
      guard †.

You may judge for yourselves that these verses refer to
an allotment-machine,[222] keeping me from having to cite
the entire passage from Eubulus. Antiphanes says in *The
Puzzle* (fr. 192):

(A.) A man who expected to cast a net around a large
      number
of fish caught a single perch at enormous expense;
and a gray mullet who was disappointed in the perch
      brought another † equal
her. A perch willingly follows a *melanouros*.[223]
(B.) A gray mullet, sir, a *melanouros*—I don't know
      what you're talking about;
you're not making sense. (A.) Then I'll explain it
      clearly.[224]
There is a man who, when he gives what he has, is
      unaware that he has given it
to those he has given it to, nor that he has what he
      did not need at all.
(B.) Someone giving something didn't give it, and he's
      got it even though he doesn't?
I don't understand a word of this. (A.) Well, that's
      exactly what
the riddle said. Because now you don't know what
      you know,

οὐδ᾽ ὅσα δέδωκας οὐδ᾽ ὅσ᾽ ἀντ᾽ αὐτῶν ἔχεις.
τοιοῦτο τοῦτ᾽ ἦν. (Β.) τοιγαροῦν κἀγώ τινα
εἰπεῖν πρὸς ὑμᾶς βούλομαι γρῖφον. (Α.) λέγε.
(Β.) πίννη καὶ τρίγλη φωνὰς ἰχθῦ δύ᾽ ἔχουσαι |

e    πόλλ᾽ ἐλάλουν, περὶ ὧν δὲ πρὸς ὅν τ᾽ ᾤοντο
     λέγειν τι,
οὐκ ἐλάλουν· οὐδὲν γὰρ ἐμάνθανεν, ὥστε πρὸς ὃν
     μὲν
ἦν αὐταῖς ὁ λόγος, πρὸς δ᾽ αὑτὰς πολλὰ
     λαλούσας—
αὐτὰς ἀμφοτέρας ἡ Δημήτηρ ἐπιτρίψαι.

ἐν δὲ Σαπφοῖ ὁ Ἀντιφάνης αὐτὴν τὴν ποιήτριαν προ-
βάλλουσαν ποιεῖ γρίφους τόνδε τὸν τρόπον, ἐπιλυο-
μένου τινὸς οὕτως. ἡ μὲν γάρ φησιν·

   (Σα.) ἔστι φύσις θήλεια βρέφη σῴζουσ᾽ ὑπὸ
     κόλποις |

f    αὑτῆς, ὄντα δ᾽ ἄφωνα βοὴν ἵστησι γεγωνὸν
   καὶ διὰ πόντιον οἶδμα καὶ ἠπείρου διὰ πάσης
   οἷς ἐθέλει θνητῶν, τοῖς δ᾽ οὐδὲ παροῦσιν ἀκούειν
   ἔξεστιν· κωφὴν δ᾽ ἀκοῆς αἴσθησιν ἔχουσιν.

ταῦτά τις ἐπιλυόμενός φησιν·

   (Β.) ἡ μὲν φύσις γὰρ ἦν λέγεις ἐστὶν πόλις,
   βρέφη δ᾽ ἐν αὐτῇ διατρέφει τοὺς ῥήτορας.

or what you've given, or what you got in return for it.
That's what it was. (B.) Alright, I want
to tell *you* a riddle. (A.) Go ahead.
(B.) A pinna and red mullet—two fish that have
        voices—
were having a long discussion, but were not talking
        about what they thought they
were, or to the person they thought they were. For
        he understood nothing, and as a consequence
        the conversation
was with him, but they were having a long discussion
        with one another—
and I hope Demeter smashes them both!

In *Sappho* (fr. 194, encompassing all three passages) Antiphanes represents the poetess herself as posing riddles
in this way, while a male character tries to solve them, as
follows. For she says:

(Sappho) It is a female creature that keeps its
        children safe beneath the folds
of its garment. And though they are mute, they raise
        a resounding cry
through the sea-surge and the whole mainland
to whichever mortals they wish, and even those who
        are not there
can hear them, deaf though their perception is.

The man trying to solve the riddles says the following:

(B.) Yes—because the object you're describing is a
        city,
and the children she nourishes inside herself are the
        politicians.

157

οὗτοι κεκραγότες δὲ τὰ διαπόντια
τἀκ τῆς Ἀσίας καὶ τἀπὸ Θρᾴκης λήμματα ‖
έλκουσι δεῦρο. νεμομένων δὲ πλησίον
αὐτῶν κάθηται λοιδορουμένων τ' ἀεὶ
ὁ δῆμος οὐδὲν οὔτ' ἀκούων οὔθ' ὁρῶν.
(Σα.) < ... > πῶς γὰρ γένοιτ' ἄν, ὦ πάτερ,
ῥήτωρ ἄφωνος; (Β.) ἢν ἁλῷ τρὶς παρανόμων.
< ... > καὶ μὴν ἀκριβῶς ᾠόμην
ἐγνωκέναι τὸ ῥηθέν. ἀλλὰ δὴ λέγε.

451

ἔπειτα ποιεῖ τὴν Σαπφὼ διαλυομένην τὸν γρῖφον
οὕτως·

(Σα.) θήλεια μέν νυν ἐστὶ φύσις ἐπιστολή,
βρέφη δ' ἐν αὐτῇ περιφέρει τὰ γράμματα· |
ἄφωνα δ' ὄντα <ταῦτα> τοῖς πόρρω λαλεῖ
οἷς βούλεθ'· ἕτερος δ' ἂν τύχῃ τις πλησίον
ἑστὼς ἀναγιγνώσκοντος οὐκ ἀκούσεται.

b

Δίφιλος δ' ἐν Θησεῖ τρεῖς ποτε κόρας Σαμίας φησὶν
Ἀδωνίοισιν γριφεύειν παρὰ πότον· προβαλεῖν δ' αὐ-
ταῖσι τὸν γρῖφον, "τί πάντων ἰσχυρότατον;" καὶ τὰν
μὲν εἰπεῖν, "ὁ σίδηρος," καὶ φέρειν τούτου λόγου τὰν
ἀπόδειξιν, διότι τούτῳ πάντ' ὀρύσσουσίν τε καὶ
τέμνουσι καὶ χρῶντ' εἰς ἅπαντα. εὐδοκιμούσᾳ δ' ἐπ-
άγειν τὰν δευτέραν | φάσκειν τε τὸν χαλκέα πολὺ
κρείττω φέρειν ἰσχύν· ἐπεὶ τοῦτον κατεργαζόμενον καὶ

c

---

225 Referring to the *graphē paranomōn*, an Athenian legal
procedure that allowed for the prosecution of a person who proposed a law or decree contrary to an existing law or decree. Anyone convicted three times on such a charge lost the right to participate in the city's political deliberations.     226 Important
evidence for silent reading already in the 4th century BCE.

They shout and bring the overseas
revenues from Asia and Thrace
to us here. And while they're splitting the money up
among themselves and constantly calling each other
     names,
the people sit nearby, and don't hear or see anything.
(Sappho) . . . For how, old sir, could
a politician lack a voice? (B.) If he's convicted three
     times of making an illegal proposal!²²⁵
. . . And yet I thought I'd figured out
exactly what you said. But tell me (the answer).

Then he represents Sappho as offering the correct solution
to the riddle, as follows:

(Sappho) The female creature is a writing tablet,
and the children she carries around inside herself are
     the letters.
Even though they're mute, they speak to anyone they
     want
who's far away. And if someone else happens to be
     standing
nearby, he won't hear the man who's reading.²²⁶

Diphilus in *Theseus* (fr. 49) claims that once upon a time
three Samian girls were telling riddles at the Adonia festival over drinks, and one of them posed the riddle, "What's
the strongest thing in the world?" The first girl said "Iron,"
and offered as an explanation for her answer that it can dig
or cut anything, and is used for purposes of all sorts. She
got a positive response for this; but the second girl spoke
next and said that a blacksmith is much more powerful, because in the course of his work he bends iron, no matter

τὸν σίδηρον τὸν σφοδρὸν κάμπτειν, μαλάσσειν, ὅ τι
ἂν χρήζῃ ποιεῖν. τὰν δὲ τρίταν ἀποφῆναι πέος ἰσχυρότατον πάντων, διδάσκειν δ' ὅτι καὶ τὸν χαλκέα
στένοντα πυγίζουσι τούτῳ. Ἀχαιὸς δ' ὁ Ἐρετριεὺς
γλαφυρὸς ὢν ποιητὴς περὶ τὴν σύνθεσιν ἔσθ' ὅτε καὶ
μελαίνει τὴν φράσιν καὶ πολλὰ αἰνιγματωδῶς ἐκφέρει, ὥσπερ ἐν Ἴριδι σατυρικῇ. λέγει γάρ·

            λιθάργυρος |
d     ὄλπη παρηωρεῖτο χρίματος πλέα
      τὸν Σπαρτιάτην γραπτὸν ἐν διπλῷ ξύλῳ
      κύρβιν.

τὸν γὰρ λευκὸν ἱμάντα βουληθεὶς εἰπεῖν, ἐξ οὗ ἡ
ἀργυρᾶ λήκυθος ἐξήρτητο, Σπαρτιάτην γραπτὸν
ἔφη[24] ἀντὶ τοῦ Σπαρτιάτιν σκυτάλην. ὅτι δὲ λευκῷ
ἱμάντι περιειλοῦντες τὴν σκυτάλην οἱ Λάκωνες ἔγραφον ἃ ἠβούλοντο εἴρηκεν ἱκανῶς Ἀπολλώνιος ὁ Ῥόδιος ἐν τῷ Περὶ Ἀρχιλόχου. καὶ Στησίχορος δ' ἐν
Ἑλένῃ

      < . . . > λιθαργύρεον ποδανιπτῆρα

ἔφη. Ἴων δὲ ἐν Φοίνικι ἢ Καινεῖ δρυὸς ἱδρῶτα εἴρηκε
τὸν ἰξὸν ἐν τούτοις·

────────────

[24] ἔφη κύρβιν ACE: κύρβιν del. Olson

────────────────────────────

[227] An oxide of lead, created by heating lead in air, and used for
vessels because of its yellowish or reddish color.
[228] The thong—Plutarch refers to it instead as a long strip of
papyrus—was removed from the dispatch-stick after the message
was written on it, and was sent off by itself; it could be read only

how strong it is, and softens it, and does whatever he wants with it. But the third girl insisted that the strongest object in the world is a dick, and explained that when someone sticks his dick up the blacksmith's ass, it makes him groan. Although Achaeus of Eretria (*TrGF* 20 T 7) is a poet who composes elegantly, he occasionally uses obscure language and expresses himself in a confusing fashion, as for example in the satyr play *Iris* (*TrGF* 20 F 19), where he says:

> A flask made of
> litharge[227] and full of ointment was suspended
> alongside
> the inscribed Spartiate tablet on a double
> peg.

Because when he wanted to refer to the white thong from which the silver oil-flask was hanging, he referred to it as an "inscribed Spartiate" rather than as a "Spartan message-staff". As for the fact that the Spartans wrapped their message-staffs in white thongs and wrote what they wanted on them,[228] Apollonius of Rhodes discusses this at length in his *On Archilochus*. So too Stesichorus in *Helen* (*PMG* 188) used the phrase

> a foot-washing basin made of litharge.

Ion in *Phoenix or Caineus* (*TrGF* 19 F 40) referred to mistletoe as "oak-sweat" in the following passage:

when wrapped around another stick of precisely the same diameter, and thus provided a modestly secure means for the Spartans to communicate with their military commanders in the field. Cf. Plu. *Lys.* 19.5–7.

δρυός μ' ἱδρὼς

e  καὶ θαμνομήκης ῥάβδος | ἤ τ' Αἰγυπτία
βόσκει λινουλκὸς χλαῖνα θήραγρος πέδη.

Θεοδέκτην δὲ τὸν Φασηλίτην φησὶν Ἕρμιππος ἐν τοῖς
Περὶ τῶν Ἰσοκράτους Μαθητῶν ἱκανώτατον γεγονέναι
ἀνευρεῖν τὸν προβληθέντα γρῖφον καὶ αὐτὸν προβαλεῖν ἑτέροις ἐπιδεξίως, οἷον τὸν περὶ τῆς σκιᾶς· ἔφη
γὰρ εἶναί τινα φύσιν, ἣ περὶ τὴν γένεσιν καὶ φθίσιν
ἐστὶ μεγίστη, περὶ δὲ τὴν ἀκμὴν ἐλαχίστη. λέγει δ'
οὕτως· |

f  τίς φύσις οὔθ' ὅσα γαῖα φέρει τροφὸς οὔθ' ὅσα
  πόντος
οὔτε βροτοῖσιν ἔχει γυίων αὔξησιν ὁμοίαν,
ἀλλ' ἐν μὲν γενέσει πρωτοσπόρῳ ἐστὶ μεγίστη,
ἐν δὲ μέσαις ἀκμαῖς μικρά, γήρᾳ δὲ πρὸς αὐτῷ
μορφῇ καὶ μεγέθει μείζων πάλιν ἐστὶν ἁπάντων;

κἂν τῷ Οἰδίποδι δὲ τῇ τραγῳδίᾳ τὴν νύκτα καὶ τὴν
ἡμέραν εἴρηκεν αἰνιττόμενος·

εἰσὶ κασίγνηται δισσαί, ὧν ἡ μία τίκτει ‖
452  τὴν ἑτέραν, αὐτὴ δὲ τεκοῦσ' ὑπὸ τῆσδε τεκνοῦται.

τοιοῦτόν τι καὶ Καλλισθένης ἐν ταῖς Ἑλληνικαῖς
φησιν, ὡς Ἀρκάδων πολιορκούντων Κρῶμνον (πο-
λίχνιον δ' ἐστὶν ἱδρυμένον πλησίον Μεγάλης πόλεως)

---

229 Mistletoe berries were boiled and used to produce an ad-
hesive substance ("birdlime"), which was smeared on the end of
sticks and used to trap small birds; cf. Ar. Av. 527 with Dunbar ad
loc.    230 I.e. a hunting-net? Flax was not widely grown in
Greece, and linen made from it was instead imported from Egypt.
231 Called Cromne below.

Oak-sweat, and
a stick as long as a bush is wide,[229] and my Egyptian
    cloak
of spun flax,[230] the shackle I use to catch wild
    creatures, keep me fed.

According to Hermippus in his *On Isocrates' Students* (fr.
77 Wehrli), Theodectas of Phaselis (*TrGF* 72 T 10) was
quite talented at figuring out any riddle presented to him
and at posing clever riddles for others, for example the one
about the shadow; because he said that there was a creature that is biggest when it is born and when it dies, but
smallest at its prime. He puts it as follows (*TrGF* 72 F 18):

What creature is not among those the nourishing
    earth or the sea produces,
and has limbs that do not grow like those of mortal
    beings,
but is instead largest at its first-sown birth,
tiny at its mid-most prime, and in extreme old age
once again larger than at any other point in shape and
    size?

And in his tragedy *Oedipus* (*TrGF* 72 F 4) he refers in a
riddling way to night and day:

There are twin sisters, one of whom gives birth to
    the other, and after giving birth she is herself born
        from the one she bore.

Callisthenes in his *History of Greece* (*FGrH* 124 F 13) offers a story along the following lines: When the Arcadians
were besieging Cromnus[231]—this is a small fortified site

163

Ἱππόδαμος ὁ Λάκων εἷς ὢν τῶν πολιορκουμένων δι-
εκελεύετο τῷ παρὰ Λακεδαιμονίων πρὸς αὐτοὺς ἥκοντι
κήρυκι, δηλῶν ἐν αἰνιγμῷ τὴν περὶ αὐτοὺς κατάστα-
σιν, ἀπαγγέλλειν τῇ μητρὶ λύεσθαι τὸ γύναιον δέχ᾽
ἡμερῶν τὸ ἐν Ἀπολλωνίῳ δεδεμένον, ὡς οὐκ ἔτι |
b  λύσιμον ἐσόμενον ἐὰν αὗται παρέλθωσι. καὶ διὰ ταύτης τῆς γνώμης ἐμήνυεν σαφῶς τὸ μήνυμα· αὕτη γάρ
ἐστιν ἐν τῷ Ἀπολλωνίῳ παρὰ τὸν τοῦ Ἀπόλλωνος
θρόνον διὰ γραφῆς ἀπομεμιμημένος Λιμὸς ἔχων γυναικὸς μορφήν. φανερὸν οὖν ἐγένετο πᾶσιν ὅτι δέκα
ἡμέρας ἔτι καρτερῆσαι δύνανται οἱ πολιορκούμενοι
διὰ τὸν λιμόν· συνέντες οὖν οἱ Λάκωνες τὸ λεχθὲν
ἐβοήθησαν κατὰ κράτος τοῖς ἐν τῇ Κρώμνῃ. πολλοὶ δὲ
⟨τῶν⟩[25] γρίφων καὶ τοιοῦτοί τινές εἰσιν οἷον·

ἄνδρ᾽ εἶδον πυρὶ χαλκὸν ἐπ᾽ ἀνέρι κολλήσαντα |
c  οὕτω συγκόλλως ὥστε σύναιμα ποεῖν.

τοῦτο δὲ σημαίνει σικύας προσβολήν. καὶ τὸ Πανάρ-
κους δ᾽ ἐστὶ τοιοῦτον, ὥς φησι Κλέαρχος ἐν τῷ Περὶ
Γρίφων, ὅτι βάλοι ξύλῳ τε καὶ οὐ ξύλῳ καθημένην
ὄρνιθα καὶ οὐκ ὄρνιθα ἀνήρ τε κοὐκ ἀνὴρ λίθῳ τε καὶ
οὐ λίθῳ· τούτων γάρ ἐστι τὸ μὲν νάρθηξ, τὸ δὲ
νυκτερίς, τὸ δὲ εὐνοῦχος, τὸ δὲ κίσηρις. καὶ Πλάτων δ᾽
ἐν πέμπτῳ Νόμων μνημονεύει· τοὺς τῶν τεχνυδρίων

25 add. Kaibel

---

232 Poralla #389; the events in question took place in 364 BCE.
Although Athenaeus does not say as much, the story assumes that
Hippodamus was speaking from the city's walls, in full hearing of
the Arcadians.

233 Heated cupping glasses were used to draw blood to the

164

located near Megalopolis—Hippodamus of Sparta,[232] who
was one of the people trapped by the siege, used a riddle to
make their situation clear, by ordering the herald the Spartans had sent to them to take a message to his mother, telling her that she needed to set the woman who was tied up
inside Apollo's precinct free within ten days, since after ten
days were up, it would no longer be possible to free her. He
used this oblique way of speaking to get his message across
clearly; because the woman in question was the figure
Famine, who was depicted in a woman's form in a painting
beside Apollo's throne within his precinct. It was thus apparent to everyone that the people under siege could hold
out for only ten more days, because they were running out
of food; and the Spartans, who understood what they were
told, accordingly came in full force to relieve the men in
Cromne. Many riddles are of this type, for example:

> I saw a man who was using fire to glue bronze to
>     another man
>   so tightly that he bound them together by blood.

This refers to the application of a cupping glass.[233] Panar-
ces' riddle is of the same sort, according to Clearchus in his
*On Riddles* (fr. 94 Wehrli): On a stick that was no stick sat
a bird that was no bird, and a man who was no man hit it
with a stone that was no stone; the objects in question are
a fennel-stalk, a bat, a eunuch, and a pumice-stone. Plato
too mentions this riddle in Book V of the *Laws*;[234] phi-

---

surface of the skin for blood-letting and the like; cf. 6.257a n.;
10.424b; Olson on Ar. *Pax* 541–2.
[234] The reference is in fact to Book V of the *Republic* (479b–c),
where Plato is discussing not philosophers but the essential ambi-
guity of evaluative adjectives.

φιλοσόφους τοῖς ἐν ταῖς ἑστιάσεσιν ἔφη ἐπαμφο-
d τερίζουσιν ἐοικέναι καὶ τῷ τῶν παίδων | αἰνίγματι τῷ
περὶ τοῦ εὐνούχου τῆς βολῆς πέρι τῆς νυκτερίδος, ᾧ
καὶ ἐφ᾽ οὗ αὐτὸν αὐτὴν αἰνίττονται βαλεῖν. καὶ τὰ
Πυθαγόρου δὲ αἰνίγματα τοιαῦτά ἐστιν, ὥς φησι Δημήτριος ὁ Βυζάντιος ἐν τετάρτῳ Περὶ Ποιημάτων·
καρδίαν μὴ ἐσθίειν ἀντὶ τοῦ ἀλυπίαν ἀσκεῖν. πῦρ
μαχαίρᾳ μὴ σκαλεύειν ἀντὶ τοῦ τεθυμωμένον ἄνδρα
μὴ ἐριδαίνειν· πῦρ γὰρ ὁ θυμός, ἡ δὲ ἔρις μάχαιρα.
ζυγὸν μὴ ὑπερβαίνειν ἀντὶ τοῦ πᾶσαν πλεονεξίαν
e φεύγειν καὶ στυγεῖν, ζητεῖν δὲ | τὸ ἴσον. λεωφόρους²⁶
μὴ στείχειν ἀντὶ τοῦ γνώμῃ ⟨τῶν⟩²⁷ πολλῶν μὴ ἀκο-
λουθεῖν· εἰκῇ γὰρ ἕκαστος ὅ τι ἂν δόξῃ ἀποκρίνεται·
τὴν δ᾽ εὐθεῖαν ἄγειν ἡγεμόνι χρώμενον τῷ νῷ. μὴ
καθῆσθαι ἐπὶ χοίνικα ἀντὶ τοῦ μὴ σκοπεῖν τὰ ἐφ᾽
ἡμέραν, ἀλλὰ τὴν ἐπιοῦσαν ἀεὶ προσδέχεσθαι. ⟨ἀπο-
δημοῦντα ἐπὶ τοῖς ὅροις μὴ ἐπιστρέφεσθαι·²⁸ ἀντὶ τοῦ
. . . ⟩· ὅρια γὰρ καὶ πέρας ζωῆς ὁ θάνατος· τοῦτον οὖν
οὐκ ἐᾷ μετὰ λύπης καὶ φροντίδος προσίεσθαι. τῷ δὲ
Θεοδέκτῃ παραπλησίως ἔπαιζε γρίφους καὶ Δρομέας
f ὁ Κῷος, ὥς φησι Κλέαρχος, | καὶ Ἀριστώνυμος ὁ
ψιλοκιθαριστής, ἔτι δὲ Κλέων ὁ Μίμαυλος ἐπικα-
λούμενος, ὅσπερ καὶ τῶν Ἰταλικῶν μίμων ἄριστος

²⁶ λεωφόρους ὁδοὺς ACE: ὁδοὺς om. D.L. 8.17
²⁷ add. Schweighäuser
²⁸ add. Schweighäuser (cf. D.L. 8.17)

---

235 Longer versions of very similar material are preserved at
Arist. fr. 159 (from Porphyry's *Life of Pythagoras*); D.L. 8.17–18.
236 Perhaps to be identified with the otherwise unknown parasite mentioned by Hegesander of Delphi at 4.132c.

losophers who occupy themselves with trivial matters, he claimed, are like people who pose ambiguous questions at banquets, or like the children's riddle about the eunuch and how he throws something at the bat, asking what he hit it with and what it was sitting on. Pythagoras' puzzles are also of this type, according to Demetrius of Byzantium in Book IV of *On Poems* (*FHG* ii.624):[235] "Don't eat your heart" means "Try not to get upset"; "Don't poke at the fire with a knife" means "Don't pick a fight with a man who's already angry" (because "the fire" stands for "anger", and "a knife" stands for "an argument"); "Don't cheat a scale" means "Avoid and abhor any type of greed, and aim to be fair"; "Don't walk on the main roads" means "Don't follow popular opinion" (because everyone gives what he takes to be the right answer, without thinking about it) "but follow a straight course and be guided by your intelligence"; "Don't sit on a measuring-cup" means "Don't think about the short term; always anticipate tomorrow"; "When you're leaving a place, don't turn back at the border" means . . . (because death is the boundary and edge of life, and he thus forbids us to approach it with grief or worry). According to Clearchus (fr. 93 Wehrli), Dromeas of Cos[236] played with riddles in much the same way that Theodectas did,[237] as was also true of Aristonymus the solo lyre-player,[238] as well as of Cleon (nicknamed "the Mime-Actor"),[239] who was the best Italian mime-actor to perform without a

[237] Cf. 10.451e–2a.

[238] Stephanis #398; cf. 12.538e. For solo lyre-playing, see 14.637f–8a.

[239] Stephanis #1457.

γέγονεν αὐτοπρόσωπος ὑποκριτής· καὶ γὰρ Νυμφο-
δώρου περιῆν ἐν τῷ μνημονευομένῳ μίμῳ. τούτου δὲ
καὶ Ἰσχόμαχος ὁ κῆρυξ ἐγένετο ζηλωτής, ὃς ἐν τοῖς
κύκλοις ἐποιεῖτο τὰς μιμήσεις· ὡς δ᾽ εὐδοκίμει, μετα-
βὰς ἐν τοῖς θαύμασιν ὑπεκρίνετο μίμους. τοιοῦτοι δ᾽
453  ἦσαν οὓς ἐποίουν γρίφους, ‖ οἷον ἀγροίκου τινὸς
ὑπερπλησθέντος καὶ κακῶς ἔχοντος, ὡς ἠρώτα αὐτὸν
ὁ ἰατρὸς μὴ εἰς ἔμετον ἐδείπνησεν, "οὐκ ἔγωγε," εἰπεῖν,
"ἀλλ᾽ εἰς τὴν κοιλίαν." καὶ πτωχῆς τινος τὴν γαστέρα
πονούσης, ἐπεὶ ὁ ἰατρὸς ἐπυνθάνετο μὴ ἐν γαστρὶ ἔχει,
"πῶς γάρ", εἶπε, "τριταία μὴ βεβρωκυῖα;" τῶν
Ἀριστωνύμ⟨ου . . . ⟩ων δ᾽ ἦν εὐπαρύφων λόγων. καὶ
Σωσιφάνης ὁ ποιητὴς εἰς Κηφισοκλέα τὸν ὑποκριτὴν
εἶπεν λοιδορῶν αὐτὸν ὡς εὐρύστομον· "ἐνέβαλον γὰρ
ἄν σου", φησίν, "εἰς τὰ ἰσχία λίθον, εἰ μὴ καταρ-
b  ραίνειν ἔμελλον ‖ τοὺς περιεστηκότας." ἀρχαιότατος δ᾽
ἐστὶ λογικὸς γρῖφος καὶ τῆς τοῦ γριφεύειν φύσεως
οἰκειότατος· "τί πάντες οὐκ ἐπιστάμενοι διδάσκομεν;"
καί "τί ταὐτὸν οὐδαμοῦ καὶ πανταχοῦ;" καὶ πρὸς
τούτοις "τί ταὐτὸν ἐν οὐρανῷ καὶ ἐπὶ γῆς καὶ ἐν
θαλάττῃ;" τοῦτο δ᾽ ἐστὶν ὁμωνυμία· καὶ γὰρ ἄρκτος
καὶ ὄφις καὶ αἰετὸς καὶ κύων ἐστὶν ἐν οὐρανῷ καὶ ἐν γῇ
καὶ ἐν θαλάσσῃ. τὸ δὲ χρόνον σημαίνει· ἅμα γὰρ
παρὰ πᾶσιν ὁ αὐτὸς καὶ οὐδαμοῦ διὰ τὸ μὴ ἐν ἑνὶ τόπῳ

---

240 Stephanis #1894; cf. 1.19f.
241 Stephanis #1304.    242 Stephanis #1400.
243 Sc. because he was a *lakkoprōktos* (literally "cistern-ass"),
as a result of having been buggered so often and so hard.
244 Cf. Ar. V. 21–3.    245 Sc. because *arktos* ("bear") can
also refer to the constellation known today as the Great Bear or
Big Dipper, as well as to a type of crab; *ophis* ("serpent") can also

mask; he was even better than Nymphodorus[240] in the mime-style just referred to. The herald Ischomachus[241] was his follower; originally he did impersonations in the marketplace, but after he got a reputation, he changed course and performed mimes in stage-shows. The riddles they performed were of the following sort: for example, a country bumpkin ate too much and felt sick, and when the doctor asked him if he had eaten until he threw up, he said: "No; actually, I was tossing my food *down*." And when an old beggar-woman had an upset stomach, and the doctor asked if perhaps she was pregnant, she said: "How's that possible, when my belly's been empty for three days now?" Of Aristonymus' . . . was of the crudest remarks. When the poet Sosiphanes (*TrGF* 92 T 3) was insulting the actor Cephisocles[242] for being a loud-mouth, he said: "I would have thrown a stone at your rear end, if there weren't a risk of splattering the bystanders."[243] There is a very old type of riddle that involves logic and is closely connected to the essential character of posing such questions: "What do we all teach, even though we don't know it?", and "What's simultaneously nowhere and everywhere?", and in addition "What's found in the sky, on the earth, and in the sea?"[244] The final example involves words with multiple meanings; because an *arktos*, an *ophis*, an *aietos*, and a *kuōn* can all be found in the sky, the earth, and the sea.[245] (The one before that) alludes to time, which is simultaneously everywhere and nowhere, because it does not exist in any specific spot.

refer to the constellation Draco, as well as to various kinds of eel; *aietos* ("eagle") can also refer to the constellation Aquila, as well as to the eagle ray; and *kuōn* ("dog") can also refer to Sirius (the "Dog Star"), as well as to a dogfish.

c τὴν φύσιν | ἔχειν. τὸ δὲ προάγον ἐστὶ ψυχὰς ἔχειν·
τοῦτο γὰρ οὐθεὶς ἡμῶν ἐπιστάμενος διδάσκει τὸν
πλησίον.

Ὁ δὲ Ἀθηναῖος Καλλίας (ἐζητοῦμεν γὰρ ἔτι πρότερον περὶ αὐτοῦ) μικρὸν ἔμπροσθεν γενόμενος τοῖς
χρόνοις Στράττιδος ἐποίησε τὴν καλουμένην Γραμματικὴν Θεωρίαν οὕτω διατάξας. πρόλογος μὲν αὐτῆς
ἐστιν ἐκ τῶν στοιχείων, ὃν χρὴ λέγειν[29] διαιροῦντας
κατὰ τὰς παραγραφὰς καὶ τὴν τελευτὴν καταστρο-
φικῶς ποιουμένους εἰς τἄλφα·

d ⟨τὸ ἄλφα⟩, βῆτα, γάμμα, | δέλτα, θεοῦ γὰρ εἶ,
ζῆτ᾽, ἦτα, θῆτ᾽, ἰῶτα, κάππα, λάβδα, μῦ,
νῦ, ξεῖ, τὸ οὖ, πεῖ, ῥῶ, τὸ σίγμα, ταῦ, ⟨τὸ⟩ ὖ,
παρὸν ⟨τὸ⟩ φεῖ, ⟨τὸ⟩ χεῖ τε τῷ ψεῖ εἰς τὸ ὦ.

ὁ χορὸς δὲ γυναικῶν ἐκ τῶν σύνδυο πεποιημένος αὐτῷ
ἐστιν ἔμμετρος ἅμα καὶ μεμελοπεποιημένος τόνδε τὸν
τρόπον· βῆτα ἄλφα βα, βῆτα εἶ βε, βῆτα ἦτα βη,
βῆτα ἰῶτα βι, βῆτα οὖ βο, βῆτα ὖ βυ, βῆτα ὦ βω, καὶ

---

[29] ἐκ τῶν στοιχείων, ὃν χρὴ λέγειν ἐκ τῶν στοιχείων A: ἐκ
τῶν στοιχείων[2] del. Petitus

---

[246] I.e. "a personality". Or perhaps the Greek means "having
breath", in which case what follows must mean "because even
though none of us knows about this (i.e. about whether his breath
stinks or not), whoever stands close to him knows at once."

[247] Strattis appears to belong to the very end of the 5th century
BCE or the beginning of the 4th (his *Anthroporestes* dates to after
408, and his *Atalantus or Atalanta* is said to have been staged
"much later" than Aristophanes' *Frogs* in 405), whereas the comic
playwright Callias dates to the 440s and 430s or so (test. 3–*5) and
is thus perhaps someone different from the poet referred to here

And the initial example refers to having a soul;[246] because even though none of us knows his soul, he informs anyone who comes in contact with him about it.

Callias of Athens (Call. Com. test. *7)—we explored some questions having to do with him previously (7.276a; 10.448b)—was a bit earlier than Strattis (test. 3)[247] and wrote the so-called *Literal Review*, which he organized as follows. The play's prologue consists of letters, and when you read it aloud, you need to follow the punctuation and bring it all full circle, ending with *alpha*:

> The letter *alpha, bēta, gamma, delta, ei* (which
>      belongs to a god),[248]
> *zēta, ēta, thēta, iōta, kappa, labda, mu,*
> *nu, xei,* the letter *ou, pei, rhō,* the letter *sigma, tau,*
>      the letter *u,*
> also the letters *phei* and *chei,* followed by the letter
>      *psei* and ending in the letter *ō.*

His chorus[249] consisted of women who represented pairs of letters and sang in meter, in a lyric style, in the following way: *bēta alpha ba, bēta ei be, bēta ēta bē, bēta iōta bi, bēta ou bo, bēta u bu, bēta ō bō,* and likewise in the antistro-

(= *TrGF* 233). The plays by Euripides and Sophocles mentioned below and supposedly influenced by the *Literal Review*, on the other hand, date to 431 BCE and perhaps the early 420s, respectively.

[248] Sc. to Apollo, upon whose temple an image of the letter E was somehow suspended (Plu. *Mor.* 384d–94c, esp. 384f–5a).

[249] "Chorus" is apparently used here and below to refer not just to the 24 individuals (one per letter) who sang and danced in the *orchestra*, but to their initial entrance song (normally called the *parodos*).

πάλιν ἐν ἀντιστρόφῳ τοῦ μέλους καὶ τοῦ μέτρου·
γάμμα ἄλφα ‹γα›, γάμμα εἶ ‹γε›, γάμμα ἦτα ‹γη›,
γάμμα ἰῶτα ‹γι›, γάμμα οὖ ‹γο›, γάμμα ὖ ‹γυ›,
e    γάμμα ὦ ‹γω›, καὶ ἐπὶ τῶν λοιπῶν συλλαβῶν | ὁμοίως
ἑκάστων τό τε μέτρον καὶ τὸ μέλος ἐν ἀντιστρόφοις
ἔχουσι πᾶσαι ταὐτόν. ὥστε τὸν Εὐριπίδην μὴ μόνον
ὑπονοεῖσθαι τὴν Μήδειαν ἐντεῦθεν πεποιηκέναι πᾶσαν, ἀλλὰ καὶ τὸ μέλος αὐτὸ μετενηνοχότα φανερὸν
εἶναι. τὸν δὲ Σοφοκλέα διελεῖν φασιν ἀποτολμῆσαι τὸ
ποίημα τῷ μέτρῳ τοῦτ᾿ ἀκούσαντα καὶ ποιῆσαι ἐν τῷ
Οἰδίποδι οὕτως·

ἐγὼ οὔτ᾿ ἐμαυτὸν οὔτε σ᾿ ἀλγυνῶ ‹ ... › ταῦτ᾿
‹ ... › ἐλεγχθείς.[30]

διόπερ οἱ λοιποὶ τὰς ἀντιστρόφους ἀπὸ τούτου παρ-
f    εδέχοντο πάντες, ὡς ἔοικεν, εἰς τὰς τραγῳδίας. | καὶ
μετὰ τὸν χορὸν εἰσάγει πάλιν ἐκ τῶν φωνηέντων
ῥῆσιν οὕτως (ἣν δεῖ κατὰ τὰς παραγραφὰς ὁμοίως
τοῖς πρόσθεν λέγοντα διαιρεῖν, ἵν᾿ ἡ τοῦ ποιήσαντος
ὑπόκρισις σῴζηται κατὰ τὴν δύναμιν)·

(Α.) ἄλφα μόνον, ὦ γυναῖκες, εἶ τε δεύτερον
λέγειν μόνον χρή. (Χο.) καὶ τρίτον μόνον γ᾿
ἐρεῖς.

[30] Sophocles actually wrote ἐγὼ οὔτ᾿ ἐμαυτὸν οὔτε σ᾿ ἀλγυνῶ. τί ταῦτ᾿ ἄλλως ἐλέγχεις;

---

250 An almost imcomprehensibly odd assertion (also made at
7.276a, where the information is specifically said to be drawn from
Book I of Clearchus' On Riddles, which must again be Athenaeus'
source here).

phic portion of the song and the meter: *gamma alpha ga, gamma ei ge, gamma ēta gē, gamma iōta gi, gamma ou go, gamma u gu, gamma ō gō*, and so on similarly through each of the other syllables, all of which have the same metrical and lyrical structure organized in antistrophic form. Euripides is accordingly not only suspected of having composed his entire *Medea* using this as his source, but has also patently borrowed the song itself.[250] And people say that after Sophocles (test. 175b) heard this song, he got up the nerve to put his work into verse and wrote the following in his *Oedipus* (332–3):

> I will cause pain neither to myself nor to you if convicted
> of these crimes.[251]

As a consequence, apparently, all the other (poets) adopted antistrophic songs into their tragedies from this source. After the chorus,[252] moreover, he introduces a speech made up of vowels (you need to follow the punctuation when you read it aloud, as with the passage discussed above,[253] so that the delivery-style intended by the poet is preserved to the extent possible); it goes as follows:

> (A.) You must pronounce "*alpha*" all by itself, ladies, and after that
> "*ei*" all by itself. (Chorus) You'll pronounce the third one all by itself.

---

[251] Sc. of stealing poetic material? But the argument is obscure (and, to the extent it is clear, ridiculous).

[252] I.e. the chorus' opening processional song; see above.

[253] At 10.453c–d.

(A.) ἧτ᾽ ἄρα φήσω. (Χο.) τό τε τέταρτόν αὖ
  μόνον
ἰῶτα, πέμπτον οὖ, τό θ᾽ ἕκτον ῦ μόνον
λέγε. (A.) λοίσθιον ⟨λέγειν⟩ δὲ φωνῶ σοι τὸ ὦ
τῶν ἑπτὰ φωνῶν, ἑπτὰ δ᾽ ἐν μέτροις μόνον. ‖

454    καὶ τοῦτο λέξασ᾽ εἶτα δὴ σαυτῇ λάλει.

Δεδήλωκε δὲ καὶ διὰ τῶν ἰαμβείων γράμμα πρῶτος
οὗτος ἀκολαστότερον μὲν κατὰ τὴν διάνοιαν, πε-
φρασμένον δὲ τὸν τρόπον τοῦτον·

κύω γὰρ, ὦ γυναῖκες. ἀλλ᾽ αἰδοῖ, φίλαι,
ἐν γράμμασι σφῶν τοὔνομ᾽ ἐξερῶ βρέφους.
ὀρθὴ μακρὰ γραμμή ᾽στιν· ἐκ δ᾽ αὐτῆς μέσης
μικρὰ παρεστῶσ᾽ ἑκατέρωθεν ὑπτία.
ἔπειτα κύκλος πόδας ἔχων βραχεῖς δύο.

ὅθεν ὕστερον, ὡς ⟨ἂν⟩[31] ὑπονοήσειέ τις, Μαιάνδριος
b  μὲν ὁ | συγγραφεὺς μικρὸν διὰ τῆς ἑρμηνείας τῇ
μιμήσει παρεγκλίνας συνέγραψεν ἓν τῶν Παραγγελ-
μάτων φορτικώτερον τοῦ ῥηθέντος, Εὐριπίδης δὲ τὴν
ἐν τῷ Θησεῖ τὴν ἐγγράμματον ἔοικε ποιῆσαι ῥῆσιν.
βοτὴρ δ᾽ ἐστὶν ἀγράμματος αὐτόθι δηλῶν τοὔνομα τοῦ
Θησέως ἐπιγεγραμμένον οὕτως·

ἐγὼ πέφυκα γραμμάτων μὲν οὐκ ἴδρις,
μορφὰς δὲ λέξω καὶ σαφῆ τεκμήρια.

[31] add. Meineke

---

[254] Literally "a letter"; but the style in this section is extremely
awkward, and the author (presumably the routinely opaque
Clearchus) is plainly referring to a set of letters rather than only
one.      [255] I.e. ΨΩ, which Dalechamp took to be the first two
letters of ψώα ("rotten stench" and thus here "fart").

(A.) Right; I'll say "*ēta*". (Chorus) And then
    pronounce the fourth all
by itself, "*iōta*"; and the fifth, "*ou*"; and the sixth, "*u*",
all by itself. (A.) I urge you to pronounce "*ō*" as the
    last
of the seven vowels, seven in meter all by themselves.
And after you've pronounced that one, say it to
    yourself.

This author was the first to use iambic verse to describe
a word[254] that has a rather crude meaning, but is alluded to
in the following fashion:

For I'm pregnant, ladies. But since I'm embarrassed,
    my friends,
I'll tell you the baby's name by spelling it.
There's a big letter that stands up straight, and
    emerging from its middle
on either side are small parts that lean backward.
Then there's a circle with two tiny feet.[255]

This is the source, one might suspect, on which the prose-
author Maeandrius drew later on (although he deviated a
bit from the original when he imitated it, by way of interpretation) when he made one of his *Precepts* (*FGrH* 491 F
6) even cruder than the passage discussed above. Euripides as well appears to have used this as the basis for the
speech that describes the shape of individual letters in his
*Theseus* (fr. 382). An illiterate shepherd is there, trying to
describe an inscription that reads "Theseus", as follows:

I don't know how to read or write,
but I'll describe their shapes and offer you a clear
    account.

κύκλος τις ὡς τόρνοισιν ἐκμετρούμενος,
οὗτος δ' ἔχει σημεῖον ἐν μέσῳ σαφές· |
c  τὸ δεύτερον δὲ πρῶτα μὲν γραμμαὶ δύο,
ταύτας διείργει δ' ἐν μέσαις ἄλλη μία·
τρίτον δὲ βόστρυχός τις ὡς εἰλιγμένος·
τὸ δ' αὖ τέταρτον ἡ μὲν εἰς ὀρθὸν μία,
λοξαὶ δ' ἐπ' αὐτῆς τρεῖς κατεστηριγμέναι
εἰσίν· τὸ πέμπτον δ' οὐκ ἐν εὐμαρεῖ φράσαι·
γραμμαὶ γάρ εἰσιν ἐκ διεστώτων δύο,
αὗται δὲ συντρέχουσιν εἰς μίαν βάσιν·
τὸ λοίσθιον δὲ τῷ τρίτῳ προσεμφερές.

d  τὸ δ' αὐτὸ πεποίηκε καὶ Ἀγάθων ὁ τραγῳδιοποιὸς | ἐν
τῷ Τηλέφῳ· ἀγράμματος γάρ τις κἀνταῦθα δηλοῖ τὴν
τοῦ Θησέως ἐπιγραφὴν οὕτως·

γραφῆς ὁ πρῶτος ἦν μεσόμφαλος κύκλος·
ὀρθοί τε κανόνες ἐζυγωμένοι δύο,
Σκυθικῷ τε τόξῳ ⟨τὸ⟩ τρίτον ἦν προσεμφερές·
ἔπειτα τριόδους πλάγιος ἦν προσκείμενος·
ἐφ' ἑνός τε κανόνος ἦσαν ⟨ . . . ⟩ δύο·
ὅπερ δὲ τὸ τρίτον, ἦν τελευταῖον πάλιν.

καὶ Θεοδέκτης δ' ὁ Φασηλίτης ἄγροικόν τινα ἀγράμ-
e  ματον | παράγει καὶ τοῦτον τὸ τοῦ Θησέως ὄνομα
διασημαίνοντα·

γραφῆς ὁ πρῶτος ἦν † μαλακόφθαλμος †
κύκλος.
ἔπειτα δισσοὶ κανόνες ἰσόμετροι πάνυ,

---

256 I.e. ΘΗΣΕΥΣ ("Theseus").

176

There's a circle neatly measured out, as if turned on a
     lathe,
with a prominent mark in the middle.
As for the second letter, there are two lines, first of
     all,
and one more, in the middle, that connects them.
The third resembles a curling lock of hair;
as for the fourth, one line stands up straight,
and three crooked ones are propped up
against it. The fifth letter's not easy to describe:
there are two lines that are separate from one
     another,
although they merge into a single base.
And the last letter's like the third.[256]

The tragic poet Agathon has a similar passage in his *Tele-phus* (*TrGF* 39 F 4). For there as well an illiterate person
describes an inscription that reads "Theseus," as follows:

The first letter in the inscription was a circle with a
     dot in the center;
there were also two upright bars attached to one
     another,
and the third letter looked like a Scythian bow.
Next was a trident turned sideways;
and two . . . were on a single bar.
The third letter appeared again as the last.

Theodectas of Phaselis (*TrGF* 72 F 6) also brings an illiter-ate peasant onstage, and he too describes Theseus' name:

The first letter in the inscription was a circle † with a
     soft eye †.
Then there were two bars of exactly the same length,

177

τούτους δὲ πλάγιος διαμέτρου συνδεῖ κανών,
τρίτον δ' ἑλικτῷ βοστρύχῳ προσεμφερές.
ἔπειτα τριόδους πλάγιος ὡς ἐφαίνετο,
πέμπται δ' ἄνωθεν ἰσόμετροι ῥάβδοι δύο,
αὗται δὲ συντείνουσιν εἰς βάσιν μίαν· |

f    ἕκτον δ' ὅπερ καὶ πρόσθεν εἶθ', ὁ βόστρυχος.

καὶ Σοφοκλῆς δὲ τούτῳ παραπλήσιον ἐποίησεν ἐν
Ἀμφιαράῳ σατυρικῷ τὰ γράμματα παράγων ὀρχού-
μενον.

Νεοπτόλεμος δὲ ὁ Παριανὸς ἐν τῷ Περὶ Ἐπιγραμμάτων ἐν Χαλκηδόνι φησὶν ἐπὶ τοῦ Θρασυμάχου
τοῦ σοφιστοῦ μνήματος ἐπιγεγράφθαι τόδε τὸ ἐπί-
γραμμα·

τοὔνομα θῆτα ῥῶ ἄλφα σὰν ῦ μῦ ἄλφα χεῖ οὖ
     σάν,
πατρὶς Χαλκηδών· ἡ δὲ τέχνη σοφίη.

τὸ δὲ Καστορίωνος τοῦ Σολέως, ὡς ὁ Κλέαρχός φησιν,
εἰς τὸν Πᾶνα ποίημα τοιοῦτόν ἐστι· τῶν ποδῶν ‖
455   ἕκαστος ὅλοις ὀνόμασιν περιειλημμένος πάντας ὁμοίως ἡγεμονικοὺς καὶ ἀκολουθητικοὺς ἔχει τοὺς πόδας,
οἷον·

σὲ τὸν βολαῖς νιφοκτύποις δυσχείμερον
ναίονθ' ἕδραν, θηρονόμε Πάν, χθόν' Ἀρκάδων,
κλήσω γραφῇ τῇδ' ἐν σοφῇ πάγκλειτ' ἔπη

---

257 Presumably the Thrasymachus of Chalcedon who appears
in Plato's *Republic* (85 A 8 D–K). The epigram violates the otherwise firm rule that the deceased's native land is not named unless
he is buried abroad, casting doubt on its authenticity.
258 I.e. ΘΡΑΣΥΜΑΧΟΣ ("Thrasymachus").

and a sideways bar in between connected them.
The third letter resembled a twisting lock of hair.
Then came what looked like a trident turned
    sideways;
and fifth were two bars of equal length on top,
which converged into a single base.
And the sixth was what I described earlier, the lock of
    hair.

Sophocles as well has a similar passage in the satyr play
*Amphiaraus* (fr. 121), where he brings a man onstage who
dances the letters.

    Neoptolemus of Parium in his *On Epigrams* (fr. 7
Mette) claims that the following epigram (anon. *FGE*
1568–9) is inscribed on the tomb of the sophist Thrasymachus[257] in Chalcedon:

My name is *thēta, rhō, alpha, san, u, mu, alpha, xei,
    ou, san*;[258]
    my fatherland is Chalcedon; and my trade is
      wisdom.

According to Clearchus (fr. 88 Wehrli), Castorion of Soli's
poem in honor of Pan (*SH* 310) is composed in the following way. Each foot consists of complete words, and all the
feet it contains can stand either at the head of the line or
within it, for example:

You who inhabit an abode made wintry by bolts
of rattling snow, Pan, tender of wild beasts, the land
    of Arcadia,
I shall invoke you by knitting together in this clever
    composition,

συνθείς, ἄναξ, δύσγνωστα μὴ σοφῷ κλύειν,
μωσοπόλε θήρ, κηρόχυτον ὃς μείλιγμ᾽ ἱείς,

καὶ τὰ λοιπὰ τὸν αὐτὸν τρόπον. τούτων δὲ ἕκαστον τῶν
ποδῶν, ὡς ἂν τῇ τάξει θῇς, τὸ αὐτὸ μέτρον ἀποδώσει,
οὕτως·

σὲ τὸν βολαῖς νιφοκτύποις δυσχείμερον, |
b      νιφοκτύποις σὲ τὸν βολαῖς δυσχείμερον.

καὶ ὅτι τῶν ποδῶν ἕκαστός ἐστι ἑνδεκαγράμματος.
ἔστι καὶ μὴ τοῦτον τὸν τρόπον ἀλλ᾽ ἑτέρως ποιῆσαι,
ὥστε πλείω πρὸς τὴν χρῆσιν ἐκ τοῦ ἑνὸς ἔχειν οὕτω
λέγοντας·

μέτρον φράσον μοι τῶν ποδῶν ⟨μέτρον λαβών⟩.
λαβὼν μέτρον μοι τῶν ποδῶν μέτρον φράσον.
οὐ βούλομαι γὰρ τῶν ποδῶν μέτρον λαβεῖν.
λαβεῖν μέτρον γὰρ τῶν ποδῶν οὐ βούλομαι.

Πίνδαρος δὲ πρὸς τὴν ἀσιγμοποιηθεῖσαν ᾠδήν, |
c   ὡς ὁ αὐτός φησι Κλέαρχος, οἱονεὶ γρίφου τινὸς ἐν
μελοποιίᾳ προβληθέντος, ὡς πολλῶν τούτῳ προσ-
κρουόντων διὰ τὸ ἀδύνατον εἶναι ἀποσχέσθαι τοῦ
σίγμα καὶ διὰ τὸ μὴ δοκιμάζειν, ἐποίησε·[32]

[32] A truncated version of the text, which ought to read ἀοιδὰ
διθυράμβων / καὶ τὸ σὰν κίβδηλον ἀνθρώποισιν ἀπὸ στομάτων.

---

[259] Counting what is printed in our text as *iota*-subscript as a
letter.

180

    lord, widely-renowned phrases that are difficult for
        dull listeners,
poetic beast, you who produce a soothing song
        moulded from wax.

The rest is similar. But each foot will produce the same
metrical pattern, no matter where you place it in the line,
as follows:

    You who inhabit an abode made wintry by bolts,
    You who an abode inhabit by bolts made wintry.

In addition, each foot contains eleven letters.[259] It is also
possible to compose in a different way than this, allowing
for the creation of a number of lines out of one, by putting
it thus:

    Tell me the meter after you measure the feet.
    After you measure the feet, tell me the meter.
    Because I do not wish to measure the feet.
    Because to measure the feet I do not wish.

According to the same Clearchus (fr. 88 Wehrli, continued),[260] Pindar was referring to the asigmatic style of poetry, and a sort of riddle, as it were, is posed in his lyrics,
since many people became upset with him as a result of his
inability to avoid the letter *sigma* and because they disap-
proved of this tendency, when he wrote (fr. 70b.1–3, lacunose):[261]

---

[260] Cf. 10.448c–d (also quoting Clearchus and referring to,
but not quoting, Pindar).

[261] Quoted again at 11.467b (also lacunose).

πρὶν μὲν ἔρπε σχοινοτένειά τ᾽ ἀοιδὰ ⟨ ... ⟩
καὶ τὸ σὰν κίβδηλον ἀνθρώποις.

ταῦτα σημειώσαιτ᾽ ἄν τις πρὸς τοὺς νοθεύοντας
Λάσου τοῦ Ἑρμιονέως τὴν ἄσιγμον ᾠδήν, ἥτις ἐπι-
γράφεται Κένταυροι. καὶ ὁ εἰς τὴν Δήμητρα δὲ τὴν ἐν
Ἑρμιόνῃ ποιηθεὶς τῷ Λάσῳ ὕμνος ἄσιγμός ἐστιν, ὡς
d φησιν Ἡρακλείδης | ὁ Ποντικὸς ἐν τρίτῳ Περὶ Μου-
σικῆς, οὗ ἐστιν ἀρχή·

Δάματρα μέλπω Κόραν τε Κλυμένοι᾽ ἄλοχον.

ἔστιν εὐπορῆσαι καὶ ἄλλων γρίφων·

ἐν Φανερᾷ γενόμαν, πάτραν δέ μου ἁλμυρὸν
    ὕδωρ
ἀμφὶς ἔχει· μήτηρ δ᾽ ἔστ᾽ Ἀριθμοῖο πάις.

Φανερᾷ μὲν οὖν λέγει τῇ Δήλῳ, ἥτις ὑπὸ θαλάσσης
περιέχεται, μήτηρ δ᾽ ἡ Λητώ, ἥτις Κοίου ἐστὶ θυ-
γάτηρ· Μακεδόνες δὲ τὸν ἀριθμὸν κοῖον προσαγο-
e ρεύουσι. | καὶ ἐπὶ τῆς πτισάνης·

κριθῆς ἀφλοίου χυλὸν ὀργάσας πίε.

πεποίηται δὲ τῆς πτισάνης τοὔνομα ἀπὸ τοῦ πτίσσειν
καὶ ἀνεῖν. καὶ ἐπὶ τοῦ κοχλίου· φέρεται δὲ τοῦτο καὶ ἐν
τοῖς Τεύκρου Ὁρισμοῖς·

---

262 At 14.624e–f, Athenaeus, again citing Heracleides, quotes
a slightly different—but still asigmatic—version of the fragment.
263 I.e. Hades (as god of the dead, better left unnamed). Kora
is a Doric form of Korē ("the Girl"), i.e. Demeter's daughter
Persephone.          264 Apollo or Artemis.          265 Because
"Delos" is literally "clear, apparent", and the adjective *phaneros*
(feminine *phanera*) means "visible, evident" *vel sim.*

Before this, song walked a straight line . . .
and people regarded the letter *san* as dishonest.

One might point to this passage in responding to those who
question the authenticity of the asigmatic song entitled
*Centaurs* attributed to Lasus of Hermione (*PMG* 704).
The hymn Lasus wrote in honor of Demeter of Hermione
is also asigmatic, according to Heracleides of Pontus in
Book III of *On Music* (fr. 161 Wehrli). Its opening line is
(*PMG* 702.1):[262]

I celebrate Demeter and Kora, wife of the Well-
Known One.[263]

One can also find many other riddles:

I was born on Phanera, and saltwater enfolds my
fatherland. But my mother is Number's child.

By Phanera the speaker[264] means Delos,[265] which is surrounded by the sea, while the speaker's mother is Leto,
who is the daughter of Coius;[266] and the Macedonians use
the word *koios* to mean "number". And referring to barley-
gruel:

Soften up the juice of husked barley and drink it.

The noun *ptisanē* ("barley-gruel") is formed from *ptissein*
("to pound, rough-mill [grain]") and *anein* (also "to pound,
rough-mill [grain]").[267] And referring to a snail; this one is
preserved in Teucrus' *Definitions* (*FGrH* 274 F 3):

---

[266] Cf. Hes. *Th.* 404–6.

[267] *ptisanē* is in fact related to *ptissein*, but has no connection
to *anein*.

ζῷον ἄπουν ἀνάκανθον ἀνόστεον ὀστρακόνωτον
ὄμματά τ᾽ ἐκκύπτοντα προμήκεα κεἰσκύπτοντα.

Ἀντιφάνης δ᾽ ἐν Αὑτοῦ Ἐρῶντί φησι· |

f    τροφαλίδας τε λινοσάρκους, μανθάνεις; τυρὸν
λέγω.

Ἀναξανδρίδης Αἰσχρᾷ·

ἀρτίως διηρτάμηκε, καὶ τὰ μὲν διανεκῆ
σώματος μέρη δαμάζετ᾽ ἐν πυρικτίτοισι γᾶς·
Τιμόθεος ἔφη ποτ᾽, ἄνδρες, τὴν χύτραν, οἶμαι,
λέγων.

Τιμοκλῆς δ᾽ ἐν Ἥρωσιν·

(Α.) ὡς δ᾽ ἦν ἠρμένη
βίου τιθήνη, πολεμία λιμοῦ, φύλαξ
φιλίας, ἰατρὸς ἐκλύτου βουλιμίας, ‖
456    τράπεζα. (Β.) περιέργως ⟨γε⟩, νὴ τὸν οὐρανόν·
ἐξὸν φράσαι "τράπεζα" συντόμως.

Πλάτων δ᾽ ἐν τῷ Ἀδώνιδι χρησμὸν δοθῆναι λέγων
Κινύρᾳ ὑπὲρ Ἀδώνιδος τοῦ υἱοῦ φησιν·

ὦ Κινύρα, βασιλεῦ Κυπρίων, ἀνδρῶν
δασυπρώκτων,
παῖς σοι κάλλιστος μὲν ἔφυ θαυμαστότατός τε
πάντων ἀνθρώπων, δύο δ᾽ αὐτὸν δαίμον᾽ ὀλεῖτον, |
b    ἡ μὲν ἐλαυνομένη λαθρίοις ἐρετμοῖς, ὁ δ᾽
ἐλαύνων.

---

268 Cf. the very similar riddle at 2.63b with n.
269 Because the cheese in question was set in linen netting to
dry.    270 = PMG 798.

An animal with no foot, or spine, or bones, but with a
  back made of shell,
and that pops its long eyes in and out.[268]

Antiphanes says in *The Man Who Was in Love with Himself* (fr. 51):

  and linen-fleshed curdlings. Do you understand? I'm
    referring to cheese.[269]

Anaxandrides in *Aeschra* (fr. 6):

  He's just now finished the butchering, and the long-
    cut
  portions of flesh are being subdued in fire-formed
    bits of earth;
  thus Timotheus at some point, gentlemen, referring,
    I believe, to a cookpot.[270]

Timocles in *Heroes* (fr. 13):

      (A.) And thus was carried away
 the nurse of life, enemy of starvation, guardian
 of friendship, healer of unbounded ravenousness—
 the table. (B.) Elaborately expressed, by heaven—
 when you could've just said "the table"!

Plato in his *Adonis* (fr. 3) reports that Cinyras received an
oracle about his son Adonis, and says:

  Cinyras, king of the hairy-assed Cyprians,
  your son is the most amazingly beautiful person
  in the entire world. But two divinities will bring
    about his ruin,
  the goddess by being rowed with secret oars, the god
    by rowing.

λέγει δ᾿ Ἀφροδίτην καὶ Διόνυσον· ἀμφότεροι γὰρ
ἤρων τοῦ Ἀδώνιδος. καὶ τὸ τῆς Σφιγγὸς δὲ αἴνιγμα
Ἀσκληπιάδης ἐν τοῖς Τραγῳδουμένοις τοιοῦτον εἶναί
φησιν·

    ἔστι δίπουν ἐπὶ γῆς καὶ τετράπον, οὗ μία φωνή,
    καὶ τρίπον, ἀλλάσσει δὲ φύσιν μόνον ὅσσ᾿ ἐπὶ
        γαῖαν
    ἑρπετὰ γίνονται καὶ ἀν᾿ αἰθέρα καὶ κατὰ πόντον.
    ἀλλ᾿ ὁπόταν πλείστοισιν ἐρειδόμενον ποσὶ βαίνῃ,
    ἔνθα τάχος γυίοισιν ἀφαυρότατον πέλει αὐτοῦ. |

c  γριφώδη δ᾿ ἐστὶ καὶ Σιμωνίδῃ ταῦτα πεποιημένα, ὥς
φησι Χαμαιλέων ὁ Ἡρακλεώτης ἐν τῷ Περὶ Σιμωνί-
δου·

    μιξονόμου τε πατὴρ ἐρίφου καὶ σχέτλιος ἰχθὺς
    πλησίον ἠρείσαντο καρήατα· παῖδα δὲ νυκτὸς
    δεξάμενοι βλεφάροισι Διωνύσοιο ἄνακτος
    βουφόνον οὐκ ἐθέλουσι τιθηνεῖσθαι θεράποντα.

φασὶ δ᾿ οἱ μὲν ἐπί τινος τῶν ἀρχαίων ἀναθημάτων ἐν
Χαλκίδι τοῦτ᾿ ἐπιγεγράφθαι, πεποιῆσθαι δ᾿ ἐν αὐτῷ
d  τράγον καὶ δελφῖνα, περὶ ὧν εἶναι τὸν λόγον | τοῦτον.
οἱ δὲ εἰς ἐπιγόνειον[33] ψαλτήριον δελφῖνα καὶ τράγον
εἰργασμένον εἰρῆσθαι, καὶ εἶναι τὸν βουφόνον καὶ τοῦ
Διονύσου θεράποντα τὸν διθύραμβον. οἱ δέ φασιν ἐν

---

33 ἐπιγόνειον West: ἐπιτόνιον ACE

---

271 Sc. and had sex with him, Aphrodite (who was "rowed") being a passive partner, Dionysus (who did the "rowing") an active
one. For Adonis and Aphrodite, cf. 2.69b–d with n.
272 The solution is "Man"; cf. 2.49c with n.

186

He is referring to Aphrodite and Dionysus; because they were both in love with Adonis.[271] Asclepiades in his *Stories Told in Tragedy* (*FGrH* 12 F 7a = *AP* 14.64) claims that the riddle of the Sphinx went as follows:

> There is a creature upon the earth that has two feet
>> and four, a single voice,
> and three feet as well; of all that moves on land,
> and through the air, and in the sea, it alone alters its
>> nature.
> But when it makes its way propped on the largest
>> number of feet,
> then the swiftness in its limbs is the weakest.[272]

The following passage composed by Simonides (fr. 69 Diehl) also has a riddling character, according to Chamaeleon of Heracleia in his *On Simonides* (fr. 34 Wehrli):

> The father of a kid that grazes on anything and a
>> miserable fish
> lean their heads close to one another. But when they
>> take a child
> of night in with their eyes, they are unwilling to tend
>> to
> the ox-slaying servant of King Dionysus.

Some authorities claim that this text was inscribed on one of the ancient dedications in Chalcis, and that a billy-goat and a dolphin were depicted on this dedication and these lines describe them. Others maintain that the reference is to a dolphin and a billy-goat carved on an *epigoneion* harp,[273] and that the "ox-slaying servant of Dionysus" is a

---

[273] Cf. 4.183c (whence West's correction of the text).

Ἰουλίδι τὸν τῷ Διονύσῳ θυόμενον βοῦν ὑπό τινος τῶν νεανίσκων παίεσθαι πελέκει. πλησίον δὲ τῆς ἑορτῆς οὔσης εἰς χαλκεῖον δοθῆναι τὸν πέλεκυν· τὸν οὖν Σιμωνίδην ἔτι νέον ὄντα βαδίσαι πρὸς τὸν χαλκέα κομιούμενον αὐτόν. ἰδόντα δὲ καὶ τὸν τεχνίτην κοιμώμενον καὶ τὸν ἀσκὸν καὶ τὸν καρκίνον εἰκῇ κείμενον

e καὶ ἐπαλλήλως ἔχοντα τὰ ἔμπροσθεν, | οὕτως ἐλθόντα εἰπεῖν πρὸς τοὺς συνήθεις τὸ προειρημένον πρόβλημα. τὸν μὲν γὰρ τοῦ ἐρίφου πατέρα τὸν ἀσκὸν εἶναι, σχέτλιον δὲ ἰχθὺν τὸν καρκίνον, νυκτὸς δὲ παῖδα τὸν ὕπνον, βουφόνον δὲ καὶ Διονύσου θεράποντα τὸν πέλεκυν. πεποίηκε δὲ καὶ ἕτερον ἐπίγραμμα ὁ Σιμωνίδης, ὃ παρέχει τοῖς ἀπείροις τῆς ἱστορίας ἀπορίαν·

φημὶ τὸν οὐκ ἐθέλοντα φέρειν τέττιγος ἄεθλον
τῷ Πανοπηιάδῃ δώσειν μέγα δεῖπνον Ἐπειῷ. |

f λέγεται δὲ ἐν τῇ Καρθαίᾳ διατρίβοντα αὐτὸν διδάσκειν τοὺς χορούς, εἶναι δὲ τὸ χορηγεῖον ἄνω πρὸς Ἀπόλλωνος ἱερῷ μακρὰν τῆς θαλάσσης. ὑδρεύεσθαι οὖν καὶ τοὺς ἄλλους καὶ τοὺς περὶ τὸν Σιμωνίδην κάτωθεν, ἔνθα ἦν ἡ κρήνη. ἀνακομίζοντος δ᾽ αὐτοῖς τὸ ὕδωρ ὄνου, ὃν ἐκάλουν Ἐπειὸν διὰ τὸ μυθολογεῖσθαι τοῦτο δρᾶν ἐκεῖνον καὶ ἀναγεγράφθαι ἐν τῷ τοῦ Ἀπόλλωνος ἱερῷ τὸν Τρωικὸν μῦθον, ἐν ᾧ ὁ Ἐπειὸς

457 ὑδροφορεῖ τοῖς Ἀτρείδαις, || ὡς καὶ Στησίχορός φησιν·

---

274 Simonides' home-town, on the island of Ceos.
275 Sc. to be sharpened.
276 From which the bellows were made.
277 Because the word (karkinos) also means "crab".

dithyramb. And others say that when an ox is sacrificed to Dionysus in Iulis,[274] it is struck with an ax by one of the young men. The festival was approaching, and the ax was sent to the blacksmith's shop;[275] Simonides, who was still young, accordingly went there to fetch it. When he saw the craftsman asleep, and his bellows and tongs scattered on the ground with their business ends facing one another, he went to his friends and told them the riddle quoted above; because the "father of a kid" is a goat-skin sack;[276] the "miserable fish" is the tongs;[277] the "child of night" is sleep; and the "ox-slaying servant of Dionysus" is the ax. Simonides also wrote another epigram (fr. 70 Diehl) that baffles those unfamiliar with history:

> I declare that he who is unwilling to endure the
>     cicada's task
> will provide a large dinner for Epeius son of
>     Panopeus.

The story goes that he was spending time in Carthaea training their choruses, and the chorus-school was on high ground next to Apollo's temple, a long way from the sea. Everyone, including Simonides' students, accordingly had to fetch their water from down below, where the spring was. A donkey brought their water up for them, and they called it Epeius, because legend had it that Epeius used to do this, and because there was a painting in Apollo's temple depicting the story of the Trojan War, in which he could be seen fetching water for the Atreidae, as Stesichorus (*PMG* 200) says:

ᾤκτιρε γὰρ αὐτὸν ὕδωρ
    αἰεὶ φορέοντα Διὸς κούρα βασιλεῦσιν.

ὑπαρχόντων οὖν τούτων ταχθῆναί φασι τῷ μὴ παρα-
γινομένῳ τῶν χορευτῶν εἰς τὴν ὡρισμένην ὥραν παρ-
έχειν τῷ ὄνῳ χοίνικα κριθῶν. τοῦτ' οὖν κἂν τῷ ποιή-
ματι λέγεσθαι, καὶ εἶναι τὸν μὲν οὐ φέροντα τὸ τοῦ
τέττιγος ἄεθλον τὸν οὐκ ἐθέλοντα ᾄδειν, Πανοπηιάδην
δὲ τὸν ὄνον, μέγα δὲ δεῖπνον τὴν χοίνικα τῶν κριθῶν.
τοιοῦτόν ἐστι καὶ τὸ Θεόγνιδος τοῦ ποιητοῦ· |

b    ἤδη γάρ με κέκληκε θαλάσσιος οἴκαδε νεκρός,
    τεθνηκὼς ζωῷ φθεγγόμενος στόματι.

σημαίνει γὰρ κόχλον. τοιοῦτον δ' ἐστὶν καὶ τὸ ῥήματα
λέγειν ἀνθρώπων ὀνόμασιν ὅμοια, οἷον·

    λαβὼν ἀριστόνικον ἐν μάχῃ κράτος.

καὶ τὸ περιφερόμενον·

    πέντ' ἄνδρες δέκα ναυσὶ κατέδραμον εἰς ἕνα
       χῶρον, |
c    ἐν δὲ λίθοις ἐμάχοντο, λίθον δ' οὐκ ἦν
       ἀνελέσθαι·

---

278 Epeius son of Panopeus was distinguished enough to compete in Patroclus' funeral games (*Il.* 23.664–99, 829–40), and ultimately built the wooden horse that brought the war to an end (*Od.*
8.492–3). Stesichorus thus presumably used the phrase "carrying
water" figuratively, to mean "working for in a subordinate position".

279 Literally "a *choenix*" (a standard dry measure).

For the daughter of Zeus
  pitied him, since he was always carrying water for
    the kings.[278]

Under these circumstances, they say, any member of the
chorus who failed to arrive on time had to provide the
donkey with a measure[279] of barley. This is accordingly
what the poem means, and the man "who does not en-
dure the cicada's task" is someone unwilling to sing; "the
son of Panopeus" is the donkey; and the "large dinner" is
the measure of barley. The passage by the poet Theognis
(1229–30) is similar:

For now the corpse from the sea summons me home,
  speaking with a living voice, though dead.

Because the reference is to a conch-shell.[280] Using words
that are identical with the names of individual persons is
similar, for example (adesp. tr. fr. 97):

getting the upper hand, which brings glorious victory
  (*aristonikos*)[281] in battle.

Also the commonplace:

Ten men in five ships[282] descended to a single place
and fought among stones, although no stone could be
  lifted.

[280] Sc. which is being used as a trumpet.
[281] Cf. the personal name Aristonicus (e.g. 10.435b).
[282] Or perhaps "five men in ten ships", which would fit the par-
adoxical character of the rest of the riddle.

δίψῃ δ᾽ ἐξώλλυντο, ὕδωρ δ᾽ ὑπερεῖχε γενείου.

τίνα δὲ κόλασιν ὑπέμενον Ἀθήνησιν οἱ μὴ λύσαντες
τὸν προτεθέντα γρῖφον, εἴ γε ἔπινον φιάλην ⟨ἄλμῃ⟩[34]
κεκερασμένην, ὡς καὶ ὁ Κλέαρχος προεῖπεν ἐν τῷ ὅρῳ;
⟨ . . . ⟩ κἂν τῷ πρώτῳ δὲ Περὶ Παροιμιῶν γράφει
οὕτως· τῶν γρίφων ἡ ζήτησις οὐκ ἀλλοτρία φιλοσο-
φίας ἐστί, καὶ οἱ παλαιοὶ τὴν τῆς παιδείας ἀπόδειξιν
d ἐν τούτοις ἐποιοῦντο. προέβαλλον | γὰρ παρὰ τοὺς
πότους οὐχ ὥσπερ οἱ νῦν ἐρωτῶντες ἀλλήλους, τίς τῶν
ἀφροδισιαστικῶν συνδυασμῶν ἢ τίς ἢ ποῖος ἰχθὺς
ἥδιστος ἢ τίς ἀκμαιότατος, ἔτι δὲ τίς μετ᾽ Ἀρκτοῦρον
ἢ μετὰ Πλειάδα ἢ τίς μετὰ Κύνα μάλιστα βρωτός; καὶ
ἐπὶ τούτοις ἆθλα μὲν τοῖς νικῶσι φιλήματα μίσους
ἄξια τοῖς ἐλευθέραν αἴσθησιν ἔχουσι, ζημίαν δὲ τοῖς
ἡττηθεῖσιν τάττουσιν ἄκρατον πιεῖν, ὃν ἥδιον τῆς
Ὑγιείας πίνουσι· κομιδῇ γάρ ἐστι ταῦτά γέ τινος τοῖς
Φιλαινίδος καὶ τοῖς Ἀρχεστράτου συγγράμμασιν |
e ἐνῳκηκότος, ἔτι δὲ περὶ τὰς καλουμένας Γαστρο-

---

283 Diels suggested that the solution to the riddle is that the
men fought among reefs, upon which they were stranded after
their boats sank, and that they died of thirst in the middle of the
sea. Caponigro, on the other hand, took the men to be almonds in
their shells, and the stones teeth, and argued that the man who ate
the almonds followed them with a cup of water.

284 Sc. of a proverb. Cf. 10.448c (although Clearchus is not
quoted there as saying anything of the sort), 458f–9b (where the
question is at last taken up, after another long digression).

285 In mid-September, mid-May, and mid-July, respectively.

They were perishing of thirst, but the water rose
above their chins.[283]

How were Athenians who failed to solve the riddle they
were set punished, if they drank a libation-bowl (of wine)
mixed with saltwater, as Cleachus said above in his definition?[284] . . . So too in Book I of *On Proverbs* (fr. 63.I Wehrli)
he writes as follows: Inquiry into riddles is not alien to philosophy, and the ancients used them to show off their education. For as they were drinking, they used to pose questions—not, however, as people do today, when they ask
one another which sexual position, or which fish or variety
of fish is the most delicious or the most precisely in season, and then which one is particularly good eating after
Arcturus rises, or the Pleiades, or the Dog-Star.[285] And
they reward those who answer these questions correctly
with kisses that would disgust anyone of decent sensibili-
ties, and penalize those who get their question wrong by
requiring them to drink unmixed wine, which they enjoy
more than the cup dedicated to Hygieia ("Health"). For
such behavior is, in fact, characteristic of an individual
who has spent time with the treatises of Philaenis and
Archestratus[286] (test. 4 Olson–Sens) and who has, moreover, devoted himself to the so-called *Gastrologies*.[287] In-

[286] Philaenis of Samos or Leucas (probably early 4th century BCE) wrote an explicit treatise on sexual behavior referred to
also at 5.220f; 8.335b, d–e (quoting Chrysippus). Archestratus was
a gastronomic poet particularly interested in seafood; almost everything known of him is preserved in Athenaeus (e.g. 9.384b,
399d–e).

[287] Cf. 8.337b (the first *Gastrology* said to have been composed by Archestratus' teacher, the otherwise obscure Terpsion).

λογίας ἐσπουδακότος· ἀλλὰ μᾶλλον τὰς τοιαύτας,
τῷ πρώτῳ ἔπος ⟨ἢ⟩[35] ἰαμβεῖον εἰπόντι τὸ ἐχόμενον
ἕκαστον λέγειν καὶ τῷ κεφάλαιον εἰπόντι ἀντειπεῖν τὸ
ἑτέρου ποιητοῦ τινος, ⟨ὅτι⟩[36] εἰς τὴν αὐτὴν εἶπε γνώ-
μην· ἔτι δὲ λέγειν ἕκαστον ἰαμβεῖον. πρός τε τούτοις
ἕκαστον εἰπεῖν ὅσων ἂν προσταχθῇ συλλαβῶν ἔμμετρον, καὶ ὅσα ἀπὸ τῆς τῶν γραμμάτων καὶ συλλαβῶν ἔχεται θεωρίας. ὁμοίως δὲ τοῖς εἰρημένοις ἡγε-
μόνος ἕκαστον[37] λέγειν ὄνομα τῶν ἐπὶ Τροίαν ἢ τῶν
Τρώων, καὶ πόλεως ὄνομα τῶν ἐν τῇ Ἀσίᾳ λέγειν ἀπὸ |
f    τοῦ δοθέντος γράμματος, τὸν δ' ἐχόμενον τῶν ἐν τῇ
Εὐρώπῃ καὶ τοὺς λοιποὺς ἐναλλάξαι, ἄν τε Ἑλληνίδος
ἄν τε βαρβάρου τάξῃ τις. ὥστε τὴν παιδιὰν μὴ
ἄσκεπτον οὖσαν μηνύματα γίνεσθαι τῆς ἑκάστου
πρὸς παιδείαν οἰκειότητος· ἐφ' οἷς ἆθλον ἐτίθεσαν
στέφανον καὶ εὐφημίαν, οἷς μάλιστα γλυκαίνεται τὸ
φιλεῖν ἀλλήλους.

458    Ταῦτα μὲν οὖν Κλέαρχος ‖ εἴρηκε. καὶ ἃ προβάλλειν δεῖ τοιαῦτά τινα εἶναι ἡγοῦμαι· στίχον εἰπεῖν
Ὁμηρικὸν ἀπὸ τοῦ ἄλφα ἀρχόμενον καὶ εἰς τὸ αὐτὸ
στοιχεῖον καταλήγοντα·

ἀγχοῦ δ' ἱσταμένη ἔπεα πτερόεντα προσηύδα.
ἀλλ' ἄγε νῦν μάστιγα καὶ ἡνία σιγαλόεντα.
ἀσπίδας εὐκύκλους λαισήϊά τε πτερόεντα.

[35] add. Meineke
[36] add. Kaibel
[37] ἕκαστον Olson: ἑκάστου A

stead, they preferred riddles of the following sort: After the first man recited a line of epic or iambic poetry, everyone had to respond by giving the line that came next; or if the first man offered the gist of a passage, they had to cite in turn something from another poet that expressed the same opinion, and each man had to quote an iambic line as well. In addition, everyone had to recite a poetic line that contained a specified number of syllables, or a set number of lines that featured a particular combination of letters and syllables. Along the same lines as the riddles mentioned earlier, everyone might be required to give the name of a commander of the forces that attacked Troy, or of the Trojan forces; or he might be asked to name a city in Asia that began with a specific letter, while the next man and those who followed would take turns giving the names of cities in Europe, either Greek or barbarian, as ordered. The game thus required considerable thinking and was informative about how well-educated each member of the group was. The prizes they set for these contests were garlands and congratulations, which made their mutual affection even more enjoyable.

This is what Clearchus has to say. In my estimation, the challenges they were expected to pose were of the following sort: To recite a Homeric line that begins with *alpha* and ends with the same letter:

> And standing close beside him she spoke winged words. (*Il.* 4.92)
> But come now, the whip and the shining reins. (*Il.* 5.226)
> circular shields and flapping animal-skins. (*Il.* 5.453)

καὶ πάλιν ὁμοίως ἰαμβεῖα·

ἀγαθὸς ἀνὴρ λέγοιτ᾽ ἂν ὁ φέρων τἀγαθά.
ἀγαθὸς ἂν εἴη χὠ φέρων καλῶς κακά. |

b  Ὁμηρικοὶ ἀπὸ τοῦ ε̄ ἐπὶ τὸ ε̄·

εὗρε Λυκάονος υἱὸν ἀμύμονά τε κρατερόν τε.
ἐν πόλει ὑμετέρῃ, ἐπεὶ οὐκ ἄρ᾽ ἔμελλον ἐγώ γε.

ὁμοίως καὶ ἰαμβεῖα·

εὐκαταφρόνητός ἐστι πενία, Δερκύλε.
ἐπὶ τοῖς παροῦσι τὸν βίον < . . . > διάπλεκε.

Ὁμήρου ἀπὸ η̄ ἐπὶ τὸ η̄·

ἡ μὲν ἄρ᾽ ὣς εἰποῦσ᾽ ἀπέβη γλαυκῶπις Ἀθήνη. |
c  ἡ δ᾽ ἐν γούνασι πῖπτε Διώνης δῖ᾽ Ἀφροδίτη.

ἴαμβοι·

ἡ τῶν φίλων σοι πίστις ἔστω κεκριμένη.

ἀπὸ τοῦ ῑ ἐπὶ τὸ ῑ Ὁμήρου·

Ἰλίου ἐξαπολοίατ᾽ ἀκήδεστοι καὶ ἄφαντοι.
Ἱππόλοχος δ᾽ ἔμ᾽ ἔτικτε, καὶ ἐκ τοῦ φημι
   γενέσθαι.

ἀπὸ τοῦ σ̄ εἰς τὸ σ̄·

συμπάντων Δαναῶν, οὐδ᾽ ἢν Ἀγαμέμνονα εἴπῃς.

And again iambic lines (adesp. com. fr. 121.1–2) in the same way:

> He who bears good fortune well would be called a
>     good man.
> He who bears troubles well would also be good.

Homeric lines beginning and ending with *epsilon*:

> She found Lycaon's faultless, powerful son. (*Il.* 4.89)
> in your city; since I was unlikely. (*Il.* 5.686)

Also iambic lines (adesp. com. fr. 121.3–4) in the same way:

> It's easy to look down on poverty, Dercylus.
> Weave your life using the materials you have.

Lines from Homer beginning and ending with *ēta*:

> After speaking thus, gray-eyed Athena departed. (*Il.*
>     5.133)
> Bright Aphrodite fell upon Dione's knees. (*Il.* 5.370)

Iambic lines (adesp. com. fr. 121.5):

> Let it be determined how faithful your friends are.

Lines beginning and ending with *iōta* from Homer:

> Might they vanish from Ilium, uncared-for and
>     obscure. (*Il.* 6.60)
> Hippolochus sired me, and I claim to be his child. (*Il.*
>     6.206)

Beginning and ending with *sigma*:

> of all the Danaans—not even if you name
>     Agamemnon. (*Il.* 1.90)

σοφός ἐστιν ὁ φέρων τἀπὸ ⟨τῆς⟩ τύχης καλῶς. |

d  ἀπὸ τοῦ ῶ εἰς τὸ ῶ·

ὡς δ' ὅτ' ἀπ' Οὐλύμπου νέφος ἔρχεται οὐρανὸν
εἴσω.
ὠρθωμένην πρὸς ἅπαντα τὴν ψυχὴν ἔχω.

προβάλλειν δὲ δεῖ καὶ στίχους ἀσίγμους, οἷον·

πάντ' ἐθέλω δόμεναι, καὶ ἔτ' οἴκοθεν ἄλλ'
ἐπιθεῖναι.

καὶ πάλιν στίχους Ὁμηρικοὺς ἀπὸ τῆς πρώτης συλλαβῆς καὶ τῆς ἐσχάτης δηλοῦντας ὄνομα, οἷον·

Αἴας δ' ἐκ Σαλαμῖνος ἄγεν δυοκαίδεκα νῆας. |

e  ⟨Αἴας⟩.[38]

Φυλείδης, ὃν τίκτε διίφιλος ἱππότα Φυλεύς.

⟨Φυλεύς⟩.[39]

ἰητῆρ' ἀγαθώ, Ποδαλείριος ἠδὲ Μαχάων.

Ἴων. εἰσὶ καὶ ἄλλοι στίχοι Ὁμηρικοὶ δηλοῦντες σκευ-
ῶν ὀνόματα ἀπὸ τῆς πρώτης καὶ ἐσχάτης συλλαβῆς,
οἷον·

ὀλλυμένων Δαναῶν ὀλοφύρεται ἐν φρεσὶ θυμός.

ὅλμος.

[38] add. Kaibel
[39] add. Kaibel

198

Wise is he who bears easily what fortune gives.
  (adesp. com. fr. 121.6)

Beginning and ending with *ōmega*:

As when a cloud rises into the sky from Olympus. (*Il.* 16.364)
My spirit meets every challenge head-on. (adesp. com. fr. 121.7)

They were also expected to call for asigmatic lines, for example:

I am willing to turn them all over, and to add even more from my house. (*Il.* 7.364)

Likewise Homeric lines whose first and last syllables combined produce a name, for example:

Ajax brought twelve ships from Salamis (*Il.* 2.557),

yielding "Ajax".

Phyleides, whom the horseman Phyleus, dear to Zeus, sired (*Il.* 2.628),

yielding "Phyleus".

A pair of fine physicians, Podaleirius and Machaon (*Il.* 2.732),

yielding "Ion". There is also another set of Homeric lines whose first and last syllables combined produce the names of utensils, for example:

The heart in your breast mourns for the Danaans, who are perishing (*Il.* 8.202),

yielding "mortar".

μυθεῖται κατὰ μοῖραν, ἅ πέρ κ᾽ οἴοιτο καὶ ἄλλος.

μύλος.

λυγρὸς ἐών, μή πού τι κακὸν καὶ μεῖζον ἐπαύρῃ.

f λύρη. | ἄλλοι στίχοι δηλοῦντες ἀπὸ τῆς ἀρχῆς καὶ τοῦ
τέλους τῶν ἐδωδίμων τί·

ἀργυρόπεζα Θέτις, θυγάτηρ ἁλίοιο γέροντος.

ἄρτος.

μή τι σὺ ταῦτα ἕκαστα διείρεο μηδὲ μετάλλα.

μῆλα.

Ἐπεὶ δὲ ἱκανὴν παρέκβασιν πεποιήμεθα περὶ τῶν
γρίφων, λεκτέον ἤδη καὶ τίνα κόλασιν ὑπέμενον οἱ μὴ
λύσαντες τὸν προτεθέντα γρῖφον. ἔπινον οὗτοι ἅλμην
παραμισγομένην τῷ αὑτῶν ποτῷ καὶ ἔδει προσενέγ-
459 κασθαι⁴⁰ τὸ ποτήριον ἀπνευστί, ὡς Ἀντιφάνης ‖ δηλοῖ
ἐν Γανυμήδει διὰ τούτων·

(A.) οἴμοι περιπλοκὰς
λίαν ἐρωτᾷς. (Λα.) ἀλλ᾽ ἐγὼ σαφῶς φράσω·
τῆς ἁρπαγῆς τοῦ παιδὸς εἰ ξύνοισθά τι,
ταχέως λέγειν χρὴ πρὶν κρέμασθαι. (A.) πότερά
μοι

⁴⁰ μὴ προσενέγκασθαι A: μὴ del. Olson

---

288 Returning to the topic proposed at 10.457c (cf. 10.448c).
289 Ganymede (the son of Laomedon, king of Troy) was kidnapped by Zeus; cf. Il. 5.265–7; 20.232–5 (cf. 13.566c–d); h.Ven.
202–17 (although in all these passages his father is called Tros); Il.
Parv. fr. 29 Bernabé; E. Tr. 820–2.

What he says is right, and he thinks what anyone else
would (*Od.* 17.580),

yielding "millstone".

sorry creature that you are, lest perhaps some even
greater trouble come to you (*Od.* 18.107),

yielding "lyre". Other lines have first and last syllables that
produce an edible object:

silver-footed Thetis, daughter of the old man of the
sea (*Il.* 1.538),

yielding "bread".

Do not inquire into each of these matters or ask me
about them (*Il.* 1.550),

yielding "apples".

Having digressed at considerable length on the topic of
riddles, I must now say something about how they were
punished if they failed to solve the riddle they were set.[288]
People in this situation drank saltwater mixed into their
wine and were expected to empty the cup without taking a
breath, as Antiphanes makes clear in the following passage
from *Ganymede* (fr. 75):[289]

> (A.) Poor me! You're asking much too
> complicated questions. (Laomedon) Alright, I'll say it
> clearly:
> if you know anything about the kidnapping of my
> child,
> you need to tell me quickly, before you're hung up.
> (A.) Are you posing

γρῖφον προβάλλεις τοῦτον εἰπεῖν, δέσποτα,
τῆς ἁρπαγῆς τοῦ παιδὸς εἰ ξύνοιδά τι,
ἢ τί δύναται τὸ ῥηθέν; (Λα.) ἔξω τις δότω
ἱμάντα ταχέως. (Α.) εἶέν· οὐκ ἔγνων ἴσως.
ἔπειτα τοῦτο ζημιοῖς με; μηδαμῶς· |
b   ἄλμης δ' ἐχρῆν τι παραφέρειν ποτήριον.
(Λα.) οἶσθ' οὖν ὅπως δεῖ τοῦτό σ' ἐκπιεῖν; (Α.)
      ἐγώ;
κομιδῇ γε. (Λα.) πῶς; (Α.) ἐνέχυρον ἀποφέροντά
      ⟨σου⟩.
(Λα.) οὔκ, ἀλλ' ὀπίσω τὼ χεῖρε ποιήσαντα δεῖ
ἕλκειν ἀπνευστί.

τοσαῦτα καὶ περὶ τῶν γρίφων εἰπόντων τῶν δειπνο-
σοφιστῶν, ἐπειδὴ καὶ ἡμᾶς ἑσπέρα καταλαμβάνει
ἀναπεμπαζομένους τὰ εἰρημένα, τὸν περὶ τῶν ἐκπωμάτων λόγον εἰς αὔριον ἀναβαλώμεθα. κατὰ γὰρ τὸν
Μεταγένους Φιλοθύτην·

c   κατ' ἐπεισόδιον | μεταβάλλω τὸν λόγον, ὡς ἂν
καιναῖσι παροψίσι καὶ πολλαῖς εὐωχήσω τὸ
      θέατρον

περὶ τῶν ἐκπωμάτων τὸν λόγον ἑξῆς ποιούμενος.

this to me as a riddle to solve, master, (when you ask)
if I know anything about the kidnapping of your
child?
If not, what's the point of what you said? (Laomedon)
Someone hurry up and
bring me out a strap! (A.) Okay—maybe I didn't
figure it out.
So are you punishing me for this? Don't!
You should've been passing a cup of saltwater
around.
(Laomedon) Well, do you know how you have to
drink it? (A.) Me?
I certainly do. (Laomedon) How? (A.) I have to get a
guarantee of safety from you!
(Laomedon) No; you have to put your hands behind
your back
and empty it without taking a breath.

This is the extent of the learned banqueters' remarks about
riddles.[290] But since evening is overtaking us, as we mull
over their comments, let us defer a report of their conversation about drinking-vessels until tomorrow. For to quote
Metagenes' *The Man Who Loved Sacrifices* (fr. 15),[291]

I vary my plot interlude by interlude, in order
to feast my audience on many novel appetizers,

by offering my account of drinking-vessels next.

[290] The speaker of these closing words is the overall narrator
"Athenaeus", addressing his friend Timocrates.
[291] Cf. 10.411b n.

459d    Ἄγε δή, τίς ἀρχὴ τῶν λόγων γενήσεται;,

κατὰ τὸν κωμῳδιοποιὸν Κηφισόδωρον, ἑταῖρε Τιμό
κρατες. συναχθέντων γὰρ ἡμῶν καθ᾽ ὥραν μετὰ σπου
δῆς διὰ τὰ ἐκπώματα ὁ Οὐλπιανός, ἔτι καθημένων
ἁπάντων, πρὶν καί τι διαλεχθῆναι ἔφη· παρὰ μὲν τῷ
Ἀδράστῳ, ἄνδρες φίλοι, καθίσαντες οἱ ἀριστεῖς
δειπνοῦσιν, ὁ δὲ Πολύιδος ἱερὰ θύων ἐν ὁδῷ παραπο
ρευόμενον τὸν Πετεὼ κατέσχεν καὶ κατακλίνας ἐν τῇ
πόᾳ θαλλίαν τε κατακλάσας ἀντὶ τραπέζης παρέθηκε
460   τῶν τυθέντων. καὶ τῷ Αὐτολύκῳ ‖ ἐλθόντι

&lt; . . . &gt; Ἰθάκης ἐς πίονα δῆμον

ἡ τροφὸς καθημένῳ δηλονότι—οὕτως γὰρ ἐδείπνουν οἱ
τότε—τὸν Ὀδυσσέα, φησὶν ὁ ποιητής,

---

[1] I.e. both by anticipation of the discussion of cups of all sorts
announced at 10.459b and recorded in this Book (see 11.460a–b
with n.), and by the prospect of the drinking party that was to accompany it.    [2] I.e. before they reclined on their couches,
when the actual drinking began; cf. 11.461e.

[3] Athenaeus repeatedly cites Antimachus of Colophon's
*Thebaid* in Book XI (also 468a–b, 475d–e, 482f, 486a), and Wyss
accordingly identified this as fr. 18 Matthews. For other fragments
of scholarly discussions of the question of whether the ancients sat
to eat, see 1.11f, 17f.

[4] Polyidus was an Corinthian seer, while Peteus was an early

# BOOK XI

Alright—where should my account begin?,

to quote the comic poet Cephisodorus (fr. 13), my friend
Timocrates. Because we had gathered on time and with
considerable excitement, motivated by the drinking vessels;[1] and while everyone was still seated,[2] and before
there had been any conversation, Ulpian said: In Adrastus'
house, my friends, the nobles eat dinner seated,[3] whereas
when Polyidus was making a sacrifice beside a road, he
stopped Peteus, who was traveling along it; had him lie
down on the grass; broke up some twigs to serve as a
table; and served him a portion of the meat.[4] And when
Autolycus[5] came (*Od.* 19.399)

to the rich land of Ithaca

and was sitting there, obviously—because that is how
people in those days ate dinner—the nurse, according to
Homer, set Odysseus (*Od.* 19.400–2):[6]

king of Athens; but the story to which Athenaeus refers is otherwise unattested.          [5] Odysseus' maternal grandfather, who
gave the hero his name in the incident to which these verses refer.

[6] The quotation helps document Ulpian's claim that people in ancient times ate while seated rather than reclining, but dis-
rupts the syntax of the sentence and seems to have been spliced
awkwardly into it.

παῖδα νέον γεγαῶτα κιχήσατο θυγατέρος ἧς·
τόν ῥά οἱ Εὐρύκλεια φίλοις ἐπὶ γούνασι θῆκε
παυομένῳ δόρποιο,

ἐκάθισεν ἐπὶ τῶν γονάτων καὶ οὐχὶ παρὰ τοῖς γόνασιν
ἔστησεν. ἡμεῖς οὖν μὴ διατρίβωμεν, ἀλλ' ἤδη κατα-
b κλινώμεθα, ἵν' ἡμῖν ὁ Πλούταρχος | περὶ ὧν ἐπαγ-
γέλλεται ποτηρίων ἀποδοὺς τὸν λόγον καὶ τὰς κύλικας
πλήρεις ἅπασι προπίῃ. ποτήρια δὲ πρῶτον οἶδα ὀνο-
μάσαντα τὸν Ἀμόργιον ποιητὴν Σιμωνίδην ἐν Ἰάμβοις οὕτως·

ἀπὸ τράπεζαν εἷλέ † νιν † ποτήρια.

καὶ ὁ τὴν Ἀλκμαιωνίδα δὲ ποιήσας φησίν·

νέκυς δὲ χαμαιστρώτου ἔπι τείνας
εὐρείης στιβάδος, παρέθηκ' αὐτοῖσι θάλειαν
δαῖτα ποτήριά τε, στεφάνους δ' ἐπὶ κρασὶν
ἔθηκεν.

ἅπερ ὠνομάσθη ἀπὸ τῆς πόσεως, ὡς τὸ ἔκπωμα οἱ
c Ἀττικοί, ἐπεὶ ὑδροποτεῖν καὶ οἰνοποτεῖν | λέγουσιν.
Ἀριστοφάνης ἐν Ἱππεῦσιν·

γαμφηλῇσι δράκοντα κοάλεμον αἱματοπώτην.

κἂν τῷ αὐτῷ δὲ ἔφη·

---

7 Plutarch begins to speak only at 11.461e, after the group
finally lies down. Although a discussion of cups is promised at
10.459b, the words are those of the external narrator Athenaeus
rather than of Plutarch.

8 For the *kulix* (a common term for a drinking cup), see
11.480b–1c.

He found his daughter's new-born son;
Eurycleia set the child on his knees
as he was finishing dinner,

on his knees, rather than beside his knees. So let us not
waste any time, but lie down at once, so that Plutarch can
offer us a speech about cups (*potēria*), as he promises,[7] and
can toast us all with full *kulikes*.[8] It is my understanding
that the first author to use the term *potēria* is the poet
Simonides of Amorgus in the *Iambs* (Semon. fr. 26 West[2]),
as follows:

He removed the table † him † *potēria*.

So too the author of the *Alcmaeonis* (fr. 2 Bernabé) says:

He stretched their corpses out on a broad
camp-bed spread on the ground, set a rich meal and
*potēria* beside them, and placed garlands on their
heads.

The word is derived from *posis* ("drink");[9] compare the
use of *ekpōma* ("drinking vessel") by Attic authors, who
employ the verbs *hudropotein* ("to drink water") and
*oinopotein* ("to drink wine"). Aristophanes in *Knights*
(198):

a stupid blood-drinking (*haimatopōtēs*) serpent in its
beak.

He also said in the same play (124):

[9] *potēria*, *posis*, and all the words cited below, along with the
common verb *pinō* ("to drink"), can in fact be traced to a single
Indo-European root that refers to drinking.

πολλῷ γ᾽ ὁ Βάκις διεχρῆτο[1] τῷ ποτηρίῳ.

καὶ Φερεκράτης ἐν Τυραννίδι·

   < ... > κρείττων < ... > μί᾽ ἐστὶ χιλίων
     ποτηρίων.

ὁ δὲ Ἀνακρέων ἔφη·

   οἰνοπότης δὲ πεποίημαι.

ἔστι δὲ τὸ ῥῆμα καὶ παρὰ τῷ ποιητῇ· οἰνοποτάζων |
d  γὰρ εἴρηκε. καὶ Σαπφὼ δ᾽ ἐν τῷ δευτέρῳ ἔφη·

   † πολλὰ[2] † δ᾽ ἀνάριθμα ποτήρια κἀλέφαις.

καὶ Ἀλκαῖος·

   ἐκ δὲ ποτήριον πώνῃς Διννομένη παρίσδων.

τιμᾶται δὲ καὶ ἐν Ἀχαίᾳ Δημήτηρ Ποτηριοφόρος κατὰ
τὴν Ἀνθέων χώραν, ὡς Αὐτοκράτης ἱστορεῖ ἐν δευτέρᾳ
Ἀχαϊκῶν. ἄξιον δὲ εἶναι νομίζω ζητῆσαι ὑμᾶς πρὸ τοῦ
καταλόγου τῶν ποτηρίων, ὧν πλῆρές ἐστι τὸ κυλικεῖον
τοδί—εἴρηται γὰρ οὕτως ἡ τῶν ποτηρίων σκευοθήκη
παρ᾽ Ἀριστοφάνει μὲν ἐν Γεωργοῖς |

e   ὥσπερ κυλικείου τουθόνιον προπέπταται.

ἔστι καὶ παρὰ Ἀναξανδρίδῃ ἐν Μελιλώτῳ· < ... >.
Εὔβουλος δ᾽ ἐν Λήδᾳ·

---

[1] The manuscripts of Aristophanes have ἐχρῆτο.
[2] *POxy.* 1232 has ἀργύρα τ᾽ ἀνάριθμα.

---

[10] An extract from a much larger fragment quoted at 11.481b–
d.     [11] The question is identified only at the end of 11.460f,
after the digression on cupstands.

Bakis certainly got a lot of use out of that *potērion*!

Also Pherecrates in *Tyranny* (fr. 152.10):[10]

> But that "single cup" is larger than 1000 normal
> *potēria*!

And Anacreon (eleg. fr. 4 West²) said:

> I've turned into a wine-drinker (*oinopotēs*).

Homer also uses the word; for he says *oinopotazōn* ("when drinking wine") (*Il.* 20.84). Sappho as well said in Book II (fr. 44.10):

> † many † countless *potēria* and ivory.

Also Alcaeus (fr. 376):

> You sit beside Dinnomene and drain your *potērion*.

Demeter Potēriophoros ("Cup-Bearer") is worshipped in Achaea in the area around Anthea, according to Autocrates in Book II of the *History of Achaea* (*FGrH* 297 F 1). Another question I feel we should take up before your catalogue of cups, which fill this cupstand (*kulikeion*) here[11]—this is the term Aristophanes uses in *Farmers* (fr. 106) for a cabinet that holds *potēria*:

> It's stretched out in front, like the linen curtain on a
> *kulikeion*.

The word is also found in Anaxandrides' *Melilot* (fr. 30):[12]
... Eubulus in *Leda* (fr. 62):

---

[12] The quotation has fallen out of the text.

ὡσπερεὶ σπονδὴν διδοὺς
ἐν τῷ κυλικείῳ συντέτριφεν τὰ ποτήρια.

κἀν Ψαλτρίᾳ δ᾽ ἔφη·

τὰ κυλικεῖα δὲ
ἐξεῦρεν ἡμῖν.

ἐν δὲ Σεμέλῃ ἢ Διονύσῳ·

Ἑρμῆς ὁ Μαίας λίθινος, ὃν προσεύγμασιν
ἐν τῷ κυλικείῳ λαμπρὸν ἐκτετριμμένον. |

f  Κρατῖνος δ᾽ ὁ νεώτερος ἐν Χείρωνι·

πολλοστῷ δ᾽ ἔτει
ἐκ τῶν πολεμίων οἴκαδ᾽ ἥκω, συγγενεῖς
καὶ φράτερας καὶ δημότας εὑρὼν μόλις
εἰς τὸ κυλικεῖον ἐνεγράφην· Ζεὺς ἔστι μοι
Ἑρκεῖος, ἔστι Φράτριος, τὰ τέλη τελῶ.

Ἄξιον δ᾽ ἐστὶ ζητῆσαι εἰ οἱ ἀρχαῖοι μεγάλοις
ἔπινον ποτηρίοις. Δικαίαρχος μὲν γὰρ ὁ Μεσσήνιος ‖
461  ὁ Ἀριστοτέλους μαθητὴς ἐν τῷ Περὶ Ἀλκαίου μικροῖς
φησιν αὐτοὺς ἐκπώμασι κεχρῆσθαι καὶ ὑδαρέστερον
πεπωκέναι. Χαμαιλέων δ᾽ ὁ Ἡρακλεώτης ἐν τῷ Περὶ
Μέθης, εἴ γε τῆς φωνῆς μνημονεύω, φησίν· εἰ δὲ οἱ
ταῖς ἐξουσίαις χρώμενοι καὶ τῷ πλουτεῖν προτιμῶσι

---

[13] I.e. the people who would normally be able to attest to the
fact that the long-lost speaker was an Athenian.

[14] Zeus Herkeios ("of the Courtyard") was the patron god of an
individual household, while Zeus Phratrios was the patron god of
the phratry (an ill-understood Athenian kinship group).

[15] Resuming the construction temporarily abandoned at
11.460d.

Just like someone making a treaty,
he smashed the cups that were in the *kulikeion*.

In *The Harp-Girl* (fr. 116) as well he said:

And he found
the *kulikeia* for us.

And in *Semele or Dionysus* (fr. 95):

Hermes the son of Maia, made of stone, whom with
    prayers
polished till he shines in the *kulikeion*.

Cratinus Junior in *Cheiron* (fr. 9):

After many years I've
escaped from our enemies and come home; since I
    had trouble
locating any relatives or members of my phratry or
    my deme,[13]
I enrolled myself in the *kulikeion*. This is my Zeus
Herkeios and my Zeus Phratrios,[14] and where I pay
    my dues.

A question that deserves discussion[15] is whether the ancients used large cups when they drank. Because Aristotle's student Dicaearchus of Messene in his *On Alcaeus*
(fr. 98 Wehrli) claims that they used small drinking vessels
and drank their wine mixed with a considerable amount of
water. Chamaeleon of Heracleia in his *On Drunkenness*
(fr. 9 Wehrli), on the other hand—if I can remember how
he puts it—says: If powerful, wealthy people prize the
drunkenness discussed here, that comes as no surprise.

τὴν μέθην ταύτην, οὐδὲν θαυμαστόν. οὐκ ἔχοντες γὰρ
ἑτέραν ἡδονὴν ταύτης καλλίω οὐδὲ μᾶλλον εὐχερῆ
καταφεύγουσιν εἰκότως ἐπὶ τὸν οἶνον· ὅθεν δὴ καὶ
τὰ μεγάλα τῶν ἐκπωμάτων ἐπιχώρια γέγονε τοῖς
b δυνάσταις. | οὐ γὰρ παλαιὸν οὐδὲ τοῦτό γέ ἐστι παρὰ
τοῖς Ἕλλησιν, ἀλλὰ νεωστὶ εὑρέθη πεμφθὲν ἐκ τῶν
βαρβάρων· ἐκεῖνοι γὰρ ἀπεστερημένοι τῆς παιδείας
ὁρμῶσιν ἐπὶ τὸν πολὺν οἶνον καὶ πορίζονται τροφὰς
περιέργους καὶ παντοίας. ἐν δὲ τοῖς περὶ τὴν Ἑλλάδα
τόποις οὔτ᾽ ἐν γραφαῖς οὔτ᾽ < . . . > ἐπὶ τῶν πρότερον
εὑρήσομεν ποτήριον εὐμέγεθες εἰργασμένον πλὴν τῶν
ἐπὶ τοῖς ἡρωικοῖς· τὸ γὰρ ῥυτὸν ὀνομαζόμενον μόνοις
τοῖς ἥρωσιν ἀπεδίδοσαν. ὃ καὶ δόξει τισὶν ἔχειν
c ἀπορίαν, εἰ μή τις ἄρα φήσειε διὰ τὴν | ὀξύτητα τῆς
ἐπιφανείας τῶν δαιμόνων καταδειχθῆναι τοῦτο. χαλε-
ποὺς γὰρ καὶ πλήκτας τοὺς ἥρωας νομίζουσι καὶ
μᾶλλον νύκτωρ ἢ μεθ᾽ ἡμέραν· ὅπως οὖν μὴ διὰ τὸν
τρόπον, ἀλλὰ διὰ τὴν μέθην φαίνωνται τοιοῦτοι, δημι-
ουργοῦσιν αὐτοὺς πίνοντας ἐκπώμασι μεγάλοις. καί
μοι δοκοῦσι λέγειν οὐ κακῶς οἱ φάσκοντες τὸ μέγα
ποτήριον φρέαρ ἀργυροῦν εἶναι. ἐν τούτοις ἀγνοεῖν
ἔοικεν ὁ Χαμαιλέων ὅτι οὔκ ἐστι μικρὸν τὸ παρ᾽
Ὁμήρῳ διδόμενον τῷ Κύκλωπι ὑπ᾽ Ὀδυσσέως κισσύ-
d βιον· | οὐ γὰρ ἂν τρὶς πιὼν οὕτως κατηνέχθη ὑπὸ
μέθης τηλικοῦτος ὤν. ἦν οὖν καὶ τότε μεγάλα ποτήρια,

---

16 Drinking-horns; cf. 11.496f–7e, especially 11.497e, where
this observation is attributed to Theophrastus (another member
of Aristotle's school).

17 Cf. 5.192a (apparently referring to the same passage, which
is most naturally taken as drawn from Chamaeleon, although it
patently interrupts the course of the discussion here).

Because the fact that they have no pleasure that is finer or easier to indulge in than this means that they take refuge in wine, as one might expect; as a consequence, the largest drinking vessels tend to belong to rulers. For this is not an ancient custom among the Greeks, but a new discovery foisted upon them by the barbarians, whose lack of education inclines them to drink large amounts and to fix themselves all kinds of odd food. But nowhere in Greece, either in paintings or . . . , will we find a large cup manufactured in ancient times, with the exception of those referred to in heroic tales; because they gave what are referred to as *rhyta*[16] exclusively to heroes. Some people will regard this as puzzling, unless they have it explained to them that this image reflects the fierceness typical of appearances by minor divinities. For heroes are thought to be harsh and violent, and to be seen more often at night than during the day; and in order that they might appear to act thus not by inclination, but because they are drunk, they are depicted as drinking out of large vessels. In my opinion, authorities who claim that a large cup is a "silver well" are correct.[17] In this passage, Chamaeleon seems unaware that the *kissubion* Odysseus offers the Cyclops in Homer (*Od.* 9.346)[18] is not a small vessel; if it were, he would not have got so drunk after three drinks, given his size.[19] These were accordingly large cups, unless one tries to pin the re-

[18] Quoted at 11.477b, in the middle of an extended discussion of the vessel, to which the remarks that follow properly belong as well.

[19] A virtually identical remark appears at 11.481e.

εἰ μὴ αἰτιάσεταί τις τὴν δύναμιν τοῦ οἴνου, ἣν αὐτὸς
Ὅμηρος ἐξηγήσατο, ἢ τὸ ἄηθες τῆς πόσεως τοῦ
Κύκλωπος, ἐπεὶ τὰ πολλὰ ἐγαλακτοπότει. ἢ τάχα καὶ
βαρβαρικὸν ἦν τὸ ἔκπωμα, εἴπερ μέγα ἦν, ἐκ τῆς
Κικόνων εἰλημμένον λείας. τί οὖν ἔχομεν λέγειν περὶ
τοῦ Νέστορος ποτηρίου, ὃ μόλις ἂν νέος βαστάσαι
ἴσχυεν,

&lt; . . . &gt; Νέστωρ δ᾽ ὁ γέρων ἀμογητὶ ἄειρε,

e  περὶ οὗ καὶ αὐτοῦ διδάξει τι ἡμᾶς | ὁ Πλούταρχος; ὥρα
οὖν κατακλίνεσθαι.

Καὶ κατακλιθέντων, ἀλλὰ μήν, ὁ Πλούταρχος ἔφη,
κατὰ τὸν Φλιάσιον ποιητὴν Πρατίναν,

οὐ γᾶν αὐλακισμέναν
ἀρῶν, ἀλλ᾽ ἄσκαφον ματεύων,

κυλικηγορήσων ἔρχομαι, οὐ τῶν Κυλικράνων εἷς
ὑπάρχων, οὓς χλευάζων Ἕρμιππος ὁ κωμῳδιοποιὸς ἐν
τοῖς Ἰάμβοις φησίν·

εἰς τὸ Κυλικράνων βαδίζων σπληνόπεδον
ἀφικόμην·
εἶδον οὖν τὴν Ἡράκλειαν, καὶ μάλ᾽ ὡραίαν
πόλιν.

---

20 Most of the passage is quoted at 11.465b–c.

21 In fact, Homer's Cyclopes are quite familiar with wine, as
Polyphemus himself makes clear (*Od.* 9.357–8).

22 Whence also, in a slightly round-about fashion, the wine itself (*Od.* 9.196–201). Homer never says where the *kissubion* is
from, but the most obvious reading of the story is that Odysseus
finds it in the Cyclops' cave.

214

sponsibility on the strength of the wine, which Homer
himself described (*Od.* 9.209–11),[20] or on the Cyclops'
lack of experience with drinking, since he generally consumed milk (cf. *Od.* 9.248–9, 297).[21] Or perhaps this was a
barbarian vessel, if it was in fact large, and was part of the
plunder taken from the Ciconians[22] (cf. *Od.* 9.41–2). What
then can we say about Nestor's cup, which young men
could barely lift, even though (*Il.* 11.637)

> the aged Nestor hoisted it easily,

and about which Plutarch will offer us some instruction?[23]
It is accordingly now time for us to take our couches.[24]

After we lay down, Plutarch said: I am indeed here
to discuss cups (*kulikēgorēsōn*)[25] and, to quote the poet
Pratinas of Phlius (*PMG* 710), am

> not plowing land that has already
>   been broken, but seeking virgin soil.

I am nonetheless not one of the Culicranoi[26] the comic
poet Hermippus makes fun of in his *Iambs* (fr. 4 West[2]),
when he says:

> As I went along I came to the splenetic plain of the
>   Culicranoi;
> I thus saw Heracleia, which is quite a lovely city.

---

[23] The question of Nestor's cup is taken up at great length at
11.477f–93e (drawing in particular on Asclepiades of Myrlea).

[24] Cf. 11.459d with n.

[25] For the verb (attested outside of Athenaeus only at Poll.
6.29), cf. 11.480b.

[26] As if the name were cognate with *kulix* (cf. 11.480b–1c, to
which the material that follows would seem properly to belong).

Ἡρακλεῶται δ᾿ εἰσὶν οὗτοι οἱ ὑπὸ τῇ Οἴτῃ κατοικοῦν
τες, ὥς φησι Νίκανδρος ὁ Θυατειρηνός, ὀνομασθῆναι
f φάσκων αὐτοὺς ἀπό τινος Κύλικος | γένος Λυδοῦ, ἑνὸς
τῶν Ἡρακλεῖ συστρατευσαμένων. μνημονεύει δ᾿ αὐ
τῶν καὶ Σκυθῖνος ὁ Τήιος ἐν τῇ ἐπιγραφομένῃ
Ἱστορίῃ λέγων οὕτως· Ἡρακλῆς λαβὼν Εὔρυτον καὶ
τὸν υἱὸν ἔκτεινε φόρους πρήσσοντας παρ᾿ Εὐβοέων.
Κυλικρῆνας ἐξεπόρθησε λῃζομένους καὶ αὐτόθι πόλιν
462 ἐδείματο Ἡράκλειαν ‖ τὴν Τρηχινίαν καλεομένην.
Πολέμων δ᾿ ἐν τῷ πρώτῳ τῶν Πρὸς Ἀδαῖον καὶ Ἀντί
γονόν φησιν οὕτως· τῆς δ᾿ Ἡρακλείας τῆς ὑπὸ τὴν
Οἴτην καὶ Τραχῖνος τῶν οἰκητόρων μεθ᾿ Ἡρακλέους
τινὲς ἀφικόμενοι ἐκ Λυδίας Κυλικρᾶνες, οἱ δ᾿ Ἀθα
μᾶνες, ἀφ᾿ ὧν οἱ τόποι διαμένουσιν· οἷς οὐδὲ τῆς
πολιτείας μετέδοσαν οἱ Ἡρακλεῶται συνοικοῦσιν, ἀλ
λοφύλους ὑπολαβόντες. Κυλικρᾶνες δὲ λέγονται, ὅτι
τοὺς ὤμους κεχαραγμένοι κύλικας ἦσαν. οἶδα δὲ καὶ
b Ἑλλάνικον ἐν Ἐθνῶν Ὀνομασίαις λέγοντα | ὅτι Λι
βύων τῶν νομάδων τινὲς οὐδὲν ἄλλο κέκτηνται ἢ
κύλικα καὶ μάχαιραν καὶ ὑδρίαν, καὶ ὅτι οἰκίας ἔχου
σιν ἐξ ἀνθερίκου πεποιημένας μικρὰς ὅσον σκιᾶς
ἕνεκα, ἃς καὶ περιφέρουσιν ὅπου ἂν πορεύωνται. πολ
λοῖς δὲ καὶ ὁ ἐν Ἰλλυριοῖς τόπος διαβόητός ἐστιν ὁ
καλούμενος Κύλικες, παρ᾿ ᾧ ἐστι τὸ Κάδμου καὶ
Ἁρμονίας μνημεῖον, ὡς ἱστορεῖ Φύλαρχος ἐν τῇ δευ
τέρᾳ καὶ εἰκοστῇ τῶν Ἱστοριῶν. καὶ Πολέμων δ᾿ ἐν τῷ
Περὶ τοῦ Μορύχου ἐν Συρακούσαις φησὶν ἐπ᾿ ἄκρᾳ τῇ

---

27 Cadmus and Harmonia were the king and queen of Thebes,
but were forced into exile as a result of Dionysus' wrath; A.R.
4.516–17 and [Apollod.] Bib. 3.5.4 agree that they settled in
Illyria, and Apollonius refers specifically to their tomb.

The Heracleots in question live in the foothills of Mt. Oeta, according to Nicander of Thyateira (*FGrH* 343 F 12), who claims that they got their name from a certain Cylix; he was a Lydian by birth and was one of the men who fought alongside Heracles. Scythinus of Teos also mentions them in his work entitled the *History* (*FGrH* 13 F 1), where he says the following: After Heracles captured Eurytus and his son, who were trying to extract tribute from the Euboeans, he killed them. He sacked the territory of the Culicranoi, who survive by raiding others, and founded the city known as Trachinian Heracleia there. Polemon says the following in Book I of his *Response to Adaeus and Antigonus* (fr. 56 Preller): Some of the inhabitants of the Heracleia located in the foothills of Oeta and of Trachis were Culicranes who came from Lydia with Heracles, while others were Athamanes, from whom the area continues (to get its name). When the Athamanes tried to settle there, the Heracleots refused to share political power with them, and instead treated them like aliens; they are known as Culicranes because they had cups (*kulikes*) tattooed on their shoulders. I am also aware that Hellanicus in *Names of Ethnic Groups* (*FGrH* 4 F 67) claims that some Libyan nomads own nothing but a *kulix*, a knife, and a water-jar, and have tiny houses made of asphodel-stem which are just large enough to offer provide some shade, and which they carry around with them wherever they go. Many people also know of the existence of an area in Illyria known as Cylices, where the tomb of Cadmus and Harmonia[27] is located, according to Phylarchus in Book XXII of his *History* (*FGrH* 81 F 39). So too Polemon in his *On Morychus* (fr. 75 Preller) says that there is a hearth in the temple of Olympian Earth located outside the city walls in Syracuse,

c  νήσῳ πρὸς τῷ Γῆς Ὀλυμπίας | ἱερῷ ἐκτὸς τοῦ τείχους
ἐσχάραν τινὰ εἶναι, ἀφ᾽ ἧς, φησί, τὴν κύλικα ναυστο-
λοῦσιν ἀναπλέοντες μέχρι τοῦ γενέσθαι τὴν ἐπὶ τοῦ
νεὼ τῆς Ἀθηνᾶς ἀόρατον ἀσπίδα· καὶ οὕτως ἀφιᾶσιν
εἰς τὴν θάλασσαν κεραμέαν κύλικα, καθέντες εἰς αὐτὴν ἄνθεα καὶ κηρία καὶ λιβανωτὸν ἄτμητον καὶ ἄλλα
ἄττα μετὰ τούτων ἀρώματα.

Ὁρῶν οὖν ὑμῶν καὶ αὐτὸς τὸ συμπόσιον κατὰ τὸν
Κολοφώνιον Ξενοφάνη πλῆρες ὂν πάσης θυμηδίας· |

d    νῦν γὰρ δὴ ζάπεδον καθαρὸν καὶ χεῖρες ἁπάντων
καὶ κύλικες· πλεκτοὺς δ᾽ ἀμφιτιθεῖ στεφάνους,
ἄλλος δ᾽ εὐῶδες μύρον ἐν φιάλῃ παρατείνει·
κρητὴρ δ᾽ ἕστηκεν μεστὸς εὐφροσύνης·
ἄλλος δ᾽ οἶνος ἑτοῖμος, ὃς οὔποτέ φησι
    προδώσειν,
μείλιχος ἐν κεράμοις, ἄνθεος ὀζόμενος·
ἐν δὲ μέσοις ἁγνὴν ὀδμὴν λιβανωτὸς ἵησιν,
ψυχρὸν δ᾽ ἐστὶν ὕδωρ καὶ γλυκὺ καὶ καθαρόν· |
e  παρκέαται δ᾽ ἄρτοι ξανθοὶ γεραρή τε τράπεζα
τυροῦ καὶ μέλιτος πίονος ἀχθομένη·
βωμὸς δ᾽ ἄνθεσιν ἂν τὸ μέσον πάντῃ
    πεπύκασται,
μολπῇ δ᾽ ἀμφὶς ἔχει δώματα καὶ θαλίη.
χρὴ δὲ πρῶτον μὲν θεὸν ὑμνεῖν εὔφρονας ἄνδρας
εὐφήμοις μύθοις καὶ καθαροῖσι λόγοις, |

[28] The construction is left dangling here, but the thread of the argument resumes at 11.463c.

at the very tip of the island, and that when they put out to sea, they take a *kulix* from there and keep it with them until the shield on the temple of Athena is no longer visible. At that point, they drop the cup (which is made of terracotta) into the sea, after putting flowers, honeycomb, solid chunks of frankincense, and various other spices as well, into it.

Since I can see for myself, then, that your party is full of happiness of every sort,[28] as in the description offered by Xenophanes of Colophon (fr. B 1 West[2]):

> For now the floor is clean, as are everyone's hands
>     and the cups. (One slave) places woven garlands
>         around (our heads),
> while another offers us fragrant perfume in a bowl;
>     and a mixing-bowl full of good cheer stands in the
>         middle.
> Another type of wine, sweet as honey and smelling of
>         flowers,
>     is ready in the jars, and promises that we will
>         never run out of it.
> In our midst is frankincense that produces a sacred
>         scent;
>     and the water is cold, delicious, and pure.
> Golden-brown loaves of bread have been set beside
>         us, along with a table full of honor
>     and heavy with cheese and dense honey.
> In the middle is an altar covered on all sides with
>         flowers;
>     song and dance and celebration fill the house.
> Reasonable men should begin by offering a hymn in
>         the god's honor,
>     using respectable vocabulary and clean words,

f    σπείσαντάς τε καὶ εὐξαμένους τὰ δίκαια
      δύνασθαι
    πρήσσειν· ταῦτα γὰρ ὦν ἐστι προχειρότερον,
οὐχ ὕβρεις· πίνειν δ᾽ ὁπόσον κεν ἔχων ἀφίκοιο
οἴκαδ᾽ ἄνευ προπόλου μὴ πάνυ γηραλέος.
ἀνδρῶν δ᾽ αἰνεῖν τοῦτον ὃς ἐσθλὰ πιὼν
      ἀναφαίνει,
    ὡς ᾖ μνημοσύνη καὶ τόνος ἀμφ᾽ ἀρετῆς,
οὔ τι μάχας διέπειν Τιτήνων οὐδὲ Γιγάντων
    οὐδὲ < . . . > κενταύρων, πλάσμα<τα> τῶν
      προτέρων,
ἢ στάσιας σφεδανάς· τοῖς οὐδὲν χρηστὸν
      ἔνεστιν· ‖

463       θεῶν <δὲ> προμηθείην αἰὲν ἔχειν ἀγαθήν.

καὶ ὁ χαρίεις δ᾽ Ἀνακρέων φησίν·

    οὐ φιλέω, ὃς κρητῆρι παρὰ πλέῳ οἰνοποτάζων
    νείκεα καὶ πόλεμον δακρυόεντα λέγει,
    ἀλλ᾽ ὅστις Μουσέων τε καὶ ἀγλαὰ δῶρ᾽
      Ἀφροδίτης
    συμμίσγων ἐρατῆς μνήσκεται εὐφροσύνης. |

b   καὶ Ἴων δὲ ὁ Χῖός φησιν·

    χαιρέτω ἡμέτερος βασιλεὺς σωτήρ τε πατήρ τε·
    ἡμῖν δὲ κρητῆρ᾽ οἰνοχόοι θέραπες

---

29 Most of verses 2–3 are quoted again at 11.496c, in a discussion of the vessel known as a *prochutēs*; despite Athenaeus (or his
source) there, the word in this passage clearly means "pouring
vessel, pitcher", not "drinking vessel, cup".

after they pour a libation and pray for the power to
    do
  what is right; for this is what one ought to prefer,
rather than ugly words and actions. Then they should
    drink as much as a person can and still
  make it home without a servant's assistance, unless
    he is extremely old.
They should also praise the man who behaves well
    when he drinks,
  so that excellence is recalled and aspired to.
But they ought not to spend their time describing
    battles fought by Titans, or Giants,
  or centaurs, stories our ancestors made up,
or their violent quarrels; topics of this sort are
    worthless.
    Instead, they should always have good forethought
    for the gods.

So too the witty Anacreon says (eleg. fr. 2 West[2]):

I dislike the man who talks of quarrels and war,
    which is full of tears,
  as he drinks wine beside a full mixing-bowl;
better someone who combines the Muses' glorious
    gifts with those of
  Aphrodite, and fixes his mind on the cheer we all
    desire.

Ion of Chios (fr. 27 West[2])[29] as well says:

Hail to our king, savior, and father!
    Let the servants who pour the wine mix up a

κιρνάντων προχύταισιν ἐν ἀργυρέοις· † ὁ δὲ
χρυσὸς
οἶνον ἔχων χειρῶν νιζέτω εἰς ἔδαφος. † |
σπένδοντες δ' ἁγνῶς Ἡρακλεῖ τ' Ἀλκμήνῃ τε,
Προκλεῖ Περσείδαις τ' ἐκ Διὸς ἀρχόμενοι
πίνωμεν, παίζωμεν· ἴτω διὰ νυκτὸς ἀοιδή,
ὀρχείσθω τις· ἑκὼν δ' ἄρχε φιλοφροσύνης.
ὅντινα δ' εὐειδὴς μίμνει θήλεια πάρευνος,
κεῖνος τῶν ἄλλων κυδρότερον πίεται.

ἐποιοῦντο δὲ καὶ οἱ ἑπτὰ καλούμενοι σοφοὶ συμπο-
τικὰς ὁμιλίας. παραμυθεῖται γὰρ ὁ οἶνος καὶ τὴν τοῦ
γήρως δυσθυμίαν φησὶ Θεόφραστος ἐν τῷ Περὶ Μέθης, διόπερ συνιοῦσι καὶ ἡμῖν ἐπὶ τὰς Διονυσιακὰς
ταύτας λαλιὰς

οὐδὲ εἷς ἂν εὐλόγως
< ... > φθονήσαι νοῦν ἔχων,

κατὰ τοὺς Ἀλέξιδος Ταραντίνους,

οἳ τῶν πέλας
οὐδέν' ἀδικοῦμεν οὐδέ. ἆρ' <οὐκ> οἶσθ' ὅτι
τὸ καλούμενον ζῆν τοῦτο διατριβῆς χάριν |
ὄνομ' ἐστίν, ὑποκόρισμα τῆς ἀνθρωπίνης
μοίρας; ἐγὼ γάρ, εἰ μὲν εὖ τις ἢ κακῶς
φήσει με κρίνειν, οὐκ ἔχοιμ' ἂν <σοι> φράσαι·

---

30 Procles (a descendant of Heracles) was the mythical
founder of one of the Spartan royal houses, while Perseus established the royal dynasty in Argos.

31 Thales of Miletus, Bias of Priene, Cleobulus of Rhodian
Lindos, Pittacus of Mitylene, Solon of Athens, Chilon of Sparta,
and Periander of Corinth (all early 6th century BCE).

bowl for us using silver pitchers (*prochutai*); † and
    the gold
      having wine of hands let it wash onto the floor! †
Let us pour holy libations to Heracles and Alcmene,
    and to Procles and the descendants of Perseus,[30]
      although we begin with Zeus;
and let us drink and enjoy ourselves! Let the songs go
    on all night;
      and let someone dance, and volunteer to lead the
      celebration!
If anyone has a beautiful woman waiting in his bed,
    he will drink more boldly than the rest.

The so-called Seven Wise Men[31] also held drinking parties. For wine offers consolation for the misery of old age,
according to Theophrastus in his *On Drunkenness* (fr. 569
Fortenbaugh), which is why,[32] when we gather for these
Dionysiac conversations,

                no one with any sense would have
    reasonable grounds for resenting our behavior,

to quote Alexis' *Men of Tarentum* (fr. 222, including what
follows),

                  since we're not hurting
    the people around us. Don't you realize that this
    "life", as it's called, is just a word designed
    to amuse us, a nice way of referring to our fate
    as human beings? Whether someone will say
    I'm right or I'm wrong, I can't tell you that.

[32] See 11.462c n., 463e with n.

ἔγνωκα δ' οὖν οὕτως ἐπισκοπούμενος,
εἶναι μανιώδη πάντα τἀνθρώπων ὅλως,
ἀποδημίας δὲ τυγχάνειν ἡμᾶς ἀεὶ
τοὺς ζῶντας, ὥσπερ εἰς πανήγυρίν τινα,
ἀφειμένους ἐκ τοῦ θανάτου καὶ τοῦ σκότους
εἰς τὴν διατριβὴν εἰς τὸ φῶς τε τοῦθ', ὃ δὴ
ὁρῶμεν. ὃς δ' ἂν πλεῖστα γελάσῃ καὶ πίῃ |
e     καὶ τῆς Ἀφροδίτης ἀντιλάβηται τὸν χρόνον
τοῦτον ὃν ἀφεῖται, κἂν τύχῃ γ', ἐράνου τινός,
πανηγυρίσας ἥδιστ' ἀπῆλθεν οἴκαδε.

καὶ κατὰ τὴν καλὴν οὖν Σαπφώ·[3]

    ἔλθε, Κύπρι,
χρυσίαισιν ἐν κυλίκεσσιν ἄβρως
συμμεμείγμενον θαλίαισι νέκταρ
    οἰνοχόεισα

τούτοις τοῖς ἑταίροις ἐμοῖς τε καὶ σοῖς.

Πρὸς οὓς λεκτέον ὅτι τρόποι εἰσὶ πόσεων κατὰ
πόλεις ἴδιοι, ὡς Κριτίας παρίστησιν ἐν τῇ Λακεδαιμονίων Πολιτείᾳ διὰ τούτων· ὁ μὲν Χῖος καὶ Θάσιος ἐκ
μεγάλων κυλίκων ἐπιδέξια, ὁ δ' Ἀττικὸς ἐκ μικρῶν
f     ἐπιδέξια, ὁ δὲ Θετταλικὸς | ἐκπώματα προπίνει ὅτῳ ἂν
βούλωνται μεγάλα. Λακεδαιμόνιοι δὲ τὴν παρ' αὑτῷ
ἕκαστος πίνει, ὁ δὲ παῖς ὁ οἰνοχόος ὅσον ἂν ἀποπίῃ.

---

3 These verses are also preserved in a papyrus, which offers
ἔνθα δὴ σὺ † συ αν † ἔλοισα Κύπρι in v. 12 and ἐμμείχμενον
(ὀμμείχμενον Norsa) at the beginning of v. 14.

---

33 Aphrodite.     34 I.e. those who might be tempted to
criticize a party of this sort (11.463c).     35 I.e. passing a single cup around the circle counter-clockwise.

But I've thought about it, and I've come to the
      following conclusion:
human existence is entirely, completely insane,
and as long as we're alive, we're enjoying
a reprieve, like going to a festival;
we've been released from death and darkness,
and allowed to have a party in this light
we see. And whoever laughs the most, and drinks the
      most,
and grabs Aphrodite during the time
he's released, or a dinner party if he gets the
      chance—
he's the happiest when he goes home after the
      festival.

So to quote the lovely Sappho (fr. 2.13–16):

      Come, Cypris,[33]
and daintily pour nectar mixed
with celebrations into gold
   cups

for these friends of yours and mine.

In response to such people,[34] we should note that
drinking-styles vary by city, as Critias establishes in his
*Constitution of the Spartans* (88 B 33 D–K), in the following passage: Chians and Thasians (drink) from left to
right,[35] from large cups; Athenians (drink) from left to
right, from small cups; and Thessalians propose toasts with
large vessels to anyone they want. The Spartans, however,
drink from individual cups, and the slave who pours the
wine (replaces) whatever they drink. Anaxandrides in *Rus-*

τοῦ δ᾽ ἐπιδέξια πίνειν μνημονεύει καὶ Ἀναξανδρίδης ἐν
Ἀγροίκοις οὕτως· ‖

464    (Α.) τίνα δὴ παρεσκευασμένοι
πίνειν τρόπον νῦν ἐστε; λέγετε. (Β.) τίνα τρόπον
ἡμεῖς; τοιοῦτον οἷον ἂν καὶ σοὶ δοκῇ.
(Α.) βούλεσθε δήπου τὸν ἐπιδέξι᾽, ὦ πάτερ,
λέγειν ἐπὶ τῷ πίνοντι; (Β.) τὸν ἐπιδέξια
λέγειν; Ἄπολλον, ὥσπερ ἐπὶ τεθνηκότι;

παραιτητέον δ᾽ ἡμῖν τὰ κεράμεα ποτήρια· καὶ γὰρ
Κτησίας, παρὰ Πέρσαις, φησίν, ὃν ἂν βασιλεὺς ἀτι-
μάσῃ, κεραμέοις χρῆται. Χοιρίλος δ᾽ ὁ ἐποποιός |
b  φησι·

    χθέζινον[4] ὄλβον ἔχω κύλικος τρύφος ἀμφὶς
        ἐαγός,
    ἀνδρῶν δαιτυμόνων ναυάγιον, οἷά τε πολλὰ
    πνεῦμα Διωνύσοιο πρὸς Ὕβριος ἔκβαλεν ἀκτάς.

ἐγὼ δὲ εὖ οἶδα ὅτι ἥδιστα πολλάκις ἐστὶ τὰ κεράμεα
ἐκπώματα, ὡς καὶ τὰ παρ᾽ ἡμῖν ἐκ τῆς Κόπτου καταγό-
μενα· μετὰ γὰρ ἀρωμάτων συμφυραθείσης τῆς γῆς
c  ὀπτᾶται. καὶ Ἀριστοτέλης δὲ ἐν τῷ | Περὶ Μέθης, αἱ
Ῥοδιακαί, φησί, προσαγορευόμεναι χυτρίδες διά τε

---

[4] χθέζινον Olson: χερσὶν ACE

---

[36] Simply a respectful form of address for any older man;
Speaker A and Speaker B are not necessarily related.

[37] A reference to the *perideipnon*, an ill-attested funeral rite in
the course of which the dead man was eulogized.

[38] Coptos was a major transit-point in Upper Egypt for goods

*tics* (fr. 1) refers to the practice of drinking from left to right, as follows:

> (A.) What style are you ready
> to drink in now? Tell me! (B.) What style are we
> ready for? Whatever style you'd like.
> (A.) I suppose, father,[36] that you want us to go from
> left to right
> and speak in honor of the man who's drinking? (B.)
> Go
> from left to right and speak? Apollo! Like over a
> corpse?[37]

We should refuse to use ceramic cups; Ctesias (*FGrH* 688 F 40), in fact, claims that in Persia anyone the king is unhappy with uses vessels of this sort. And the epic poet Choerilus (fr. 9 Bernabé) says:

> In my hands is yesterday's happiness—a fragment of a
> shattered cup,
> a bit of driftwood left by dinner-party guests, like
> those Dionysus'
> gusts cast up in large numbers on the coast of
> Outrage.

But I am well aware that people often prefer ceramic drinking vessels, for example those brought downriver to us from Coptos;[38] because the clay is mixed with spices before the cups are fired. So too Aristotle says in his *On Drunkenness* (fr. 672, encompassing both quotations): What are referred to as Rhodian cookpots are brought to

moving between the Red Sea region and Alexandria (the hometown of Plutarch, who is speaking here).

227

τὴν ἡδονὴν εἰς τὰς μέθας παρεισφέρονται καὶ διὰ τὸ
θερμαινομένας τὸν οἶνον ἧττον ποιεῖν μεθύσκειν·
σμύρνης γὰρ καὶ σχοίνου καὶ τῶν τοιούτων ἑτέρων εἰς
ὕδωρ ἐμβληθέντων ἕψονται καὶ παραχεόντων εἰς τὸν
οἶνον ἧττον μεθύσκουσιν. κἂν ἄλλῳ δὲ μέρει φησίν· αἱ
Ῥοδιακαὶ χυτρίδες γίνονται σμύρνης, σχοίνου, ἀνή-
θου, κρόκου, βαλσάμου, ἀμώμου, κινναμώμου συνεψη-
θέντων· ἀφ᾽ ὧν τὸ γινόμενον τῷ οἴνῳ παραχυθὲν οὕτω

d ⟨τὰς⟩[5] μέθας | ἵστησιν ὥστε καὶ τῶν ἀφροδισίων
παραλύειν τὰ πνεύματα πέττον. οὐ δεῖ οὖν ἡμᾶς
ἐκμανῶς πίνειν ἀποβλέποντας εἰς τὸ πλῆθος τῶν
καλῶν τούτων καὶ παντοδαπῶν κατὰ τὰς τέχνας
ἐκπωμάτων. τὴν δὲ μανίαν τοὺς πολλούς φησιν ὁ
Χρύσιππος ἐν τῇ Εἰσαγωγικῇ Περὶ Ἀγαθῶν Καὶ
Κακῶν Πραγματείᾳ τοῖς πλείστοις προσάπτειν.
καλεῖσθαι γοῦν τὴν μὲν γυναικομανίαν, τὴν δ᾽
ὀρτυγομανίαν· τινὲς δὲ καὶ δοξομανεῖς καλοῦσι τοὺς
φιλοδόξους, καθάπερ τοὺς φιλογύνας γυναικομανεῖς

e καὶ τοὺς φιλόρνιθας | ὀρνιθομανεῖς, τὸ αὐτὸ
σημαινόντων τῶν ὀνομάτων τούτων, ὥστε καὶ τὰ
λοιπὰ μὴ ἀλλοτρίως καλεῖσθαι τὸν τρόπον τοῦτον. καὶ
γὰρ ὁ φίλοψος καὶ ὁ ὀψοφάγος οἷον ὀψομανής ἐστι καὶ
ὁ φίλοινος οἰνομανὴς καὶ ὡσαύτως ἐπὶ τῶν ὁμοίων,
οὐκ ἀλλοτρίως τῆς μανίας κειμένης ἐπ᾽ αὐτοῖς ὡς
ἁμαρτάνουσι μανικῶς καὶ τῆς ἀληθείας ἐπὶ πλεῖστον
ἀπαρτωμένοις. ἡμεῖς οὖν, ὡς καὶ παρ᾽ Ἀθηναίοις
ἐγίνετο, ἅμα ἀκροώμενοι τῶν γελωτοποιῶν τούτων καὶ

[5] add. Kaibel

---

[39] Cf. the word *erōtomanēs* ("crazy about love") at 13.599e.

drinking parties both because people enjoy using them and because they make the wine less intoxicating when warmed up; for they add myrrh, aromatic rush, and other similar substances to the water before bringing it to a boil, and when they pour the water into the wine, they get less drunk. And in another section he says: Rhodian cookpots are prepared by boiling together myrrh, aromatic rush, anise, saffron, costmary, Siam cardamom, and cinnamon. When the liquid produced using these substances is poured into the wine, it prevents one from getting drunk so effectively that it even paralyzes sexual desire by modifying the forces that inspire it. We should not, therefore, drink insanely (*ekmanōs*), as we gaze at this massive collection of beautiful drinking vessels produced in every imaginable way. As for the word *mania* ("madness, insanity"), Chrysippus in his *Introductory Treatise on Goods and Evils* (fr. 667, *SVF* iii.167) says that people routinely attach it to a large number of other terms.[39] They refer, for example, to *gunaikomania* ("being crazy about women") and *ortugomania* ("being crazy about quail"); and some refer to individuals who are eager for a good reputation (*doxa*) as *doxomaneis*, much as they refer to those who like women (*gunaikes*) as *gunaikomaneis* or those who like birds (*ornithes*) as *ornithomaneis*, these being parallel terms, so that it comes as no surprise that others are formed this way as well. And in fact someone who likes fish (*opson*) and eats it greedily is *opsomanēs*, as it were; someone who likes wine (*oinos*) is *oinomanēs*; and so on in similar cases, where it is unsurprising that the word *mania* is applied to the individuals in question, since they make crazy mistakes and are substantially detached from reality. So let us then have something to drink, as we listen to these comics and mimes, and to the

f   μίμων, ἔτι δὲ τῶν ἄλλων τεχνιτῶν ὑποπίνωμεν. | λέγει
δὲ περὶ τούτων ὁ Φιλόχορος οὑτωσί· Ἀθηναῖοι τοῖς
Διονυσιακοῖς ἀγῶσι τὸ μὲν πρῶτον ἠριστηκότες καὶ
πεπωκότες ἐβάδιζον ἐπὶ τὴν θέαν καὶ ἐστεφανωμένοι
ἐθεώρουν, παρὰ δὲ τὸν ἀγῶνα πάντα οἶνος αὐτοῖς
ᾠνοχοεῖτο καὶ τραγήματα παρεφέρετο, καὶ τοῖς χοροῖς
εἰσιοῦσιν ἐνέχεον πίνειν καὶ διηγωνισμένοις ὅτ᾿
ἐξεπορεύοντο ἐνέχεον πάλιν· μαρτυρεῖν δὲ τούτοις καὶ
Φερεκράτη τὸν κωμικόν, ὅτι μέχρι τῆς καθ᾿ ἑαυτὸν
ἡλικίας οὐκ ἀσίτους εἶναι τοὺς θεωροῦντας.

465   Φανόδημος ‖ δὲ πρὸς τὸ ἱερόν φησι τοῦ ἐν Λίμναις
Διονύσου τὸ γλεῦκος φέροντας τοὺς Ἀθηναίους ἐκ τῶν
πίθων τῷ θεῷ κιρνάναι, εἶτ᾿ αὐτοὺς προσφέρεσθαι·
ὅθεν καὶ Λιμναῖον κληθῆναι τὸν Διόνυσον, ὅτι μιχθὲν
τὸ γλεῦκος τῷ ὕδατι τότε πρῶτον ἐπόθη κεκραμένον.
διόπερ ὀνομασθῆναι τὰς νύμφας[6] καὶ τιθήνας τοῦ
Διονύσου, ὅτι τὸν οἶνον αὐξάνει τὸ ὕδωρ κιρνάμενον.
ἡσθέντες οὖν τῇ κράσει ἐν ᾠδαῖς ἔμελπον τὸν
Διόνυσον, χορεύοντες καὶ ἀνακαλοῦντες Εὔαν τε[7] καὶ
b   Διθύραμβον καὶ Βακχευτὰν | καὶ Βρόμιον. καὶ
Θεόφραστος δ᾿ ἐν τῷ Περὶ Μέθης φησὶν ὅτι τοῦ
Διονύσου τροφοὶ αἱ νύμφαι κατ᾿ ἀλήθειαν· αἱ γὰρ
ἄμπελοι πλεῖστον ὑγρὸν χέουσι τεμνόμεναι καὶ κατὰ

6 τὰς πηγὰς νύμφας ACE: πηγὰς del. Kaibel
7 Εὔαν τε Kaibel (cf. Hsch. ε 6709): Εὐάνθη A

40 Quoted at 11.485d.
41 Sc. as part of the Pithoigia festival; cf. 10.437b–c (again citing Phanodemus).

other artists as well, just as the Athenians did. Philochorus
(*FGrH* 328 F 171) says the following about them: During
their Dionysiac contests, the Athenians used to have
lunch and something to drink before attending the show,
and they watched the performances with garlands on their
heads. Wine was poured for them and snacks were served
throughout the entire competition, and when the choruses
entered, they offered them a drink, and after they finished
and were on their way out, they offered them another. The
comic author Pherecrates (fr. 101)[40] also attests to the fact
that up to his own time the spectators never went hungry.
Phanodemus (*FGrH* 325 F 12) reports that the Athenians
brought grape-must drawn from their storage-jars to the
sanctuary of Dionysus in the Marshes (*en Limnais*), mixed
it for the god, and then consumed it themselves.[41] This is
why Dionysus has the epithet Limnaios ("of the Marsh"),
because this is the first time that grape-must was combined with water and drunk mixed with something else.
This is the reason the nymphs are referred to as Dionysus'
nurses, because when water is mixed with the wine, it in-
creases its volume.[42] So because they liked the mixing,
they sang songs in Dionysus' honor, dancing and invoking
him as Euas, Dithurambos, Bakcheutas, and Bromios.[43]
Theophrastus in his *On Drunkenness* (fr. 573 Fortenbaugh) also claims that the nymphs are in fact Dionysus'
nurses; because when grapevines are pruned, they emit
a considerable quantity of liquid and seemingly weep.

[42] Cf. 2.38c–d; 15.693d–e (citing Philochorus). This comment
interrupts the flow of Phanodemus' narrative and has presumably
been inserted into it by Athenaeus.

[43] These are all cult-titles of the god.

φύσιν δακρύουσι. διόπερ καὶ Εὐριπίδης ἕνα τῶν τοῦ
Ἡλίου ἵππων φησὶν εἶναι

> Βακχίου φιλανθέμου
> Αἴθοπα πεπαίνοντ᾽ ὀρχάτους ὀπωρινούς·
> ἐξ οὗ βροτοὶ καλοῦσιν οἶνον αἴθοπα.

καὶ Ὀδυσσεὺς ὤπασεν

> μελιηδέα οἶνον ἐρυθρόν, |

c

> ἓν δέπας ἐμπλήσας, ὕδατος δ᾽[8] ἀνὰ εἴκοσι μέτρα
> χεῦ᾽, ὀδμὴ δ᾽ ἡδεῖα ἀπὸ κρητῆρος ὀδώδει.

Τιμόθεος δ᾽ ἐν Κύκλωπι·

> ἔγχευε δ᾽ ἐν μὲν δέπας κίσσινον μελαίνας
> σταγόνος ἀμβρότας ἀφρῷ βρυάζον,
> εἴκοσιν δὲ μέτρ᾽ ἐνέχευ᾽, ἀνέμισγε
> δ᾽ αἷμα Βακχίου νεορρύτοισιν
> δακρύοισι νυμφᾶν.

οἶδα δέ τινας, ἄνδρες θιασῶται, καὶ μέγα φρονήσαν-
τας οὐχ οὕτως ἐπὶ πλούτῳ ὡς ἐπὶ τῷ κεκτῆσθαι πολλὰ
ἐκπώματα ἀργυρᾶ τε καὶ χρυσᾶ. ὧν εἷς ἐστι καὶ

d Πυθέας | ὁ Ἀρκὰς ἐκ Φιγαλείας, ὃς καὶ ἀποθνήσκων
οὐκ ὤκνησεν ὑποθέσθαι τοῖς οἰκείοις ἐπιγράψαι αὐτοῦ
τῷ μνήματι τάδε·

---

8 δ᾽ is absent from the traditional text of Homer.

---

44 Sc. that carry his sun-chariot through the sky. But the connection between this remark and the argument that surrounds it is
unclear; cf. 1.26b.

This is why Euripides (fr. 896) claims that one of Helios' horses[44] is

> Aethops, who ripens the rows of vines
> that belong to the flower-loving Bacchic god in the
>     autumn;
> mortals accordingly refer to wine as *aithops* ("fiery").

And Odysseus provided[45] (*Od.* 9.208–10)

> honey-sweet red wine,
> filling a single goblet; and he poured 20 measures of
>     water
> over it, and a delicious smell rose from the mixing-
>     bowl.

Timotheus in *Cyclops* (*PMG* 780):

> He poured in a single ivy-wood[46] goblet of dark,
> ambrosial drops—the goblet was filled with foam—
> and poured 20 measures over it, mixing together
> the Bacchic god's blood with the fresh-shed
> tears of the nymphs.

I am aware, my fellow-revellers, that some people are less proud of being rich than they are of owning large numbers of silver and gold drinking vessels. One example is Pytheas of Arcadian Phigaleia who, when he was dying, did not hesitate to require his family to inscribe the following on his tomb (*FGE* 315–18):

---

[45] Sc. to the Cyclops. But in Homer the subject is actually Maron, from whom Odysseus got the wine.

[46] *kissinos*; apparently intended as a learned gloss of the problematic Homeric word *kissubion* (discussed at 11.476f–7e).

Πυθέα μνῆμα τόδ᾽ ἔστ᾽, ἀγαθοῦ καὶ σώφρονος
    ἀνδρός,
ὃς κυλίκων ἔσχεν πλῆθος ἀπειρέσιον
ἀργυρέων χρυσοῦ τε καὶ ἠλέκτροιο φαεινοῦ,
τῶν προτέρων πάντων πλείονα πασάμενος.

τοῦτο δ᾽ ἱστορεῖ Ἁρμόδιος ὁ Λεπρεάτης ἐν τῷ Περὶ |
e Τῶν Κατὰ Φιγάλειαν Νομίμων. Ξενοφῶν δ᾽ ἐν ὀγδόῳ
Παιδείας περὶ Περσῶν λέγων γράφει καὶ ταῦτα· καὶ
μὴν ἐκπώματα ἢν μὲν ὡς πλεῖστα ἔχωσιν, τούτῳ
καλλωπίζονται· ἢν δ᾽ ἐξ ἀδίκων φανερῶς ᾖ μεμηχανη-
μένα, οὐδὲν τούτῳ αἰσχύνονται· πολὺ γὰρ ηὔξηται ἐν
αὐτοῖς ἡ ἀδικία τε καὶ αἰσχροκέρδεια. ὁ δὲ Οἰδίπους
δι᾽ ἐκπώματα τοῖς υἱοῖς κατηράσατο, ὡς ὁ τὴν κυκλι-
κὴν Θηβαΐδα πεποιηκὼς φησιν, ὅτι αὐτῷ παρέθηκαν
ἔκπωμα ὃ ἀπηγορεύκει, λέγων οὕτως· |

f      αὐτὰρ ὁ διογενὴς ἥρως ξανθὸς Πολυνείκης
       πρῶτα μὲν Οἰδιπόδῃ καλὴν παρέθηκε τράπεζαν
       ἀργυρέην Κάδμοιο θεόφρονος· αὐτὰρ ἔπειτα
       χρύσεον ἔμπλησεν καλὸν δέπας ἡδέος οἴνου.
       αὐτὰρ ὅ γ᾽ ὡς φράσθη παρακείμενα πατρὸς ἑοῖο
       τιμήεντα γέρα, μέγα οἱ κακὸν ἔμπεσε θυμῷ, ‖
466    αἶψα δὲ παισὶν ἑοῖσι ἐπ᾽ ἀμφοτέροισιν ἐπαρὰς
       ἀργαλέας ἠρᾶτο· θοὴν δ᾽ οὐ λάνθαν᾽ Ἐρινύν·
       ὡς οὔ οἱ πατρώϊ᾽ ἐνηέϊ <ἐν> φιλότητι
       δάσσαιντ᾽, ἀμφοτέροισι δ᾽ ἀεὶ πόλεμοί τε μάχαι
           τε.

This is the tomb of Pytheas, a good, thoughtful man
    who owned an enormous number of cups
made of silver, as well as of gold and glistening
        electrum,
        having acquired a larger collection than anyone
            before him.

Harmodius of Lepreum reports this in his *On the Customs
in Phigaleia* (*FGrH* 319 F 3). Xenophon in Book VIII
(8.18) of the *Education* writes the following in the course
of his discussion of the Persians: Moreover, if they own a
particularly large number of drinking vessels, they are extremely proud of the fact. And if they have accomplished
this in a patently dishonest way, they feel no shame on that
account; because they regard crime and greed as quite
glorious. According to the author of the *Thebaid* (fr. 2
Bernabé), which is part of the epic cycle, Oedipus cursed
his sons on account of some drinking vessels, because they
set a vessel beside him that he had forbidden them to use.
The poet puts it as follows:

But the divinely-sired hero, blond Polynices,
first placed a beautiful silver table which had
        belonged
to reverent Cadmus beside Oedipus, and then
filled a fine gold goblet with delicious wine.
But when (Oedipus) noticed his father's precious
possession set beside him, tremendous grief invaded
        his heart,
and immediately he called down fearsome curses
on both his sons—nor did the swift Fury ignore
        him—
asking that they not divide their inheritance in gentle
friendship, but both have endless wars and battles.

Καικίλιος δὲ ὁ ῥήτωρ ὁ ἀπὸ Καλῆς ἀκτῆς ἐν τῷ Περὶ Ἱστορίας Ἀγαθοκλέα φησὶ τὸν τύραννον ἐκπώματα χρυσᾶ ἐπιδεικνύντα τοῖς ἑταίροις φάσκειν ἐξ ὧν ἐκε-
b ράμευσε κατεσκευακέναι ταῦτα. | ὁ δὲ παρὰ Σοφοκλεῖ ἐν τοῖς Λαρισαίοις Ἀκρίσιος καὶ αὐτὸς ἐκπώματα ὅσα πλεῖστα εἶχεν, ὥς φησιν ὁ τραγικός·

> πολὺν δ' ἀγῶνα πάγξενον κηρύσσεται,
> χαλκηλάτους λέβητας ἐκτιθεὶς φέρειν
> καὶ κοῖλα χρυσόκολλα καὶ πανάργυρα
> ἐκπώματ', εἰς ἀριθμὸν ἑξήκοντα δίς. |

c Ποσειδώνιος δ' ἐν ἕκτῃ καὶ δεκάτῃ[9] τῶν Ἱστοριῶν Λυσίμαχόν φησι τὸν Βαβυλώνιον, καλέσαντα ἐπὶ δεῖπνον Ἵμερον τὸν τυραννήσαντα οὐ μόνον Βαβυ-λωνίων ἀλλὰ καὶ Σελευκέων μετὰ τριακοσίων, μετὰ τὸ τὰς τραπέζας ἀρθῆναι τετράμνουν ἑκάστῳ τῶν τριακο-σίων ἔκπωμα δοῦναι ἀργυροῦν, καὶ σπονδοποιησάμε-νον προπιεῖν ἅμα πᾶσιν· καὶ ἀποφέρεσθαι ἔδωκε τὰ ποτήρια. Ἀντικλείδης δ' ὁ Ἀθηναῖος ἐν τῷ ἕκτῳ καὶ δεκάτῳ Νόστων περὶ Γρᾶ διηγούμενος τοῦ τὴν ἀποι-κίαν εἰς Λέσβον στείλαντος σὺν ἄλλοις βασιλεῦσι,

9 ἕκτῃ καὶ δεκάτῃ (i.e. ις΄) Müller: εἴκοσι καὶ ἕκτῃ (i.e. κς΄) A

---

47 Literally "that he had worked as a potter", as again at 11.781d. Agathocles ruled Syracuse for several decades at the end of the 4th century BCE and the beginning of the 3rd; his father had owned a large pottery workshop.

48 Doubtless the contest at which Acrisius, who was in exile in Larisa, was accidentally killed by a discus thrown by Perseus.

49 Emended from the manuscript's "Book XXVI" by Müller on the ground that the passage ought to stand immediately after the

The orator Caecilius of Calacte in his *On History* (*FGrH* 183 F 2) claims that when the tyrant Agathocles showed off his gold drinking vessels to his inner circle, he used to say that he had had to get his hands dirty[47] to produce them. The Acrisius who appears in Sophocles' *Men of Larisa* (fr. 378) also owned an enormous number of drinking vessels, according to the tragic poet:

> He is announcing a great contest,[48] open to all
>     comers,
> and is setting out as the prizes basins of hammered
>     bronze,
> hollow cups inlaid with gold, and drinking vessels of
>     solid silver, twice 60 in number.

Posidonius in Book XVI[49] of his *History* (*FGrH* 87 F 13 = fr. 65 Edelstein–Kidd) reports that Lysimachus of Babylon invited Himerus, who controlled not just Babylon, but Seleucia as well, to dinner along with 300 other people. After the tables had been removed,[50] he presented each of his 300 guests with a silver drinking vessel that weighed four pounds;[51] poured a libation; toasted them all simultaneously; and gave them their cups to take home. Anticleides of Athens in Book XVI of the *Homecomings* (*FGrH* 140 F 4),[52] in the course of his discussion of Gras, who along with some other kings led the colony that set off

---

description of Himerus' drunken ambition and death in *FGrH* 87 F 11 = fr. 63 Edelstein–Kidd (quoted at 10.439d–e). The anecdote thus apparently belongs in 129 BCE.
[50] Sc. at the end of the meal, when the drinking party was about to begin.   [51] Literally "four *minas*"; cf. 11.782a n.
[52] Plu. *Mor.* 163a–d offers another version of the story.

καὶ ὅτι χρησμὸς ἦν αὐτοῖς δηλώσας καθεῖναι δια-
πλέοντας τῷ Ποσειδῶνι εἰς τὸ πέλαγος παρθένον,
γράφει καὶ ταῦτα· μυθολογοῦσι δὲ τῶν[10] ἐν Μηθύμνῃ
τινὲς περὶ τῆς ἀφεθείσης εἰς τὴν θάλασσαν παρθένου
d   καὶ φασὶν | ἐρασθέντα αὐτῆς τῶν ἡγεμόνων τινά, ᾧ ἦν
τοὔνομα Ἔναλος, ἐκκολυμβῆσαι βουλόμενον ἀνασῶ-
σαι τὴν παιδίσκην. τότε μὲν οὖν ὑπὸ κύματος αὐτοὺς
ἀμφοτέρους κρυφθέντας ἀφανεῖς γενέσθαι, χρόνῳ δ᾽
ὕστερον ἤδη τῆς Μηθύμνης οἰκουμένης παραγενέσθαι
τὸν Ἔναλον καὶ διηγεῖσθαι τὸν τρόπον ⟨ . . . ⟩, καὶ ὅτι
ἡ μὲν παρθένος παρὰ ταῖς Νηρῇσι διέτριβεν, αὐτὸς δὲ
τὰς τοῦ Ποσειδῶνος ἔβοσκεν ἵππους· καί ποτε καὶ
κύματος[11] ‖

## ΕΚ ΤΟΥ ΙΑ

781b   ἐπιφερομένου μεγάλου συγκολυμβήσαντα αὐτὸν ἐκ-
c   βῆναι | ἔχοντα κύπελλον χρυσοῦ οὕτω θαυμασίου ὡς
τὸν παρ᾽ αὐτοῖς αὐτῷ παραβαλλόμενον οὐδὲν διάφορον εἶναι χαλκοῦ. τιμιώτατον δ᾽ ἦν πάλαι τὸ τῶν
ἐκπωμάτων κτῆμα. Ἀχιλλεὺς οὖν ὡς ἐξαίρετόν τι εἶχεν
ἀνάθημα δέπας,

οὐδέ τις ἄλλος
οὔτ᾽ ἀνδρῶν πίνεσκεν ἀπ᾽ αὐτοῦ ⟨ . . . ⟩
οὔτέ τεῳ σπένδεσκε ⟨ . . . ⟩, ὅτε μὴ Διί.

10 δὲ περὶ τῶν A: περὶ del. Meineke
11 A number of leaves were missing from the manuscript from
which the text in A was drawn, and the text that follows is drawn
from the Epitome (which has its own system of Casaubon page-
numbers). Manuscript A resumes following the section numbered
784d.

for Lesbos, reports that they had an oracle specifying that as they were crossing the sea, they were to drop a young woman into it for Poseidon. He then writes as follows: Some of the inhabitants of Methymna[53] tell a story about the young woman who was thrown into the sea, and say that one of the leaders of the expedition, who was named Enalus,[54] had fallen in love with the girl and wanted to swim out and rescue her. At that point they were both covered by a wave and disappeared; but later on, after Methymna had been settled, Enalus appeared and described how . . . , and (told them) that the girl was living with the Nereids, and that he himself was a groom for Poseidon's horses. And then when a large wave

## FROM BOOK ELEVEN

came along, he dived down along with it and emerged holding a goblet made of such extraordinary gold that what they had was no better than bronze in comparison to it. In ancient times, owning drinking vessels brought enormous prestige. Achilleus accordingly treated his goblet as a special, sacred object (*Il.* 16.225–7):[55]

> and neither did any other
> man drink from it . . .
> nor did he pour libations to anyone . . . except to
>     Zeus.

[53] A city on Lesbos, where the colony was heading.

[54] Literally "In-the-Sea", an unsurprising name for a minor sea-divinity.

[55] The passage is referred to again at 11.783a–b.

καὶ ὁ Πρίαμος δὲ τὸν υἱὸν λυτρούμενος τοῖς ἐπισημο-
τάτοις κειμηλίοις καὶ δέπας δίδωσι περικαλλές. αὐτός
γε μὴν ὁ Ζεὺς τῆς Ἡρακλέους γενέσεως ἄξιον ἡγεῖται
δῶρον Ἀλκμήνῃ δοθῆναι ποτήριον, ὅπερ Ἀμφιτρύωνι
εἰκασθεὶς δίδωσιν, |

d     ἁ δ᾽ ὑποδεξαμένα θαήσατο χρύσεον αἶψα
       ποτήριον.

τὸν δὲ Ἥλιον ὁ Στησίχορος ποτηρίῳ διαπλεῖν φησι
τὸν ὠκεανόν, ᾧ καὶ τὸν Ἡρακλέα περαιωθῆναι ἐπὶ τὰς
Γηρυόνου βόας ὁρμῶντα. οἴδαμεν δὲ καὶ τὸ Βαθυ-
κλέους τοῦ Ἀρκάδος ποτήριον, ὃ σοφίας ἆθλον ὁ
Βαθυκλῆς τῷ κριθέντι ἀρίστῳ τῶν καλουμένων
⟨ἑπτὰ⟩[12] σοφῶν ἀπέλιπε. τὸ δὲ Νέστορος ποτήριον
πολλοὶ κεραμεύουσι· πλεῖστοι γὰρ περὶ αὐτοῦ συν-
εγράψαντο. καὶ θεοφιλὲς δὲ τὸ ποτήριον·

                χρυσέοις (γοῦν) δεπάεσσιν
⟨ . . . ⟩ ἀλλήλους

δεξιοῦνται. ἐλευθέριον δέ, φησί, καὶ ἐμμελῶς ἐν οἴνῳ
διάγειν, μὴ κωθωνιζόμενον μηδὲ Θρακίῳ νόμῳ ἄμυ-

---

[12] add. Meineke

---

56 The dead Hector.

57 Alcmene's mortal husband. For the story, cf. 11.474f (citing
Pherecydes and Herodorus of Heracleia), 475b–c (citing Charon
of Lampsacus).

58 Quoted at 11.469e–f, in the course of an extended discussion of the story.

59 The Sun-god, who used the cup as a way to get back to his
rising-place in the East at night. It was thus available to take

240

So too Priam, when he tries to ransom his son[56] with his most brilliant treasures, offers (*Il.* 24.234) a beautiful goblet. Zeus himself, moreover, regards a cup as an appropriate gift to offer Alcmene in return for producing Heracles, and presents it to her, disguised as Amphitryon[57] (adesp. *PMG* 952):

> And she accepted the gold cup and was immediately astonished by it.

Stesichorus (*PMG* 185)[58] claims that Helios[59] used to sail across the ocean in a drinking cup, and that Heracles as well used it to get to the other side when he set off after the cattle of Geryon. I am also familiar with the cup that belonged to Bathycles of Arcadia, which he left behind as a prize for whoever was judged the best of the so-called Seven Wise Men.[60] Many people get their hands dirty[61] with Nestor's cup, by which I mean that a large number of people produced treatises discussing it.[62] The gods also like cups; at any rate they toast (*Il.* 4.3–4)

> one another with gold goblets.

A mark of a free man, says (Athenaeus), is to drink one's wine carefully, not consuming large amounts at one time or gulping the wine without pausing to breathe, as the

---

Heracles to the furthest western edge of the world, where Geryon lived.      [60] For the Seven Wise Men, see 11.463c n. For the story of Bathycles' cup, see D.L. 1.28–9; the prize went to Thales (cf. 11.495d).

[61] For the image, cf. 11.466a with n.

[62] See 11.461d n.

στιν οἰνοποτεῖν, ἀλλὰ τῷ πόματι φάρμακον ὑγείας
ἐγκιρνάναι τὸν λόγον. |

e     Ὅτι διὰ σπουδῆς εἶχον οἱ ἀρχαῖοι ἐγκόλαπτον
ἱστορίαν ἔχειν ἐν ἐκπώμασιν· ἐν ταύτῃ δὲ τῇ τέχνῃ
εὐδοκίμησαν Κίμων καὶ Ἀθηνοκλῆς. ἐχρῶντο δὲ καὶ
λιθοκολλήτοις ἐκπώμασι. Μένανδρος δέ πού φησι καὶ
ποτήριον τορνευτὸν καὶ τορευτά. Ἀντιφάνης·

> ἄλλοι δὲ καὶ δὴ βακχίου παλαιγενοῦς
> ἀφρῷ † σκιὰ καὶ † χρυσοκόλλητον δέπας
> μεστόν, κύκλῳ χορεῦον, ἕλκουσι γνάθοιν
> ὁλκοῖς ἀπαύστοις, παντελῶς ἐστραμμένον |
f     τἄνω κάτω δεικνύντες.

φησὶ πρός τινα Νικόμαχος·

> ὦ <χαῖρε> χρυσόκλυστα καὶ χρυσοῦς ἐμῶν.

Φιλιππίδης·

> τὰ ποτήρι' ἂν ἴδῃς τὰ παρεσκευασμένα,
> ἅπαντα χρυσᾶ, τρόφιμε, νὴ τὸν οὐρανόν,
> ὑπερήφαν', ἀγὼ μὲν παρεξέστην ἰδών·
> κρατῆρες ἀργυροῖ, κάδοι μείζους ἐμοῦ.

    Ὅτι Παρμενίων συγκεφαλαιούμενος ἐν ταῖς Πρὸς
Ἀλέξανδρον Ἐπιστολαῖς τὰ Περσικὰ λάφυρα, ποτη-
782 ρίων, ‖ φησί, χρυσῶν σταθμὸς τάλαντα Βαβυλώνια

---

63 Wilamowitz suggested that a poetic quotation lurks behind
these words.

64 Also mentioned in the catalogue of famous engravers at
11.782b.

65 There were 60 *minas* in an Attic talent, and a Babylonian

Thracians do, but mixing conversation into the drinking,
like a drug intended to keep you healthy.[63]

The ancients were interested in having stories engraved on their drinking vessels; Cimon and Athenocles[64]
were famous for work of this sort. They also used vessels
with inset jewels. Menander (fr. 438) refers somewhere to
a cup produced on a lathe and to those decorated with
relief work. Antiphanes (fr. 234):

> Others use jaws that never cease to work
> to drain a goblet inlaid with gold that dances in a
>     circle
> and is full of ancient-born, Bacchic liquid
> with foam † and a shadow †, and exhibit it turned
> completely upside-down.

Nicomachus (fr. 4) says to someone:

> Hello there, you who vomit up gold-inlaid (cups) and
>     gold . . .

Philippides (fr. 28):

> If you see the cups they've got ready,
> young master—they're all made of gold, by heaven,
> and they're gorgeous; I was knocked out when I saw
>     them.
> Silver mixing-bowls! Wine-jars bigger than me!

Parmenion in his *Letters to Alexander*, totaling up the
spoils taken from the Persians, says: The weight of the gold
cups: 73 Babylonian talents, 52 *minas*.[65] The weight of the

---

talent was 20% larger and thus weighed about 72 pounds (Hdt.
3.89.2; Ael. *VH* 1.22). For Parmenion, see 11.508e n.

ἑβδομήκοντα καὶ τρία, μναῖ πεντήκοντα καὶ δύο. ποτηρίων λιθοκολλήτων σταθμὸς τάλαντα Βαβυλώνια
πεντήκοντα καὶ ἕξ, μναῖ τριάκοντα καὶ τέσσαρες. ἔθος
δ᾽ ἦν πρότερον ἐν τῷ ποτηρίῳ ὕδωρ ἐμβάλλεσθαι, μεθ᾽
ὃ τὸν οἶνον. Ξενοφάνης·

  οὐδέ κεν ἐν κύλικι πρότερον κεράσειέ τις οἶνον
  ἐγχέας, ἀλλ᾽ ὕδωρ καὶ καθύπερθε μέθυ.

Ἀνακρέων·

  φέρ᾽ ὕδωρ φέρ᾽ οἶνον, ὦ παῖ, φέρε <δ᾽>
    ἀνθεμόεντας ἡμὶν
  στεφάνους ἔνεικον, ὡς δὴ πρὸς Ἔρωτα
    πυκταλίζω.

πρὸ δὲ τούτων Ἡσίοδος·

  κρήνης τ᾽ αἰενάου καὶ ἀπορρύτου, ἥ τ᾽ ἀθόλωτος,
  τρὶς ὕδατος προχέειν, τὸ δὲ τέτρατον ἱέμεν οἴνου.

b Θεόφραστος· ἐπεὶ καὶ τὰ περὶ τὴν | κρᾶσιν ἐναντίως
εἶχε τὸ παλαιὸν τῷ νῦν παρ᾽ Ἕλλησιν ὑπάρχοντι· οὐ
γὰρ τὸ ὕδωρ ἐπὶ τὸν οἶνον ἐπέχεον, ἀλλ᾽ ἐπὶ τὸ ὕδωρ
τὸν οἶνον, ὅπως ἐν τῷ πίνειν ὑδαρεστέρῳ χρῶντο τῷ
ποτῷ καὶ τούτου ποιησάμενοι τὴν ἀπόλαυσιν ἧττον
ὀρέγοιντο τοῦ λοιποῦ. καὶ τὸ πλεῖστον δὲ εἰς τοὺς
κοττάβους κατανήλισκον.

Ἔνδοξοι δὲ τορευταὶ Ἀθηνοκλῆς, Κράτης, Στρα-
τόνικος, Μυρμηκίδης ὁ Μιλήσιος, Καλλικράτης ὁ

---

66 Presumably from *On Drunkenness* (the title of the work
having been removed by the Epitomator, like most of the titles in
this section).

cups set with jewels: 56 Babylonian talents, 34 *minas*. It was standard practice in the past to put water in one's cup first, and add the wine afterward. Xenophanes (fr. B 5 West[2]):

> No one would pour wine into his cup first and then
>     mix it; instead, water with wine on top of it.

Anacreon (*PMG* 396):

> Bring water, slave! Bring wine! Come!—bring us
>     garlands
> woven of flowers, so that I can box with Eros!

And before them Hesiod (*Op*. 595–6):

> Pour three parts of water drawn from a spring that
>     flows continually
> without stopping and is clear, and add the fourth part,
>     of wine.

Theophrastus (fr. 571):[66] Since in ancient times the method of mixing wine was the opposite of what prevails among Greeks today. Because they did not pour the water into the wine, but the wine into the water, so that when they were drinking they could consume something more diluted, and so that after they enjoyed this, they would have a diminished appetite for more. They also wasted most of it playing cottabus.[67]

Athenocles,[68] Crates, Stratonicus, Myrmecides of Miletus, Callicrates of Sparta,[69] and Mys were famous en-

---

[67] A drinking-party game that involved throwing one's wine-lees at a target; cf. 11.479c–e with nn.; 15.665b–8f.

[68] Mentioned in a similar context at 11.781e.

[69] Poralla #406.

Λάκων καὶ Μῦς, οὗ εἴδομεν σκύφον Ἡρακλεωτικὸν
τεχνικῶς ἔχοντα Ἰλίου ἐντετορευμένην πόρθησιν,
ἔχοντα ἐπίγραμμα τόδε·

> γραμμὰ Παρρασίοιο, τέχνα Μυός. εἰμὶ δὲ ἔργον
> Ἰλίου αἰπεινᾶς, ἃν ἕλον Αἰακίδαι. |

c    Ὅτι κλεινοὶ λέγονται παρὰ Κρησὶν οἱ ἐρώμενοι.
σπουδὴ δὲ αὐτοῖς παῖδας ἁρπάζειν· καὶ τοῖς καλοῖς
παρ᾽ αὐτοῖς ἄδοξόν ἐστιν ἐραστοῦ μὴ τυχεῖν. καλοῦνται δὲ οἱ ἁρπασθέντες παρασταθέντες. διδόασι δὲ τῷ
ἁρπασθέντι στολὴν καὶ βοῦν καὶ ποτήριον· ἣν καὶ
πρεσβύτεροι γενόμενοι φέρουσιν, ἵνα δῆλοι ὦσι κλεινοὶ γενόμενοι.

> ὁρᾷς δ᾽,[13] ὅταν πίνωσιν ἄνθρωποι, τότε
> πλουτοῦσι, διαπράττουσι, νικῶσιν δίκας,
> εὐδαιμονοῦσιν, ὠφελοῦσι τοὺς φίλους. |

d    αὔξει γὰρ καὶ τρέφει μεγαλύνει τε τὴν ψυχὴν ἡ ἐν τοῖς
πότοις διατριβή, ἀναζωπυροῦσα καὶ ἀνεγείρουσα
μετὰ φρονήσεως τὸν ἑκάστου νοῦν, ὥς φησιν ὁ Πίν-
δαρος·

> ἀνίκ᾽ ἀνθρώπων καματώδεες οἴχονται μέριμναι
> στηθέων ἔξω· πελάγει δ᾽ ἐν πολυχρύσοιο
> πλούτου

---

[13] The traditional text of Aristophanes omits δ᾽ and punctuates
ὁρᾷς;

---

70 For the painter Parrhasius (*PAA* 767505; late 5th/early 4th
century BCE), cf. 12.543c–4a; 15.687b–c. The sculptor Mys is *PAA*
663415.

gravers. I saw a Heracleot *skuphos* produced by the latter that featured a finely engraved Sack of Troy and had the following inscribed upon it (anon. *FGE* 1852–3):

> Parrhasius[70] sketched the design, while Mys did the
> work. I depict events
> at lofty Ilium, which the Aeacidae[71] captured.

On Crete, boys who have adult male lovers are known as *kleinoi*.[72] The Cretans are very interested in kidnapping boys, and it is embarrassing in their country for the good-looking ones not to have an adult lover. The boys who have been kidnapped are known as *parastathentes* ("companions" *vel sim.*). When they kidnap a boy, they give him a robe, an ox, and a cup;[73] after they get older, they still wear the robe, as a way of making it obvious that they are *kleinoi*.

> When people drink, you see, that's when
> they get rich, are successful, win their lawsuits,
> are happy, and help their friends. (Ar. *Eq.* 92–4)

Because spending time drinking expands, nourishes, and enlarges one's soul, by invigorating an individual's mind and waking it up, making him think, as Pindar (fr. 124b.5–8) says:[74]

> when the cares that wear human beings out vanish
> from their breasts. All of us alike swim in a sea

---

[71] I.e. Achilleus and his son Neoptolemus.

[72] Literally "famous ones".

[73] Cf. 11.502b (citing Hermonax).

[74] The four verses that precede these (Pi. fr. 124a) are preserved at 11.480c, where see n.

πάντες ἴσᾳ νέομεν ψευδῆ πρὸς ἀκτάν·
ὃς μὲν ἀχρήμων, ἀφνεὸς τότε, τοὶ δ᾽ αὖ
    πλουτέοντες.

εἶτ᾽ ἐπάγει·

< ... > ἀέξονται φρένας ἀμπελίνοις τόξοις
    δαμέντες.

Ἀγκύλη. ποτήριον πρὸς τὴν τῶν κοττάβων παιδιὰν
χρήσιμον. Κρατῖνος·

πιεῖν δὲ θάνατος οἶνον ἢν ὕδωρ ἐπῇ.
ἀλλ᾽ ἴσον ἴσῳ μάλιστ᾽ ἀκράτου δύο χοᾶς
πίνουσ᾽ ἀπ᾽ ἀγκύλης, ἐπονομάζουσα < ... >, |
ἵησι λάταγας τῷ Κορινθίῳ πέει.

e

καὶ Βακχυλίδης·

        εὖτε
τὴν ἀπ᾽ ἀγκύλης ἵησι < ... > τοῖς νεανίαις,
λευκὸν ἀντείνασα πῆχυν.

ἐντεῦθεν ἐννοοῦμεν τοὺς παρ᾽ Αἰσχύλῳ ἀγκυλητοὺς
κοττάβους. λέγονται δὲ καὶ δόρατα ἀγκυλητὰ καὶ
μεσάγκυλα ἄλλα ἀπὸ ἀγκύλης ἤτοι τῆς δεξιᾶς χειρός.
καὶ ἡ κύλιξ δὲ ἀγκύλη[14] διὰ τὸ ἐπαγκυλοῦν τὴν δεξιὰν

---

[14] ἡ ἀγκύλη CE: ἡ del. Kaibel

---

[75] This quotation must originally have served to introduce
(and justify) the long catalogue of cups that makes up most of the
rest of this Book.

[76] This is a misinterpretation, as the passages cited below—in
all of which the word is more easily taken as having its normal
sense "bend of the wrist"—make clear. For the drinking-game
known as cottabus, see 11.479c–e with nn.; 15.665b–8f.

of gilded wealth toward a treacherous coast;
he who is now poor was once rich, while the wealthy
    for their part . . .

After which he continues (fr. 124b.9):

will grow haughty, mastered by the grapevine's
    arrows.[75]

*Ankulē*. A cup used to play cottabus.[76] Cratinus (fr. 299):[77]

It would kill her to drink wine with water in it.
Instead, she drinks two pitchers of strong stuff, mixed
one-to-one; and she calls out his name and tosses her
    wine-lees
from her *ankulē* in honor of the Corinthian dick.

Also Bacchylides (fr. 17):[78]

    when
she extends her white forearm and makes
the from-the-*ankulē* toss for the young men.

On this basis we can make sense of the Aeschylean (fr. 179.4)[79] *ankulētoi kottaboi*. Certain spears are referred to as *ankulēta*, while others are *mesankula*, the words being derived from *ankulē* in the sense "right hand".[80] The cup

---

[77] The subject is Stheneboea, who is in love with the Corinthian stranger Bellerophon; cf. 10.427d–e (quoting the passage from Euripides from which Cratinus' fourth verse is adapted) with n.

[78] Quoted also, in slightly more complete form, at 15.667c.

[79] From a fragment quoted at 15.667c–d.

[80] In fact, the adjectives are derived from *ankulē* in the sense "throwing-thong"; cf. 12.534e with n.

χεῖρα ἐν τῇ προέσει. ἦν γὰρ τοῖς παλαιοῖς πεφρον-
τισμένον καλῶς καὶ εὐσχημόνως κότταβον προΐεσθαι·
καὶ οἱ πολλοὶ ἐπὶ τούτῳ μᾶλλον ἐφρόνουν μέγα ἢ ἐπὶ
τῷ εὖ ἀκοντίζειν. ὠνομάσθη οὖν ἀπὸ τοῦ τῆς χειρὸς
σχηματισμοῦ, ὃν ποιούμενοι εὐρύθμως ἐρρίπτουν εἰς
f   τὸ κοττάβιον. | καὶ οἴκους δὲ ἐπιτηδείους κατεσκεύ-
αζον εἰς ταύτην τὴν παιδιάν.

Ὅτι παρὰ Τιμαχίδᾳ αἰακὶς ἡ κύλιξ καλεῖται.
Ἄκατος. ποτήριον ἐοικὸς πλοίῳ. Ἐπικράτης·

κατάβαλλε τἀκάτεια, ⟨καὶ τὰ⟩ κιλίκια
αἴρου τὰ μείζω, κεὐθὺ τοῦ καρχησίου
ἄνελκε τὴν γραῦν, τὴν νέαν δ' ἐπουρίσας
πλήρωσον, εὐτρεπῆ τε τὸν κοντὸν ποοῦ
καὶ τοὺς κάλως ἔκλυε καὶ χάλα πόδα. ||

783   Ἄωτον. παρὰ Κυπρίοις τὸ ἔκπωμα, ὡς Πάμφιλος.
Φιλητᾶς δὲ ποτήριον οὖς οὐκ ἔχον.
Ἄροκλον. ἡ φιάλη παρὰ τῷ Κολοφωνίῳ Νικάνδρῳ.
Ἄλεισον καὶ δέπας τὸ αὐτό. Ὅμηρος ἐν Ὀδυσσείᾳ
περὶ Πεισιστράτου·

ἐν δ' οἶνον ἔχευε

χρυσείῳ δέπαϊ.

εἶτα παρακατιὼν τὸ αὐτό·

---

81 Cf. 11.479d–e (material very similar to this and what follows, drawn from Hegesander of Delphi).
82 Literally "skiff". Cf. 11.702a.
83 *akateia* (punning on *akatos* in the sense "drinking cup").
84 *karchēsion*, another cup-name (11.474e–5c).
85 The fragment is omitted by Schmidt.
86 As if the word were formed from a privative *alpha* + *ous*

(*kulix*) as well is called an *ankulē* because the right hand
bends at the wrist (*epankuloun*) during the throw. For the
ancients had given careful thought to how to throw cottabus gracefully and elegantly; many people were prouder of
this than of throwing a javelin well.[81] (The cup) thus got its
name from the motion of the hand produced when they
tossed (its contents) at the target in a smooth motion. They
also built rooms specifically for this game.

A cup (*kulix*) is referred to as an *aiakis* in Timachidas
(fr. 20 Blinkenberg).

*Akatos*.[82] A cup that resembles a boat. Epicrates (fr. 9):

Drop the small sails,[83] and raise the larger ones
made of goat-hair! Hoist the old woman
straight up the masthead,[84] fill the younger one up,
and full speed ahead! Get the pole ready,
let out the reefs, and ease off on the sheets!

*Aōton*. A Cyprian term for a drinking vessel, according
to Pamphilus.[85] Philetas (fr. 2 Dettori = fr. 30 Spanoudakis) describes it as a cup that lacks a handle.[86]

*Aroklon*. Used by Nicander of Colophon (fr. 129
Schneider) to refer to a bowl (*phialē*).

*Aleison* and *depas* ("goblet") describe the same object.
Homer in the *Odyssey* (3.40–1), referring to Pisistratus:

> He poured wine into
a gold *depas*.

Then further on, in regard to the same vessel (*Od.* 3.50):

("ear, handle")—as it in fact almost certainly is. Cf. 11.483a (citing
Simaristus, who may thus be Philetas' source); Hsch. α 8997,
9000; Suda α 2860.

251

τοὔνεκα σοὶ < ... > δώσω χρύσειον ἄλεισον.

καὶ ἑξῆς τὸ αὐτὸ πάλιν·

δῶκε δὲ Τηλεμάχῳ καλὸν δέπας.

φησὶν οὖν Ἀσκληπιάδης ὁ Μυρλεανός· δοκεῖ μοι
φιαλῶδες εἶναι τὸ δέπας· σπένδουσι γὰρ ἐν αὐτῷ. |
b λέγει γοῦν Ὅμηρος δέπας, δι᾽ οὗ Διὶ μόνῳ σπένδεσκεν
Ἀχιλλεύς. καλεῖται δὲ δέπας ἤτοι ὅτι δίδοται πᾶσι
τοῖς σπένδειν βουλομένοις εἴτε καὶ τοῖς πίνειν, ἢ ὅτι
δύο ὦπας εἶχε· ταῦτα δὲ ἂν εἴη τὰ ὦτα. τὸ δὲ ἄλεισον
ἤτοι ἀπὸ τοῦ ἄγαν λεῖον εἶναι ἢ ὅτι ἁλίζεται ἐν αὐτῷ
τὸ ὑγρόν. ὅτι δὲ δύο ὦτα εἶχε δῆλον·

ἦ τοι ὁ καλὸν ἄλεισον ἀναιρήσεσθαι ἔμελλε,
χρύσεον ἄμφωτον.

ἀμφικύπελλον δὲ λέγων αὐτὸ οὐδὲν ἄλλο σημαίνει ἢ
ὅτι ἦν ἀμφίκυρτον. Σιληνὸς δὲ ἀμφικύπελλόν φησι τὸ
μὴ ἔχον ὦτα. ἄλλοι δὲ τὴν ἀμφὶ ἀντὶ τῆς περὶ εἶναι, ἵν᾽
ἦ περίποτον, τὸ πανταχόθεν πίνειν ἐπιτήδειον. Παρ-
c θένιος δὲ διὰ τὸ περικεκυρτῶσθαι τὰ ὠτάρια· | κυφὸν
γὰρ εἶναι τὸ κυρτόν. Ἀνίκητος δὲ τὸ μὲν κύπελλόν

---

87 The subject at this point is Athena disguised as Mentor.

88 Presumably in *On Nestor's Cup* (a vessel described by
Homer specifically as a *depas*), cited at length at 11.488a–93c.

89 Quoted at 11.781c.

90 Cf. *EM* p. 61.32–5, where a closely related view is assigned
to Apollonius the son (or student) of Archibius.

91 These are all false etymologies.

92 The adjective is used exclusively in Homer of the *depas*. A
jumble of closely related material is preserved at 11.482e–3a,
where *Od.* 22.9–10 is quoted again.

I will accordingly give you the gold *aleison*.

And shortly thereafter, referring again to the same vessel (*Od.* 3.63):[87]

And she gave Telemachus the beautiful *depas*.

Asclepiades of Myrlea[88] accordingly says: In my opinion, a *depas* resembles a *phialē* ("bowl"); because they use it to pour libations. Homer (*Il.* 16.225–7)[89] refers, for example, to the *depas* Achilleus used to pour libations for Zeus alone. The vessel is referred to as a *depas* either because it is offered to everyone (*didotai pasi*) who wants to make a libation or have a drink, or because it had two faces (*duo ōpas*), which is to say two handles (*ōtas*). It is referred to as an *aleison* either because it is extremely shallow (*agan leion*),[90] or because the liquid is collected (*halizetai . . . hugron*) in it.[91] That it had two handles is apparent (*Od.* 22.9–10):

He was in fact just about to lift a beautiful gold
two-handled *aleison*.

When he refers to it as *amphikupellos*[92] (e.g. *Od.* 3.63), he means specifically that both ends were hollow (*amphikurtos*).[93] Silenus, however, claims that a vessel that is *amphikupellos* lacks handles, while other authorities assert that *amphi-* is used in place of *peri-*, making the compound equivalent to *peripotos*, i.e. "suitable for drinking from from every side". Parthenius (says) that the adjective reflects the fact that the handles are convex; because *kuphos* means "convex". Whereas Anicetus claims that *kupellos*

[93] Cf. 11.482e with n.

φησι φιάλην εἶναι, τὸ δ' ἀμφικύπελλον ὑπερφίαλον,
τὸ ὑπερήφανον καὶ καλόν. εἰ μὴ ἄρα τὸ ποικίλον τῇ
κατασκευῇ ἄλεισον θέλει τις ἀκούειν, ἔξω λειότητος
ὄν. Πείσανδρος δέ φησιν Ἡρακλέα Τελαμῶνι τῆς ἐπὶ
Ἴλιον στρατείας ἀριστεῖον ἄλεισον δοῦναι.

Ὅτι ἐστὶ ποτήριον Ἀμαλθείας κέρας καὶ ἐνιαυτὸς
καλούμενον. |

d    Ἄμφωτις.[15] ξύλινον ποτήριον, ᾧ χρῆσθαι τοὺς
ἀγροίκους Φιλητᾶς φησι, τοὺς ἀμέλγοντας εἰς αὐτὸ
καὶ οὕτως πίνοντας.

Ἄμυστις. καλεῖται μὲν οὕτω πόσις τις, ἣν ἔστιν
ἀπνευστὶ πίνειν μὴ μύσαντα. καλοῦσι δ' οὕτω καὶ τὰ
ποτήρια, ἀφ' ὧν ἔστι πιεῖν εὐμαρῶς. καὶ τὸ ῥῆμα δὲ
ἐξημύστισε φασί, τὸ ἐφ' ἓν πνεῦμα πιεῖν, ὡς ὁ κωμικὸς
Πλάτων·

λύσας † δὲ ἀργὴν † στάμνον εὐώδους ποτοῦ
ἵησιν εὐθὺς κύλικος εἰς κοῖλον κύτος·

[15] Hsch. α 4166 has the word (followed by a very similar
definition) in the form ἄμφωξις.

---

[94] As if the word were formed from privative-*alpha* + *leios*
("smooth, plain"). These are all false etymologies.

[95] I.e. during Heracles' expedition against the city, which
ended with the death of Priam's father Laomedon. Telamon (the
father of Salaminian Ajax) entered Troy before Heracles during
the sack, and Heracles was so insulted that he almost killed him
([Apollod.] *Bib*. 2.6.4). Cf. *PMG* 899 (quoted at 15.695c).

[96] An error, more likely by the Epitomator than by Athenaeus
himself, who apparently cited Callixeinus' mention at 5.198a (in a
description of an extraordinary procession organized by Ptolemy

is a term for a *phialē* ("bowl"), and that *amphikupellos* is equivalent to *hyperphialos* ("proud, overbearing"), i.e. "magnificent and beautiful". Alternatively, one might choose to take *aleison* to mean an elaborately crafted object, which thus cannot be referred to as *leios*.[94] Pisander (fr. 11 Bernabé) claims that Heracles gave an *aleison* to Telamon as a prize for his outstanding service during the expedition against Troy.[95]

There is a type of cup referred to as an Amaltheia's horn and an *eniautos* ("year").[96]

*Amphōtis*. According to Philetas (fr. 1 Dettori = fr. 29 Spanoudakis), a wooden cup used by peasants, who milk into it and therefore drink from it.

*Amustis*. This is a term for a style of drinking, specifically when someone drinks with his mouth wide open[97] without stopping to take a breath. Cups from which one can drink easily are also referred to this way. In addition, people use the term *exēmustise*, meaning "to drink without pausing for a breath", for example the comic author Plato (fr. 205):

> After he opens a † white † cask of fragrant drink,
> he pours it straight into the cup's hollow cavity.

II Philadelphus) of a man who "was carrying a golden horn of Amaltheia; he was called 'The Year'." Cf. 11.472a, 474e, 483e–f. Amaltheia's horn (used to feed the infant Zeus) was much like our horn of plenty (e.g. Cratin. fr. 261 with K–A ad loc.; adesp. com. fr. 708; Anacr. *PMG* 361.1–2); cf. 11.497c, 503b; 12.542a; 14.643a.

[97] *mē musanta*, with *amustis* thus understood to be derived from privative-*alpha* + *muō* ("close one's mouth").

ἔπειτ᾽ ἄκρατον κοὐ τεταργανωμένον
ἔπινε κἀξημύστισεν. |

e  ἔπινον δὲ τὴν ἄμυστιν μετὰ μέλους, μεμετρημένου
πρὸς ὠκύτητα χρόνου. ὡς Ἀμειψίας·

(Α.) αὔλει μοι μέλος,
σὺ δ᾽ ᾆδε πρὸς τήνδ᾽· ἐκπίομαι δ᾽ ἐγὼ τέως.
(Β.) αὔλει σύ, καὶ <σὺ> τὴν ἄμυστιν λάμβανε.
"οὐ χρὴ πόλλ᾽ ἔχειν θνητὸν ἄνθρωπον,
ἀλλ᾽ ἐρᾶν καὶ κατεσθίειν· σὺ δὲ κάρτα φείδῃ."

Ἀντιγονίς. ἔκπωμα ἀπὸ τοῦ βασιλέως Ἀντιγόνου,
ὡς ἀπὸ Σελεύκου Σελευκὶς καὶ ἀπὸ Προυσίου Πρου-
σιάς[16]. |

f  Ἀναφαία. ἡ θερμοποτὶς παρὰ Κρησίν.
Ἀρύβαλλος. ποτήριον κάτωθεν εὐρύτερον, ἄνω δὲ
συνηγμένον, ὡς τὰ συσπαστὰ βαλάντια, ἃ καὶ αὐτὰ
διὰ τὴν ὁμοιότητα ἀρυβάλλους τινὲς καλοῦσιν. Ἀριστοφάνης Ἱππεῦσι·

κατασπένδειν κατὰ τῆς κεφαλῆς ἀρυβάλλῳ
ἀμβροσίαν.

οὐ πόρρω δέ ἐστι τοῦ ἀρυστίχου ὁ ἀρύβαλλος· ἀπὸ
τοῦ ἀρύτειν καὶ βάλλειν. λέγουσι δὲ καὶ πρόχουν
ἄρυστιν. Σοφοκλῆς·

---

16 Προυσιάς Schweighäuser (cf. 11.475f): προυσίς CE

---

98 The quotation = anon. *PMG* 913; but the final phrase may
be the speaker's own addition to it.
99 Cf. 11.497f (citing Apollodorus of Athens).
100 An unlikely but not impossible etymology.

Then he began to drink unmixed wine that lacked
    any taste
of vinegar, and drained the cup without pausing for a
    breath (*exēmustisen*).

They drank this way to music, keeping track of who drank
the fastest. For example Amipsias (fr. 21):

> (A.) Play some pipe-music for me!
> And you—sing along with her! Meanwhile, I'm going
>     to empty my cup.
> (B.) You—play the pipes! And you—get the *amustis*!
> "A mortal creature doesn't need much—
> just making love and eating a lot. But you're really
>     cheap!"[98]

*Antigonis.* A drinking vessel named after King Antigonus, in the same way that a *Seleukis* is named after
Seleucus, and a *Prousias* is named after Prousius.[99]

*Anaphaia.* A Cretan term for a cup used for hot drinks.

*Aruballos.* A cup that is wider at the bottom and narrower at the top, like the type of purses that are closed
with a drawstring, which some authorities refer to as *aru-
balloi* because of the resemblance. Aristophanes in
*Knights* (1094–5):

> and to be using an *aruballos* to pour ambrosia
> over your head.

An *aruballos* is not much different from an *arustichos*;
the word is formed from *arutein* ("to draw, dip [liquid]")
and *ballein* ("to throw").[100] People also refer to a pitcher
(*prochous*) as an *arustis*. Sophocles (fr. 764):

κακῶς σὺ πρὸς θεῶν ὀλουμένη, ‖
784    ἢ τὰς ἀρύστεις ὧδ' ἔχουσ' ἐκώμασας.

ἐστὶ δὲ καὶ πόλις Ἰώνων Ἄρυστις.

Ἀργυρίς. εἶδος ποτηρίου, οὐ μόνον ἐξ ἀργύρου.
Ἀναξίλας·

   < ... > καὶ πίνειν ἐξ ἀργυρίδων χρυσῶν.

Βατιάκιον, λαβρώνιος, τραγέλαφος, πρίστις. ποτηρίων ὀνόματα. Περσικὴ δὲ φιάλη ἡ βατιάκη. Ἀλεξάνδρου δὲ τοῦ βασιλέως ἐν ταῖς Ἐπιστολαῖς ταῖς Πρὸς
τοὺς Ἐν τῇ Ἀσίᾳ Σατράπας φέρεταί τις ἐπιστολὴ ἐν ᾗ
ταῦτα γέγραπται· βατιάκαι ἀργυραῖ κατάχρυσοι
τρεῖς. κόνδυα ἀργυρᾶ ἑκατὸν καὶ ἑβδομήκοντα καὶ ἕξ·
τούτων ἐπίχρυσα τριάκοντα καὶ τρία. τισιγίτης ἀργυ-
b  ροῦς εἷς. | μύστροι ἀργυροῖ κατάχρυσοι τριάκοντα καὶ
δύο. λαγυνοθήκη ἀργυρᾶ μία. οἰνοφόρον βαρβαρικὸν
ἀργυροῦν ποικίλον ἕν. ἄλλα ποτήρια παντοδαπὰ
μικρὰ εἴκοσι καὶ ἐννέα, ῥυτὰ[17] καὶ βατιάκαι Λυκιουργεῖς ἐπίχρυσοι καὶ θυμιατήρια καὶ τρυβλία.

Βῆσσα. ποτήριον παρ' Ἀλεξανδρεῦσι πλατύτερον
ἐκ τῶν κάτω μερῶν, ἐστενωμένον ἄνωθεν.

Βαυκαλίς. ἐν Ἀλεξανδρείᾳ καὶ αὕτη, ὡς Σώπατρος
ὁ παρῳδός· † βαυκαλὶς ἡ τετράκυκλος †. καὶ πάλιν·

νᾶμα μελισσῶν ἡδὺ μὲν ὄρθρου
καταβαυκαλίσαι τοῖς ὑπὸ πολλῆς
κραιπαλοβόσκου δίψης κατόχοις. |

[17] ἄλλα ποτήρια μικρὰ ῥυτὰ CE: ἄλλα ποτήρια μικρὰ del.
Wilamowitz

You goddamned bitch—
wandering the streets drunk holding your *arusteis*
    like this!

There is also a city in Ionia known as Arustis.

*Arguris.* A type of cup, not made exclusively of silver
(*arguros*). Anaxilas (fr. 39):

    and to drink from gold *argurides*.

*Batiakion, labrōnios, tragelaphos, pristis.* Names of
cups.[101] A *batiakē* is a Persian bowl (*phialē*). A letter from
King Alexander preserved in his *Letters to the Satraps in
Asia* contains the following passage: Gilded silver *batiakai*:
three. Silver *kondua*: 176, 33 of them gilded. One silver
*tisigitēs*. Gilded silver spoons: 32. One silver *lagynos*-case.
One elaborately decorated silver barbarian-style wine-jar.
Other small cups of all sorts: 29, including *rhyta*, gilded
Lycian-made *batiakai*, incense-burners, and bowls.

*Bēssa.* An Alexandrian term for a cup that is wider
toward the bottom and narrower on top.[102]

*Baukalis.* This is another Alexandrian vessel, for example the parodist Sopater (fr. 24, unmetrical): † the four-
ringed *baukalis* †. Again (fr. 25):

    It's nice, first thing in the morning, to *baukalis*-down
    a bee-stream[103] as a way of dealing with the
        oppressive
    thirst that results from an all-night drinking party,

---

[101] In origin this must be a gloss on Diph. fr. 81.1 (quoted at
11.484e).    [102] Perhaps to be connected with the drinking-
horn shaped like the Egyptian dancer Bēsas mentioned in the
epigram preserved at 11.497d.    [103] I.e. some honey.

c  κατασκευάζουσι δέ, φησίν, οἱ ἐν Ἀλεξανδρείᾳ τὴν
ὕαλον μεταρρυθμίζοντες πολλαῖς καὶ ποικίλαις ἰδέαις
ποτηρίων, παντὸς τοῦ πανταχόθεν κατακομιζομένου
κεράμου τὴν ἰδέαν μιμούμενοι. Λύσιππον τὸν ἀνδρι-
αντοποιόν φασι Κασάνδρῳ χαριζόμενον, ὅτε συν-
ῴκισε τὴν Κασάνδρειαν, φιλοδοξοῦντι καὶ βουλομένῳ
ἴδιόν τινα εὑρέσθαι κέραμον διὰ τὸ πολὺν ἐξάγεσθαι
τὸν Μενδαῖον οἶνον ἐκ τῆς πόλεως, φιλοτιμηθῆναι καὶ
πολλὰ καὶ παντοδαπὰ γένη παραθέμενον κεραμίων ἐξ
ἑκάστου ἀποπλασάμενον ἴδιον ποιῆσαι πλάσμα. |

d  Βῖκος. Ξενοφῶν Ἀναβάσεως πρώτῳ· Κῦρος ἔπεμπε
βίκους οἴνου ἡμιδεεῖς. ἐστὶ δὲ φιαλῶδες ποτήριον
κατὰ τὸν Παριανὸν Πολυδεύκην.

Βομβυλιός. θηρίκλειον Ῥοδιακόν, οὗ περὶ τῆς ἰδέας
Σωκράτης φησίν· οἱ μὲν ἐκ φιάλης πίνοντες ὅσον
θέλουσι τάχιστ᾽ ἀπαλλαγήσονται, οἱ δ᾽ ἐκ βομβυλιοῦ
κατὰ μικρὸν στάζοντος ⟨ . . . ⟩ ἐστὶ δὲ καὶ ζῷόν τι.

Βρομάδες. ἔκπωμα ὅμοιον τοῖς μακροτέροις τῶν
σκύφων.

Γραμματικόν. ἔκπωμα τὸ γράμματα ἔχον ἐγκε-
χαραγμένα. Ἄλεξις·[18]

_____

[18] Manuscript A resumes at this point.

_____

[104] Cassander founded Cassandreia in 316 BCE (D.S. 19.52),
and if this story is not apocryphal, it must belong at the very end of
Lysippus' career. Mendaean wine was one of the most famous ancient varieties (e.g. Eub. fr. 123.4, quoted at 1.23b).

[105] In fact, a *bikos* is a transport-jar most often used for wine,
as the quotation from Xenophon makes clear.

The inhabitants of Alexandria, (Athenaeus) reports, work with glass, transforming it into cups of a wide variety of shapes and imitating the look of all the types of pottery imported from every corner of the world. They say that the sculptor Lysippus did a favor for Cassander when Cassander founded Cassandreia and wanted to establish his reputation by inventing a distinctive pottery shape, since he was exporting Mendaean wine from his city on a massive scale;[104] Lysippus got hard to work, assembled a large number of pots of various sorts, made casts of them all, and produced a distinctive form.

*Bikos*. Xenophon in Book I (9.25) of the *Anabasis*: Cyrus used to send *bikoi* half-full of wine. According to Polydeuces of Parium, this is a cup that resembles a *phialē* ("bowl").[105]

*Bombulios*. A Rhodian Thericleian[106] (cup), about whose shape Socrates (Antisth. *SSR* V A 64) says: People who drink as much as they want from a bowl (*phialē*) will finish sooner, whereas those who drink from a *bombulios*, whose contents trickle out slowly . . . The word also refers to a living creature.[107]

*Bromiades*.[108] A drinking vessel that resembles the larger types of *skuphoi*.

*Grammatikon*. A drinking vessel with letters (*grammata*) engraved on it. Alexis (fr. 272):

---

[106] For Thericleian pottery, see 11.470d–2d.
[107] A bumblebee.
[108] Cognate with the divine name Bromius (i.e. Dionysus).

466d   (Α.) τὴν ὄψιν εἴπω τοῦ ποτηρίου γέ σοι
πρώτιστον. ἦν γὰρ στρογγύλον, μικρὸν πάνυ,
παλαιόν, ὦτα συντεθλασμένον σφόδρα, |

e   ἔχον κύκλῳ τε γράμματ'. (Β.) ἆρά γ' ἔνδεκα
χρυσᾶ, Διὸς Σωτῆρος; (Α.) οὐκ ἄλλου μὲν οὖν.

τοιοῦτον εἴδομεν ποτήριον γραμματικὸν ἀνακείμενον
ἐν Καπύῃ τῆς Καμπανίας τῇ Ἀρτέμιδι, ἀργυροῦν, ἐκ
τῶν Ὁμηρικῶν ἐπῶν κατεσκευασμένον καὶ ἐντετυπω-
μένα ἔχον τὰ ἔπη χρυσοῖς γράμμασιν, ὡς τὸ Νέστορος ὄν. Ἀχαιὸς δ' ὁ τραγικὸς ἐν Ὀμφάλῃ καὶ αὐτὸς
περὶ γραμματικοῦ ποτηρίου ποιεῖ τοὺς σατύρους τάδε
λέγοντας· |

f   ὁ δὲ σκύφος με τοῦ θεοῦ καλεῖ πάλαι
τὸ γράμμα φαίνων· δέλτ', ἰῶτα καὶ τρίτον
οὗ, νῦ τό τ' ῦ πάρεστι, κοὐκ ἀπουσίαν
ἐκ τοὐπέκεινα σὰν τό τ' οὖ κηρύσσεται.

ἐν τούτοις λείπει τὸ ῦ στοιχεῖον, ἐπεὶ πάντες οἱ ἀρχαῖοι τῷ ō ἀπεχρῶντο οὐ μόνον ἐφ' ἧς νῦν τάττεται ‖
467 δυνάμεως, ἀλλὰ καὶ ὅτε τὴν δίφθογγον ἔδει σημαίνειν
διὰ τοῦ ō μόνου γράφουσι. παραπλησίως δὲ καὶ τὸ ē
γράφουσιν καὶ ὅταν καθ' αὑτὸ μόνον ἐκφωνῆται καὶ

---

109 Cf. 11.489b–c (from the extended discussion of Nestor's
cup), where the same information is expressed, but in almost
entirely different words.

110 A less complete version of the first verse is quoted also at
11.498e.

111 Spelling ΔΙΟΝΤΣΟ ("[Property] of Dionysus"; see below).

## BOOK ELEVEN

(A.) First of all, let me tell you what the cup
looked like. It was globular; quite small;
old; its handles were badly damaged;
and it had letters around the exterior. (B.) Eleven
        letters?
of gold? saying "Property of Zeus the Savior?" (A.)
        That's the name.

I saw a *grammatikon* cup of this type dedicated to Artemis
in Capua in Campania; it was made of silver, the design was
inspired by the Homeric poems, and it had the verses engraved on it in gold letters that identified it as Nestor's
property.[109] The tragic author Achaeus in *Omphale* (*TGrF*
20 F 33)[110] also represents the satyrs as saying the following about a *grammatikon* cup:

> The god's *skuphos* has been summoning me for a long
>         time now
> by showing me its inscription: *delta*; *iota*; third comes
> *ou*; *nu* and *u* are there; and after them
> *san* and *ou* announce their presence.[111]

The letter *upsilon* is missing in this passage, since the
ancients universally did not use the letter *omicron* only
for the purpose it serves today, but use *omicron* alone
when they want to indicate the diphthong.[112] Similarly,
they write the letter *epsilon* both when the vowel is pro-

---

[112] I.e. the combination of *omicron-upsilon* (which is what one
would expect as the genitive ending of "Dionysus", rather than the
bare *omicron*—which the speaker of this fragment refers to mis-
leadingly as an "*ou*").

ὅταν συζευγνυμένου τοῦ ῑ. κἂν τοῖς προκειμένοις οὖν
οἱ σάτυροι τοῦ Διονύσου τὴν τελευταίαν συλλαβὴν
διὰ τοῦ ō μόνου ὡς βραχέος ἐγκεχαραγμένου ἐδήλω-
σαν ὅτι συνυπακούεσθαι δεῖ καὶ τὸ ῡ, ἵν᾽ ᾖ Διονύσου.
τὸ δὲ σὰν ἀντὶ τοῦ σίγμα Δωρικῶς εἰρήκασιν· οἱ γὰρ
μουσικοί, καθάπερ πολλάκις Ἀριστόξενός φησι, τὸ
b   σίγμα λέγειν | παρῃτοῦντο διὰ τὸ σκληρόστομον εἶναι
καὶ ἀνεπιτήδειον αὐλῷ. τὸ δὲ ρ̄ διὰ τὸ εὔκολον πολλάκις παραλαμβάνουσι. καὶ τοὺς ἵππους τοὺς τὸ σ̄
ἐγκεχαραγμένον ἔχοντας σαμφόρας καλοῦσιν. Ἀριστοφάνης Νεφέλαις·

   οὔτ᾽ αὐτὸς οὔθ᾽ ὁ ζύγιος οὔθ᾽ ὁ σαμφόρας.

καὶ Πίνδαρος δέ φησι·

   πρὶν μὲν ἕρπε σχοινοτένειά τ᾽ ἀοιδὰ ‹ ... ›
   καὶ τὸ σὰν κίβδηλον ‹ ... › ἀπὸ στομάτων.[19]

μνημονεύει δὲ τοῦ γραμματικοῦ ἐκπώματος ὡς οὕτως
καλουμένου Εὔβουλος ἐν Νεοττίδι οὕτως· |

c   (A.) μισῶ κάκιστον γραμματικὸν ἔκπωμ᾽ ἀεί·
   ἀτὰρ ὡς ὅμοιον οὑμὸς υἱὸς ᾤχετο
   ἔχων φιάλιον τῷδε. (B.) πολλὰ γίνεται
   ὅμοια.

[19] The text is also preserved in a papyrus, which has ἀοιδὰ
διθυράμβων and κίβδηλον ἀνθρώποισιν ἀπὸ στομάτων.

---

[113] What Aristoxenus meant, however, was that the poets tried
to avoid using the *sound* represented by the letter *sigma/san*, not
that they tried to avoid saying "*sigma*". On the poets' occasional
attempts to compose asigmatically, see 10.455b–d.
[114] Cf. 10.448d (where the passage is merely alluded to),

nounced by itself and when it forms a diphthong with *iōta*. In the passage cited above, therefore, the satyrs made it clear in regard to the final syllable of the genitive form of *Dionusos* that, although the inscription features only what would appear to be the short vowel *omicron*, the letter *upsilon* needs to be heard along with it, yielding *Dionusou* ("[Property] of Dionysus"). They use the Doric *san* rather than *sigma*; because, as Aristoxenus notes repeatedly (fr. 87 Wehrli), the poets tried to avoid saying "*sigma*", since the letter is difficult to pronounce and ill-suited to the pipes.[113] They frequently incorporate *rho*, on the other hand, because it is easily pronounced. They refer to horses with a *sigma*-brand as *samphoroi* ("*san*-bearers"). Aristophanes in *Clouds* (122):

> neither you yourself, nor your yoke-horse, nor your
>     *samphoras*.

Pindar (fr. 70b.1–3, lacunose)[114] as well says:

> Before an extended song . . . and the false
> *san* emerged . . . from their mouths.

Eubulus in *Neottis* (fr. 69) refers to a *grammatikon* drinking vessel specifically by this name, as follows:

> (A.) I've always hated a nasty *grammatikon* drinking
>     vessel.
> But the little bowl my son had when he left
> was a lot like this one! (B.) Lots of them look
> the same.

455b–c (quoting a slightly different, but still asigmatic version of the lines).

265

Γυάλας. Φιλητᾶς ἐν Ἀτάκτοις Μεγαρέας οὕτω
φησὶ καλεῖν τὰ ποτήρια, γυάλας. Παρθένιος δ᾽ ὁ τοῦ
Διονυσίου ἐν πρώτῳ Περὶ τῶν Παρὰ τοῖς Ἱστορικοῖς
Λέξεων Ζητουμένων φησί· γυάλας. ποτηρίου εἶδος, ὡς
Μαρσύας γράφει ὁ ἱερεὺς τοῦ Ἡρακλέους οὕτως· ὅταν
εἰσίῃ ὁ βασιλεὺς εἰς τὴν πόλιν, ὑπαντᾶν οἴνου πλήρη
γυάλαν ἔχοντά τινα, τὸν δὲ λαβόντα σπένδειν. |

d    Δῖνος.[20] Διονύσιος[21] ὁ Σινωπεὺς ἐν Σῳζούσῃ καταλέγων ὀνόματα ποτηρίων μνημονεύει καὶ τούτου λέγων οὕτως·

(Α.) ὅσα δ᾽ ἐστὶν εἴδη Θηρικλείων τῶν καλῶν,
γυάλαι δικότυλοι, τρικότυλοι, δῖνος μέγας
χωρῶν μετρητήν, κυμβίον, σκύφοι, ῥυτά.
(Β.) ποτήρι᾽ ἡ γραῦς, ἄλλο δ᾽ οὐδὲ ἓν βλέπει.

Κλεάνθης δ᾽ ὁ φιλόσοφος ἐν τῷ Περὶ Μεταλήψεως |
e    ἀπὸ τῶν κατασκευασάντων φησὶν ὀνομασθῆναι τήν τε
Θηρίκλειον κύλικα καὶ τὴν Δεινιάδα. Σέλευκος δ᾽ εἰπὼν ἐκπώματος εἶναι γένος τὸν δῖνον παρατίθεται
Στράττιδος ἐκ Μηδείας·

οἶσθ᾽ ᾧ προσέοικεν, ὦ Κρέων, τὸ βρέγμα σου;
ἐγᾦδα· δίνῳ περικάτω τετραμμένῳ.

Ἀρχέδικος δ᾽ ἐν Διαμαρτάνοντι παράγων οἰκέτην τινὰ
περὶ ἑταιρίδων διαλεγόμενόν φησι·

20 Δεῖνος A (as all three manuscripts throughout this section)
21 ὅτι καὶ τοῦτο ποτηρίου ὄνομα Διονύσιος A: ὅτι . . .
ὄνομα del. Dindorf

---

115 Sc. of Macedon.
116 Quoted again, at greater length, at 11.471b.

*Gualas*. Philetas in the *Miscellany* (fr. 3 Dettori = fr. 31 Spanoudakis) says that this is a Megarian term for cups, *gualas*. Dionysius' student Parthenius says in Book I of *On Problematic Words in the Historians: Gualas*. A type of cup, as Marsyas the priest of Heracles (*FGrH* 135/6 F 21) writes in the following passage: Whenever the king[115] enters the city, someone is to meet him holding a *gualas* full of wine, and he is to take it and pour a libation.

*Dinos*. Dionysius of Sinope in *The Girl Who Was Rescued* (fr. 5) offers a list of names of cups and mentions this one, saying the following:

(A.) All the types of nice Thericleian cups:
*gualai* with a capacity of two *kotuloi*, or three; a big
    *dinos*
that could hold an amphora; a *kumbion*; *skuphoi*;
    drinking horns.
(B.) The old woman's got an eye for cups—but
    nothing else!

The philosopher Cleanthes in his *On Substitution* (fr. 591, *SVF* i.133)[116] says that Thericleian cups and *Deiniades* got their names from the people who manufactured them. Seleucus (fr. 48 Müller) first identifies the *dinos* as a type of drinking vessel, and then cites a passage from Strattis' *Medea* (fr. 35):

Do you know what your forehead looks like, Creon?
I do: like a *dinos* turned upside-down!

Archedicus in *The Man Who Made Mistakes* (fr. 1) brings a slave onstage discussing courtesans, and says:

(A.) Νικοστράτην τιν' ἤγαγον πρῴην σφόδρα
γρυπήν, Σκοτοδίνην ἐπικαλουμένην, ὅτι |

f  δῖνον ποτ' ἦρεν ἀργυροῦν ἐν τῷ σκότῳ.
(B.) δῖνον; < ... > δεινόν, ὦ θεοί.

ἐστὶ καὶ γένος ὀρχήσεως, ὡς Ἀπολλοφάνης ἐν Δαλίδι
παρίστησιν·

(A.) οὑτοσὶ δῖνος. (B.) τί δῖνος; (A.) καὶ
καλαθίσκος οὑτοσί.

Τελέσιλλα δὲ ἡ Ἀργεία καὶ τὴν ἅλω καλεῖ δῖνον.
Κυρηναῖοι δὲ τὸν ποδονιπτῆρα δῖνον ὀνομάζουσιν, ὡς
Φιλητᾶς φησιν ἐν Ἀτάκτοις. ||

468  Δέπαστρον. Σιληνὸς καὶ Κλείταρχος ἐν Γλώσσαις
παρὰ Κλειτορίοις τὰ ποτήρια καλεῖσθαι. Ἀντίμαχος
δ' ὁ Κολοφώνιος ἐν πέμπτῳ Θηβαΐδος φησί·

πάντα μάλ', ὅσσ' Ἄδρηστος ἐποιχομένους
ἐκέλευσε
ῥεξέμεν· ἐν μὲν ὕδωρ, ἐν δ' ἀσκηθὲς μέλι χεῦαν
ἀργυρέῳ κρητῆρι, περιφραδέως κερόωντες· |

b  νώμησαν δὲ δέπαστρα θοῶς βασιλεῦσιν Ἀχαιῶν
ἐνσχερὼ ἑστηῶσι, καὶ ἐς λοιβὴν χέον εἶθαρ
χρυσείῃ προχόῳ.

καὶ πάλιν·

---

[117] Literally a "twirl, whirl".
[118] Literally a "little basket"; mentioned at 14.630a as another
type of dance.

(A.) Two days ago I brought a girl named Nicostrate,
   who had a real
hook-nose; her nickname was Scotodine, because she
once stole a silver *dinos* when it was dark (*skotos*).
(B.) A *dinos*? . . . dangerous, by the gods!

A *dinos*[117] is also a type of dance, as Apollophanes establishes in *The Fool* (fr. 1):

(A.) This here's a *dinos*. (B.) What's a *dinos*? (A.) And
   this here's a *kalathiskos*.[118]

Telesilla of Argos (*PMG* 723) also refers to a threshing-
floor as a *dinos*. The inhabitants of Cyrene call a foot-wash-
ing basin a *dinos*, according to Philetas in the *Miscellany*
(fr. 4 Dettori = fr. 21 Spanoudakis).

*Depastron*. Silenus and Cleitarchus in the *Glossary*
claim that the inhabitants of Cleitoria use this as a term
for cups. Antimachus of Colophon says in Book V of the
*Thebaid* (fr. 21 Matthews):

absolutely everything that Adrastus ordered them to
   do
as they approached. They poured water and virgin
   honey
into a silver mixing-bowl, combining them carefully;
and they quickly distributed *depastra* to the Achaean
   kings
who stood in a row, and immediately poured them
   enough for a libation
with a gold pitcher.

And again (fr. 19.8–10 Matthews):

ἄλλοι δὲ κρητῆρα πανάργυρον ἠδὲ δέπαστρα
οἰσόντων χρύσεια, τά τ᾽ ἐν μεγάροισιν ἐμοῖσι
κεῖαται.

κἀν τοῖς ἑξῆς δέ φησι·

καὶ χρύσεια δέπαστρα καὶ ἀσκηθὲς κελέβειον
ἔμπλειον μέλιτος τὸ ῥά οἱ προφερέστερον εἴη. |

c  Δακτυλωτόν. ἔκπωμα οὕτως καλούμενον παρὰ
Ἴωνι ἐν Ἀγαμέμνονι·

οἴσῃ δὲ δῶρον ἄξιον δραμήματος
ἔκπωμα δακτυλωτόν, ἄχραντον πυρί,
Πελίου μέγ᾽ ἆθλον, Κάστορος δ᾽ ἔργον ποδῶν.

Ἐπιγένης μὲν οὖν ἀκούει τὸ ἄμφωτον ποτήριον, εἰς ὃ
οἷόν τε τοὺς δακτύλους διείρειν ἑκατέρωθεν· ἄλλοι δὲ
τὸ ἐν κύκλῳ τύπους ἔχον οἷον δακτύλους, ἢ τὸ ἔχον
ἐξοχὰς οἷα τὰ Σιδώνια ποτήρια, ἢ τὸ λεῖον. "ἄχραντον
δὲ πυρί" παρὰ τὸ Ὁμηρικόν·

d  < . . . > ἄπυρον | κατέθηκε λέβητα,

τὸ ἐπιτήδειον εἰς ψυχρῶν ὑδάτων ὑποδοχὴν ἢ τὸ πρὸς
ψυχροποσίαν εὔθετον. τινὲς δὲ τὸ κέρας. περὶ δὲ τὴν
Μολοσσίδα οἱ βόες ὑπερφυῆ ἱστοροῦνται κέρατα

---

119 The cup in question belonged to Pelias, king of Iolcus, and
was offered as the prize in the footrace at his funeral games (cf.
below), which Castor won. It is now being offered to someone else
for a cognate service, perhaps to a messenger who has brought
Clytemestra news of Agamemnon's return.

120 Repeated virtually word-for-word at 11.468f (at the very
end of this entry), but with the definition credited to Philemon
rather than Epigenes.

Let others fetch a solid silver mixing-bowl and
gold *depastra*, which are stored in my
house!

And in the lines immediately after this he says (fr. 23.5–6
Matthews):

and gold *depastra* and an untouched jar
full of the finest honey he had.

*Daktulōtos*. A drinking vessel is referred to this way in
Ion's *Agamemnon* (*TrGF* 19 F 1):

You will carry off a gift worthy of the race you ran,
a *daktulōtos* drinking vessel, untouched by fire,
a prize cherished by Pelias, to commemorate what
    Castor's feet accomplished.[119]

Epigenes takes this as a reference to a cup with two handles, into which one can insert one's fingers (*daktuloi*) from
either side. But other authorities (maintain) that it is a
cup with impressions resembling fingers all around it,[120] or
one with embossed decoration, like Sidonian cups, or one
that is smooth. "Untouched by fire" is an allusion to the
Homeric phrase (*Il.* 23.267):

he set as a prize a basin that had never felt the fire,

i.e., one suitable for having cold water poured into it, or appropriate for cold drinks. But some authorities (believe)
that a drinking horn is in question.[121] The cows in Molossia

---

[121] The comment is repeated below, suggesting that several
scholarly sources have been crudely combined here.

ἔχειν· περὶ ὧν τῆς κατασκευῆς Θεόπομπος ἱστορεῖ· ἐξ
ὧν πιθανὸν καὶ αὐτὸν ἐσχηκέναι. πλησίον δὲ τῆς
Μολοσσίας ἡ Ἰωλκός, ἐν ᾗ ὁ ἐπὶ Πελίᾳ ἀγὼν ἐτέθη.
βέλτιον δὲ λέγειν, φησὶν ὁ Δίδυμος ἐν τῷ τοῦ δρά-
ματος ἐξηγητικῷ, ὅτι παρήκουσεν Ὁμήρου λέγοντος· |

e    πέμπτῳ δ᾽ ἀμφίθετον φιάλην ἀπύρωτον ἔθηκεν.

ἔδοξε γὰρ ἔκπωμα εἶναι· ἐστὶ δὲ χαλκίον ἐκπέταλον
λεβητῶδες, ἐπιτηδείως ἔχον πρὸς ὑδάτων ψυχρῶν
ὑποδοχάς. δακτυλωτὸν δ᾽ οἷον κύκλῳ τὴν φιάλην
κοιλότητας ἔχουσαν ἔνδοθεν οἷον δακτύλων, ἢ ἐπεὶ
περιείληπται τοῖς τῶν πινόντων δακτύλοις. τινὲς δὲ
"ἀπύρωτον φιάλην" τὸ κέρας· οὐ γὰρ γίνεται διὰ
πυρός. λέγοι δ᾽ ἂν ἴσως κατὰ μεταφορὰν ἔκπωμα τὴν
φιάλην. Φιλήμων δ᾽ ἐν τοῖς Ἀττικοῖς Ὀνόμασιν ἢ
f    Γλώτταις προθεὶς "καλπίς" | φησι· δακτυλωτὸν ἔκ-
πωμα καὶ τὸ ἄμφωτον, εἰς ὅ ἐστιν οἷόν τε τοὺς
δακτύλους ἑκατέρωθεν διείρειν. οἱ δὲ τὸ ἔχον κύκλῳ
δακτυλοειδεῖς τύπους τινάς.

Ἐλέφας. οὕτως ἐκαλεῖτο ποτήριόν τι, ὡς Δαμόξενός
φησιν ἐν Αὑτὸν Πενθοῦντι·

    (Α.) εἰ δ᾽ οὐχ ἱκανόν σοι, τὸν ἐλέφανθ᾽ ἥκει
        φέρων
    ὁ παῖς. (Β.) τί δ᾽ ἐστι τοῦτο, πρὸς θεῶν; (Α.)
        ῥυτὸν ‖

---

122 Cf. 11.468c with n.
123 Literally "elephant" or (more appropriate here) "elephant's tusk".

are reported to have exceptionally long horns—Theopompus (*FGrH* 115 F 284) describes how they are made (into drinking vessels)—and it is plausible that the speaker had one of these; Iolcus, where Pelias' funeral games were held, is near Molossia. A better interpretation, according to Didymus in his commentary on the play (p. 89 Schmidt), is that Ion misunderstood Homer when he said (*Il.* 23.270):

> and he set a two-handled *phialē* untouched by fire as
> fifth prize.

Because he took this to be a drinking vessel, whereas it is in fact an open bronze vessel that resembles a basin and is suited to having cold water poured into it. The *phialē* is *daktulōtos* in that it has depressions all around its interior, like those produced by fingers (*daktuloi*), or else because people grasp it with their fingers when they drink from it. Some authorities claim that a "*phialē* untouched by fire" is a drinking-horn, because fire is not used to produce drinking-horns. But perhaps he is referring metaphorically to the *phialē* as a drinking vessel. Philemon in his *Attic Vocabulary* or *Glossary* begins with the lemma *kalpis* and says: A *daktulōtos* drinking vessel with two handles, into which one can insert one's fingers from either side; but other authorities believe that this is a cup with impressions resembling fingers all around it.[122]

*Elephas*.[123] This was a term for a cup of some sort, as Damoxenus says in *The Man Who Mourned for Himself* (fr. 1):

> (A.) If that's not enough for you, the slave's here
> with the *elephas*. (B.) What's that, by the gods? (A.) A
> drinking-horn

469    δίκρουνον ἡλίκον τι τρεῖς χωροῦν χοᾶς,
      Ἄλκωνος ἔργον. προὔπιεν δέ μοι ποτὲ
      ἐν Κυψέλοις Ἀδαῖος.

μνημονεύει τοῦ ποτηρίου τούτου καὶ Ἐπίνικος ἐν Ὑποβαλλομέναις, οὗ τὸ μαρτύριον παρέξομαι ἐν τῷ περὶ
τοῦ ῥυτοῦ λόγῳ.

Ἔφηβος. τὸ καλούμενον ποτήριον ἐμβασικοίταν
οὕτως φησὶ καλεῖσθαι Φιλήμων ὁ Ἀθηναῖος ἐν τῷ
Περὶ Ἀττικῶν Ὀνομάτων ἢ Γλωσσῶν. Στέφανος δ᾽ ὁ
κωμικὸς ἐν Φιλολάκωνί φησι· |

b    (Σω.) τούτῳ προέπιεν ὁ βασιλεὺς κώμην τινά.
      (Β.) καινόν τι τοῦτο γέγονε νῦν ποτήριον;
      (Σω.) κώμη μὲν οὖν τις ἐστὶ περὶ τὴν Θουρίαν.
      (Β.) εἰς τὰς Ῥοδιακὰς ὅλος ἀπηνέχθην ἐγὼ
      καὶ τοὺς ἐφήβους, Σωσία, τοὺς δυσχερεῖς.

Ἡδυποτίδες. ταύτας φησὶν ὁ Σάμιος Λυγκεὺς Ῥο-
δίους ἀντιδημιουργήσασθαι πρὸς τὰς Ἀθήνησι Θηρικλείους, Ἀθηναίων μὲν[22] τοῖς πλουσίοις διὰ τὰ βάρη
χαλκευσαμένων τὸν ῥυθμὸν τούτου, Ῥοδίων δὲ διὰ τὴν
c    ἐλαφρότητα τῶν ποτηρίων | καὶ τοῖς πένησι τοῦ καλ-
λωπισμοῦ τούτου μεταδιδόντων. μνημονεύει δ᾽ αὐτῶν
καὶ Ἐπιγένης ἐν Ἡρωΐνῃ διὰ τούτων·

<hr />

[22] μὲν αὐτοῖς πλουσίως A: μὲν αὐτὰς τοῖς πλουσίοις
Musurus: μὲν τοῖς πλουσίοις tantum Olson

<hr />

[124] At 11.497a.
[125] The word "ephebe" is normally used to describe a young
man who is just on the edge of becoming an adult; cf. 11.494f.
[126] The verb more often means "toasted", hence the joke that
follows.

with two mouths and big enough to hold three *choes*;
Alcon made it, and Adaeus once toasted
me with it in Cypsela.

Epinicus in *Women Who Try to Pass off Supposititious
Children* (fr. 2.4) also mentions this cup; I will cite his testimony when I discuss drinking-horns.[124]

*Ephēbos*.[125] Philemon of Athens in his *On Attic Vocabulary* or *Glossary* says that this is another name for the
cup referred to as an *embasikoitas*. The comic author
Stephanus says in *The Man Who Loved Sparta* (fr. 1):

(Sosias) The king presented him[126] with a village.
(B.) Is this some new kind of cup?
(Sosias) No—it's an actual village near Thuria.
(B.) I was totally carried away, Sosias, to the Rhodian
cups and the aggravating *ephēboi*.

*Hēdupotides*.[127] Lynceus of Samos (fr. 16a Dalby)[128]
claims that the Rhodians produced these to compete with
the Thericleian cups made in Athens; but whereas the
Athenians produced this shape only for the rich, because
of the amount of metal required, the Rhodians offered the
poor an opportunity to participate in this fashion as well,
since their cups were so light. Epigenes mentions them in
*The Heroine* (fr. 5.3–4), in the following passage:[129]

[127] Literally "cups for delicious drinks" *vel sim.*
[128] Clearly another fragment of the *Letter to Diagoras* cited at
e.g. 3.109d–e; 7.285e–f, 295a–b; 14.654a.
[129] Two additional verses of the same fragment, along with an
abbreviated and slightly different version of the third, are quoted
at 11.502e.

ψυκτήρια, κύαθον, κυμβία, ῥυτὰ τέτταρα,
ἡδυποτίδας τρεῖς, ἠθμὸν ἀργυροῦν.

Σῆμος δ' ἐν πέμπτῃ Δηλιάδος ἀνακεῖσθαί φησιν ἐν
Δήλῳ χρυσῆν ἡδυποτίδα Ἐχενίκης ἐπιχωρίας γυναι-
κός, ἧς μνημονεύει καὶ ἐν τῇ ὀγδόῃ. Κρατῖνος δ' ὁ
νεώτερός φησι·

παρ' Ἀρχεφῶντος ἡδυποτίδας δώδεκα.

d  Ἡράκλειον. Πείσανδρος ἐν δευτέρῳ Ἡρακλείας | τὸ
δέπας ἐν ᾧ διέπλευσεν ὁ Ἡρακλῆς τὸν ὠκεανὸν εἶναι
μέν φησιν Ἡλίου, λαβεῖν δ' αὐτὸ παρ' Ὠκεανοῦ τὸν
Ἡρακλέα. μήποτε δὲ ἐπεὶ μεγάλοις ἔχαιρε ποτηρίοις ὁ
ἥρως, διὰ τὸ μέγεθος παίζοντες οἱ ποιηταὶ καὶ συγ-
γραφεῖς πλεῖν αὐτὸν ἐν ποτηρίῳ ἐμυθολόγησαν.
Πανύασις δ' ἐν πρώτῳ Ἡρακλείας παρὰ Νηρέως φησὶ
τὴν τοῦ Ἡλίου φιάλην κομίσασθαι τὸν Ἡρακλέα καὶ
διαπλεῦσαι εἰς Ἐρύθειαν. ὅτι δὲ εἷς ἦν ὁ Ἡρακλῆς τῶν
πλεῖστον πινόντων προείπομεν. ὅτι δὲ καὶ ὁ Ἥλιος ἐπὶ
e  ποτηρίου | διεκομίζετο ἐπὶ τὴν δύσιν Στησίχορος μὲν
οὕτως φησίν·

Ἀέλιος δ' Ὑπεριονίδας δέπας ἐσκατέβαινε
χρύσεον, ὄφρα δι' ὠκεανοῖο περάσας
ἀφίκοιθ' ἱαρᾶς ποτὶ βένθεα νυκτὸς ἐρεμνᾶς,
ποτὶ ματέρα κουριδίαν τ' ἄλοχον παῖδας τε
φίλους,

---

130 She was a member of a politically prominent local family,
and the cup appears to be mentioned in several Delian temple
inscriptions.

cooling-vessels, a ladle, *kumbia*, four drinking-horns, three *hēdupotides*, a silver wine-strainer.

Semus in Book V of the *History of Delos* (*FGrH* 396 F 9) reports that a gold *hēdupotis* that belonged to a local woman named Echenice[130] is dedicated on Delos; he mentions her in Book VIII as well (*FGrH* 396 F 15). Cratinus Junior (fr. 14) says:

a dozen *hēdupotides* from Archephon.[131]

*Hērakleion.* Pisander in Book II of the *Epic of Heracles* (fr. 5 Bernabé) claims that the goblet in which Heracles sailed across the ocean belonged to Helios, although Heracles got it from Ocean. But perhaps the fact that the hero liked large cups led poets and prose-authors to play on the idea of their size and come up with the story that he sailed in one. Panyasis in Book I of the *Epic of Heracles* (fr. 9 Bernabé) says that Heracles got Helios' *phialē* from Nereus and sailed over to Erytheia.[132] I noted earlier (10.412b, 441a–b) that Heracles was an extremely heavy drinker. Stesichorus (*PMG* 185)[133] claims that Helios used to travel to the West in a cup, as follows:

Hyperion's son Aelios embarked in a gold
goblet, in order to cross the ocean
and come to the depths of the sacred, gloomy night,
and to his mother, and the wife he married when she
        was a girl, and the children he loved.

131 *PAA* 211865; described as a parasite at 6.244a–d (citing Macho).
132 Sc. to steal Geryon's cattle (one of his 12 Labors).
133 Alluded to (but not quoted) also at 11.781d, where see n.

ὁ δ᾿ ἐς ἄλσος ἔβα δάφναισι κατάσκιον |
f     ποσὶ παῖς Διός.

καὶ Ἀντίμαχος δ᾿ οὑτωσὶ λέγει·

    τότε δὴ χρυσέῳ ἐν δέπαι
Ἥλιον πόμπευεν ἀγακλυμένη Ἐρύθεια.

καὶ Αἰσχύλος ἐν Ἡλιάσιν·

    ἔνθ᾿ ἐπὶ δυσμαῖς
† ισου † πατρὸς Ἡφαιστοτευχὲς
δέπας, ἐν τῷ διαβάλλει
πολὺν οἰδματόεντα
† φέρει δρόμου πόρον οὐθεις †
μελανίππου προφυγὼν
ἱερᾶς νυκτὸς ἀμολγόν. ||

470  Μίμνερμος δὲ Ναννοῖ ἐν εὐνῇ φησι χρυσῇ κατεσκευ-
ασμένῃ πρὸς τὴν χρείαν ταύτην ὑπὸ Ἡφαίστου τὸν
Ἥλιον καθεύδοντα περαιοῦσθαι πρὸς τὰς ἀνατολάς,
αἰνισσόμενος τὸ κοῖλον τοῦ ποτηρίου. λέγει δ᾿ οὕτως·

Ἥλιος μὲν γὰρ ἔλαχεν πόνον ἤματα πάντα,
    οὐδέ ποτ᾿ ἄμπαυσις γίνεται οὐδεμία
ἵπποισίν τε καὶ αὐτῷ, ἐπὴν ῥοδοδάκτυλος Ἠὼς
    ὠκεανὸν προλιποῦσ᾿ οὐρανὸν εἰσαναβῇ. |
b   τὸν μὲν γὰρ διὰ κῦμα φέρει πολυήρατος εὐνή,
    ποικίλη, Ἡφαίστου χερσὶν ἐληλαμένη,
χρυσοῦ τιμήεντος, ὑπόπτερος, ἄκρον ἐφ᾿ ὕδωρ
    εὕδονθ᾿ ἁρπαλέως χώρου ἀφ᾿ Ἑσπερίδων

Meanwhile the son of Zeus strode into the sacred
>     grove
shaded with laurel trees.

Antimachus (fr. 86 Matthews) as well says the following:

>     At that time, in fact, renowned Erytheia
> was sending Ēelios off in a gold goblet.

Aeschylus too in *The Daughters of Helios* (fr. 69):

>     there in the West
> [corrupt] his father's goblet, fashioned
> by Hephaestus, in which he traverses
> the vast, wave-swollen
> † he bears of a course a way no one †
> after escaping the gloom of sacred
> night with its dark horses.

Mimnermus in *Nanno* (fr. 12 West²) makes a riddling allusion to the hollow shape of the cup, claiming that Helios
goes to sleep in a gold bed Hephaestus made specifically
for this purpose, and travels to the East in it. He puts it as
follows:

> Ēelios had eternal hard work assigned to him,
>     nor is there ever any rest
> for him or his horses, once rosy-fingered Dawn
>     leaves the ocean and mounts into the sky.
> For he is carried through the waves on a lovely,
>     elaborately crafted
>     bed forged by Hephaestus' hands
> from precious gold and equipped with wings. As he
>     sleeps, it takes
>     him rapidly over the water's surface, from the
>         Hesperides' country

279

γαῖαν ἐς Αἰθιόπων, ἵνα δὴ θοὸν ἅρμα καὶ ἵπποι
  ἑστᾶσ᾽, ὄφρ᾽ Ἠὼς ἠριγένεια μόλη·
ἔνθ᾽ ἐπέβη ἑτέρων ὀχέων Ὑπερίονος υἱός.

Θεόλυτος δ᾽ ἐν δευτέρῳ Ὥρων ἐπὶ λέβητός φησιν |
c αὐτὸν διαπλεῦσαι, τοῦτο πρῶτον εἰπόντος τοῦ τὴν
Τιτανομαχίαν ποιήσαντος. Φερεκύδης δ᾽ ἐν τῇ τρίτῃ
τῶν Ἱστοριῶν προειπὼν περὶ τοῦ Ὠκεανοῦ ἐπιφέρει· ὁ
δ᾽ Ἡρακλῆς ἕλκεται ἐπ᾽ αὐτὸν τὸ τόξον ὡς βαλῶν, καὶ
ὁ Ἥλιος παύσασθαι κελεύει, ὁ δὲ δείσας παύεται.
Ἥλιος δὲ ἀντὶ τούτου δίδωσιν αὐτῷ τὸ δέπας τὸ
χρύσεον, ὃ αὐτὸν ἐφόρει σὺν ταῖς ἵπποις, ἐπὴν δύνῃ,
διὰ τοῦ ὠκεανοῦ τὴν νύκτα πρὸς ἕωην, ἵν᾽ ἀνίσχει.²³
ἔπειτα πορεύεται Ἡρακλῆς ἐν τῷ δέπᾳ τούτῳ ἐς τὴν
d Ἐρύθειαν. | καὶ ὅτε δὲ ἦν ἐν τῷ πελάγει, Ὠκεανὸς
πειρώμενος αὐτοῦ κυμαίνει τὸ δέπας φανταζόμενος. ὁ
δὲ τοξεύειν αὐτὸν μέλλει, καὶ αὐτὸν δείσας Ὠκεανὸς
παύσασθαι κελεύει.

Ἠθάνιον. Ἑλλάνικος ἐν Αἰγυπτιακοῖς οὕτως γρά-
φει· Αἰγυπτίων ἐν τοῖς οἴκοις κεῖται φιάλη χαλκῆ καὶ
κύαθος χαλκοῦς καὶ ἠθάνιον χάλκεον.

Ἡμίτομος. ἔκπωμά τι παρ᾽ Ἀττικοῖς ἀπὸ τοῦ σχήματος ὀνομασθέν, φησὶν Πάμφιλος ἐν Γλώσσαις.

e Θηρίκλειος. ἡ κύλιξ | αὕτη ἐγκάθηται περὶ τὰς
λαγόνας ἱκανῶς βαθυνομένη ὦτά τε ἔχει βραχέα ὡς

---

²³ ἀνίσχει ὁ ἥλιος A: ὁ ἥλιος del. Kaibel

---

134 I.e. from the extreme West to the extreme East.

135 What follows is garbled and appears to represent two versions of the story run awkwardly together.

to the land of the Ethiopians,[134] where his swift
    chariot and horses
stand waiting until early-born Dawn arrives.
Then Hyperion's son embarks into a different vehicle.

Theolytus in Book II of the *Annals* (*FGrH* 478 F 1), on the
other hand, claims that (Heracles) crossed the ocean in a
cauldron, the first person to say this having been the author of the *Titanomachy* (fr. 8 Bernabé). Pherecydes in
Book III of his *History* (*FGrH* 3 F 18a) first discusses
Ocean and then continues:[135] Heracles aimed his bow
at him, as if intending to shoot him; but Helios ordered
him to stop, and he was frightened and did so. In return,
Helios gave Heracles the gold goblet that carried him and
his horses, after he set, through the ocean by night to
Dawn's country, where he rises. Heracles then traveled to
Erytheia in this goblet. While he was at sea, Ocean tested
him by appearing and trying to swamp the goblet; Heracles was on the verge of shooting him with his bow, but
Ocean was frightened and told him to stop.

*Ēthanion*.[136] Hellanicus in the *History of Egypt* (*FGrH*
4 F 53) writes as follows: In their homes the Egyptians
have a bronze *phialē*, a bronze ladle, and a bronze
*ēthanion*.

*Hēmitomos*.[137] An Attic drinking vessel that gets its
name from its shape, according to Pamphilus in the *Glossary* (fr. VIIII Schmidt).

Thericleian. This *kulix* has concave sides, is fairly deep,
and has short handles, inasmuch as it is a *kulix*. Alexis in

---

[136] "small strainer".
[137] Literally "half-section".

ἂν κύλιξ οὖσα. καὶ μήποτε Ἄλεξις ἐν Ἡσιόνῃ Θηρικλείῳ ποιεῖ τὸν Ἡρακλέα πίνοντα, ὅταν οὑτωσὶ λέγῃ·

γενόμενος δ' ἔννους μόλις
ᾔτησε κύλικα, καὶ λαβὼν ἑξῆς πυκνὰς
ἕλκει καταντλεῖ, κατά τε τὴν παροιμίαν
ἀεί ποτ' εὖ μὲν ἀσκός, εὖ δὲ θύλακος
ἄνθρωπός ἐστιν.

ὅτι δὲ κύλιξ ἐστὶν ἡ Θηρίκλειος σαφῶς παρίστησιν |
f Θεόφραστος ἐν τῇ Περὶ Φυτῶν Ἱστορίᾳ. διηγούμενος
γὰρ περὶ τῆς τερμίνθου φησί· τορνεύεσθαι δὲ ἐξ αὐτῆς
καὶ κύλικας Θηρικλείους, ὥστε μηδένα ⟨ἂν⟩ διαγνῶ-
ναι πρὸς τὰς κεραμέας. κατασκευάσαι δὲ λέγεται τὴν
κύλικα ταύτην Θηρικλῆς ὁ Κορίνθιος κεραμεύς, ἀφ' οὗ
καὶ τοὔνομα ἔχει, γεγονὼς τοῖς χρόνοις κατὰ τὸν
κωμικὸν Ἀριστοφάνη. μνημονεύει δὲ τῆς κύλικος Θεόπομπος μὲν ἐν Νεμέᾳ οὕτως·

(Σπ.) χώρει σὺ δεῦρο, Θηρικλέους πιστὸν τέκνον,
γενναῖον εἶδος· ὄνομά σοι τί θώμεθα; ‖
471 ἆρ' εἰ κάτοπτρον φύσεος, ἢν πλήρες δοθῇς;
οὐδέν ποτ' ἄλλο. δεῦρο δή, γεμίσω σ' ἐγώ.
γραῦ Θεολύτη, γραῦ. (Θε.) τί με καλεῖς σύ; (Σπ.)
φιλτάτη,
ἵν' ἀσπάσωμαι. δεῦρο παρ' ἐμέ, Θεολύτη,
παρὰ τὸν νέον ξύνδουλον. οὑτωσὶ καλῶς.

---

138 Aristophanes lived c.448–388 BCE.

*Hesione* (fr. 88) perhaps represents Heracles as drinking from a Thericleian when he says the following:

> The moment he regained consciousness,
> he asked for a *kulix*; and as soon as he got it, he drank
>     down
> and emptied off plenty of them. As the proverb says,
> this guy's always good at being a wineskin, and
>     equally good
> at being a grain-sack.

Theophrastus in his *Inquiry into Plants* (5.3.2) establishes beyond any doubt that a Theracleian is a type of *kulix*. For in the course of his description of the terebinth tree he says: Thericleian *kulikes* can be produced on a lathe from the wood of this tree, and no one would be able to distinguish them from the ceramic variety. The Corinthian potter Thericles is said to have manufactured this type of *kulix*, to which he lent his name; he was a contemporary of the comic author Aristophanes.[138] Theopompus in *Nemea* (fr. 33) mentions this *kulix*, as follows:

> (Spinther) Come over here, trustworthy child of
>     Thericles,
> noble shape! What should we call you?
> Maybe "a mirror of an individual's character", if
>     you're full when you're handed to him?
> That's definitely it. Come here, let me fill you up!
> Old Theolyte! Old woman! (Theolyte) Why are you
>     calling me? (Spinther) So
> I can say hello to you, sweetheart. Come here to me,
>     Theolyte;
> meet your new fellow-slave! Like that; very nice.

(Θε.) Σπινθὴρ τάλας, πειρᾶς με; (Σπ.) ναί,
   τοιοῦτό τι·
φιλοτησίαν δὲ ⟨τήνδε⟩ σοι προπίομαι.
δέξαι· πιοῦσα δ᾽ ὁπόσον ἄν σοι θυμὸς ᾖ, |

b   ἐμοὶ παράδος τὸ πρῶτον.

Κλεάνθης δ᾽ ἐν τῷ Περὶ Μεταλήψεως συγγράμματί
φησι· τὰ τοίνυν εὑρήματα καὶ ὅσα τοιαῦτα ἔτι καὶ τὰ
λοιπά ἐστιν, οἷον Θηρίκλειος, Δεινιάς, Ἰφικρατίς· ταῦτα γὰρ πρότερον συνιστορεῖν τοὺς εὑρόντας. φαίνεται
δ᾽ ἔτι καὶ νῦν· εἰ δὲ μὴ ποιεῖ τοῦτο, μεταβεβληκὸς ἂν
εἴη μικρὸν τοὔνομα. ἀλλά, καθάπερ εἴρηται, οὐκ ἔστιν
πιστεῦσαι τῷ τυχόντι. ἄλλοι δ᾽ ἱστοροῦσι Θηρίκλειον
ὀνομασθῆναι τὸ ποτήριον διὰ τὸ δορὰς θηρίων αὐτῷ

c  ἐντετυπῶσθαι. | Πάμφιλος δ᾽ ὁ Ἀλεξανδρεὺς ἀπὸ τοῦ
τὸν Διόνυσον τοὺς θῆρας κλονεῖν σπένδοντα ταῖς
κύλιξι ταύταις κατ᾽ αὐτῶν. μνημονεύει τοῦ ἐκπώματος
καὶ Ἀντιφάνης ἐν Ὁμοίοις οὕτως·

  ὡς δ᾽ ἐδείπνησαν (συνάψαι βούλομαι γὰρ τὰν
    μέσῳ)
  καὶ Διὸς Σωτῆρος ἦλθε Θηρίκλειον ὄργανον,
  τῆς τρυφερᾶς ἀπὸ Λέσβου σεμνογόνου σταγόνος
  πλῆρες, ἀφρίζον, ἕκαστος δεξιτερᾷ δ᾽ ἔλαβεν.

καὶ Εὔβουλος ἐν μὲν Δόλωνι·

  διένιψα δ᾽ οὐδὲν σκεῦος οὐδεπώποτε· |

---

139 Cf. 11.467d–e.
140 Sc. to provide a reliable etymology in such cases.
141 Called *Women Who Looked Like One Another* at 4.158c.
Meineke combined these verses with the passage from the same
play preserved at 14.642a to produce fr. 172.

(Theolyte) Spinther, you bastard—are you making a
     pass at me? (Spinther) Yeah—something like
     that.

I'm proposing a toast to you, with this friendship cup.
Take it—and after you drink as much as you want,
give it back right away!

Cleanthes in his treatise *On Substitution* (fr. 591, *SVF*
i.133):[139] the inventions, therefore, and whatever else
belongs in the same category, such as a Thericleian, a
Deinias, or an Iphicratis; because in the past these carried
their inventors' identities with them. This is true even today; and if this is not the case, the name may have changed
a bit. But, as has been noted, you cannot trust people at
random.[140] Other authorities report that this style of cup
came to be referred to as a Thericleian because the skins of
wild animals (*thēria*) were embossed on it. But Pamphilus
of Alexandria (fr. X Schmidt) (claims that the name came)
from the fact that Dionysus drives the wild animals crazy
(*thēras klonein*) by pouring libations over them with this
type of *kulix*. Antiphanes in *Men Who Looked Like Each
Other*[141] (fr. 172.1–4) mentions this vessel, as follows:

They dined this way—I want to give a summary
     account of what happened in the middle—
and a Thericleian vessel dedicated to Zeus the Savior
     came,
full of the luxurious, nobly-born drop
from Lesbos, and foaming. Each man took it in his
     right hand.

Also Eubulus in *Dolon* (fr. 30):

I never, ever washed a dish;

d  καθαρώτερον γὰρ τὸν κέραμον ἠργαζόμην
   ἢ Θηρικλῆς τὰς κύλικας, ἡνίκ᾽ ἦν νέος.

ἐν δὲ Κυβευταῖς·

          ἄρτι μὲν μάλ᾽ ἀνδρικὴν
   τῶν Θηρικλείων ὑπεραφρίζουσαν † παρα †,
   κωθωνοχειλῆ, ψηφοπεριβομβήτριαν,
   μέλαιναν, εὐκύκλωτον, ὀξυπύνδακα,
   στίλβουσαν, ἀνταυγοῦσαν, ἐκνενιμμένην,
   κισσῷ κάρα βρύουσαν, ἐπικαλούμενοι |
e  εἷλκον Διὸς Σωτῆρος.

Ἀραρὼς δ᾽ ἢ Εὔβουλος ἐν Καμπυλίωνι·

   ὦ γαῖα κεραμί, τίς σε Θηρικλῆς ποτε
   ἔτευξε κοίλης λαγόνος εὐρύνας βάθος;
   ἦ που κατειδὼς τὴν γυναικείαν φύσιν,
   ὡς οὐχὶ μικροῖς ἥδεται ποτηρίοις.

Ἄλεξις δ᾽ ἐν Ἱππεῖ·

   καὶ Θηρίκλειός τις κύλιξ, στέφανον κύκλῳ
   ἔχουσα χρυσοῦν· οὐ γὰρ ἐπίτηκτόν τινα.

καὶ ἐν Ἱππίσκῳ·

   μεστὴν ἀκράτου Θηρίκλειον ἔσπασε
   κοίλην ὑπερθύουσαν. |

f  Τίμαιος δ᾽ ἐν τῇ ὀγδόῃ καὶ εἰκοστῇ τῶν Ἱστοριῶν

---

142 Athenaeus also expresses doubts about the authorship of
the play at 13.562c, but assigns it unambiguously to Eubulus at
7.295e; 13.571f; 14.642c.

143 Referred to as *Agonis or The Brooch* at 8.339c; 15.678e
(simply *The Brooch* also at 3.120b; 11.502e–3a).

because I used to make my pottery cleaner
than Thericles made his *kulikes*, when I was young.

And in *Dice-Players* (fr. 56):

A moment ago they were draining a
muscular Thericleian with foam running over the top
[corrupt]
and a brim like a Spartan flask, which rattles when a
pebble's rolled around inside it,
and is black and round and pointed on the bottom,
and shines and gleams and has been carefully
washed,
and is covered on top with ivy; and they were
invoking
Zeus the Savior.

Araros or Eubulus (fr. 42) in *Campylion*:[142]

Potter's earth, what Thericles was it who made
you, drawing broad the depth of your hollow side?
Perhaps someone familiar with a woman's nature,
who knew they don't like tiny cups!

Alexis in *The Knight* (fr. 101):

And a Thericleian *kulix*, with a gold garland
around it; because it wasn't just gilded!

And in *The Brooch*[143] (fr. 5):

He drained a hollow Thericleian cup that was full
to overflowing of unmixed wine.

Timaeus in Book XXVIII of the *History* (*FGrH* 566 F 33)

Θηρικλείαν καλεῖ τὴν κύλικα γράφων οὕτως· Πολύξε-
νός τις τῶν ἐκ Ταυρομενίου μεθεστηκότων ταχθεὶς ἐπὶ
τὴν πρεσβείαν ἕτερά τε δῶρα παρὰ τοῦ Νικοδήμου καὶ
κύλικα Θηρικλείαν λαβὼν ἐπανῆκεν. Ἀδαῖος δ᾽ ἐν τοῖς
Περὶ Διαθέσεως τὸ αὐτὸ ὑπολαμβάνει Θηρίκλειον
εἶναι καὶ καρχήσιον. ὅτι δὲ διαφέρει σαφῶς παρ-
472 ίστησι ‖ Καλλίξεινος ἐν τοῖς Περὶ Ἀλεξανδρείας
φάσκων τινὰς ἔχοντας Θηρικλείους πομπεύειν, τοὺς δὲ
καρχήσια. ὁποῖον δ᾽ ἐστὶ τὸ καρχήσιον ἐν τοῖς ἑξῆς
λεχθήσεται. καλεῖται δέ τις καὶ Θηρίκλειος κρατήρ, οὗ
μνημονεύει Ἄλεξις ἐν Κύκνῳ·

> φαιδρὸς δὲ κρατὴρ Θηρίκλειος ἐν μέσῳ
> ἕστηκε, λευκοῦ νέκταρος παλαιγενοῦς
> πλήρης, ἀφρίζων· ὃν λαβὼν ἐγὼ κενὸν
> τρίψας, ποήσας λαμπρόν, ἀσφαλῆ βάσιν
> στήσας, συνάψας καρπίμοις κισσοῦ κλάδοις
> ἔστεψα. |

b θηλυκῶς δὲ τὴν Θηρίκλειον εἶπε Μένανδρος ἐν Θεο-
φορουμένῃ·

> μέσως μεθύων ⟨τὴν⟩ Θηρίκλειον ἔσπασε.

καὶ ἐν Μηναγύρτῃ·

---

144 The events in question probably belong to the early 330s
BCE and involve Timoleon's military and political intervention on
Sicily.   145 A reference to two details from the long description of Ptolemy II's procession in Alexandria, the first preserved
also at 5.199b, the other alluded to also at 11.474e. Cf. 11.783c n.

146 At 11.474e–5c.   147 But the definite article—which
is the only evidence of what Menander took to be the grammatical
gender of the object in question (doubtless a *kulix*)—must be supplied, and the masculine would do just as well.

refers to a Thericleian *kulix*, writing as follows: Polyxenus, who was one of the people from Tauromenium who had changed sides, was assigned to go on the embassy, and he returned with gifts from Nicodemus that included a Thericleian *kulix*.[144] Adaeus in his *On the Sense of Words* understands a Thericleian to be identical to a *karchēsion*. But Callixeinus establishes beyond any doubt that they are different in his *On Alexandria* (*FGrH* 627 F 2a), when he says that some members of the procession carried Thericleians, while others carried *karchēsia*.[145] What a *karchēsion* is will be discussed below.[146] There is also something known as a Thericleian mixing-bowl, which Alexis mentions in *Cycnus* (fr. 124):

> A shining Thericleian mixing-bowl stood
> in the middle, full of ancient-born, white
> nectar, and foaming over. I took it when it was empty
> and polished it, buffed it, and set it firmly on
> its base, and wove together some berry-covered ivy
>     twigs,
> which I wrapped around it.

Menander in *The Girl Who Was Possessed by a God* (*Theophor.* fr. 4 Körte–Thierfelder) referred to a Thericleian in the feminine:[147]

> Although he was half-way drunk, he drained the
>     Thericleian.

And in *The Mendicant Priest of Rhea* (fr. 235):[148]

[148] Nothing in the fragment as it is preserved in the manuscripts suggests the gender of the Thericleian.

< ... > προπίνων Θηρίκλειον τρικότυλον.

καὶ Διώξιππος ἐν Φιλαργύρῳ·

> (A.) τῆς Θηρικλείου τῆς μεγάλης χρεία 'στί μοι.
> (B.) εὖ οἶδα. (A.) καὶ τῶν Ῥοδιακῶν· ἥδιστα γὰρ
> ἐκ τῶν τοιούτων † αἴσχεα † ποτηρίων
> εἴωθα πίνειν.

Πολέμων δ' ἐν πρώτῳ Περὶ τῆς Ἀθήνησιν Ἀκρο-
c πόλεως | οὐδετέρως ὠνόμασεν εἰπών· τὰ χρυσᾶ Θηρί-
κλεια ὑπόξυλα Νεοπτόλεμος ἀνέθηκεν. Ἀπολλόδωρος
δ' ὁ Γελῷος ἐν Φιλαδέλφοις ἢ Ἀποκαρτεροῦντί φησιν·

> ἐφεξῆς στρώματ', ἀργυρώματα,
> Θηρίκλειοι ⟨καὶ⟩ τορευτὰ πολυτελῆ ποτήρια
> ἕτερα.

Ἀριστοφῶν δ' ἐν Φιλωνίδῃ·

> (A.) τοιγαροῦν ἐμοὶ μὲν ἀρτίως ὁ δεσπότης
> δι' ἀρετὴν τῶν Θηρικλείων εὐκύκλωτον ἀσπίδα, |
d ὑπεραφρίζουσαν, τρυφῶσαν, ἴσον ἴσῳ
> κεκραμένην,
> προσφέρων ἔδωκεν. (B.) οἶμαι, χρηστότητος
> οὕνεκα.
> (A.) εἶτ' ἐλευθέραν ἀφῆκε βαπτίσας ἐρρωμένως.

Θεόφιλος δ' ἐν Βοιωτίᾳ·

---

149 Cf. 11.469b, where this verse is referred to (but not quoted).

150 The question of the grammatical gender of the word is abruptly abandoned in what follows, presumably marking Athenaeus' return to his initial source.

offering a Thericleian that held three *kotylai* as a
toast.

Also Dioxippus in *The Miser* (fr. 4):

(A.) I need the big (fem.) Thericleian.
(B.) I realize that. (A.) The Rhodians[149] too—because
I tend
to be happiest when I'm drinking out of cups
[corrupt]
like that.

But Polemon in Book I of *On the Athenian Acropolis* (fr. 1
Preller) used the word as a neuter, saying: Neoptolemus
dedicated the gold (neut.) Thericleians with wooden
cores.[150] Apollodorus of Gela says in *Men Who Loved
Their Brothers or The Man Who Starved to Death* (fr. 4):

after that, bed-clothes, silver vessels,
Thericleians, and other expensive cups
with relief work.

Aristophon in *Philonides* (fr. 13):

(A.) So as a reward for my courage, my master just
now
brought a perfectly round Thericleian shield,
foaming over at the top, dainty, and mixed one-to-
one,
and gave it to me. (B.) Because you were so helpful, I
suppose.
(A.) And then he gave me a vigorous soaking—and
set me free!

Theophilus in *The Girl from Boeotia* (fr. 2):

291

τετρακότυλον δὲ κύλικα κεραμεᾶν τινα
τῶν Θηρικλείων, πῶς δοκεῖς, κεράννυει
καλῶς, ἀφρῷ ζέουσαν· οὐδ' ἂν Αὐτοκλῆς
οὕτως μὰ τὴν γῆν εὐρύθμως τῇ δεξιᾷ
ἄρας ἐνώμα. |

e  ἐν δὲ Προιτίσι·

καὶ κύλικα < ... > Θηρίκλειον εἰσφέρει
πλέον ἢ κοτύλας χωροῦσαν ἔπτ' Ἀγαθῆς Τύχης.

Ἴσθμιον. Πάμφιλος ἐν τοῖς Περὶ Ὀνομάτων Κυπρίους τὸ ποτήριον οὕτως καλεῖν.
Κάδος. Σιμμίας ποτήριον, παρατιθέμενος Ἀνα-
κρέοντος·

ἠρίστησα μὲν ἰτρίου λεπτοῦ <μικρὸν> ἀποκλάς,
οἴνου δ' ἐξέπιον κάδον.

Ἐπιγένης δ' ἐν Μνηματίῳ φησίν·

(Α.) κρατῆρες, κάδοι,
ὁλκεῖα, κρουνεῖ. (Β.) ἔστι † δὲ † κρουνεῖα; (Α.)
ναί.

f  < ... > ἀλλὰ τί καθ' | ἔκαστον δεῖ λέγειν;
ὄψει γὰρ αὐτός. (Β.) βασιλέως υἱὸν λέγεις
<Καρῶν> ἀφῖχθαι; (Α.) δηλαδή, Πιξώδαρον.

Ἡδύλος Ἐπιγράμμασι·

---

151 Unidentified; the name is a common one.

152 Quoted also at 14.646d (in the context of a discussion of
*itrion*, "sesame-cake"). A *kados* is generally a "jar", not a "cup".

153 Smaller portions of the fragment are quoted also at
11.480a, 486b–c.   154 The word (cognate with *krounos*,
"spring"; presumably another vessel associated with drinking

One of those ceramic Thericleian *kulikes*
that holds four *kotulai*, if you can believe it—he's
    mixing it
nicely, so it bubbles and foams. Not even Autocles,[151]
by earth, could pick it up and move it that smoothly
with his right hand!

And in *The Daughters of Proetis* (fr. 10):

And he brings in a Thericleian *kulix* dedicated to
Good Luck that holds more than seven *kotulai*.

*Isthmion*. Pamphilus in his *On Nouns* (fr. XI Schmidt)
says that this is a Cyprian term for a cup.

*Kados*. Simmias (identifies this as) a cup, citing
Anacreon (*PMG* 373.1–2):[152]

I broke off a bit of crisp sesame-cake and had it for
    lunch,
and I drank a *kados* of wine.

Epigenes says in *The Tomb* (fr. 6):[153]

                     (A.) Mixing-bowls, *kadoi*,
basins, *krouneia*.[154] (B.) There are † but † *krouneia*?
    (A.) Yeah—
but why should I list them individually?
You'll see for yourself. (B.) You say the Carian king's
son's arrived? (A.) Absolutely; his name's Pixodarus.[155]

Hedylus in the *Epigrams* (*HE* 1853–6):

wine) is not attested elsewhere, hence perhaps the lack of an entry
for it in Athenaeus' catalogue.
[155] Satrap of Caria 340/39–335/4 BCE.

πίνωμεν, καὶ γάρ τι νέον, καὶ γάρ τι παρ' οἶνον ‖
εὕροιμ' ἂν λεπτὸν καί τι μελιχρὸν ἔπος.
ἀλλὰ κάδοις Χίου με κατάβρεχε καὶ λέγε,
    "παῖζε,
Ἡδύλε." μισῶ ζῆν ἐς κενὸν οὐ μεθύων.

καὶ ἐν ἄλλῳ·

ἐξ ἠοῦς εἰς νύκτα καὶ ἐκ νυκτὸς πάλι Σωκλῆς
    εἰς ἠοῦν πίνει τετραχόοισι κάδοις,
εἶτ' ἐξαίφνης που τυχὸν οἴχεται· ἀλλὰ παρ'
    οἶνον
Σικελίδεω παίζει πουλὺ μελιχρότερον, |
ἔστι δὲ † δὴ πολὺ † στιβαρώτερος· ὡς δ'
    ἐπιλάμπει
ἡ χάρις ὥστε, φίλος, καὶ γράφε καὶ μέθυε.

Κλείταρχος δ' ἐν ταῖς Γλώσσαις τὸ κεράμιόν φησιν
Ἴωνας κάδον καλεῖν. Ἡρόδοτος δ' ἐν τῇ τρίτῃ, φοι-
νικήιον, φησίν, οἴνου κάδον.

Καδίσκος. Φιλήμων ἐν τῷ προειρημένῳ συγγράμ-
ματι ποτηρίου εἶδος. ἀγγεῖον δ' ἐστὶν ἐν ᾧ τοὺς
Κτησίους Δίας ἐγκαθιδρύουσιν, ὡς Ἀντικλείδης φη-
σὶν ἐν τῷ Ἐξηγητικῷ γράφων | οὕτως· Διὸς Κτησίου

---

156 Unidentified.

157 I.e. the epigrammatist Asclepiades of Samos; cf. Theoc.
7.40 with Gow ad loc.

158 A diminutive form of *kados* (above).

159 His *Attic Vocabulary* or *Glossary*, cited at 11.469a.

160 If the author's name is emended to Autocleides (to match
the reference to Autocleides' *Expository Treatise* at Plu. *Nic.* 23)
here, it ought to be emended at 9.409f–10a as well.

Let's drink! Because when I'm drinking, I'm capable
 of inventing
  something new and clever and as sweet as honey
   to say.
So drench me with *kadoi* of Chian wine, and say:
  "Write a poem,
   Hedylus!" I hate being sober and living for
    nothing.

And in another passage (*HE* 1857–62):

From dawn to nightfall, and again from nightfall to
  dawn,
  Socles[156] drinks, using *kadoi* that hold four *choes*;
and then suddenly, somehow or other—he's gone!
   But when he's drinking,
  he writes poetry that's much more delicious than
    what Sicelidas[157] produces,
and he's † a whole lot † sturdier. As long as you've got
  the gift, my friend, stay drunk and write!

Cleitarchus in his *Glossary* reports that the Ionians refer to
a wine-jar (*keramion*) as a *kados*. And Herodotus says in
Book III (20.1): a *kados* of date-wine.

*Kadiskos*.[158] Philemon in the treatise cited earlier[159]
(identifies this as) a type of cup. This is a vessel people use
when they establish a cult of Zeus Ktēsias, according to
Anticleides in his *Expository Treatise* ([Anticleides] *FGrH*
140 F 22 = Autocleides *FGrH* 353 F *1),[160] where he
writes as follows: Cult-images of Zeus Ktēsias should be

σημεῖα ἱδρύεσθαι χρὴ ὧδε· καδίσκον καινὸν δίωτον
ἐπιθηματοῦντα στέψαι τὰ ὦτα ἐρίῳ λευκῷ καὶ ἐκ τοῦ
ὤμου τοῦ δεξιοῦ καὶ ἐκ τοῦ μετώπου ‹ . . . › τοῦ
κροκίου, καὶ ἐσθεῖναι ὅ τι ἂν εὕρῃς καὶ εἰσχέαι ἀμβροσίαν. ἡ δ᾽ ἀμβροσία ὕδωρ ἀκραιφνές, ἔλαιον, παγκαρ-
πία· ἅπερ ἔμβαλε. μνημονεύει τοῦ καδίσκου καὶ
Στράττις ὁ κωμικὸς ἐν Λημνομέδᾳ λέγων οὕτως·

Ἑρμῆς, ὃν ἕλκουσ᾽ οἱ μὲν ἐκ προχοιδίου,
οἱ δ᾽ ἐκ καδίσκου ‹γ᾽› ἴσον ἴσῳ κεκραμένον. |

d  Κάνθαρος. ὅτι μὲν πλοίου ὄνομα κοινόν, ὅτι δὲ καὶ
ποτήριόν τι οὕτω καλεῖται Ἀμειψίας ἐν Ἀποκοττα-
βίζουσί φησι·

ἡ Μανία, φέρ᾽ ὀξύβαφα καὶ κανθάρους.

Ἄλεξις δ᾽ ἐν Κρατείᾳ—ὁ δὲ λόγος περί τινος ἐν
καπηλείῳ πίνοντος·

εἶθ᾽ ὁρῶ τὸν Ἑρμαΐσκον τῶν ἁδρῶν τούτων τινὰ
κάνθαρον καταστρέφοντα, πλησίον δὲ κείμενον
στρωματέα καὶ γύλιον αὐτοῦ. |

e  Εὔβουλος δ᾽ ἐν Παμφίλῳ πολλάκις μεμνημένος τοῦ
ὀνόματός φησιν·

ἐγὼ δέ, καὶ γὰρ ἔτυχεν ὢν κατ᾽ ἀντικρὺ
τῆς οἰκίας καινὸν καπηλεῖον μέγα,

---

161 Alluded to (but not quoted) at 1.32b, where "Hermes" is
said to be a beverage of some type.
162 Cf. Ar. *Pax* 143, quoted at 11.486e.
163 Quoted at slightly greater length at 15.667f.

established as follows. Place a lid on a new two-handled *kadiskos*; wrap the handles with white wool, and from the right shoulder and the front . . . of the piece of wool; put whatever you find into it; and pour in ambrosia. Ambrosia is clean water, olive oil, and fruit of all sorts; place these items inside it. The comic author Strattis in *Lemnomeda* (fr. 23)[161] also mentions a *kadiskos*, saying the following:

> Hermes, which some people drink from a little
>         pitcher,
> while others drink it mixed one-to-one from a
>         *kadiskos*.

*Kantharos*. That this is the name of a boat is a commonplace.[162] But Amipsias in *Cottabus-Players* (fr. 2.1)[163] says that there is also a type of cup referred to this way:

> Mania! Bring some vinegar cruets and *kantharoi*!

Alexis in *Crateia*[164] (fr. 120)—the plot involves a person drinking in a bar:

> Then I see Hermaïscus turning one of these fat
> *kantharoi* upside-down, and his bed-clothes and
> backpack are lying next to him.

Eubulus in *Pamphilus* (fr. 80, encompassing all three quotations) uses the word repeatedly and says:

> And as for me—because a big new wineshop
> happened to be directly opposite the house—

[164] Athenaeus generally refers elsewhere to the play as *Crateia or The Pharmacist* (3.107a; 6.254a; 8.340a; 15.678c; simply as *Crateia* also at 8.340c).

ἐνταῦθ' ἐπετήρουν τὴν τροφὸν τῆς παρθένου,
κεράσαι κελεύσας τὸν κάπηλόν μοι χοᾶ
ὀβολοῦ, παραθεῖναί θ' ὡς μέγιστον κάνθαρον.

καὶ πάλιν·

ὁ δὲ κάνθαρος πάλαι κενός· ὡς ξηραίνεται.

καὶ ἔτι·

f ἅμα δὲ λαβοῦσ' ἠφάνικε πηλίκον | τινὰ
οἴεσθε μέγεθος † ἀρεσιαν † μέγαν πάνυ
καὶ ξηρὸν ἐποίησ' εὐθέως τὸν κάνθαρον.

Ξέναρχος δ' ἐν Πριάπῳ φησὶ τάδε·

(A.) σὺ δὲ μηκέτ' ἔγχει, παιδάριον, εἰς ἀργυροῦν,
εἰς τὸ βαθὺ δ' ἐπανάγωμεν· εἰς τὸν κάνθαρον, ||
474 παιδάριον, ἔγχει. (B.) νὴ Δί', εἰς τὸν κάνθαρον.

Ἐπιγένης Ἡρωίνῃ·

ἀλλ' οὐδὲ κεραμεύουσι νῦν τοὺς κανθάρους,
ὦ τάλαν, ἐκείνους τοὺς ἁδρούς, ταπεινὰ δὲ
καὶ γλαφυρὰ πάντες < . . . > ὡσπερεὶ
αὐτὰ τὰ ποτήρι', οὐ τὸν οἶνον πιόμενοι.

Σωσικράτης Φιλαδέλφοις·

λεπτὴ δὲ κυρτοῖς ἐγγελῶσα κύμασιν
αὔρα, κόρη Σκείρωνος, ἡσύχῳ ποδὶ |
b προσῆγε πρᾴως καὶ καλῶς τὸν κάνθαρον.

---

165 Probably a comment by the nurse, who is still thirsty.

166 I.e. blowing from the direction of the so-called Scironian
Rocks, from the Megarid into the Saronic Gulf (Thphr. Vent. 62;
Hsch. σ 894). The passage is most naturally taken as referring to a
ship rather than a cup.

I kept an eye out there for the girl's nurse;
and I told the bartender to mix me a pitcher of wine
that cost an obol, and to set the biggest *kantharos* he
 had beside me.

And again:[165]

The *kantharos* has been empty for a long time now!
 How dry it is!

And also:

As soon as she took hold of a remarkably big
 [corrupt],
really big, she's made it disappear;
and she immediately drained the *kantharos*.

Xenarchus in *Priapus* (fr. 10) says the following:

(A.) Don't pour any more into the silver cup, boy;
let's head off into the deep sea! Pour it into the
*kantharos*, boy! (B.) Right, by Zeus! Into the
 *kantharos*!

Epigenes in *The Heroine* (fr. 4):

But nowadays they're not manufacturing those fat
*kantharoi*, fool; they're all making
fancy shallow ones, as if
they were planning to drink the cups rather than the
 wine.

Sosicrates in *Men Who Loved Their Brothers* (fr. 2):

A light breeze—Sciron's daughter[166]—laughing
among the curling waves, gently and carefully,
on quiet foot, brought the *kantharos*.

299

Φρύνιχος Κωμασταῖς·

εἶτα κεραμεύων ἂν οἴκοι σωφρόνως
 Χαιρέστρατος
ἑκατὸν ⟨ἂν⟩ τῆς ἡμέρας † ἔκλαιεν † οἴνου
 κανθάρους.

Νικόστρατος Διαβόλῳ·

(Α.) ἡ ναῦς δὲ πότερον εἰκόσορός ἐστ᾽ ἢ κύκνος,
ἢ κάνθαρος; τουτὶ γὰρ ἂν πύθωμ᾽ ἔτι,
αὐτὸς περανῶ τὰ πάντ᾽. (Β.) ἀμέλει
 κυκνοκάνθαρος
ἐξ ἀμφοτέρων τούτων κεκεραμευμένος.[24]

Μένανδρος δὲ Ναυκλήρῳ·

(Α.) ἥκει λιπὼν Αἰγαῖον ἁλμυρὸν βάθος |
Θεόφιλος ἡμῖν. ὦ Στράτων, ὡς εἰς καλὸν
τὸν υἱὸν εὐτυχοῦντα καὶ σεσωμένον
πρῶτος λέγω σοι τόν τε χρυσοῦν κάνθαρον.
(Στρ.) ποῖον; (Α.) τὸ πλοῖον.

καὶ μετ᾽ ὀλίγα·

(Στρ.) τὴν ναῦν σεσῶσθαί μοι λέγεις; (Α.) ἔγωγε
 μήν·
† κείνην ναῦν Καλλικλῆς ἐποίησε
τὸν καλούμενον †, Εὐφράνωρ ⟨δ᾽⟩ ἐκυβέρνα
 Θούριος.

---

[24] The fourth verse should perhaps be deleted (thus Dindorf).

---

[167] Literally "swan".
[168] The first verse is borrowed from E. *Tr.* 1 (quoted also at

Phrynichus in *Revellers* (fr. 15):

> Then Chaerestratus, modestly producing pots at
>     home,
> would be † wailing † 100 *kantharoi* of wine per day.

Nicostratus in *The Slanderer* (fr. 9):

> (A.) The ship—is it a 20-oared *kuknos*[167]
> or a *kantharos*? If I get this additional information,
> I'll work out all the rest for myself. (B.) Don't
>     worry—it's a *kuknokantharos*
> that's formed from both of these.

Menander in *The Ship-Owner* (fr. 246, encompassing both quotations):[168]

> (A.) Theophilus has come, leaving the salty depth of
>     the Aegean
> to visit us. Straton, it's so wonderful that
> I can be the first to inform you that your son's
> good luck has held, and he's safe—as is your gold
>     *kantharos*!
> (Straton) What *kantharos*? (A.) Your ship.

And shortly after this:

> (Straton) You're saying my ship got home safe? (A.) I
>     certainly am!
> † that ship Callicles built
> the man known as; † and Euphranor of Thurii was
>     the helmsman.

1.4a), while a slightly more complete version of the fifth is preserved at Macrob. *Sat.* 5.21.15.

Πολέμων δ' ἐν τοῖς Πρὸς Ἀντίγονον Περὶ Ζωγράφων
φησίν· Ἀθήνησιν ἐν τῷ τοῦ Πειρίθου γάμῳ πεποίηκεν
d Ἵππυς²⁵ τὴν μὲν οἰνοχόην καὶ τὸ κύπελλον | λίθινα,
χρυσῷ τὰ χείλη περιτεραμνίσας, τὰς δὲ κλισίας ἐλα-
τίνας χαμᾶζε ποικίλοις στρώμασι κεκοσμημένας,
ἐκπώματα δὲ κεραμέους κανθάρους, καὶ τὸν λύχνον
ὁμοίως ⟨τὸν⟩ ἐκ τῆς ὀροφῆς ἐξηρτημένον, ἀνακε-
χυμένας ἔχοντα τὰς φλόγας. ὅτι δὲ καὶ ἀπὸ Κανθάρου
κεραμέως ὠνομάσθη τὸ ἔκπωμα Φιλέταιρός φησιν ἐν
Ἀχιλλεῖ·

Πηλεύς· ὁ Πηλεὺς δ' ἐστὶν ὄνομα κεραμέως, |
e ξηροῦ λυχνοποιοῦ, Κανθάρου, πενιχροῦ πάνυ,
ἀλλ' οὐ τυράννου νὴ Δία.

ὅτι δὲ καὶ γυναικεῖον κοσμάριόν ἐστιν κάνθαρος Ἀντιφάνης εἴρηκεν ἐν Βοιωτίᾳ.

Καρχήσιον. Καλλίξεινος ὁ Ῥόδιος ἐν τοῖς Περὶ
Ἀλεξανδρείας φησὶν ὅτι ποτήριόν ἐστιν ἐπίμηκες,
συνηγμένον εἰς μέσον ἐπιεικῶς, ὦτα ἔχον μέχρι τοῦ
πυθμένος καθήκοντα· καὶ τάχα²⁶ διὰ τὸ ἀνατετάσθαι
f οὕτως ὠνόμασται. ἀρχαιότατον | δ' ἐστὶ ποτήριον τὸ
καρχήσιον, εἴ γε ὁ Ζεὺς ὁμιλήσας Ἀλκμήνῃ ἔδωκε

---

25 Ἵππυς Dindorf: Ἱππεύς ACE
26 ἐστὶ δὲ ἱκανῶς ἐπίμηκες ποτήριον τὸ καρχήσιον, καὶ
τάχα A: ἐστὶ δὲ κτλ. om. CE, del. Kaibel

---

169 For the title of the work, see 11.497f n.
170 Plin. *Nat.* 35.141 mentions a Hippys who painted a Poseidon and a Victory, hence Dindorf's emendation of the manuscripts' Hippeus (otherwise unknown). The scene combines rus-
ticity and ostentation, as befits the wedding party of the Lapith

Polemon says in his *Response to Antigonus on Painters* (fr. 63 Preller):[169] In his Wedding of Pirithous in Athens, Hippys[170] represents the wine-pitcher and the cup as made of stone, although he gilds their lips; the couches as made of fir-limbs laid on the ground, even if covered with embroidered bed-clothes; and the drinking vessels as ceramic *kantharoi*, as also in the case of the lamp suspended from the ceiling, with its flames projecting in various directions. Philetaerus in *Achilleus* (fr. 4) claims that the drinking vessel is called after a potter named Cantharus:

Peleus; Peleus is the name of a potter[171]—
a skinny lampmaker called Cantharus, who's really
  poor.
But it's not a tyrant's name, by Zeus!

Antiphanes in *The Girl from Boeotia* (fr. 62) says that a *kantharos* is also an item of jewelry worn by women.

*Karchēsion.* Callixenus of Rhodes in his *On Alexandria* (*FGrH* 627 F 3)[172] reports that this is a tall cup that is fairly narrow in the middle and has handles that extend down to its base; perhaps it gets its name from how long and thin it is.[173] The *karchēsion* is a very old type of cup, if Zeus gave one to Alcmene after he slept with her, as a gift in re-

king Pirithous, where the guest-list included the Centaurs (cf. 11.476b with n.; 14.613a–b with n.).

[171] Punning on *pēlos* ("mud", i.e. "potter's clay"), as also at 9.383b–c and in a fragment of epic parody at 15.699b.

[172] See 11.472a n.

[173] Because the word was also used for a mast-tip; see the fragment of Asclepiades of Myrlea cited below.

δῶρον αὐτὸ τῆς μίξεως, ὡς Φερεκύδης ἐν τῇ δευτέρᾳ
ἱστορεῖ καὶ Ἡρόδωρος ὁ Ἡρακλεώτης. Ἀσκληπιάδης
δ' ὁ Μυρλεανὸς κεκλῆσθαί φησιν αὐτὸ ἀπό τινος τῶν
ἐν τῇ νηὶ κατασκευασμάτων· τοῦ γὰρ ἱστοῦ τὸ μὲν
κατωτάτω πτέρνα καλεῖται, ᾗ ἐμπίπτει εἰς τὴν ληνόν,
τὸ δ' οἷον εἰς μέσον τράχηλος, τὸ δὲ πρὸς τῷ τέλει
475    καρχήσιον. ‖ ἔχει δὲ τοῦτο κεραίας ἄνωθεν νευούσας
ἐφ' ἑκάτερα τὰ μέρη, καὶ ἐπίκειται τὸ λεγόμενον αὐτῷ
θωράκιον, τετράγωνον πάντῃ πλὴν τῆς βάσεως καὶ
τῆς κορυφῆς· αὗται δὲ προὔχουσι μικρὸν ἐπ' εὐθείας
ἐξωτέρω. ἐπὶ δὲ τοῦ θωρακίου εἰς ὕψος ἀνήκουσα καὶ
ὀξεῖα γιγνομένη ἐστὶν ἡ λεγομένη ἠλακάτη. μνημονεύει δὲ τῶν καρχησίων καὶ Σαπφὼ ἐν τούτοις·

κῆνοι δ' ἄρα πάντες
καρχάσι' ἦχον
κἄλειβον· ἀράσαντο δὲ πάμπαν ἔσλα
γάμβρῳ.

Σοφοκλῆς Τυροῖ·

προσβῆναι μέσην
τράπεζαν ἀμφὶ σῖτα καὶ καρχήσια, |

b    πρὸς τὴν τράπεζαν φάσκων προσεληλυθέναι τοὺς
δράκοντας καὶ γενέσθαι περὶ τὰ σιτία καὶ τὰ καρχή-
σια· ἔθος γὰρ ἦν τοῖς ἀρχαίοις ἐπὶ τῶν τραπεζῶν

---

174 For the story, cf. 11.781c–d, 475b–d.

175 Most likely another fragment of *On Nestor's Cup*; cf.
11.783a–b n., 477f–93e; Macrob. *Sat.* 5.21.5.

176 The first three verses of the fragment (joined to this passage by Ahrens) are quoted at 2.39a; 10.425c–d; cf. 5.192c.

turn for the sex, as Pherecydes in Book II (*FGrH* 3 F 13a) and Herodorus of Heracleia (*FGrH* 31 F 16) report.[174] Asclepiades of Myrlea[175] claims that the name comes from one of the items of gear in a ship; because the lowest part of the mast, where it sits in the mast-socket, is referred to as the *pterna* ("heel"); the central section is the *trachēlos* ("neck"); and the part near the tip is the *karchēsion*. This part supports yard-arms that bend downward on either side, and the so-called *thōrakion* ("crow's-nest"), which is rectilinear everywhere except in its base and its upper section (which extend straight out a bit further on either side), sits on top of it. On top of the *thōrakion* is the so-called *ēlakatē* ("distaff"), which extends straight up and ends in a point. Sappho (fr. 141.4–6)[176] mentions *karchēsia* in the following passage:

> So they all
> held *karchasia*
> and poured a libation; and they prayed that
> everything good might come to the
> bridegroom.[177]

Sophocles in *Tyro* (fr. 660):

> to approach the middle of
> the table, around the food and the *karchēsia*,

by which he meant that the snakes had come up the table and were in the vicinity of the food and the *karchēsia*;[178] because the ancients, as Homer represents

---

[177] Kaibel (following Macrobius) misguidedly added Cratin. fr. 40 to the text of Athenaeus at this point.

[178] Presumably a miraculous sign of some sort.

κεκραμένα τιθέναι ποτήρια, καθὰ καὶ Ὅμηρος ποιεῖ. ὠνομάσθη δὲ τὸ καρχήσιον διὰ τὸ τραχύσματα ἔχειν κεγχροειδῆ, καὶ εἴρηται κατὰ ἐναλλαγὴν τοῦ ε πρὸς τὸ ᾱ ἀντὶ τοῦ κερχήσιον· διὸ καὶ Ὅμηρος τοὺς ὑπὸ δίψους κρατουμένους καρχαλέους εἶπεν. Χάρων δ᾽ ὁ Λαμψακηνὸς ἐν τοῖς Ὥροις παρὰ Λακεδαιμονίοις φησὶν | ἔτι καὶ εἰς αὐτὸν δείκνυσθαι τὸ δέπας τὸ δοθὲν Ἀλκμήνῃ ὑπὸ Διός, ὅτε Ἀμφιτρύωνι εἰκάσθη.

Κάλπιον. ποτηρίου τι γένος Ἐρυθραίου, ὥς φησι Πάμφιλος· εἶναι δ᾽ αὐτὸ οἷόν ἐστι τὸ σκαφίον.

Κελέβη. τούτου τοῦ ἐκπώματος Ἀνακρέων μνημονεύει·

ἄγε δὴ φέρ᾽ ἡμίν, ὦ παῖ,
κελέβην, ὅκως ἄμυστιν
προπίω, τὰ μὲν δέκ᾽ ἐγχέας
ὕδατος, τὰ πέντε δ᾽ οἴνου
κυάθους.

ἄδηλον δὲ πότερον εἶδός ἐστι ποτηρίου ἢ πᾶν ποτήριον κελέβη καλεῖται ἀπὸ τοῦ χέειν εἰς αὐτὸ τὴν λοιβὴν ἤτοι λείβειν· τοῦτο δὲ ἐπὶ τοῦ ὑγροῦ συνήθως | ἔταττον, ἀφ᾽ οὗ λέγεται καὶ ὁ λέβης. Σιληνὸς δὲ καὶ Κλείταρχος τοὺς Αἰολεῖς φασιν οὕτω καλεῖν τὸ ποτήριον. Πάμφιλος δὲ τὸ ποτήριον θερμοποτίδα καλούμενον τὴν κελέβην εἶναι. Νίκανδρος δ᾽ ὁ Κολοφώνιος ἐν ταῖς Γλώσσαις ποιμενικὸν ἀγγεῖον μελιτηρὸν τὴν

---

179 Literally "rough", i.e. "rough-throated, raspy".

180 Cf. 11.474f (where this comment clearly belongs, everything in between having presumably been added from a different source) with n.

181 Quoted at slightly greater length at 10.427a.

them, made it a habit to set cups full of mixed wine on the table. The *karchēsion* got its name from the fact that it has rough sections that look like grains of millet (*kenchros*), although it is pronounced with an *alpha* substituted for the *epsilon* in the expected *kerchēsion*. This is why Homer (*Il.* 21.541) referred to people who are desperately thirsty as *karchaleoi*.[179] Charon of Lampsacus in his *Annals* (*FGrH* 262 F 2) claims that even up to his own day the goblet Zeus in disguise as Amphitryon gave to Alcmene was on display in Sparta.[180]

*Kalpion*. A type of Erythraean cup, according to Pamphilus (fr. XII Schmidt); it resembles a small bowl (*skaphion*).

*Kelebē*. Anacreon (*PMG* 356(a).1–5)[181] mentions this vessel:

> Come on, slave—bring us
> a *kelebē*, so I can drink a toast
> without pausing to breathe, after I pour in ten
> ladles of water, followed by five of
> wine.

It is unclear whether this is a specific type of cup, or whether any cup can be referred to as a *kelebē* because wine is poured (*cheein*) into it for a libation (*loibē*) or to make a libation (*leibein*); they routinely used this verb to refer to any liquid, hence the word *lebēs* ("cauldron, basin"). Silenus and Cleitarchus claim that the Aeolians use this term for a cup; Pamphilus (fr. XIII Schmidt) (says) that the cup referred to as a *thermopotis* is identical with a *kelebē*, while Nicander of Colophon in his *Glossary* (fr. 138 Schneider) (claims) that a *kelebē* is a cup used by shep-

κελέβην εἶναι. καὶ γὰρ Ἀντίμαχος ὁ Κολοφώνιος ἐν πέμπτῳ Θηβαΐδος φησί·

κήρυκας ἀθανάτοισι φέρειν μέλανος οἴνοιο
ἀσκὸν ἐνίπλειον κελέβειόν ⟨θ᾽⟩ ὅττι φέριστον |
e    οἷσιν ἐνὶ μεγάροις κεῖτο μέλιτος πεπληθός.

καὶ πάλιν·

ἀτὰρ ἀμφίθετον κελέβειον ἑλόντες
ἔμπλειον μέλιτος τὸ ῥά οἱ προφερέστερον ἦεν.

ἀλλαχοῦ δέ φησιν·

καὶ χρύσεια δέπαστρα καὶ ἀσκηθὲς κελέβειον
ἔμπλειον μέλιτος τὸ ῥά οἱ προφερέστερον εἴη.

σαφῶς γὰρ νῦν κελέβειον ἀντὶ ἀγγείου τινὸς τέθεικε, προειπὼν ποτήρια δέπαστρα. Θεόκριτος δ᾽ ὁ Συρακόσιος ἐν ταῖς Φαρμακευτρίαις φησίν·

στέψον τὰν κελέβαν φοινικέῳ οἰὸς ἀώτῳ. |

f    καὶ Εὐφορίων·

ἠὲ πόθεν ποταμῶν κελέβη ἀποήφυσας ὕδωρ;

Ἀνακρέων·

οἰνοχόει δ᾽ ἀμφίπολος μελιχρὸν
οἶνον τρικύαθον κελέβην ἔχουσα.

Διονύσιος δ᾽ ὁ Λεπτὸς ἐξηγούμενος Θεοδωρίδα τὸ εἰς τὸν Ἔρωτα μέλος τὴν κελέβην φησὶ τίθεσθαι ἐπὶ τοῦ

---

182 Quoted also at 11.468b.
183 Literally "the Skinny". The note is expanded a bit (but with

herds to hold honey. And in fact Antimachus of Colophon says in Book V of the *Thebaid* (fr. 22 Matthews):

> heralds to bring a skin-bag full of dark
> wine for the immortals, and the best *kelebeion*
> that lay within his house, full of honey.

And again (fr. 20.2–3 Matthews):

> but taking a two-handled *kelebeion*
> full of honey, the finest one he had.

And elsewhere he says (fr. 23.5–6 Matthews):[182]

> and gold goblets and an untouched *kelebeion*
> full of the finest honey he had.

He thus clearly used *kelebeion* here to refer to a storage vessel of some sort, since he mentioned goblets before this. Theocritus of Syracuse says in his *Women Practicing Witchcraft* (*Id.* 2.2):

> Cover the *keleba* with purple sheep's wool!

Also Euphorion (fr. 131, p. 52 Powell):

> Or from what river did you draw water with a *kelebē*?

Anacreon (*PMG* 383):

> A slave-girl holding a three-*kuathos kelebē*
> pours wine as sweet as honey.

Dionysius Leptos,[183] in the course of explicating Theodoridas' lyric poem in honor of Eros (*SH* 741), says that

no reference to Dionysius or Theodoridas) at 11.496d. For Thericleians, cf. 11.470d–2e.

309

ὀρθοῦ ποτηρίου οἷον Προυσιάδος καὶ Θηρικλείου. ‖

476  Κέρας. τοὺς πρώτους λέγεται τοῖς κέρασι τῶν βοῶν
πίνειν· ἀφ' οὗ τὸν Διόνυσον κερατοφυῆ πλάττεσθαι ἔτι
τε ταῦρον καλεῖσθαι ὑπὸ πολλῶν ποιητῶν. ἐν δὲ Κυ-
ζίκῳ καὶ ταυρόμορφος ἵδρυται. ὅτι δὲ τοῖς κέρασιν
ἔπινον δῆλον ἐκ τοῦ καὶ μέχρι νῦν λέγεσθαι, ὅταν
συμμίσγωσι τῷ οἴνῳ τὸ ὕδωρ, κεράσαι φάσκοντες.
καὶ τὸ ἀγγεῖον δ' ἐν ᾧ κιρνᾶται ὁ οἶνος κρατὴρ ἀπὸ
b  τοῦ συγκιρνᾶσθαι ἐν αὐτῷ τὸ ὕδωρ, ‖ <ἢ>[27] ἀπὸ τοῦ
κέρατος, οἷον κερατήρ, ἀπὸ τοῦ εἰς τὸ κέρας ἐγχεῖσθαι
τὸ πόμα. διαμένει δὲ ἔτι καὶ νῦν ἡ τῶν κεράτων
κατασκευή· καλοῦσι γοῦν ἔνιοι ταῦτα ῥυτά. καὶ τῶν
ποιητῶν δὲ πολλοὶ παράγουσι πίνοντας τοὺς ἀρχαίους
κέρασι. Πίνδαρος μὲν ἐπὶ τῶν Κενταύρων λέγων·

<ἀνδρ>οδάμαν<τα> δ' ἐπεὶ Φῆρες δάεν
ῥιπὰν μελιαδέος οἴνου,
c  ἐσσυμένως ἀπὸ μὲν λευκὸν ‖ γάλα χερσὶ
τραπεζᾶν
ὤθεον, αὐτόματοι δ' ἐξ ἀργυρέων κεράτων
πίνοντες ἐπλάζοντο.

καὶ Ξενοφῶν δ' ἐν τῇ ἑβδόμῃ τῆς Ἀναβάσεως διηγούμενος τὸ παρὰ τῷ Θρακὶ Σεύθῃ συμπόσιον γράφει

---

[27] add. Kaibel

184 Literally "horn".
185 Cf. E. Ba. 100 with Dodds ad loc., 920–1.
186 This is the correct etymology; cf. 3.123a.
187 Cf. 11.496f–7e.

the word *kelebē* is used of a tall cup like a Prousias or a Thericleian.

*Keras*.[184] It is said that people originally drank using cows' horns; as a consequence, statues of Dionysus have horns, and many poets also refer to him as a bull.[185] In Cyzicus he is worshipped in the form of a bull. That people used to drink using horns (*kerades*) is apparent from the vocabulary used even today, in that when they combine the water and the wine, they say that they are mixing (*kerasai*) them. In addition, the vessel in which the wine is mixed (*kirnatai*) is referred to as a *kratēr*, because the water is mixed (with wine) in it;[186] alternatively, the word may be from *keras* ("horn"), as if it were *keratēr*, from the fact that what they drink is poured into the horn. Drinking-horns are still manufactured today, although some people refer to them as *rhuta*.[187] Many poets also represent the ancients as drinking out of horns. Pindar, referring to the Centaurs (fr. 166):

> When the Phēres[188] caught the man-taming
> scent of the honey-sweet wine,
> they quickly shoved the white milk off the tables
> with their hands, and began to reel about uninvited,
> > drinking
> from silver horns.

Likewise Xenophon in Book VII (2.23) of his *Anabasis*, in the course of describing the party given by Seuthes the

---

[188] Another name for the Centaurs. The reference is to the wedding of Pirithous (11.474c–d n.), where the Centaurs ran wild.

οὕτως· ἐπεὶ δὲ Ξενοφῶν σὺν τοῖς μετ᾽ αὐτοῦ εἰσῆλθε
πρὸς τὸν Σεύθην, ἠσπάζοντο μὲν πρῶτον ἀλλήλους
καὶ κατὰ τὸν Θρᾴκιον νόμον κέρατα οἴνου προύτεινον.
ἐν δὲ τῇ ἕκτῃ περὶ Παφλαγόνων διηγούμενός φησι·
κατακείμενοι δ᾽ ἐν στιβάσιν ἐδείπνουν καὶ ἔπινον
κερατίνοις ποτηρίοις. Αἰσχύλος δ᾽ ἐν Περραιβίσι τοὺς
Περραιβοὺς παρίστησιν ἀντὶ ποτηρίων τοῖς κέρασι
χρωμένους διὰ τούτων·

ἀργυρηλάτοις
κέρασι χρυσᾶ στόμια προσβεβλημένοις.

καὶ Σοφοκλῆς Πανδώρᾳ·

καὶ πλῆρες ἐκπιόντι χρύσεον κέρας |
d   τρίψει † γέμοντα † μαλθακῆς ὑπ᾽ ὠλένης.

Ἕρμιππος Μοίραις·

οἶσθα νῦν ὅ μοι πόησον; τήνδε νῦν μή μοι δίδου,
ἐκ δὲ τοῦ κέρατος αὖ μοι δὸς πιεῖν ἅπαξ μόνον.

Λυκοῦργος δ᾽ ὁ ῥήτωρ ἐν τῷ Κατὰ Δημάδου Φίλιππόν
φησι τὸν βασιλέα προπίνειν κέρατι τούτοις οἷς ἐφι-
λοφρονεῖτο. τοὺς δὲ Παιόνων βασιλεῖς φησι Θεόπομπος ἐν δευτέρᾳ Φιλιππικῶν, τῶν βοῶν τῶν παρ᾽ αὐτοῖς
γινομένων μεγάλα κέρατα φυόντων, ὡς χωρεῖν τρεῖς
καὶ τέτταρας χόας, ἐκπώματα ποιεῖν ἐξ αὐτῶν, τὰ

---

189 In fact, the quotation (slightly different from what the
manuscripts of Xenophon preserve) represents Xenophon's description of how his negotiations with Seuthes began, and the dinner (a substantial portion of the description of which is quoted at
4.150f–1e) took place the next day. Cf. 1.15e for similar confusion
involving Xenophon's account of Seuthes' party.

Thracian,[189] writes as follows: When Xenophon and his companions entered Seuthes' house, they began by greeting one another and drinking horns of wine in one another's honor, in the Thracian style. And in Book VI (1.4), in the course of describing the Paphlagonians,[190] he says: They lay down on camp-beds and had dinner, and drank out of cups made of horn. Aeschylus in *The Women of Perrhaebia* (fr. 185) establishes that the Perrhaebi use horns rather than cups, in the following passage:

> horns of hammered
> silver with gold rims attached.

Also Sophocles in *Pandora* (fr. 483):

> and after he empties a full gold horn,
> she'll smash it † teeming † under her soft arm.

Hermippus in *Fates* (fr. 44):

> Do you know what you need to do for me? Don't
>     offer me this one now;
> instead, let me drink just once out of the horn.

The orator Lycurgus in his *Against Demades* (fr. 59 Conomis) claims that King Philip would drink toasts from a horn in honor of people he was well-disposed to. But Theopompus in Book II of the *History of Philip* (*FGrH* 115 F 38) says that because Paeonian cows produce horns large enough to hold three or four *choes*, their kings make

---

[190] Xenophon is actually describing the behavior of the Greeks while they were in Paphlagonian territory, although he notes that they had not brought the drinking-horns they used with them, but had found them in the country.

313

e χείλη περιαργυροῦντας καὶ χρυσοῦντας. | καὶ Φιλό-
ξενος δ᾽ ὁ Κυθήριος ἐν τῷ ἐπιγραφομένῳ Δείπνῳ
φησίν·

πίνετο νεκτάρεον
πῶμ᾽ ἐν χρυσέαις προτομαῖς
† τε ἄλλων † κεράτων,
† ἔβρεχον δὲ κατὰ μικρόν †.

Ἀθηναῖοι δὲ καὶ ἀργυρᾶ ποιοῦντες κέρατα ἔπινον ἐξ
αὐτῶν. ἔστι γοῦν τοῦτο εὑρεῖν ἐν τοῖς Δημιοπράτοις
ἀναγεγραμμένον οὕτως· < ... > ἐκ στήλης ἀνακειμένης
ἐν ἀκροπόλει ἡ τὰ ἀναθήματα περιέχει· κέρας ἔκπωμα
ἀργυροῦν, καὶ περισκελὶς πρόσεστι.

Κέρνος. ἀγγεῖον κεραμεοῦν, ἔχον ἐν αὐτῷ πολλοὺς
κοτυλίσκους κεκολλημένους, ἐν οἷς, φησίν, μήκωνες
f λευκοί, πυροί, | κριθαί, πισοί, λάθυροι, ὦχροι, φακοί. ὁ
δὲ βαστάσας αὐτὸ οἷον λικνοφορήσας τούτων γεύεται,
ὡς ἱστορεῖ Ἀμμώνιος ἐν τρίτῳ Περὶ Βωμῶν καὶ Θυ-
σιῶν.

Κισσύβιον. τὸ μόνωτον ποτήριον Φιλήμων. Νεοπτόλεμος δ᾽ ὁ Παριανὸς ἐν τρίτῳ Γλωσσῶν τὸ κίσσινον ποτήριον σημαίνειν παρ᾽ Εὐριπίδῃ ἐν Ἀνδρο-
μέδᾳ· ||

477
πᾶς δὲ ποιμένων ἔρρει λεώς,
ὁ μὲν γάλακτος κίσσινον φέρων σκύφος,
πόνων ἀναψυκτήρ᾽, ὁ δ᾽ ἀμπέλων γάνος.

---

191 The quotation has fallen out of the text.
192 For what follows, cf. 11.478c–d, which makes it clear that
this material is drawn from Polemon's *On the Sacred Fleece*.

drinking vessels out of them, covering the lips with silver or gold. So too Philoxenus of Cythera says in his poem entitled *The Dinner Party* (Philox. Leuc. *PMG* 836(d)):

A nectar-like drink
 was being consumed from gold animal-head cups
  † and of others † made from horns,
 † and they were drenching little by little †.

The Athenians used to make silver horns and drink from them. The following, for example, can be found inscribed in the records of the public auctions thus:[191] . . . from a stele set up on the Acropolis that contains a list of the dedications (*IG* II² 1407.38): a silver drinking-horn, and a decorative band is attached to it.

*Kernos*.[192] A ceramic vessel that contains a large number of smaller cups attached to one another, in which, he reports (Polemon fr. 88 Preller), are white poppy-seed, grains of wheat and barley, peas, vetch-seeds, birds' pease, and lentils. The man who carries it, in the same way that someone might carry a sacred winnowing-shovel, tastes these, according to Ammonius in Book III of *On Altars and Sacrifices* (*FGrH* 361 F 2).

*Kissubion*. A cup with a single handle, according to Philemon. Neoptolemus of Parium in Book III of the *Glossary* (fr. 10a Mette) (claims) that the word is used in Euripides' *Andromeda* (fr. 146) to refer to a cup made of ivy wood (*kissinos*):

 All the shepherd-folk wandered in;
 one man brought an ivy-wood bowl (*kissinos skuphos*)
  full of milk,
 which offers refreshment after hard work, another
  the gleaming product of the vines.

τὸ γὰρ κισσύβιον, φησί, λέγεται ἐπὶ συνόδου ἀγροι-
κικῆς, ἔνθα προσήκει μάλιστα τὸ ξύλινον ποτήριον.
Κλείταρχος δέ φησιν Αἰολεῖς τὸν σκύφον κισσύβιον
καλεῖν· Μαρσύας δὲ κύπελλον καὶ τὸ ξύλινον ποτήριον. Εὔμολπος δὲ γένος τι ποτηρίου, ἴσως, φησίν,
κατ᾽ ἀρχὰς ἐκ κισσίνου κατασκευασθὲν ξύλου. Νίκαν-
b δρος δὲ ὁ Κολοφώνιος ἐν τῷ | πρώτῳ τῶν Αἰτωλικῶν
γράφει· ἐν τῇ ἱεροποιίῃ τοῦ Διδυμαίου Διὸς κισσοῦ
σπονδοποιέονται πετάλοισιν, ὅθεν τὰ ἀρχαῖα ἐκπώματα κισσύβια φωνέεται. Ὅμηρος·

> κισσύβιον μετὰ χερσὶν ἔχων μέλανος οἴνοιο.

Ἀσκληπιάδης δ᾽ ὁ Μυρλεανὸς ἐν τῷ Περὶ τῆς Νεστορίδος, σκύφει, φησί, καὶ κισσυβίῳ τῶν μὲν ἐν ἄστει
καὶ μετρίων οὐδεὶς ἐχρῆτο, συβῶται δὲ καὶ νομεῖς καὶ
οἱ ἐν ἀγρῷ· Πολύφημος μὲν τῷ κισσυβίῳ, θατέρῳ δὲ
c Εὔμαιος. Καλλίμαχος δ᾽ ἔοικε | διαμαρτάνειν ἐν τῇ
συγχρήσει τῶν ὀνομάτων, λέγων ἐπὶ τοῦ Ἰκίου ξένου
τοῦ παρὰ τῷ Ἀθηναίῳ Πόλλιδι συνεστιασθέντος
αὐτῷ·

> καὶ γὰρ ὁ Θρηϊκίην μὲν ἀνήνατο χανδὸν ἄμυστιν
> ζωροποτεῖν[28], ὀλίγῳ δ᾽ ἥδετο κισσυβίῳ.

[28] 10.442f (supported by a papyrus) has ἀπέστυγε χανδὸν
ἄμυστιν / οἰνοποτεῖν.

---

[193] Quoted again at 11.498f (along with Od. 14.112–13, which
is more relevant to the discussion there).

[194] Sc. at Od. 9.346–61. Homer never says where the cup
comes from, but the obvious implication of the text is that Odysseus found it in the Cyclops' cave.

Because the word *kissubion*, he says, is used in connection
with gatherings of country-folk, when a wooden cup is
most appropriate. Cleitarchus claims that the Aeolians refer to a bowl (*skuphos*) as a *kissubion*, whereas Marsyas
(*FGrH* 135/6 F 22) says that another word for a wooden
cup is *kupellos*. Eumolpus (identifies) this as a type of cup,
perhaps, he says, originally made of ivy (*kissinos*) wood.
Nicander of Colophon writes in Book I of his *History of
Aetolia* (fr. 1 Schneider): In the ritual in honor of Didy-
mean Zeus, they pour libations from ivy (*kissos*) leaves,
which is why ancient drinking vessels are referred to as
*kissubia*. Homer (*Od.* 9.346):

> holding a *kissubion* of dark wine in my hands.

Asclepiades of Myrlea says in his *On Nestor's Cup*:[193] No
one from the city or who was even moderately well-to-do
used a bowl (*skuphos*) or a *kissubion*. Instead it was swine-
herds, shepherds, and country-folk: Polyphemus used a
*kissubion*,[194] while Eumaeus (*Od.* 14.112) used a *skuphos*.
Callimachus (fr. 178.11–14 Pfeiffer)[195] seemingly uses the
words incorrectly, when he says of the stranger from Icus
who was entertained along with him[196] in the house of
Pollis of Athens:

> For he in fact hated drinking strong wine greedily in
>     a long
> Thracian draft, but liked a small *kissubion*.

[195] Verses 11–12 are quoted also at 10.442f, while verses 15–
16 are quoted at 1.32b–c.
[196] I.e. the poem's narrator.

317

τῷ μὲν ἐγὼ τόδ' ἔλεξα περιστείχοντος ἀλείσου
τὸ τρίτον.

ὁ γὰρ λέγων ἄλεισον τὸ αὐτὸ καὶ κισσύβιον τὴν
ἀκριβῆ θέσιν τῶν ὀνομάτων οὐ διαφυλάττει. εἰκάσειε |

d δ' ἄν τις τὸ κισσύβιον τὸ πρῶτον ὑπὸ ποιμένων
ἐργασθῆναι ἐκ κισσίνου ξύλου. ἄλλοι δὲ ἐτυμολο-
γοῦσιν αὐτὸ ἀπὸ τοῦ χεῖσθαι, τὸ δ' ἐστὶ χωρεῖν·

οὐδὸς δ' ἀμφοτέρους ὅδε χείσεται.

καὶ ἡ τοῦ ὄφεως κατάδυσις χειή, ἡ καταδεχομένη τὸ
ζῷον· καὶ κήθιον τὸ χήτιον τὸ χωροῦν τοὺς ἀστρα-
γάλους. Διονύσιος δ' ὁ Σάμιος ἐν τοῖς Περὶ τοῦ
Κύκλου τὸ Ὁμηρικὸν κισσύβιον κυμβίον ἔφη γράφων

e οὕτως· | καὶ αὐτὸν Ὀδυσσεὺς ὁρῶν ταῦτα ποιοῦντα
πληρώσας τοῦ οἴνου κυμβίον δίδωσι πιεῖν.

Κιβώριον. Ἡγήσανδρος ὁ Δελφὸς Εὐφορίωνά
φησι τὸν ποιητὴν παρὰ Πρυτάνιδι δειπνοῦντα καὶ
ἐπιδεικνυμένου τοῦ Πρυτάνιδος κιβώριά τινα δοκοῦν-
τα πεποιῆσθαι πολυτελῶς, τοῦ κώθωνος εὖ μάλα προ-
βεβηκότος, λαβὼν ἓν τῶν κιβωρίων ὡς ἐξοινῶν καὶ
μεθύων ἐνεούρησε. Δίδυμος δέ φησι ποτηρίου εἶδος
εἶναι, καὶ τάχ' ἂν εἴη τὰ λεγόμενα σκυφία διὰ τὸ

---

197 Deponent future infinitive of *chandanō* ("hold, contain").
198 The word is used at *Il.* 22.93, 95.
199 The word is not attested elsewhere in the sense "box" with
a *chi*, and the odd spelling must be a product of the awkward attempt to derive *kissubion* from *cheisthai*.
200 Cited again at 11.481e. The Cycle in question is the Epic
Cycle (including but not limited to the *Iliad* and the *Odyssey*).

To him I said the following, as the bowl (*aleison*) was
    going around
  for the third time.

For anyone who refers to an *aleison* and a *kissubion* as
identical is not respecting the precise sense of the words.
One might conjecture that *kissubia* were originally made
of ivy (*kissinos*) wood by shepherds. But other authorities
derive the word from *cheisthai*,[197] in the sense "to have
room for" (*Od.* 18.17):

This threshold will accommodate (*cheisetai*) us both.

The place snakes descend to, that gives the creature somewhere to hide, is also a *cheiē* ("hole");[198] and the little
*chētos*[199] used to store knucklebones is a *kēthion* ("dice-
box"). Dionysius of Samos in his *On the Cycle* (*FGrH* 15
F 4a)[200] wrote as follows, claiming that the Homeric *kissubion* is a *kumbion*:[201] And when Odysseus sees him doing
this, he fills a *kumbion* with the wine and offers it to him to
drink.

*Kibōrion.* Hegesander of Delphi (fr. 21, *FHG* iv.417)
claims that the poet Euphorion was having dinner with
Prytanis, and Prytanis showed him some *kibōria* that
seemed to be very expensively made. After the party had
gone on for a long time, Euphorion, who had consumed
a large amount of wine and was drunk, took one of the
*kibōria* and urinated in it. Didymus (p. 75 Schmidt) says
that this was a type of cup; perhaps it is to be identified

---

[201] Apparently a comment on *Od.* 9.345–6; what Odysseus has
just seen Polyphemus do is snatch two more members of his crew
and prepare them for dinner (*Od.* 9.344).

f  κάτωθεν εἰς στενὸν | συνῆχθαι ὡς τὰ Αἰγύπτια κιβώ-
ρια.

Κόνδυ. ποτήριον Ἀσιατικόν. Μένανδρος Κόλακι·

κοτύλας χωροῦν δέκα
ἐν Καππαδοκίᾳ κόνδυ χρυσοῦν, Στρουθία.

Ἵππαρχος Ἀνασῳζομένοις·

(Α.) προσέχεις τι τούτῳ τῷ στρατιώτῃ; † τοῦ δε
δειου †
ἀργύριον οὗτος; οὐδαμόθεν, εὖ οἶδ᾽ ἐγώ,
ἀλλ᾽ ἢ δαπίδιον ἓν ἀγαπητὸν ποικίλον,
Πέρσας ἔχον καὶ γρῦπας ἐξώλεις τινὰς ‖
478  τῶν Περσικῶν. (Β.) ἐς κόρακας, ὦ μαστιγία.
(Α.) καὶ κόνδυ καὶ ψυκτήριον καὶ κυμβίον.

Νικόμαχος δ᾽ ἐν πρώτῳ Περὶ Ἑορτῶν Αἰγυπτίων
φησί· τὸ δὲ κόνδυ ἐστὶ μὲν Περσικόν, τὴν δὲ ἀρχὴν †
ἦν Ἕρμιππος ἀστρολογικὸς ὡς ὁ κόσμος ἐξ οὗ τῶν
θεῶν τὰ θαύματα καὶ τὰ καρπώσιμα γίνεσθαι ἐπὶ γῆς
† διὸ ἐκ τούτου σπένδεσθαι. Παγκράτης δ᾽ ἐν πρώτῳ
Βοκχορηΐδος·

αὐτὰρ ὅ γε σπείσας ἐκ κόνδυος ἀργυφέοιο |
b  νέκταρ ἐπ᾽ ἀλλοδαπὴν οἶμον ἔβαινε πόδα.

Κονώνειος. Ἴστρος ὁ Καλλιμάχειος ἐν πρώτῳ Πτο-
λεμαΐδος τῆς Ἐν Αἰγύπτῳ Πόλεως γράφει οὕτως·
κυλίκων Κονωνείων ζεῦγος καὶ Θηρικλείων χρυσο-
κλύστων ζεῦγος.

---

202 Cf. 3.72a–b.
203 Quoted at greater length at 10.434b–c.
204 See 11.486c (on the supposed origin of the name).

with what are called *skuphia* because the lower part tapers
to a nub like an Egyptian bean (*kibōrion*).[202]

*Kondu*. An Asiatic cup. Menander in *The Flatterer*
(*Kol.* fr. 2.1–2 Körte–Thierfelder):[203]

> in Cappadocia, Strouthias,
> a gold *kondu* that held ten ladles.

Hipparchus in *Men Who Were Returning Home Safely*
(fr. 1):

> (A.) Are you paying any attention to this soldier?
> [corrupt]
> silver . . . this guy? From nowhere, I'm sure of that—
> except one nice embroidered rug
> with Persians and some damned Persian
> griffins on it. (B.) To hell with you, you lowlife!
> (A.) And a *kondu*, a wine-cooling vessel, and a
>     *kumbion*.

Nicomachus says in Book I of *On Egyptian Festivals*
(*FGrH* 662 F 1): The *kondu* is a Persian vessel, but originally † which the astrologer Hermippus (*SH* 486 = fr. 102
Wehrli) that the created order from which the marvels and
profitable deeds of the gods occurred on earth, † which is
why it is used to pour libations. Pancrates in Book I of the
*Bocchoreïs* (*SH* 602):

> But after he poured a libation of nectar from a silver
> *kondu*, he set off on a journey to another land.

*Konōneios*.[204] Callimachus' student Istrus writes as follows in Book I of *The Egyptian City of Ptolemaïs* (*FGrH*
334 F 47): a pair of *Konōneis kulikes* and a pair of gilded
Thericleians.

Κότυλος. τὰ μόνωτα ποτήρια κότυλοι, ὧν καὶ Ἀλκαῖος μνημονεύει. Διόδωρος δ' ἐν τῷ πρὸς Λυκόφρονα
παρὰ Σικυωνίοις καὶ Ταραντίνοις ἐπιπολάζειν φησὶ τὸ
ἔκπωμα, εἶναι δ' αὐτὸ λουτηρίῳ ἐοικὸς βαθεῖ· ἔχει δὲ
καὶ οὖς ἐνιαχῇ. μνημονεύει δὲ αὐτοῦ καὶ Ἴων ὁ Χῖος

< . . . > κότυλον οἴνου πλέον

c λέγων. | Ἕρμιππος δὲ ἐν Θεοῖς·

τόν τε κότυλον πρῶτον ἤνεγκ' ἐνέχυρον τῶν
γειτόνων.

καὶ Πλάτων ἐν Διὶ Κακουμένῳ

< . . . > τὸν κότυλον φέρει

φησί. καὶ Ἀριστοφάνης ἐν Βαβυλωνίοις· < . . . >.
Εὔβουλος δ' ἐν Ὀδυσσεῖ ἢ Πανόπταις·

ὁ δ' ἱερεὺς Εὐήγορος
ἐν μέσοις αὐτοῖσιν ἑστὼς τὴν καλὴν σκευὴν
ἔχων
οἶνον ἐξέσπενδε κοτύλῳ.

Πάμφιλος δὲ ποτηρίου φησὶν εἶναι γένος, ἴδιον δ'
εἶναι Διονύσου. Πολέμων δ' ἐν τῷ Περὶ τοῦ Δίου
Κῳδίου φησί· μετὰ δὲ ταῦτα τὴν τελετὴν ποιεῖ καὶ
αἱρεῖ τὰ ἐκ τῆς θαλάμης καὶ νέμει ὅσοι ἄνω τὸ κέρνος
d περιενηνοχότες. τοῦτο | δ' ἐστὶν ἀγγεῖον κεραμεοῦν
ἔχον ἐν αὐτῷ πολλοὺς κοτυλίσκους κεκολλημένους·

---

205 Cf. 11.478e (clearly drawn from the same passage).
206 The quotation has fallen out of the text, but is preserved at
Poll. 10.85.

*Kotulos*. *Kotuloi* are cups with a single handle, and are mentioned by Alcaeus (fr. 417). Diodorus in his *To Lycophron* (Gloss. Ital. 128 K–A) says that this vessel is common in Sicyon and Tarentum, and resembles a deep *loutērion*; sometimes it has a handle.[205] Ion of Chios (*TrGF* 19 F 51) also mentions it, saying:

a *kotulos* full of wine.

Hermippus in *Gods* (fr. 29):

And first he brought the *kotulos* as security from his neighbors.

And Plato says in *Zeus Abused* (fr. 48):

He brings the *kotulos*.

Also Aristophanes in *Babylonians* (fr. 68):[206] ... Eubulus in *Odysseus or Men Who See Everything* (fr. 71):

The priest Euagorus
was standing in their midst holding a beautiful vessel
and pouring a libation of wine from a *kotulos*.

Pamphilus (fr. XVII Schmidt) claims that this is a type of cup associated with Dionyus in particular. Polemon says in his *On the Sacred Fleece* (fr. 88 Preller):[207] After this, he carries out the ritual, removing what is in the sacred chamber and dividing the contents among everyone who has helped hold the *kernos* up and carry it around. The latter is a ceramic vessel that contains a large number of smaller cups (*kotuliskoi*) attached to one another; in these are

---

[207] Cf. 11.476e–f (a slightly condensed version of the same material) with n.

ἔνεισι δ' ἐν αὐτοῖς ὅρμινοι, μήκωνες λευκοί, πυροί,
κριθαί, πισοί, λάθυροι, ὦχροι, φακοί, κύαμοι, ζειαί,
βρόμος, παλάθιον, μέλι, ἔλαιον, οἶνος, γάλα, οἷον
ἔριον ἄπλυτον. ὁ δὲ τοῦτο βαστάσας οἷον λικνοφορήσας τούτων γεύεται.

Κοτύλη. Ἀριστοφάνης Κωκάλῳ· † ἄλλαι ὑπο-
πρεσβύτεραι γρᾶες Θασίου μέλανος μεστὸν κεραμευ-
ομέναις κοτύλαις μεγάλαις ἔγχεον ἐς σφέτερον δέμας
e  οὐδὲν ἀκόσμον, ἔρωτι βιαζόμεναι μέλανος | οἴνου
ἀκράτου. † Σιληνὸς καὶ Κλείταρχος ἔτι τε Ζηνόδοτος
τὴν κύλικα·

πάντῃ δ' ἀμφὶ νέκυν κοτυλήρυτον ἔρρεεν αἷμα.

καί·

πολλὰ μεταξὺ πέλει κοτύλης καὶ χείλεος ἄκρου.

Σιμάριστος δὲ τὸ λεπτὸν ποτήριον οὕτως καλεῖσθαι.
Διόδωρος δὲ τὸν παρά τισι κότυλον κοτύλην ὠνομακέναι τὸν ποιητήν·

< ... > πύρνον καὶ κοτύλην·[29]

ὃν κύλικα μὲν οὐκ εἶναι, οὐ γὰρ ἔχειν ὦτα, παραπλήσιον δ' ὑπάρχειν λουτηρίῳ βαθεῖ, ποτηρίου δὲ
f  εἶδος εἶναι. δύνασθαι δὲ | καὶ τὸν παρὰ τοῖς Αἰτωλοῖς
καί τισι τῶν Ἰώνων λεγόμενον κότυλον, ὃν ὅμοιον
ὄντα τῷ προειρημένῳ ἐν οὓς ἔχειν. μνημονεύει δ' αὐτοῦ
Κράτης ἐν Παιδιαῖς καὶ Ἕρμιππος ἐν Θεοῖς. Ἀθηναῖοι

[29] The traditional text of Homer has κοτύλην καὶ πύρνον.

---

208 Cf. Zenob. 5.71 (who, however, has *kulikos* for Athenaeus'
*kotulēs*).          209 Literally "the poet".

sage, white poppy-seed, grains of wheat and barley, peas, vetch-seeds, birds' pease, lentils, beans, emmer, oats, a cake of dried fruit, honey, olive oil, wine, milk, and a bit of unwashed sheep's wool. The man who carries it, in the same way that someone might carry a sacred winnowing-shovel, tastes these items.

*Kotulē*. Aristophanes in *Cocalus* (fr. 364, unmetrical and lacunose): † Other elderly hags were using large ceramic *kotuloi* to pour . . . full of dark Thasian (wine) into their bodies, not at all indecorous, driven by their desire for unmixed dark wine. † Silenus and Cleitarchus, along with Zenodotus, (identify this with) a *kulix* (*Il.* 23.34):

> And blood was flowing everywhere around the corpse
>   by the cupful (*kotulēruton*).

Also:[208]

> There's many a slip 'twixt the *kotulē* and the lip.

Simaristus (claims) that this is a term for a small, fine cup. Diodorus says that Homer[209] (*Od.* 15.312) refers to what some people call a *kotulos* as a *kotulē*:

> wheat-bread and a *kotulē*.

This, (he says,) is not a *kulix*, since it lacks handles, but resembles a deep *loutērion* and is a type of cup;[210] it might also be what the Aetolians and some Ionians refer to as a *kotulos*, which resembled the vessel discussed above, but has a single handle. Crates mentions it in *Children's Games* (fr. 29), as does Hermippus in *Gods* (fr. 29).[211]

---

[210] Cf. 11.478b (where the work in question is identified as Diodorus' *To Lycophron*) with n.     [211] Quoted at 11.478c.

δὲ μέτρον τι καλοῦσι κοτύλην. Θουκυδίδης· ἐδίδοσαν
μὲν αὐτῶν ἑκάστῳ ἐπὶ ὀκτὼ μῆνας κοτύλην ὕδατος καὶ
δύο κοτύλας σίτου. Ἀριστοφάνης Προάγωνι·

> ὁ δ' ἀλφίτων < ... > πριάμενος τρεῖς χοίνικας
> κοτύλης δεούσας ἑκτέα λογίζεται. ||

479   Ἀπολλόδωρος δὲ ποτηρίου τι γένος ὑψηλὸν καὶ ἔγκοι-
λον. πᾶν δὲ τὸ κοῖλον κοτύλην, φησίν, ἐκάλουν οἱ
παλαιοί, ὡς καὶ τὸ τῶν χειρῶν κοῖλον· ὅθεν καὶ κοτυλήρυτον αἷμα τὸ ἀμφοτέραις ταῖς χερσὶν ἀρυσθῆναι
δυνάμενον. καὶ ἐν κοτύλῃ δέ τις παιδιὰ καλεῖται, ἐν ᾗ
κοιλάναντες τὰς χεῖρας δέχονται τὰ γόνατα τῶν νενι-
κηκότων οἱ νενικημένοι καὶ βαστάζουσιν αὐτούς. Διόδωρος δ' ἐν Ἰταλικαῖς Γλώσσαις καὶ Ἡράκλειτος, ὥς
φησι Πάμφιλος, τὴν κοτύλην καλεῖσθαι καὶ ἡμίναν,
παρατιθέμενος Ἐπιχάρμου·

b   καὶ πιεῖν ὕδωρ διπλάσιον χλιαρόν, ἡμίνας δύο.

καὶ Σώφρων· κατάστρεψον, τέκνον, τὰν ἡμίναν. κοτυ-
λίσκην δ' εἴρηκε Φερεκράτης ἐν Κοριαννοῖ·

> < ... > (Β.) τὴν κοτυλίσκην. (Α.) μηδαμῶς.

Ἀριστοφάνης ἐν Ἀχαρνεῦσι·

> κοτυλίσκιον τὸ χεῖλος ἀποκεκρουμένον.

---

212 Sc. per day; referring to the Athenian prisoners held in the
stone-quarries in Syracuse after the failure of the Sicilian Expedition.   213 A reference to *Il.* 23.34 (quoted at 11.478e).

214 Thus presumably Crates in *Children's Games*, cited above.

215 That the word is cited from Epicharmus and Sophron but
from no one else leaves little doubt that it is a bit of Western Greek
vocabulary.   216 Quoted also at 14.648d.

The Athenians refer to a unit of measure as a *kotulē*.
Thucydides (7.87.2): For eight months they gave each of
them a *kotulē* of water and two *kotulai* of grain.[212] Aristophanes in *The Proagon* (fr. 481):

> He bought three *choinikes* of barley-groats
> minus one *kotulē*, but he's charging me for a *hekteus*!

Apollodorus (*FGrH* 244 F 254) (identifies this as) a type of
high, deep cup. The ancients, he says, referred to anything hollow, for example the hollow of one's hands, as a
*kotulē*; blood that can be scooped up in one's cupped hands
is accordingly referred to as *kotulērutos*.[213] There is also
a game known as "In a *kotulē*", in which the losers have
to cup their hands, take the knees of the winners in them,
and pick them up.[214] According to Pamphilus (fr. VIII
Schmidt), Diodorus in the *Italian Glossary* and Heraclei-
tus (say) that a *kotulē* is also referred to as a *hēmina*.[215] He
cites a passage from Epicharmus (fr. 289):[216]

> and to drink twice as much warm water, two *hēminai*.

Also Sophron (fr. 100): Turn the *hēmina* upside-down,
child! Pherecrates uses the diminutive *kotuliskē* in
*Corianno* (fr. 75.4):[217]

> (B.) the *kotuliskē*. (A.) Don't!

Aristophanes in *Acharnians* (459):[218]

> a little *kotuliskē* with a chipped rim.

---

[217] An extract from a fragment quoted at greater length at
11.481a–b (where the manuscripts, however, offer the accusative
form of *kuliskē* rather than of *kotuliskē*).          [218] The manuscripts of Aristophanes have *kuliskion* or variants thereof, rather
than Athenaeus' *kotuliskion* (which is probably correct).

κοτύλη δὲ καλεῖται καὶ ἡ τοῦ ἰσχίου κοιλότης, καὶ αἱ τοῦ πολύποδος ἐν ταῖς πλεκτάναις ἐπιφύσεις παραγώγως κοτυληδόνες. καὶ τὰ κύμβαλα δ᾽ Αἰσχύλος ἐν Ἠδωνοῖς κοτύλας εἴρηκεν·

ὁ δὲ χαλκοδέτοις κοτύλαις ὀτοβεῖ.

c Μαρσύας δέ φησι | τὸ ἐν τῷ ἰσχίῳ ὀστοῦν καλεῖσθαι ἄλεισον καὶ κύλικα. κοτυλίσκος δὲ καλεῖται ὁ ἱερὸς τοῦ Διονύσου κρατηρίσκος, καὶ οἷς χρῶνται οἱ μύσται, ὡς Νίκανδρός φησιν ὁ Θυατειρηνὸς παρατιθέμενος τὸ ἐκ Νεφελῶν Ἀριστοφάνους·

< ... > μηδὲ στέψω κοτυλίσκον.

Σιμμίας δὲ ἀποδίδωσι τὴν κοτύλην ἄλεισον.

Κοτταβίς. Ἁρμόδιος ὁ Λεπρεάτης ἐν τῷ Περὶ τῶν Κατὰ Φιγάλειαν Νομίμων διεξιὼν περὶ τῶν ἐπιχωρίων δείπνων γράφει καὶ ταῦτα· καθαγισάντων ταῦτα ἐν d κεραμέα κοτταβίδι πιεῖν ἑκάστῳ | μικρόν, καὶ ὁ προσφέρων ἀνεῖπεν "εὐδειπνίας." Ἡγήσανδρος δ᾽ ὁ Δελφὸς ἐν Ὑπομνήμασιν, ὧν ἀρχή, Ἐν τῇ ἀρίστῃ πολιτείᾳ, φησίν· ὁ καλούμενος κότταβος παρῆλθεν εἰς τὰ συμπόσια τῶν περὶ Σικελίαν, ὥς φησιν Δικαίαρχος, πρῶτον εἰσαγαγόντων. τοσαύτη δὲ ἐγένετο σπουδὴ περὶ τὸ ἐπιτήδευμα ὥστε εἰς τὰ συμπόσια παρεισφέρειν ἆθλα κοτταβεῖα καλούμενα. εἶτα κύλικες αἱ πρὸς τὸ πρᾶγμα

219 A reference to *Il.* 5.305–6.    220 From the lost original version of the play (rather than the revised version preserved for us today).    221 An extract from a much longer fragment quoted at 4.148f–9d (this section at 4.149a–b).

222 Cf. 11.782e–f (from the Epitomator, with no mention of Hegesander) with n. For cottabus, see 15.665d–8f.

The hollow part of the hip-joint is also called the *kotulē*,[219] and the sucker-pads on an octopus' tentacles are referred to (e.g. *Od.* 5.433) with a term derived from this, *kotulē-dones*. In addition, Aeschylus in *Edonians* (fr. 57.6) refers to cymbals as *kotulai*:

> and another creates an uproar with bronze-edged
> *kotulai*.

But Marsyas (*FGrH* 135/6 F 23) says that the hip-bone is referred to as an *aleison* or *kulix*. The small sacred mixing-bowl of Dionysus used by the initiates is called a *kotuliskos*, according to Nicander of Thyateira (*FGrH* 343 F 13), who cites the verse from Aristophanes' *Clouds* (fr. 395):[220]

> and that I not garland a *kotuliskos*.

Simmias glosses *kotulē* as *aleison*.

   *Kottabis.* Harmodius of Lepreum in his *On the Customs in Phigaleia* (*FGrH* 319 F 1.15–16),[221] in the course of offering details of the local dining practices, writes the following: After they dedicated these items, each guest was given a little wine to drink in a ceramic *kottabis*; the man who served it would say "Enjoy your dinner!" Hegesander of Delphi in his *Commentaries*, which begin with the words "In the best state", says (fr. 32, *FHG* iv.419):[222] What is known as cottabus was a later addition to drinking parties; according to Dicaearchus (fr. 97 Wehrli), the Sicilians were the first to introduce it. They were so devoted to this activity that they also introduced prizes, known as *kottabeia*, to their parties. Subsequently, the cups that ap-

χρήσιμαι μάλιστ' εἶναι δοκοῦσαι κατεσκευάζοντο, κα-
e λούμεναι κοτταβίδες. πρὸς δὲ | τούτοις οἶκοι κατεσκευ-
άζοντο κυκλοτερεῖς, ἵνα πάντες εἰς τὸ μέσον τοῦ
κοττάβου τεθέντος ἐξ ἀποστήματος ἴσου καὶ τόπων
ὁμοίων ἀγωνίζοιντο περὶ τῆς νίκης. οὐ γὰρ μόνον
ἐφιλοτιμοῦντο βάλλειν ἐπὶ τὸν σκοπόν, ἀλλὰ καὶ
καλῶς ἕκαστα αὐτῶν· ἔδει γὰρ εἰς τὸν ἀριστερὸν
ἀγκῶνα ἐρείσαντα καὶ τὴν δεξιὰν ἀγκυλώσαντα
ὑγρῶς ἀφεῖναι τὴν λάταγα· οὕτω γὰρ ἐκάλουν τὸ
πῖπτον ἐκ τῆς κύλικος ὑγρόν. ὥστε ἔνιοι μεῖζον ἐφρόνουν ἐπὶ τῷ καλῶς κοτταβίζειν τῶν ἐπὶ τῷ ἀκοντίζειν
μέγα φρονούντων.

Κρατάνιον. μήποτε τὸ νῦν καλούμενον κρανίον
f ἔκπωμα οὕτως ὠνόμαζον | οἱ ἀρχαῖοι. Πολέμων γοῦν ἢ
ὅστις ἐστὶν ὁ ποιήσας τὸν ἐπιγραφόμενον Ἑλλαδικὸν
περὶ τοῦ ἐν Ὀλυμπίᾳ λέγων Μεταποντίνων ναοῦ
γράφει καὶ ταῦτα· ναὸς Μεταποντίνων, ἐν ᾧ φιάλαι
ἀργυραῖ ἑκατὸν καὶ τριάκοντα καὶ δύο, οἰνοχόαι ἀργυραῖ δύο, ἀποθυστάνιον ἀργυροῦν, φιάλαι τρεῖς ἐπί-
480 χρυσοι. ναὸς Βυζαντίων, ‖ ἐν ᾧ Τρίτων κυπαρίσσινος
ἔχων κρατάνιον ἀργυροῦν, Σειρὴν ἀργυρᾶ, καρχήσια
δύο ἀργυρᾶ, κύλιξ ἀργυρᾶ, οἰνοχόη χρυσῆ, κέρατα
δύο. ἐν δὲ τῷ ναῷ τῆς Ἥρας τῷ παλαιῷ φιάλαι
ἀργυραῖ τριάκοντα, κρατάνια ἀργυρᾶ δύο, χύτρος
ἀργυροῦς, ἀποθυστάνιον χρυσοῦν, κρατὴρ χρυσοῦς,
Κυρηναίων ἀνάθημα, βατιάκιον ἀργυροῦν.

Κρουνεῖα. Ἐπιγένης Μνηματίῳ·

peared to be best suited to the business began to be produced; these were known as *kottabides*. In addition, round rooms began to be constructed, so that when the target[223] was placed in the middle, everyone would be able to compete for the prize from an equal distance and identical locations. They were anxious not only to hit the mark, but to carry out the entire activity gracefully; because the participants had to lean on their left elbow, bend their right wrist, and toss the *latax*—this was their term for the liquid that fell from the cup—fluidly. As a consequence, some people were prouder of playing cottabus well than others were of throwing the javelin.

*Kratanion*. Perhaps this is the term the ancients used for the drinking vessel referred to today as a *kranion*. Polemon (fr. 22 Preller), at any rate—or whoever the author of the work entitled *An Account of Hellas* is—writes the following about the treasury of the Metapontians at Olympia: A treasury belonging to the Metapontians, within which are: 132 silver *phialai*; 2 silver wine-pitchers; a silver *apothustanion*; and three gilt *phialai*. A treasury belonging to the Byzantines, within which are: a Triton made of cypress-wood, holding a silver *kratanion*; a silver Siren; two silver *karchēsia*; a silver *kulix*; a gold wine-pitcher; and two drinking-horns. Inside the old temple of Hera are: 30 silver *phialai*; two silver *kratania*; a silver cook-pot; a gold *apothustanion*; a gold mixing-bowl, dedicated by the people of Cyrene; and a silver *batiakion*.

*Krouneia*. Epigenes in *The Tomb* (fr. 6.1–2):[224]

---

[223] Literally "the *kottabos*".

[224] An excerpt from a longer fragment quoted at 11.472e–f (but with the second verse corrupt); cf. 11.486b–c.

(Α.) κρατῆρες, κάδοι,
ὁλκεῖα, κρουνεῖ. (Β.) ἔστι γὰρ κρουνεῖα; (Α.) ναί.

b     Κυαθίς. κοτυλῶδες ἀγγεῖον. | Σώφρων ἐν τῷ ἐπι-
γραφομένῳ μίμῳ Γυναῖκες Αἲ τὰν Θεόν Φαντι Ἐξε-
λᾶν· ὑποκατώρυκται δὲ ἐν κυαθίδι τρικτὺς ἀλεξιφαρ-
μάκων.

    Κύλιξ. Φερεκράτης Δουλοδιδασκάλῳ·

> νυνὶ δ' ἀπόνιζε τὴν κύλικα δώσων πιεῖν,
> ἔγχει τ' ἐπιθεὶς τὸν ἠθμόν.

ταῦτα δ' ἐστὶ κεράμεα ποτήρια καὶ λέγεται ἀπὸ τοῦ
κυλίεσθαι τῷ τροχῷ· ἀφ' ὧν καλεῖται τό τε κυλικεῖον,
ἐν ᾧ τίθεται τόπῳ τὰ ποτήρια, κἂν ἀργυρᾶ τυγχάνῃ
c ὄντα, καὶ τὸ κυλικηγορεῖν, ὅταν ἐπὶ τῇ | κύλικί τις
ἀγορεύῃ. Ἀθηναῖοι δὲ καὶ τὴν ἰατρικὴν πυξίδα καλοῦσι κυλιχνίδα διὰ τὸ τῷ τόρνῳ κεκυλίσθαι. ἐγένοντο δ'
ἐπίσημοι κύλικες αἵ τε Ἀργεῖαι καὶ αἱ Ἀττικαί. καὶ
τῶν μὲν Ἀττικῶν μνημονεύει Πίνδαρος ἐν τοῖσδε·

> ὦ Θρασύβουλ', ἐρατᾶν ὄχημ' ἀοιδᾶν
> τοῦτό ‹τοι› πέμπω μεταδόρπιον. ἐν ξυνῷ κεν εἴη
> συμπόταισίν τε γλυκερὸν καὶ Διωνύσοιο καρπῷ
> καὶ κυλίκεσσιν Ἀθηναίαισι κέντρον.

αἱ δ' Ἀργεῖαι δοκοῦσι καὶ τὸν τύπον ἔχειν διάφορον
d πρὸς τὰς | Ἀττικάς. φοξαὶ γοῦν ἦσαν τὸ χεῖλος, ὡς
Σιμωνίδης φησὶν ὁ Ἀμόργιος·

---

225 A false etymology.
226 Cf. 11.460d–f.
227 Cf. 11.461e with n.     228 Other portions of the fragment are preserved at 11.782d; 14.641b–c.

(A.) Mixing-bowls, *kadoi*,
basins, *krouneia*. (B.) There are really *krouneia*? (A.)
Yeah.

*Kuathis*. A vessel that resembles a *kotulē*. Sophron in
the mime entitled *Women Who Claim to Be Driving out
the Goddess* (fr. 3): A three-fold sacrifice of healing drugs
has been buried beneath it in a *kuathis*.

*Kulix*. Pherecrates in *The Slave Teacher* (fr. 45):

Now wash out the *kulix*, so you can give me a drink;
and put a strainer over it and pour some wine.

These are ceramic cups which get their name from the fact
that they are turned (*kuliesthai*) on a potter's wheel;[225] they
in turn are the source of the terms *kulikeion* (the place
where cups are stored, even if they are made of silver)[226]
and *kulikēgorein* (when someone makes a speech while
drinking from a *kulix*).[227] The Athenians also refer to a
physician's storage box as a *kulichnis*, because it has been
turned (*kekulisthai*) on a lathe. Argive and Attic *kulikes*
were much sought-after. Pindar (fr. 124a)[228] mentions the
Attic variety in the following passage:

Thrasybulus, I send you this carriage
of lovely songs as an after-dinner treat. At your party
it might be
a pleasant spur for your guests, for Dionysus'
fruit, and for your Athenian *kulikes*.

The Argive variety apparently have a different shape than
the Attic. They had a pointed (*phoxai*) rim, at any rate, according to Simonides of Amorgos (Semon. fr. 27 West[2]):

αὕτη δὲ φοξὴ χεῖλος ‹Ἀργείη κύλιξ›,[30]

ἡ εἰς ὀξὺ ἀνηγμένη, οἷοί εἰσιν οἱ ἄμβικες καλούμενοι.
τὸ γὰρ φοξὸν ἐπὶ τούτου τάττουσι, καθότι Ὅμηρος ἐπὶ
τοῦ Θερσίτου·

φοξὸς ἔην κεφαλήν.

καὶ ἔστιν οἷον φαοξός, ὁ πρὸς τὰ φάη ὀξὺς ὁρώμενος.
διάφοροι δὲ κύλικες γίνονται καὶ ἐν τῇ τοῦ συσσίτου
e ἡμῶν Ἀθηναίου πατρίδι Ναυκράτει· | εἰσὶν γὰρ φια-
λώδεις μέν, οὐ κατὰ τόρνον, ἀλλ᾿ ὥσπερ δακτύλῳ
πεποιημέναι, καὶ ἔχουσιν ὦτα τέσσαρα, πυθμένα εἰς
πλάτος ἐκτεταμένον (πολλοὶ δ᾿ ἐν τῇ Ναυκράτει κερα-
μεῖς ἀφ᾿ ὧν καὶ ἡ πλησίον τῶν κεραμείων πύλη
Κεραμικὴ καλεῖται) καὶ βάπτονται εἰς τὸ δοκεῖν εἶναι
ἀργυραῖ. ἐπαινοῦνται δὲ καὶ αἱ Χῖαι κύλικες, ὧν μνημονεύει Ἕρμιππος ἐν Στρατιώταις·

Χία δὲ κύλιξ ὑψοῦ κρέμαται
περὶ πασσαλόφιν.

Γλαύκων δ᾿ ἐν ταῖς Γλώσσαις Κυπρίους φησὶ τὴν
f κοτύλην κύλικα | καλεῖν. Ἑρμῶναξ δ᾿ ἐν Συνωνύμοις
οὕτως γράφει· ἄλεισον, ποτήριον, κύπελλον, ἄμφωτις,
σκύφος, κύλιξ, κώθων, καρχήσιον, φιάλη. Ἀχαιὸς δὲ ὁ
Ἐρετριεὺς ἐν Ἀλκμαίωνι ἀντὶ τοῦ κύλικες παραγώγως
κυλιχνίδας εἴρηκε διὰ τούτων·

ἀλλ᾿ ὡς τάχιστα μέλανα δεῦρ᾿ ἀμνὸν φέρειν
κοινόν τε χρὴ κρατῆρα καὶ κυλιχνίδας.

[30] The final two words of the quotation (which are necessary to
the sense in Athenaeus and must have been lost accidentally) are
preserved at Σ Il. 2.219 (cited below).

This is an Argive *kulix* with a pointed rim,

that is, one with a sharp tip, like what are referred to as *ambikes*. Because this is how they use the adjective *phoxos*, as Homer does in his description of Thersites (*Il.* 2.219):

He had a pointed (*phoxos*) head.

The word is, as it were, *phaoxos*, "someone who appears sharp around his eyes" (*phaē oxus*).[229] Excellent *kulikes* can also be found in Naucratis, the native city of our fellow-guest Athenaeus. They resemble *phialai*, but are made not on a lathe, but by hand, as it were; and they have four handles and a broadly extended base—there are many potters in Naucratis, and the gate nearest to the potters' quarter is called the Ceramic Gate because of them—and are painted to make them resemble silver. Chian *kulikes* also have a good reputation; Hermippus mentions them in *Soldiers* (fr. 55):

A Chian *kulix* is hanging high up
on a wall-peg.

Glaucon in his *Glossary* says that the Cyprians refer to a *kotulē* as a *kulix*. Hermonax writes as follows in *Synonyms: aleison, potērion, kupellon, amphōtis, skuphos, kulix, kōthōn, karchēsion, phialē*. Achaeus of Eretria in *Alcmaeon* (*TrGF* 20 F 14) uses the derivative form *kulichnides* rather than *kulikes* in the following passage:

But as fast as you can, you need to bring a black lamb
here, and a mixing-bowl we can share, and some
   *kulichnides*.

[229] A false etymology.

481   καὶ Ἀλκαῖος ‖ κυλίχνας·

πώνωμεν· τί τὰ λύχν᾽ ὀμμένομεν; δάκτυλος
   ἀμέρα·
κὰδ δ᾽ ἄερρε κυλίχναις μεγάλαις, ἆιτα,
   ποικίλαις·
οἶνον γὰρ Σεμέλας καὶ Δίος ⟨υἶος⟩ λαθικάδεα
ἀνθρώποισιν ἔδωκ᾽. ἔγχεε κέρναις ἕνα καὶ ⟨ . . . ⟩
   πλήαις.

καὶ ἐν τῷ δεκάτῳ·

λάταγες ποτέονται κυλίχναν ἀπὺ Τηίαν,

ὡς διαφόρων γινομένων καὶ ἐν Τέῳ κυλίκων.
Φερεκράτης Κοριαννοῖ·

(Α.) ἐκ τοῦ βαλανείου γὰρ δίεφθος ἔρχομαι,
ξηρὰν ἔχουσα τὴν φάρυγα. (Β.) δώσω πιεῖν.
(Α.) γλίσχρον γέ μούστὶ τὸ σίαλον νὴ τὼ θεώ. ‖
b   (Β.) † εἰ λάβω κυρισοι † τὴν κυλίσκην. (Α.)
   μηδαμῶς
μικράν γε· κινεῖται γὰρ εὐθύς μοι χολή,
ἐξ οὗπερ ἔπιον ἐκ τοιαύτης φάρμακον.
ἐς τὴν ἐμὴν νῦν ἔγχεον τὴν μείζονα.

ὅτι δὲ μεγάλοις ποτηρίοις αἱ γυναῖκες ἐχρῶντο ὁ
αὐτὸς εἴρηκε Φερεκράτης ἐν Τυραννίδι διὰ τούτων·

εἶτ᾽ ἐκεραμεύσαντο τοῖς μὲν ἀνδράσιν ποτήρια ‖
c   πλατέα, τοίχους οὐκ ἔχοντ᾽ ἀλλ᾽ αὐτὸ τοὔδαφος
   μόνον,

---

230 Quoted at slightly greater length at 10.430c–d; cf. 10.430a.
231 Dionysus.    232 Part of verse 4 is quoted also (in a
slightly different form) at 11.479b.

And Alcaeus (fr. 346.1–5)[230] (used the form) *kulichnes*:

> Let's drink! Why are we waiting for the lamps?
>     There's only a sliver of daylight left.
> Take down the fancy large *kulichnai*, sweet boy;
> for the son of Semele and Zeus[231] gave human beings
>     wine
> to help them forget their troubles. Mix it one . . .
> filling it!

Also in Book X (fr. 322):

> Drops of wine are flying from Teian *kulichnes*;

for excellent *kulikes* can also be found on Teos.
Pherecrates in *Corianno* (fr. 75):[232]

> (A.) Because I'm coming from the bathhouse, having
>     been boiled to death;
> my throat's dry. (B.) I'll give you something to drink.
> (A.) My spit's sticky, by the two goddesses!
> (B.) † If I get [corrupt] † the *kuliskē*. (A.) Don't (use)
> the little one! My stomach's been upset
> ever since I drank medicine out of a cup like that.
> This time pour my drink into this bigger one I've got!

The same Pherecrates claims that women used large cups,
in the following passage from *Tyranny* (fr. 152):[233]

> Then they had flat cups made for their
> husbands with no sides, just a bottom

[233] Although the word *kulikes* occurs in the fourth line of this
fragment, it is only marginally relevant to the topic at hand. The
final verse is quoted also at 11.460c.

κοὐχὶ χωροῦντ᾽ οὐδὲ κόγχην, ἐμφερῆ
γευστηρίοις·
σφίσι δέ ⟨γ᾽⟩ αὐταῖσιν βαθείας κύλικας ὥσπερ
ὁλκάδας
οἰναγωγούς, περιφερεῖς, λεπτάς, μέσας
γαστροίδας,
οὐκ ἀβούλως, ἀλλὰ πόρρωθεν κατεσκευασμέναι
αὖθ᾽, ὅπως ἀνεκλογίστως πλεῖστος οἶνος ἐκποθῇ. |

d  εἶθ᾽ ὅταν τὸν οἶνον αὐτὰς αἰτιώμεθ᾽ ἐκπιεῖν,
λοιδοροῦνται κὠμνύουσι μὴ πιεῖν ἀλλ᾽ ἢ μίαν.
ἡ δὲ κρείττων ἡ μί᾽ ἐστὶ χιλίων ποτηρίων.

Κυμβία. τὰ κοῖλα ποτήρια καὶ μικρὰ Σιμάριστος.
Δωρόθεος δέ· γένος ποτηρίων βαθέων τὰ κυμβία καὶ
ὀρθῶν, πυθμένα μὴ ἐχόντων μηδὲ ὦτα. Πτολεμαῖος δὲ
ὁ τοῦ Ἀριστονίκου τὰ κυφά. Νίκανδρος δ᾽ ὁ Θυατειρηνὸς τὸ χωρὶς ὠτίων ποτήριον ὠνομακέναι Θεόπομ-
πον ἐν Μήδῳ. Φιλήμων Φάσματι·

ἔπιεν ἡ Ῥόδη
e  κυμβίον | ἀκράτου· κατασέσεις᾽ ὑμᾶς ἄνω.

Διονύσιος δ᾽ ὁ Σάμιος ἐν ἕκτῳ Περὶ τοῦ Κύκλου τὸ
αὐτὸ οἴεται εἶναι κισσύβιον καὶ κυμβίον· φησὶ γὰρ ὡς
Ὀδυσσεὺς πληρώσας κυμβίον ἀκράτου ὤρεξε τῷ Κύκλωπι. οὐκ ἔστι δὲ μικρὸν τὸ διδόμενον αὐτῷ κισσύ-

---

234 Or "son".

235 Cf. 11.477d–e (a reference to the same passage) with n.

236 Homer uses the word *kissubion*, hence Athenaeus' conclu-
sion that Dionysius equated the two terms.

that wouldn't even hold a sip, like sampling-bowls.
But for themselves they ordered *kulikes* as deep as
    wine-transport
ships, nice and round, with thin walls that swell out in
    the middle into pot-bellies.
And that wasn't a mistake; they'd planned it long
ago, so they could drink lots of wine and no one
    would notice.
Then whenever we accuse them of consuming it all,
they call us names and swear they only had a single
    cup.
But that "single cup" is bigger than 1000 normal
    ones!

*Kumbia*. Small concave cups, according to Simaristus.
Dorotheus: *Kumbia* are a type of tall, deep cup with
no base or handles. Ptolemy the student[234] of Aristonicus
(Aristonic. test. 4 Razzetti) (claims that these are) cups
with a slumped shape. Nicander of Thyateira (*FGrH* 343 F
14) (says that) Theopompus in *The Mede* (fr. 32) uses the
word to refer to a cup that lacks handles. Philemon in *The
Phantom* (fr. 87):

> Rhode drank
> a *kumbion* of unmixed wine; she's knocked you onto
>     your feet.

Dionysius of Samos in Book VI of *On the Cycle* (*FGrH* 15
F 4b)[235] believes that a *kissubion* is identical to a *kumbion*;
because he says that after (*Od.* 9.346) Odysseus filled a
*kumbion*[236] of unmixed wine, he offered it to the Cyclops.
The *kissubion* offered to the Cyclops in Homer cannot be a
small vessel; because (if it were), he would not have be-

βιον παρ' Ὁμήρῳ· οὐ γὰρ ἂν τρὶς πιὼν μέγιστος ὢν τὸ
σῶμα ταχέως ἂν ὑπὸ τῆς μέθης κατηνέχθη. τοῦ κυμ-
βίου μνημονεύει καὶ Δημοσθένης ἐν τῷ Κατὰ Μειδίου
ἀκολουθεῖν αὐτῷ φάσκων ῥυτὰ καὶ κυμβία. καὶ ἐν τῷ
f  Κατὰ Εὐέργου | καὶ Μνησιβούλου. φησὶ δὲ Δίδυμος ὁ
γραμματικὸς ἐπίμηκες εἶναι τὸ ποτήριον καὶ στενὸν
τῷ σχήματι, παρόμοιον πλοίῳ. καὶ Ἀναξανδρίδης ἐν
Ἀγροίκοις·

(Α.) μεγάλ' ἴσως ποτήρια
προπινόμενα καὶ μέστ' ἀκράτου κυμβία
ἐκάρωσεν ὑμᾶς. (Β.) ἀνακεχαίτικεν μὲν οὖν.

Ἄλεξις Ἱππεῖ·

(Α.) τά τε κυμβία
482  ⟨ἆρ'⟩ ἦν ‖ πρόσωπ' ἔχοντα χρυσᾶ παρθένων;
(Β.) νὴ τὸν Δί', ἦν γάρ. (Α.) ὦ τάλαιν' ἐγὼ
κακῶν.

Ἐρατοσθένης δ' ἐν τῇ Πρὸς Ἀγήτορα τὸν Λάκωνα
Ἐπιστολῇ ὡς κυαθῶδες ἀγγεῖον τὸ κυμβίον παρα-
δίδωσι γράφων οὕτως· θαυμάζουσι δὲ οἱ αὐτοὶ καὶ πῶς
κύαθον μὴ κεκτημένος, ἀλλὰ κυμβίον μόνον, φιάλην
προσεκέκτητο. δοκεῖ δή μοι τὸ μὲν τῆς τῶν ἀνθρώπων
χρείας ἕνεκα, τὸ δὲ τῆς τῶν θεῶν τιμῆς εἰς τὴν κτῆσιν
παρειληφέναι. κυάθῳ μὲν οὖν οὐδὲν ἐχρῶντο τότε οὐδὲ
b  κοτύλῃ· | κρατῆρα γὰρ ἵστασαν τοῖς θεοῖς, οὐκ ἀργυ-
ροῦν οὐδὲ λιθοκόλλητον, ἀλλὰ γῆς Κωλιάδος. τοῦτον
δ' ὁσάκις ἐπί τι πληρώσαιεν, ἀποσπείσαντες τοῖς
θεοῖς ἐκ τῆς φιάλης ᾠνοχόουν ἐφεξῆς, τὸν νεοκράτα

---

237 Kaibel misguidedly inserted additional references to
Demosthenes drawn from Macrob. 5.21.9 here.

come drunk so quickly after having had three drinks, given how large he is. Demosthenes in his *Against Meidias* (21.158) mentions a *kumbion*, saying that drinking-horns and *kumbia* accompany him everywhere.[237] So too in his *Against Euergus and Mnesibulus* (47.58). The grammarian Didymus (p. 75 Schmidt) argues that the cup has a long, narrow shape, like a ship. Also Anaxandrides in *Rustics* (fr. 3):

> (A.) Perhaps the big cups that were
> offered as toasts and the *kumbia* full of unmixed wine
> stunned you. (B.) Actually, they knocked us off our
> feet!

Alexis in *The Knight* (fr. 100):

> (A.) And did the *kumbia*
> have girls' faces made of gold on them?
> (B.) Yes, by Zeus, they did. (A.) Oh miserable me!
> What problems I've got!

Eratosthenes in his *Letter in Response to Agetor of Sparta* (p. 201 Bernhardy), on the other hand, writes as follows, implying that a *kumbion* is a vessel that resembles a *kuathos*: The same people are amazed at the fact that, if he did not own a *kuathos*, but only a *kumbion*, he also owned a *phialē*. In my opinion, the former was for human beings to use, whereas he had acquired the latter in addition in order to honor the gods. In those days, they did not use a ladle (*kuathos*) or a cup (*kotulē*); instead, they set up a mixing-bowl—and not one made of silver or with inset jewels, but one made of clay from Colias—in honor of the gods. And every time they filled it for some reason, they poured a libation to the gods with the *phialē*, and then poured wine

341

βάπτοντες τῷ κυμβίῳ, καθὰ καὶ νῦν παρ' ὑμῖν ποιοῦσιν ἐν τοῖς φιδιτίοις. εἰ δέ ποτε πλεῖον πιεῖν βουλη-
θεῖεν, προσπαρετίθεσαν τοὺς καλουμένους κοτύλους,
κάλλιστα καὶ εὐποτώτατα ἐκπωμάτων. ἦσαν δὲ καὶ
οὗτοι τῆς αὐτῆς κεραμείας. ὅταν δ' Ἔφιππος ἐν Ἐφή-
βοις λέγῃ· |

c      οὐ κύλικας ἐπὶ τὰ δεῖπνα Χαιρήμων φέρει;
     οὐ κυμβίοισι πεπολέμηκ' Εὐριπίδης;,

οὐ τὸν τραγικὸν λέγει ποιητήν, ἀλλά τινα ὁμώνυμον
αὐτῷ, ἤτοι φίλοινόν τινα ἢ αἰτίαν ἔχοντα οὐ χρηστήν,
ὥς φησιν Ἀντίοχος ὁ Ἀλεξανδρεὺς ἐν τῷ Περὶ τῶν Ἐν
τῇ Μέσῃ Κωμῳδίᾳ Κωμῳδουμένων Ποιητῶν· τὸ γὰρ
ἐπάγεσθαι κατὰ τὰς ἑστιάσεις κυμβία καὶ δοκεῖν
τούτοις διαμάχεσθαι εἰς ἑκάτερα τείνει. μνημονεύει δ'
αὐτοῦ καὶ Ἀναξανδρίδης ἐν Νηρηίσιν· |

d                    (Α.) δὸς δὴ τὸν χοᾶ
     αὐτῷ σύ, Κῶμε, καὶ τὸ κυμβίον φέρων.
     (Β.) Εὐριπίδης τις τήμερον γενήσεται.

καὶ Ἔφιππος ἐν Ὁμοίοις ἢ Ὀβελιαφόροις·

     Διονυσίου δὲ δράματ' ἐκμαθεῖν δέοι
     καὶ Δημοφῶντος ἅττ' ἐπόησεν εἰς Κότυν,
     ῥήσεις τε κατὰ δεῖπνον Θεόδωρός μοι λέγοι,
     Λάχητί τ' οἰκήσαιμι τὴν ἑξῆς θύραν,

---

238 I.e. in Sparta. For the Spartan messes, see 4.138b–41f, esp.
141a–e.      239 Sc. as the mixing-bowl.
240 PAA 444547; known only from the passages quoted below.
Chaeremon is perhaps the tragic poet (TrGF 71).
241 Dionysius is Dionysius I, tyrant of Syracuse and would-be
tragic poet (PAA 350340; TrGF 76 T 5). Nothing else is known of
Demophon (PAA 321650) or Laches (PAA 602162). But the Cotys

for everyone, one person after the next, using the *kumbion* to dip out the wine they had just mixed, just as people do nowadays in your country[238] at the men's messes. And if they ever wanted to drink more, they also set out what were known as *kotuloi*, which were their finest vessels and the easiest to drink from. These were made from the same material.[239] When Ephippus says in *Ephebes* (fr. 9):

> Doesn't Chaeremon bring *kulikes* to dinner parties?
> Doesn't Euripides wage war with *kumbia*?,

he is not referring to the tragic poet, but to another individual by the same name,[240] either someone who likes wine or someone with a bad reputation, according to Antiochus of Alexandria in his *On the Poets Ridiculed in Middle Comedy*; because the charge of bringing *kumbia* to feasts and of having a reputation for using them as weapons would apply in either case. Anaxandrides also mentions this Euripides in *Nereids* (fr. 33):

> (A.) Give him the pitcher,
> Comus—and bring the *kumbion* too!
> (B.) He's going to turn into a Euripides today!

Also Ephippus in *Men Who Looked Like One Another or Spitbearers* (fr. 16):

> May I have to memorize Dionysius' plays,
> along with everything Demophon wrote about Cotys;
> may Theodorus recite speeches to me during dinner;
> may I live next door to Laches;[241]

in question is presumably the 4th-century BCE king of Thrace (see 4.131a n.), while Theodorus must be the mid-4th-century tragic actor (O'Connor #230; Stephanis #1157; *PAA* 506155).

κυμβία τε παρέχοιμ᾽ ἑστιῶν Εὐριπίδῃ.

ὅτι δὲ καὶ πλοῖον ἡ κύμβη Σοφοκλῆς ἐν Ἀνδρομέδᾳ φησίν· |

e　ἵπποισιν ἢ κύμβαισι ναυστολεῖς χθόνα;

κύββα ποτήριον Ἀπολλόδωρος Παφίους.

Κύπελλον. τοῦτο πότερόν ἐστιν ταὐτὸν τῷ ἀλείσῳ καὶ τῷ δέπαι ‹καὶ μόνον› ὀνόματι διαλλάσσει·

τοὺς μὲν ἄρα χρυσέοισι κυπέλλοις υἷες Ἀχαιῶν
δειδέχατ᾽ ἄλλοθεν ἄλλος ἀνασταδόν;

ἢ διάφορος ἦν ὁ τύπος καὶ οὐχ ὥσπερ τὸ δέπας καὶ τὸ ἄλεισον ἀμφικύπελλον, οὕτω δὲ καὶ τοῦτο † κυφὸν δὲ μόνον †; ἀπὸ γὰρ τῆς κυφότητος τὸ κύπελλον, ὥσπερ
f　καὶ τὸ ἀμφικύπελλον. | ἢ ὅτι παραπλήσιον ἦν ταῖς πέλλαις, συνηγμένον μᾶλλον εἰς τὴν κυφότητα; ἢ ἀμφικύπελλα οἷον ἀμφίκυρτα ἀπὸ τῶν ὤτων, διὰ τὸ τοιαῦτα εἶναι τῇ κατασκευῇ. φησὶ γὰρ καὶ ὁ ποιητής·

ἦ τοι ὁ καλὸν ἄλεισον ἀναιρήσεσθαι ἔμελλε,
χρύσεον ἄμφωτον.

Ἀντίμαχος δ᾽ ἐν πέμπτῳ Θηβαΐδος·

πᾶσιν δ᾽ ἡγεμόνεσσιν ἐποιχόμενοι κήρυκες
χρύσεα καλὰ κύπελλα τετυγμένα νώμησαντο.

---

242 Cited also at 11.483a.
243 Cf. 11.783a–c (perhaps from the same source, and certainly a closely related discussion).
244 These are false etymologies.
245 Cf. *EM* p. 90.43–6 (citing Aristarchus).
246 Quoted also at 11.783b.

and may I furnish Euripides with *kumbia* when I'm
giving a feast!

Sophocles in *Andromeda* (fr. 127) says that a *kumbē* is also
a boat:

Do you travel the earth on horseback or on *kumbai*?

Apollodorus (*FGrH* 244 F 224)[242] (reports that) the
Paphians (refer to) a cup as a *kubba*.

*Kupellon*. Is this the same as an *aleison* or a *depas*,[243]
and is the only difference the name:

The sons of the Achaeans then stood up and toasted
them
from all sides with gold *kupella* (*Il.* 9.670–1)?

Or is the shape different, and is a *kupellon* not *amphi-
kupellon*, like a *depas* or an *aleison*, but is it thus † but only
bulging †? Because the word *kupellos* is derived from
*kuphotēs* ("bentness, squatness"), as is *amphikupellos*.[244]
Or did it resemble *pellai*, although it was more compressed
and thus more squat? Or are they called *amphikupella* in
the sense *amphikurta* ("gibbous, convex on both sides"),
referring to the handles, because this is how they are constructed?[245] For Homer says (*Od.* 22.9–10):[246]

He was in fact just about to lift a beautiful gold
two-handled *aleison*.

Antimachus in Book V of the *Thebaid* (fr. 24 Matthews):

The heralds approached all the commanders
and distributed beautiful *kupella* made of gold.

345

Σιληνὸς δέ φησι· κύπελλα ἐκπώματα σκύφοις ὅμοια,
ὡς καὶ Νίκανδρος ὁ Κολοφώνιος, < . . . >· ||

483  < . . . > κύπελλα δὲ νεῖμε συβώτης.

Εὔμολπος δὲ ποτηρίου γένος, ἀπὸ τοῦ κυφὸν εἶναι.
Σιμάριστος δὲ τὸ δίωτον ποτήριον Κυπρίους, τὸ δὲ
δίωτον καὶ τετράωτον Κρῆτας. Φιλητᾶς δὲ Συρακοσί-
ους κύπελλα καλεῖν τὰ τῆς μάζης καὶ τῶν ἄρτων ἐπὶ
τῆς τραπέζης καταλείμματα.

Κύμβη. Φιλήμων ἐν ταῖς Ἀττικαῖς Φωναῖς κύλικος
εἶδος. Ἀπολλόδωρος δ᾽ ἐν τῷ Περὶ Ἐτυμολογιῶν Παφίους τὸ ποτήριον καλεῖν κύββα.

b  Κώθων. Λακωνικὸν ποτήριον, | οὗ μνημονεύει Ξενο-
φῶν ἐν πρώτῳ Κύρου Παιδείας. Κριτίας δ᾽ ἐν Λακεδαιμονίων Πολιτείᾳ γράφει οὕτως· χωρὶς δὲ τούτων τὰ
σμικρότατα ἐς τὴν δίαιταν· ὑποδήματα ἄριστα Λακω-
νικὰ <καὶ> ἱμάτια φορεῖν ἥδιστα καὶ χρησιμώτατα·
κώθων Λακωνικός, ἔκπωμα ἐπιτηδειότατον εἰς στρα-
τείαν καὶ εὐφορώτατον ἐν γυλιῷ. οὗ δὲ ἕνεκα στρατιω-
τικόν, πολλάκις ἀνάγκη ὕδωρ πίνειν οὐ καθαρόν.
πρῶτον μὲν οὖν τὸ μὴ λίαν κατάδηλον εἶναι τὸ πόμα·
c  εἶτα ἄμβωνας ὁ κώθων ἔχων ὑπολείπει | τὸ οὐ καθαρὸν
ἐν αὐτῷ. καὶ Πολέμων δ᾽ ἐν τῇ < . . . >31 τῶν Πρὸς
Ἀδαῖον καὶ Ἀντίγονον, ὅτι κεραμέοις ἀγγείοις ἐχρῶν-

31 ἐν τῷ πρώτῳ Preller

---

247 The quotation has fallen out of the text, along with the reference to Homer that followed.
248 Cited also at 11.482e.
249 Sc. deserve commendation.
250 Sc. when one is drinking from a *kōthōn*. Cf. Plu. *Lyc.* 9.4–5.

But Silenus says: *Kupella* are drinking vessels that resemble *skuphoi*, for example Nicander of Colophon (fr. 140 Schneider):[247] . . . (*Od.* 20.253):

The swineherd distributed *kupella*.

Eumolpus, on the other hand, (claims that a *kupellon* is) a type of cup (and that the name comes from the fact that it is *kuphos* ("squat"). Simaristus (says that) the Cyprians (use the term *kupellon* for) a two-handled cup, while the Cretans (use it for) a two- or four-handled cup. But Philetas (fr. 10 Dettori = fr. 38 Spanoudakis = Gloss. Ital. 29 K–A) (claims that) the Syracusans refer to the scraps of barley-cake and bread left on the table as *kupella*.

*Kumbē*. Philemon in his *Attic Vocabulary* (says that this is) a type of *kulix*. Apollodorus in his *On Etymologies* (*FGrH* 244 F 224)[248] (reports that) the Paphians refer to a cup as a *kubba*.

*Kōthōn*. A Spartan cup, mentioned by Xenophon in Book I (2.8) of the *Education of Cyrus*. Critias writes as follows in the *Constitution of the Spartans* (88 B 34 D–K): Apart from these matters, the smallest details of their way of life.[249] The best shoes, as well as the robes that are most comfortable to wear and convenient, are the Spartan variety; the *kōthōn*, a drinking vessel particularly well-suited to military campaigning and easily carried in a backpack, is also characteristic of Sparta. The reason it is well-suited to military use is that soldiers are frequently forced to drink dirty water. In the first place, then, it is not easy to see what one is drinking;[250] second, the fact that the *kōthōn* has a rim that curves in means that the muck is trapped inside it. So too Polemon in Book . . . of his *Response to Adaeus and Antigonus* (fr. 61 Preller) writes as follows, (arguing) that

347

το οἱ Λακεδαιμόνιοι γράφει οὕτως· ἀλλὰ μὴν ὅτι
ἀρχαϊκὸν ἦν τὸ τοιοῦτον τῆς ἀγωγῆς γένος, ὃ καὶ νῦν
δρᾶται παρά τισι τῶν Ἑλλήνων· ἐν Ἄργει μὲν ἐν ταῖς
δημοσίαις θοίναις, ἐν Λακεδαίμονι δὲ κατὰ τὰς ἑορ-
τάς, ἔν τε τοῖς ἐπινικίοις καὶ τοῖς γάμοις τῶν παρθένων, πίνουσιν ἐκ κεραμέων ποτηρίων· ἐν δὲ τοῖς ἄλλοις
συμποσίοις καὶ φιδιτίοις ἐν πιθάκναις < ... > μνη-
d μονεύει | αὐτοῦ καὶ Ἀρχίλοχος ἐν Ἐλεγείοις ὡς ποτη-
ρίου οὕτως·

ἀλλ' ἄγε σὺν κώθωνι θοῆς διὰ σέλματα νηὸς
    φοίτα καὶ κοίλων πώματ' ἄφελκε κάδων,
ἄγρει δ' οἶνον ἐρυθρὸν ἀπὸ τρυγός· οὐδὲ γὰρ
    ἡμεῖς
    νηφέμεν ἐν φυλακῇ τῇδε δυνησόμεθα,

ὡς τῆς κύλικος λεγομένης κώθωνος. Ἀριστοφάνης
Ἱππεῦσιν·

        εἰς τὰς ἱππαγωγοὺς εἰσεπήδων ἀνδρικῶς,
e    πριάμενοι κώθωνας, οἱ δὲ <καὶ> σκόροδα | καὶ
    κρόμμυα.

Ἡνίοχος Γοργόσι·

    πιεῖν πιεῖν τις ἐγχείτω λαβὼν
† πυριγενῆ κυκλοτερῆ βραχύωτον παχύστομον
κώθωνα παῖδα φάρυγος.

Θεόπομπος Στρατιώτισιν·

ἐγὼ γὰρ <ἂν> κώθωνος ἐκ στρεψαύχενος
πίοιμι τὸν τράχηλον ἀνακεκλασμένη;

the Spartans used ceramic vessels: In fact, this sort of education, which some Greeks practice even today, was traditional: at the public feasts in Argos, and at the public festivals in Sparta, as well as at their victory celebrations and the wedding feasts for their girls, they drink out of ceramic cups. Whereas at their other parties and at the men's messes in casks . . . Archilochus in the *Elegies* (fr. 4.6–9 West[2]) refers to a *kōthōn* as a type of cup, as follows:

> But come now—take a *kōthōn* and make your way
>    through the rowing-benches of the swift
> ship; draw something to drink from the hollow
>    jars;
> and separate the red wine from the lees. Because we
>    are not
> going to be able to stay sober during this watch,

treating the *kōthōn* like what is generally called a *kulix*. Aristophanes in *Knights* (599–600):

> They bought *kōthōnes* and jumped bravely into
> the horse-transports, while others purchased garlic
>    and onions.

Heniochus in *Gorgons* (fr. 1):

> Let someone fetch † a fire-born, rounded, short-
>    handled,
> thick-lipped *kōthōn*, a slave to serve my throat,
> and pour me something to drink, to drink!

Theopompus in *Female Soldiers* (fr. 55):

> Because I'd bend my neck back
> and drink out of a throat-twisting *kōthōn*?

Ἄλεξις Ἐρίθοις·

εἶτα τετρακότυλον ἐπεσόβει κώθωνά μοι,
παλαιὸν οἴκων κτῆμα.

ἀπὸ δὲ τοῦ ποτηρίου τούτου καὶ ἀκρατοκώθωνας καλοῦσι τοὺς πλέονα ἄκρατον σπῶντας, ὡς Ὑπερείδης
f ἐν τῷ Κατὰ Δημοσθένους. Καλλίξεινος δ' | ἐν τετάρτῳ
Περὶ Ἀλεξανδρείας ἀναγράφων τὴν τοῦ Φιλαδέλφου
πομπὴν καὶ καταλέγων πολλὰ ἐκπώματα γράφει καὶ
τάδε· κώθωνες διμέτρητοι δύο. περὶ δὲ τοῦ κωθωνίζεσθαι καὶ ὅτι χρήσιμός ἐστι διὰ χρόνου ὁ κωθω-
νισμὸς Μνησίθεος ὁ Ἀθηναῖος ἰατρὸς ἐν τῇ Περὶ
Κωθωνισμοῦ Ἐπιστολῇ φησιν οὕτως· συμβαίνει τοὺς
μὲν πολὺν ἄκρατον ἐν ταῖς συνουσίαις πίνοντας
484 μεγάλα βλάπτεσθαι καὶ τὸ σῶμα καὶ τὴν ψυχήν. || τὸ
μέντοι κωθωνίζεσθαι διά τινων ἡμερῶν δοκεῖ μοι ποιεῖν τινα καὶ τοῦ σώματος κάθαρσιν καὶ τῆς ψυχῆς
ἄνεσιν. γίγνονται γάρ τινες ἡμῖν ἐκ τῶν καθ' ἡμέραν
συμποσίων ἐπιπόλαιοι δριμύτητες· ταύταις οὖν ἐστι
τῶν μὲν πόρων οἰκειότατος ὁ διὰ τῆς οὐρήσεως, τῶν δὲ
καθάρσεων ἡ διὰ τῶν κωθωνισμῶν πρέπει μάλιστα.
κατανίζεται γὰρ τὸ σῶμα τοῖς οἴνοις· ὑγρὸν γὰρ καὶ
θερμὸν ὁ οἶνος· τὸ δὲ ἀφ' ἡμῶν διηθούμενον οὖρόν
ἐστιν δριμύ. τὰ γοῦν ἱμάτια τούτῳ χρώμενοι ῥύμματι |

---

251 Athenaeus generally refers elsewhere to the play as
*The All-Night Festival or Day-Laborers* (3.96a; 4.170b; 6.248a;
12.516d; simply as *The All-Night Festival* also at 9.385f).

252 A quotation of E. *Med.* 49.      253 Cf. 6.246a.

254 Another extract from the work quoted at length at 5.196a–
203b (5.199e–f for the specific passage quoted here) and alluded
to repeatedly in this Book; cf. 11.783c n.

Alexis in *Day-Laborers*[251] (fr. 181):

> Then he started shooing a four-*kotuloi kōthōn*, "the
> ancient
> property of my house,"[252] at me.

The name of this cup is the source of the term *akrato-
kōthōnes*, which they apply to people who gulp down large
quantities of unmixed wine (*akratos*), as for example
Hyperides in his *Against Demosthenes* (p. 24 Jensen).[253]
Callixeinus in Book IV of *On Alexandria* (*FGrH* 627 F
2c)[254] writes the following in the course of offering an account of Philadelphus' procession and listing a large number of drinking vessels: two *kōthōnes* with a capacity of two
amphoras. As for drinking large amounts (*kōthōnizesthai*)
and the fact that doing so occasionally is good for one's
health, the Athenian physician Mnesitheus says the following in his *Letter on the Subject of Drinking Large Amounts*
(*Kōthōnismos*) (fr. 45 Bertier): The fact is that some people suffer considerable physical and mental damage when
they drink large quantities of unmixed wine at parties. In
my opinion, however, drinking large amounts (*kōthōnizesthai*) from time to time cleanses the body somehow and
relaxes the mind. Our routine drinking parties leave us
with certain superficial acridities. The most effective
means of excreting these is via urination, whereas the best
means of clearing them out is by drinking large amounts.
For wine washes the body clean, since it is moist and warm,
whereas the urine that is filtered out of us is acrid. Fullers,
for example, use it as a detergent to wash robes. Keep

b πλύνουσιν οἱ γναφεῖς. τρία δὲ παραφύλαττε ὅταν
κωθωνίζῃ· μὴ πονηρὸν οἶνον πίνειν μηδὲ ἄκρατον
μηδὲ τραγηματίζεσθαι ἐν τοῖς κωθωνισμοῖς. ὅταν δ᾽
ἱκανῶς ἔχῃς ἤδη, μὴ κοιμῶ πρὶν ἂν ἐμέσῃς πλέον ἢ
ἔλαττον. εἶτα ἐὰν μὲν ἐμέσῃς ἱκανῶς, ἀναπαύου
μικρὸν περιχεάμενος· ἐὰν δὲ μὴ δυνηθῇς ἱκανῶς κενῶ-
σαι σαυτόν, πλείονι χρῆσαι τῷ λουτρῷ καὶ εἰς τὴν
πύελον κατακλίθητι σφόδρα εἰς θερμὸν ὕδωρ. Πολέ-
μων δ᾽ ἐν πέμπτῳ τῶν Πρὸς Ἀδαῖον καὶ Ἀντίγονον |

c φησι· Διόνυσος Τέλειος καθήμενος ἐπὶ πέτρας· ἐξ
εὐωνύμων δ᾽ αὐτοῦ σάτυρος φαλακρός, ἐν τῇ δεξιᾷ
κώθωνα μόνωτον ῥαβδωτὸν κρατῶν.

Λαβρώνια. ἐκπώματος Περσικοῦ εἶδος ἀπὸ τῆς ἐν
τῷ πίνειν λαβρότητος ὠνομασμένον. πλατὺ δ᾽ ἐστὶ τῇ
κατασκευῇ καὶ μέγα· ἔχει δὲ καὶ ὦτα μεγάλα. Μένανδρος Ἁλιεῖ·

εὐποροῦμεν, οὐδὲ μετρίως· ἐκ Κυΐνδων χρυσίον, |
d Περσικαὶ στολαὶ δ᾽ ἐκεῖναι πορφυραῖ, τορεύματα
ἔνδον ἔστ᾽, ἄνδρες, † ποτηρίδια τορεύματα †
κἀκτυπωμάτων πρόσωπα, τραγέλαφοι, λαβρώνια.

ἐν δὲ Φιλαδέλφοις·

ἤδη δ᾽ ἐπιχύσεις διάλιθοι, λαβρώνιοι,
Πέρσαι δ᾽ ἔχοντες μυιοσόβας εἱστήκεσαν.

Ἵππαρχος δ᾽ ἐν Θαΐδι·

(Α.) ὁ λαβρώνιος δ᾽ ἔσθ᾽ οὗτος ὄρνις; (Β.)
Ἡράκλεις· |

three things in mind when you drink large amounts (*kōthō-nizēi*). Do not drink low-quality wine or unmixed wine, and do not eat snacks when you are drinking large amounts (*en tois kōthōnismois*). When you have finally had enough, do not go to sleep until you vomit at least a bit; afterward, if you vomit enough, take a bath and rest a little. But if you are unable to empty your stomach sufficiently, take a longer bath and lie in the tub in particularly warm water. Polemon says in Book V of his *Response to Adaeus and Antigonus* (fr. 60 Preller): Dionysus Teleios sitting on a rock; to his left is a bald satyr holding a one-handled, ribbed *kōthōn* in his right hand.

*Labrōnia*. A type of Persian drinking vessel that gets its name from the greediness (*labrotēs*) with which people drink.[255] It is broad and large in its design, and has big handles. Menander in *The Fisherman* (fr. 26):[256]

> We're rich—really rich! Inside the house, gentlemen,
> is Cyindian gold, the famous purple Persian
> robes, engraved cups, † little engraved cups †
> and figures worked in relief, goat-stag cups, *labrōnia*.

And in *Men Who Loved Their Brothers* (fr. 395):

> Now there are wine-jugs set with precious stones,
>       and *labrōnia*;
> and Persians are standing there holding fly-whisks.

Hipparchus in *Thaïs* (fr. 3):

> (A.) This *labrōnios*—is it a bird? (B.) Heracles!

[255] A false etymology; cf. 7.310f (a very similar etymology offered for *labrax*, "sea-bass").    [256] The end of the fourth verse is quoted also at 11.500e (where the manuscripts, however, offer *labrōnioi* rather than *labrōnia*).

e    ποτήριον χρυσοῦς διακοσίους ἄγον.
     (Α.) ὦ περιβοήτου, φιλτάτη, λαβρωνίου.

Δίφιλος Τιθραύστῃ καὶ ἄλλα γένη καταλέγων ποτηρίων φησί·

     (Α.) πρίστις, τραγέλαφος, βατιάκη, λαβρώνιος.
     † ἀνδραπόδιον † δὴ ταῦθ’, ὁρᾷς, ἥκιστά γε,
     ἐκπωμάτων δ’ ὀνόματα. (Β.) πρὸς τῆς Ἑστίας.
     (Α.) ὁ λαβρώνιος χρυσῶν δέ, παῖδες, εἴκοσι.

f    Δίδυμος δ’ ὅμοιον εἶναί φησιν αὐτὸ βομβυλιῷ | ἢ
βατιακίῳ.
     Λάκαιναι. κυλίκων εἶδος οὕτως λεγόμενον ἢ ἀπὸ
τοῦ κεράμου, ὡς τὰ Ἀττικὰ σκεύη, ἢ ἀπὸ τοῦ σχήματος ἐπιχωριάσαντος ἐκεῖ, ὥσπερ ⟨ ... ⟩ αἱ Θηρίκλειαι
λέγονται. Ἀριστοφάνης Δαιταλεῦσι·

     Συβαρίτιδάς τ’ εὐωχίας καὶ “Χῖον ἐκ Λακαινᾶν”
     † κυλίκων μέθυ ἡδέως καὶ φίλως †.

     Λεπαστή. οἱ μὲν ὀξύνουσι τὴν τελευταίαν, ὡς καλή,
485  οἱ δὲ παροξύνουσιν, ὡς μεγάλη. ‖ τοῦτο δὲ τὸ ποτήριον ὠνομάσθη ἀπὸ τῶν εἰς τὰς μέθας καὶ τὰς ἀσω-
τίας πολλὰ ἀναλισκόντων, οὓς λαφύκτας καλοῦμεν.
κύλικες δ’ ἦσαν μεγάλαι. Ἀριστοφάνης Εἰρήνῃ·

---

257 Cf. 11.784a (originally a gloss on this verse).
258 Or "slaves".        259 Literally "Spartans". Discussion of
the *lagunos* belongs here alphabetically, but is omitted and taken
up instead at 11.499b–e.
260 The first three verses of the fragment are quoted at
12.527c.
261 Like the connection of the word to *lapsai* (< *laptō*) below, a
false etymology.

It's a cup, and it weighs 200 gold staters!
(A.) Oh, my dear—what a famous *labrōnios*!

Diphilus in *Tithraustes* (fr. 81) lists various types of cups
and says:

> (A.) A *pristis*, a goat-stag cup, a *batiakē*, a
>     *labrōnios*.[257]
> † a slave † in fact, you see, these aren't at all;
> they're the names of drinking vessels. (B.) By Hestia!
> (A.) And the *labrōnios*, children,[258] cost 20 gold
>     coins!

Didymus (p. 75 Schmidt) says that it resembles a *bombulios* or a *batiakion*.

*Lakainai*.[259] A type of *kulix* that gets its name either
from the fabric, like Attic vessels, or from the shape, which
is indigenous there, just as . . . Thericleians get their name.
Aristophanes in *Banqueters* (fr. 225.3–4):[260]

> and Sybaritic feasts and "Chian (wine) from
>     *Lakainai*"
> † of cups wine in a pleasant, friendly way †.

*Lepastē*. Some authorities place an acute accent on the
final syllable, as with *kalé* (*"beautiful"*), *whereas others
place it on the penult, as with* megálē (*"large"*). This cup
got its name from the people who spend large amounts of
money on drinking parties and other profligate behavior,
and whom we refer to as *laphuktai*.[261] They were large
*kulikes*.[262] Aristophanes in *Peace* (916):

---

[262] Thus Aristophanes of Byzantium and Apollodorus of Athens, cited at 11.485d.

† τί δῆτα πίοις οἴνου κύλικα † λεπαστήν;[32]

ἀφ᾽ ἧς ἔστι λάψαι, τουτέστιν ἀθρόως πιεῖν, κατεναν-
τίον τῷ λεγομένῳ βομβυλίῳ. φησὶν γάρ που ὁ αὐτός·

τὸ δ᾽ αἷμα λέλαφας τοὐμόν, ὦναξ δέσποτα,

οἷον "ἄθρουν μ᾽ ἐξέπιες". ἐν δὲ Γηρυτάδῃ·

                                        ἦν δὲ

b       τὸ πρᾶγμ᾽ ἑορτή· περιέφερε † δὲ | κύκλῳ
            λεπαστὴν ἡμῖν †
        ταχὺ προσφέρων παῖς † ἐνέχει τε † σφόδρα
            κυανοβενθῆ,

τὸ βάθος παρίστησιν ὁ κωμικὸς τοῦ ποτηρίου. Ἀντιφάνης δὲ ἐν Ἀσκληπιῷ·

    τὴν δὲ γραῦν τὴν ἀσθενοῦσαν πάνυ πάλαι, τὴν
        βρυτικήν,
    ῥίζιον τρίψας τι μικρὸν δελεάσας τε γεννικῇ
    τὸ μέγεθος κοίλῃ λεπαστῇ, τοῦτ᾽ ἐπόησεν
        ἐκπιεῖν.

Φιλύλλιος Αὔγῃ·

                        πάντα γὰρ ἦν
    μέστ᾽ ἀνδρῶν ‹καὶ› μειρακίων
    πινόντων· ὁμοῦ † δ᾽ ἄλλων †

---

[32] A garbled and unmetrical version of the line, which ought
most likely to read τί δῆτ᾽, ἐπειδὰν ἐκπίῃς οἴνου νέου λεπαστήν;

---

[263] Literally "to lap up".        [264] Cf. 11.784d.
[265] For *bruton* as a word for beer, cf. 10.447b–c.

† Why indeed might you drink a *kulix* of wine † a
  *lepastē*?

The name is the source of the verb *lapsai*,[263] i.e., "to drink
all at once", which is the opposite (of how one drinks) with
what is referred to as a *bombulios*.[264] Because the same
author says somewhere (Ar. fr. 615):

You've lapped up (*lelaphas*) my blood, lord and
  master!,

as if to say "You've drunk me up with one gulp!" And in
*Gerytades* (fr. 174) the comic author emphasizes the depth
of the cup:

                    The occasion
was a festival. A slave was bringing † a *lepastē* around
  in a circle to us †
and serving us rapidly † and was pouring it in † very
  dark blue depths.

Antiphanes in *Asclepius* (fr. 47):

And as for the old woman who'd been sick for a really
  long time, the one who drinks a lot of beer
  (*brutikē*),[265]
he ground up a little bit of root and used a hollow
  *lepastē* of generous
proportions as a lure to make her drink it up.

Philyllius in *Auge* (fr. 5):

                  Because the whole place was
full of men and boys
drinking; and along with them † of others †

γρᾳδίων ἦν μεγάλαισιν οἴ-
νου χαίροντα λεπασταῖς.

Θεόπομπος Παμφίλῃ·

c   σπόγγος, | λεκάνη, πτερόν, λεπαστὴ πάνυ πυκνή,
ἣν ἐκπιοῦσ᾽ ἄκρατον Ἀγαθοῦ Δαίμονος
τέττιξ κελαδεῖ.

καὶ ἐν Μήδῳ·

ὥς ποτ᾽ ἐκήλησεν Καλλίστρατος υἷας Ἀχαιῶν,
κέρμα φίλον διαδούς, ὅτε συμμαχίαν ἐρέεινεν·
οἷον δ᾽ οὐ κήλησε δέμας λεπτὸν Ῥαδάμανθυν |
d   Λύσανδρον κώθωνι, πρὶν αὐτῷ δῶκε λεπαστήν.

Ἀμερίας δέ φησι τὴν οἰνοχόην λεπαστὴν καλεῖσθαι.
Ἀριστοφάνης δὲ καὶ Ἀπολλόδωρος γένος εἶναι κύλικος. Φερεκράτης Κραπατάλλοις· † τῶν θεατῶν δ᾽ ὅστις
διψῇ λεπαστὴν λαψάμενος μεστὴν ἐκκαρυβδίσαι. †
Νίκανδρος δ᾽ ὁ Κολοφώνιός φησι Δόλοπας οὕτω
καλεῖν τὴν κύλικα. Λυκόφρων δ᾽ ἐν τῷ ἐνάτῳ Περὶ
Κωμῳδίας παραθέμενος τὰ Φερεκράτους καὶ αὐτὸς
e   εἶναί | φησι γένος κύλικος τὴν λεπαστήν. Μόσχος δ᾽

---

266 The standard equipment used to make oneself vomit and
then clean up afterwards.

267 Dactylic hexameter, and containing a certain amount of
Homeric language.

268 Probably a reference to the organization of the Second
Delian League in 378/7 BCE; Callistratus is *PAA* 561575.
Rhadamanthys was a Cretan lawgiver and eventually a judge in
Elysium (*Od.* 4.563–4); but who the Lysander to whom he is as-
similated is, is unclear.

269 Cf. 11.464f.

there was . . . of old women
    enjoying large
      *lepastai* of wine.

Theopompus in *Pamphile* (fr. 41):

a sponge, a basin, a feather,[266] and a solidly built
    *lepastē*,
which she used to drink unmixed wine dedicated to
    the Good Divinity,
and is now singing like a cicada.

And in *The Mede* (fr. 31):[267]

As Callistratus once bewitched the sons of the
    Achaeans,
by handing out small change of the type they like,
    when he was asking for an alliance;[268]
it was only the thin Rhadamanthys—that's
    Lysander—that he
didn't charm with his *kōthōn*, until he gave him a
    *lepastē*.

Amerias (p. 10 Hoffmann) says that a wine-pitcher is
referred to as a *lepastē*, whereas Aristophanes (Ar. Byz.
fr. 411 Slater) and Apollodorus (*FGrH* 244 F 258) claim
that it is a type of *kulix*. Pherecrates in *Small Change* (fr.
101, corrupt and unmetrical):[269] † Anyone in the audience
who's thirsty, after he laps up a full *lepastē*, to swallow
down like Charybdis †. Nicander of Colophon (fr. 142
Schneider) says that this is the word the Dolopes use for
a *kulix*. Lycophron in Book IX of *On Comedy* (fr. 85
Strecker) cites the passage from Pherecrates (fr. 101,
quoted above) and expresses his own opinion that a *lepastē*
is a type of *kulix*. Moschus in the explanatory notes to the

ἐν ἐξηγήσει Ῥοδιακῶν Λέξεων κεραμεοῦν ἀγγεῖόν
φησιν αὐτὸ εἶναι, ἐοικὸς ταῖς λεγομέναις πτωματίσιν,
ἐκπεταλώτερον δέ. Ἀρτεμίδωρος δ᾽ ὁ Ἀριστοφάνειος
ποτήριον ποιόν. Ἀπολλοφάνης δὲ Κρησί·

καὶ λεπαστά μ᾽ ἀδύοινος εὐφρανεῖ δι᾽ ἀμέρας.

Θεόπομπος Παμφίλῃ·

λεπαστὴ μάλα συχνή, |

f    ἣν ἐκπιοῦσ᾽ ἄκρατον Ἀγαθοῦ Δαίμονος
περίστατον βοῶσα τὴν κώμην ποεῖ.

Νίκανδρος δ᾽ ὁ Θυατειρηνός, κύλιξ, φησί, μείζων,
παρατιθέμενος Τηλεκλείδου ἐκ Πρυτάνεων·

καὶ μελιχρὸν οἶνον ἕλκειν
ἐξ ἡδύπνου λεπαστῆς. ‖

486    Ἕρμιππος Μοίραις·

ἢν ἐγὼ πάθω τι τήνδε τὴν λεπαστὴν ἐκπιών,
τῷ Διονύσῳ πάντα τἀμαυτοῦ δίδωμι χρήματα.

Λοιβάσιον. κύλιξ, ὥς φησι Κλείταρχος καὶ Νίκανδρος ὁ Θυατειρηνός, < ... > ᾧ τὸ ἔλαιον ἐπισπένδουσι
τοῖς ἱεροῖς, σπονδεῖον δὲ ᾧ τὸν οἶνον, καλεῖσθαι
λέγων καὶ λοιβίδας τὰ σπονδεῖα ὑπὸ Ἀντιμάχου τοῦ
Κολοφωνίου.

---

270 Presumably from his work on culinary terms; cf. 1.5b n.
271 Doric dialect.    272 Strikingly similar to fr. 41 (quoted
at 11.485b–c, and supposedly from the same play).
273 A third verse probably from the same fragment is quoted at
4.170d.    274 Cognate with *leibō*, "pour".
275 Cognate with *spendō*, "make a drink-offering".

360

*Rhodian Vocabulary* says that it is a ceramic vessel that resembles what are referred to as *ptōmatides*, but has a more extended shape. Aristophanes' student Artemidorus[270] (says that it is) a cup of some type. Apollophanes in *Cretans* (fr. 7):[271]

> And a *lepastē* of sweet wine will keep me happy all
>     day long.

Theopompus in *Pamphile* (fr. 42):[272]

>                              and a really large *lepastē*,
>     which she used to drink unmixed wine dedicated to
>         the Good Divinity,
> and is now making the village aghast with her racket.

Nicander of Thyateira (*FGrH* 343 F 15) says: A rather large *kulix*, and cites a passage from Teleclides' *Prytaneis* (fr. 27.1–2):[273]

> and to drink honey-sweet wine
> from a *lepastē* that puts you pleasantly to sleep.

Hermippus in *Fates* (fr. 45):

> If I die before I finish drinking the contents of this
>     *lepastē*,
> I leave all my money to Dionysus.

*Loibasion*.[274] A *kulix*, according to Cleitarchus and Nicander of Thyateira (*FGrH* 343 F 16) . . . which they use to pour libations of olive oil during rituals, whereas a *spondeion*[275] is used for libations of wine; he notes that *spondeia* are referred to as *loibides* by Antimachus of Colophon (fr. 26 Matthews).

Λέσβιος. ὅτι ποτηρίου εἶδος, Ἡδύλος παρίστησιν
ἐν Ἐπιγράμμασιν οὑτωσὶ λέγων· |

b    ἡ διαπινομένη Καλλίστιον ἀνδράσι, θαῦμα
    κοὐ ψευδές, νῆστις τρεῖς χόας ἐξέπιεν·
   ἧς τόδε σοί, Παφίη, † ζωρεσμιτρησι † θυωθὲν
    κεῖται πορφυρέης Λέσβιον ἐξ ὑέλου.
   ἣν ⟨σὺ⟩ σάου πάντως ὡς καὶ † πάντων ἀπ'
    ἐκείνης †
   σοὶ τοῖχοι γλυκερῶν σῦλα φέρωσι πότων.

Λουτήριον. Ἐπιγένης Μνηματίῳ ἐν τῷ τῶν ποτηρίων καταλόγῳ φησί·

                (Α.) κρατῆρες, κάδοι, |

c  ὁλκεῖα, ⟨κρουνεῖ '. (Β.) ἔστι γὰρ⟩ κρουνεῖα; (Α.)
    ναί.
   λουτήρι'. ἀλλὰ τί καθ' ἕκαστον δεῖ λέγειν;
   ὄψει γὰρ αὐτός.

Λυκιουργεῖς. φιάλαι τινὲς οὕτως καλοῦνται ἀπὸ
Λύκωνος τοῦ κατεσκευασμένου, ὡς καὶ Κονώνειοι αἱ
ὑπὸ Κόνωνος ποιηθεῖσαι. μνημονεύει τοῦ Λύκωνος
Δημοσθένης ἐν τῷ Περὶ τοῦ Στεφάνου κἀν τῷ Πρὸς
Τιμόθεον Ὑπὲρ Χρέως λέγων οὕτως· φιάλας Λυκιουρ-
γεῖς δύο. ἐν δὲ τῷ Πρὸς Τιμόθεον γράφει· δίδωσιν

---

276 Literally "Lesbian".
277 Aphrodite, called "Paphian" from her cult-center Paphos
on Cyprus.    278 Cognate with *louō*, "wash".
279 A slightly longer version of the fragment (which however
omits the word *loutēri(a)* at the beginning of the third verse) is
quoted at 11.472e–f; cf. 11.480a.
280 In fact, Lycon is not mentioned in the text of either speech

*Lesbios*.[276] Hedylus in the *Epigrams* (*HE* 1837–42) (establishes) that this is a type of cup, saying the following:

> Callistion, who keeps up with the men when she
>       drinks—an amazing boast,
>    but true—drank three pitchers on an empty
>       stomach.
> This is her *Lesbion*, Paphian goddess,[277] made of red
>       glass
>    and full of the sweet scent of [corrupt], which is
>       dedicated to you.
> Therefore keep her wholly safe, so that also † of
>       everything from her †
>    your walls might be loaded with the plunder of
>       her happy drinking parties.

*Loutērion*.[278] Epigenes in *The Tomb* (fr. 6.1–4),[279] in his list of cups, says:

>                 (A.) Mixing-bowls, *kadoi*,
> basins, *krouneia*. (B.) There are really *krouneia*? (A.)
>       Yeah—
> and *loutēria*. But why should I list them individually?
>    You'll see for yourself.

*Lukiourgeis*. Certain *phialai* are referred to this way, the name coming from Lycon, who produced them, just as *Konōneioi* are *phialai* made by Conon. Demosthenes mentions Lycon in his *On the Crown* and his *Against Timotheus on Account of a Debt*:[280] two *Lukiourgeis phialai*. And in his *Against Timotheus* he writes: Along

as we have it, and the brief quotation that follows comes from [D.] 49.31.

ἀποθεῖναι τῷ Φορμίωνι μετὰ τῶν χρημάτων καὶ ἄλλας
d φιάλας Λυκιουργεῖς | δύο. Ἡρόδοτος δ᾽ ἐν ἑβδόμῃ·
προβόλους δύο Λυκιουργίδας ἡμιεργέας. ὅτι ἀκόντιά
ἐστι πρὸς λύκων θήραν ἐπιτήδεια ⟨ἢ⟩ ἐν Λυκίᾳ εἰργασμένα. ὅπερ ἐξηγούμενος Δίδυμος ὁ γραμματικὸς
τὰς ὑπὸ Λυκίου φησὶ κατεσκευασμένας· ἦν δὲ οὗτος τὸ
γένος Βοιώτιος ἐξ Ἐλευθερῶν, υἱὸς Μύρωνος τοῦ ἀν-
δριαντοποιοῦ, ὡς Πολέμων φησὶν ἐν πρώτῳ Περὶ
Ἀκροπόλεως. ἀγνοεῖ δ᾽ ὁ γραμματικὸς ὅτι τὸν τοιοῦτον σχηματισμὸν ἀπὸ κυρίων ὀνομάτων οὐκ ἄν τις
e εὕροι γινόμενον, ἀλλ᾽ ἀπὸ πόλεων | ἢ ἐθνῶν· Ἀρι-
στοφάνης τε γὰρ ἐν Εἰρήνῃ φησί·

τὸ δὲ πλοῖον ἔσται Ναξιουργὴς κάνθαρος.

Κριτίας τε ἐν τῇ Λακεδαιμονίων Πολιτείᾳ· κλίνη Μι-
λησιουργὴς καὶ δίφρος Μιλησιουργής, κλίνη Χιουρ-
γὴς καὶ τράπεζα Ῥηνιοεργής. Ἡρόδοτός τε ἐν τῇ
ἑβδόμῃ φησί· προβόλους δύο Λυκοεργέας. μήποτ᾽ οὖν
καὶ παρὰ ⟨τῷ Ἡροδότῳ ὡς καὶ παρὰ⟩[33] τῷ Δημοσθέ-
νει γραπτέον Λυκιοεργέας, ἵν᾽ ἀκούηται τὰ ἐν Λυκίᾳ
εἰργασμένα.

Μέλη. οὕτω καλεῖταί τινα ποτήρια, ὧν μνημονεύει
Ἀνάξιππος ἐν Φρέατι λέγων οὕτως· |

[33] add. Schweighäuser

---

[281] The text of Herodotus—quoted again below, in a different
form—is defective at this point, and does not include the word
translated "half-finished" here (presumably an intrusive gloss on
*lukiourgides*).

[282] *PAA* 610500 (fl. *c.*450–430 BCE?); the floruit of Lycius' father Myron (*PAA* 663220) is *c.*470–440 BCE.

with these objects, he gives Phormio two additional *phialai*, which were *Lukiourgeis*, to store. Herodotus in Book VII (76):[281] two half-finished *lukiourgides* spears. These are javelins of a type used to hunt wolves (*lukoi*), or else they were made in Lycia. The grammarian Didymus, in his explication of the passage (pp. 314–15 Schmidt), says that these are *phialai* produced by Lycius;[282] Lycius' family was from Boeotian Eleutherai, and his father was the sculptor Myron, according to Polemon in Book I of *On the Acropolis* (fr. 2 Preller). The grammarian is unaware that such formations are nowhere attested as based on personal names, but are always drawn from the names of cities or peoples. Thus Aristophanes says in *Peace* (143):

And my ship will be a *Naxiourgēs* ("Naxian-made")
        beetle-craft.[283]

And Critias in the *Constitution of the Spartans* (88 B 35 D–K):[284] a *Milēsiourgēs* ("Milesian-made") couch and a *Milēsiourgēs* stool; a *Chiourgēs* ("Chian-made") couch, and a *Rhēniourgēs* ("Rhenian-made") table. And Herodotus in Book VII (76): two *Lykoergeis* spears. Perhaps, therefore, one ought to write *Lukioergeis* in Herodotus,[285] just as in Demosthenes, so that the reference is to spears manufactured in Lycia.

*Melē*. This is a term for certain cups, which are mentioned by Anaxippus in *The Well* (fr. 8), as follows:

[283] *kantharos*; cf. 11.473d.
[284] Cf. Critias fr. B 2 West² (quoted at 1.28b–c).
[285] As in the other quotation of the passage, above.

f     σὺ δὲ τὴν μέλην, Συρίσκε, ταυτηνὶ λαβὼν
    ἔνεγκον ἐπὶ τὸ μνῆμ᾽ ἐκείνῃ, μανθάνεις;
    καὶ κατάχεον.

Μετάνιπτρον. ἡ μετὰ τὸ δεῖπνον ἐπὴν ἀπονίψωνται
διδομένη κύλιξ. Ἀντιφάνης Λαμπάδι·

                        Δαίμονος
Ἀγαθοῦ μετάνιπτρον, ἐντραγεῖν, σπονδή, κρότος. ‖

487   Δίφιλος Σαπφοῖ·

    Ἀρχίλοχε, δέξαι τήνδε τὴν μετανιπτρίδα
    μεστὴν Διὸς Σωτῆρος, Ἀγαθοῦ Δαίμονος.

ἔνιοι δὲ τὴν μετὰ τὸ νίψασθαι πόσιν, ὡς Σέλευκος ἐν
Γλώσσαις. Καλλίας δ᾽ ἐν Κύκλωψι·

    καὶ δέξαι τηνδὶ μετανιπτρίδα τῆς Ὑγιείας.

Φιλέταιρος Ἀσκληπιῷ·

    ἐνέσεισε μεστὴν ἴσον ἴσῳ μετανιπτρίδα
    μεγάλην, ἐπειπὼν τῆς Ὑγιείας τοὔνομα.

Φιλόξενος δ᾽ ὁ διθυραμβοποιὸς ἐν τῷ ἐπιγραφομένῳ
b  Δείπνῳ μετὰ τὸ ἀπονίψασθαι τὰς χεῖρας | προπίνων
τινί φησι·

        σὺ δὲ τάνδ᾽ † εκβακχια †
    εὔδροσον πλήρη μετανιπτρίδα δέξαι·

---

286 A separate, partially overlapping version of the fragment is
quoted at 11.487b.

287 I.e. dedicating the contents to the goddess by that name.

And you, Syriscus—take this *melē*
and carry it to the tomb for her, do you understand?
And pour out the contents.

*Metaniptron*. The *kulix* offered after (*meta*) dinner,
when they wash their hands (*aponipsōntai*). Antiphanes in
*Lampas* (fr. 135.1–2):[286]

> a *metaniptron* dedicated to
> the Good Divinity, (something) to nibble on, a
> libation, applause.

Diphilus in *Sappho* (fr. 70):

> Archilochus, take this *metaniptris*
> full of Zeus the Savior, the Good Divinity!

But some authorities claim that the word refers to the wine
they drink after they wash their hands (*meta to nipsasthai*),
for example Seleucus in the *Glossary* (fr. 59 Müller).
Callias in *Cyclopes* (fr. 9):

> And accept this *metaniptris* here dedicated to
> Hygieia ("Health").

Philetaerus in *Asclepius* (fr. 1):

> He brandished a large *metaniptris* full of wine mixed
> one-to-one, pronouncing the name of Hygieia
> ("Health") over it.[287]

The dithyrambic poet Philoxenus in his poem entitled
*The Dinner Party* (PMG 836(c)) toasts someone after they
wash their hands and says:

> But you—accept this [corrupt]
> *metaniptris* drenched in dew and full;

πραΰ τί τοι Βρόμιος
γάνος τόδε δοὺς ἐπὶ τέρ-
ψιν πάντας ἄγει.

Ἀντιφάνης Λαμπάδι·

τράπεζα † φυστημινεις † ἀλλὰ μὴν Δαίμονος
Ἀγαθοῦ μετάνιπτρον.

Νικόστρατος Ἀντερώσῃ·

μετανιπτρίδ᾽ αὐτῷ τῆς Ὑγιείας ἔγχεον.

Μαστός. Ἀπολλόδωρος ὁ Κυρηναῖος, ὡς Πάμφιλός
φησι, Παφίους τὸ ποτήριον οὕτως καλεῖν.
c    Μαθαλίδας Βλαῖσος ἐν | Σατούρνῳ φησίν·

ἑπτὰ μαθαλίδας ἐπίχεε ἡμῖν τῷ γλυκυτάτῳ.

Πάμφιλος δέ φησι· μήποτε ἐκπώματός ἐστιν εἶδος, ἢ
μέτρον οἷον κύαθος. Διόδωρος δὲ κύλικα ἀποδίδωσι.
Μάνης. ποτηρίου εἶδος. Νίκων Κιθαρῳδῷ·

καὶ πάνυ τις εὐκαίρως "προπίνω", φησί, "⟨σοί⟩,
πατριῶτα." μάνην δ᾽ εἶχε κεραμεοῦν ἁδρόν,
χωροῦντα κοτύλας πέντ᾽ ἴσως. ἐδεξάμην.

παρέθετο τὰ ἰαμβεῖα καὶ Δίδυμος καὶ Πάμφιλος. |
d καλεῖται δὲ μάνης καὶ τὸ ἐπὶ τοῦ κοττάβου ἐφεστηκός,

---

288 Dionysus.

289 A separate, partially overlapping version of the fragment is
quoted at 11.486f.

290 An identical verse is quoted at 15.693a, as part of a larger
fragment assigned to Nicostratus' *Pandrosus* (= fr. 18.2).

291 Literally "breast" (presumably from its shape).

by offering this gentle, refreshing drink,
    Bromius[288] induces everyone
        to enjoy themselves.

Antiphanes in *Lampas* (fr. 135.1–2):[289]

    a table [corrupt] but certainly a *metaniptron*
        dedicated to
    the Good Divinity.

Nicostratus in *The Female Rival in Love* (fr. 3):[290]

    Pour him a *metaniptris* dedicated to Hygieia
        ("Health")!

*Mastos*.[291] According to Pamphilus (fr. XXI Schmidt),
Apollodorus of Cyrene (fr. 5 Dyck) (claims that) the inhabitants of Cyrene use this as a term for a cup.
    Blaesus uses the word *mathalides* in *Saturnus* (fr. 2):

    Pour us seven *mathalides* of your sweetest wine!

Pamphilus (fr. XIX Schmidt) says: Perhaps this is a type
of drinking vessel, or a unit of measure, like a *kuathos*.
Diodorus glosses it "*kulix*".
    *Manēs*. A type of cup. Nico in *The Citharode* (fr. 1):

    And at just the right moment someone says: "I drink
        to you,
    my fellow-countryman!" He had a large ceramic
        *manēs*
    that held maybe five *kotylai*. I accepted it.

Didymus (pp. 73–5 Schmidt) and Pamphilus (fr. XX
Schmidt) both cited these lines. The term *manēs* is also
used for the object that rests on top of the cottabus-stand,

ἐφ' οὗ τὰς λάταγας ἐν παιδιᾷ ἔπεμπον· ὅπερ ὁ Σοφοκλῆς ἐν Σαλμωνεῖ χάλκειον ἔφη κάρα, λέγων οὕτως·

τάδ' ἐστὶ κνισμὸς καὶ φιλημάτων ψόφος·
τῷ καλλικοσσαβοῦντι νικητήρια
τίθημι καὶ βαλόντι χάλκειον κάρα.

Ἀντιφάνης Ἀφροδίτης Γοναῖς·

(A.) ἐγὼ διδάξω· καθ' ὅσον ἂν τὸν κότταβον
ἀφεὶς ἐπὶ τὴν πλάστιγγα ⟨ ... ⟩
(B.) ⟨ ... ⟩ ποίαν; (A.) τοῦτο τοὐπικείμενον |
e   ἄνω τὸ μικρόν (B.) τὸ πινακίσκιον λέγεις;
(A.) τοῦτ' ἐστὶ πλάστιγξ—οὗτος ὁ κρατῶν
γίγνεται.
(B.) πῶς δ' εἴσεταί τις τοῦτ'; (A.) ἐὰν θίγῃ μόνον
αὐτῆς, ἐπὶ τὸν μάνην πεσεῖται καὶ ψόφος
ἔσται πάνυ πολύς. (B.) πρὸς θεῶν, τῷ κοττάβῳ
πρόσεστι καὶ Μάνης τις ὥσπερ οἰκέτης;

Ἕρμιππος Μοίραις·

ῥάβδον δ' ὄψει (φησί) τὴν κοτταβικὴν
ἐν τοῖς ἀχύροισι κυλινδομένην,
μάνης δ' οὐδὲν λατάγων ἀίει·
f   τὴν δὲ τάλαιναν πλάστιγγ' | ἂν ἴδοις
παρὰ τὸν στροφέα τῆς κηπαίας
ἐν τοῖσι κορήμασιν οὖσαν.

---

292 An extract from a longer fragment quoted at 15.666f–7a.
293 A common Athenian slave-name.
294 An extract from a longer fragment quoted at 15.668a.
295 Literally "the chaff, the husks".

370

at which they throw their wine-lees in the course of the game. Sophocles in *Salmoneus* (fr. 537) referred to this as a "bronze head", putting it as follows:

> What you have here is titillation and the sound of
>> kisses;
> I'm setting this as the prize for whoever's the best
> cottabus-player and hits the bronze head.

Antiphanes in *The Birth of Aphrodite* (fr. 57.5–13):[292]

> (A.) I'll teach you. To the extent that someone throws
>> his
> *kottabos* onto the disk—
> (B.) What disk? (A.) This little object
> set on top— (B.) Are you talking about the little
>> platter?
> (A.) That's the disk;—this guy wins.
> (B.) How's anyone going to know? (A.) If he just
>> touches
> it, it'll fall onto the *manēs*, and there'll be
> an enormous clatter. (B.) By the gods—does the
>> *kottabos*
> also have a Manēs[293] to serve it?

Hermippus says in *Fates* (fr. 48.5–10):[294]

> You'll see the cottabus-stand
> rolling around in the dust,[295]
> and the *manēs* no longer pays attention to the wine-
>> lees.
> You'd also notice the poor disk
> lying in the trash beside
>> the hinge of the back door.

Νεστορίς. περὶ τῆς ἰδέας τοῦ Νέστορος ποτηρίου
φησὶν ὁ ποιητής·

πὰρ δὲ δέπας περικαλλές, ὃ οἴκοθεν ἦγ' ὁ
  γεραιός,
χρυσείοις ἥλοισι πεπαρμένον· οὔατα δ' αὐτοῦ
τέσσαρ' ἔσαν, δοιαὶ δὲ πελειάδες ἀμφὶς ἕκαστον
χρύσειαι νεμέθοντο, δύω δ' ὑπὸ πυθμένες ἦσαν. ‖
ἄλλος μὲν μογέων ἀποκινήσασκε τραπέζης
πλεῖον ἐόν, Νέστωρ δ' ὁ γέρων ἀμογητὶ ἄειρεν.

488

ἐν τούτοις ζητεῖται πρῶτον μὲν τί ποτ' ἐστὶ τὸ χρυσείοις ἥλοισι πεπαρμένον, ἔπειτα τί τὸ οὔατα δ' αὐτοῦ
τέσσαρ' ἔσαν· τὰ γὰρ ἄλλα ποτήριά φησιν ὁ Μυρλεανὸς Ἀσκληπιάδης ἐν τῷ Περὶ τῆς Νεστορίδος δύο
ὦτα ἔχειν. πελειάδας δὲ πῶς ἄν τις ὑπόθοιτο νεμο-
μένας περὶ ἕκαστον τῶν ὤτων; πῶς δὲ καὶ λέγει δύο
πυθμένας εἶναι τοῦ ποτηρίου; ἰδίως δὲ καὶ τοῦτο
λέγεται ὅτι οἱ μὲν ἄλλοι μογοῦντες ‖ ἐβάσταζον τὸ
ποτήριον, Νέστωρ δ' ὁ γέρων ἀμογητὶ ἄειρεν. ταῦτα
προθέμενος ὁ Ἀσκληπιάδης ζητεῖ περὶ τῶν ἥλων, πῶς
πεπαρμένους αὐτοὺς δεῖ δέχεσθαι. οἱ μὲν οὖν λέγουσιν
ἔξωθεν δεῖν ἐμπείρεσθαι τοὺς χρυσοῦς ἥλους τῷ
ἀργύρῳ ἐκπώματι κατὰ τὸν τῆς ἐμπαιστικῆς τέχνης
λόγον, ὡς καὶ ἐπὶ τοῦ Ἀχιλλέως σκήπτρου·

b

---

296 Literally "the poet".    297 The passage is quoted at
even greater length at 11.492e–3a.
298 Sc. that are mentioned by Homer.

*Nestoris*. As for what Nestor's cup looked like, Homer[296] says (*Il.* 11.632–7):[297]

And (she set) beside them an exquisitely beautiful
　　goblet, which the old man had brought from
　　home.
It was pierced with gold studs, and had four
handles, with a pair of gold doves feeding
on either side of each; and there were two bases
　　beneath it.
Another man would have had difficulty raising it from
　　the table
when it was full. But the aged Nestor hoisted it easily.

The first question that arises in connection with this passage is what "pierced with gold studs" means, and after that, what the claim that it "had four handles" means; because the other cups[298] have two handles, according to Asclepiades of Myrlea in his *On the Nestoris*. And how is one to understand the doves that are feeding under each handle? And what does he mean by saying that the cup had two bases? This is another odd remark, when he claims that other people lifted the cup only with difficulty, "but the aged Nestor hoisted it easily". Asclepiades first poses these questions, and then takes up the problem of the studs, that is, how we ought to understand the assertion that the cup was pierced by them. Some authorities claim that the gold studs must be driven into the silver cup from the outside, in the style of embossed work, as also in the case of Achilleus' staff (*Il.* 1.245–6):

ὡς φάτο χωόμενος[34], ποτὶ δὲ σκῆπτρον βάλε
γαίη
χρυσείοις ἥλοισι πεπαρμένον.

ἐμφαίνεται γὰρ ὡς τῶν ἥλων ἐμπεπερονημένων |
c καθάπερ ἐπὶ τῶν ῥοπάλων. καὶ ἐπὶ τοῦ ξίφους τοῦ
Ἀγαμέμνονος·

ἀμφὶ δ' ἄρ' ὤμοισιν βάλετο ξίφος· ἐν δέ οἱ ἧλοι
χρύσειοι πάμφαινον, ἀτὰρ περὶ κουλεὸν ἦεν
ἀργύρεον.

Ἀπελλῆς μὲν οὖν ὁ τορευτὴς ἐπεδείκνυεν, φησίν, ἡμῖν
ἔν τισι Κορινθιακοῖς ἔργοις τὴν τῶν ἥλων θέσιν·
ἐξοχὴ δ' ἦν ὀλίγη τοῖς κολαπτῆρσιν ἐπηρμένη καὶ
οἱονεὶ κεφαλίδας ἥλων ἀποτελοῦσα. πεπάρθαι δὲ λέγεται τοὺς ἥλους ὑπὸ τοῦ ποιητοῦ οὐχ ὅτι ἔξωθεν πρόσ-
d κεινται καὶ | πεπαρμένοι εἰσίν, ἀλλ' ὅτι ἐμπεπαρμένοις
ἐοίκασιν ἔξω τε ὀλίγῳ προὔχουσι, μετέωροι τῆς ἄλλης
ἐπιφανείας ὄντες. καὶ περὶ τῶν ὤτων οὕτως διορί-
ζονται, ὅτι εἶχεν μὲν δύο ὦτα ἄνω, καθότι καὶ τἄλλα
ποτήρια, ἄλλα δὲ δύο κατὰ τὸ κύρτωμα μέσον ἐξ
ἀμφοῖν τοῖν μεροῖν μικρά, παρόμοια ταῖς Κοριν-
θιακαῖς ὑδρίαις. ὁ δὲ Ἀπελλῆς ἐντέχνως ἄγαν ὑπέδειξε
τὴν τῶν τεσσάρων ὤτων σχέσιν ἔχουσαν ὧδε. ἐκ μιᾶς
οἱονεὶ ῥίζης, ἥτις τῷ πυθμένι προσκυρεῖ, καθ' ἑκάτε-
e ρον τὸ οὖς διασχιδεῖς εἰσι | ῥάβδοι ἐπ' ἀμφοῖν, οὐ
πολὺ ἀπ' ἀλλήλων διεστῶσαι διάστημα. αὗται μέχρι
τοῦ χείλους διήκουσαι τοῦ ποτηρίου καὶ μικρὸν ἔτι
μετεωριζόμεναι κατὰ μὲν τὴν ἀπόστασιν τοῦ ἀγγείου
φυλάττουσι τὴν διάσχισιν, κατὰ δὲ τὸ ἀπολῆγον πρὸς

---

[34] The traditional text of Homer has Πηλείδης.

Thus he spoke, in anger; and he hurled the staff,
    which was pierced
with gold studs, to the ground.

Because it is apparent that the studs are attached (to the staff) in the same way they sometimes are to clubs. So too in the case of Agamemnon's sword (*Il.* 11.29–31):

And he threw a sword about his shoulder. The gold
    studs
shone on it, and it was silver around the
scabbard.

The metal-worker Apelles, he says, showed us how the studs were placed in some pieces he produced in Corinth: there were tiny bumps that had been produced by a punch, and which terminated in what might have been nail-heads. Homer says that the cup was pierced by the studs not because they are attached to it from the outside and driven through, but because they seem to have been driven in from the interior and project out a bit, so that they are elevated above the rest of the surface. As for the handles, they offer the following conclusions: It had two handles on top, like the other cups, and two other, smaller handles on its two sides, in the middle, where the belly swells out, like those on Corinthian water-jars. Apelles very artfully showed the position of the four handles, which was as follows: From a single root, as it were, attached to the base, extend split coils of clay on either side of the vessel, one per handle and not very far apart from one another. These stretch as high as the lip of the cup, and in fact rise a bit above it; as long as they are separated from the vessel, they maintain their distance from one another, whereas near

τὴν τοῦ χείλους ἔρεισιν πάλιν συμφυεῖς ⟨εἰσιν⟩. καὶ
γίνεται τὸν τρόπον τοῦτον τέτταρα ὦτα. τοῦτο δὲ οὐκ
ἐπὶ πάντων, ἀλλ' ἐπ' ἐνίων ποτηρίων τὸ εἶδος τῆς
κατασκευῆς θεωρεῖται, μάλιστα δὲ τῶν λεγομένων
Σελευκίδων. τὸ δ' ἐπὶ τῶν δυεῖν πυθμένων ζητούμενον, |
f   πῶς λέγεται τὸ δύω δ' ὑπὸ πυθμένες ἦσαν, διαλύουσιν
οὕτως τινές. τῶν ποτηρίων τινὰ μὲν ἕνα πυθμένα ἔχειν
τὸν φυσικὸν καὶ συγκεχαλκευμένον τῷ ὅλῳ ποτηρίῳ,
καθότι τὰ λεγόμενα κυμβία καὶ τὰς φιάλας καὶ εἴ τι
φιαλῶδές ἐστι τὴν ἰδέαν· τινὰ δὲ δύο, ὥσπερ τὰ
ᾠοσκύφια καὶ τὰ κανθάρια καὶ τὰς Σελευκίδας καὶ τὰ
καρχήσια καὶ τὰ τούτοις ὅμοια· ἕνα μὲν γὰρ εἶναι
πυθμένα τὸν κατὰ τὸ κύτος συγκεχαλκευμένον ὅλῳ τῷ
ἀγγείῳ, ἕτερον δὲ τὸν πρόσθετον, ἀπὸ ὀξέος ἀρχόμενον, καταλήγοντα δ' εἰς πλατύτερον, ἐφ' οὗ ἵσταται
489   τὸ ποτήριον. ‖ καὶ τὸ τοῦ Νέστορος οὖν δέπας φασὶν
εἶναι τοιοῦτον. δύναται δὲ καὶ δύο πυθμένας ὑπο-
τίθεσθαι, τὸν μὲν οἷον τοῦ ποτηρίου φέροντα τὸν ὅλον
ὄγκον καὶ κατὰ μείζονα κυκλοειδῆ περιγραφὴν ἔξαρ-
σιν ἔχοντα τοῦ ὕψους σύμμετρον, τὸν δὲ κατ' ἐλάττω
κύκλον συνεχόμενον ἐν τῷ μείζονι, καθ' ὅσον συν-
νεύειν συμβέβηκεν εἰς ὀξὺν τὸν φυσικὸν τοῦ ποτηρίου
πυθμένα, ὥστε ὑπὸ δυοῖν πυθμένοιν φέρεσθαι τὸ
ἔκπωμα. Διονύσιος δὲ ὁ Θρᾷξ ἐν Ῥόδῳ λέγεται τὴν
Νεστορίδα κατασκευάσαι τῶν μαθητῶν αὐτῷ συν-
b   ενεγκάντων | τἀργύριον· ὅπερ Προμαθίδας ὁ Ἡρακλε-
ώτης ἐξηγούμενος τὴν κατὰ τὸν Διονύσιον διάταξίν
φησιν σκύφον εἶναι παρακειμένως ἔχοντα τὰ ὦτα,
καθάπερ αἱ δίπρῳροι τῶν νεῶν, περὶ δὲ τὰ ὦτα τὰς
περιστεράς· ὡσπερεὶ δέ τινα ῥοπάλια δύο ὑποκεῖσθαι

---

[299] This sentence is quoted again at 11.503e–f.

the end, when they are about to touch the lip, they come back together. There are thus four handles. This style of construction is not seen in the case of all cups, but only in certain types, notably what are referred to as *Seleukides*. As for the question concerning the two bases, that is, what it means to say that "there were two bases beneath it", some authorities resolve the matter as follows: Some cups have a single base that is an organic part of the vessel as a whole and is attached directly to it, as for example what are referred to as *kumbia, phialai,* and anything shaped like a *phialē*. But others have two bases, such as *ōioskuphia, kantharia, Seleukides, karchēsia,* and the like; because the first base is the one that is located beneath the bowl and is attached directly to the vessel as a whole, whereas the second base is the one that has been added to it, and that begins with a pointed section and ends in a broader part, upon which the cup stands.[299] Nestor's goblet, they claim, was of the latter sort. But it is also possible that two bases are meant, the first, as it were, supporting the entire weight of the cup and at its point of maximum circumference extending as far out as the vessel is tall, while the other disk, which has a smaller circumference, is attached to the larger one, at the point where the natural base of the cup contracts to a nub, with the result that the cup is supported by two bases. Dionysius Thrax (test. 5 Linke) is said to have constructed a model of the *Nestoris*, the silver having been contributed by his students; Promathidas of Heracleia (*FGrH* 430 F 8), in his description of Dionysius' design, says that it was a *skuphos* with pairs of handles set beside one another, like ships with two prows, and that the doves were placed on either side of the handles. Objects

τῷ ποτηρίῳ πλάγια διὰ μήκους· ταῦτα δ' εἶναι τοὺς
δύο πυθμένας. ὁποῖόν τι καὶ νῦν ἔστιν ἰδεῖν ἐν Καπύῃ
πόλει τῆς Καμπανίας ἀνακείμενον τῇ Ἀρτέμιδι ποτήριον, ὅπερ λέγουσιν ἐκεῖνοι Νέστορος γεγονέναι· ἐστὶ

c δὲ ἀργύρεον, χρυσοῖς γράμμασιν | ἐντετυπωμένα ἔχον
τὰ Ὁμηρικὰ ἔπη.

Ἐγὼ δέ, φησὶν ὁ Μυρλεανός, τάδε λέγω περὶ τοῦ
ποτηρίου. οἱ παλαιοὶ καὶ τὰ περὶ τὴν ἥμερον τροφὴν
πρῶτοι διαταξάμενοι τοῖς ἀνθρώποις, πειθόμενοι τὸν
κόσμον εἶναι σφαιροειδῆ, λαμβάνοντες ἔκ τε τοῦ
ἡλίου καὶ τῆς σελήνης σχήματος ἐναργεῖς τὰς φαντα-
σίας, καὶ τὰ περὶ τὴν ἰδίον[35] τροφὴν τῷ περιέχοντι
κατὰ τὴν ἰδέαν τοῦ σχήματος ἀφομοιοῦν εἶναι δίκαιον
ἐνόμιζον. διὸ τὴν τράπεζαν κυκλοειδῆ κατεσκεύασαν-

d το καὶ τοὺς τρίποδας τοὺς τοῖς θεοῖς | καθαγιζομένους,
φθόεις κυκλοτερεῖς καὶ ἀστέρας ἔχοντας, οὓς καὶ
καλοῦσι σελήνας. καὶ τὸν ἄρτον δ' ἐκάλεσαν ὅτι τῶν
σχημάτων ὁ κύκλος ἀπήρτισται καὶ ἔστι τέλειος. καὶ
τὸ ποτήριον οὖν τὸ δεχόμενον τὴν ὑγρὰν τροφὴν
κυκλοτερὲς ἐποίησαν κατὰ μίμημα τοῦ κόσμου. τὸ δὲ
τοῦ Νέστορος καὶ ἰδιαίτερόν ἐστιν. ἔχει γὰρ καὶ
ἀστέρας, οὓς ἥλοις ὁ ποιητὴς ἀπεικάζει διὰ τὸ τοὺς
ἀστέρας περιφερεῖς εἶναι τοῖς ἥλοις ὁμοίως καὶ ὥσπερ
ἐμπεπηγέναι τῷ οὐρανῷ, καθὼς καὶ Ἄρατός φησιν ἐπ'
αὐτῶν· |

35 ἰδίον Schweighäuser: ἀίδιον A

300 Cf. 11.466c with n.
301 "the created order", i.e. "the world, the universe" vel sim.
302 For the phoïs (a cheese-and-honey cake), see 14.647d–e.

resembling two rods were attached to the bottom of the cup, running horizontally lengthwise; these were the two bases. A cup like this is on display today in the city of Capua in Campania; it is dedicated to Artemis, and the locals claim that it is actually Nestor's cup. It is made of silver and has the Homeric lines embossed on it in gold letters.[300]

But I for my part, says the Myrlean, have the following to say about the cup. The ancients were the first to organize a civilized style of dining for human beings, and because they believed that the *kosmos*[301] was shaped like a sphere, given that they got their clearest impression of its form from the sun and the moon, they thought it right to make everything associated with their own dining style resemble what the world that surrounded them looked like. They accordingly made their tables and the tripods they dedicated to the gods round, and made their pastries (*phoïdes*)[302] circular and decorated them with stars (which they refer to as *selēnai*[303]). They also adopted the term *artos* ("loaf of bread"), because its circular shape is regular (*apērtistai*)[304] and perfect; and they made the cup that held their liquid nourishment round, to imitate the shape of the *kosmos*. Nestor's cup, however, is rather unusual, since it has stars, which the poet compares to studs on account of the fact that stars are round, just as studs are, and seem to have been stuck into the sky, just as Aratus (*Phaen.* 453) says in regard to them:

---

[303] Literally "moons"; cf. Hsch. σ 379 "*selēnas*: sacrificial cakes (*popana*) that resemble a star, baked cakes".

[304] A false etymology.

e  οὐρανῷ αἰὲν ἄρηρεν[36] ἀγάλματα νυκτὸς ἰούσης.

περιττῶς δὲ καὶ τοῦτ' ἔφρασεν ὁ ποιητής, τοὺς χρυσοῦς ἥλους παρατιθεὶς τῇ τοῦ ἀργύρου ἐκπώματος
φύσει, τὴν τῶν ἀστέρων καὶ τοῦ οὐρανοῦ ἐκτυπῶν
κατὰ τὴν ἰδέαν τῆς χρόας οὐσίαν· ὁ μὲν γὰρ οὐρανὸς
ἀργύρῳ προσέοικεν, οἱ δὲ ἀστέρες χρυσῷ διὰ τὸ
πυρῶδες. ὑποθέμενος οὖν κατηστερισμένον τὸ τοῦ
Νέστορος ποτήριον μεταβαίνει καὶ ἐπὶ τὰ κράτιστα
τῶν ἀπλανῶν ἀστέρων, οἷς δὴ τεκμαίρονται τὰ περὶ
f  τὴν ζωὴν οἱ ἄνθρωποι. | λέγω δὲ τὰς πελειάδας· ὅταν
γὰρ εἴπῃ·

    δύο[37] δὲ πελειάδες ἀμφὶς ἕκαστον
  χρύσειαι νεμέθοντο,

πελειάδας οὐ σημαίνει τὰς ὄρνιθας, ἅς τινες ὑπονο-
οῦσι περιστερὰς εἶναι, ἁμαρτάνοντες· ἕτερον γὰρ
εἶναί φησιν Ἀριστοτέλης πελειάδα καὶ ἕτερον περι-
στεράν. πελειάδας δ' ὁ ποιητὴς καλεῖ νῦν τὰς Πλειάδας, πρὸς ἃς σπόρος τε καὶ ἀμητὸς καὶ τῶν καρπῶν,
ἀρχὴ γενέσεως καὶ συναιρέσεως, καθά φησι καὶ Ἡσί-
οδος·

  Πληιάδων Ἀτλαγενέων ἐπιτελλομενάων ‖
490  ἄρχεσθ' ἀμητοῖ, ἀρότοιο δὲ δυσομενάων.

καὶ Ἄρατος·

  αἱ μὲν ὁμῶς ὀλίγαι καὶ ἀφεγγέες, ἀλλ'
   ὀνομασταὶ

---

36 The traditional text of Aratus has εὖ ἐνάρηρεν.
37 The traditional text of Homer has δοιαί (as at 11.487f).

380

always fixed in the sky, as ornaments of the passing
night.

Homer was very careful about how he described this, con-
trasting the gold studs to the rest of the vessel, which was
made of silver, and creating an impression of the stars and
the sky that matches what can be seen of their actual color;
because the sky resembles silver, while the fiery nature of
the stars makes them look like gold. After hinting, then,
that Nestor's cup is covered with stars, the poet moves on
to the most important fixed stars, which human beings use
as a source of information about their lives. I refer to the
"doves"; for when he says (*Il.* 11.634–5):

> with a pair of gold doves (*peleiades*) feeding
> on either side of each,

he does not mean the birds known as *peleiades*, which
some authorities take to be pigeons (*peristerai*); this is an
error, since Aristotle (*HA* 544$^b$1–2) says that a *peleias* is different from a *peristeras*. Instead, the poet is here using the
term *peleiades* to refer to the Pleiades, which fix the times
for sowing and harvesting crops, the point at which they
begin to be generated and gathered in, just as Hesiod (*Op.*
383–4) says:

> Begin your harvest when the Pleiades, daughters of
> Atlas,
> are on the rise, and your plowing when they start to
> set.

Also Aratus (*Phaen.* 264–7):

> Although few and faint, they are nonetheless much-
> discussed

ἦρι καὶ ἑσπέριαι, Ζεὺς δ' αἴτιος, εἰλίσσονται,
ὅς[38] σφισι καὶ θέρεος καὶ χείματος ἀρχομένοιο
σημαίνειν ἐπένευσεν ἐπερχομένου τ' ἀρότοιο.

τὰς οὖν τῆς τῶν καρπῶν γενέσεως καὶ τελειώσεως
προσημαντικὰς Πλειάδας οἰκείως ἐνετόρευσε τῷ τοῦ
σοφωτάτου Νέστορος ὁ ποιητὴς ποτηρίῳ· καὶ γὰρ |
b    τοῦτο τῆς ἑτέρας τροφῆς δεκτικὸν ἀγγεῖον. διὸ καὶ τῷ
Διὶ τὴν ἀμβροσίαν τὰς Πελειάδας φέρειν φησί·

τῇ μέν τ' οὐδὲ ποτητὰ παρέρχεται οὐδὲ Πέλειαι
τρήρωνες, ταί τ' ἀμβροσίην Διὶ πατρὶ φέρουσιν.

οὐ γὰρ τὰς πελειάδας τὰς ὄρνεις φέρειν νομιστέον τῷ
Διὶ τὴν ἀμβροσίαν, ὡς <οἱ>[39] πολλοὶ δοξάζουσιν
(ἄσεμνον γάρ), ἀλλὰ τὰς Πλειάδας· οἰκεῖον γὰρ τὰς
προσημαινούσας τῷ τῶν ἀνθρώπων γένει τὰς ὥρας,
ταύτας καὶ τῷ Διὶ φέρειν τὴν ἀμβροσίαν. διόπερ ἀπὸ
τῶν πτηνῶν αὐτὰς χωρίζει λέγων· |

c    τῇ μέν τ' οὐδὲ ποτητὰ παρέρχεται οὐδὲ Πέλειαι.

ὅτι δὲ τὰς Πλειάδας τὸ ἐνδοξότατον τῶν ἀπλανῶν
ἄστρων ὑπείληφε, δῆλον ἐκ τοῦ προτάττειν αὐτὰς
κατὰ τὴν τῶν ἄλλων συναρίθμησιν·

ἐν δὲ τὰ τείρεα πάντα, τά τ' οὐρανὸς
ἐστεφάνωται,

---

[38] Although the manuscripts of Aratus are divided, with some supporting Athenaeus, the proper reading is most likely ὅ σφισι.
[39] add. Dobree

> as they move around in the morning and the evening,
>       and Zeus is responsible,
> since he gave his consent that they were to mark the
>       beginning
> of summer and winter, and the arrival of plowing-
>       season.

Homer thus quite aptly embossed the Pleiades, which herald the birth and the maturity of our crops, on the cup of the supremely wise Nestor; for this vessel held other types of food as well. This is why he claims that the Peleiades bring Zeus his ambrosia (*Od.* 12.62–3):

> Not even birds can get by via this route, not even the
>       timid
> Peleiai, which bring ambrosia to father Zeus.

Because one ought not to imagine that the birds known as *peleiades* bring Zeus his ambrosia, as many authorities suppose—this would be undignified—but that the Pleiades do; for it is appropriate that the figures who herald the beginning of the seasons to human beings also bring Zeus his ambrosia. This is why Homer distinguishes them from the birds, by saying (*Od.* 12.62):

> Not even birds can get by via this route, not even the
>       Peleiai.

As for the fact that he judged the Pleiades to be the most important of the fixed stars, this is apparent from the fact that he puts them first when he enumerates them along with the others (*Il.* 18.485–7):

> And in it were all the signs with which the sky is
>       wreathed,

Πληϊάδας θ᾽ Ὑάδας τε τό τε σθένος Ὠρίωνος
Ἄρκτον θ᾽, ἣν καὶ Ἄμαξαν ἐπίκλησιν καλέουσιν. |

d ἐπλανήθησαν δ᾽ οἱ πολλοὶ νομίζοντες τὰς Πελειάδας
ὄρνεις εἶναι πρῶτον μὲν ἐκ τοῦ ποιητικοῦ σχηματισμοῦ τοῦ κατὰ τὴν πρόσθεσιν τοῦ γράμματος· ἔπειτα δ᾽ ὅτι τὸ τρήρωνες μόνον ἐδέξαντο εἶναι ἐπίθετον
πελειάδων, ἐπεὶ διὰ τὴν ἀσθένειαν εὐλαβὴς ἡ ὄρνις
αὕτη· τρεῖν δ᾽ ἐστὶ τὸ εὐλαβεῖσθαι. πιθανὸν δ᾽ ἐστὶ τὸ
ἐπίθετον καὶ ἐπὶ τῶν Πλειάδων τιθέμενον· μυθεύονται
γὰρ καὶ αὗται τὸν Ὠρίωνα φεύγειν, διωκομένης τῆς
e μητρὸς αὐτῶν Πληιόνης ὑπὸ τοῦ Ὠρίωνος. | ἡ δὲ τοῦ
ὀνόματος ἐκτροπή, καθ᾽ ἣν αἱ Πλειάδες λέγονται Πέλειαι καὶ Πελειάδες, παρὰ πολλοῖς ἐστι τῶν ποιητῶν.
πρώτη δὲ Μοιρὼ ἡ Βυζαντία καλῶς ἐδέξατο τὸν νοῦν
τῶν Ὁμήρου ποιημάτων ἐν τῇ Μνημοσύνῃ ἐπιγρα-
φομένη φάσκουσα τὴν ἀμβροσίαν τῷ Διὶ τὰς Πλειάδας κομίζειν· Κράτης δ᾽ ὁ κριτικὸς σφετερισάμενος
αὐτῆς τὴν δόξαν ὡς ἴδιον ἐκφέρει τὸν λόγον. καὶ
Σιμωνίδης δὲ τὰς Πλειάδας Πελειάδας εἴρηκεν ἐν
τούτοις·[40]

f δίδωτι δ᾽ εὖ < . . . > | Ἑρμᾶς ἐναγώνιος,
Μαιά<δο>ς εὐπλοκάμοιο παῖς,
ἔτικτε δ᾽ Ἄτλας ἑπτὰ ἰοπλοκάμων φιλᾶν
θυγατρῶν
τάν γ᾽ ἔξοχον εἶδος, ταὶ καλέονται
Πελειάδες οὐράνιαι.

[40] The fragment as Athenaeus preserves it is badly corrupt.

---

[305] Quoted at 11.491a–c.    [306] Literally "Memory", but
presumably referring to the goddess by that name, who was the
mother of the Muses (e.g. Hes. *Th.* 52–61). Cf. 11.503f with n.

the Pleiades, the Hyades, mighty Orion,
and the Bear, which some refer to by the name "the
    Wagon".

Many authorities went wrong by taking the Peleiades to be
birds, being misled first by the poetic form of the word,
which involves the addition of a letter, and then because
they assumed that the adjective *trērōn* ("*timid*") is an epithet applied exclusively to doves, since this bird is cautious
as a consequence of its lack of strength, and the verb *trein*
means "to be cautious". But the epithet can reasonably be
applied to the Pleiades as well, since the traditional story is
that they are trying to get away from Orion, who is chasing
their mother Pleionē. The variation in the name, by which
the Pleiades are referred to as Peleiai and Peleiades, occurs in many poets. The first to correctly grasp what the
Homeric lines mean was Moero of Byzantium (fr. 1, p. 21
Powell),[305] who said in her poem entitled *Mnemosyne*[306]
that the Pleiades bring Zeus his ambrosia. The literary
scholar Crates (fr. 59 Broggiato) appropriated her interpretation and published it as if it were his own argument.
Simonides (*PMG* 555)[307] as well refers to the Pleiades as
Peleiades in the following passage:

Hermes god of contests, the child of
fair-tressed Maia, grants well . . . ;
she was the most beautiful of the seven beloved dark-
    haired
daughters born to Atlas, who are referred to as
the heavenly Peleiades.

[307] The second verse in particular is preserved by other
sources in a significantly different—and seemingly better—form.

σαφῶς γὰρ τὰς Πλειάδας οὔσας Ἄτλαντος θυγατέρας
Πελειάδας καλεῖ, καθάπερ καὶ Πίνδαρος·

> ἐστὶ δ᾽ ἐοικὸς
> ὀρειᾶν γε Πελειάδων
> μὴ τηλόθεν Ὠαρίωνα νεῖσθαι.

σύνεγγυς γάρ ἐστιν ὁ Ὠρίων τῇ ἀστροθεσίᾳ τῶν
Πλειάδων· διὸ καὶ ὁ περὶ ταύτας μῦθος, ὅτι φεύγουσι
μετὰ τῆς μητρὸς τῆς Πληιόνης τὸν Ὠρίωνα. ὀρείας δὲ
λέγει τὰς Πλειάδας ἐν ἴσῳ τῷ οὐρείας κατὰ παράλει-
491 ψιν τοῦ ῠ, ἐπειδὴ κεῖνται ἐπὶ ‖ τῆς οὐρᾶς τοῦ Ταύρου.
καὶ Αἰσχύλος δ᾽ ἐκφανέστερον προσπαίζων τῷ ὀνόματι κατὰ τὴν ὁμοφωνίαν·

> αἱ δ᾽ ἔπτ᾽ Ἄτλαντος παῖδες ὠνομασμέναι
> πατρὸς μέγιστον ἆθλον οὐρανουστεγῆ
> κλαίεσκον, ἔνθα νυκτέρων φαντασμάτων
> ἔχουσι μορφὰς ἄπτεροι Πελειάδες.

ἀπτέρους γὰρ αὐτὰς εἴρηκε διὰ τὴν πρὸς τὰς ὄρνεις
ὁμωνυμίαν. ἡ δὲ Μοιρὼ καὶ αὐτὴ τὸν τρόπον τοῦτόν
φησι· |

b      Ζεὺς δ᾽ ἄρ᾽ ἐνὶ Κρήτῃ τρέφετο μέγας, οὐδ᾽ ἄρα
>      τίς νιν
> ἤείδει μακάρων· ὁ δ᾽ ἀέξετο πᾶσι μέλεσσι.
> τὸν μὲν ἄρα τρήρωνες ὑπὸ ζαθέῳ τράφον ἄντρῳ
> ἀμβροσίην φορέουσαι ἀπ᾽ Ὠκεανοῖο ῥοάων·

---

308 Cf. 11.490e.

He thus patently refers to the Pleiades, who are Atlas' daughters, as Peleiades, as Pindar (*N.* 2.10–12) does as well:

> It is reasonable
> that Orion not travel far from
> the mountain-dwelling Peleiades;

for Orion is located close to the constellation of the Pleiades, hence the traditional story about them, which is that they are trying to get away from Orion along with their mother Pleionē. His reference to the Pleiades as *oreiai* ("mountain-dwelling") is equivalent to calling them *oureiai*, with the *upsilon* omitted, because they are located next to Taurus' tail (*oura*). So too Aeschylus (fr. 312), playing even more openly on the name and relying on the similar pronunciation:

> They who are called the seven daughters of Atlas
> wailed constantly for their father's immense labor
> in supporting the roof of the sky, where they have the
>     shape
> of night-time visions, the wingless Peleiades.

For he referred to them as wingless because of the fact that they share a name with the birds. Moero herself (fr. 1, p. 21 Powell)[308] puts it as follows:

> Zeus, then, grew up on Crete, and none of the
>     blessed ones
> knew about him; but all his limbs grew ever larger.
> The timid ones, then, fed him within the sacred cave,
> bringing ambrosia from Ocean's streams;

νέκταρ δ᾽ ἐκ πέτρης μέγας αἰετὸς αἰὲν ἀφύσσων
γαμφηλῇς φορέεσκε ποτὸν Διὶ μητιόεντι.
τῷ καὶ νικήσας πατέρα Κρόνον εὐρύοπα Ζεὺς
ἀθάνατον ποίησε καὶ οὐρανῷ ἐγκατένασσεν.
ὡς δ᾽ αὔτως τρήρωσι Πελειάσιν ὤπασε τιμήν, |
c     αἳ δή τοι θέρεος καὶ χείματος ἄγγελοί εἰσιν.

καὶ Σιμμίας δ᾽ ἐν τῇ Γοργοῖ φησιν·

    αἰθέρος ὠκεῖαι πρόπολοι πίλναντο Πέλειαι.

Ποσείδιππός τ᾽ ἐν τῇ Ἀσωπίᾳ·

    οὐδέ τοι ἀκρόνυχοι ψυχραὶ δύνουσι Πέλειαι.

Λαμπροκλῆς δ᾽ ὁ διθυραμβοποιὸς καὶ ῥητῶς αὐτὰς
εἶπεν ὁμωνυμεῖν ταῖς περιστεραῖς ἐν τούτοις·

               αἵ τε ποταναῖς
ὁμώνυμοι πελειάσιν αἰθέρι κεῖσθε.

καὶ ὁ τὴν εἰς Ἡσίοδον δὲ ἀναφερομένην ποιήσας
Ἀστρονομίαν αἰεὶ Πελειάδας αὐτὰς λέγει |

d     < ... > τὰς δὲ βροτοὶ καλέουσι Πελειάδας.

καὶ πάλιν·

    < ... > χειμέριαι δύνουσι Πελειάδες.

καὶ πάλιν·

and a great eagle always scooped up nectar from a
      rock
and fetched it in its beak for wily Zeus to drink.
After he defeated his father Cronus, therefore, wide-
      voiced Zeus
made the eagle immortal and settled him in heaven.
So too he bestowed an honor on the timid Peleiades,
who bring news of summer and winter.

Simmias as well says in his *Gorgo* (fr. 7, p. 112 Powell):

The Peleiai, swift servants of the upper air, were
      drawing near.

Also Posidippus in his *Story of Aesop* (Posidipp. 145 Austin–Bastianini = *SH* 698):

Nor indeed are the cold Peleiai, who rise at dusk,
      setting.

The dithyrambic poet Lamprocles (*PMG* 736) said expressly that they share a name with the pigeons (*peristerai*), in the following passage:

         And you who share a name
with winged doves (*peleiades*) are set in the sky.

So too the author of the *Astronomy* attributed to Hesiod (fr. 288) always calls them Peleiades:

whom mortals refer to as Peleiades.

And again (fr. 289):

The wintry Peleiades are setting.

And again (fr. 290):

⟨ . . . ⟩ τῆμος ἀποκρύπτουσι Πελειάδες.

οὐδὲν οὖν ἄπιστον καὶ Ὅμηρον τὰς Πλειάδας κατὰ ποιητικὸν νόμον Πελειάδας ὠνομακέναι. ἀποδεδειγμένου οὖν τοῦ ὅτι Πλειάδες ἦσαν ἐντετορευμέναι τῷ ποτηρίῳ, καθ’ ἕκαστον τῶν ὤτων δύο ὑποθετέον εἴτε βούλεταί τις ὀρνιθοφυεῖς κόρας εἴτ’ αὖ καὶ ἀνθρωπο-
e ειδεῖς, ἄστροις δὲ πεποικιλμένας. | τὸ μέντοι

> ἀμφὶς ἕκαστον

χρύσειαι νεμέθοντο

οὐχ ὡς περὶ ἓν ἕκαστον ἀκουστέον· γενήσονται γὰρ οὕτως ὀκτὼ τὸν ἀριθμόν· ἀλλ’ ἐπείπερ ἔσχισται μὲν ἑκάτερον τῶν ὤτων εἰς δύο σχίσεις, τούτων δ’ αὖ συνάφεια κατὰ τὴν τελευταίαν ὑπόληξιν, ἕκαστον μὲν ἂν λέγοιτο καθὸ τέτταρες αἱ πᾶσαι σχίσεις τῶν ὤτων, ἑκάτερον δὲ καθὸ συμφυῆ πάλιν ἐπὶ τέλει γίνεται τῆς ἀποστάσεως αὐτῶν. ὅταν οὖν εἴπῃ·

> δοιαὶ δὲ πελειάδες ἀμφὶς ἕκαστον
> χρύσειαι νεμέθοντο, δύω δ’ ὑπὸ πυθμένες ἦσαν,

f καθ’ ἑκατέραν | τὴν σχίσιν τῶν ὤτων ἀκουσόμεθα μίαν Πελειάδα· ἃς δοιὰς εἶπεν καθὸ συμφυεῖς εἰσιν ἀλλήλαις καὶ συνεζευγμέναι. τὸ γὰρ δοιοὶ καὶ δοιαὶ σημαίνει καὶ τὸ κατ’ ἀριθμὸν εἶδος, τὸ δύο, οἷον·

> δοιοὺς δὲ τρίποδας, δέκα δὲ χρυσοῖο τάλαντα.

καί·

at the time when the Peleiades disappear.

It is therefore not at all unbelievable that Homer as well refers to the Pleiades, as poets do, as Peleiades. Now that it has been demonstrated that the Pleiades were engraved on the cup, we must assume that there were two of them per handle, regardless of whether one wants to conceive of them as girls who resemble birds, or as having a human shape but covered with stars. The phrase

with gold (doves) feeding
on either side of each,

moreover, should not be understood as referring to each individual handle-section; because in that case there will be eight of them. But since each handle is divided into two parts, and they connect again at the very end, the word "each" must be used in a way consistent with the fact that the total number of handle-sections is four, although each pair comes together again when they are done being separated. So when he says (*Il.* 11.634–5):

with a pair of gold doves feeding
on either side of each; and there were two bases
beneath it,

we should understand that there is only one Peleiad per handle-section, and that he referred to them as a "pair" only because they are connected and associated with one another. For the words *doioi* and *doiai* refer to numerical character, i.e. "two", for example (*Od.* 4.129):

two (*doioi*) tripods, and ten talents of gold.

And (*Od.* 16.253):

< . . . > δοιὼ θεράποντε.

σημαίνει δὲ καὶ τὸ συμφυὲς καὶ τὸ συνεζευγμένον κατ᾽
ἀριθμόν, ὡς ἐν τούτοις·

> δοιοὺς δ᾽ ἄρ᾽ ὑπήλυθε θάμνους
ἐξ ὁμόθεν πεφυῶτας· ὁ μὲν φυλίης, ὁ δ᾽ ἐλαίης. ||

492 γενήσονται οὖν ἐπὶ τῶν ὤτων τέσσαρες Πελειάδες.
ἔπειθ᾽ ὅταν ἐπενέγκῃ τὸ

> δοιαὶ δὲ πελειάδες ἀμφὶς ἕκαστον
χρύσειαι νεμέθοντο, δύω δ᾽ ὑπὸ πυθμένες ἦσαν,

ἀκουστέον οὐ πυθμένας δύο, ἀλλ᾽ οὐδὲ κατὰ διαίρεσιν
ἀναγνωστέον, ὡς ὁ Θρᾷξ Διονύσιος, ἀλλὰ κατὰ σύν-
θετον ὑποπυθμένες, ὅπως ἐπὶ τῶν Πελειάδων ἀκούω-
μεν, ὅτι τέσσαρες μὲν ἦσαν ἐπὶ τῶν ὤτων, δύο δὲ
ὑποπυθμένες, τουτέστιν ὑπὸ τῷ πυθμένι οἷον ὑπο-
b πυθμένιοι· ὥστε διακρατεῖσθαι τὸ δέπας ὑπὸ | δυεῖν
Πελειάδων ὑποκειμένων τῷ πυθμένι, ἐξ δὲ τὰς πάσας
γενέσθαι Πλειάδας, ἐπείπερ ὁρῶνται τοσαῦται, λέγονται δὲ ἑπτά, καθότι καὶ Ἄρατός φησιν·

> ἑπτάποροι δὴ ταί γε μετ᾽ ἀνθρώποις[41]
> καλέονται[42],
> ἐξ οἷαί περ ἐοῦσαι ἐπόψιαι ὀφθαλμοῖσιν.

[41] Although the manuscripts of Aratus are divided, with
some supporting Athenaeus, the proper reading is most likely
ἀνθρώπους.

[42] The manuscripts of Aratus have ὑδέονται (a much rarer
word with a similar sense).

two (*doiō*) servants.

The word also signifies something that has merged and been closely associated when counted, as in the following passage (*Od.* 5.476–7):

> he crawled in beneath a pair (*doioi*) of bushes
> that had grown together; one was wild olive, the
> other domesticated.

There must accordingly be four Peleiades. Then when he adds the comment (*Il.* 11.634–5):

> with a pair of gold doves feeding
> on either side of each; and there were two (*duō*)
> bases beneath it (*hupo puthmenes ēsan*),

we should not take this to mean that there were two bases, and neither should we read the words separately, as Dionysius Thrax does. Instead, we need to read this as the compound adjective *hupoputhmenes* ("under-base") and thus understand, as regards the Peleiades, that there were four of them on the handles, while two more were "under-base", which is to say that they were placed on the base underneath (*hupo tōi puthmeni*), as if the word were *hupoputhmenioi*. The goblet was thus supported by a pair of Peleiades located beneath the base, and there were a total of six Peleiades, since this is how many are visible, although there are said to be seven, as Aratus (*Phaen.* 257–61) notes:

> People in fact refer to them as moving along seven
>     paths,
> although only six are visible to the eye.

393

οὐ μέν πως ἀπόλωλεν ἀπευθὴς ἐκ Διὸς ἀστήρ,
ἐξ οὗ καὶ γενεῆθεν ἀκούομεν, ἀλλὰ μάλ' αὕτως
εἴρεται. ἑπτὰ δὲ κεῖναι ἐπιρρήδην καλέονται.[43] |

c  τὸ ὁρώμενον οὖν ἐν τοῖς ἄστροις καὶ ἐν τῇ φαινομένῃ
κατασκευῇ προσηκόντως ἐτόρευσεν. τοῦτο μέντοι καὶ
ἐπὶ τοῦ Διὸς σημαίνειν πείθονται τὸν ποιητὴν ὅταν
λέγῃ·

τῇ μέν τ' οὐδὲ ποτητὰ παρέρχεται οὐδὲ πέλειαι
τρήρωνες, ταί τ' ἀμβροσίην Διὶ πατρὶ φέρουσιν,
ἀλλά τε καὶ τῶν αἰὲν ἀφαιρεῖται λὶς πέτρη·
ἀλλ' ἄλλην ἐνίησι πατὴρ ἐναρίθμιον εἶναι, |

d  ὑπὸ τῆς ὀξύτητος τῶν πλαγκτῶν πετρῶν καὶ τῆς
λειότητος ἀφαιρεῖσθαι λέγων μίαν τῶν Πλειάδων,
ἄλλην δὲ πρὸς τοῦ Διὸς ἐνίεσθαι χάριν τοῦ σῴζειν τὸν
ἀριθμὸν αὐτῶν, ποιητικῶς αἰνιττόμενος ὅτι τῶν Πλειάδων ἐξ ὁρωμένων ὅμως ὁ ἀριθμὸς αὐτῶν οὐκ ἀπόλ-
λυται, λέγονται δὲ καὶ τῷ ἀριθμῷ καὶ τοῖς ὀνόμασιν
ἑπτά. πρὸς δὲ τοὺς λέγοντας οὐκ οἰκείως τῷ ποτηρίῳ
ἐντετυπῶσθαι τὰς Πλειάδας, ξηρῶν τροφῶν οὔσας
σημαντικάς, λεκτέον ὅτι τὸ δέπας ἀμφοτέρων τῶν
e  τροφῶν | ἐστιν δεκτικόν· κυκεὼν γὰρ ἐν αὐτῷ γίνεται·
τοῦτο δ' ἐστὶ πόσις ἐν τῷ κράματι τυρὸν ἔχουσα καὶ
ἄλφιτον. ἄμφω δὲ ταῦτα κυκώμενα καὶ οὕτω πινόμενα
λέγει ὁ ποιητής·

---

[43] After this verse, Athenaeus offers ἐξ οἷαί περ ἐοῦσαι
ἐπόψιαι ὀφθαλμοῖσιν (= v. 258, repeated in error).

---

309 The word Homer uses for Nestor's cup.

310 Portions of this passage are quoted and discussed also at
1.10a–b, 24f–5a.

It is by no means the case that any star has vanished
    without notice from the sky
from the time when we first heard of them. But that
    is precisely what
is said, and they are explicitly referred to as seven.

(Homer) thus accurately engraved what is seen among the
stars into the pattern visible (on Nestor's cup). (Some authorities) are in fact convinced that the poet is referring to
Zeus' behavior, when he says (*Od.* 12.62–5):

Not even birds can get by via this route, including the
    timid
Peleiai that bring ambrosia to father Zeus;
for the smooth rock always takes away one of them.
But the father adds another, to maintain their
    number.

For by saying that one of Pleiades is taken away by the
sharpness and smoothness of the Wandering Rocks, but
that Zeus adds another, to keep up their number, he alludes poetically to the fact that although only six Pleiades
are visible, their number nonetheless remains the same,
and they are said to be seven in both number and name. In
response to those who claim that it is inappropriate for
the Pleiades to be engraved on the cup, since they mark
the seasons for the production of dry foods, it should be
noted that a *depas*[309] is used to hold both types of food; because *kukeōn*, which is a drink made from a mixture of
cheese and barley-groats, is produced in it. Homer refers
to both ingredients as being mixed together (*kukōmena*)
and drunk like that (*Il.* 11.624, 628–32, 638–41):[310]

τοῖσι δὲ τεῦχε κυκειὼ ἐυπλόκαμος Ἑκαμήδη,

\* \* \*

ἥ σφωιν < ... > μὲν ἐπιπροΐηλε τράπεζαν
< ... > ἐύξοον, αὐτὰρ ἐπ' αὐτῆς
χάλκειον κάνεον, ἐπὶ δὲ κρόμνον ποτῷ[44] ὄψον
ἠδὲ μέλι χλωρόν, παρὰ δ' ἀλφίτου ἱεροῦ ἀκτήν, |
f     πὰρ δὲ δέπας περικαλλές, ὃ οἴκοθεν ἦγ' ὁ
      γεραιός,

\* \* \*

ἐν τῷ ῥά σφι κύκησε γυνὴ εἰκυῖα θεῆσιν
οἴνῳ Πραμνείῳ, ἐπὶ δ' αἴγειον κνῆ τυρόν
κνήστι χαλκείῃ, ἐπὶ δ' ἄλφιτα λευκὰ πάλυνεν·
πινέμεναι δ' ἐκέλευεν[45], ἐπεί ῥ' ὥπλισσε κυκειῶ.

τὸ δὲ

    ἄλλος μὲν μογέων ἀποκινήσασκε τραπέζης ‖
493     πλεῖον ἐόν, Νέστωρ δ' ὁ γέρων ἀμογητὶ ἄειρεν

οὐκ ἀκουστέον ἐπὶ μόνων Μαχάονος καὶ Νέστορος, ὡς
οἴονταί τινες, τὸ ὃς ἀντὶ τοῦ ὃ λαμβάνοντες ἐπὶ τοῦ
Μαχάονος·

ἀλλ' ὃς μὲν μογέων ἀποκινήσασκε τραπέζης,

ἐκ τοῦ μογέων δηλοῦσθαι νομίζοντες, ἐπειδὴ τέτρωται.

---

44 Contrast the reading ποτοῦ at 1.24f with n.
45 Although the manuscripts of Aratus are divided, with
some supporting Athenaeus, the proper reading is most likely
ἐκέλευσεν.

---

311 The warrior drinking with Nestor at this point in the story.
312 The expected form of the masculine nominative singular
relative pronoun.

Fair-tressed Hecamede made them a *kukeiōn*,

          \*     \*     \*

and she set . . . a polished table beside
. . .             them, and a bronze bread-basket
upon it, along with an onion and pale honey,
to eat as they drank; and (she set) beside them sacred
     barley-groats,
as well as an exquisitely beautiful cup, which the old
     man had brought from home.

          \*     \*     \*

In it, then, the woman who resembled goddesses
     mixed them a *kukeiōn*
using Pramneian wine; and she grated goat-cheese
     over it
with a bronze grater, and sprinkled white barley-
     groats on top,
and encouraged them to drink after she prepared the
     *kukeiōn*.

But as for the remark (*Il.* 11.636–7):

Another (*allos*) man would have had difficulty raising
     it from the table
when it was full. But the aged Nestor hoisted it easily,

this should not be taken as referring exclusively to
Machaon[311] and Nestor, as some authorities believe, taking *hos* as standing for *ho*,[312] in reference to Machaon,
and reading (*Il.* 11.636):

But he (*all' hos*) would have had difficulty raising it
     from the table,

on the ground that the reference to the "difficulty" makes

ὅτι δὲ καθ᾽ Ὅμηρον ὁ Μαχάων οὐ τέτρωται ἐν ἄλλοις
δειχθήσεται. ἀγνοοῦσιν δ᾽ ὅτι τὸ ἄλλος Ὅμηρος οὐκ
ἐπὶ μόνων Μαχάονος καὶ Νέστορος ἔθηκε, δύο γὰρ
b   οὗτοι πίνουσιν, | ἀλλ᾽ εἶπεν ἂν "ἕτερος"· τοῦτο γὰρ ἐπὶ
δύο τάσσεσθαι πέφυκεν, ὡς καὶ ἐπὶ τούτων·

οἴσετε δ᾽ ἄρν᾽, ἕτερον λευκόν, ἑτέρην δὲ
    μέλαιναν.

ἔπειτα δὲ τὸ ὅς ἀντὶ προτακτικοῦ τοῦ ὁ Ὅμηρος
οὐδέποτε τίθησι· τοὔμπαλιν δὲ ἀντὶ τοῦ ὅς ὑποτακτι-
κοῦ παραλαμβάνει τὸ προτακτικὸν ὅ, οἷον·

ἔνθα δὲ Σίσυφος ἔσκεν, ὁ κέρδιστος γένετ᾽
    ἀνδρῶν.

ἐλλείπει οὖν τό τις μόριον· τὸ γὰρ πλῆρές ἐστιν· ἄλλος
c   μέν τις μογέων ἀποκινήσασκε | τραπέζης πλεῖον ἐόν,
Νέστωρ δ᾽ ὁ γέρων ἀμογητὶ ἄειρεν, ὡς παντὸς ἀνθρώπου μόλις ἂν ἀποκινήσαντος ἀπὸ τῆς τραπέζης τὸ
ποτήριον, τοῦ δὲ Νέστορος αὐτὸ ῥᾳδίως βαστάζοντος
δίχα πόνου καὶ κακοπαθείας. τὸ γὰρ ποτήριον ὑφίστα-
ται μέγα κατὰ τὸ κύτος καὶ βαρὺ τὴν ὁλκήν, ὅπερ
φιλοπότης ὢν ὁ Νέστωρ ἐκ τῆς συνεχοῦς συνηθείας
ῥᾳδίως βαστάζειν ἔσθενε. Σωσίβιος δ᾽ ὁ λυτικὸς προ-
θεὶς τὰ ἔπη·

ἄλλος μὲν μογέων ἀποκινήσασκε τραπέζης |
d   πλεῖον ἐόν, Νέστωρ δ᾽ ὁ γέρων ἀμογητὶ ἄειρεν,

---

313 I.e. elsewhere in the work of Asclepiades of Myrlea (or
whoever is being excerpted here), not elsewhere in the *Learned
Banqueters*.

it clear (that this interpretation is right), since Machaon had been wounded. That Homer does not actually claim that Machaon has been wounded will be demonstrated elsewhere.[313] These people, however, are unaware that Homer did not use *allos* ("another man") to refer to Machaon and Nestor alone; for there are two of them drinking, and in that case he would have said *heteros* ("the other"), since this is the word employed when two individuals are involved, as in the following passage (*Il.* 3.103):

> Fetch lambs, one (*heteros*) a white male, the other
> (*heterē*) a black female!

In addition, Homer never uses *hos* in place of an initial *ho*. On the other hand, he does use a properly initial *ho* in place of a subordinate *hos*, for example (*Il.* 6.153):

> There dwelt Sisyphus, who (*ho*) was the canniest man
> that ever lived.

The missing element is thus *tis*; because the full sense is, "Any other (*allos . . . tis*) man would have had difficulty raising it from the table when it was full. But the aged Nestor hoisted it easily," meaning that anyone else would have had difficulty raising the cup from the table, but Nestor picked it up easily, without trouble or effort. For the cup has a large bowl and is heavy, but because Nestor liked to drink, he had considerable practice at picking it up and was thus strong enough to do so easily. Sosibius (*FGrH* 595 F 26), whose specialty is resolving literary puzzles, begins by citing these verses (*Il.* 11.636–7):

> Another man would have had difficulty raising it from
> the table
> when it was full. But the aged Nestor hoisted it easily,

γράφει κατὰ λέξιν· νῦν τὸ μὲν ἐπιτιμώμενόν ἐστι τῷ
ποιητῇ ὅτι τοὺς μὲν λοιποὺς εἶπε μογέοντας ἀείρειν τὸ
δέπας, τὸν δὲ Νέστορα μόνον ἀμογητί. ἄλογον δ᾽
⟨ἂν⟩[46] ἐδόκει Διομήδους καὶ Αἴαντος, ἔτι δ᾽ Ἀχιλλέως
παρόντων εἰσάγεσθαι τὸν Νέστορα γενναιότερον, τῇ
ἡλικίᾳ προβεβηκότα. τούτων τοίνυν οὕτως κατηγορου-
μένων τῇ ἀναστροφῇ χρησάμενοι ἀπολύομεν τὸν ποι-
ητήν. ἀπὸ γὰρ τούτου τοῦ ἑξαμέτρου· |

e     πλεῖον ἐόν, Νέστωρ δ᾽ ὁ γέρων ἀμογητὶ ἄειρεν,

ἀπὸ τοῦ μέσου ἐξελόντες τὸ γέρων τάξομεν τοῦ πρώτου στίχου πρὸς τὴν ἀρχὴν ὑπὸ τὸ ἄλλος μέν, εἶτα τὸ
ἐξ ἀρχῆς συνεροῦμεν· ἄλλος μὲν γέρων μογέων ἀποκινήσασκε τραπέζης πλεῖον ἐόν, ὁ δὲ Νέστωρ ἀπονητὶ
ἄειρεν. νῦν οὖν οὕτω τεταγμένων ὁ Νέστωρ φαίνεται
τῶν μὲν λοιπῶν πρεσβυτῶν μόνος τὸ δέπας ἀμογητὶ
ἀείρων. ταῦτα καὶ ὁ θαυμάσιος λυτικὸς Σωσίβιος, ὃν
οὐκ ἀχαρίτως διέπαιξε διὰ τὰς πολυθρυλήτους ταύτας
f  καὶ τὰς τοιαύτας | λύσεις Πτολεμαῖος ὁ Φιλάδελφος
βασιλεύς. λαμβάνοντος γὰρ αὐτοῦ σύνταξιν βασιλι-
κήν, μεταπεμψάμενος τοὺς ταμίας ἐκέλευσεν, ἐὰν
παραγένηται ὁ Σωσίβιος ἐπὶ τὴν ἀπαίτησιν τῆς συν-
τάξεως, λέγειν αὐτῷ ὅτι ἀπείληφε. καὶ μετ᾽ οὐ πολὺ
παραγενομένῳ καὶ αἰτοῦντι εἰπόντες δεδωκέναι αὐτῷ
τὰς ἡσυχίας εἶχον, ὁ δὲ τῷ βασιλεῖ προσελθὼν κατ-
εμέμφετο τοὺς ταμίας. Πτολεμαῖος ⟨δὲ⟩ μεταπεμψάμενος αὐτοὺς καὶ ἥκειν κελεύσας μετὰ τῶν βιβλίων, ‖

<hr>

[46] add. Olson

[314] Ptolemy II of Egypt (reigned 285/3–246 BCE), founder of
the Museum and of the Library at Alexandria.

and then writes specifically as follows: The poet is criticized nowadays for saying that the others would have lifted the goblet only with difficulty, whereas Nestor alone hoisted it effortlessly. And it might seem illogical, when Diomedes and Ajax, as well as Achilleus, are there, to refer to Nestor, who was an extremely old man, as being better than them. But by making use of the technique of *anastrophē* ("inversion, rearrangement"), I find the poet not guilty of these charges that are brought against him. For if we remove the word *gerōn* ("aged") from the middle of the following hexameter (*Il.* 11.637):

when it was full. But the aged Nestor hoisted it easily,

and put it near the beginning of the first line (*Il.* 11.636), after *allos men*, we will then construe the beginning: Another old man would have had difficulty raising it from the table when it was full, but Nestor hoisted it without any trouble. So if the words are arranged thus, Nestor is presented as the only individual within the subset of old men who can hoist the goblet effortlessly. Thus Sosibius (*FGrH* 595 T 4), the extraordinary resolver of literary puzzles, of whom King Ptolemy Philadelphus[314] made witty fun because of this famous solution and others like it. Sosibius was drawing a royal stipend, and Ptolemy summoned his paymasters and told them that, if Sosibius came to ask for his money, they were to tell him that he had already received it. Shortly thereafter Sosibius appeared and asked to be paid, and they told him that they had given him his money, and refused to discuss the matter further. Sosibius therefore went to the king and complained about his paymasters, and Ptolemy summoned them and told them to bring with them the books that listed everyone who re-

494 ἐν οἷς αἱ ἀναγραφαί εἰσι τῶν τὰς συντάξεις λαμ-
βανόντων, λαβὼν ταύτας εἰς χεῖρας καὶ[47] κατιδὼν
ἔφη καὶ αὐτὸς ἀπειληφέναι αὐτὸν οὕτως· ἦν ὀνόματα
ἐγγεγραμμένα ταῦτα, Σωτῆρος Σωσιγένους Βίωνος
Ἀπολλωνίου[48]. εἰς ἃ ἀποβλέψας ὁ βασιλεὺς εἶπεν, "ὦ
θαυμάσιε λυτικέ, ἐὰν ἀφέλῃς τοῦ Σωτῆρος τὸ σω- καὶ
τοῦ Σωσιγένους τὸ -σι- καὶ τοῦ Βίωνος τὴν πρώτην
συλλαβὴν[49] καὶ τὴν τελευταίαν τοῦ Ἀπολλωνίου,
εὑρήσεις σαυτὸν ἀπειληφότα κατὰ τὰς σὰς ἐπινοίας.
καὶ

b ταῦτ' οὐχ | ὑπ' ἄλλων, ἀλλὰ τοῖς αὑτοῦ[50]
πτεροῖς,

κατὰ τὸν θαυμάσιον Αἰσχύλον, ἀλίσκῃ, ἀπροσδι-
ονύσους λύσεις πραγματευόμενος."

Ὅλμος. ποτήριον κερατίου τρόπον εἰργασμένον.
Μενεσθένης ἐν τετάρτῳ Πολιτικῶν γράφει οὕτως· Ἀλ-
βατάνης δὲ στρεπτὸν καὶ ὅλμον χρυσοῦν. ὁ δὲ ὅλμος
ἐστὶ ποτήριον κερατίου τρόπον εἰργασμένον, ὕψος ὡς
πυγονιαῖον.

47 εἰς χεῖρας ὁ βασιλεὺς καὶ A: ὁ βασιλεὺς om. CE, del.
Kaibel       48 Ἀπολλωνίου Lehrs: Ἀπόλλωνος Δίωνος A:
Ἀπόλλωνος tantum CE
49 συλλαβὴν βι A: βι om. CE, del. Herwerden
50 The correct reading is almost certain the plural αὐτῶν.

315 The story is slightly garbled; what the list should contain is
the names of everyone who had recently been paid, not everyone
who regularly drew a royal stipend.
316 Referring to an eagle hit by an arrow fletched with its own
feathers. Cf. Ar. Av. 808 with Dunbar ad loc.

ceived a stipend.[315] He took the books in his hands and inspected them, and said that he too believed that Sosibius had got his money, for the following reason: The names on the list were Soterus, Sosigenes, Bion, and Apollonius, and after the king looked them over, he said: "My extraordinary puzzle-solver, if you take the So- from Soterus, the -si- from Sosigenes, the initial syllable from Bion, and the final syllable from Apollonius, you will find, by applying your own methods, that you have already got your money. You are caught

> thus not by others, but by means of your own feathers,

to quote the marvellous Aeschylus (fr. 139.4),[316] since you spend your time producing unpoetic solutions[317] to poetic problems."

*Holmos*. A cup made in the same style as a small drinking-horn.[318] Menesthenes writes as follows in Book IV of the *Politics* (*FHG* iv.451–2): a chain-mail collar from Albatane and a gold *holmos*. A *holmos* is a cup made in the same style as a small drinking-horn, and is about 15 inches[319] tall.

---

[317] Literally "nothing-to-do-with-Dionysus solutions".

[318] This definition is repeated word-for-word below, and the most economical explanation would seem to be that Athenaeus has drawn it straight—and clumsily—from Menesthenes. A *holmos* is normally a "mortar".

[319] Literally "a *pugōn*" (also known as a "bare cubit"), the distance from the elbow to the first joint of the fingers, = 5/6 of a cubit.

'Οξύβαφον. ἡ μὲν κοινὴ συνήθεια οὕτως καλεῖ τὸ
ὄξους δεκτικὸν σκεῦος. ἐστὶ δὲ καὶ ὄνομα ποτηρίου, οὗ
c  μνημονεύει Κρατῖνος μὲν ἐν Πυτίνῃ | οὕτως·

πῶς τις αὐτόν, πῶς τις ἂν
ἀπὸ τοῦ πότου παύσειε, τοῦ λίαν πότου;
ἐγῷδα· συντρίψω γὰρ αὐτοῦ τοὺς χοᾶς
καὶ τοὺς καδίσκους συγκεραυνώσω σποδῶν
καὶ τἆλλα πάντ' ἀγγεῖα τὰ περὶ τὸν πότον,
κοὐδ' ὀξύβαφον οἰνηρὸν ἔτι κεκτήσεται.

ὅτι δέ ἐστι τὸ ὀξύβαφον εἶδος κύλικος μικρᾶς κεραμέας σαφῶς παρίστησιν Ἀντιφάνης ἐν Μύστιδι διὰ
τούτων· γραῦς ἐστι φίλοινος ἐπαινοῦσα κύλικα μεγάλην καὶ ἐξευτελίζουσα τὸ ὀξύβαφον ὡς βραχύ. εἰ-
d  πόντος | οὖν τινος πρὸς αὐτήν·

<(Α.) σὺ δ' ἀλλὰ πῖθι,

λέγει>[51].

(Β.) τοῦτο μέν σοι πείσομαι·
καὶ γὰρ ἐπαγωγόν, ὦ θεοί, τὸ σχῆμά πως
τῆς κύλικός ἐστιν ἄξιόν τε τοῦ κλέους
τοῦ τῆς ἑορτῆς. οὗ μὲν ἦμεν ἄρτι γὰρ
ἐξ ὀξυβαφίων κεραμεῶν ἐπίνομεν·
τούτῳ δέ, τέκνον, πολλὰ κἀγάθ' οἱ θεοὶ
τῷ δημιουργῷ δοῖεν ὃς ἐποίησέ σε,
τῆς συμμετρίας καὶ τῆς † ἀσφαλείας[52] † οὕνεκα.

51 add. Schweighäuser
52 At 10.446c Athenaeus offers the correct reading ἀφελείας.

404

*Oxubaphon*. Common usage refers in this way to a vessel that holds vinegar (*oxos*). But this is also the name of a cup mentioned by Cratinus in *Wine-Flask* (fr. 199), as follows:

> How, how could someone
> put a stop to his drinking, his excessive drinking?
> I know—I'll crush his pitchers,
> and smash his wine-buckets and all
> the other vessels he uses when he drinks to bits;
> he won't even own an *oxubaphon* that holds wine
>     after this!

Antiphanes in *The Female Initiate* (fr. 161)[320] establishes unambiguously that an *oxubaphon* is a type of small ceramic cup, in the following passage. After someone says to a woman:

(A.) But as for you—drink!,

she says:

> (B.) I'll do what you say;
> because the fact is, by the gods, that the cup's shape
> is rather attractive, and it fits the festival's
> reputation. Because where we were just now,
> we were drinking out of ceramic *oxubapha*!
> May the gods grant many blessings, my child,
> to the craftsman who produced you,
> on account of your symmetrical shape and †
>     security †.

[320] Quoted also at 10.446c (but with the correct reading in the final verse).

κἂν τοῖς Βαβυλωνίοις οὖν τοῖς Ἀριστοφάνους ἀκου-
σόμεθα ποτήριον τὸ ὀξύβαφον, ὅταν ὁ Διόνυσος λέγῃ |
e περὶ τῶν Ἀθήνησι δημαγωγῶν ὡς αὐτὸν ᾔτουν ἐπὶ
τὴν δίκην ἀπελθόντα ὀξυβάφω δύο· οὐ γὰρ ἄλλο τι
ἡγητέον εἶναι ἢ ὅτι ἐκπώματα ᾔτουν. καὶ τὸ τοῖς
ἀποκοτταβίζουσι δὲ ὀξύβαφον τιθέμενον εἰς ὃ τὰς
λάταγας ἐγχέουσιν οὐκ ἄλλο τι ἂν εἴη ἢ ἐκπέταλον
ποτήριον. μνημονεύει δὲ τοῦ ὀξυβάφου ὡς ποτηρίου
καὶ Εὔβουλος ἐν Μυλωθρίδι·

καὶ πιεῖν χωρὶς † μέτρω †
ὀξύβαφον εἰς τὸ κοινόν· εἶθ᾽ ὑπώμνυτο
ὁ μὲν οἶνος ὄξος αὐτὸν εἶναι γνήσιον, |
f      τὸ δ᾽ ὄξος οἶνον αὐτὸ μᾶλλον θατέρου.

Οἰνιστήρια. οἱ μέλλοντες ἀποκείρειν τὸν σκόλλυν
ἔφηβοι, φησὶ Πάμφιλος, εἰσφέρουσι τῷ Ἡρακλεῖ
μέγα ποτήριον πληρώσαντες οἴνου, ὃ καλοῦσιν οἰνι-
στηρίαν, καὶ σπείσαντες τοῖς συνελθοῦσι διδόασι
πιεῖν.

Ὄλλιξ. Πάμφιλος ἐν Ἀττικαῖς Λέξεσι τὸ ξύλινον
ποτήριον ἀποδίδωσι.

Παναθηναϊκόν. Ποσειδώνιος ὁ φιλόσοφος ἐν ἕκτῃ
καὶ τριακοστῇ τῶν Ἱστοριῶν ὡς οὕτω καλουμένων
495  τινῶν ποτηρίων μέμνηται γράφων οὕτως· ‖ ἦσαν δὲ
καὶ ὀνύχινοι σκύφοι καὶ συνδέσεις τούτων μέχρι δικο-
τύλων· καὶ Παναθηναϊκὰ μέγιστα, τὰ μὲν δίχοα, τὰ δὲ
καὶ μείζονα.

---

321 Sc. because Dionysus was the god of wine and drinking.
322 Cf. 15.667e–f.
323 See 11.469a n.

In Aristophanes' *Babylonians* (fr. 75) as well, therefore, we will take the word *oxubaphon* to refer to a cup, when Dionysus describes how the Athenian demagogues asked him for two *oxubapha* after he went to court for his trial; for it is impossible to conclude that they asked for anything other than drinking vessels.[321] So too the *oxubaphon* set out for people playing cottabus to dump their wine-lees into[322] could scarcely be anything other than a broad, shallow cup. Eubulus in *The Girl Who Worked a Mill* (fr. 65) also refers to an *oxubaphon* as a cup:

> and to drink separately † two measures †
>    an *oxubaphon* in common. Then the wine offered a
>       motion
>    that the trial be postponed, on the ground that it was
>       itself legitimate vinegar,
>    while the vinegar argued that it was more wine than
>       it was the opposite.

*Oinistēria*. According to Pamphilus (fr. XXIV Schmidt), ephebes[323] who are about to cut their long hair short fill a large cup referred to as an *oinistēria* with wine (*oinos*) as an offering to Heracles, and after they pour a libation, they offer a drink to the people who accompany them.

*Ollix*. Pamphilus in *Attic Vocabulary* (fr. XXV Schmidt) defines this as a wooden cup.

*Panathenaïkon* ("Panathenaic [cup]"). The philosopher Posidonius in Book XXXVI of his *History* (*FGrH* 87 F 25 = fr. 76 Edelstein–Kidd) mentions certain cups as referred to this way, writing as follows: There were also *skuphoi* made of onyx, and sets of these that held as much as two *kotuloi*; also very large *Panathenaïka*, some with a capacity of two *choes*, others even larger.

Πρόαρον. κρατὴρ ξύλινος, εἰς ὃν τὸν οἶνον κιρνᾶσιν οἱ Ἀττικοί.

κοίλοις ἐν προάροις,

φησὶ Πάμφιλος.

Πελίκαι. Καλλίστρατος ἐν Ὑπομνήμασι Θραττῶν Κρατίνου ἀποδίδωσι κύλικα. Κράτης δ᾽ ἐν δευτέρῳ Ἀττικῆς Διαλέκτου γράφει οὕτως· οἱ χόες πελίκαι, καθάπερ εἴπομεν, ὠνομάζοντο. ὁ δὲ τύπος ἦν τοῦ
b ἀγγείου πρότερον μὲν τοῖς Παναθηναϊκοῖς | ἐοικώς, ἡνίκα ἐκαλεῖτο πελίκη, ὕστερον δὲ ἔσχεν οἰνοχόης σχῆμα, οἷοί εἰσιν οἱ ἐν τῇ ἑορτῇ παρατιθέμενοι, ὁποίους δή ποτε ὄλπας ἐκάλουν, χρώμενοι πρὸς τὴν τοῦ οἴνου ἔγχυσιν, καθάπερ Ἴων ὁ Χῖος ἐν Εὐρυτίδαις φησίν·

ἐκ ζαθέων πιθακνῶν ἀφύσαντες ὄλπαις
οἶνον ὑπερφίαλον κελαρύζετε.

νυνὶ δὲ τὸ μὲν τοιοῦτον ἀγγεῖον καθιερωμένον τινὰ τρόπον ἐν τῇ ἑορτῇ παρατίθεται μόνον, τὸ δ᾽ ἐς τὴν χρείαν πῖπτον μετεσχημάτισται, ἀρυταίνῃ μάλιστα
c ἐοικός, ὃ δὴ καλοῦμεν χόα. τὴν δὲ | ὄλπην Κλείταρχος Κορινθίους μέν φησι καὶ Βυζαντίους καὶ Κυπρίους τὴν λήκυθον ἀποδιδόναι, Θεσσαλοὺς δὲ τὴν πρόχοον. Σέλευκος δὲ πελίχναν Βοιωτοὺς μὲν τὴν κύλικα, Εὐφρόνιος δὲ ἐν Ὑπομνήμασι τοὺς χόας.

---

324 Seemingly formed from pro- ("forward, forth") + aruō ("draw liquid").

325 A fragment of some anonymous epic or elegiac poet quoted by Pamphilus for the sake of this word.     326 I.e., presumably, the Choes festival in Athens; cf. 10.437b–d.

*Proaron*.[324] A wooden mixing-bowl, in which the inhabitants of Attica mix wine. Pamphilus (fr. XXX Schmidt) says
(*SH* 1011):[325]

in hollow *proara*.

*Pelikai*. Callistratus in the *Commentary on Cratinus'*
*Thracian Women* (p. 325 in Nauck (ed.), *Aristophanis*
*Byzantii . . . fragmenta* = Cratin. fr. 88) defines this as a
*kulix*. But Crates in Book II of the *Attic Dialect* (*FGrH* 362
F 8 = fr. 108 Broggiato) writes as follows: Pitchers (*choes*)
were referred to, as I noted, as *pelikai*. The shape of the
vessel was previously like that of a *Panathenaïkon* (at
which time it was referred to as a *pelikē*), but later it took
on the look of an *oinochoē* ("wine-pitcher"), like those set
beside people at the festival.[326] These were the type they
referred to in those days as *olpai*, and which were used to
pour wine, as Ion of Chios says in *The Sons of Eurytus*
(*TrGF* 19 F 10):

Draw potent wine from sacred jars
and pour it gurgling forth from *olpai*!

Whereas nowadays the use of vessels of this type is re-
stricted, as it were, and they are only set beside us at
the festival, while the shape of the type that has come
into common use (and which we refer to as a *chous*)
has evolved, and is more like an *arutaina* ("dipper").
Cleitarchus claims that the Corinthians, Byzantines, and
Cypriots refer to a *lēkuthos* as an *olpē*, while the Thessalians use this as a term for a *prochoos*. But Seleucus
(says) that the Boeotians refer to a *kulix* as a *pelichna*,
whereas Euphronius in the *Commentaries* (fr. 107
Strecker) (says) that they use the term for *choes*.

Πέλλα. ἀγγεῖον σκυφοειδές, πυθμένα ἔχον πλατύτερον, εἰς ὃ ἤμελγον τὸ γάλα. Ὅμηρος·

ὡς ὅτε μυῖαι
σταθμῷ ἔνι βρομέωσι ἐυγλαγέας[53] κατὰ πέλλας.

τοῦτο δὲ Ἱππῶναξ λέγει πελλίδα· |

d  ἐκ πελλίδος πίνοντες· οὐ γὰρ ἦν αὐτῇ
κύλιξ, ὁ παῖς γὰρ ἐμπεσὼν κατήραξε,

δῆλον, οἶμαι, ποιῶν ὅτι ποτήριον μὲν οὐκ ἦν, δι'
ἀπορίαν δὲ κύλικος ἐχρῶντο τῇ πελλίδι. καὶ πάλιν·

ἐκ δὲ τῆς πέλλης
ἔπινον· ἄλλοτ' αὐτός, ἄλλοτ' Ἀρήτη
προὔπινεν.

Φοῖνιξ δ' ὁ Κολοφώνιος ἐν τοῖς Ἰάμβοις ἐπὶ φιάλης
τίθησι τὴν λέξιν λέγων οὕτως·

Θαλῆς γάρ, ὅστις ἀστέρων < ... >
< ... > ὀνήιστος
καὶ τῶν τότ', ὡς λέγουσι, πολλὸν ἀνθρώπων
ἐὼν ἄριστος, ἔλαβε πελλίδα χρυσῆν. |

e  καὶ ἐν ἄλλῳ δὲ μέρει φησίν·

ἐκ πελλίδος ⟨γὰρ⟩ τάργανον κατηγυίης
χωλοῖσι δακτύλοισι τῇτέρῃ σπένδει,
τρέμων οἷόν περ ἐν βορηίῳ νωδός.

---

[53] The traditional text of Homer has περιγλαγέας.

410

*Pella*. A vessel shaped like a *skuphos*, but with a broader base, which was used for milking. Homer (*Il.* 16.641–2):

> as when flies
> buzz around the *pellai* full of milk in a barn.

Hipponax (fr. 21 Degani) refers to this vessel as a *pellis*:

> drinking from a *pellis*; because she didn't have
> a *kulix*, since her slave had tripped and broken it,

thus making it clear, I think, that a *pellis* was not a cup, but was something they used when they lacked a *kulix*. And again (fr. 22 Degani):

> They were drinking from
> the *pellē*, and sometimes he was toasting Arete, and
>         sometimes
> she was toasting him.

Phoenix of Colophon in his *Iambs* (fr. 4, p. 234 Powell) uses the word to refer to a *phialē*, putting it as follows:

> Because Thales, who of stars . . .
> . . . and was the most useful
> and far and away the best, so they say, of people
> in those times, got a gold *pellis*.[327]

And elsewhere (fr. 5, p. 235 Powell) he says:

> For he pours a libation of vinegar from a broken
> *pellis* with the gnarled fingers of one hand,
> shivering like a broken-down old man in a north
>         wind.

[327] For Thales' prize, cf. 11.781d n.

Κλείταρχος δὲ ἐν ταῖς Γλώσσαις πελλητῆρα μὲν καλεῖν Θεσσαλοὺς καὶ Αἰολεῖς τὸν ἀμολγέα, πέλλαν δὲ
τὸ ποτήριον. Φιλητᾶς δ᾿ ἐν Ἀτάκτοις τὴν κύλικα
Βοιωτούς.

Πενταπλόα. μνημονεύει αὐτῆς Φιλόχορος ἐν δευ-
f τέρᾳ Ἀτθίδος. Ἀριστόδημος δ᾿ ἐν τρίτῳ | Περὶ Πιν-
δάρου τοῖς Σκίροις φησὶν Ἀθήναζε ἀγῶνα ἐπιτελεῖ-
σθαι τῶν ἐφήβων δρόμου· τρέχειν δ᾿ αὐτοὺς ἔχοντας
ἀμπέλου κλάδον κατάκαρπον τὸν καλούμενον ὦσχον.
τρέχουσι δ᾿ ἐκ τοῦ ἱεροῦ τοῦ Διονύσου μέχρι τοῦ τῆς
Σκιράδος Ἀθηνᾶς ἱεροῦ, καὶ ὁ νικήσας λαμβάνει
κύλικα τὴν λεγομένην πενταπλόαν καὶ κωμάζει μετὰ
496 χοροῦ. ‖ πενταπλόα δ᾿ ἡ κύλιξ καλεῖται καθ᾿ ὅσον
οἶνον ἔχει καὶ μέλι καὶ τυρὸν καὶ ἀλφίτων καὶ ἐλαίου
βραχύ.

Πέταχνον. ποτήριον ἐκπέταλον, οὗ μνημονεύει
Ἄλεξις ἐν Δρωπίδῃ· πρόκειται δὲ τὸ μαρτύριον. μνημονεύει αὐτοῦ καὶ Ἀριστοφάνης ἐν Δράμασι λέγων·

< . . . > πάντες δ᾿ ἔνδον πεταχνοῦνται.

Πλημοχόη. σκεῦος κεραμεοῦν βεμβικῶδες ἑδραῖον
ἡσυχῇ, ὃ κοτυλίσκον ἔνιοι προσαγορεύουσιν, ὥς φησι
Πάμφιλος. χρῶνται δὲ αὐτῷ ἐν Ἐλευσῖνι τῇ τελευταίᾳ
b τῶν μυστηρίων ἡμέρᾳ, ἣν καὶ ἀπ᾿ αὐτοῦ | προσ-
αγορεύουσι Πλημοχόας· ἐν ᾗ δύο πλημοχόας πληρώσαντες τὴν μὲν πρὸς ἀνατολάς, τὴν δὲ πρὸς δύσιν

---

328 Celebrated on 12 Skirophorion (late June/early July); see
Austin–Olson on Ar. *Th.* 834–5.
329 Literally "fivefold", for the five edible substances it held.
330 I.e., presumably, "getting drunk"; cf. Phot. p. 426.9.

Cleitarchus in his *Glossary* (claims that) the Thessalians and Aeolians refer to a milk-pail as a *pellētēr*, and to a cup as a *pella*. But Philetas in the *Miscellany* (fr. 5 Dettori = fr. 33 Spanoudakis) (claims that) the Boeotians use the term for a *kulix*.

*Pentaploa*. Philochorus mentions this in Book II of the *History of Attica* (*FGrH* 328 F 15). Aristodemus in Book III of *On Pindar* (*FGrH* 383 F 9) says that a footrace for ephebes is held at the Skira festival in Athens,[328] and that they run holding a bit of grapevine with grape-clusters attached, which is referred to as an *ōschos*. They run from the temple of Dionysus to the temple of Athena Skiras, and the winner gets the *kulix* known as a *pentaploa* and celebrates with a chorus. The *kulix* is referred to as *pentaploa*[329] because of the fact that it contains wine, honey, cheese, barley-groats, and a little olive oil.

*Petachnon*. A broad, shallow cup mentioned by Alexis in *Dropides* (fr. 60); the passage was cited earlier (3.125f). Aristophanes also refers to it in *Dramas* (fr. 301), saying:

Everyone inside is petachnizing.[330]

*Plēmochoē*.[331] A ceramic vessel that resembles a top, but is relatively stable; some people employ the term *kotuliskos* for it, according to Pamphilus (fr. XXVIII Schmidt). It is used at Eleusis on the final day of the Mysteries, which is accordingly referred to as Plēmochoai.[332] On this day they fill two *plēmochoai*, and standing facing east in the case of one, and facing west in the case of

---

[331] The first element in the name is cognate with the verb *pimplēmi*, "fill".    [332] Poll. 10.74 preserves similar information, but in almost entirely different words.

< . . . > ἀνιστάμενοι ἀνατρέπουσίν τε ἐπιλέγοντες
ῥῆσιν μυστικήν. μνημονεύει αὐτῶν καὶ ὁ τὸν Πειρί-
θουν γράψας, εἴτε Κριτίας ἐστὶν ὁ τύραννος ἢ Εὐριπίδης, λέγων οὕτως·

　ἵνα πλημοχόας τάσδ' εἰς χθόνιον
　　χάσμ' εὐφήμως προχέωμεν.

Πρίστις. ὅτι ποτηρίου εἶδος προείρηται ἐν τῷ περὶ
τοῦ βατιακίου λόγῳ.

c　Προχύτης. εἶδος ἐκπώματος, | ὡς Σιμάριστος ἐν
τετάρτῳ Συνωνύμων. Ἴων δ' ὁ Χῖος ἐν Ἐλεγείοις·

　ἡμῖν δὲ κρητῆρ' οἰνοχόοι θέραπες
　κιρνάντων προχύταισιν ἐν ἀργυρέοις.

Φιλητᾶς δ' ἐν Ἀτάκτοις ἀγγεῖον ξύλινον, ἀφ' οὗ τοὺς
ἀγροίκους πίνειν. μνημονεύει αὐτοῦ καὶ Ἀλέξανδρος
ἐν Ἀντιγόνῃ[54]. Ξενοφῶν δ' ἐν ὀγδόῳ Παιδείας προ-
χοίδας τινὰς λέγει κύλικας γράφων ὧδε (ὁ δὲ λόγος
ἐστὶν αὐτῷ περὶ Περσῶν)· ἦν δὲ αὐτοῖς νόμιμον μὴ
d　προχοίδας εἰσφέρεσθαι εἰς τὰ | συμπόσια, δῆλον ὅτι
νομίζοντες τὸ μὴ ὑπερπίνειν ἧττον ἂν καὶ σώματα καὶ
γνώμας σφάλλειν· νῦν δὲ τὸ μὲν μὴ εἰσφέρεσθαι ἔτι
αὖ καταμένει· τοσοῦτον δὲ πίνουσιν ὥστε ἀντὶ τοῦ
εἰσφέρειν αὐτοὶ ἐκφέρονται, ἐπειδὰν μηκέτι δύνωνται
ὀρθούμενοι ἐξιέναι.

---

[54] Ἀντιγόνῃ Kaibel: τιγονι A

---

[333] Not accepted as Euripidean by Kannicht in *TrGF*.

[334] At 11.784a, where see n.

[335] An excerpt from a much longer fragment quoted at
11.463b–c, where see n.

the other . . . and turn them upside down, reciting a for-
mula associated with the Mysteries. They are mentioned
by the author of the *Pirithous*, who may be either the tyrant Critias (*TrGF* 43 F 2 = 88 B 17 D–K) or Euripides (fr.
592 Nauck²),[333] and who says the following:

> in order that we may silently pour these
>   *plēmochoes* into the chasm in the earth.

*Pristis*. That this is a type of cup was noted earlier, in
our discussion of the *batiakion*.[334]

*Prochutēs*. A type of drinking vessel, according to
Simaristus in Book IV of *Synonyms*. Ion of Chios in the
*Elegiacs* (fr. 27.2–3 West²):[335]

> Let the servants who pour the wine mix a
> bowl for us using silver *prochutai*.

Philetas in the *Miscellany* (fr. 6 Dettori = fr. 34 Spanoudakis) (claims that) this is a wooden vessel from which country people drink. Alexander mentions it in *Antigone* (Alex.
Aet. fr. dub. 22, p. 129 Powell = Alexand. Com. fr. dub. 4).
Xenophon in Book VIII (8.10) of the *Education* mentions a
type of *kulikes* known as *prochoides*, writing as follows—
his topic is the Persians: They did not regard it as appropriate for *prochoides* to be brought into their drinking
parties, obviously believing that if they did not drink too
much, they would suffer less physical and mental damage.
Nowadays, on the other hand, the rule about not bringing
(these specific vessels) in is still respected, but they drink
so much that rather than bringing anything in, they are
themselves carried out when they can no longer stand up
straight and leave.

Προυσίας. ὅτι τὸ ποτήριον τοῦτο ἔξορθόν ἐστι
προείρηται. καὶ ὅτι τὴν προσηγορίαν ἔσχεν ἀπὸ
Προυσίου τοῦ Βιθυνίας βασιλεύσαντος καὶ ἐπὶ τρυφῇ
καὶ μαλακίᾳ διαβοήτου γενομένου ἱστορεῖ Νίκανδρος
e ὁ Καλχηδόνιος | ἐν τετάρτῳ Προυσίου Συμπτωμάτων.

Ῥέοντα. οὕτως ποτήριά τινα ἐκαλεῖτο. μνημονεύει
δ᾽ αὐτῶν Ἀστυδάμας ἐν Ἑρμῇ λέγων οὕτως·

κρατῆρε μὲν πρώτιστον ἀργυρῶ δύο,
φιάλας δὲ πεντήκοντα, δέκα δὲ κυμβία,
ῥέοντα δώδεχ᾽, ὧν τὰ μὲν δέκ᾽ ἀργυρᾶ
ἦν, δύο δὲ χρυσᾶ, γρύψ, τὸ δ᾽ ἕτερον Πήγασος.

Ῥυσίς. φιάλη χρυσῆ, Θεόδωρος. Κρατῖνος ἐν Νό-
μοις·

ῥυσίδι[55] σπένδων.

Ῥοδιάς. Δίφιλος Αἱρησιτείχει (τὸ δὲ δρᾶμα τοῦτο
f Καλλίμαχος | ἐπιγράφει Εὐνοῦχον) λέγει δὲ οὕτως·

55 At 11.502a Athenaeus offers the correct reading χρυσίδι.

---

336 Cf. 11.475f (where this is, however, merely implied rather
than stated specifically).

337 Cf. 11.783e.

338 Quoted again, in a more complete form and with a different spelling of the name of the vessel (see next n.), at 11.502b.

339 The text ought, however, to read *chrusis* (as at 11.502b; cf.
Hsch. χ 791), meaning that Athenaeus' entire entry ought almost
certainly to be deleted as a scholarly misunderstanding based on a
manuscript error. Theodorus was the author of an *Attic Vocabulary* cited several times elsewhere in the *Learned Banqueters*
(14.646c; 15.677b, 678d; cf. 15.691c), and it seems unlikely that

*Prousias*. That this cup stands upright was noted earlier.[336] That it got its name from Prousias, who was the king of Bithynia and was notorious for his addiction to luxury and his effeminate behavior, is recorded by Nicander of Calchedon in Book IV of the *Adventures of Prousias* (*FGrH* 700 F 1).[337]

*Rheonta*. This was the name of cups of some sort. Astydamas mentions them in *Hermes* (*TrGF* 60 F 3), putting it as follows:

> two silver mixing-bowls, first of all,
> and 50 *phialai*, ten *kumbia*,
> and a dozen *rheonta*, ten of them made of
> silver, two of gold—one a griffin, the other a Pegasus.

*Rhusis*. A gold *phialē*, (according to) Theodorus (*FGrH* 346 F 4). Cratinus in *The Laws* (fr. 132.1):[338]

> pouring a libation using a *rhusis*.[339]

*Rhodias*.[340] Diphilus in *The Man Who Captured Walls* (fr. 5.1–2)[341]—Callimachus (fr. 440 Pfeiffer) gives the title of this play as *The Eunuch*—says the following:

---

he had any authority for the word *rhusis* outside of the text of Cratinus.

[340] See also 11.497f (citing Polemon fr. 57 Preller).

[341] Quoted again immediately below in a more complete (and slightly different) form and with a more detailed discussion of the relationship of the play to *The Eunuch*. Although K–A treat these as a single fragment from a single play, they ought perhaps to be treated instead as separate fragments from related plays, as Athenaeus suggests.

πιεῖν γέ τι
ἀδρότερον, ἢ τῶν Ῥοδιακῶν ἢ τῶν ῥυτῶν.

μνημονεύει αὐτῶν καὶ Διώξιππος ἐν Φιλαργύρῳ καὶ
Ἀριστοτέλης ἐν τῷ Περὶ Μέθης Λυγκεύς τε ὁ Σάμιος
ἐν ταῖς Ἐπιστολαῖς.

Ῥυτόν. ἔχει τὸ ῠ βραχὺ καὶ ὀξύνεται. Δημοσθένης
ἐν τῷ Κατὰ Μειδίου, ῥυτὰ καὶ κυμβία, φησί, καὶ
φιάλας. Δίφιλος δ᾽ ἐν Εὐνούχῳ ἢ Στρατιώτῃ (ἐστὶ δὲ
τὸ δρᾶμα διασκευὴ τοῦ Αἱρησιτείχους)· ‖

497　　ἔσθ᾽ ὑποχέασθαι πλείονας· πιεῖν γέ τι
ἀδρότερον, ἢ τῶν Ῥοδιακῶν ἢ τῶν ῥυτῶν.

Ἐπίνικος δ᾽ ἐν Ὑποβαλλομέναις·

(Α.) καὶ τῶν ῥυτῶν τὰ μέγιστα τῶν ὄντων τρία
πίνειν δεήσει τήμερον πρὸς κλεψύδραν
κρουνιζόμενον. (Β.) ἀμφότερα δ᾽ οἰωνίζομαι.
(Α.) † ἐστιν δ᾽ ἐλέφας. (Β.) ἐλέφαντας περιάγει;
　　(Α.) ῥυτὸν
χωροῦντα δύο χοᾶς, ὃν οὐδ᾽ ἂν ἐλέφας ἐκπίοι. |
b　　ἐγὼ τοῦτο πέπωκα πολλάκις. †
(Β.) οὐδὲν ἐλέφαντος γὰρ διαφέρεις οὐδὲ σύ.
(Α.) ἕτερον τριήρης· τοῦτ᾽ ἴσως χωρεῖ χοᾶ.

περὶ δὲ τοῦ τρίτου λέγων φησίν·

---

342 The entire fragment is quoted at 11.472b.
343 Cf. 11.469b.　　344 A type of ceramic drinking-horn, as
the discussion that follows makes clear. The word is cognate with
the verb *rheō*, "flow".　　345 Referred to in passing also at
11.469a (where the drinking vessel known as an *elephas* is being
discussed), 500f (on the *triērēs*, "trireme"), with a cross-reference
in both cases to this passage.

418

>                     to drink a bit
> harder than from *Rhodiaka* or drinking-horns.

Dioxippus in *The Miser* (fr. 4.2)[342] also mentions them, as do Aristotle in his *On Drunkenness* (fr. 673) and Lynceus of Samos in his *Letters* (fr. 16b Dalby).[343]

*Rhuton*.[344] The word has a short *upsilon* and an acute accent on the final syllable. Demosthenes says in his *Against Meidias* (21.158): *rhuta*, *kumbia*, and *phialai*. Diphilus in *The Eunuch or The Soldier* (fr. 5)—the play is a revised version of *The Man Who Captured Walls*:

> We can have more (cups) poured; to drink a bit
> harder than from *Rhodiaka* or drinking-horns.

Epinicus in *Women Who Try to Pass off Supposititious Children* (fr. 2, encompassing both quotations):[345]

> (A.) And today he'll have to drink the contents of the
>           three
> biggest *rhuta* there are, while the waterclock's
> running. (B.) I'd call those both bad omens.
> (A.) † There's an *elephas*. (B.) He's surrounding us
>           with elephants? (A.) a *rhuton*
> that can hold two *choes*; not even an elephant could
>           drink that much.
> I've drained it many times myself. †
> (B.) Because you're no different from an elephant.
> (A.) The next one's a *triērēs*; it holds maybe a *chous*.

And when he discusses the third one, he says:

(A.) ὁ Βελλεροφόντης ἐστὶν ἀπὸ τοῦ Πηγάσου
τὴν πύρπνοον Χίμαιραν εἰσηκοντικώς.
εἶέν· δέχου καὶ τοῦτο.

ἐκαλεῖτο δὲ τὸ ῥυτὸν πρότερον κέρας. δοκεῖ δὲ σκευο-
ποιηθῆναι ὑπὸ πρώτου τοῦ Φιλαδέλφου Πτολεμαίου
βασιλέως φορήματα γενέσθαι τῶν Ἀρσινόης εἰκόνων·
c τῇ γὰρ | εὐωνύμῳ χειρὶ τοιοῦτον φέρει δημιούργημα
πάντων τῶν ὡραίων πλῆρες, ἐμφαινόντων τῶν δημι-
ουργῶν ὡς καὶ τοῦ τῆς Ἀμαλθείας ἐστὶν ὀλβιώτερον
τὸ κέρας τοῦτο. μνημονεύει αὐτοῦ Θεοκλῆς ἐν Ἰθυ-
φάλλοις οὕτως·

ἐθύσαμεν γὰρ σήμερον Σωτήρια
    πάντες οἱ τεχνῖται·
μεθ᾽ ὧν πιὼν τὸ δίκερας ὡς τὸν φίλτατον
    βασιλέα πάρειμι.

Διονύσιος δ᾽ ὁ Σινωπεὺς ἐν Σῳζούσῃ καταλέγων τινὰ
d ποτήρια καὶ τοῦ ῥυτοῦ ἐμνήσθη, ὡς προεῖπον. | Ἡδύ-
λος δ᾽ ἐν Ἐπιγράμμασι περὶ τοῦ κατασκευασθέντος
ὑπὸ Κτησιβίου τοῦ μηχανοποιοῦ ῥυτοῦ μνημονεύων
φησί·

ζωροπόται καὶ τοῦτο φιλοζεφύρου κατὰ νηὸν
    τὸ ῥυτὸν αἰδοίης δεῦτ᾽ ἴδετ᾽ Ἀρσινόης,
ὀρχηστὴν Βησᾶν Αἰγύπτιον, ὃς λιγὺν ἦχον
    σαλπίζει κρουνοῦ πρὸς ῥύσιν οἰγομένου,

---

346 Cf. the similar remark at 11.476b.        347 Ptolemy
Philadelphus is Ptolemy II of Egypt (reigned 285/3–246 BCE);
Arsinoe I was his queen.        348 For Amaltheia's horn, see
11.783c n.        349 For Ctesibius, cf. 4.174b–e with nn. For the
temple of Arsinoe referred to in this epigram, cf. 7.318b–d.

(A.) It's Bellerophon spearing the fire-breathing
Chimaera from Pegasus' back.
Alright—take this one too!

*Rhuta* were referred to in the past as *kerata* ("horns").[346]
The shape was apparently first produced by King Ptolemy
Philadelphus to be carried by Arsinoe in the statues of
her;[347] because in her left hand she carries an object of this
sort, full of ripe fruit of all types, as if the artists were trying
to show that this horn she has contains more wealth than
the one that belonged to Amaltheia.[348] Theocles mentions
this vessel in the *Ithyphallics* (p. 173 Powell), as follows:

> For today all us craftsmen made the sacrifice
>     that's part of the Soteria festival;
> I drank the double-horn along with them, and
>     I'm here to visit our beloved king.

Dionysius of Sinope in *The Girl Who Was Being Rescued*
(fr. 5) listed a number of types of cups and mentioned the
*rhuton*, as I noted earlier (11.467d). Hedylus in the *Epigrams* (*HE* 1843–52) refers to the *rhuton* made by the
engineer Ctesibius[349] and says:

> Come, lovers of strong wine, and behold this *rhuton*
>     in the temple of the venerable Arsinoe, dear to
>         the West Wind;
> it represents the Egyptian dancer Besas,[350] who
>         trumpets a shrill
>     blast when the stream is opened up, allowing the
>         wine to flow.

[350] A minor Egyptian fertility god, popular in the Greek world
in the Hellenistic period. Cf. 11.784b with n.

οὐ πολέμου σύνθημα, διὰ χρυσέου δὲ γέγωνεν
κώδωνος κώμου σύμβολα καὶ θαλίης,
Νεῖλος ὁκοῖον ἄναξ μύσταις φίλον ἱεραγωγοῖς
εὗρε μέλος θείων πάτριον ἐξ ὑδάτων. |
e  ἀλλὰ Κτησιβίου σοφὸν εὕρεμα τίετε τοῦτο—
δεῦτε, νέοι—νηῷ τῷδε παρ' Ἀρσινόης.

Θεόφραστος δ' ἐν τῷ Περὶ Μέθης τὸ ῥυτόν φησιν
ὀνομαζόμενον ποτήριον τοῖς ἥρωσι μόνοις ἀποδίδο-
σθαι. Δωρόθεος δ' ὁ Σιδώνιός φησιν τὰ ῥυτὰ κέρασιν
ὅμοια εἶναι, διατετρημένα δ' εἶναι, ἐξ ὧν κρουνιζόντων
λεπτῶς κάτωθεν πίνουσιν, ὠνομάσθαι τε ἀπὸ τῆς
ῥύσεως.

Σαννάκια[56]. Κράτης ἐν πέμπτῳ Ἀττικῆς Διαλέκτου
ἔκπωμά φησιν εἶναι οὕτως καλούμενον· ἐστὶ δὲ Περ-
f  σικόν. | Φιλήμων δ' ἐν τῇ Χήρᾳ βατιακιῶν[57] μνησθεὶς
καὶ τῇ γελοιότητι τοῦ ὀνόματος προσπαίξας φησί·

ἱπποτραγέλαφοι, βατιάκια,[58]
σαννάκια.

56 Σαννάκια Kaibel: Σαννάκρα ACE
57 βατιακιῶν Olson: βατιακῶν A
58 ACE have σαννάκρα (del. Kaibel) at the beginning of the
line.

---

351 One basic function of the *salpinx* (referred to obliquely
above in the verb *salpizei*, "trumpets") was to provide battle-
signals.
352 Cf. 11.461b–c (where this idea is assigned, however, to the
*On Drunkenness* of Chamaeleon).

This is no signal for war;[351] through its gold bell
  resounds the summons to celebrations and
    festivities,
like the beloved traditional song King Nile produces
  from his sacred waters for those who celebrate his
    mysteries.
But honor this clever invention of Ctesibius—
  come, young men!—in this temple of Arsinoe.

But Theophrastus in his *On Drunkenness* (fr. 575 Fortenbaugh) claims that the cup known as a *rhuton* is assigned
exclusively to heroes.[352] Dorotheus of Sidon[353] says that
*rhuta* are similar to drinking-horns (*kerata*), but have holes
drilled through them, allowing people to drink out of the
bottom as the wine slowly leaks out, and that they get their
name from the trickle (*rhusis*) of liquid.

  *Sannakia*. Crates in Book V of the *Attic Dialect* (*FGrH*
362 F 10 = fr. 110 Broggiato)[354] claims that a type of drinking vessel is referred to this way; it comes from Persia.
Philemon in his *The Widow* (fr. 90) first mentions *batiakia*[355] and then makes a joke about how ridiculous the
name is, saying:

  horse-goat-stag cups,[356] *batiakia*,
*sannakia*.

[353] Probably an error; the intended reference seems more
likely to be to the lexicographer and grammarian Dorotheus of
Ascalon than to the astronomer-poet Dorotheus of Sidon.

[354] Most likely simply drawing on Philemon (quoted below),
since the word appears to be otherwise unattested.

[355] Drinking vessels of some sort; cf. 11.784a–b.

[356] Cf. 11.500e–f (on "goat-stag cups").

Σελευκίς. ὅτι ἀπὸ Σελεύκου τοῦ βασιλέως τὴν
προσηγορίαν ἔσχεν τὸ ἔκπωμα προείρηται, ἱστοροῦν-
τος τοῦτο καὶ Ἀπολλοδώρου τοῦ Ἀθηναίου. Πολέμων
δ᾽ ἐν πρώτῳ τῶν Πρὸς Ἀδαῖον, ποτήρια, φησί, παρα-
πλήσια Σελευκίς, Ῥοδιάς, Ἀντιγονίς. ||

498

Σκαλλίον. κυλίκιον μικρόν, ᾧ σπένδουσιν Αἰολεῖς,
ὡς Φιλητᾶς φησιν ἐν Ἀτάκτοις.

Σκύφος. τούτου τινὲς τὴν γενικὴν σὺν τῷ σ̄ προ-
φέρονται διὰ παντός, οὐκ εὖ· ὅτε γὰρ ἀρσενικόν ἐστιν
ὁ σκύφος, ὡς λύχνος, ἄνευ τοῦ σ̄ προοισόμεθα, ὅτε δὲ
οὐδέτερον τὸ σκύφος, σὺν τῷ σ̄ κλινοῦμεν σκύφος
σκύφους, ὡς τεῖχος τείχους. οἱ δ᾽ Ἀττικοὶ τὴν εὐθεῖαν
καὶ ἀρσενικῶς καὶ οὐδετέρως λέγουσιν. Ἡσίοδος δ᾽ ἐν
τῷ δευτέρῳ Μελαμποδίας σὺν τῷ π̄ σκύφον λέγει·

τῷ δὲ Μάρης θοὸς ἄγγελος ἦλθε δι᾽ οἴκου, |
b      πλήσας δ᾽ ἀργύρεον σκύπφον φέρε, δῶκε δ᾽
       ἄνακτι.

καὶ πάλιν·

καὶ τότε μάντις μὲν δεσμὸν βοὸς αἴνυτο χερσίν,
Ἴφικλος δ᾽ ἐπὶ νῶτ᾽ ἐπεμαίετο· τῷ δ᾽ ἐπ᾽ ὄπισθεν

---

357 Generally referred to elsewhere as the *Response to Adaeus
and Antigonis* (e.g. 5.210a; 11.462a); called the *Response to
Antigonis on Painters* at 11.474c.      358 Cf. Hsch. σ 817.

359 I.e. as *skuphous* (as if the word were a third-declension
neuter like *genos*).      360 Sc. in the genitive singular, *skuphou*.

361 *skuphos* and *teixos* are the nominative singular forms,
while *skuphous* and *teichous* are the genitive singular forms.

362 I.e., presumably, they offer both masculine accusative singular *skuphon* and the metrically indistinguishable neuter accusative singular *skuphos*.

*Seleukis.* That this drinking vessel got its name from King Seleucus was noted earlier (11.783e); the source of the information is Apollodorus of Athens (*FGrH* 244 F 273). And Polemon says in Book I of his *Response to Adaeus*[357] (fr. 57 Preller): The *Seleukis, Rhodias,* and *Antigonis* are similar types of cups.

*Skallion.* A tiny little *kulix* used by Aeolians to pour libations, according to Philetas in the *Miscellany* (fr. 7 Dettori = fr. 35 Spanoudakis).[358]

*Skuphos.* Some authorities pronounce the genitive of this word with a *sigma*[359] in all circumstances. This is incorrect; because when *skuphos* is treated as masculine, like *luchnos* ("lamp"), we should pronounce it without the *sigma*,[360] whereas when it is treated as neuter, we should decline it with the *sigma, skuphos, skuphous,* like *teixos* ("wall"), *teichous.*[361] But Attic authors give the accusative in both masculine and neuter forms.[362] Hesiod in Book II of the *Melampodia* (fr. 271) offers *skupphos,* with a *pi:*[363]

> Marēs went through the house for him as
> a swift messenger,
> and he filled a silver *skupphos,* and brought it and
> gave it to the king.

And again (fr. 272):

> And then the seer took a thong of ox-hide in his
> hands,
> while Iphiclus grabbed him by the back. And from
> behind him,

[363] The additional consonant allows the word to be used more easily in dactylic hexameter, as in the passages cited below.

σκύπφον ἔχων ἑτέρῃ, ἑτέρῃ δὲ σκῆπτρον ἀείρας
ἔστειχεν Φύλακος καὶ ἐνὶ δμώεσσιν ἔειπεν.

ὁμοίως δὲ καὶ Ἀναξίμανδρος ἐν τῇ Ἡρωολογίᾳ λέγων |
c ὧδε· Ἀμφιτρύων δὲ τὴν λείην δασάμενος τοῖς συμ-
μάχοις καὶ τὸν σκύπφον ἔχων ὃν εἵλετο αὐτῷ. καὶ
πάλιν· τὸν δὲ σκύπφον Τηλεβόῃ δίδωσι Ποσειδῶν
παιδὶ τῷ ἑαυτοῦ, Τηλεβόης δὲ Πτερέλεῳ· τοῦτον ἑλὼν
ἀπέπλεεν. ὁμοίως εἴρηκε καὶ Ἀνακρέων·

ἐγὼ δ᾽ ἔχων σκύπφον Ἐρξίωνι
τῷ λευκολόφῳ μεστὸν ἐξέπινον,

ἀντὶ τοῦ προέπινον· κυρίως γάρ ἐστι τοῦτο προπίνειν,
τὸ ἑτέρῳ πρὸ ἑαυτοῦ δοῦναι πιεῖν. καὶ ὁ Ὀδυσσεὺς δὲ
παρὰ τῷ Ὁμήρῳ τῇ |

d Ἀρήτῃ δ᾽ ἐν χερσὶ[59] τίθει δέπας ἀμφικύπελλον.

καὶ ἐν Ἰλιάδι·

πλησάμενος δ᾽ οἴνοιο δέπας δείδεκτ᾽ Ἀχιλῆα.

πληροῦντες γὰρ προέπινον ἀλλήλοις μετὰ προσαγο-
ρεύσεως. Πανύασσις τρίτῳ Ἡρακλείας φησίν·

59 The traditional text of Homer has χειρί.

---

364 For Amphitryon's expedition against the Teleboans, see
[Apollod.] *Bib.* 2.4.7; Paus. 1.37.6. For the vessel itself, cf. Plaut.
*Amphitr.* 260–1. The two passages from Anaximander appear to
be closely related, with the second tracing the history of the cup
referred to in the first.

365 Returning to the discussion of different forms of the word
*skuphos/skupphos*, after the brief excursus on the meaning of
*propinō*.

holding a *skupphos* in one hand, and wielding a staff
    in the other,
came Phylacus, and he spoke among his slaves.

Likewise Anaximander in his *Story of the Heroes* (*FGrH* 9
F 1, encompassing both quotations), saying the following:[364] after Amphitryon divided the plunder among his
allies and was holding the *skupphos* he had taken for himself. And again: Poseidon gave the *skupphos* to his son
Teleboes, and Teleboes gave it Ptereleus; and after he got
it, he began to sail away. Likewise Anacreon (*PMG* 433)
says:

But I was holding a full *skupphos* and was
draining it (*exepinon*) in honor of white-crested
    Erxion.

He uses this verb in place of *proepinon*, because this is,
strictly speaking, what drinking a toast (*propinein*) involves, that is, giving the other person something to drink
(*piein*) before (*pro*) one drinks oneself. So too the Homeric Odysseus (*Od.* 13.57)

placed a two-handled goblet in Arete's hands.

And in the *Iliad* (9.224):

He filled a goblet with wine and toasted Achilleus.

Because they used to fill their cups and toast (*proepinon*)
one another as they exchanged words. Panyassis says in
Book III of *The Epic of Heracles* (fr. 7 Bernabé):[365]

τοῦ κεράσας κρητῆρα μέγαν χρυσοῖο φαεινὸν
σκύπφους αἰνύμενος θαμέας ποτὸν ἡδὺν ἔπινεν.

Εὐριπίδης δ' ἐν Εὐρυσθεῖ ἀρσενικῶς ἔφη·

< . . . > σκύφος τε μακρός.

καὶ Ἀχαιὸς δ' ἐν Ὀμφάλῃ· |

ὁ δὲ σκύφος με τοῦ θεοῦ καλεῖ.

Σιμωνίδης δὲ

< . . . > οὐατόεντα σκύφον

ἔφη. Ἴων δ' ἐν Ὀμφάλῃ·

οἶνος οὐκ ἔνι
ἐν τῷ σκύφει,

τὸ σκύφει ἰδίως ἀπὸ τοῦ σκύφος σχηματίσας οὐδετέρως ἔφη. ὁμοίως καὶ Ἐπίχαρμος ἐν Κύκλωπι·

< . . . > φέρ' ἐγχέας ἐς τὸ σκύφος.

καὶ Ἄλεξις ἐν Λευκαδίᾳ·

οἴνου γεραιοῖς χείλεσιν μέγα σκύφος.

καὶ Ἐπιγένης ἐν Βακχίδι·

τὸ σκύφος ἔχαιρον δεχόμενος.

Φαίδιμός τε ἐν πρώτῳ Ἡρακλείας·

δουράτεον σκύφος εὐρὺ μελιζώροιο ποτοῖο. |

---

366 An extract from a longer quotation preserved at 11.466f
(which makes it clear that the verb must be treated as something
approaching a perfect).

After he mixed a large, glistening gold mixing-bowl of
    this, he took
numerous *skupphoi* and drank the sweet drink.

Euripides in *Eurystheus* (fr. 379) used the word as a masculine:

    and a large *skuphos*.

So too Achaeus in *Omphale* (*TrGF* 20 F 33.1):[366]

    The god's *skuphos* (masc.) has been summoning me.

And Simonides (*PMG* 631) said:

    a *skuphos* (masc.) with handles.

But Ion in *Omphale* (*TrGF* 19 F 26) said:

            There's no wine
    in the *skuphos*,

producing an eccentric dative form *skuphei* from *skuphos*,
and treating the word as neuter. Likewise Epicharmus in
*Cyclops* (fr. 72):

    Pour (some wine) into the *skuphos* (neut.) and bring
       it (to me)!

Also Alexis in *The Girl from Leucas* (fr. 135):

    a large *skuphos* (neut.) of wine with aged lips.

And Epigenes in *Bacchis* (fr. 3):

    I was happy when I got the *skuphos* (neut.).

Also Phaedimus in Book I of the *Epic of Heracles* (*SH* 669):

    a broad wooden *skuphos* (neut.) full of wine sweet as
       honey.

f  καὶ παρ᾽ Ὁμήρῳ δ᾽ Ἀριστοφάνης ὁ Βυζάντιος γρά-
φει·[60]

> πλησάμενος δ᾽ ἄρα οἱ δῶκε σκύφος, ᾧ περ
> ἔπινεν.

Ἀρίσταρχος δέ·

> πλησάμενος δ᾽ ἄρα οἱ δῶκε σκύφον, ᾧ περ
> ἔπινεν.

Ἀσκληπιάδης δ᾽ ὁ Μυρλεανὸς ἐν τῷ Περὶ τῆς Νεστορίδος φησὶν ὅτι τῷ σκύφει καὶ τῷ κισσυβίῳ τῶν μὲν ἐν
ἄστει καὶ μετρίων οὐδεὶς ἐχρῆτο, συβῶται δὲ καὶ
νομεῖς καὶ οἱ ἐν ἀγρῷ, ὡς ὁ Εὔμαιος

> πλησάμενος δῶκε σκύφος, ᾧ περ ἔπινεν,
> οἴνου ἐνίπλειον.

καὶ Ἀλκμὰν δέ φησι· ||

499

> πολλάκι δ᾽ ἐν κορυφαῖς ὀρέων, ὅκα
> σιοῖσι ϝάδη πολύφανος ἑορτά,
> χρύσιον ἄγγος ἔχοισα, μέγαν σκύφον,
> οἷά τε ποιμένες ἄνδρες ἔχοισιν,
> χερσὶ λεόντεον ἐν γάλα θεῖσα
> τυρὸν ἐτύρησας μέγαν ἄτρυφον Ἀργειφόντᾳ.

Αἰσχύλος δ᾽ ἐν Περραιβίσι φησί·

---

[60] The traditional text of Homer has καὶ οἱ πλησάμενος δῶκε
σκύφος, ᾧπερ ἔπινεν.

---

367 Presumably a reference to *Od.* 14.112. But neither Aristophanes' version of the text nor Aristarchus' is accepted by mod-

430

So too in the text of Homer[367] Aristophanes of Byzantium (p. 201 Slater) writes:

> So he filled a *skuphos* (neut.), from which he himself
> drank, and gave it to him.

But Aristarchus (writes):

> So he filled a *skuphos* (masc.), from which he himself
> drank, and gave it to him.

Asclepiades of Myrlea in his *On Nestor's Cup*[368] says that no one from the city or who was even moderately well-to-do used a *skuphos* or a *kissubion*. Instead it was swine-herds, shepherds, and country-folk, as for example Eumaeus (*Od.* 14.112–13)

> filled a *skuphos* (neut.), from which he himself
> drank, and gave it to him,
> full of wine.

Alcman (*PMG* 56) as well says:

> Often on the mountain-tops, when
> the festival full of torches delights the gods,
> you held a gold vessel, a large *skuphos*,
> the type that shepherds own,
> and you took lion-milk into your hands,
> and made a large, solid cheese for Argeiophontes.[369]

And Aeschylus says in *Women of Perrhaebi* (fr. 184):

ern editors, who instead print it in the form in which it is given by
Asclepiades of Myrlea, below.
  368 Also quoted at 11.477b, where see n.
  369 Hermes.

ποῦ μοι τὰ πολλὰ δῶρα κἀκροθίνια;
ποῦ χρυσότευκτα κἀργυρᾶ σκυφώματα;

Στησίχορος δὲ τὸ παρὰ Φόλῳ τῷ κενταύρῳ ποτήριον
σκύφιον δέπας καλεῖ ἐν ἴσῳ τῷ σκυφοειδές· λέγει δ'
ἐπὶ τοῦ Ἡρακλέους· |

b    σκύφιον δὲ λαβὼν δέπας ἔμμετρον ὡς
         τριλάγυνον
     πί᾽ ἐπισχόμενος, τό ῥά οἱ παρέθηκε Φόλος
         κεράσας.

καὶ Ἄρχιππος δὲ ἐν Ἀμφιτρύωνι οὐδετέρως εἴρηκε.
λάγυνον δὲ μέτρου λέγουσιν εἶναι ὄνομα παρὰ τοῖς
Ἕλλησιν, ὡς χοὸς καὶ κοτύλης· χωρεῖν δ' αὐτὸ κοτύλας Ἀττικὰς δώδεκα. καὶ ἐν Πάτραις δέ φασι τοῦτ'
εἶναι τὸ μέτρον τὴν λάγυνον. ἀρσενικῶς δὲ εἴρηκε τὸν
λάγυνον Νικόστρατος μὲν ἐν Ἑκάτῃ·

         (Α.) τῶν κατεσταμνισμένων |
c    ἡμῖν λαγύνων πηλίκοι τινές; (Β.) τρίχους.

καὶ πάλιν·

     τὸν μεστὸν ἡμῖν φέρε λάγυνον.

καὶ ἐν τῇ ἐπιγραφομένῃ Κλίνῃ·

---

370 The fragment is identified at 11.499e as coming from the
*Geryoneis*.

371 Pholus entertained Heracles in the course of his Labors,
but the wine he served attracted the other centaurs, and a battle between them and Heracles resulted ([Apollod.] *Bib.* 2.5.4,
associating the visit to Pholus' cave with the capture of the Ery-
manthian Boar).

Where are my many gifts and dedications?
Where are my *skuphōmata* made of gold and silver?

Stesichorus (*PMG* 181)[370] refers to the cup in the house of
Pholus the centaur[371] as a *skuphion depas*, meaning that it
looks like a *skuphos*. He says about Heracles:

He took the *skuphion depas* that held about three
     *lagunoi*,
and which Pholus had mixed and set beside him, and
     put it to his lips and drank.

Archippus in *Amphitryon* (fr. 7) also uses the word in the
neuter.[372] They say that a *lagunos* is the name of a Greek
unit of measure, like a *chous* and a *kotulē*, and is equivalent
to twelve Attic *kotulai*.[373] They also say that this unit, the
*lagunos* (fem.), is used in Patras. But Nicostratus in *Hecate*
(fr. 10, encompassing both quotations) has the word as
masculine:

          (A.) How large (masc.) are the *lagunoi*
we transferred from the wine-jars? (B.) They hold
     three *choes*.

And again:

Bring us the full *lagunos* (masc.)!

And in his play entitled *The Couch* (fr. 14):

[372] A quotation has perhaps fallen out of the text. This is
clearly a final fragment of the source that deals with the grammatical gender of *skuphos* quoted at 11.498a–f, and sits awkwardly in
the discussion here.

[373] About three quarts.

καὶ δυσχερὴς λάγυνος οὗτος πλησίον
ὄξους.

Δίφιλος ἐν Ἀνασωζομένοις·

λάγυνον ἔχω κενόν, ὦ γραῦ, θύλακον δὲ μεστόν.

Λυγκεὺς δ' ὁ Σάμιος ἐν τῇ Πρὸς Διαγόραν Ἐπιστολῇ
γράφει· καθ' ὃν χρόνον ἐπεδήμησας ⟨ἐν⟩[61] Σάμῳ, Δια-
γόρα, πολλάκις οἶδά σε παραγινόμενον εἰς τοὺς παρ'
ἐμοὶ πότους, ἐν οἷς λάγυνος κατ' ἄνδρα κείμενος |
d οἰνοχοεῖτο, πρὸς ἡδονὴν διδοὺς ἑκάστῳ ποτήριον.
Ἀριστοτέλης δ' ἐν τῇ Θετταλῶν Πολιτείᾳ θηλυκῶς
λέγεσθαί φησιν ὑπὸ Θετταλῶν τὴν λάγυνον. καὶ Ῥια-
νὸς ὁ ἐποποιὸς ἐν Ἐπιγράμμασιν·

ἥμισυ μὲν πίσσης κωνίτιδος, ἥμισυ δ' οἴνου,
    Ἀρχῖν', ἀτρεκέως ἥδε λάγυνος ἔχει,
λεπτοτέρης δ' οὐκ οἶδ' ἐρίφου κρέα· πλὴν ὅ γε
        πέμψας
    αἰνεῖσθαι πάντων ἄξιος Ἱπποκράτης.

οὐδετέρως δὲ Δίφιλος ἐν Ἀδελφοῖς εἴρηκεν· |

e                    ὦ τοιχωρύχον
ἐκεῖνο καὶ τῶν δυναμένων λαγύνιον·
ἔχον βαδίζειν εἰς τὰ γεύμαθ' ὑπὸ μάλης,
καὶ τοῦτο πωλεῖν μέχρι ἂν ὥσπερ ἐν ἐράνῳ

61 add. Musurus

---

374 The sense of the fragment is obscure, and the fact that the
diminutive *lagunion* is used as neuter shows nothing about what
Diphilus took to be the grammatical gender of *lagunos*.

This *lagunos* (masc.) full of vinegar that's next to us
  is also disgusting.

Diphilus in *Men Trying to Get Home Safe* (fr. 12):

I've got an empty *lagunos* (masc./neut.), old woman,
  and a full grain-sack.

Lynceus of Samos writes in his *Letter to Diagoras* (fr. 6
Dalby): During the time you visited Samos, Diagoras, I
know that you were often at my drinking parties; at them, a
*lagunos* (masc.) lay beside each man, full of wine, offering
every person a cup whenever he felt like one. But Aristotle
in his *Constitution of the Thessalians* (fr. 503) claims that
the Thessalians use the word as feminine. Likewise the
epic poet Rhianus in the *Epigrams* (fr. 75, p. 21 Powell =
HE 3246–9):

This *lagunos* (fem.), Archinus, contains precisely one-
    half
      pine-cone resin, and one-half wine,
  and I've never seen meat from a skinnier kid. But
      Hippocrates, who
    sent these gifts, deserves our praise on all
      accounts.

Diphilus in *Brothers* (fr. 3), on the other hand, uses it as
neuter:[374]

What a crooked
  *lagunion* that is, that belongs to powerful people!
To go to the wine-sampling area with it under her
    arm,
  and sell it until, just like what happens at dinner
    parties,

εἷς λοιπὸς ἦ κάπηλος ἠδικημένος
ὑπ᾽ οἰνοπώλου.

τὸ δ᾽ ἐν Γηρυονηίδι Στησιχόρου

⟨ . . . ⟩ ἔμμετρον ὡς τριλάγυνον

τὴν τῶν τριῶν γενῶν ἀμφιβολίαν ἔχει. Ἐρατοσθένης
δέ φησι λέγεσθαι τὴν πέτασον καὶ τὴν στάμνον ὑπό
τινων. τὸ δὲ σκύφος ὠνομάσθη ἀπὸ τῆς σκαφίδος. καὶ
τοῦτο δ᾽ ἐστὶν ὁμοίως ἀγγεῖον ξύλινον στρογγύλον
f  γάλα καὶ ὀρὸν | δεχόμενον, ὡς καὶ παρ᾽ Ὁμήρῳ
λέγεται·

ναῖον δ᾽ ὀρῷ ἄγγεα πάντα,
γαυλοί τε σκαφίδες τε, τετυγμένα, τοῖς
ἐνάμελγεν.

εἰ μὴ σκύφος οἷον σκύθος τις διὰ τὸ τοὺς Σκύθας
περαιτέρω τοῦ δέοντος μεθύσκεσθαι· Ἱερώνυμος δ᾽ ὁ
Ῥόδιος ἐν τῷ Περὶ Μέθης καὶ τὸ μεθύσαι Σκυθίσαι
500  φησί· συγγενὲς γὰρ εἶναι τὸ φ ‖ τῷ θ. ὕστερον δὲ κατὰ
μίμησιν εἰργάσαντο κεραμέους τε καὶ ἀργυροῦς σκύφους. ὧν πρῶτοι μὲν ἐγένοντο καὶ κλέος ἔλαβον οἱ

---

375 An extract from a longer fragment quoted at 11.499b (but
without the title of the work).    376 Sc. because it is simply
an element in the compound adjective *trilagunos*.

377 Both nouns are normally masculine; but the comment appears otherwise out of place here.

378 The etymology of *skuphos* is obscure, and whether there is
a connection with *skaphos* (cognate with *skaptō*, "dig") is unclear.

379 For Scythian drinking, see 10.427a–c; cf. 12.524c. This discussion of the supposed—in fact chimerical—relationship between the words *skuphos* and *skuthos* (resumed below, after a

there's only one bartender left who's been cheated
by a wine-merchant!

But as for the phrase

that held about three *lagunoi*

in Stesichorus' *Geryoneis* (*PMG* 181.1),[375] it is unclear
which of the three genders the word belongs to.[376] Eratosthenes (fr. 82, p. 54 Strecker) claims that some people
use *petasos* ("broad-brimmed hat") and *stamnos* ("wine-
jar") as feminines.[377] The *skuphos* gets its name from the
*skaphis*,[378] which is also a round wooden vessel used to
hold milk and whey, as Homer says (*Od.* 9.222–3):

> and all the vessels ran with whey,
> the milk-pails and the *skaphides*, which he had made,
> and into which he did his milking.

Unless a *skuphos* is, as it were, a *skuthos*, because of the
fact that the Scythians get more drunk than they should.[379]
Hieronymus of Rhodes in his *On Drunkenness* (fr. 27
Wehrli) glosses *methusai* ("to be drunk") as *Skuthisai* ("to
act like a Scythian"); for *phi* and *theta* are cognate
sounds.[380] Later on they produced ceramic and silver
*skuphoi* that imitated them.[381] The earliest and best-

---

brief interruption; see the next note) is clearly drawn from a different source than what precedes it. Cf. 11.500b (citing Parmenon).        [380] This explains why *skuphos* and *skuthos* are (allegedly) the same word, marking the reference to Hieronymus as
a clumsy Athenaean insertion into his source document.

[381] I.e. the wooden *skaphides* mentioned above, in a source-
document to which Athenaeus now returns, and to which *skuphoi*
are supposed to be both etymologically and historically related.

Βοιώτιοι λεγόμενοι, χρησαμένου κατὰ τὰς στρατείας
πρώτου Ἡρακλέους τῷ γένει· διὸ καὶ Ἡρακλεωτικοὶ
πρός τινων καλοῦνται. ἔχουσι μέντοι πρὸς τοὺς ἄλλους διαφοράν· ἔπεστι γὰρ ἐπὶ τῶν ὤτων αὐτοῖς ὁ
λεγόμενος Ἡράκλειος δεσμός. μνημονεύει δὲ τῶν Βοι-
ωτίων σκύφων Βακχυλίδης ἐν τούτοις ποιούμενος τὸν
b λόγον πρὸς τοὺς Διοσκόρους, καλῶν | αὐτοὺς ἐπὶ
ξένια·

οὐ βοῶν πάρεστι σώματ᾽, οὔτε χρυσός,
    οὔτε πορφύρεοι τάπητες,
    ἀλλὰ θυμὸς εὐμενής,
Μοῦσά τε γλυκεῖα, καὶ Βοιωτίοισιν
    ἐν σκύφοισιν οἶνος ἡδύς.

διήνεγκαν δὲ μετὰ τοὺς Βοιωτίους οἱ Ῥοδιακοὶ λεγόμενοι Δαμοκράτους δημιουργήσαντος· τρίτοι δ᾽ εἰσὶν
οἱ Συρακόσιοι. καλεῖται δ᾽ ὁ σκύφος ὑπὸ Ἠπειρωτῶν,
ὥς φησι Σέλευκος, λυρτός, ὑπὸ δὲ Μηθυμναίων, ὡς
Παρμένων φησὶν ἐν τῷ Περὶ Διαλέκτου, σκύθος. ἐκα-
c λεῖτο δὲ καὶ Δερκυλλίδας ὁ Λακεδαιμόνιος | Σκύφος,
ὥς φησιν Ἔφορος ἐν τῇ ὀκτωκαιδεκάτῃ λέγων οὕτως·
Λακεδαιμόνιοι ἀντὶ Θίμβρωνος Δερκυλλίδαν ἔπεμψαν
εἰς τὴν Ἀσίαν, ἀκούοντες ὅτι πάντα πράττειν εἰώθασιν
οἱ περὶ τὴν Ἀσίαν βάρβαροι μετὰ ἀπάτης καὶ δόλου.
διόπερ Δερκυλλίδαν ἔπεμψαν ἥκιστα νομίζοντες
ἐξαπατηθήσεσθαι· ἦν γὰρ οὐδὲ ἐν τῷ τρόπῳ Λακω-
νικὸν οὐδ᾽ ἁπλοῦν ἔχων, ἀλλὰ πολὺ τὸ πανοῦργον καὶ

---

382 Cf. 4.137e n.; 6.237e; 9.372a.

383 "Scythian"; cf. 11.499f–500a.

384 X. *HG* 3.1.8 reports that Dercyllidas (Poralla #228) was actually nicknamed Sisyphus, after the arch-trickster of Greek my-
thology. But Athenaeus' version of the story would seem intended

known of these were the so-called Boeotians; Heracles was the first to use this type, during his military campaigns, and some authorities accordingly refer to them as Heracleotic *skuphoi*. They are actually different from the others, because they have the so-called Heracles-band on their handles. Bacchylides (fr. 21) mentions Boeotian *skuphoi* in the following passage, in which he addresses the Dioscuri and invites them to dinner:[382]

There are no sides of beef here, no gold,
    and no purple tapestries.
    But there is a kind heart,
and a sweet Muse, and delicious wine
    in Boeotian *skuphoi*.

After the Boeotians, the next most distinguished variety were the so-called Rhodians, which were manufactured by Damocrates; the Syracusan type came third. According to Seleucus (fr. 47 Müller), the Epirotes refer to a *skuphos* as a *lurtos*, whereas the Methymnians, according to Parmenon in his *On Dialect*, call it a *skuthos*.[383] The Spartan Dercyllidas was also known as Skuphos,[384] according to Ephorus in Book XVIII (*FGrH* 70 F 71), where he says the following: The Spartans sent Dercyllidas rather than Thimbron[385] to Asia, since they heard that the barbarians in Asia tended to do everything by means of treachery and deceit. They accordingly sent Dercyllidas, because they felt that he was very unlikely to be tricked, since he did not behave like a Spartan at all and was not straightforward,

to lend further support to the notion that *skuphos* and *skuthos* are in origin the same word, meaning that Dercyllidas was really nicknamed "the Scythian".

[385] Poralla #374.

τὸ θηριῶδες. διὸ καὶ Σκύφον αὐτὸν οἱ Λακεδαιμόνιοι προσηγόρευον.

d     Ταβαίτη. Ἀμύντας | ἐν τῷ πρώτῳ τῶν τῆς Ἀσίας Σταθμῶν περὶ τοῦ ἀερομέλιτος καλουμένου διαλεγόμενος γράφει οὕτως· σὺν τοῖς φύλλοις δρέποντες συντιθέασιν εἰς παλάθης Συριακῆς τρόπον πλάττοντες, οἱ δὲ σφαίρας ποιοῦντες. καὶ ἐπειδὰν μέλλωσι προσφέρεσθαι, ἀποκλάσαντες ἀπ' αὐτῶν ἐν τοῖς ξυλίνοις ποτηρίοις, οὓς καλοῦσι ταβαίτας, προβρέχουσι καὶ διηθήσαντες πίνουσι. καὶ ἔστιν ὅμοιον ὡς ἄν τις μέλι πίνοι διείς, τούτου δὲ καὶ πολὺ ἥδιον.

e     Τραγέλαφος. οὕτω τινὰ καλεῖται | ποτήρια, ὧν μνημονεύει Ἄλεξις μὲν ἐν Κονιατῇ·

> κυμβία,
> φιάλαι, τραγέλαφοι, κύλικες.

Εὔβουλος δ' ἐν Κατακολλωμένῳ·

> ἀλλ' εἰσὶ φιάλαι πέντε, τραγέλαφοι δύο.

Μένανδρος δ' ἐν Ἁλιεῖ φησι·

> < . . . > τραγέλαφοι, λαβρώνιοι.

Ἀντιφάνης Χρυσίδι·

> (Α.) <τῷ> σατραποπλούτῳ δ', ὡς λέγουσι,
>     νυμφίῳ,
> κεκτημένῳ τάλαντα, παῖδας, ἐπιτρόπους,
> ζεύγη, καμήλους, στρώματ', ἀργυρώματα,

---

386 Sc. in wine.

387 Literally a "goat-stag (cup)". Cf. the "horse-goat-stag cup" mentioned in Philem. fr. 90 (quoted at 11.497f).

but was instead quite wily and brutal. This is why the Spartans called him Skuphos.

*Tabaitē*. Amyntas in Book I of his *Way-Stations in Asia* (*FGrH* 122 F 1) writes as follows in his discussion of what is referred to as oak-manna: They strip it off, along with the leaves, and compress and mould it in the same way you would to make a Syrian cake of dried fruit, although others make it into balls. When they are ready to serve it, they break off chunks of the cakes and soak them ahead of time in wooden cups, which they refer to as *tabaitai*, and then strain the liquid and drink it. It is like drinking honey that has been soaked,[386] but is considerably sweeter.

*Tragelaphos*.[387] This is a term for certain cups mentioned by Alexis in *The Plasterer* (fr. 111):

> *kumbia,*
> *phialai, tragelaphoi, kulikes.*

Eubulus in *The Man Who Was Glued to the Spot* (fr. 47):

> But there are five *phialai*, two *tragelaphoi*.

And Menander says in *The Fisherman* (fr. 26.4):[388]

> *tragelaphoi, labrōnioi.*

Antiphanes in *Chrysis* (fr. 223):

> (A.) for the bridegroom who's as rich as a satrap,
>     people say,
> who owns talents of silver, slaves, overseers,
> ox-teams, camels, bed-clothes, silver vessels,

[388] An excerpt from a longer fragment quoted at 11.484c–d, where see n.

φιάλας, τριήρεις, τραγελάφους, καρχήσια, |

f    γαυλοὺς ὁλοχρύσους (B.) πλοῖα; (A.) τοὺς
       κάδους μὲν οὖν

καλοῦσι γαυλοὺς πάντες οἱ προγάστορες.

Τριήρης. ὅτι καὶ τριήρης εἶδος ἐκπώματος Ἐπίνικος ἐν Ὑποβαλλομέναις δεδήλωκε· προείρηται δὲ τὸ
μαρτύριον.

Ὑστιακόν. ποτήριον ποιὸν Ῥίνθων ἐν Ἡρακλεῖ·

ἐν ὑστιακῷ τε καθαρὸν ἐλατῆρα ⟨ ... ⟩
καθαρῶν τ' ἀλήτων κἀλφίτων ἀπερρόφεις.

Φιάλη. Ὅμηρος μὲν ὅταν λέγῃ·

⟨ ... ⟩ ἀμφίθετον φιάλην ἀπύρωτον ἔθηκεν, ‖

501  καὶ

⟨ ... ⟩ χρυσῆν φιάλην καὶ δίπλακα δημόν,

οὐ τὸ ποτήριον λέγει, ἀλλὰ χαλκίον τι καὶ ἐκπέταλον
λεβητῶδες, ἴσως δύο ὦτα ἔχον ἐξ ἀμφοτέρων τῶν
μερῶν. Παρθένιος δ' ὁ τοῦ Διονυσίου ἀμφίθετον ἀκούει τὴν ἀπύθμενον φιάλην. Ἀπολλόδωρος δ' ὁ Ἀθηναῖος ἐν τῷ Περὶ τοῦ Κρατῆρος ῥησειδίῳ τὴν κατὰ τὸν

---

389 As Speaker B's question makes clear, the word *gaulos* is
more often used of a type of large Phoenician merchant-ship; cf.
*triēreis* (literally "triremes") .

390 Literally a "trireme"; cf. *akatos* (literally "skiff"), *gaulos*
(above), and *kantharos* (also the name of a type of boat).

391 A broad, flat cake of some sort; cf. Olson on Ar. *Ach.* 245–6.
The passage in fact suggests that *hustiakon* was a word for a mixing-bowl or mortar, presumably in Tarentum, where Rhinton was
from.

*phialai, triēreis, tragelaphoi, karchēsia,*
*gauloi*[389] made of solid gold. (B.) You mean ships?
    (A.) All the fat guys
refer to wine-jars (*kadoi*) as *gauloi*.

*Triērēs*.[390] Epinicus in *Women Who Try to Pass off Sup-
positititious Children* (fr. 2.8) makes it clear that a *triērēs* is
a type of drinking vessel; the passage was cited earlier
(11.497b).

*Hustiakon*. Rhinton in *Heracles* (fr. 3) (refers to this as)
a cup of some sort:

> you swallowed down an *elatēr*[391] made of bran-free
>     flour
> in a *hystiakon* and . . . of white meal and barley-
>     groats.

*Phialē*. When Homer (*Il.* 23.270) says:

> He set an *amphithetos phialē* that had never been
>     placed over a fire (*apurōtos*),

and (cf. *Il.* 23.243):

> a gold *phialē* and fat folded double,

he is not referring to a cup, but to a shallow bronze vessel that resembles a cauldron and perhaps has two handles
on either side.[392] Dionysius' student Parthenius understands *amphithetos* to mean a *phialē* that lacks a base. But
Apollodorus of Athens in his short essay[393] *On the Mixing-*

---

[392] I.e. as if *amphithetos* meant "[with handles] set on either
side".

[393] Literally "speech".

πυθμένα μὴ δυναμένην τίθεσθαι καὶ ἐρείδεσθαι, ἀλλὰ
κατὰ τὸ στόμα. τινὲς δέ φασιν, ὃν τρόπον ἀμφιφορεὺς
λέγεται ὁ ἀμφοτέρωθεν κατὰ τὰ ὦτα δυνάμενος |
b φέρεσθαι, οὕτως καὶ τὴν ἀμφίθετον φιάλην. Ἀρίσταρχος δὲ τὴν δυναμένην ἐξ ἀμφοτέρων τῶν μερῶν τίθεσθαι, κατὰ τὸν πυθμένα καὶ κατὰ τὸ στόμα. Διονύσιος
δ᾽ ὁ Θρᾷξ τὴν στρογγύλην, τὴν ἀμφιθέουσαν κυκλο-
τερεῖ τῷ σχήματι. Ἀσκληπιάδης δ᾽ ὁ Μυρλεανός, ἡ
μὲν φιάλη, φησί, κατ᾽ ἀντιστοιχίαν ἐστὶ πιάλη, ἡ τὸ
πιεῖν ἅλις παρέχουσα· μείζων γὰρ τοῦ ποτηρίου. ἡ δὲ
ἀμφίθετος καὶ ἀπύρωτος ἢ ψυχρήλατος ἢ ἐπὶ πῦρ οὐκ
c ἐπιτιθεμένη, καθότι καὶ λέβητα καλεῖ ὁ ποιητὴς | τὸν
μὲν ἐμπυριβήτην, τὸν δὲ ἄπυρον·

          κὰδ δὲ λέβητ᾽ ἄπυρον, βοὸς ἄξιον, ἀνθεμόεντα,

τὸν δεχόμενον ἴσως ὕδωρ ψυχρόν, ὥστε καὶ τὴν
φιάλην εἶναι χαλκίῳ προσεοικυῖαν ἐκπετάλῳ, δεχομέ-
νην ψυχρὸν ὕδωρ. τὴν δ᾽ ἀμφίθετον πότερα δύο βάσεις
ἔχειν δεῖ νομίζειν ἐξ ἑκατέρου μέρους, ἢ τὸ μὲν ἀμφὶ
σημαίνει τὸ περί, τοῦτο δ᾽ αὖ τὸ περιττόν; ὥστε
λέγεσθαι τὴν περιττῶς πεποιημένην ἀμφίθετον, ἐπεὶ

---

394 The actual meaning of the word is uncertain.
395 Perhaps another fragment of *On Nestor's Cup*.
396 Literally "the poet".
397 Literally "fire-less", i.e. "never exposed to fire". Cf. the
similar remarks at 2.37f.
398 "about", but also "beyond".

*Bowl* (FGrH 244 F 220) (takes it to be) a *phialē* that cannot be set on its base and made to stand firm that way,
but one that must be set on its rim. Whereas some authorities claim that, in the same way that a vessel that can be
picked up from both sides and transported (*amphote-
rōthen pheresthai*) by means of its handles is called an
*amphiphoreus* ("amphora"), so too in the case of an *amphithetos phialē*. Thus Aristarchus (argues that) this is a
*phialē* that can be set (*tithesthai*) on either end, that is, on
its base, but also on its rim. Dionysius Thrax (fr. 28 Linke),
on the other hand, (maintains that) this is a round *phialē*,
which runs around (*amphitheousa*) in a circular shape.[394]
But Asclepiades of Myrlea says:[395] A *phialē* is, via substitution of a letter, a *pialē*, that is, a cup that provides one
with enough to drink (*piein halis*); because it is larger than
an ordinary cup. As for a *phialē* that is *amphithetos* and
*apurōtos*, the latter means that it has either been cold-
forged or has never been placed over a fire, in the same
way that Homer[396] refers to a cauldron as either (*Il.*
23.702) *empuribētēs* ("having gone over a fire") or
*apuros*[397] (*Il.* 23.885):

> And he set down an *apuros* cauldron, which was
> worth an ox and had a floral design worked
> into it,

perhaps meaning one used to hold cold water, so that the
*phialē* in question resembles a shallow bronze vessel and is
used to hold cold water. As for a *phialē* that is *amphithetos*,
should we imagine that it has two bases, one on either
side? Or is *amphi* used here in the sense of *peri*,[398] which is
in turn to be understood *peritton* ("extraordinary")? In
that case, an exquisitely made *phialē* could be referred to

445

τὸ ποιῆσαι θεῖναι πρὸς τῶν ἀρχαίων ἐλέγετο. δύναται |
d δὲ καὶ ἡ ἐπὶ τὸν πυθμένα καὶ τὸ στόμα τιθεμένη· ἡ δὲ
τοιαύτη θέσις τῶν φιαλῶν Ἰωνική ἐστι καὶ ἀρχαία. ἔτι
γοῦν καὶ νῦν οὕτως Μασσαλιῆται τιθέασι τὰς φιάλας
ἐπὶ πρόσωπον. Κρατίνου δ' εἰπόντος ἐν Δραπέτισιν·

δέχεσθε φιάλας τάσδε βαλανειομφάλους,

Ἐρατοσθένης ἐν τῷ ἑνδεκάτῳ Περὶ Κωμῳδίας τὴν
λέξιν ἀγνοεῖν φησι Λυκόφρονα· τῶν γὰρ φιαλῶν οἱ
ὀμφαλοὶ καὶ τῶν βαλανείων οἱ θόλοι παρόμοιοι, εἰς δὲ
e τὸ εἶδος οὐκ ἀρύθμως παίζονται. Ἀπίων δὲ | καὶ
Διόδωρός φησι· φιάλαι ποιαί, ὧν ὁ ὀμφαλὸς παραπλήσιος ἠθμῷ. ὁ δὲ Μυρλεανὸς Ἀσκληπιάδης ἐν τοῖς
Περὶ Κρατίνου, βαλανειόμφαλοι, φησίν, λέγονται, ὅτι
οἱ ὀμφαλοὶ αὐτῶν καὶ τῶν βαλανείων οἱ θόλοι ὅμοιοί
εἰσιν. καὶ Δίδυμος δὲ τὰ αὐτὰ εἰπὼν παρατίθεται
⟨τὰ⟩[62] Λυκόφρονος οὕτως ἔχοντα· ἀπὸ τῶν ὀμφαλῶν
τῶν ἐν ταῖς γυναικείαις πυέλοις, ὅθεν τοῖς σκαφίοις
ἀρύουσιν. Τίμαρχος δ' ἐν τετάρτῳ Περὶ τοῦ Ἐρατο-
σθένους Ἑρμοῦ, πεπαῖχθαί τις ἂν οἰηθείη, φησί, τὴν
f λέξιν, διότι τὰ | πλεῖστα τῶν Ἀθήνησι βαλανείων
κυκλοειδῆ ταῖς κατασκευαῖς ὄντα τοὺς ἐξαγωγοὺς ἔχει
κατὰ μέσον, ἐφ' οὗ χαλκοῦς ὀμφαλὸς ἔπεστιν. Ἴων δ'
ἐν Ὀμφάλῃ·

62 add. Toup

399 Quoted again below, at 11.501f.

400 The two are cited together again at 14.642d–e.

401 Cf. Powell pp. 58–9 (who mistakenly cites this passage as
coming from Timarchus' Book X); Susemihl proposed reading
"Timachidas" rather than "Timarchus".

as *amphithetos*, since the ancients used *theinai* ("to put, set, place") to mean *poiēsai* ("to make"). But the reference might be instead to a *phialē* that is set on either its base or its lip, which is an ancient Ionian way of storing *phialai*. Even today, in fact, the Massaliotes store their *phialai* upside-down. When Cratinus in *Runaway Slave-Girls* (fr. 54)[399] said:

> Take these *balaneiomphaloi phialai*!,

Eratosthenes in Book XI of *On Comedy* (fr. 25, p. 31 Strecker) claims that Lycophron misunderstands the word; because the central bosses (*omphaloi*) on *phialai* resemble bathhouse (*balaneia*) drains, and this is thus a fairly sophisticated joke about the form of the vessel. Apion (*FGrH* 616 F 49), along with Diodorus,[400] says: a type of *phialai*, the central boss on which resembles a wine-strainer. But Asclepiades of Myrlea says in his *On Cratinus* (Cratin. test. *40): They are referred to as *balaneiomphaloi* because their central bosses resemble bathhouse (*balaneia*) drains. Didymus (pp. 42–4 Schmidt) too says the same thing and then cites Lycophron's comment, which runs as follows: (The image is drawn) from the *omphaloi* in women's bathtubs, which are drained using bowls. Timarchus says in Book IV of *On Eratosthenes' Hermes*:[401] This might be taken as a play on words, because the majority of Athenian bathhouses are round and have drain-holes in the middle, with a bronze *omphalos* set on top. Ion in *Omphale* (*TrGF* 19 F 20):

447

ἴτ᾽ ἐκφορεῖτε, παρθένοι, κύπελλα καὶ
    μεσομφάλους.

οὕτω δ᾽ εἴρηκε τὰς βαλανειομφάλους, ὧν Κρατῖνος
μνημονεύει·

δέχεσθε φιάλας τάσδε βαλανειομφάλους.

καὶ Θεόπομπος δ᾽ ἐν Ἀλθαίᾳ ἔφη· ‖

502    λαβοῦσα πλήρη χρυσέαν μεσόμφαλον
    φιάλην· Τελέστης δ᾽ ἄκατον ὠνόμαζέ νιν,

ὡς τοῦ Τελέστου ἄκατον τὴν φιάλην εἰρηκότος. Φερεκράτης δὲ ἢ ὁ πεποιηκὼς τοὺς εἰς αὐτὸν ἀναφερο-
μένους Πέρσας φησί·

στεφάνους τε πᾶσι κὠμφαλωτὰς χρυσίδας.

Ἀθηναῖοι δὲ τὰς μὲν ἀργυρᾶς φιάλας ἀργυρίδας λέγουσι, χρυσίδας δὲ τὰς χρυσᾶς. τῆς δὲ ἀργυρίδος[63]
Φερεκράτης μὲν ἐν Πέρσαις οὕτως μνημονεύει· |

b    οὗτος σύ, ποῖ τὴν ἀργυρίδα τηνδὶ φέρεις;

χρυσίδος δὲ Κρατῖνος ἐν Νόμοις·

χρυσίδι σπένδων † γέγραφε † τοῖς ὄφεσι πιεῖν
    διδούς.

---

63 ἀργυρίδος φιάλης A: φιάλης del. Meineke

---

402 Quoted once already in this discussion, at 11.501d.
403 = *PMG* 811. For *akatos* (literally "skiff") as a cup-name, cf.
11.782f.
404 For doubts about the authorship of *Persians*, see 3.78d n.

Come, girls—bring forth goblets and cups with
    central bosses (*mesomphaloi*)!

This is how he refers to the *balaneiomphaloi* vessels mentioned by Cratinus (fr. 54):[402]

Take these *balaneiomphaloi phialai*!

So too Theopompus said in *Althaea* (fr. 4):

Taking a full gold *phialē* with a central boss
    (*mesomphalos*);
Telestes used to refer to it as an *akatos*,

as if Telestes referred to a *phialē* as an *akatos*.[403] Pherecrates (fr. 134)—or whoever the author of the *Persians* attributed to him is[404]—says:

and garlands and *chrusides* with bosses (*omphalōtai*)
    for everyone.

The Athenians refer to their silver (*argurai*) *phialai* as
*argurides*, and to their gold (*chrusai*) *phialai* as *chrusides*.
Pherecrates in *Persians* (fr. 135) mentions an *arguris*, as
follows:

Hey you—where are you taking this *arguris*?

And Cratinus mentions a *chrusis* in *Laws* (fr. 132):[405]

pouring a libation with a *chrusis* † he has written †
    giving snakes a drink.

[405] The first two words of the fragment are quoted also, with
the name of the vessel given in a slightly different form, at
11.496e, where see n.

καὶ Ἕρμιππος ἐν Κέρκωψι·

χρυσίδ᾽ οἴνου πανσέληνον ἐκπιὼν ὑφείλετο.

καὶ ὅ γε ἐ < . . . >[64]

## ΕΚ ΤΟΥ ΙΑ

ἐκαλεῖτο δέ τις καὶ βαλανωτὴ φιάλη, ἧς τῷ πυθμένι χρυσοῖ ὑπέκειντο ἀστράγαλοι. Σῆμος δ᾽ ἐν Δήλῳ ἀνακεῖσθαί φησι χαλκοῦν φοίνικα, Ναξίων ἀνάθημα, καὶ καρυωτὰς φιάλας χρυσᾶς. Ἀναξανδρίδης δὲ φιάλας Ἄρεος καλεῖ τὰ ποτήρια ταῦτα. Αἰολεῖς δὲ τὴν φιάλην ἄρακιν καλοῦσι.

Φθοῖς. πλατεῖαι φιάλαι ὀμφαλωτοί. Εὔπολις·

σὺν φθοῖσι προσπεπωκώς.

ἔδει δὲ ὀξύνεσθαι ὡς Καρσί, παισί, φθειρσί.

Φιλοτησία. κύλιξ τις, ἣν κατὰ φιλίαν προὔπινον, ὥς φησι Πάμφιλος. Δημοσθένης δέ φησι· καὶ φιλοτησίας προὔπινεν. Ἄλεξις·

φιλοτησίαν σοι τήνδ᾽ ἐγὼ
ἰδίᾳ τε καὶ κοινῇ κύλικα προπίομαι.

64 A folio was missing at this point from the manuscript from which the text in A was drawn, and the section of text that follows is drawn from the Epitome.

406 Cognate with *balanos*, "acorn".

407 Cf. Antiph. fr. 110.1 (quoted at 10.433c–d).

408 Sc. in the dative plural, as in *phthoisi* in the quotation above (although modern editors place a circumflex on the penult rather than an acute on the ultima, as is recommended here).

Also Hermippus in *Cercopes* (fr. 38):

> After he drank wine out of a *chrusis* as round as a full
> moon, he stole it.

And who was . . .

## FROM BOOK ELEVEN

There was also a type of *phialē* referred to as a *balanōtē*,[406] which had gold feet that resembled knucklebones set beneath its base. Semus (*FGrH* 396 F 18) says that a bronze palm-tree given by the Naxians was among the dedications on Delos, and was accompanied by gold *phialai* decorated with dates. Anaxandrides (fr. dub. 82)[407] calls cups of this sort Ares' *phialai*. The Aeolians refer to a *phialē* as an *arakis*.

*Phthois*. Flat *phialai* with a central boss. Eupolis (fr. 382):

> having collapsed along with the *phthoides*.

The word ought to have an acute accent on the final syllable,[408] like *Karsí* ("Carians"), *paisí* ("children"), and *phtheirsí* ("fleas").

*Philotēsia*. A type of *kulix*, which they used to drink toasts of friendship (*philia*), according to Pamphilus (fr. XXXVIII Schmidt). Demosthenes (19.128) says: and he drank toasts out of *philotēsia*. Alexis (fr. 293):

> I'll toast you with this *philotēsia*
> *kulix* both individually and as a group.

ἐκαλεῖτο δὲ καὶ τὸ ἑταιρικὸν συνευωχούμενον φιλο-
τήσιον. Ἀριστοφάνης·

> ἑπτάπους γοῦν ἡ σκιά 'στιν
> † ἡ 'πὶ τὸ δεῖπνον· ὡς ἤδη καλεῖ μ'
> ὁ χορὸς ὁ φιλοτήσιος.

διὰ δὲ τὴν τοιαύτην πρόποσιν ἐκαλεῖτο καὶ κύλιξ
φιλοτησία, ὡς ἐν Λυσιστράτῃ·

> δέσποινα Πειθοῖ καὶ κύλιξ φιλοτησία.

Χόννοι. παρὰ Γορτυνίοις ποτηρίου εἶδος, ὅμοιον
Θηρικλείῳ, χάλκεον· ὃ δίδοσθαι τῷ ἁρπασθέντι ὑπὸ
τοῦ ἐραστοῦ φησιν Ἑρμῶναξ.

Χαλκιδικά. ποτήρια, ἴσως ἀπὸ τῆς Χαλκίδος τῆς
Θρᾳκικῆς, εὐδοκιμοῦντα.

Χυτρίδες. < Ἄλεξις ἐν Ὑπο>βολιμαίῳ·[65] |

IA

502b
> ἐγὼ Πτολεμαίου τοῦ βασιλέως τέτταρα
> χυτρίδι' ἀκράτου τῆς τ' ἀδελφῆς προσλαβὼν
> τῆς τοῦ βασιλέως ταῦτ', ἀπνευστί τ' ἐκπιὼν
> ὡς ἄν τις ἥδιστ' ἴσον ἴσῳ κεκραμένον, |

---

[65] Manuscript A resumes at this point.

---

[409] For the context, cf. 11.782c.

[410] Probably supported in the original form of the text by a reference to the *Chalkidikon potērion* mentioned at Ar. *Eq.* 237.

[411] Properly "small pots" (diminutive of *chutra*, normally
"cooking pot").

A group of friends having a feast together was also described as *philotēsios*. Aristophanes (fr. 695):

> That shadow † that calls us to dinner,
>    at any rate, is seven feet long; so now my chorus
>       of friends (*philotēsios*) is summoning me.

It was referred to as a *philotēsia kulix* because of toasting of this sort, for example in *Lysistrata* (203):

> Lady Persuasion and *philotēsia kulix*.

*Chonnoi*. The inhabitants of Gortyn (refer thus to) a type of cup that resembles a Thericleian and is made of bronze; it is given by an adult lover to the boy he kidnaps,[409] according to Hermonax.

*Chalkidika*. Cups with a good reputation, perhaps from Chalcis in Thrace.[410]

*Chutrides*.[411] Alexis in *The Suppositious Child* (fr. 246):[412]


## BOOK ELEVEN

> Now that I've had four *chutridia* of strong wine
>    in honor of King Ptolemy,[413] and the same number in
>       honor
>    of the king's sister, emptying them without pausing
>       for a breath,
> mixed one-to-one, the most delicious proportion
>    possible,


[412] Much of the third and the fourth verses are quoted also at 10.431b.　　[413] I.e. Ptolemy II Philadelphus (reigned 285/3–246 BCE), whose sister Arsinoe (verse 3) was also his wife.

c     καὶ τῆς Ὁμονοίας δύο, τί νῦν μὴ κωμάσω
    ἄνευ λυχνούχου πρὸς τὸ τηλικοῦτο φῶς;

Ἡρόδοτος δ' ἐν τῇ πέμπτῃ τῶν Ἱστοριῶν νόμον φησὶ
θέσθαι Ἀργείους καὶ Αἰγινήτας Ἀττικὸν μηδὲν προσ-
φέρειν πρὸς τὰς θυσίας μηδὲ κέραμον, ἀλλ' ἐκ χυτρί-
δων ἐπιχωρίων τὸ λοιπὸν αὐτόθι εἶναι πίνειν. καὶ
Μελέαγρος δ' ὁ κυνικὸς ἐν τῷ Συμποσίῳ οὑτωσὶ
γράφει· κἂν τοσούτῳ πρόποσιν αὐτῷ βαρεῖαν διέδωκε,
χυτρίδια βαθέα δώδεκα.

d     Ψυγεὺς ἢ ψυκτήρ. Πλάτων | Συμποσίῳ· "ἀλλὰ φέρε,
παῖ", φάναι, "τὸν ψυκτῆρα ἐκεῖνον," ἰδόντα αὐτὸν
πλέον ἢ ὀκτὼ κοτύλας χωροῦντα. τοῦτον οὖν ἐμπλη-
σάμενον πρῶτον μὲν αὐτὸν ἐκπιεῖν, ἔπειτα τῷ Σωκρά-
τει κελεύειν ἐγχεῖν. παραμηκύνειν ἐγχειροῦντος τοῦ
Ἀρχεβούλου, εὐκαιρότατα προχέων ὁ παῖς τοῦ οἰνα-
ρίου ἀνατρέπει τὸν ψυκτῆρα. Ἄλεξις ἐν Εἰσοικιζομένῳ
φησί· † τρικότυλον ψυγέα †. Διώξιππος Φιλαργύρῳ·

    παρ' Ὀλυμπίχου δὲ Θηρικλείους ἔλαβεν ἕξ,
    † ἰτάτους † δύο ψυκτῆρας.

e     Μένανδρος δ' ἐν τῷ ἐπιγραφομένῳ | δράματι Χαλκεῖα
φησιν·

                            τοῦτο δὴ τὸ νῦν ἔθος,
"ἄκρατον" ἐβόων, "τὴν μεγάλην." ψυκτῆρά τις
προὔπινεν αὐτοῖς ἀθλίους ἀπολλύων.

---

414 Literally a "cooler", i.e. a vessel that was packed with ice,
snow, or chilled water, and in which a wine-jar was floated.
415 About two quarts.

plus two more in honor of Concord—why shouldn't I
  wander the streets drunk
with no lamp, in light as bright as this?

Herodotus in Book V (88.2) of his *History* claims that the
Argives and the Aeginetans passed a law that nothing made
in Attica, including pottery, was to be brought to their sacrifices, and that in the future people there would be required to drink from local *chutrides*. Meleager the Cynic
as well in his *Symposium* (fr. 1 Riese) writes as follows: In
so grave a situation, he assigned him a toast to match: a
dozen deep *chutridia*.

*Psugeus* or *psuktēr*.[414] Plato in the *Symposium* (213e,
condensed): "But come, slave", he said, "—that *psuktēr*
there!", since he saw that it held more than eight *kotulai*.[415]
So after he filled it, he first drained it himself, and then
ordered them to pour wine into it for Socrates. When
Archebulus was trying to make (the party) last longer, the
slave who was doing the pouring knocked over the *psuktēr*
of wine in the nick of time. Alexis says in *The Man Who
Was Moving In* (fr. 65, unmetrical): † a *psugeus* that holds
three *kotylai* †. Dioxippus in *The Miser* (fr. 5):

He got six Thericleians from Olympichus,
[corrupt] two *psuktēres*.

Menander says in his play entitled *The Chalkeia Festival*
(fr. 401):

As people do nowadays,
  they started shouting: "Unmixed wine!" "The big
    cup!" Someone kept toasting
them with a *psuktēr* and murdered the poor bastards.

Ἐπιγένης δ᾽ ἐν Ἡρωίνῃ καταλέγων πολλὰ ποτήρια
καὶ τοῦ ψυγέως οὕτως μνημονεύει·

τὴν Θηρίκλειον δεῦρο καὶ τὰ Ῥοδιακὰ
κόμισον λαβὼν τοὺς παῖδας. εἶτ᾽ οἴσεις μόνος
ψυκτῆρα, κύαθον, κυμβία.

Στράττις Ψυχασταῖς·

ὁ δέ τις ψυκτῆρ᾽, ὁ δέ τις κύαθον
χαλκοῦν κλέψας ἀπορῶν κεῖται,
κοτύλῃ δ᾽ ἀνὰ χοίνικα μάττει.

f  Ἄλεξις | δ᾽ ἐν Ἱππίσκῳ ψυκτηρίδιον καλεῖ διὰ τούτων·

ἀπήντων τῷ ξένῳ
εἰς τὴν κατάλυσιν † ησονην † αἴθων ἀνήρ.
τοῖς παισί τ᾽ εἶπα (δύο γὰρ ἦγον οἴκοθεν)
τἀκπώματ᾽ εἰς τὸ φανερὸν ἐκκελιτρωμένα
θεῖναι· κύαθος δ᾽ ἦν ἀργυροῦς † τἀκπώματα †
ἦγεν δύο δραχμάς, κυμβίον δὲ τέτταρας, ||

503  ⟨ ... ⟩ ψυκτηρίδιον τὲ δύ[66] ὀβολούς,
Φιλιππίδου λεπτότερον.

Ἡρακλέων δὲ ὁ Ἐφέσιος, ὃν ἡμεῖς, φησί, ψυγέα
καλοῦμεν, ψυκτηρίαν τινὲς ὀνομάζουσιν. τοὺς δ᾽ Ἀττι-

66 δέκ᾽ 6.230c

---

416 A more complete version of the third verse (with a minor
variant), followed by a fourth, is quoted at 11.469c.
417 Obscure (perhaps a proverb).

456

Epigenes in *The Heroine* (fr. 5.1–3)[416] lists many types of cups and refers as follows to a *psugeus*:

> Get the slaves, and bring the Thericleian
> and the *Rhodiaka* here! And you all by yourself bring
> a *psuktēr*, a ladle, *kumbia*!

Strattis in *Men Who Keep Cool* (fr. 62):

> One guy steals a *psuktēr*, while another steals
> a bronze ladle and lies there confused.
> A cup kneads by the *choinix*.[417]

Alexis in *The Brooch* (fr. 2.1–8)[418] refers to the vessel as a *psuktēridion* in the following passage:

> I was meeting the stranger
> at the place I was staying [corrupt] an impetuous
> man.
> And I told my slaves—I brought two of them from
> home—
> to clean my drinking vessels and set them out where
> everyone
> could see them. There was a silver ladle, † the
> drinking vessels †
> weighed two drachmas; a *kumbion* weighed four
> . . . ; and a *psuktēridion* that weighed two obols
> and was thinner than Philippides.

Heracleon of Ephesus (fr. 7 Berndt) says: What we call a *psugeus* is referred to by some people as a *psuktēria*; Attic-

---

[418] Verses 3–9 of the fragment are quoted at 6.230b–c (with a slight variant in verse 7), where see nn. Philippides is *PA* 14351. For the title of the play, see 11.471e n.

κοὺς καὶ κωμῳδεῖν τὸν ψυγέα ὡς ξενικὸν ὄνομα.
Εὔφρων ἐν Ἀποδιδούσῃ·

   (Πυ.) ἐπὰν δὲ καλέσῃ ψυγέα τὴν ψυκτηρίαν,
   τὸ τευτλίον δὲ σεῦτλα, φακέαν τὴν φακῆν,
   τί δεῖ ποεῖν; σὺ γὰρ εἶπον. (Β.) ὥσπερ χρυσίου |
b   φωνῆς ἀπότεισον, Πυργόθεμι, καταλλαγήν.

Ἀντιφάνης Ἱππεῦσι·

   (Α.) πῶς οὖν διαιτώμεσθα; (Β.) τὸ μὲν ἐφίππιον
   στρῶμ᾽ ἐστὶν ἡμῖν, ὁ δὲ καλὸς πῖλος κάδος,
   ψυκτήρ· τί βούλει; πάντ᾽, Ἀμαλθείας κέρας.

ἐν δὲ τῇ Καρίνῃ σαφῶς δηλοῦται, ὅτι τούτῳ ἐχρῶντο
οἰνοχοοῦντες κυάθῳ· εἰπὼν γὰρ

            τρίποδα καὶ κάδον
παραθέμενος ψυκτῆρά τ᾽ οἴνου < . . . >
μεθύσκεται,

ἐν τοῖς ἑξῆς ποιεῖ αὐτὸν λέγοντα·

c            πότος | ἔσται < . . . >
σφοδρότερος· οὐκοῦν, εἰ φράσαι τις, οὐκέτι
ἔξεστι κυαθίζειν γὰρ < . . . >
τὸν δὲ κάδον ἔξω καὶ τὸ ποτήριον λαβὼν
ἀπόφερε τἆλλα πάντα.

---

419 For Amaltheia's horn (a horn of plenty), cf. 11.783c n.

speakers in fact make fun of *psugeus* as a foreign word.
Euphro in *The Girl Who Was Repaying a Debt* (fr. 3):

> (Pyrgothemis) When you call a *psuktēria* a *psugeus*,
> a *teutlion* ("beet") a *seutla*, and *phakē* ("lentil-soup")
>     *phakea*—
> what am I supposed to do? That's how you talk! (B.)
>     Repay me,
> Pyrgothemis, with a novel word of your own, as if you
>     were changing money.

Antiphanes in *Knights* (fr. 108):

> (A.) So how are we going to live? (B.) The saddle-
>     cloth
> is what we'll lie on; the nice helmet's our wine-jar
> or our *psuktēr*. What do you want? We've got
>     everything—Amaltheia's horn.[419]

In *The Female Dirge-Singer* he makes it absolutely clear
that they used this vessel by pouring wine into it with a
ladle. Because after he says (fr. 112):

> He had a table and
> a wine-jug and a *psuktēr* of wine set beside him,
> and he's getting drunk,

he represents the man as saying in the lines that follow
immediately afterward (fr. 113):

> It's going to be a
> really wild party. So if anyone claims, it's
> no longer possible to ladle it out because . . .
> take the wine-jug and the cup outside,
> and remove everything else!

Διονύσιος δὲ ὁ τοῦ Τρύφωνος ἐν τῷ Περὶ Ὀνομάτων, τὸν ψυγέα, φησίν, ἐκάλουν οἱ ἀρχαῖοι δῖνον. Νίκανδρος δ' ὁ Θυατειρηνὸς καλεῖσθαί φησι ψυκτήρια καὶ τοὺς ἀλσώδεις καὶ συσκίους τόπους τοὺς τοῖς θεοῖς ἀνειμένους, ἐν οἷς ἔστιν ἀναψῦξαι. Αἰσχύλος Νεανίσκοις·

< . . . > αὔρας ὑποσκίοισιν[67] ἐν ψυκτηρίοις.

d  Εὐριπίδης | Φαέθοντι·

ψυκτήρια
δένδρη φίλαισιν ὠλέναισι δέξεται.

καὶ ὁ τὸν Αἰγίμιον δὲ ποιήσας εἴθ᾽ Ἡσίοδός ἐστιν ἢ Κέρκωψ ὁ Μιλήσιος·

ἔνθά ποτ᾽ ἔσται ἐμὸν ψυκτήριον, ὄρχαμε λαῶν.

Ὠιδός. οὕτως ἐκαλεῖτο τὸ ποτήριον, φησὶ Τρύφων ἐν τοῖς Ὀνοματικοῖς, τὸ ἐπὶ τῷ σκολίῳ διδόμενον, ὡς Ἀντιφάνης παρίστησιν ἐν Διπλασίοις·

(Α.) τί οὖν ἐνέσται τοῖς θεοῖσιν; (Β.) οὐδὲ ἕν, |
e  ἂν μὴ κεράσῃ τις. (Α.) ἴσχε, τὸν ᾠδὸν λάμβανε.
ἔπειτα μηδὲν τῶν ἀπηρχαιωμένων

---

67 ὑποσκίοισιν CE: ὑπηκόοισιν A (which may be what Aeschylus wrote, but is unlikely to be what Athenaeus offered here)

Tryphon's student Dionysius says in his *On Nouns*: The ancients referred to a *psugeus* as a *dinos*. Nicander of Thyateira (*FGrH* 343 F 17) claims that shady, tree-filled spots dedicated to the gods in which you could cool off (*anapsuxai*) were also referred to as *psuktēria*. Aeschylus in *Young Men* (fr. 146):

> breezes in cool, shaded places (*psuktēria*).

Euripides in *Phaethon* (fr. 782):

> Cooling (*psuktēria*)
> trees will receive you in their loving arms.

So too the author of the *Aegimius*, whether this is Hesiod (fr. 301) or Cercops of Miletus:

> In this place someday will be my *psuktērion*,
>      marshaller of the host!

*Ōidos*. According to Tryphon in his *On Terminology* (fr. 115 Velsen), this was the term for the cup offered when a skolion is sung,[420] as Antiphanes establishes in *Men Who Were Twice as Big* (fr. 85):

> (A.) What'll be in it, then, for the gods? (B.) Nothing,
> unless someone mixes some wine. (A.) Hold on. Take
>      hold of the *ōidos*;
> and then don't recite one of these

---

[420] For skolia, see 15.693f–6a.

ATHENAEUS

τούτων περάνῃς, τὸν Τελαμῶνα, μηδὲ τὸν
Παιῶνα, μηδ᾽ Ἁρμόδιον.

Ὠοσκύφια. περὶ τῆς ἰδέας τῶν ποτηρίων Ἀσκληπιάδης ὁ Μυρλεανὸς ἐν τῷ Περὶ τῆς Νεστορίδος
φησὶν ὅτι δύο πυθμένας ἔχει, ἕνα μὲν τὸν κατὰ τὸ
κύτος αὐτῷ συγκεχαλκευμένον, ἕτερον δὲ τὸν πρόσθετον ἀπ᾽ ὀξέος ἀρχόμενον, καταλήγοντα δὲ εἰς πλα-
f    τύτερον, ἐφ᾽ | οὗ ἵσταται τὸ ποτήριον.

Ὠόν. Δίνων ἐν τρίτῃ Περσικῶν φησιν οὕτως· ἐστὶ
δὲ ποτίβαζις ἄρτος κρίθινος καὶ πύρινος ὀπτὸς καὶ
κυπαρίσσου στέφανος καὶ οἶνος κεκραμένος ἐν ᾠῷ
χρυσῷ, οὗ αὐτὸς βασιλεὺς πίνει.

Τοσαῦτα εἰπὼν ὁ Πλούταρχος καὶ ὑπὸ πάντων
κροταλισθεὶς ᾔτησε φιάλην, ἀφ᾽ ἧς σπείσας ταῖς
Μούσαις καὶ τῇ τούτων Μνημοσύνῃ μητρὶ προὔπιε
πᾶσι φιλοτησίαν. ἐπειπὼν <δέ>·

504    φιάλαν ‖ ὡς εἴ τις ἀφνειᾶς ἀπὸ χειρὸς ἑλὼν
ἔνδον ἀμπέλου καχλάζοισαν < ... >
δωρήσεται,

οὐ μόνον

---

421 Telamon was the father of Salaminian Ajax; a skolion that
praises him is preserved at 15.695c. Cf. 11.783c n. For singing
paeans (hymns in honour of Paian, a god often associated with
Apollo) at dinner parties and symposia, see Alcm. PMG 98;
Antiph. fr. 3.1 (quoted at 15.692f); Pl. Smp. 176a with Dover ad
loc. Harmodius of Aphidnae (PAA 203425) and his lover Aris-
togiton assassinated Hipparchus son of Pisistratus in 514 and were
remembered (inaccurately) as having freed Athens from the
tyrants and established a democracy; see 13.602a; Th. 1.20.2;

old-fashioned pieces, the Telamon, or the
Paean, or the Harmodius.[421]

*Ōioskuphia*.[422] As for the shape of these cups, Asclepiades of Myrlea in his *On Nestor's Cup*[423] says that they
have two bases, one beneath the belly and organically inte-
grated with it, while the cup stands on the other, which is
attached to it, and which begins with a slender shaft and
ends up being much broader.

*Ōion*.[424] Dinon in Book III of the *History of Persia*
(*FGrH* 690 F 4) says the following: There is *potibazis*,
which is baked barley- and wheat-bread, and a wreath
made of cypress, and wine mixed in a gold *ōion*, which the
king himself drinks.

After Plutarch completed these extended remarks
and was applauded by everyone, he asked for a *phialē*; after he poured a libation to the Muses and their mother
Mnemosyne,[425] and toasted everyone with a *philotēsia*
("friendship cup"), he continued (Pi. *O.* 7.1–3):

> As when someone takes a *phiala* boiling
> within with . . . of the vine and offers it
> from his wealthy hand,

not only (Pi. *O.* 7.4)

6.53.3–59; Olson on Ar. *Ach*. 978–9. Four skolia praising them are
preserved at 15.695a–b; cf. Antiph. fr. 3.1 (quoted at 15.692f).

[422] Literally "egg-*skuphia*".

[423] Quoted in context at 11.488f–9a.

[424] Literally "egg".

[425] Cf. 11.490e n.; appropriately invoked here to celebrate
Plutarch's achievement in presenting his long catalogue of names
of cups and related texts.

νεανίᾳ γαμβρῷ προπίνων,

ἀλλὰ καὶ πᾶσι τοῖς φιλτάτοις, ἔδωκε τῷ παιδὶ περισοβεῖν κελεύσας[68], τὸ κύκλῳ πίνειν τοῦτ᾽ εἶναι λέγων,
παρατιθέμενος Μενάνδρου ἐκ Περινθίας·

οὐδεμίαν ἡ γραῦς ὅλως
κύλικα παρῆκεν, ἀλλὰ πίνει τὴν κύκλῳ.

καὶ πάλιν ἐκ Θεοφορουμένης·

καὶ ταχὺ
πάλιν τὸ πρῶτον περισόβει ποτήριον
αὐτοῖς ἀκράτου. |

b   καὶ Εὐριπίδης δ᾽ ἐν Κρήσσαις·

τὰ δ᾽ ἄλλα χαῖρε κύλικος ἑρπούσης κύκλῳ.

αἰτοῦντος δὲ τοῦ γραμματικοῦ Λεωνίδου μεῖζον ποτήριον καὶ εἰπόντος, κρατηρίζωμεν, ἄνδρες φίλοι ‹ . . . ›
οὕτως δὲ τοὺς πότους Λυσανίας φησὶν ὁ Κυρηναῖος
Ἡρόδωρον εἰρηκέναι ἐν τούτοις· ἐπεὶ δὲ θύσαντες πρὸς
δεῖπνον καὶ κρατῆρα καὶ εὐχὰς καὶ παιῶνας ἐτρά-
ποντο. καὶ ὁ τοὺς μίμους δὲ πεποιηκώς, οὓς αἰεὶ διὰ
χειρὸς ἔχειν Δοῦρίς φησι τὸν σοφὸν Πλάτωνα, λέγει
c   που "κἠκρατηρίχημες" ἀντὶ τοῦ ἐπεπώκειμεν. | ἀλλὰ
μήν, πρὸς θεῶν, ὁ Ποντιανὸς ἔφη, οὐ δεόντως ἐκ

68 περισοβεῖν ἐν κύκλῳ κελεύσας A: ἐν κύκλῳ del. Nauck

426 *perisobein*; cf. 4.130c, where the verb is used in a very similar context.

427 *kratēr*, "mixing-bowl".

toasting his young son-in-law,

but also all his family and friends; and he gave it to the slave and ordered him "to shoo it around",[426] which he claimed meant "to drink around the circle", citing a passage from Menander's *The Girl from Perinthus* (*Perinth.* fr. 4 Sandbach):

> The old woman didn't ignore a single *kulix*, but drank from every one that went around the circle.

And again in *The Girl Who Was Possessed by a God* (*Theoph.* fr. 3 Sandbach):

> And again he begins by quickly shooing around (*perisobei*) a cup of unmixed wine to them.

So too Euripides in *Cretan Women* (fr. 468):

> Otherwise, take joy in the cup making its way around the circle!

When the grammarian Leonidas asked for a larger cup and said: We ought to be drinking straight from the mixing-bowl, my friends . . . Lysanias of Cyrene claims that Herodorus (*FGrH* 31 F 59) uses this term[427] for a drinking party in the following passage: when, after making sacrifice, they turned their attention to dinner, the *kratēr*, prayers, and paeans. So too the author of the mimes that, according to Duris (*FGrH* 76 F 72 = Sophr. test. 5), the wise Plato always had with him, somewhere says (Sophr. fr. 101) "and we drank straight from the mixing-bowl" to mean "we got drunk". No, by the gods, said Pompeianus;

μεγάλων πίνετε ποτηρίων, τὸν ἥδιστον καὶ χαριέστα-
τον Ξενοφῶντα πρὸ ὀφθαλμῶν ἔχοντες, ὃς ἐν τῷ
Συμποσίῳ φησίν· ὁ δ' αὖ Σωκράτης εἶπεν· "ἀλλὰ
πίνειν μέν, ὦ ἄνδρες, καὶ ἐμοὶ πάνυ δοκεῖ. τῷ γὰρ ὄντι
ὁ οἶνος ἄρδων τὰς ψυχὰς τὰς μὲν λύπας ὥσπερ ὁ
μανδραγόρας ἀνθρώπους κοιμίζει, τὰς δὲ φλόγας
ἐγείρει. δοκεῖ μέντοι μοι καὶ τὰ τῶν ἀνθρώπων σώματα τὰ αὐτὰ πάσχειν ἅπερ καὶ τὰ τῶν ἐν γῇ φυομέ-
d  νων. καὶ γὰρ ἐκεῖνα, | ὅταν μὲν ὁ θεὸς αὐτὰ ἄγαν
ἀθρόως ποτίζῃ, οὐ δύναται ὀρθοῦσθαι οὐδὲ ταῖς ὥραις
διαπλοῦσθαι· ὅταν δὲ ὅσῳ ἥδεται τοσοῦτο πίνῃ, καὶ
μάλα ὀρθά τε αὔξεται καὶ θάλλοντα ἀφικνεῖται εἰς τὴν
καρπογονίαν. οὕτω δὴ καὶ ἡμεῖς, ἢν μὲν ἀθρόον τὸ
ποτὸν ἐγχεώμεθα, ταχὺ ἡμῶν καὶ τὰ σώματα καὶ αἱ
γνῶμαι σφαλοῦνται, καὶ οὐδ' ἀναπνεῖν μὴ ὅτι λέγειν
δυνησόμεθα· ἢν δὲ ἡμῖν οἱ παῖδες μικραῖς κύλιξι
μικρὰ ἐπιψακάζωσιν, ἵνα καὶ ἐγὼ Γοργιείοις ῥήμασιν
e  εἴπω, οὕτως οὐ βιαζόμενοι μεθύειν | ὑπὸ τοῦ οἴνου,
ἀλλ' ἀναπειθόμενοι πρὸς τὸ παιγνιωδέστερον ἀφιξό-
μεθα." εἰς ταῦτά τις ἀποβλέπων τὰ τοῦ καλοῦ Ξενοφῶντος ἐπιγινώσκειν δυνήσεται ἣν εἶχε πρὸς αὐτὸν ὁ
λαμπρότατος Πλάτων ζηλοτυπίαν, ἢ τάχα φιλονίκως
εἶχον ἀρχῆθεν πρὸς ἑαυτοὺς οἱ ἄνδρες οὗτοι, αἰσθό-
μενοι τῆς ἰδίας ἑκάτερος ἀρετῆς, καὶ ἴσως καὶ περὶ
πρωτείων διεφέροντο, οὐ μόνον ἐξ ὧν περὶ Κύρου
εἰρήκασι τεκμαιρομένοις ἡμῖν, ἀλλὰ κἀκ τῶν αὐτῶν
ὑποθέσεων. Συμπόσια μὲν γὰρ γεγράφασιν ἀμφό-
f  τεροι, | καὶ ἐν αὐτοῖς ὁ μὲν τὰς αὐλητρίδας ἐκβάλλει, ὁ

---

428 Much of what follows (to 11.509e) appears to be taken
(perhaps via a secondary source) from Herodicus the Cratetean
(pp. 24–5, 30–40 Düring); cf. 5.218e–19a (from the same essay).

you should not drink from large cups, at least not if you fo-
cus your attention on the delightful, witty Xenophon, who
says in his *Symposium* (2.24–6): But Socrates responded:
"Well, gentlemen, I too am very much of the opinion that
we ought to be drinking. Because by watering our souls,
wine does in fact put our cares to sleep, as mandrake does
to people generally, while also rousing our fires. It seems to
me, in fact, that human bodies are affected in the same way
as plants growing in the earth are. Because when the latter get too much rain at any one time, they cannot stand
up straight or open their blossoms at the right moment;
whereas if they get exactly the right amount to drink, they
grow quite straight and are flourishing when they reach the
point where they produce their crop. So too with us: if we
constantly pour ourselves one drink after another, our bodies and our minds will soon cease to function, and we will
become incapable of speaking or even breathing. But if the
slaves sprinkle only a little on us (if I may use a Gorgianic
expression) using tiny cups, the wine will not force us to get
drunk, and we will instead be persuaded to attain a rather
playful condition." Anyone who studies this passage from
the noble Xenophon will be able to recognize how jealous
the distinguished Plato was of him—or perhaps how com-
petitive these men were with each other from the very
first, since they both saw where they excelled personally.[428]
And it may be that they were also divided by their desire to
be the most important, as we can tell not only from what
they have to say about Cyrus, but also from their essays
on similar topics. Because they both wrote *Symposia*, but
within them one author expels pipe-girls from the party,

δὲ εἰσάγει. καὶ ὁ μέν, ὡς πρόκειται, παραιτεῖται πίνειν
μεγάλοις ποτηρίοις, ὁ δὲ τὸν Σωκράτην παράγει τῷ
ψυκτῆρι πίνοντα μέχρι τῆς ἔω. κἂν τῷ Περὶ Ψυχῆς δὲ
ὁ Πλάτων καταλεγόμενος ἕκαστον τῶν παρατυχόντων
οὐδὲ κατὰ μικρὸν τοῦ Ξενοφῶντος μέμνηται. καὶ περὶ
τοῦ Κύρου οὖν ὁ μὲν λέγει ὡς ἐκ πρώτης ἡλικίας
ἐπεπαίδευτο πάντα τὰ πάτρια, ὁ δὲ Πλάτων ὥσπερ
505   ἐναντιούμενος ἐν τρίτῳ Νόμων φησί· || μαντεύομαι δὲ
περὶ Κύρου τὰ μὲν ἄλλα στρατηγὸν αὐτὸν ἀγαθὸν
εἶναι καὶ φιλόπονον, παιδείας δ᾽ ὀρθῆς οὐδὲ ἧφθαι τὸ
παράπαν, οἰκονομίᾳ δ᾽ οὐδ᾽ ἡτινιοῦν προσεσχηκέναι.
ἔοικε δ᾽ ἐκ νέου στρατεύεσθαι, παραδούς τε τοὺς
παῖδας ταῖς γυναιξὶ τρέφειν. πάλιν ὁ μὲν Ξενοφῶν
συναναβὰς Κύρῳ εἰς Πέρσας μετὰ τῶν μυρίων Ἑλλήνων καὶ ἀκριβῶς εἰδὼς τὴν προδοσίαν τοῦ Θεσσαλοῦ
Μένωνος, ὅτι αὐτὸς αἴτιος ἐγένετο τοῖς περὶ Κλέαρχον
b    τῆς ἀπωλείας τῆς ὑπὸ Τισσαφέρνου γενομένης, | καὶ
οἷός τις ἦν τὸν τρόπον, ὡς χαλεπός, ὡς ἀσελγής,
διηγησαμένου· ὁ καλὸς Πλάτων μονονουχὶ εἰπών·

   οὐκ ἔστ᾽ ἔτυμος λόγος οὗτος,

ἐγκώμια αὐτοῦ διεξέρχεται, ὁ τοὺς ἄλλους ἀπαξαπλῶς
κακολογήσας, ἐν μὲν τῇ Πολιτείᾳ Ὅμηρον ἐκβάλλων

---

429 For the story, see X. *An.* 2.5.27–34, 2.6.1. Clearchus was
lured to dinner by the satrap Tissaphernes and murdered along
with most of the men who accompanied him—except Meno,
whom Xenophon denounces at length (and claims was ultimately
tortured to death by the King) at 2.6.21–9.

430 The first line of the *Palinode* (rejecting the tradition that
Helen went to Troy), quoted also at 5.216b, in a very similar context, and at greater length by Plato himself (*Phdr.* 243a).

while the other includes them. And—as was noted above
(11.504d)—one author declines to drink out of large cups,
while the other represents Socrates as drinking from a
cooling-vessel (*psuktēr*) until the sun comes up (Pl. *Smp*.
213e–14a, 223c). And in his *On the Soul* (*Phd*. 59b) Plato
lists everyone who was there, but makes no mention whatsoever of Xenophon. On the subject of Cyrus, at any rate,
the one author (X. *Cyr*. 1.3.1) claims that he was educated
in all the traditional subjects from his earliest childhood,
whereas Plato in Book III (694c–d) of the *Laws*, as if deliberately contradicting him, says: As for Cyrus, I gather that
he is a generally good general and willing to work hard,
but has never received any formal education whatsoever,
and has never paid the slightest attention to how to manage his household. He seems to have been on campaign
constantly ever since he was a young man, and to have
turned his children over to his women to raise. Again,
Xenophon marched inland to attack the Persians along
with Cyrus and accompanied by 10,000 Greeks, and had
precise knowledge of how Meno of Thebes betrayed them;
and he described how Meno was responsible for the death
at Tissaphernes' hands of the men who were with Clearchus, and what a harsh and depraved individual he was.[429]
The noble Plato, on the other hand, all but admitting that
(Stesich. *PMG* 192.1):[430]

This tale is not true,

offers an extended encomium of the man[431]—although he
relentlessly slanders other people, expelling Homer and
mimetic poetry generally in his *Republic* (e.g. 606e–7a),

[431] Sc. in the dialogue that bears his name.

καὶ τὴν μιμητικὴν ποίησιν, αὐτὸς δὲ τοὺς διαλόγους
μιμητικῶς γράψας, ὧν τῆς ἰδέας οὐδ᾽ αὐτὸς εὑρετής
ἐστιν. πρὸ γὰρ αὐτοῦ τοῦθ᾽ εὗρε τὸ εἶδος τῶν λόγων ὁ
Τήιος Ἀλεξαμενός, ὡς Νικίας ὁ Νικαεὺς ἱστορεῖ καὶ

c   Σωτίων. | Ἀριστοτέλης δ᾽ ἐν τῷ Περὶ Ποιητῶν οὕτως
γράφει· οὐκοῦν οὐδὲ ἐμμέτρους ⟨ὄντας⟩[69] τοὺς καλουμένους Σώφρονος Μίμους μὴ φῶμεν εἶναι λόγων καὶ
μιμήσεις, ἢ τοὺς Ἀλεξαμενοῦ τοῦ Τηίου τοὺς πρότερον[70] γραφέντας τῶν Σωκρατικῶν διαλόγους[71], ἄντι-
κρυς φάσκων ὁ πολυμαθέστατος Ἀριστοτέλης πρὸ
Πλάτωνος διαλόγους γεγραφέναι τὸν Ἀλεξαμενόν.
διαβάλλει δὲ ὁ Πλάτων καὶ Θρασύμαχον τὸν Χαλκη-
δόνιον σοφιστὴν ὅμοιον εἶναι λέγων τῷ ὀνόματι, ἔτι δ᾽

d   Ἱππίαν καὶ Γοργίαν | καὶ Παρμενίδην καὶ ἐνὶ διαλόγῳ
τῷ Πρωταγόρᾳ πολλούς, ὁ τοιαῦτα ἐν τῇ Πολιτείᾳ
εἰπών· ὅταν, οἶμαι, δημοκρατουμένη πόλις ἐλευθερίας
διψήσασα κακῶν οἰνοχόων τύχῃ καὶ ἀκράτου αὐτῆς
μεθυσθῇ. λέγεται δὲ ὡς καὶ ὁ Γοργίας αὐτὸς ἀναγνοὺς
τὸν ὁμώνυμον αὐτῷ διάλογον πρὸς τοὺς συνήθεις ἔφη·
"ὡς καλῶς οἶδε Πλάτων ἰαμβίζειν." Ἕρμιππος δὲ ἐν
τῷ Περὶ Γοργίου, ὡς ἐπεδήμησε, φησί, ταῖς Ἀθήναις
Γοργίας μετὰ τὸ ποιήσασθαι τὴν ἀνάθεσιν τῆς ἐν

e   Δελφοῖς ἑαυτοῦ χρυσῆς εἰκόνος, εἰπόντος | τοῦ Πλά-

---

69 add. Kaibel
70 πρότερον Bergk: πρώτους A
71 διαλόγους Bake: διαλόγων A

---

432 If these dialogues ever existed, no trace of them survives
except here; in a papyrus fragment that once again cites Aristotle's
testimony (*POxy.* xlv 3219 fr. 1 = Sophr. test. 4); and at D.L. 3.48
(citing Favorinus, who knew Herodicus).

despite the fact that he himself wrote dialogues that imitate real life! Nor did he invent the genre; because this
type of literature was first produced before him, by Alexamenus of Teos, according to Nicias of Nicaea (*FHG*
iv.464) and Sotion (fr. 14 Wehrli). And Aristotle in his *On
Poets* (fr. 15) writes as follows: Should we, then, deny that
the so-called *Mimes* of Sophron (test. 3), which lack a metrical character, are imitations of actual conversations, or
that the same is true of the dialogues of Alexamenus of
Teos, which were written before those that feature Socrates?—which amounts to the deeply learned Aristotle saying outright that Alexamenus wrote dialogues before Plato
did.[432] Plato also mounts an ugly personal attack on the
sophist Thrasymachus of Chalcedon, by saying that he deserved his name,[433] as well as on Hippias, Gorgias, Parmenides, and many others in his dialogue *Protagoras*, and
by saying something along the following lines in his *Republic* (562c–d):[434] whenever, I suppose, a democratically governed city thirsty for freedom has bad wine-pourers, and
gets drunk on its strong wine. The story goes that when
Gorgias himself read the dialogue named after him, he
said to his friends: "Plato's quite talented at writing abuse-
poetry!" Hermippus says in his *On Gorgias* (fr. 63 Wehrli):
When Gorgias visited Athens after dedicating the gold
statue of himself in Delphi,[435] and Plato saw him and said:

[433] Literally "Bold Fighter"; cf. Arist. *Rh.* 1400b19–20.

[434] Quoted more accurately at 10.433f, 443f–4a.

[435] For the statue, cf. Paus. 10.18.7 (= 82 A 7 D–K). Gorgias
visited Athens in 427 BCE.

τωνος ὅτε εἶδεν αὐτόν, "ἥκει ἡμῖν ὁ καλός τε καὶ
χρυσοῦς Γοργίας," ἔφη ὁ Γοργίας· "ἦ καλόν γε αἱ
Ἀθῆναι καὶ νέον τοῦτον Ἀρχίλοχον ἐνηνόχασιν." ἄλλοι δέ φασιν ὡς ἀναγνοὺς ὁ Γοργίας τὸν Πλάτωνος
διάλογον πρὸς τοὺς παρόντας εἶπεν ὅτι οὐδὲν τούτων
οὔτ᾽ εἶπεν οὔτ᾽ ἤκουσε[72]. ταῦτά φασι καὶ Φαίδωνα
εἰπεῖν ἀναγνόντα τὸν Περὶ Ψυχῆς. διὸ καλῶς ὁ Τίμων
περὶ αὐτοῦ ἔφη·

ὡς ἀνέπλασσε Πλάτων ὁ πεπλασμένα θαύματα
εἰδώς.

f Παρμενίδῃ μὲν γὰρ καὶ ἐλθεῖν | εἰς λόγους τὸν τοῦ
Πλάτωνος Σωκράτην μόλις ἡ ἡλικία συγχωρεῖ, οὐχ
ὡς καὶ τοιούτους εἰπεῖν ἢ ἀκοῦσαι λόγους. τὸ δὲ
πάντων σχετλιώτατον καὶ τὸ εἰπεῖν οὐδεμιᾶς κατεπει-
γούσης χρείας ὅτι παιδικὰ γεγόνοι τοῦ Παρμενίδου
Ζήνων ὁ πολίτης αὐτοῦ. ἀδύνατον δὲ καὶ Φαῖδρον οὐ
μόνον κατὰ Σωκράτην εἶναι, ἢ πού γε καὶ ἐρώμενον
αὐτοῦ γεγονέναι. ἀλλὰ μὴν οὐ δύνανται Πάραλος καὶ
506 Ξάνθιππος οἱ Περικλέους υἱοὶ[73] ‖ Πρωταγόρᾳ δια-
λέγεσθαι, ὅτε ‹τὸ›[74] δεύτερον ἐπεδήμησε ταῖς Ἀθήναις, οἱ ἔτι πρότερον τελευτήσαντες. πολλὰ δ᾽ ἔστι καὶ
ἄλλα λέγειν περὶ αὐτοῦ καὶ δεικνύναι ὡς ἔπλαττε τοὺς
διαλόγους. ὅτι δὲ καὶ δυσμενὴς ἦν πρὸς ἅπαντας,

[72] οὔτ᾽ ἤκουσε παρὰ Πλάτωνος ACE: παρὰ Πλάτωνος del.
Rossi    [73] υἱοὶ τελευτήσαντες τῷ λοιμῷ ACE: τελευτήσαντες τῷ λοιμῷ del. Kaibel    [74] add. Kaibel

[436] Famous above all else for his abuse-poetry.
[437] I.e. of the sort made in the dialogue that bears Parmenides'
name. Plato (*Prm.* 127b–c) claims that Zenon was about 65, and

"Our fine, gold Gorgias has arrived!", Gorgias responded: "And this is a fine new Archilochus[436] that Athens has produced!" Other authorities claim that after Gorgias read Plato's dialogue, he told the people present that he had not spoken or heard a word of this, and they say that Phaedo had the same reaction after he read *On the Soul*. Timo's (*SH* 793) remark about him is thus quite apt:

> What fabrications the marvellous forger Plato
> produced!

Their relative dates would barely allow Plato's Socrates to have a conversation with Parmenides, and certainly not to make and listen to speeches of this sort.[437] But the nastiest feature of all is that he claims—when there was absolutely no need to do so—that Parmenides' fellow-citizen Zeno had also been his boyfriend.[438] It is likewise impossible that Phaedrus was Socrates' contemporary, to say nothing of being a young man he was in love with. Nor could Pericles' sons Paralus and Xanthippus[439] have had a conversation with Protagoras the second time he visited Athens, since they were already dead before then. Much else could also be said about him, to show that his dialogues are fabrications.[440] As for the fact that he was hostile to everyone,

that Socrates was very young when the two men met, putting the encounter around 450 BCE. Why Herodicus thought this impossible is unclear, and it is tempting to believe that he has simply ignored Plato's attempt at chronological verisimilitude.

[438] *Prm.* 127b; this is, however, merely presented as a rumor.

[439] Paralus is *PAA* 765275, while Xanthippus is *PAA* 730515. Both died of the plague in 430 BCE.

[440] Cf. 5.215c–18e (5.218b–e on the dramatic date of the *Protagoras*).

δῆλον καὶ ἐκ τῶν ἐν τῷ Ἴωνι ἐπιγραφομένῳ, ἐν ᾧ
πρῶτον μὲν κακολογεῖ πάντας τοὺς ποιητάς, ἔπειτα
καὶ τοὺς ὑπὸ τοῦ δήμου προαγομένους, Φανοσθένη τὸν
Ἄνδριον κἀπολλόδωρον τὸν Κυζικηνόν, ἔτι δὲ τὸν
Κλαζομένιον Ἡρακλείδην. ἐν δὲ τῷ Μένωνι καὶ τοὺς
b μεγίστους | παρ' Ἀθηναίοις γενομένους Ἀριστείδην
καὶ Θεμιστοκλέα, Μένωνα δὲ ἐπαινεῖ τὸν τοὺς Ἕλληνας προδόντα. ἐν δὲ τῷ Εὐθυδήμῳ ⟨Εὐθύδημον⟩[75] καὶ
τὸν ἀδελφὸν αὐτοῦ Διονυσόδωρον προπηλακίζων καὶ
καλῶν ὀψιμαθεῖς ἔτι τε ἐριστὰς ὀνομάζων ὀνειδίζει
αὐτοῖς καὶ τὴν ἐκ Χίου τῆς πατρίδος φυγήν, ἀφ' ἧς ἐν
Θουρίοις κατῳκίσθησαν. ἐν δὲ τῷ Περὶ Ἀνδρείας
Μελησίαν τὸν Θουκυδίδου τοῦ ἀντιπολιτευσαμένου
Περικλεῖ καὶ Λυσίμαχον τὸν Ἀριστείδου τοῦ δικαίου,
c τῆς τῶν πατέρων ἀρετῆς ἀναξίους εἶναι φάσκων. | ἃ δὲ
περὶ Ἀλκιβιάδου εἴρηκεν ἐν τῷ Συμποσίῳ οὐδ' εἰς φῶς
λέγεσθαί ἐστιν ἄξιον, ἔν τε τῷ προτέρῳ τῶν εἰς αὐτὸν
διαλόγων· ὁ γὰρ δεύτερος ὑπό τινων Ξενοφῶντος εἶναι
λέγεται, ὡς καὶ ἡ Ἀλκυὼν Λέοντος τοῦ Ἀκαδημαϊκοῦ,
ὥς φησι Νικίας ὁ Νικαεύς. τὰ μὲν οὖν κατὰ Ἀλκι-

---

[75] add. Dindorf

---

441 *PA* 14083, *PAA* 143545, and *PAA* 486295, respectively. All
three men were elected to serve as Athenian generals, despite being from other cities, and there is in fact no hint of disparagement
in Socrates' remarks.

442 Aristides "the Just" (*PAA* 165170; 530s/520s–*c*.467 BCE)
and Themistocles (*PAA* 502610; *c*.525–459 BCE) were two of Athens' most distinguished early 5th-century political and military
leaders.        443 See 11.505a–b n.

444 Melesias is *PAA* 639150, while Lysimachus is *PAA* 616305.

this is also apparent from what goes on in his work entitled *Ion*, in which he disparages (533c–4e) first all the poets, and then (541c–d) the individuals the people selected for important offices: Phanosthenes of Andros, Apollodorus of Cyzicus, and even Heraclides of Clazomenae.[441] In his *Meno* (he attacks) the greatest Athenians who ever lived, Aristides and Themistocles,[442] but praises Meno,[443] who betrayed the Greeks. In his *Euthydemus* he tramples Euthydemus and his brother Dionysodorus, calling them pedants, as well as referring to them as quibblers, and criticizes them for having been driven into exile from their native island of Chios (271c), which they left to settle in Thurii. And in his *On Courage* (*La.* 179c–d) (he abuses) Melesias, the son of the Thucydides who was Pericles' political opponent, as well as Lysimachus the son of Aristides the Just,[444] claiming that they failed to live up to their fathers' reputations. But as for what he says about Alcibiades[445] in his *Symposium*, that ought not even to be mentioned in public, any more than what is said in the first dialogue addressed to him; because some authorities claim that the second dialogue was written by Xenophon,[446] just as the *Alcyon* is sometimes assigned to Leon of the Academy, according to Nicias of Nicaea (*FHG* iv.464).[447] I pass

---

[445] *PAA* 121625. Cf. the very similar remarks below and at 5.182a with n.   [446] *Alcibiades II* is universally regarded today as spurious.   [447] D.L. 3.62 (citing Favorinus, who knew Herodicus) makes very similar comments. The *Alcyon* was also attributed in antiquity to Lucian, and is included in the seventh volume of the Loeb edition of that author (pp. 303–17, with an introduction that takes up the problem of the identity of the obscure "Leon of the Academy").

βιάδου λεχθέντα σιωπῶ· ὅτι δὲ τὸν Ἀθηναίων δῆμον
εἰκαῖον εἴρηκε κριτὴν ἔτι τε πρόκωπον, Λακεδαιμονίους δὲ ἐπαινῶν ἐπαινεῖ καὶ τοὺς πάντων Ἑλλήνων
ἐχθροὺς Πέρσας. καὶ τὸν ἀδελφὸν δὲ τοῦ Ἀλκιβιάδου

d Κλεινίαν μαινόμενόν | τε ἀποφαίνει καὶ τοὺς υἱοὺς
αὐτοῦ ἠλιθίους Μειδίαν τε ὀρτυγοκόπον, καὶ τὸν τῶν
Ἀθηναίων δῆμον εὐπρόσωπον μὲν εἶναι, δεῖν δ' αὐτὸν
ἀποδύσαντας θεωρεῖν· ὀφθήσεται γάρ, φησί, περί-
βλεπτον ἀξίωμα περικείμενος κάλλους οὐκ ἀληθινοῦ.
ἐν δὲ τῷ Κίμωνι οὐδὲ τῆς Θεμιστοκλέους φείδεται
κατηγορίας οὐδὲ τῆς Ἀλκιβιάδου καὶ Μυρωνίδου, ἀλλ'
οὐδ' αὐτοῦ τοῦ Κίμωνος. καὶ ὁ Κρίτων δ' αὐτοῦ
<Κρίτωνος, ἡ δὲ Πολιτεία καὶ>[76] Σοφοκλέους περιέχει
καταδρομήν, ὁ δὲ Γοργίας οὐ μόνον ἀφ' οὗ τὸ ἐπί-

e γραμμα, ἀλλὰ καὶ Ἀρχελάου τοῦ Μακεδονίας | βασι-
λέως, ὃν οὐ μόνον ἐπονείδιστον γένος ἔχειν, ἀλλ' ὅτι
καὶ ἀπέκτεινε τὸν δεσπότην. οὗτος δ' ἐστὶ Πλάτων, ὃν
Σπεύσιππός φησι φίλτατον ὄντα Φιλίππῳ[77] τῆς βασιλείας αἴτιον γενέσθαι. γράφει γοῦν Καρύστιος ὁ Περγαμηνὸς ἐν τοῖς Ἱστορικοῖς Ὑπομνήμασιν οὕτως·

---

76 add. Wilamowitz

77 Ἀρχελάῳ Φιλίππῳ ACE: Ἀρχελάῳ del. Gomperz

---

448 The reference is in fact to Pericles' sons (*Alc. I* 118e).

449 *PAA* 637170; mentioned also *inter alia* at Ar. *Av.* 1297–9, where see Dunbar's n.

450 This final remark is not in the text of Plato.

451 No work by this title is included in the Platonic corpus.

452 For Themistocles and Alcibiades, see 11.506b n. and 11.506c n., respectively. Myronides (*PAA* 663265; cf. Ar. *Lys.* 801–3 [ignored in *PAA*] with Henderson *ad loc.*) was an Athenian

over in silence the criticisms he offers of Alcibiades. But (I do note) that he calls the Athenian people rash, even over-eager judges, and that in the course of praising the Spartans he also praises the Persians, the universal enemies of the Greeks. He also portrays Alcibiades' brother Cleinias as a lunatic (*Alc. I* 118e), his sons as fools,[448] and Meidias[449] as a gambler (*Alc. I* 120a); and (he says) that although the Athenian people have a pretty face, you need to see them with their clothes off (*Alc. I* 132a). Because it will be apparent, he says, that they are wrapped in an admirable reputation that has nothing to do with genuine beauty.[450] In his *Cimon*[451] he spares no criticism of Themistocles, or of Alcibiades and Myronides, or even of Cimon himself.[452] So too his *Crito* contains an attack on Crito himself, while his *Republic* attacks Sophocles,[453] and his *Gorgias* attacks not just the man who gave the work its title, but also the Macedonian king Archelaus,[454] who is said not only to be from a quite unsavory family, but to have killed his master (471a–b). And this is the Plato who, Speusippus claims, was Philip's[455] good friend and was responsible for him becoming king! Carystius of Pergamum, at any rate, writes as follows in his *Historical Commentary* (fr. 1, *FHG* iv.356–7

general in the early 450s BCE. Cimon (*PAA* 569795) was one of Athens' most important political and military leaders in the early 470s–461 (when he was ostracized), and then again after his return in the late 450s.

[453] Apparently a reference to *R.* 329b–c, which can scarcely, however, be understood as a personal attack, any more than Plato's characterization of Crito can.

[454] Archelaus I, reigned *c.*413–399 BCE.

[455] Philip II of Macedon (reigned 360/59–336 BCE).

Σπεύσιππος πυνθανόμενος Φίλιππον βλασφημεῖν
περὶ Πλάτωνος εἰς ἐπιστολὴν ἔγραψέ τι τοιοῦτον·
ὥσπερ ἀγνοοῦντας τοὺς ἀνθρώπους ὅτι καὶ τὴν ἀρχὴν
τῆς βασιλείας Φίλιππος διὰ Πλάτωνος ἔσχεν. Εὐ-
f φραῖον γὰρ ἀπέστειλε τὸν | Ὠρείτην πρὸς Περδίκκαν
Πλάτων, ὃς ἔπεισεν ἀπομερίσαι τινὰ χώραν Φιλίππῳ.
διατρέφων δ' ἐνταῦθα δύναμιν, ὡς ἀπέθανε Περδίκκας,
ἐξ ἑτοίμου δυνάμεως ὑπαρχούσης ἐπέπεσε τοῖς
πράγμασι. τοῦτο δ' εἴπερ οὕτως ἀληθείας ἔχει, θεὸς ἂν
εἰδείη. ὁ δὲ καλὸς αὐτοῦ Πρωταγόρας πρὸς τῷ κατα-
δρομὴν ἔχειν πολλῶν ποιητῶν καὶ σοφῶν ἀνδρῶν
ἐκθεατριζόμενον ἔχει καὶ τὸν Καλλίου βίον μᾶλλον
τῶν Εὐπόλιδος Κολάκων. ἐν δὲ τῷ Μενεξένῳ οὐ μόνον
Ἱππίας ὁ Ἠλεῖος χλευάζεται, ἀλλὰ καὶ ὁ Ῥαμνούσιος
Ἀντιφῶν καὶ ὁ μουσικὸς Λάμπρος. ἐπιλίποι δ' ἄν με ἡ
507 ἡμέρα, εἰ πάντας ἐθελήσαιμι ‖ ἐπελθεῖν τοὺς κακῶς
ἀκούσαντας ὑπὸ τοῦ σοφοῦ. ἀλλὰ μὴν οὐδ' Ἀντισθένη
ἐπαινῶ· καὶ γὰρ καὶ οὗτος πολλοὺς εἰπὼν κακῶς οὐδ'
αὐτοῦ τοῦ Πλάτωνος ἀπέσχετο, ἀλλὰ καλέσας αὐτὸν
φορτικῶς Σάθωνα τὸν ταύτην ἔχοντα τὴν ἐπιγραφὴν
διάλογον ἐξέδωκεν. Ἡγήσανδρος δὲ ὁ Δελφὸς ἐν τοῖς
Ὑπομνήμασι περὶ τῆς πρὸς πάντας τοῦ Πλάτωνος
κακοηθείας λέγων γράφει καὶ ταῦτα· μετὰ τὴν Σωκράτους τελευτὴν ἐπὶ πλεῖον τῶν συνήθων ἀθυμούν-
των ἔν τινι συνουσίᾳ Πλάτων συμπαρὼν λαβὼν τὸ |

456 Speusippus was Plato's nephew (as well as his successor as
head of the Academy), hence his eagerness to stand up for him.

457 Perdiccas III ruled Macedon 367/5–360/59 BCE; he died in
a campaign against the Illyrians. For Euphraeus in Perdiccas'
court, cf. 11.508d–e.

458 Cf. 5.218b–c (also drawn from Herodicus).

478

= Speusipp. test. 48 Tarán): When Speusippus[456] heard
that Philip was making hostile comments about Plato, he
wrote something along the following lines in a letter: as if
people were unaware that Plato was responsible for Philip
getting initial control of his kingship! For Plato sent
Euphraeus of Oreus to Perdiccas,[457] and Euphraeus convinced him to give Philip control of a bit of territory. Philip
maintained troops there, and when Perdiccas died, because Philip had an army ready to go, he seized political
power. As for whether this is true or not, only a god would
know. But his lovely *Protagoras*, in addition to disparag-
ing numerous poets and other clever men, holds Callias'
life-style up for public consideration more than Eupolis'
*Flatterers* (test. ii) does.[458] And in his *Menexenus* it is not
just Hippias of Elis who is made fun of,[459] but also (236a)
Antiphon of Rhamnous and the musician Lamprus.[460]
There would not be enough hours in the day for me, however, if I wanted to list everyone about whom the philosopher makes ugly comments. Nor do I have any praise for
Antisthenes (*SSR* V A 147);[461] because the fact is that he
too made nasty remarks about many people and did not
leave even Plato himself alone, but referred to him in low-
class way as Sathō ("dick") and published a dialogue with
this as its title. Hegesander of Delphi in his *Commentaries*
(fr. 1, *FHG* iv.412–13) discusses Plato's nasty attitude toward everyone, writing as follows: After Socrates' death,
his friends were extremely discouraged. Plato was at one of

---

[459] Hippias is not, in fact, mentioned in the dialogue.

[460] Antiphon is *PAA* 138625, while Lamprus is *PAA* 601647.

[461] A heavily condensed version of material preserved also at
5.220c–e, esp. d–e.

b ποτήριον παρεκάλει μὴ ἀθυμεῖν αὐτούς, ὡς ἱκανὸς
αὐτὸς εἴη ἡγεῖσθαι τῆς σχολῆς, καὶ προέπιεν Ἀπολ-
λοδώρῳ. καὶ ὃς εἶπεν· "ἥδιον ἂν παρὰ Σωκράτους τὴν
τοῦ φαρμάκου κύλικα εἰλήφειν ἢ παρὰ σοῦ τὴν τοῦ
οἴνου πρόποσιν." ἐδόκει γὰρ Πλάτων φθονερὸς εἶναι
καὶ κατὰ τὸ ἦθος οὐδαμῶς εὐδοκιμεῖν· καὶ γὰρ Ἀρί-
στιππον πρὸς Διονύσιον ἀποδημήσαντα ἔσκωπτεν,
αὐτὸς τρὶς εἰς Σικελίαν ἐκπλεύσας, ἅπαξ μὲν τῶν
ῥυάκων χάριν, ὅτε καὶ τῷ πρεσβυτέρῳ Διονυσίῳ συγ-
c γενόμενος ἐκινδύνευσεν, δὶς δὲ πρὸς τὸν | νεώτερον
Διονύσιον. Αἰσχίνου τε πένητος ὄντος καὶ μαθητὴν
ἕνα ἔχοντος Ξενοκράτην, τοῦτον περιέσπασεν. καὶ
Φαίδωνι δὲ τὴν τῆς δουλείας ἐφιστὰς δίκην ἐφωράθη·
καὶ τὸ καθόλου πᾶσι τοῖς Σωκράτους μαθηταῖς ἐπεφύ-
κει μητρυιᾶς ἔχων διάθεσιν. διόπερ Σωκράτης οὐκ
ἀηδῶς περὶ αὐτοῦ στοχαζόμενος ἐνύπνιον ἔφησεν
ἑωρακέναι πλειόνων παρόντων. "δοκεῖν γάρ", ἔφη "τὸν
Πλάτωνα κορώνην γενόμενον ἐπὶ τὴν κεφαλήν μου
ἀναπηδήσαντα τὸ φαλακρόν μου κατασκαριφᾶν καὶ
κρώζειν περιβλέπουσαν. | δοκῶ οὖν σε, ὦ Πλάτων,
d πολλὰ κατὰ τῆς ἐμῆς ψεύσεσθαι κεφαλῆς." ἦν δὲ ὁ
Πλάτων πρὸς τῇ κακοηθείᾳ καὶ φιλόδοξος, ὅστις
ἔφησεν· "ἔσχατον τὸν τῆς φιλοδοξίας χιτῶνα ἐν τῷ

---

462 Apollodorus (*PAA* 143280) was a member of Socrates' circle, and *inter alia* serves as the narrator for the *Symposium*.

463 For Aristippus of Cyrene (another member of Socrates'
circle) in the court of Dionysius I of Syracuse (d. 367 BCE), see
12.544a–e with n. For the hostility between Aristippus and Plato,
see also 8.343c–d; cf. 11.508c–d.

464 Sc. from an eruption on Mt. Aetna.

their parties and took the cup; told them not to worry, since he was capable of leading the school himself; and toasted Apollodorus.[462] Apollodorus responded: "I would rather have taken the cup of poison from Socrates than accept this toast of wine from you;" because Plato was regarded as jealous and as having a thoroughly bad reputation as far as his personal behavior was concerned. He made hostile jokes about Aristippus (*SSR* IV A 26), for example, when the latter went to visit Dionysius,[463] despite the fact that he sailed to Sicily three times himself, once to see the lava,[464] when he and the elder Dionysius almost lost their lives, and twice to visit the younger Dionysius.[465] And despite the fact that Aeschines (*SSR* III A 4) was poor and had only one student, Xenocrates,[466] Plato took Xenocrates away from him. He was also caught red-handed bringing the suit against Phaedo that charged him with being a slave, and he was in general as cruel as a stepmother to all Socrates' students. This is why Socrates in the presence of many witnesses described a dream he had and offered a rather amusing conjecture about him. "Because I imagined", he said, "that Plato had turned into a raven and had hopped up on top of my head, and was pecking at my bald-spot and looking in all directions and cawing. So I suspect, Plato, that you're going to bury me in lies!" In addition to being unpleasant, Plato was very concerned about his reputation. This is the man who, according to Dioscurides in his *Memoirs* (*FGrH* 594 F 7), said: "The final garment we

---

[465] Dionysius II of Syracuse (reigned 367–357 BCE).

[466] *PAA* 732995; he became head of the Academy after Speusippus.

θανάτῳ αὐτῷ ἀποδυόμεθα, ἐν διαθήκαις, ἐν ἐκκομι-
δαῖς, ἐν τάφοις," ὥς φησι Διοσκουρίδης ἐν τοῖς
Ἀπομνημονεύμασιν. καὶ τὸ πόλιν δὲ θελῆσαι κτίσαι
καὶ τὸ νομοθετῆσαι τίς οὐ φήσει πάθος εἶναι φιλοδοξίας; δῆλον δ᾽ ἐστὶ τοῦτο ἐξ ὧν ἐν τῷ Τιμαίῳ λέγει·
πέπονθά τι πάθος πρὸς τὴν πολιτείαν, ὥσπερ ἂν εἰ
e  ζωγράφος ἐβούλετο | τὰ ἑαυτοῦ ἔργα κινούμενα καὶ
ἐνεργὰ ἰδεῖν, οὕτω κἀγὼ τοὺς πολίτας οὓς διαγράφω.
περὶ δὲ τῶν ἐν τοῖς διαλόγοις αὐτοῦ κεκλεμμένων τί ἂν
καὶ λέγοι τις; ἡ μὲν γὰρ ψυχὴ ἡ διαπλαττομένη
ἀθάνατος ὑπ᾽ αὐτοῦ καὶ κατὰ τὴν ἀπόλυσιν χωριζο-
μένη τοῦ σώματος παρὰ προτέρῳ εἴρηται Ὁμήρῳ.
οὗτος γὰρ εἶπεν ὡς ἡ τοῦ Πατρόκλου ψυχὴ

Ἄϊδόσδε κατῆλθεν[78],
ὃν πότμον γοόωσα, λιποῦσ᾽ ἀνδροτῆτα καὶ ἥβην.

εἰ δ᾽ οὖν καὶ Πλάτωνος φήσειέν τις εἶναι τὸν λόγον,
f  οὐχ | ὁρῶ τίν᾽ ἐσχήκαμεν ἀπ᾽ αὐτοῦ ὠφέλειαν· ἐὰν γὰρ
καὶ συγχωρήσῃ τις μεθίστασθαι τὰς τῶν τετελευτη-
κότων ψυχὰς εἰς ἄλλας φύσεις ἢ πρὸς τὸν μετεωρό-
τερον καὶ καθαρώτερον ἀνέρχεσθαι τόπον, ἅτε κου-
φότητος μετεχούσας, τί πλέον ἡμῖν; ὧν γὰρ μήτ᾽
ἀνάμνησίς ἐστιν οὔ ποτε ἦμεν μήτ᾽ αἴσθησις, εἰ καὶ τὸ
σύνολον ἦμεν, τίς χάρις ταύτης τῆς ἀθανασίας; οἱ δὲ
συντεθέντες ὑπ᾽ αὐτοῦ Νόμοι καὶ τούτων ἔτι πρότερον
508  ἡ Πολιτεία ‖ τί πεποιήκασιν; καίτοι γε ἔδει καθάπερ
τὸν Λυκοῦργον τοὺς Λακεδαιμονίους καὶ τὸν Σόλωνα

---

[78] The traditional text of Homer has βεβήκει.

shed, at the moment we die, in our will, our funeral procession, and our burial, is our reputation." And will anyone
deny that a desire to found a city and establish its laws is
symptomatic of a hunger for glory? This is obvious from
what he says in his *Timaeus* (19b, heavily adapted): My
feeling about my republic is like that of a painter, who
would like to see his creations moving and active; that's
how I feel about the citizens I describe. And what could
one say about the material in his dialogues that is stolen
from other sources? Because the idea he cobbled together
of an immortal soul that is separated from the body at
death is found earlier than him, in Homer. For Homer (*Il.*
16.856–7) claimed that Patroclus' soul

> descended to Hades,
> lamenting its fate, and leaving behind manhood and
> youth.

And even if one were to attribute the doctrine to Plato, I do
not see what good he has done us. Because if one agrees
that the souls of the dead are transformed into beings of a
different sort, or ascend to his higher and purer place,
since lightness is one of their characteristics—what difference does this make to us? For if we have no recollection
or consciousness of where we were once, or even if we existed at all, what happiness do we derive from this type of
immortality? And what have the *Laws* he composed, and
the *Republic* even earlier than that, accomplished? If (his
laws) were of any value, he should have been able to convince some of the Greeks to use them, as Lycurgus convinced the Spartans, and Solon convinced the Athenians,

τοὺς Ἀθηναίους καὶ τὸν Ζάλευκον τοὺς Θουρίους, καὶ
αὐτόν, εἴπερ ἦσαν χρήσιμοι, πεῖσαί τινας τῶν Ἑλλήνων αὐτοῖς χρήσασθαι. νόμος γάρ ἐστιν, ὥς φησιν
Ἀριστοτέλης, λόγος ὡρισμένος καθ᾽ ὁμολογίαν κοι-
νὴν πόλεως, μηνύων πῶς δεῖ πράττειν ἕκαστα. ὁ δὲ
Πλάτων πῶς; οὐκ ἄτοπον τριῶν Ἀθηναίων γενομένων
νομοθετῶν τῶν γε δὴ γνωριζομένων, Δράκοντος καὶ
αὐτοῦ τοῦ Πλάτωνος καὶ Σόλωνος, τῶν μὲν τοῖς |
b  νόμοις ἐμμένειν τοὺς πολίτας, τῶν δὲ τοῦ Πλάτωνος
καὶ προσκαταγελᾶν; ὁ δ᾽ αὐτὸς λόγος καὶ περὶ τῆς
πολιτείας· εἰ καὶ πασῶν εἴη αὕτη βελτίων, μὴ πείθοι δ᾽
ἡμᾶς, τί πλέον; ἔοικεν οὖν ὁ Πλάτων οὐ τοῖς οὖσιν
ἀνθρώποις γράψαι τοὺς Νόμους, ἀλλὰ τοῖς ὑπ᾽ αὐτοῦ
διαπλαττομένοις, ὥστε καὶ ζητεῖσθαι τοὺς χρησο-
μένους. ἐχρῆν οὖν ἃ πείσει λέγων ταῦτα καὶ γράφειν
καὶ μὴ ταῦτα ποιεῖν τοῖς εὐχομένοις, ἀλλὰ τοῖς τῶν
ἐνδεχομένων ἀντεχομένοις. χωρὶς τοίνυν τούτων εἴ τις
c  διεξίοι τοὺς Τιμαίους | αὐτοῦ καὶ τοὺς Γοργίας, καὶ
τοὺς ἄλλους δὲ τοὺς τοιούτους διαλόγους, ἐν οἷς καὶ
περὶ τῶν ἐν τοῖς μαθήμασι διεξέρχεται καὶ περὶ τῶν
κατὰ φύσιν καὶ περὶ πλειόνων ἄλλων, οὐδ᾽ ὡς διὰ
ταῦτα θαυμαστέος ἐστίν. ἔχει γάρ τις καὶ παρ᾽ ἑτέρων
ταῦτα λαβεῖν ἢ βέλτιον λεχθέντα ἢ μὴ χεῖρον. καὶ
γὰρ Θεόπομπος ὁ Χῖος ἐν τῷ Κατὰ τῆς Πλάτωνος
Διατριβῆς, τοὺς πολλούς, φησί, τῶν διαλόγων αὐτοῦ

---

467 Lycurgus (Poralla #499) was the legendary founder of the
Spartan constitution, while Solon (*PAA* 827640; fl. 590s–560s
BCE) carried out important revisions of the Athenian constitution.
Zaleucus (mid-7th century BCE) is normally associated with
Epizephrian Locri (Ephor. *FGrH* 70 F 139; Arist. *Pol.* 1274a22–3;
cf. 10.429a) rather than with Thurii (founded only in 444/3).

and Zaleucus convinced the inhabitants of Thurii.[467] Because a law, according to Aristotle (*Rh.Al.* 1420$^a$25–7), is a statement ratified by general agreement of the city that tells us how we ought to do this or that. But what does this have to do with Plato? Is it not strange that of the three Athenians generally recognized to have been lawgivers, that is, Draco,[468] Plato himself, and Solon, the citizens adhere to the laws of the other two, but laugh at Plato's? The same argument applies to his republic: even if this is the best possible form, but he fails to convince us of the fact, what is the gain? Plato thus appears to have written his *Laws* not for actual human beings, but for those he made up, requiring us to institute a search for someone who might find them useful. He should accordingly have written down only the arguments he was likely to be successful with, and not have behaved like people who are merely boasting, but instead like those with a firm grasp of the possible. Quite apart from this, if one were to work through his works like the *Timaeus* and the *Gorgias* and other, similar dialogues, in which he goes on at length about his teachings having to do with nature and numerous other subjects, he deserves no particular respect on this count either. Because one could get the same material from other sources, where it is expressed better or at least no worse. In fact, Theopompus of Chios says in his *Against Plato's School* (*FGrH* 115 F 259): One would find that the ma-

---

[468] Draco (*PAA* 374190) dates to the late 6th century BCE; his law-code was notoriously severe, hence English "Draconian".

485

ἀχρείους καὶ ψευδεῖς ἄν τις εὕροι· ἀλλοτρίους δὲ τοὺς
d πλείους, ὄντας ἐκ τῶν Ἀριστίππου διατριβῶν, | ἐνίους
δὲ κἀκ τῶν Ἀντισθένους, πολλοὺς δὲ κἀκ τῶν Βρύσω-
νος τοῦ Ἡρακλεώτου. ἀλλὰ τὰ κατὰ τὸν ἄνθρωπον
ἅπερ ἐπαγγέλλεται καὶ ἡμεῖς ζητοῦμεν ἐκ τῶν ἐκείνου
λόγων, οὐχ[79] εὑρίσκομεν, ἀλλὰ συμπόσια μὲν καὶ
λόγους ὑπὲρ ἔρωτος εἰρημένους καὶ μάλα ἀπρεπεῖς,
οὓς καταφρονῶν τῶν ἀναγνωσομένων συνέθηκεν,
ὥσπερ καὶ οἱ πολλοὶ τῶν μαθητῶν αὐτοῦ τυραννικοί
τινες καὶ διάβολοι γενόμενοι. Εὐφραῖος μὲν γὰρ παρὰ
e Περδίκκᾳ τῷ βασιλεῖ διατρίβων | ἐν Μακεδονίᾳ οὐχ
ἧττον αὐτοῦ ἐβασίλευε φαῦλος ὢν καὶ διάβολος, ὃς
οὕτω ψυχρῶς συνέταξε τὴν ἑταιρίαν τοῦ βασιλέως
ὥστε οὐκ ἐξῆν τοῦ συσσιτίου μετασχεῖν, εἰ μή τις
ἐπίσταιτο γεωμετρεῖν ἢ φιλοσοφεῖν. ὅθεν Φιλίππου
τὴν ἀρχὴν παραλαβόντος Παρμενίων αὐτὸν ἐν Ὠρεῷ
λαβὼν ἀπέκτεινεν, ὥς φησι Καρύστιος ἐν Ἱστορικοῖς
Ὑπομνήμασι. καὶ Κάλλιππος δ᾽ ὁ Ἀθηναῖος, μαθητὴς
καὶ αὐτὸς Πλάτωνος, ἑταῖρος Δίωνος καὶ συμμαθητὴς
f γενόμενος καὶ συναποδημήσας αὐτῷ | εἰς Συρακού-

---

[79] ὅπερ οὐχ A: ὅπερ del. Dobree

---

469 For Aristippus, cf. 11.507b n. Antisthenes (*PAA* 136800)
was another member of Socrates' circle, and an intellectual prede-
cessor of the Stoic and Cynic movements. Bryson of Heraclea
Pontica (early 4th century BCE) was associated with the Megarian
school (although cf. Ephipp. fr. 14.3, quoted at 11.509c); the reference here = fr. 207 Döring.

470 A hostile characterization of the contents of the *Symposium*.        471 Cf. 11.506e–f with n.

472 For a very different version of the story, in which

jority of his dialogues are useless or full of lies. Most of them are actually by other authors, and are excerpts from Aristippus' treatises, while others come from Antisthenes' works, or from the works of Bryson of Heraclea in a number of cases.[469] And as for the discussions of human nature he promises, I have looked for them in his dialogues but have not discovered them. Instead, I find descriptions of drinking parties and extraordinarily inappropriate speeches about love,[470] which he composed as a means of expressing his contempt for his future readers, in the same way that many of his students turned out to be tyrants and slanderers. Because when Euphraeus spent time with King Perdiccas in Macedon,[471] he acted like a king himself, even though he came from an undistinguished family and had nothing good to say about anyone; he organized life within the king's inner circle so pedantically that it was impossible to have a meal with them, unless you understood geometry and philosophy. When Philip seized power, therefore, Parmenion arrested Euphraeus in Oreus and put him to death, according to Carystius in his *Historical Commentaries* (fr. 2, *FHG* iv.357).[472] So too Callippus of Athens,[473] another one of Plato's students, was a friend and fellow-student of Dion, and visited Syracuse with him. When

Euphraeus is a democratic hero ultimately driven to suicide, when the people of his city turn on them, see D. 9.59–62. Parmenion (who served both Philip and his son Alexander) is Berve i #606; cf. 11.781f–2a.

[473] *PAA* 559250. Callippus in fact got control of Syracuse in 353 BCE, and ruled for 13 months before being expelled by Dion's son; he was murdered in *c.* 350. Dion was also one of Plato's students (Plu. *Dio* 17.1–5; D.L. 3.46).

σας, ὁρῶν ἤδη τὸν Δίωνα ἐξιδιοποιούμενον τὴν μοναρ-
χίαν ἀποκτείνας αὐτὸν καὶ αὐτὸς τυραννεῖν ἐπιχει-
ρήσας ἀπεσφάγη. Εὐάγων δ' ὁ Λαμψακηνός, ὡς
φησιν Εὐρύπυλος καὶ Δικαιοκλῆς ὁ Κνίδιος ἐνενη-
κοστῷ καὶ πρώτῳ Διατριβῶν, ἔτι δὲ Δημοχάρης ὁ
ῥήτωρ ἐν τῷ Ὑπὲρ Σοφοκλέους Πρὸς Φίλωνα, δανεί-
σας τῇ πατρίδι ἀργύριον ἐπὶ ἐνεχύρῳ τῇ ἀκροπόλει
καὶ ἀφυστερησάσης τυραννεῖν ἐβουλεύετο, ἕως συν-
δραμόντες ἐπ' αὐτὸν οἱ Λαμψακηνοὶ καὶ τὰ χρήματα
509  ἀποδόντες ἐξέβαλον. ‖ Τίμαιος δ' ὁ Κυζικηνός, ὡς ὁ
αὐτὸς Δημοχάρης φησίν, χρήματα καὶ σῖτον ἐπιδοὺς
τοῖς πολίταις καὶ διὰ ταῦτα πιστευθεὶς εἶναι χρηστὸς
παρὰ τοῖς Κυζικηνοῖς, μικρὸν ἐπισχὼν χρόνον ἐπέθε-
το τῇ πολιτείᾳ δι' Ἀριδαίου· κριθεὶς δὲ καὶ ἁλοὺς καὶ
ἀδοξήσας ἐν μὲν τῇ πόλει ἐπέμενε πολιὸς[80] καταγεγη-
ρακώς, ἀτίμως δὲ καὶ ἀδόξως διαζῶν. τοιοῦτοι δ' εἰσὶ
καὶ νῦν τῶν Ἀκαδημαϊκῶν τινες, ἀνοσίως καὶ ἀδόξως
βιοῦντες· χρημάτων γὰρ ἐξ ἀσεβείας καὶ παρὰ φύσιν
b  κυριεύσαντες | διὰ γοητείαν νῦν εἰσιν περίβλεπτοι.
ὥσπερ καὶ Χαίρων ὁ Πελληνεύς, ὃς οὐ μόνῳ Πλάτωνι
ἐσχόλακεν, ἀλλὰ καὶ Ξενοκράτει· καὶ οὗτος οὖν τῆς
πατρίδος πικρῶς τυραννήσας οὐ μόνον τοὺς ἀρίστους
τῶν πολιτῶν ἐξήλασεν, ἀλλὰ καὶ τοῖς τούτων δούλοις
τὰ χρήματα τῶν δεσποτῶν χαρισάμενος καὶ τὰς ἐκείνων γυναῖκας συνῴκισεν πρὸς γάμου κοινωνίαν, ταῦτ'

---

[80] πολιὸς Olson: παλαιὸς ACE

---

[474] Included in the list of Plato's students at D.L. 3.46, where
his name is, however, given as Euaion.

[475] The Sophocles in question is supposed to have expelled the
philosophers from Attica; cf. 5.187d, 215c (in both cases seemingly drawing on Herodicus); 13.610e–f.

he saw that Dion was already trying to get control of the monarchy, he killed him and attempted to become tyrant himsef, and was murdered. Euagon of Lampsacus,[474] according to Eurypylus and Dicaeocles of Cnidus in Book XCI of the *Treatises*, as well as the orator Demochares in his *On Behalf of Sophocles against Philo*[475] (fr. I.1, p. 341 Baiter–Sauppe), loaned his native land money and took the acropolis as surety; when the city failed to repay him on time, he wanted to become tyrant, until the Lampsacenes joined forces against him, returned his money, and threw him out. Timaeus of Cyzicus,[476] according to the same Demochares, provided his fellow-citizens with money and grain, and accordingly came to be regarded by the Cyzicenes as a decent person; then after waiting a little while, he used Aridaeus to mount an assault on their form of government. After he was tried and convicted, and had fallen into disgrace, he remained in the city after he had become a gray-haired old man, living in dishonor and disgrace. This is what some representatives of the Academy are like even today, living in an unholy and disgraceful fashion; because they got money through fraud, by acting impiously and unnaturally, and are now prominent people. Chaeron of Pellene, for example, who studied not only with Plato, but also with Xenocrates—he was a cruel tyrant of his fatherland, and not only drove the best citizens into exile, but gave their slaves their masters' property, and

---

[476] Included in the list of Plato's students at D.L. 3.46, where his name is, however, given as Timolaus. The Aridaeus referred to below must be the Macedonian satrap of Hellespontine Phrygia (Berve i #145), whose attack on Cyzicus is mentioned at Marmor Parium *FGrH* 239 B12 (319/8 BCE); D.S. 18.51.

ὠφεληθεὶς ἐκ τῆς καλῆς Πολιτείας καὶ τῶν παρανόμων
Νόμων.

Διὸ καὶ Ἔφιππος ὁ κωμῳδιοποιὸς ἐν Ναυάγῳ Πλά-

c τωνά | τε αὐτὸν καὶ τῶν γνωρίμων τινὰς κεκωμῴδηκεν
ὡς καὶ ἐπ' ἀργυρίῳ συκοφαντοῦντας, ἐμφαίνων ὅτι καὶ
πολυτελῶς ἠσκοῦντο καὶ ὅτι τῆς εὐμορφίας τῶν καθ'
ἡμᾶς ἀσελγῶν πλείονα πρόνοιαν ἐποιοῦντο. λέγει δ'
οὕτως·

ἔπειτ' ἀναστὰς εὔστοχος νεανίας
τῶν ἐξ Ἀκαδημείας τις ὑπὸ Πλάτωνα καὶ
Βρυσωνοθρασυμαχειοληψικερμάτων
πληγεὶς ἀνάγκῃ, † λιψιγομισθω † τέχνῃ |

d συνών τις, οὐκ ἄσκεπτα δυνάμενος λέγειν,
εὖ μὲν μαχαίρᾳ ξύστ' ἔχων τριχώματα,
εὖ δ' ὑποκαθιεὶς ἄτομα πώγωνος βάθη,
εὖ δ' ἐν πεδίλῳ πόδα τιθεὶς † ὑπὸ ξυρόν †
κνήμης ἱμάντων ἰσομέτροις ἑλίγμασιν,
ὄγκῳ τε χλανίδος εὖ τεθωρακισμένος,
σχῆμ' ἀξιόχρεων ἐπικαθεὶς βακτηρίᾳ,
ἀλλότριον, οὐκ οἰκεῖον, ὡς ἐμοὶ δοκεῖ, |

e ἔλεξεν· "ἄνδρες τῆς Ἀθηναίων χθονός."

μέχρι τούτων ἡμῖν πεπεραιώσθω καὶ ἥδε ἡ συναγωγή,
φίλτατε Τιμόκρατες· ἑξῆς δὲ ἐροῦμεν περὶ τῶν ἐπὶ
τρυφῇ διαβοήτων γενομένων.

---

477 Chaeron (Moretti #432 [he was a wrestler; Berve i #818]),
supported by Alexander the Great, apparently seized power
sometime in the mid-330s BCE; cf. D. 17.10; Paus. 7.27.7.

478 For Bryson, see 11.508c–d n.; the reference to him here =
fr. 206 Döring. Thrasymachus of Chalcedon (late 5th century
BCE; D–K 85) was likewise not a member of Plato's school, although he appears as a character in the *Republic*.

forced their wives to live with them, as if they were married.[477] This is how he benefitted from the lovely *Republic* and the lawless *Laws*!

This is why the comic poet Ephippus in *The Shipwreck Victim* (fr. 14) makes fun of Plato himself and of some of his students for abusing the legal system to extort money, bringing out the fact that they dressed expensively and were more concerned with how they looked than the degenerates in our own time are. He puts it as follows:

> Then a sharp young man stood up,
> someone from the Academy who'd studied with Plato and
> was driven by the need for Brysono-Thrasyma-chian-[478]
> money-grubbing, an individual familiar with the trick
> [corrupt] and incapable of saying anything unconsidered.
> His hair was carefully trimmed with a razor;
> his beard hung carefully down, heavy and untrimmed;
> his feet were carefully set in sandals [corrupt]
> with twisted straps of equal length around his shins;
> his chest was carefully wrapped in a heavy robe;
> and he leaned his handsome frame on a staff
> and made a speech composed, in my opinion, by someone
> other than himself: "Men of the land of Athens."

Let this compilation of mine come to an end at this point, my good friend Timocrates; in what follows, I will tell you about individuals notorious for their addiction to luxury.

# INDEX

Sections numbered 11.781–784, added from the Epitome, are found following the first portion of section 11.466d.

# INDEX

511